Music
in the Social
and Religious Life
of Antiquity

Attic amphora from Dulci. Sacrificial procession, showing two kitharas
and two auloi. (Sixth century B.C.E.). State Museum, Berlin.

Music
in the Social
and Religious Life
of Antiquity

Alfred Sendrey

Rutherford • Madison • Teaneck
Fairleigh Dickinson University Press

© 1974 by Associated University Presses, Inc.

Associated University Presses, Inc.
Cranbury, New Jersey 08512

Library of Congress Cataloging in Publication Data

Sendrey, Alfred, 1884–
     Music in the social and religious life of antiquity.

     Bibliography: p.
     1.   Music—History   and   criticism—Ancient.
I.   Title.
ML162.S45   780′.901   72-160458
ISBN 0-8386-1003-X

*The illustrations in this book are reproduced with the
kind   permission   of   DEUTSCHER   VERLAG   FÜR
MUSIK (Leipzig), VERLAG HIERSEMANN (Stuttgart),
VERLAG   ASCHENDORFF   (Münster),   and   FRANKE
VERLAG (Bern).*

By the same author:

Bibliography of Jewish Music (1951)
Music in Ancient Israel (1969)
Musik in Alt-Israel (German, 1970)
The Music of the Jews in the Diaspora (1971)
David's Harp (in collab. Mildred Norton) 1964

Contents

List of Abbreviations

AbertEthos	Abert Hermann, *Die Lehre von Ethos in der griechischen Musik* (Leipzig, 1899).
AdlerHandbuch	Adler, Guido, *Handbuch der Musikgeschichte* (Berlin, 1929).
AfMw	*Archiv für Musikwissenschaft* (Berlin)
Athen	Athēnaios, *Deipnosophistēs* (The Sophists at Dinner).
BaethPsalm	Baethgen, Friedrich, *Die Psalmen übersetzt und erklärt* (Göttingen, 1897).
Behn	Behn, Friedrich, *Musikleben im Altertum und frühen Mittelalter* (Stuttgart, 1954).
BuddeGesch	Budde, Karl, *Geschichte der althebräischen Literatur* (Leipzig, 1906).
CAH	*Cambridge Ancient History* (New York, 1924).
DelitzschComm	Delitzzsch, Franz Julius, *Biblical Commentary on the Psalms* (Edinburgh, 1892).
Durant I	Durant, Will, *The History of Civilization*. Vol. 1. *Our Oriental Heritage* (New York, 1954).
Durant II	Durant, Will, *The History of Civilization*, Vol. 2. *The Life of Greece* (New York, 1959).
Durant III	Durant, Will, *The History of Civilization*, Vol. 3. *Caesar and Christ* (New York, 1944).
EngMus	Engel, Carl, *The Music of the Most Ancient Nations* (London, 1864).
ERE	Hastings, James, *Encyclopedia of Religion and Ethics* (New York, 1908–1921).
EwAnt	Ewald, Heinrich August, *The Antiquities of the Jews* (Boston, 1876).
EwDicht	Ewald, Heinrich August, *Die Dichter des Alten Bundes* (Göttingen, 1866).
FarOrg	Farmer, Henry George, *The Organ of the Ancients, From Eastern Sources (Hebrew, Syriac and Arabic)* (London, 1931).
FineShof	Finesinger, Sol, Baruch, "The Shofar," in *HUCA* (1931–32), vol. 9.
Fleischhauer	Fleischhauer, Günther, *Musikgeschichte in Bildern*. Vol. 2. *Musik des Altertums. Etrurien und Rom.* (Leipzig, 1964).
Friedländer	Friedländer, Ludwig, *Darstellungen aus der Sittengeschichte Roms* (Leipzig, 1920).
GalpSum	Galpin, Francis William, *The Music of the Sumerians and*

Their Immediate Successors the Babylonians and Assyrians (Cambridge, 1937).

GesHandw	Gesenius, Wilhelm, *Hebräisches und Chaldäisches Handwörterbuch über das A.T.* (Leipzig, 1915).
GesLex	Gesenius, Wilhelm, *A Hebrew and English Lexicon of the Old Testament, including the Biblical Chaldee* (Boston, 1906).
GesThes	Gesenius, Wilhelm, *Thesaurus philologicus, criticus linguae Hebraicae et Chaldaeae Veteris Testamenti* (vol. 2 ed. by Aemilius Roediger) (Leipzig, 1829–58.)
GraetzHist	Graetz, Heinrich Hirsch, *History of the Jews* (Engl. ed., Philadelphia, 1898).
GressMus	Gressmann, Hugo, *Musik und Musikinstrumente im Alten Testament* (Giessen, 1903).
HarrisHer	Harris, C. W., *The Hebrew Heritage: A Study of Israel's Cultural and Spiritual Origins* (New York, 1935).
Hark	Harkavy, Alexander, *The Twenty-Four Books of the Old Testament* (New York, 1916).
HerdSpirit	Herder, Johann Gottfried, *The Spirit of Hebrew Poetry* (trans. by James March). (Burlington 1833.)
HickMus	Hickmann, Hans, *Musikgeschichte in Bildern*, Vol. 2, *Musik des Altertums. Agypten* (Leipzig, 1961.)
HUCA	*Hebrew Union College Annual.*
IdelMus	Idelsohn, Abraham Zevi, *Jewish Music in its Historical Development* (New York, 1929).
IdelThes	Idelsohn, Abraham Zevi, *Hebräisch-Orientalischer Melodienschatz* (Jerusalem, Berlin, Vienna, 1914–32).
JastDict	Jastrow, Marcus, *A Dictionary of the Targumim, the Talmud Babli and Yerushalmi and the Midrashic Literature* (New York, 1943).
JBL	*Journal of Biblical Literature* (Syracuse, N. Y.)
JewEncycl	*Jewish Encyclopedia* (New York 1901–06).
JewTransl	*The Holy Scriptures. According to the Masoretic Text.* (Philadelphia, 1917).
JosAnt	Josephus Flavius, *Antiquitatum Judaeorum Libri XX* (*Antiquities of the Jews*) n.d.
JosApio	Josephus Flavius, *Contra Apionem* (*Against Apion*) n.d.
JosWars	Josephus Flavius, *De bello Judaico Libri VII* (*The Wars of the Jews*) n.d.
JQR	*Jewish Quarterly Review.*
JRAS	*Journal of the Royal Asiatic Society.*
Koller	Koller, Hermann, *Musik und Dichtung im Alten Griechenland* (Bern and Munich, 1963).
KraussSynAlt	Krauss, Samuel, *Synagogale Altertümer* (Berlin, Vienna, 1922).
KraussTA	Krauss, Samuel, *Talmudische Archäologie* (Leipzig, 1910–12).
LangdLit	Langdon, Stephen Herbert, *Babylonian Liturgies* (Paris, 1913).
LangdTerms	Langdon, Stephen Herbert, "Babylonian and Hebrew Musical Terms," in *JRAS* (1921), part 2.
LeitGes	Leitner, Franz, *Der gottesdienstliche Volksgesang im jüdischen und christlichen Altertum* (Freiburg, i.B. 1906).

MGG   *Musik in Geschichte und Gegenwart.*

MGWJ   *Monatsschrift für die Geschichte und Wissenschaft des Juden-
           tums.*

MowPsalm   Mowinckel, Sigmund, *Psalmenstudien* (Kristiania, 1913–16).

OestPsalms Oesterley, Emil Oscar William, *The Psalms in the Jewish
           Church* (London, 1910).

PfeifferMus Pfeiffer, Augustus Friedrich, *Über die Musik der alten He-
           bräer* (Erlangen, 1779).

PfeifferIntro Pfeiffer, Robert H., *Introduction to the Old Testament* (New
           York, 1941).

PG   *Patrologia Graeca.*

PGL   *Patrologia Graeco-Latina.*

PhiloMos   Philo Judaeus, *Peri biou Mouseōs* (About the Life of Moses).

PhiloTher Philo Judaeus, *Peri biou theorētikou hē iketon* (About the
           Contemplative Life).

PL   *Patrologia Latina.*

PortShilṭe Portaleone, Abraham da, *Shilṭe ha-Gibborim* (Mantua, 1612).

RiehmHand Riehm, Eduard Carl August, *Handwörterbuch des biblischen
           Altertums* (Bielefeld and Leipzig, 1893–94).

RiemannHand Riemann, Hugo, *Handbuch der Musikgeschichte*, Vol. 1, *Al-
           tertum und Mittelalter* (Leipzig, 1904).

RothHist   Roth, Cecil, *History of the Jews* (New York, 1961).

SacharHist Sachar, Abram Leon, *A History of the Jews* (New York, 1965).

SachsDance Sachs, Curt, *World History of the Dance* (New York, 1937).

SachsGeist Sachs, Curt, *Geist und Werden der Musikinstrumente* (Ber-
           lin, 1929).

SachsHist Sachs, Curt, *The History of Musical Instruments* (New York,
           1940).

SachsReal Sachs, Curt, *Reallexikon der Musikinstrumente* (New York,
           1936).

SachsRhythm Sachs, Curt, *Rhythm and Tempo* (New York, 1953).

SachsRise Sachs, Curt, *The Rise of Music in the Ancient World East and
           West* (New York, 1943).

SachsWell Sachs, Curt, *The Wellsprings of Music* (Ed. by Jaap Kunst).
           (The Hague, 1962.)

SchneidHist *The History of World Civilization from Prehistoric Times to
           the Middle Ages* (Trans. by Margaret M. Green). (New York,
           1931.)

SchneidKult Schneider, Hermann, *Die Kulturleistungen der Menschheit*
           (Leipzig, 1931).

SieversMetr Sievers, Eduard. *Metrische Studien.* Part I. "Studien zur he-
           bräischen Metrik," in *Abhandlungen der philologisch-histori-
           schen Klasse der Königlich Sächsischen Gesellschaft der Wis-
           senschaften* (1901), Vol. 21, no. 1.

SIMG   *Sammelbände der Internationalen Musikgesellschaft* (Leip-
           zig).

StainMus   Stainer, Sir John, *The Music of the Bible.* New ed. by F. W.
           Galpin. (London, 1914).

SuetNero   Suetonius, *Nero*, in *Vitae Imperatorum Romanorum.*

ThirProblems Thirtle, James William, *Old Testament Problems* (London,
           1916).

ThirTitles	Thirtle, James William, *The Titles of the Psalms* (London, 1904).
U.J.E.	*Universal Jewish Encyclopedia* (New York, 1939–42).
Ward	Ward, Cyrus Osborn, *The Ancient Lowly* (Chicago, 1907).
WegnerSesch	Wegner, Max, *Musikgeschichte in Bildern*. Vol. 2, *Musik der Altertums*. Griechenland (Leipzig, 1962).
WegnerMus	Wegner, Max, *Das Musikleben der Griechen* (Berlin, 1949).
WeissInstr	Weiss, Johann, *Die musikalischen Instrumente in den heiligen Schriften des Alten Testaments* (Graz, 1895).
WilleMus	Wille, Günther, *Musica Romana* (Amsterdam, 1967).
ZAW	*Zeitschrift der alttestamentlichen Wissenschaft.*
ZNTW	*Zeitschrift der neutestamentlichen Wissenschaft.*

List of Illustrations

Chronological Table

Prehistoric Times	– ca. 10,000
Chinese Culture	ca. 5,000 – B.C.E.

MESOPOTAMIA

Early Mesopotamia	ca. 4,500 – ca. 3,000 B.C.E.
Sumer and Akkad	– ca. 3,000 B.C.E.
Early Babylonia	3,000 – 2,000 B.C.E.
Elamites	ca. 2,850 –1,800 B.C.E.
Kassites	1,740 – 1,100 B.C.E.
Assyrian Empire	ca. 750 – ca. 606 B.C.E.
Chaldaean Empire	606 – 539 B.C.E.
Media	835 – 550 B.C.E.
Persia	ca. 600 – 330 B.C.E.

EGYPT

Old Kingdom	– 2,160 B.C.E.
Middle Kingdom	2,160 – 1,580 B.C.E.
New Kingdom	1,580 – 1,000 B.C.E.
Nubians	1,090 – 663 B.C.E.
Saïtes	663 – 382 B.C.E.
Greek Influence	from 332 B.C.E.

CRETE and GREECE

Early Crete	– ca. 2,100 B.C.E.
Middle Crete	2,100 – 1,580 B.C.E.
Late Crete	1,580 – 1,400 B.C.E.
Dorian Migration	11th cent. B.C.E.
Classical Greece	6th – 4th century B.C.E.

JUDAEA

Early History	– ca. 1,650 B.C.E.
Egyptian Sojourn	ca. 1,650 – ca. 1,200 B.C.E.
Exodus from Egypt	ca. 1,200 B.C.E.
Early Kingdom	1,012 – 933 B.C.E.
Separation of Two Jewish States	933 B.C.E.
Babylonian Captivity	537 B.C.E. – 417 B.C.E.
Destruction of the Jewish National State by the Romans	70 C.E.

ETRURIA and ROME

Etruscans	ca. 10th century – 310 B.C.E.
The Terramare people	ca. 1,000 B.C.E.
Greek Colonization	ca. 750 – B.C.E.

The Roman Monarchy	753 – 509 B.C.E.
Founding of the Republic	509 B.C.E.
Conquest of Magna Graecia	281 – 266 B.C.E.
Imperial Rome	31 B.C.E – 235 C.E.
Decline and Fall	315 C.E.

Acknowledgments

It is the author's pleasant duty to express his gratitude to the many persons who, through encouragement or active assistance, helped him to overcome the many obstacles that every author of a book such as this must encounter.

First of all, sincere thanks are due Dr. Robert Strassburg, Professor at the California State University in Los Angeles, who read the entire manuscript and was of utmost help in arriving at the final shape of the text. Furthermore, he assisted in the reading of the galley proofs, for which he deserves the author's special gratitude.

Dr. Israel J. Katz, Professor at Columbia University in New York, read a sizable portion of the manuscript. His suggestions represented an invaluable aid to the author.

Special thanks are due Mrs. Mathilde E. Finch, the editor of the manuscript. Her meticulous work greatly contributed to the uniformity and consistency of the text. For her valiant efforts she has earned the author's sincere indebtedness.

And old and trusted friend, Mr. William Gresser, was untiring in his efforts to alleviate the difficulties that cropped up along the way. For his unselfish assistance the author owes him heartfelt gratitude.

The Lucius N. Littauer Foundation in New York contributed a generous grant-in-aid toward the clerical work on the manuscript, for which the author gratefully expresses his appreciation.

ALFRED SENDREY

Los Angeles, California
September 1972.

Music
in the Social
and Religious Life
of Antiquity

Illus. 1 Dancing men. South African Cave drawing of prehistoric dancers. (After Chailley, *40,000 Years of Music*, London, 1964, p. 65.)

Illus. 2 Dancing man, "charming" reindeers. Prehistoric drawing in a cave of the Trois-Frères (Department of Ariège, France). (After Chailley, *40,000 Years of Music*, London, 1964, p. 61.)

Prologue

THEORIES ABOUT THE ORIGIN OF MUSIC

For hundreds of years the subject of music has lured writers from all walks of life. The major spokesmen came from among the music theorists, historians, philosophers, acousticians, and grammarians, as well as performing artists and composers, who occupied themselves with increasing vigor in such varied aspects of music as an art, a means of education, an ethos, a therapeutic guide, and every other facet of this seemingly infinite subject.

Styles, forms, rhythm, melody, harmony, and tone color are but mere granules among the multitudinous elements making up the musical art, and they have been treated in hundreds of scholarly essays. Biographies of famous and obscure composers, virtuosi, musicologists, and theoreticians have fully represented their activities within the historical framework of music. In short, there is almost no branch of the musical art, now thousands of years old, that has not been extensively treated. Thus, it appears that the entire study of tonal art has almost been achieved.

Yet, there is one branch of music history that has been somewhat neglected, if not severely overlooked. This branch takes into account the function of music in society, both as a folk art and as an art phenomenon. Prior to becoming an *art*, music most certainly played a major role in daily life. It need not be emphasized that different peoples, during their long cultural and social development, during the various stages of human civilization, utilized music in manifold ways. The motivating force behind musical practice is a decisive factor for an understanding of its artistic, social, spiritual, and ethical role among the folk cultures of the world. The reason for making music must first be explored, before attempting to study its roles in the course of civilization.

The present work does not intend to be a history of music in the usual sense, but rather attempts to present music within its social and religious context. Neither will it deal with the aesthetic evaluation of music as an art, but rather with its function in society. In the study of the earliest civilizations, I shall evaluate music primarily as a utilitarian phenomenon, as it developed during these earliest stages into a useful product, which contributed to man's existence from dawn to late at night, complementing and enriching the exigencies of his daily life.

It is "very difficult to say anything definite about the origin of music, because the phenomenon is quite outside the range of our observation."[1] Quite a number of scholars have tried to answer this question—when and how music originated.

One theory maintains that "music begins at the point where clearly distinguishable intervals appear."[2] The weakness of this theory becomes immediately evident when we realize that "intervals," that is, clearly recognizable differences in pitch between two tones, represent a rather advanced stage of aural perception. This is far from its real "origin."

Before approaching the thorny problem of the origin of music, let us begin by scrutinizing the earliest forms of musical activity, that is, those which were exclusively the result of the cooperative behavior of human beings.

In archaic times there was no audience, properly speaking—only performers. The practice of music was synonymous with its performance. Only after a long period of time did the sense of hearing develop to the point where it assumed a role of importance equal to the physical activity involved in performance. The significance of the individual as a "listener" emerged in the course of history, when the auditory sense gained in importance and later even became the determining factor in music's development.[3]

This earliest form of musical practice was revealed by the growing evolution of the individual's capacity to perceive and understand pitch differences of single tones as well as tones in combination. This most certainly occurred long after the origin of music itself. Gradually, the "listener" acquired equal importance with the "performer." At this point, music not only united the "makers" of music, but created a sense of communal rapport among them. This is the earliest manifestation of an "audience *versus* performers" relationship, which came to full bloom at a much later period.

We are not lacking in theories that attempt to trace the origin of music. Innumerable hypotheses have been presented by scholars of anthropology, psychology, physiology, history of civilization, and so on, which were often contradictory, at times in agreement, at times complementing each other. However, the solution to this age-old problem has remained inconclusive.

On only one point do they all agree, namely, that music is as old as civilization itself. At the most primitive stage, music-making must have utilized, in a sing-song manner, sounds of different pitch. Out of such crude-sounding utterances came human song and even human speech which, according to some theories, developed from it laboriously over a long period of time.

Although some scholars reject the hypothesis that "speech is protomorphic music," they maintain that "it is still possible to speculate whether the very ancient sound language may not represent the common source of both speech and music."[4] Thus, speech and song (music) seem to have originated from the same source, a hypothesis that has both the advantages and disadvantages of being only partially applicable.

Let us now examine to what and where the roots of primitive song can be traced. There is a strange theory, according to which music provided an outlet for social diversion and play, "which releases surplus animal spirit, stimulates emotional excitement, and helps to maintain muscular and nervous energy."[5] The weakness of this theory lies in its presupposition of the existence of human "society," that is, a relatively advanced civilization, in which entertainment and play could not be considered in terms of a "primitive" instinct, but rather as manifestations of a definite social behavior. At this stage of development, we are already very far from the "source" of music and are approaching the *conscious* use of music in an environment of social life of mankind.

The theory advanced by HERBERT SPENCER is more reasonable. He maintained, along with ROUSSEAU and HERDER, that singing was a primitive function of speech. In SPENCER'S opinion, the organs of speech, under the influence of emotions, create certain reflex actions, which manifest themselves in acts related to singing. "The vocal peculiarities which indicate excited feeling, are those which especially distinguish song from ordinary speech."[6] He admits, however, that the borderline between speech and singing is hazy at this elementary stage of civilization.

If we follow SPENCER'S thesis, this kind of "singing" is not very different from animal sounds. Therefore, modern science has abandoned the idea that singing developed from speech.[7]

On the opposite side stands the hypothesis that speech originated from singing. "It is possible that the whole language is merely a sort of levelled-down music; but it is more likely that the sound-language is the older element from which developed both speech and song."[8] This would tend to support the theory of the common origin of music and speech.

CHARLES DARWIN tried to relate the origin of music (i.e., singing) to human courtship and mating. He argued that "the progenitors of man, either males or females or both sexes, before acquiring the power of expressing their mutual love in articulate language, endeavored to charm each other with musical notes and rhythms."[9] Furthermore, he assumed that "the vocal organs were primarily used and perfected in relation to the procreation of the species,"[10] which brought him to the conclusion that "music and impressioned speech becomes intelligible to a certain extent, if we may assume that musical tones and rhythms were used by our half-human ancestors during the season of courtship."[11] According to DARWIN, "articulate speech is one of the latest, as it is certainly the highest, of the arts acquired by man, and as the instinctive power of producing musical notes and rhythms low down in the animal series, it would be altogether opposed to the principle of evolution if we were to admit that man's musical capacity has been developed from the tones used in impassioned speech."[12] These so-called musical tones express instinctively the emotions of primitive man: sexual urge, rivalry, and triumph.

DARWIN compared these primitive sounds with the similar reactions of modern man: "The impassioned orator, bard, or musician, when with his musical tones and cadences he excites the strongest emotions in his hearers, little suspects that he uses the same means by which his half-human ancestors long ago aroused each other's ardent passions during their courtship and rivalry."[13]

It is surprising that DARWIN, who delved into the mystery of the origin of man, reached such an erroneous conclusion. More than anyone else, he was certainly aware that the sexual instinct, ingrained by nature in humans, did not require an aural means (whether we use the term *singing* or not) to ensure the preservation of the species.

Anthropology furnishes yet another explanation. According to this discipline, prehistoric man tried to imitate animal sounds, bird-twitters, the neigh of horses, the howling of wolves, and other animal sounds. This theory goes so far as to assume that man "sang" before he started to speak.[14]

CARL STUMPF had his own theory, maintaining that speech originated out of primitive man's need for aural and visual signals, which manifested themselves by special actions involving sound and sight. Here, as STUMPF believed, lay the root of speech as well as music (i.e., singing).[15]

Another hypothesis, advanced by KARL BÜCHER, maintains that music, in the earliest civilizations, originated through group-work activity. Primitive man would alleviate the drudgery of work by employing accompanying rhythmical devices, among them singing. The validity of this hypothesis is highly over-estimated. Surely, at a higher level of civilization rhythmical activities consid-erably facilitated all kinds of work; but in prehistoric times "work" merely meant securing the daily necessities of life through hunting and fishing. For these activities, group work was not required and often impossible to muster. Thus, this theory did not contribute anything new toward solving the problem about the origin of music.[16]

Likewise, RICHARD WALLASCHEK advanced the theory that music was based on rhythm, without defining the rhythmical impulses that would, supposedly, lead to the creation of music.[17]

Primitive religion is considered to be another source of song. Superstitious and magical practices at a low stage of civilization are closely connected with man's daily existence. The phenomena of nature, such as lightning, thunder, storm, and hail, brought about superstitious fears. Tribes in a low state of civilization, even today, generally have "mystery-men," or "medicine-men," like the *Shaman,* who combines in one person the avocation of priest and physician, as well as prophet, sorcerer, rain-maker, and shrewd adviser. In short, these were the men who, by their comparatively superior knowledge, exercised con-siderable influence over their ignorant and superstitious tribesmen.[18] To exorcise evil spirits, or to avoid impending disaster, the *Shaman* employed certain types of incantation, the most potent of these being a form of mystical chanting, to which magical power was attributed, thus making his sorcery effective.

As primitive magic evolved into institutionalized religion, the priest took over the functions of the *Shaman.* Nevertheless, the goals and techniques of incantation remained the same. The archaic sing-song rendition, necessary for creating the proper mood during a magical act, was retained and transformed into ritual cantillation. At this stage of evolution we may describe this as "singing" in the customary sense.

Not very far from the sing-song rendering of the sorcerer or *Shaman,* but rather nearer to the chanting of the priest, was the role of music in healing. This power attributed to music has remained unchanged throughout the history of early civilizations. "Music" in the sense of singing or playing of instruments, has equal importance for healing. The Bible describes the well-known episode dealing with David's playing the lyre to soothe King Saul's melancholy, although there is no mention of singing in these Scriptural passages.

There are other examples from Antiquity, as there are from later times, that stress the belief in the healing power of music and singing. In the second century C.E., ATHENAIOS reported healings (see chapter 8, "The Healing Power of Music").

The Talmud mentions that among the Jews the belief in the healing power of music was widespread. Talmudic sages even mention a song (*shir peg'ayim*) that was supposedly effective in protecting people from epidemics.[20] (For further examples about the healing power of music see below.)

For a long time witch-doctors, as well as priests, perpetuated the idea that music had healing powers. Superstitious and magical practices connected with music could not be eradicated easily from society, either in the lower or higher stages of civilization.

In contemporary thought, the most logical and almost generally accepted theory for the origin of singing is that which is based upon the bodily functions of dancing. Dancing is a physical expression that is inherent by nature in the human race. To examine it from the viewpoint of physiology and psychology, dancing originated from primitive man's urge to transform his psychic impulses into physical acts. Joy, sorrow, excitement, aggression, and triumph are but some of the intensive motivating forces that automatically set the body in motion.

With regard to the dance-instinct, LOMBROSO gave the physiological explanation that the auditory nerve is so closely connected with the spinal cord that we may say "dancing" is a sort of reflexive motion ("Reflex-Bewegung") caused by music.[21]

Among primitive peoples, dancing is generated, or supported, by such acoustical devices as clapping the hands and stamping the feet, as well as beating rhythmically on percussive instruments. However, these devices alone do not create dance patterns, as is often assumed, but do play a decisive role in the later development of music as an art.

During the act of archaic dance, the onlookers probably excited the dancers by their ejaculative outcries which, undoubtedly, developed into a sing-song pattern. This form of rhythmic chant, inspired by primitive dancing, is one of the probable origins of singing.

CURT SACHS, the outstanding scholar in the field of the music of Antiquity, particularly stressed the interrelationship of dancing and singing. He stated that "song is an essential, inseparable element in primitive life and cannot be isolated from the conditions that are its cause, its sense, and its reason of being."[22] He rejected all the above theories, pointing out that the common error in them was the assumption that music originated from a *single* root. As SACHS states, "music, bound to the motor impulses of our bodies, to the vague images of our minds, and to our emotion in all its depth and width, eludes whatever attempt may be made to find a simple formula."[23] Furthermore, he felt that all these theories were in vain, because there were no solid historical facts to support them. With our present state of knowledge, we must give up the hope of discovering historical proofs that deal with the earliest human civilizations, for our understanding of archaic life is, and will always remain, incomplete, inaccurate, and beclouded by ambivalent evidence. The most ancient history of man is mere speculation, and does not warrant or allow logical conclusions.

Similar opinions are held by other musicologists, hence, for instance, the statement that "a definite, wholly unimpeachable solution [of the problem] will probably never be arrived at."[24]

But even SACHS did not exclude the idea that "music began with singing."[25] However primitive this song might have been, it was still an integral part of the slowly burgeoning civilization, which gave meaning to primitive man's existence and determined the nature of his poetry. It helped him in the process of healing, provided the necessary background for his ritual magic; it also inspired the dancer and intoxicated the warrior. However rudimentary man's existence might have been, music (i.e., singing) could not be eliminated from human behavior.

In summarizing the position taken by contemporary musicology, SACHS came to the conclusion that the question of origin cannot be solved. The beginnings of music are lost in the days of yore, as are the rudiments of speech, religion, and the dance. All we can achieve is to follow these manifestations back to the time when the curtain slowly rises over the earliest acts of mankind's history.[26]

Recently, new theories have emerged that have attempted to trace the origin of music, (at least in one of its manifestations, the dance), as far back as 40,000 years ago. This assumption is based upon discoveries made in caves of the Trois-Frères (in the Department of Ariège, France), as well as others in South Africa. Paintings were discovered in these caves that depicted dancing figures; the age of these paintings was estimated by the French anthropologist, JACQUES MAUDUIT, to be 40,000 years old.[27] French musicologist JACQUES CHAILLEY used this figure for the origin of music as well.[28]

Now, this assumption is quite arbitrary, because the paintings could just as well have originated 100,000 or 200,000, or any number of years ago. Even if archaeological estimates, or carbon measurements, put their age at 40,000 years, it is by no means to be taken as pure fact that such acts of dancing occurred only at that time. Certainly, the dances could have occurred perhaps even thousands of years earlier, and waited only for a gifted artist to depict them on walls in such caves as were recently discovered.

Undoubtedly they are the earliest examples known to us of the human urge to express itself in a pictorial form. To associate these prehistoric drawings with the *beginning* of music, is questionable, to say the least.

The drawing of the three dancing men, implying rhythmic impulses in a naturalistic delineation, affords a vivid portrayal of the archaic dance, which may have already reached a higher form than is generally assumed for the dance of primitive man (Illus. 1).

As for the dancing masked man, chasing reindeers or, as CHAILLEY implies, "charming" them, this is an unwarranted and subjective opinion. Moreover, the implement in the hands of the masked dancer is certainly not a musical "bow", as CHAILLEY intimates,[29] but at best a hunting bow, depicted by the artist in a rather abstract way (Illus. 2).

Thus, even these earliest preserved documents that display the archaic manifestations of music (in the form of dance) do not shatter SACHS's opinion that the origins of music went far back into a prehistoric epoch, which is, and will probably continue to be a mystery for all time, regardless of the documentation yet to be found.

NOTES TO PROLOGUE

1 Marius Schneider, *Primitive Music*, in *New Oxford History of Music* (1957), p. 5.
2. *Ibid.*
3. Richard Wallaschek, *Anfänge der Tonkunst* (Leipzig, 1903), p. 169.
4. Schneider, p. 6.
5. Waldo Selden Pratt, *The History of Music* (New York: 1935), p. 25.
6. Herbert Spencer, *The Origin and Function of Music.* In *Essays* (New York, 1904), 2:410.
7. *SachsRise*, pp. 19–20.
8. Schneider, p. 7.
9. Charles Darwin, *The Descent of Man.* 2d ed. (New York, 1874), p. 653.
10. *Ibid.*, p. 646.
11. *Ibid.*, p. 652.
12. *Ibid.*
13. *Ibid.*, p. 654.

14. *Durant,* 1:88. See also n. 8.
15. Carl Stumpf, *Die Anfänge der Musik* (Leipzig, 1911), p. 29.
16. Karl Bücher, *Arbeit und Rhythmus* (Leipzig, 1909).
17. Richard Wallaschek, *Primitive Music* (London, 1893), p. 251.
18. Carl Engel, *Musical Myths and Facts* (London, 1876), 2:85.
19. Athēnaios *Deipnosophistēs,* XIV, 634 a,b.
20. Tal. Yer., *'Erubin* X:1 (26 c).
21. Cesare Lombroso, *Klinische Beiträge zur Psychiatrie* (Leipzig, 1869), p. 145.
22. Curt Sachs, *The Wellsprings of Music* (The Hague, 1962), p. 16.
23. *SachsRise,* pp. 19–20.
24. Siegfried Nadel, "The Origins of Music." In *JQ* 16 (1931):531.
25. *SachsRise,* p. 21.
26. Sachs, *Wellsprings,* p. 39.
27. Jacques Mauduit, *40,000 ans d'art moderne* (Paris, 1904). Chailley used Illus. 1 and 2 from this work.
28. Even Virgil Thomson, in his Preface to the English version of Chailley's book says: "Mr. Chailley's forty-thousand years of music turn out to be, in the proportion of space they occupy in that text, more like two hundred." Indeed, Chailley devotes to the music of Antiquity all in all six-and-a-half pages (in the English edition), passing in silence all the musical achievements of Sumeria, Babylonia, Assyria, Egypt, Ancient Israel, Phoenicia, Lybia, and Phrygia, and ignoring completely Greek, Roman, and Byzantine musical cultures. Furthermore, he advocates such bizarre theories as "in the opinion of some, *musica* is derived from the word *moys,* water, because according to the pseudo-Sidrach, it was invented by Japhet when listening to water flowing over the rocks" (p. 12). The Muses of the Hellenes, who are responsible for the term *mousikē,* the Mousic arts (the real origin of *music*), are not mentioned at all in his treatise.
29. The musical bow was invented thousands of years later by the Hindus and transmitted to our musical practice by the Persians.

1
Sumeria *

Whenever ancient Oriental potentates considered it necessary to proclaim laws, they did so always in the name of a mighty god. This provided the guarantee that the laws would be accepted and followed. This useful practice proliferated and soon there were a multitude of gods and goddesses, big and small. Every city, every human group, and every profession had their helping and punishing gods. And just as according to such ancient conception every human activity was created and protected by some god, the mythology of all ancient peoples attributed also the creation of music, and especially of singing, to divine origin.

Both the creation of the world and the origins of music were ascribed by legends to an act of the gods, or at least as influenced by them. Most of the peoples of Antiquity had one or several gods of music. These gods had the same rank as the useful gods of nature, fertility and war, a sign of the importance of music in the lives of these nations.

The Bible designates Jubal as the "inventor" or at least the "originator" of music.

He was the father of all such as handle the harp and organ (1 Mos. 4:21).

The Egyptian god Thot was said to have written 42 books, which dealt with astronomy, acoustics and music; he was also regarded as the inventor of the lyre. Apollo was a kithara player and considered likewise to be the inventor of music; Athena was the inventor of the aulos and the trumpet; Hermes was supposed to have been the inventor of the lyre, Minerva of the flute, and Pan of the syrinx (called therefore Pan's pipe). In India the astronomer Narada was the inventor of the *Vina;* he himself was no god, but the son of the goddess of music, knowledge, and speech, Saraswati, the consort of Brahma.[1] The Japanese have a legend, according to which

* Recent excavations made in the Soghun Valley, 155 miles south of Kerman, by a Harvard team of archaeologists, discovered another Mesopotamian civilization, which was thousands of years older than the Sumerian. Tablets were found in cuneiform writing, in an early form in the Elamite language, which antedate the Sumerian written records by at least 1500 years. This makes it evident that prior to the Sumerian civilization there must have existed an earlier "Mesopotamia," maybe several of them. This is a logical conclusion, since a high culture such as that of the Sumerian could not have developed without forerunners. It is still too early to investigate this pre-Sumerian civilization, because the results of the archaeological expedition are not yet published. As for its music, and this is what concerns us in this study, nothing is known as yet.

the Sun-goddess, in resentment of the violence of an evil-disposed brother, retired into a cave, leaving the universe in darkness and anarchy; then the beneficent gods, in their concern for the welfare of mankind, devised music to lure her forth from her retreat, and their efforts soon proved successful.[2]

According to an Abyssinian legend, the inventor of music was St. Yared. He was inspired by the Holy Spirit who appeared to him in the form of a dove and taught him reading, writing, and music.[3] The Armenians assigned the invention of music to Mesrop in a somewhat later period, namely, 364 B.C.E.,[4] whereas the music of the Syriac church was invented not much earlier than the Armenian, in 370 B.C.E. by St. Ephrem.[5]

Only the Chinese and the Hebrews have not ascribed instrumental music to divine origin. They knew that an art such as music could not have been invented by or ascribed to a divine act, but required the development of innumerable generations. The Chinese did, however, believe that they received the musical scale from a miraculous bird, called Foung-hoang.[6] They also have numerous traditions with regard to the invention of the musical instruments.[7]

These are but a few names of the "inventors" of music.

The civilization of Mesopotamia started with city-states. The oldest were Susa, Kish, and ʾUr, located in the southern part of Mesopotamia. At this time, what was known as Babylonia was divided into two halves: in the south was Sumeria, and in the north was the Semitic kingdom of Akkad.

In the third millennium B.C.E., the Semitic king Sargon I conquered Sumeria and founded the great empire of Sumer and Akkad. Another great ruler, Hammurabi, united in 2100 B.C.E. all the small principalities and created the Great-Babylonian empire. This is the historical basis of the first great civilization which, through good fortune, had an extensive musical culture as well.

In Sumerian civilization, we find not only the earliest manifestations of an organized musical practice, but judging from the pictorial and written evidence, the Sumerians must have arrived, independently of Egypt, at a high level of musical art.

According to the belief of the Sumerians that their music was of divine origin, its practice took place mainly in the sacred service, in sumptuous and richly adorned temples. Nippur erected a great sanctuary to the god Enlil and his goddess Ninlil. In Uruk they worshipped mainly the virgin earth-goddess Ininni. She was called Ishtar by the Semites of Akkad, and was later introduced in the Graeco-Roman pantheon as Aphrodite-Demeter. Kish and Lagash worshipped the sorrowing mother Ninkarsag, who interceded for humanity with the cruel gods. Ningirsu was the god of the waters, Tammuz the god of vegetation, and Sim the god of the moon, who was reproduced in human form with a crescent on his head.

All these gods had their abode in their own sacred temples and were richly provided for by the population. Since it was believed that they had to be entertained, it was essential that they be kept in good spirits by music, singing, and the playing of instruments. Therefore, their musical entertainment was integrated into the daily ritual. The gift offerings destined for the gods were used, of course, by the priests and other functionaries of the temples.

The focal point around which the musical activity of the Sumerians revolved was the cult and ritual. Thus we already find in the texts of the third millennium B.C.E. constant references to religious music. The manner in which this music had to be performed was prescribed in all its minutiae.

The great temples of the god Ningirsu in Lagash, of Shamash in Sippar, of Enlil in Nippur, of Ininni in Erech were not only places of worship but also centers of learning, in which music played an important role. Here new generations of men were educated, to whom the leadership of the nation, the maintenance of the religious institutions, and the musical culture were entrusted. These cultic places of education show that knowledge was a monopoly of a selected minority and the instruction of this privileged class was mainly in the religious sphere.

Though we have only scant reports about this, there was in Sumeria besides sacred music a vigorous folk music derived from various popular customs. Just as with all agricultural peoples of Antiquity, the life of the Sumerian husbandman gave him ample opportunity for musical activity. In a Sumerian epic poem we learn that

> the shepherds do not play flutes and pipes before him (that is Dumuzi, the titular god of the city of Kullab),[8]

which leads to the assumption that the playing of flutes was widely practiced among the shepherds.

A stone slab found in Assur, dating from ca. 800 B.C.E. (now in the Museum of Berlin), contains a veritable catalogue of Sumerian and Assyrian hymns and secular songs. It quotes the initial lines of numerous poems and songs of a great variety of categories, such as liturgies, royal psalms, festive songs, and lamentations; poems describing victories and heroic deeds alternate with folk songs for shepherds and artisans, as well as recitations requiring music. It contains, furthermore, numerous love songs for both sexes. Originally, the catalogue was even more extensive, since only the upper half of the slab upon which the list was engraved, has been preserved.[9] Nevertheless, this collection of titles permits deep insight into the character of Sumerian secular music and throws light upon the various forms of life among the Sumerian people.

Music in Sumeria was a profession and a rather lucrative one. The preserved documents contain numerous names of musicians. Like the Egyptians, Greeks, and Byzantines, the Sumerians have recorded the names of the most famous musicians.[10] The number of those not mentioned must have been considerable. In the payrolls of a single year, one hundred and sixty-four *galas* (liturgical singers) are mentioned. The payroll of the precincts of the temple at Lagash refers to seventy-six *gim* (female temple-slaves), showing that the musical profession was not restricted to men alone. Certainly these females must have had other functions besides music, as was usual in all sanctuaries of Antiquity.

More meaningful are the sources describing the ritual music of the Sumerians. This is natural in view of the overwhelming importance of the cult and the temple ceremonies in the life of the Sumerians. In order to preserve the tradition, all the above-mentioned, as well as the other great temples must have had affiliated music schools, in which neophytes were educated systematically in the liturgy.[11]

The earliest orders of the sacred service were simple. They consisted of sacrifices, in which supplications to the gods were supported by musical ceremonies. The songs were accompanied by flutes, double-oboes, and lyres. Certain ceremonies required accompaniment by sacred drums. Later, this simple religious service developed into a complicated pattern of liturgical actions. It contained four or more hymns, performed with choir singing and instrumental accompaniment. In coeval records we find a minute description of the liturgical ceremony, as it was performed during the full bloom of Sumerian culture.

First of all, a chosen priest applied the magic formula necessary for the purification and consecration of the participants. Then the psalmists had to sustain the opening supplication with their singing; a professional musician (*nar*) furnished the required instrumental accompaniment. The principal psalmist (a sort of "high priest") chanted a hymn to the gods Ea, Shamash, and Marduk, to the accompaniment of double-oboes. Sacred services ended with the singing of an epic poem, which must have been well known to everyone, since the entire congregation took part in it.

How strongly music was rooted in the consciousness of the Sumerians becomes evident from a discovery of a big stone slab with double columns containing a legend about Enlil, the father of humanity. This god governed the fate of mankind with a musical instrument called an *al*, leading the warriors in the battles, announcing the destruction of his enemies, and producing, in his temple of Nippur, "sweet music" day and night. This instrument (called *al-gar* by Gudea) is placed in the "Harem" of the temple of Eninnu in Lagash, which is the mythical bridal chamber of Ningirsu and the goddess Bau. Evidently, the *al* was a sacred symbol used in the cult of Ningirsu at Lagash. What instrument this might have been is not clear, since the term cannot be found in any other document. In a hymn for the king Idin-Dagan the singer mentions that the sound of the *al-gar* is "sweet"; nevertheless, we may assume that it might have been a trumpet, since it was used in wars and its sound was compared to the howling of the storm and the roaring of the bull.[12] Even the insensitive ears of the listeners of high Antiquity could not have regarded such sounds as "sweet."

On the other hand, singing and its accompaniment as used in the regular ritual could indeed have been considered "sweet." This becomes evident if we examine closely the functions of the professional temple musicians.

The musical service in the temples was enacted by liturgists (*gala* or *kalū*) and psalmists (*nar* or *narū*) who also had to provide, besides the daily ceremonies, the supporting chant.[13] The offices of the *gala* and the *nar* were hereditary, but such offices could also be bought. Furthermore, one musician could take care of several functions. The temple musicians were members of a privileged class. The honors due them were shared by their wives. Like the musicians, they received gifts from the community on festival days.

In the temple of Ningirsu at Lagash, there was a special officer for supervising the singers, and another was responsible for the thorough preparation of the choir, which consisted of both male and female singers. Whether this officer also had to lead the choir in the sacred service is not known. The choir was divided into several classes or groups and was organized in the form of a guild. This guild represented a learned society, a sort of college, which was entrusted with the editing of the official liturgy. We possess a great deal of literature concerning such a college, affiliated with the temple of Bel in Babylon.[14]

Numerous instruments were used in the sacred service.[15] Gudea (third millennium B.C.E), for instance, gives the director of music of his newly erected temple at Lagash, the instruction that

the flute player must practice diligently and fill with joy the porch of Eninnu.

At the ritual dance, the flute was played, along with the lyre, the sistrum, and the drum. The libations and supplications offered to the gods took place in the portico of the temples. They were accompanied by the sacred drums (*a-la*). In the same place a large bell (*nig-kal-ga*) was suspended, the sounding of which, along with the sacred drum (*balag*) and the big drum (*lilis*), was meant to draw the attention of the deity to the ritual action and the participants.

The temple ceremony at Lagash, and probably also at Eridu, was accompanied by the blowing of the horn (*sim*). In secular practice, on the other hand, horn-blowing was always the signal for general rejoicing. In processions, small types of hand-drums were used: the square-shaped *a-dâp* and the round *me-se* (in Akkadian, *manzu*).

In the ritual, for accompanying singers and psalmists, string instruments were mainly used, among them the harp (*al* or *zag-sal*) and the seven-stringed lyre (*shebitu*). These instruments were preferred "owing to their sweet sound," as stated in a coeval record.[16] In Eridu they called this instrument "the sacred *al-gar* of Enki," or of Ea, the god of knowledge and of music. It was combined with the flute of seven tones during the singing of hymns of penitence and adoration.

Owing to the numerous discoveries in royal tombs and because of its importance in cultic ceremonies, the lyre may be considered the national instrument of the Sumerians (Illus. 3, 4).

Among other stringed instruments, the two-stringed lute (*zinnitu*) is mentioned most often. It might have been a long-necked instrument on which the different pitches were produced by shortening the strings with the fingers or with the help of frets.[17]

The most important stringed instrument in the sacred service, however, was the *balaggu* (in another spelling *balagdi*). As LANGDON opines, this was a sort of dulcimer, a flat wooden box to which strings were attached, which were plucked by the fingers or beaten with small sticks.

With the lapse of time the nomenclature must have changed radically, because later *balag* meant a drum-like instrument.[18] From this it is evident that *balag* did not refer to the same instrument all the time. The change of meaning was due mainly to the fact that this instrument was associated with a certain type of liturgical ceremony. In early times it was a stringed instrument used as an accompaniment for singing; later, when the ceremony required accompaniment mainly with the sacred drum, the term changed to designate a percussion instrument.[19]

In a litany to the sun-god, we find, besides the *balaggu*, reference to an instrument named *manzu*. As LANGDON thinks, this was a bagpipe. This must be an error on his part, since the earliest records containing mention of the bagpipe originate in the time of the Roman emperors.[20]

The priests spoke their oracles accompanied by the cross-stringed harp (*zag-sal*) or the lyre (*al-gar*), a practice used later by the Hebrew prophets and psalmists who used to "open their dark saying [i.e., prophecies] upon the harp" (Ps. 49:4).

The most important feast of the Sumerians was the festival of the New Year, which reached its climax with the "sacred wedding." This represented the mythical union of the king and the priestess, in the form of the god Tammuz and the giddess Inanna, symbolizing the rebirth and fertility in nature.[21] This "royal wedding" was preceded by festivities and banquets, at which music and dance were the principal activities.[22]

An important role was played by music in the Sumerian funeral services.

Only a few religious texts about these customs are preserved, but the discovery of instruments in the royal tombs are proof that the Sumerians believed in immortality and that life after death was akin to life on earth. Therefore, the Sumerians furnished the royal tombs (just as in Egypt) with all kinds of useful implements, among them musical instruments (Illus. 5). These were meant to be used in the netherworld to please the gods with their sound and to insure their clemency toward the deceased. The ceremony of the funeral lamentations was minutely prescribed (sometimes for as long as ten days after death); the playing of instruments was entrusted to women.

In the excavations of ʾUr a number of mass graves were discovered in which the ruler was buried with his entire court. In one of these tombs 63 people, in another 74, and in another 34, were found.[23] In all these tombs, the instruments discovered were lying next to the female skeletons, grouped on one side of the burial chamber, which seems to have been specifically designated for the musicians.

This mass burial has been interpreted in different ways.

According to WOOLLEY, these were no human sacrifices in honor of the deceased king, but the retinue accompanied their master voluntarily into death to continue their services in the netherworld.[24]

Close to every skeleton small drinking cups were found, which evidently contained the poison used by the members of the court for their voluntary suicide.

Another theory, presented by MOORTGATT,[25] connects these rites of burial with the cult of Tammuz. In his opinion, the deceased king was identified with the god Tammuz, who carried his retinue with him into the underworld, to celebrate, after a certain time, resurrection with all his devoted followers. This ceremony was supposed to be similar to that of the rites celebrated by the Sumerians every New Year.[26]

GALPIN believes that he has discovered an example of the instrumental accompaniment to a Sumerian song. A tone-slab of Assur, found in the region of the Middle Tigris, dating from the second millennium B.C.E., contains a hymn in Sumerian with some marginal signs, supposedly of a musical nature. GALPIN sought to decipher these signs.[27] However, he started from the erroneous supposition that these signs represent single musical notes. SACHS, on the other hand, proved that they cannot be single notes, but are symbols for rising and falling intervals. According to this belief, he attempted to make his own interpretation of these signs. He published his solution in 1924,[28] modifying and correcting it, however, at a later date,[29] and in its final form it represents the first successful attempt, confirmed repeatedly by musicology, to reconstruct music of remote Antiquity.

The pictorial design of a group of Sumerian musicians and dancers on a fragment of a vase found at Bismaya, dating from ca. 3200 B.C.E. affords a useful, if somewhat confused, picture of the musical practices of the Sumerians. On this fragment, two lyres are clearly reproduced, one with five, and the other with seven strings, plucked by the fingers. The figure behind the lyre players seems to be singing. The figure on the extreme right claps the hands just as the torso does in the upper left hand corner. The musicians are evidently accompanying a dance performance in which one of the participants, the figure in the top center of the picture, seems to be executing dance steps (Illus. 6).

Foreign conquerors, like the Chaldaeans, invaded Sumeria, burned the houses and temples of Lagash, and carried the inhabitants into captivity and slavery. The laments in metrical form, composed on this occasion and addressed to the deities of the city, are very similar to those the Hebrew psalmists wrote in times of national disaster.[30]

As may be seen, there are obvious similarities between the musical practices of the Sumerians and the Israelites. This will become even more evident when we scrutinize the musical aspects of Ancient Israel.

NOTES

1. Carl. Engel, *Musical Myths and Facts*, 1:75.
2. Ibid., 1:76.
3. Guillaume André Villoteau, *Description de l'Egypte*, Pt. 4 (Paris, 1812), p. 135.
4. Ibid.
5. Ibid., p. 154, n. 1.
6. Engel, 1:75. See also Jacques Chailley, *40,000 years of music* (London, 1964), p. 5.
7. Engel, 1:75.
8. S. W. Kramer, *From the Tablets of Sumer* (Indian Hills, Colo., 1956), p. 192.
9. Erich Ebeling, "Ein Hymnenkatalog aus Assur," in *JRAS* (1923); *GalpSum*, p. 61.
10. Henrike Hartmann, *Die Musik der sumerischen Kultur* (Frankfurt a.M., 1960), pp. 159–83.
11. *LangdLit*, pp. xii, xix.
12. Stephen Langdon, *Sumerian Liturgical Texts* (Philadelphia, 1917), p. 187.
13. *Narū* and *kalū* were the Akkadian (Semitic) forms of the same term.
14. *LangdLit*, pp. xii, xix.
15. Langdon mentions 13 instruments, the names of which are to be found in cuneiform texts (pp. xxxii–xxxiii). Hartmann enumerates 10 instruments of percussion (with variants), 12 wind-instruments (also with variants), and 5 stringed instruments, the names of which are contained in Sumerian texts.
16. *GalpSum*, p. 60.
17. *LangdLit*, p. viii.
18. *Ibid.*, p. vii, n.
19. *LangdLit*, p. vii, n.; Hartmann, p. 159.
20. *SachsHist*, p. 141.
21. Hartmann, p. 159.
22. S. W. Kramer, p. 250.
23. Hartmann, pp. 278–79.
24. *Ibid.*, p. 280.
25. A. Moortgatt, *Der Unsterblichkeitsglaube in der altorientalischen Bildkunst* (Berlin, 1949).
26. Hartmann, p. 280.
27. *GalpSum*, pp. 99–104.
28. Curt Sachs, "Die Entzifferung einer babylonischen Notenschrift," in *Sitzungsberichte der Preussischen Akademie der Wissenschaften* (1924), vol. 18.
29. *Papers read at the International Congress of Musicology* (1939) (New York, 1944), pp. 161–67. Illus. of the tone-slab, preserved in the Museum of Berlin, in *GalpSum*, p. 70, Plate IX.
30. *HarrisHer*, p. 65.

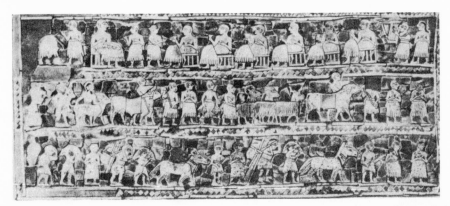

Illus. 3 The Royal Standard of ʾUr (ca. fourth millennium B.C.E.), found in Bismaya. (After Henrike Hartmann, *Die Musik der sumerischen Kultur*, Frankfurt a.M., 1960.)

Illus. 4 The musicians from the Royal Standard of ʾUr (enlarged).

Illus. 5 Gold and mosaic kithara, found in the Great Death-pit at ᵓUr. (ca. 2700 B.C.E.) In the Baghdad Museum. (After Woolley.)

Illus. 6 Sumerian musicians. Vase fragment of the fourth millennium B.C.E. The two lyres depicted have five and seven strings respectively. (After Curt Sachs, *Musik der Antike,* in *Handbuch der Musikwissenschaft,* Potsdam, 1934.)

Illus. 7 Sumerian harpist. (After Wilhelm Stauder, *Die Harfen und Leiern der Sumerer,* Frankfurt a.M., 1957.)

Illus. 8 Sumerian vertical flute. From an archaic Sumerian seal. Louvre, Paris. (After F. W. Galpin, *The Music of the Sumerians* . . . , Cambridge, 1937. Plate IV, 1.)

2

Egypt

The general Egyptian civilization, thousands of years old, and rich in science and arts, is well known in almost all its aspects through its own historical records and through foreign documents. About the music of the Egyptians, however, we know relatively little. This highly civilized nation, whose literature contains specimens of supreme quality, among them the oldest known art-poem of mankind, mainly left pictorial representations of its musical culture, and these in great abundance.

Not before science succeeded in deciphering the numerous hieroglyphic comments accompanying the iconography, was the real meaning of Egyptian musical life, which until then was shrouded in obscurity or misunderstood, unravelled.

The subjectively biased reports by foreign authors who traveled in Egypt, such as HERODOTUS, PLATO, PYTHAGORAS and others, have validity mainly for their own time, at a period when the Egyptian art was already markedly over-shadowed by that of Greece. About the earlier period, in which Egyptian music reached its zenith, these authors report only hearsay, gathered from the lips of priests or laymen with limited knowledge of musical art.

Just as in other myths of Antiquity, where the origin of music is attributed to the gods, so, too, in Egypt. In Egyptian mythology, the earth was created by the gesture of a god whose name is not revealed. This gesture, reproduced in a hieroglyphic sign, is identical with that by which the god Hesu created music. The name Hesu, translated literally, means, "singer." This gesture also describes the activity of the cheironomist, the leader of musical performances, who indicated by special movements of his hands and arms the melody, the accompaniment, and other essential details of the performance.

Thus, the creativity, be it for the universe, for music, or for a musical performance, is expressed in the pictorial language of the Egyptians by the same hieroglyphic symbol.

Besides Hesu, the Egyptian pantheon had several other gods of music, such as Hathor who besides being the goddess of music was also the goddess of love. It is difficult for us to imagine this deity as "lovely," as the Egyptians regarded her, since she was depicted as having the head, or at least the ears, of a cow, as seen in a number of illustrations. Another goddess of music was Mert. The god of the sistrum was Ihi, although the sistrum was generally one of the musical implements attributed to the goddess Bastet, or Bubastis, as the Greeks called her (Illus. 9).

37

There was even a "comedian" among the gods of music, Bes, who was also the god of dancing, and who enjoyed great popularity. He was represented as a dwarf, with contorted limbs, and seems to have been modeled on the buffoons, who belonged to the entourage of every oriental ruler. Dwarfs and grotesque characters were often brought by the Pharaohs from far-off provinces to entertain the court retinue. It is possible that the figure of the god Bes was an imitation of, or at least influenced by, such buffoons. Curiously enough, this gay fellow was worshipped in the later period of Egypt as the god of war; in this highly dignified status, he was represented having a large plume of feathers on his head (Illus. 10).

In the early epoch of Egyptian history the sound of instruments, as in other primitive civilizations, had mainly magical connotation. Musical instruments were used to ward off evil spirits who, according to the conception of the Oriental mind, could not endure noise. The instruments used in the predynastic period of Egypt scarcely deserve this term; they are better regarded as tools for creating noise.

Throughout the development of Egyptian music, and until it reached its fullest maturity, it remained in the service of religion. Its importance was attributed to its ability to influence favorably the gods of the higher and lower regions, as well as evil spirits. Thus, music had the function as an intermediary between man and the higher beings, and attained its own ethos, owing to its power in bringing about the gods' good will for human use.

For the Egyptians, music was the way to the hearts of the gods, invoking their clemency. Owing to its sacred character, in this period, it was performed mainly by priests and priestesses, the latter functioning at the same time as sacred temple dancers.

Besides its role in ritual, music played an increasingly important role in courtly life and in the entertainment of the nobles and the wealthy. Thus, soon a new type of musical culture came into being, providing ample opportunity for the livelihood of professional musicians, and assuming an importance in the social life of wide strata of the population.

We are informed about all this by a rich iconography, portraying religious conceptions of the Egyptians. As is well known, the Egyptians believed in the continuation of life after death. According to their faith, life in the netherworld was similar to that on earth. The court retinue joined the kings and the nobles for the purpose of serving the deceased after his resurrection. It has been shown earlier that this was also the belief of the Sumerians. However, while the Sumerians sacrificed to their deceased rulers hecatombs, practically their entire retinue, the Egyptians (maybe after initial human sacrifices) found a more practical "substitute." They added to the burial chamber of a Pharaoh, or of a high dignitary, his retinue *in effigie*. The persons and actions depicted in the tombs represent *reality;* they are imitating real life, they are minutely observed and exactly reproduced. The persons destined to serve their masters in the new life act in the pictorial design exactly as they did in life; all the scenes, and also the musical performances, are meant to be imitations of live actions; the musicians, singers, and dancers carry out a routine that was a copy of the actual practice. This provides unsuspected advantages for musicology, since the added hieroglyphic "footnotes" afford a vivid picture of the musical practice of the Egyptians.

Music was a widespread profession and a rather lucrative one. If we disregard the musical background of the ritual action, which had exclusively religious motivation, the professional musician had a rich field of action for his artistry. To cite only a few examples:

The work of sowing and harvesting the crops was done with the accompaniment of music (flute-playing and dancing, using concussion sticks (Illus. 11); at the vintage, singing facilitated the rhythmical motions of the wine-treaders; the toil of rowing on the Nileboats was alleviated by singing; in general, every profession requiring a regularized rhythmic activity was facilitated by singing, such as the threshing of the corn, the milling of the wheat, the work of the carpenters, and the like. At this stage, Egyptian music was pure and simple heteronomic utilitarian music, similar in nature to that found in all civilizations where manual work was alleviated by rhythmical support.

Other forms of heteronomous musical activity included the trumpet-signals and the rhythmical beating of drums, which accompanied the warriors in battles, as well as the clapping of the hands and the using of clappers, all concomitants of dancing, common to the ancient practices of the peoples of the Orient in all epochs.

The entertainment of the Pharaoh and his nobles involved the element of pleasure, and thereby approached "art for art or pleasure's sake." This stage of development, however, was reached only at a later period, when the musical performance became destined exclusively for the enjoyment of an *audience*.

In the social structure of Egypt, musicians had a privileged, sometimes even an honored position, although many of them were slaves. Some musicians not only held high positions and were favorites of the courts, but also were very popular among the people. Names of numerous court-singers and instrumentalists have been preserved. A sign of their importance is seen in the fact that they were allowed to place their tombs in the vicinity of the royal burial places. Some of them bear the title "royal director of music," a function that certainly entailed high responsibilities. Among the musicians at the court and in social life, the singers, male and female, had predominant roles; about the same importance was given to the flute-players; this instrument was frequently used for solo performances in ensemble music.

Among the numerous names of musicians in the Old Empire (2778–2160 B.C.E.), we find in the IV. Dynasty a royal musical director of the court, a leader of ritual music, a female leader of the royal music at the court and at the same time mistress of the ballet, certainly a unique case in the third millennium B.C.E. In the V. Dynasty (2563–2423 B.C.E.) there is, among others, the name of a court-musician and inspector of vocal music, and a royal music teacher. During the VI. Dynasty (2423–2242 B.C.E.) numerous amateur musicians are similarly mentioned, indicating that not merely the names of professional musicians are preserved, but that this special distinction was due to the exceptional ability of the performers. In the Middle Empire (2160–1580 B.C.E.) names of harp-singers, dancers, even of players of castanets (better, clappers) are recorded; there is also a calendar preserved with a list of the names of the contemporary musicians. In the New Empire (1580–1090 B.C.E.), there is the name of a leader of the court orchestra, and that of a female harp-singer and oboe-player. Besides, there are the names of quite a number of female temple musicians, specially singers of the temples of Amon and Ḥathor.

In the New Empire, the practice of music was mainly reserved to women.

Ladies of noble families were active as singers and musicians in temples, without being considered as belonging to the profession of musicians. It seems to have been an honorary duty for those familiar with the musical art to serve in the sacred singing and ritual processions. Especially in the temples of Amon-Re and Hathor there were numerous amateur female singers (Illus. 12).

The songstress ITI must have been very popular in the V. Dynasty. Not only is her beautiful grave placed in the vicinity of one of the royal pyramids, but a music enthusiast has adorned his own tomb with the picture of this singer, in order to be able to enjoy her voice in the netherworld[1] (see Illus. 30).

Even in the late period of Egyptian music (1085–332 B.C.E.), the names of certain musicians are preserved, among others those of a royal director of music and of one famous female player of the lyre and the lute. At this period, playing the double-oboe was mainly entrusted to females.

During the reign of the PTOLEMIES (332–30 B.C.E.) and in the period when Egypt became a Roman province, the names of Egyptian musicians decline. Instead, we find more often the names of Greek theoreticians of music, such as the mathematician EUCLID, the composer DEMETRIOS of PHALERON (who had lived in Egypt since 297), also the engineer KTESIBIOS of ALEXANDRIA (300–250 B.C.E.), to whom the invention of the *hydraulis* (the water-organ) was ascribed. In Roman times especially DIDYMOS of ALEXANDRIA (first century C.E.) and ATHENAIOS (third century C.E.) are mentioned, who gave valuable information about the practice of music of their own epoch.

It is significant that we find in Egypt the very first dynasty of musicians, the son inheriting his father's profession as his birthright. A statue of the musician SNEFRUNOFER is preserved, who may be considered to be the ancestor of a family of musicians. Several generations of this family were active as royal musicians. It is true that, according to HERODOTUS (about 450 B.C.E.), the sons generally followed their father's profession or trade. But the members of this family must have been highly qualified musicians, otherwise they could not have held such responsible positions for several generations.

In view of the high social standard of the profession of musicians, it seems strange that apparently there were in Egypt some beggar-musicians; at least, several statuettes found in the later period may be interpreted as being such pariahs.[2]

We know, however, of blind singer-musicians, who must have been outstanding artists, otherwise their names and pictures would not have been preserved (Illus. 13 and 23).

Extant documents mention itinerant "actors." These might have been folk-bards, dispensing their songs in traveling from place to place. One of them even employed a helper, a drummer who accompanied him for years on his travels.

Some female musicians and dancers were tattooed on their thighs with the image of the god Bes. The significance of this measure is not clear. It was certainly not a sign of belonging to a certain caste, since the caste system was unknown in Egypt. It must rather be assumed that they were dancers in a temple in which Bes was specially worshipped.

AMENOPHIS IV (IKHNATON) must have been a great lover of music. He not only transferred his court orchestra to his newly built capital city of Amarna but, in order to house "as suited to their status" the numerous musicians and dancers, he constructed for them in Amarna a special building, a veritable "musicians' barracks." A wall-painting shows the interior of this abode, with numerous instruments, as well as an eager musical activity, giving a good insight into the life in this musicians' hostelry (Illus. 14 and 33). In the entrance to the portico of the building there is lively activity taking place in practicing music and dancing.

IKHNATON arranged in Amarna concerts with a double-orchestra.

We see on the reliefs an Egyptian group in its typical garb and with Egyptian instruments, and an other ensemble, whose members are characterized as foreigners by their long graded frocks and their different instruments; they are probably Syrians.[3]

We do not know whether such "cultural exchange" was carried out systematically, or whether it was the single attempt of an art-loving monarch.

The manifestly widespread musical art had as its concomitant intensive musical instruction. Curiously enough, our sources are scanty about this phase of musical culture in Egypt. We have to rely therefore mostly on conjectures, or to take facts for granted in the reports of foreign writers. The "instruction" in swinging a sistrum and clapping the hands, as reproduced in a wall-painting in the Necropolis of Thebes, is at best a rhythmical exercise; it does not depict actual music instruction.

There was in Memphis a school for temple music, a foregone conclusion in view of the numerous musicians employed in the ritual. Besides, there must have been in Egypt another school, in which music was taught methodically. This becomes evident from a discovery, in which the musicians NEKARE and REWER, who lived during the V. Dynasty (2563–2423 B.C.E.), were active as music educators and teachers of traditional songs, as well as teachers for players of instruments. REWER who lived earlier, may be considered the most ancient music teacher we know of.[4]

STRABO reports that the Egyptians instructed their children in stories, songs, and a special kind of music, established by the government, which therefore had statutory power. He also reports that the poets and musicians in Egypt considered themselves "improvers of the mores":

The musicians in giving instruction in singing and playing the lyre or flute, considered this virtue as essential, since they maintain that such studies are destined to create discipline and develop the character.[5]

This seems to indicate the existence of a well-organized and effective type of music instruction. True enough, STRABO (born ca. 63 B.C.E.) reports the "tradition," since in those times the ancient music culture of the Egyptians must have changed to a considerable extent through the Greek-Roman influence. Furthermore, his assertion stating that Egyptian temples did not use instruments does not tally with the facts; history reports just the contrary.

The role of music in the cult was highly important. The musical service was carried out by large choral groups, among which were entire families of musicians. Solo singers intoned hymns, with the choir answering responsively. A particular feature of the Egyptian rites were solemn temple-dances, accompanied by instrumental music. Religious processions encircled the altar with singing and pantomimic evolutions, with a rich instrumental background.

We have a precise knowledge about the Egyptian instruments through the numerous pictorial representations in temples and burial places, and also through some specimens of preserved old-Egyptian instruments. Their forms are varied and they are well constructed and technically more advanced than those of all other civilizations of Antiquity (Illus. 15–26).

About the character of the Egyptian music, however, we possess only indirect and incomplete records. There is no trace of a musical system in Egypt, nor do we know whether the Egyptians knew any modes or had a kind of tonality.[6] Had there been an Egyptian system of music, it could be assumed that some written records would have survived to describe it. About all the sciences of those days—mathematics, geometry, astronomy, natural science, and the like— there are written documents, in which priestly scribes have deposited the knowledge of the times for their own use and for posterity. Though music was a part of these sciences, there is nothing known about a system of music. The 42 books authored by the god Thot, in which, allegedly, music has also been treated, seems to be a mere legend.

We have pictorial representations not only of single instruments, but also of their use in ensembles of larger or smaller groups, with or without singers, and led by conductors.

Among the Egyptian instruments, the family of the harps (*ben* or *bīn*) had the most important role. There were all kinds of variants, such as the horizontal and vertical angular harp, the large erect harp, the arched harp, the shoulder harp, furthermore small and medium-sized portable harps, and so on. Very much in favor was also the family of the lyres (*k•nn•r*), with numerous variants in form and equipment (Illus. 15, 16).

In the tomb of a lute-player named HARMOSIS, a well preserved three-stringed lute was discovered. Even the original strings were intact, a rare find from Antiquity.[7] This musician lived in the epoch of the Queen HATCHEPSUT (1520– 1484 B.C.E.) who, prior to the accession to the throne, is supposed to have been the leader of the Amon-singers, and therefore must have been a great lover of music.

The strings made of gut of this lute are approximately 1 mm. thick; this seems to have been the norm for other stringed instruments, although we have no record in this regard. The strings are fastened on the instrument with wooden pegs, designed to prevent the fingers from sliding off the finger board. We do not know how the strings were tuned. Pegs for the tuning of instruments in today's sense were a later accomplishment.

Small instruments were carried by hand, while larger ones were fastened on the neck or shoulder. The largest upright harps, which could not be carried, had appropriate pedestals (Illus. 21).

The predominance of stringed instruments in Egyptian pictorial representations gives us a number of clues about the character of the sacred music of the Egyptians. It must have been soft, solemn, and sedate, conforming to the *clair-obscure* of the temples, being used as a tonal background for the mystic ceremonies.

Among the wind-instruments, we find mostly the double-clarinet (with parallel pipes), the double-oboe (with pipes arranged in a certain angle) (Illus. 22), and a kind of short-oboe.[8] On the double-oboes, one pipe was destined for the melody (it had therefore finger-holes), while the other pipe created a drone-like accompaniment. When the wind-instruments were not in use, they were preserved in receptacles in the form of quivers.

The old-Egyptian name for the vertical flute was *me·et*, for the horizontal flute, *sebet*. The flutes were made of wood or reed, sometimes of bronze. Curiously enough, the Egyptians do not say anything about this, but the Greeks considered the god Osiris the "inventor" of the woodwind instruments.

In the tomb of Tut-Ankh-Amon two trumpets were discovered, one of silver, the other of gilt bronze. Both had wooden cores, which were also well preserved (Illus. 32). The trumpet (called in Egyptian hieroglyphics *ch·n·b* or *chnobe*) was mainly a signal instrument for military purposes, but was also used as a sacred instrument in the worship of Osiris; its invention was even attributed to the god himself.[9]

The tone of the Egyptian trumpets must have been uneven and certainly not pleasant to listen to, and for this reason the old-Egyptian police forbade their being played outside of the military barracks, which were located beyond the city walls. Plutarch compares their tone with "the braying of a furious mule"; Aeschylos, too, in his tragedy *Eumenides*, calls the tone of the *salpinx* "piercing" (*diatoros*). The signal instruments imported with the Roman army of occupation, the *tuba*, *bucina*, *lituus*, and *cornu*, cannot be considered Egyptian instruments. The Roman authors themselves did not have a high opinion of the sonority of their war-trumpets; they characterize the *tuba* as *horribilis*, *raucus, rudis*, or *terribilis*.[10]

The Egyptians had a multitude of percussive and rattling instruments. There were whole families of drums, ranging from the small round or cylindrical tabret (Illus. 35) and square hand-drum (Illus. 24) to the big drum in the shape of a barrel; they had small and large cymbals (Illus. 34), castanets, and other wooden clappers, including some in the form of a human hand; furthermore, they had different kinds of sistra, such as the "hooped-sistrum," the body of which resembled a stirrup, and the "*naos*-sistrum," which had the form of a small chapel (in Greek =*naos*) (Illus. 36).

During the reign of the Ptolemies, owing to Greek influence on the one hand, and the international trade of women slaves on the other, all types of foreign instruments were imported into Egypt. These were mostly of Asiatic (Syrian) origin, brought into the country by the multitude of slave girls (singers and dancers). Thus we witness the emergence of bells, rattles, the Pan's pipe, and novel forms of lyres, for example, the mammoth lyre, which had to be played simultaneously by two women (Illus. 33).

An innovation originating in the country itself was the water-organ (*hydraulis*), invented by an engineer of Alexandria, Ktesibios (second half of the third century b.c.e.), about which we possess a number of descriptions and pictorial representations. It was essentially an improvement on the pneumatic organ, about which Pollux has already informed us. However, he called it a "tyrrhenic flute," which is either an error or a confusion of terms. Of the pneumatic organ we have also several pictorial representations, which date without exception from later Roman times (Illus. 40, 41).

In the later period of Egyptian musical culture, starting with the XXII. Dynasty (950–730 b.c.e.), medium-sized and little bells have been found, which were hung upon persons and animals as magical protection against evil spirits. In Judaea, also, such bells were thought to have the same magical power and, with the same implication, they were adopted in the later Christian-Coptic rites.

During the reign of the Ptolemies, several foreign orchestral groups made their appearance in Alexandria.[11] The aim of such cultural "exchange" might have been entirely different from that which induced the Pharaoh IKHNATON to invite a Syrian orchestra to his capital city. In Amarna, it was the love of music that brought them, while in Alexandria the foreign orchestras merely served as amusement for the wealthy classes.

The Egyptians had songs in all categories, which were performed mainly with instrumental accompaniment. In great musical performances at the Court and in the houses of nobility, solo singers and choir groups participated. Quite a few pictorial representations in the tombs testify to the fact that music in the home was assiduously practiced. The most revealing of such pictures was found in the tomb of MERERUKA (in the Necropolis of Sakkarah), who must have been a great lover of music; his burial chamber gives the impression that his music studio is being depicted. This picture is the more important since it dates from the end of the Ancient Empire, providing proof that music entered private homes at this early period. In ladies' parties, too, music was eagerly practiced, and at banquets the participants were entertained with musical performances (see Illus. 29).

It is well known that Egyptian painters did not know the art of perspective; all drawings, pictures, and bas-reliefs show the persons represented in the foreground in a single line, one person behind the other. More revealing is a relic found at Sakkarah, showing in sculpture a scene of house music (see Illus. 31). Starting with the Middle Empire, wooden figurines were deposited in the burial chambers, replacing or complementing pictorial representations. These little figures indicated either the social status, the profession, or the hobby of the deceased person. There are among these statuaries artisans at work and, as in this particular case, a house concert is represented by wooden figurines that appear to be toys but in reality reproduce the scene of the actual happening. In this reproduction, the master of the house sits on an elevated chair. Close to him is his spouse. To the right and left of them are male and female harp-players. Before the head of the household there are three female singers crouching on the floor, clapping their hands. The group gives a lively reproduction of a house concert, as it was performed from the XII. Dynasty on (Middle Empire, 2160–2000 B.C.E.). Whether this Egyptian custom had its influence upon Cretic-Mycenic culture can only be surmised. We know, however, that when a musician died in Crete, he was buried with small figurines of clay representing an orchestra.[12]

In the Old Empire, a group of musicians consisted mainly of one or several harp-players and pipers, including a leader of the music. There is extant only a single picture, in which seven harps exclusively are shown.

The Egyptians did not have any musical notation. Anything the Hellenes report about a supposed Egyptian music theory is Pythagorean, i.e., later Hellenic tradition. Yet, how were the Egyptians able to develop a musical culture without having had musical notations to transmit it to later generations? This was done by the device shown in numerous pictures depicting the activity of the leaders of music.

These leaders have been misnamed "conductors." Their function was more important and more far-reaching than simply holding together the musical ensemble. Their main task was to indicate, through different motions of the arms, of the hands, of the fingers, and perhaps also by movements of the head, the essence of the musical performance. All these movements had different meanings, showing the up and down of the melodic line, indicating the intervals. Other movements served to show the harp-players which string they had to play. This technique was called *cheironomy*,[13] an artistic skill that—for want of other devices—furnished a visual and instantaneous musical notation. Thus, the most important person in Egyptian musical performances was the cheironomist, who was, at the same time, the composer and the conductor of the music performed (see Illus. 27, 28, 30).

We do not know whether cheironomy was an Egyptian invention; at any rate, it was first depicted on Egyptian monuments. It was adopted by the Hebrews and other peoples of the Near East. As the most useful technique for choral conducting, it was preserved in church singing until late medieval times.[14]

The movements and the positions of the fingers of the cheironomist have been subjected to close scrutiny by students of the music of Antiquity. CURT SACHS, and especially HANS HICKMANN, deduced from these movements that the Egyptians knew polyphonic music. HICKMANN's arguments are particularly convincing. He does not consider it real polyphony when, on wind-instruments with double pipes, one of the pipes was destined for the melody, while the other produced a sustained tone, a sort of bourdon. In several pictures, however, he found actual two-part harp-playing and two-part singing, and in one case even the possibility of three-part singing is apparent.[15]

In view of such pictorial representations, HICKMANN considers heterophony to be a proven art practice of Egypt. He defines it as a sort of improvisation: the singer and the accompanying orchestra are playing the same melody, which—according to the abilities of the singers and instrumentalists—represents a "theme with variations," so to speak. These variations, however, are not played one after the other, but *simultaneously*. The polyphony consists in the ornamentations applied by the various performers to the main melody.[16]

Thus, having established the principle of polyphony, it is relatively easy to find proofs for it.[17] One convincing example for it was found in the tomb of the lute-player HARMOSIS. His burial place is in front of that of his master, SENMOUT, who was an architect of the Queen HATCHEPSUT (1520–1484 B.C.E.). According to this picture, he was not only an instrumentalist, but also a singer, who accompanied himself on the lute. His instrument was buried in front of his sarcophagus in a special coffin. It is a small miracle that this lute has been completely preserved; even the original strings are intact. Through this lucky discovery it was possible to reconstruct the accordatura of the Egyptian lutes.

From the abovementioned and other pictures there seems to be little doubt that the origin of polyphony goes back to Egypt. This practice seems already to have been in permanent use toward the end of the Old Empire.[18]

Even more convincing are some terra-cotta figurines, originating from the times of the PTOLEMIES (first century C.E.). One of these little sculptures represents two musicians. One, seated, holds a Pan's pipe before his lips, while the other, a dwarf or a child, strikes the cymbals as an accompaniment (Illus. 41). The Pan's pipe is seemingly connected, by a curved hose, with a gadget like a pedal, which is activated by the musician with his right foot. Thus, the blowing of the Pan's pipe would be superfluous, and the open mouth of the player seems indeed to indicate that he is singing. From this, HICKMANN draws the conclusion that we are confronted here with a type of vocal and instrumental polyphony, primitive, to be sure, but nevertheless unmistakable.

Other similar figurines from the same epoch contradict, however, the supposition that the curved hose represents an air-channel to the Pan's pipe. HICK-MANN thinks that this supposed air-channel is, in reality, another instrument, the Greek *aulos*, activated by this air-bellows. This has given support to the idea that in these pieces of statuary we are confronted for the first time with the bagpipe. As far as the time element is concerned, such suppositions might not be excluded, since about this time the bagpipe made its appearance in the Roman empire.

Besides the visual leading of the music, the Egyptians seem to have us 1 also the audible marking of the beats in music. In the grave of AMENEMHET (or AMENOPHIS II) at the Necropolis of Thebes (XVIII. Dynasty, 1580–1320) a leader of music is reproduced, marking the beats with his right heel and with the snapping of the thumb and the fingers of both hands.[19]

Singing in Egypt was done by soloists or in choral groups, and mostly by females, except in professions such as, e.g., the rowing teams, who sang among themselves or—to animate the rowing men—engaged professional singers. Singing was carried out either antiphonally by alternating choir groups, or responsively, one soloist starting, the choir responding with the ritornello. Singing and playing in alternation seems to have been practiced in the earliest period of Egyptian music.

As usual in Oriental singing, we see in the pictures singers putting one hand, and sometimes both, to their ears. The meaning of this practice is not clear, despite the fact that this manner has survived until our time in the Orient (e.g., with the Arabs and the Coptic church singers of today's Egypt). There are several interpretations of this age-old usage, but none of them is too convincing.[20]

Besides singing and playing instruments, the Egyptians assiduously cultivated dancing. In all the religions of the ancient Orient, dancing was an essential element of the ritual; the same applies to Egyptian temple ceremonies. Dances were performed mainly to honor the goddess of love, Hathor; but other goddesses also were worshipped with dancing ceremonies. In the Necropolis of Thebes, there are pictorial representations of *Muu-dancers*, known throughout the entire history of Egyptian music. These were special female dancers, meeting with certain dancing evolutions the burial processions, giving the participants "the permission, by using appropriate gestures, to bury the deceased"[21] (see Illus. 39).

The *dances of Iba*, performed by maidens and boys, must have enjoyed great popularity. Dances by boys alone were supported rhythmically by girls clapping their hands.

Sometimes antiphonal singing was coupled with dancing evolutions. Such performances were carried out by two choir groups, or between a solo singer and a choir of priests or, in later periods, between the *Amon*-singers (Illus. 12), who regularly participated in the ritual of this deity. In the ceremonials of the court, too, dance had an important role. The text of a beautiful song is preserved, which to all appearance accompanied the ritual dance of the Pharaohs.[22]

The Pharaohs offered sacrifices to the gods in a dancing manner. A preserved papyrus shows such a sacrificial dance of a Pharaoh (Illus. 37). The Pharaoh offers to the gods Amon, Mut and Khonsu, while a priest recites from the mystical book "The dances of Min."[23]

In the temple at Dandera, songs were performed in honor of Hathor, goddess of the heaven and music.[24] Besides the *Dances of Iba*, performed by children,

Illus. 9 The Egyptian goddess Bastet (or Bubastis), holding a sistrum. (After Adolf Ermann, *Die Ägyptische Religion,* Berlin, 1905.)

Illus. 10 Bronze statuette of Bes, the god of dancing and war (second century B.C.E.). Museum Cairo. (After Hans Hickman, *Musikgeschichte in Bildern,* Leipzig, 1961. Illus. 15.)

Illus. 11 Dancing Egyptian harvesters, using concussion sticks (Fifth Dynasty, 2563–2423 B.C.E.). (After Curt Sachs, *The History of Musical Instruments,* New York, 1940, p. 88.)

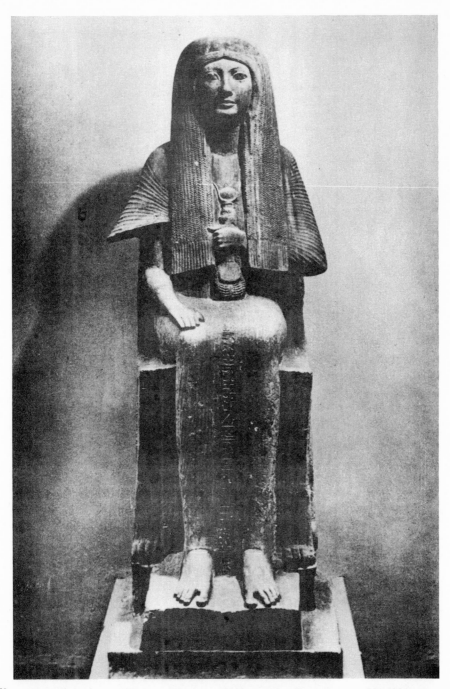

Illus. 12 The Amon-Singer Merit. (Eighteenth Dynasty, 1580–1320 B.C.E.) Rijksmuseum Leiden. (After Hans Hickmann, *Musikgeschichte in Bildern,* Leipzig, 1961. Illus. 119.)

Illus. 13 The blind singer and harpist Neferhotep (Twelfth Dynasty, 2000–1785 B.C.E.). Rijksmuseum Leiden. (After Hans Hickmann, *Musikgeschichte in Bildern*, Leipzig, 1961. Illus. 117.)

Illus. 14 Musicians' hostelry in Amarna (Eighteenth Dynasty, 1580–1320 B.C.E.). (After Davies, *Amarna*, 1903–1908.)

Illus. 15 Egyptian lyre. Probably from Der el-Medinah. (Middle Empire). Cairo Museum. (After Hans Hickmann, *Musikgeschichte in Bildern*, Leipzig, 1961. Illus. 114.)

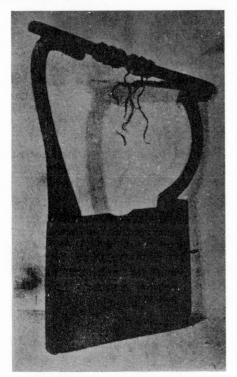

Illus. 16 Egyptian lyre. (Eighteenth Dynasty, 1580–1320 B.C.E.) (After Curt Sachs, *Die Musik der Antike*, in *Handbuch der Musikwissenschaft*, Potsdam, 1934.)

Illus. 17 Long-necked Egyptian lute (New Kingdom). Berlin Museum. (After Curt Sachs, *The History of Musical Instruments*, New York, 1940. Plate V, C.)

Illus. 18 Lute-player for Tell el-Amarna. (Reign of Thutmoses, 1425–1405 B.C.E.). (After Friedrich Behn, *Musikleben im Altertum . . .* , Stuttgart, 1934.)

Illus. 19 Statuette of a harp-playing girl. (Twenty-fifth Dynasty, 751–656 B.C.E.). British Museum. (After Sir John Stainer, *The Music of the Bible,* London, 1914.)

Illus. 20 Egyptian lyres from wall paintings in a tomb of the Nineteenth Dynasty, 1320–1200 B.C.E. (After Carl Engel, *The Music of the Most Ancient Nations,* London, 1864.)

Illus. 21 Egyptian harpers, with bow-shaped harps. Wall painting in the tomb of Rameses III. Necropolis of Thebes. (Twentieth Dynasty, 1200–1085 B.C.E.). (After Julius Wellhausen, *The Book of Psalms,* New York, 1898.)

Illus. 22 Harp-singer Bakit, accompanied with a long-necked lute and a double-oboe. Necropolis of Thebes. (New Empire, ca. 1500 B.C.E.). (After Hans Hickmann, *Musikgeschichte in Bildern,* Leipzig, 1961. Illus. 118.)

Illus. 23 Blind singer-harpist, accompanied with two flutes and a long-necked lute. Necropolis of Sakkarah. (Eighteenth Dynasty, time of Ikhnaton, 1370–1352 B.C.E.). Rijkmuseum Leiden. (After Hans Hickmann, *Musikgeschichte in Bildern,* Leipzig, 1961. Illus. 51.)

Illus. 24 Egyptian orchestra. Harp, lute, double-oboe, lyre, and squareshaped drum. Necropolis of Thebes. (After Sir Gardner Wilkinson, *The Manners and Customs of the Ancient Egyptians,* London, 1878.)

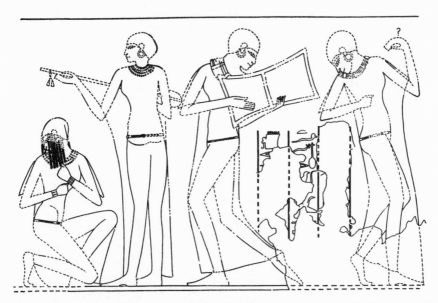

Illus. 25 Egyptian dancers and musicians, playing a long-necked lute and a square-shaped hand-drum. (After *Bulletin of the Metropolitan Museum of Art,* New York, 1928.)

Illus. 26 Singing, playing, and dancing, showing the main types of Egyptian stringed instruments: angular harp, lyre, bow-shaped harp, and long-necked lute. (Fragmented). Wall painting in the tomb of Paser. Necropolis of Thebes (Reign of Amenophis II, 1450–1425 B.C.E.). (After Hans Hickmann, *Musikgeschichte in Bildern,* Leipzig, 1961. Illus. 8.)

Illus. 27 Wind instruments: flute and double clarinet, led by a cheironomist. Wall painting in the tomb of Nencheftka (Fifth Dynasty, 2563–2423 B.C.E.). Cairo Museum. (After Hans Hickmann, *Musikgeschichte in Bildern,* Leipzig, 1961. Illus. 5.)

Illus. 28 Harp player led by a cheironomist. Wall painting in the tomb of Nencheftka (Fifth Dynasty, 2563–2423 B.C.E.). Cairo Museum. (After Hans Hickmann, *Musikgeschichte in Bildern,* Leipzig, 1961. Illus. 8.)

Illus. 29 Ladies' party with musical entertainment. Wall painting in the Necropolis of Thebes (Eighteenth Dynasty, 1580–1320 B.C.E.). British Museum. (After Hans Hickmann, *Musikgeschichte in Bildern,* Leipzig, 1961. Illus. 39.)

Illus. 30 The famous singer Iti. The name of the harp-player is Hekenu. Relief from the Necropolis of Sukkarah (Fifth Dynasty, 2563–2423 B.C.E.). Cairo Museum. (After Hans Hickmann, *Musikgeschichte in Bildern,* Leipzig, 1961. Illus. 116.)

Illus. 31 Domestic music scene. Wooden figurines from a tomb in the Necropolis of Sakkarah (Middle Empire, ca. 2000 B.C.E.). Cairo Museum. (After Hans Hickmann, *Musikgeschichte in Bildern,* Leipzig, 1961. Illus. 56.)

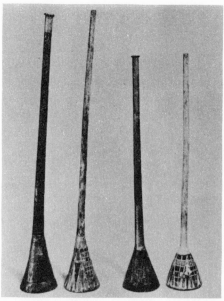

Illus. 32 Trumpets found in Tut-Ankh-Amon's tomb. From l. to r.: Silver trumpet; its wooden core; gilded bronze trumpet; its wooden core. Cairo Museum. (After Hans Hickmann, *Musikgeschichte in Bildern,* Leipzig, 1961. Illus. 88.)

Illus. 33   Female musicians in Amarna, playing different kinds of lyres, a long-necked lute, and a mammoth-lyre (Reign of the Ptolemies, 332 B.C.E.–30 C.E.). (After Davies, *Amarna*, 1903–1908.)

Illus. 34   Egyptian bronze cymbals (five-and-a-half inches in diameter. (After Sir Gardner Wilkinson, *The Manners and Customs of the Ancient Egyptians*, London, 1878.)

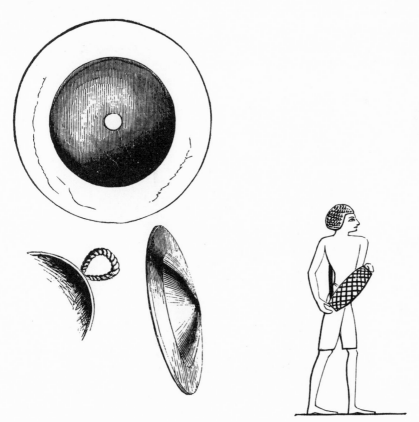

Illus. 35   Egyptian hand-drum. (After Sir Gardner Wilkinson, *The Manners and Customs of the Ancient Egyptians,* London, 1878.)

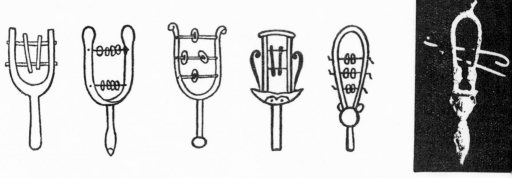

Illus. 36 Different kinds of sistra. (After F. W. Galpin, *The Music of the Sumerians . . . ,* Cambridge, 1937.)

Illus. 37 Sacrificial dance of the Egyptian Pharaoh, offering to the gods of Amon, Mut, and Khonsu. "He offers incense before the statue of the god, while a priest recites from the mysterious books of the *Dances of Min.*" (After Adolf Ermann, *Die Ägyptische Religion,* Berlin, 1905.)

Illus. 38 Egyptian ritual dances. (After *Bulletin of the Metropolitan Museum of Art,* New York, 1928.)

Illus. 39 Egyptian funeral dance. The women (on the left) perform the dance, while a group of priests (on the right) follows them with pantomimic evolutions. Necropolis of Sakkarah (Nineteenth Dynasty, 1320–1200 B.C.E.). Cairo Museum. (After Hans Hickmann, *Musikgeschichte in Bildern,* Leipzig, 1961. Illus. 32.)

Illus. 40 Primitive pneumatic organ. Sculpture in the Museum of Arles. The wind is supplied by the lung power of the two blowers, who alternately supplied the required pressure by blowing vigorously. It is more probable, however, that in view of the large pipes the two handles represent the levers of the wind pump. (Aftr Wm. H. Grattan Flood, *The Story of the Bagpipe*. London, 1911.)

the tomb of a high official named Mereruka (in the Necropolis of Sakkarah) contains a picture in which boys and girls are represented playing games and dancing. The picture shows scenes from the life of boys, carrying out gymnastic exercises and a whirling play that—according to hieroglyphic comments—has the meaning of "the crushing of the grapes." Four young girls perform a so-called mirror-dance in honor of the goddess Hathor. In the same tomb, but in another chamber, a picture shows dancing boys.

The Egyptians had pantomimic representations, which may be considered as the forerunners of the dramatic art so highly developed in Greece. Among such representations the most important ones were the mystery-plays of the cult, which were performed at the doors of the temples in open air, by actors, singers and dancing choral groups. They were not theatrical performances in the proper sense of the word, but myths presented in a dramatic form, like the mysteries, passion-plays, or moralities of the Middle Ages. In all these performances, dance was an important element. The text of one of such performances, an Osiris-passion, has been preserved.

The cast included two female actors who personified the goddess Isis and her sister Nephthis, lamenting the death of Osiris. They were called in Egypt "the great lamenting women." The text of another such mystery-play has been found in the temple at Edfu; it contains, besides recitations and songs, some indications for the *mise en scène.*[25]

In the temple of Luxor there is the complete pictorial reproduction of a performance in open air, called *"The beautiful feast of Opet."* At this festival, a barge was carried in a solemn procession, accompanied by high dignitaries, as well as by members of the clergy and the army.[26] The picture shows a group of lute-players and female dancers, making somersaults and clapping their hands, with other female singers, rattling sistra. This was a joyous popular festival, judging from the grotesque dances and the somersaulting dancers depicted. In secular feasts we often find dancers in acrobatic activities quite common at such occasions (Illus. 38). There must have been some comic dances, like those performed by the comedian among the gods, Bes, who was, as mentioned before, the god of the dance (see Illus. 10). Dances of dwarfs have also been mentioned above.

The Egyptians used so-called dance-tours, in which some action, sometimes even an abstract idea, was to be expressed. Such "tours," using various positions and gestures, were ordinarily applied when two or more people danced together.[27] They had particular names, such as "column," expressing probably through the position of the body the upright shape of a column. Other "tours" represented or imitated the wind, sweeping over the trees and bending down the reeds, or the abduction of a belle, or the mystery of birth, as explained by hieroglyphic inscriptions.

At big popular festivities the Egyptians used to bring groups of Negro dancers to perform "exotic" dances, which the populace enjoyed greatly. In the picture of the *"Beautiful feast of Opet"* there is such a group of Negro dancers and musicians represented,

whose contortions and quite un-Egyptian movements were in sharp contrast to the dignified procession of the priests, the lute-players and the other participants of the festival, adding a folkloristic feature to the otherwise strictly regulated ceremony of the feast.[28]

As mentioned before, the Egyptians believed in life after death; accordingly, the burial ceremonies took place under particularly solemn circumstances. The *Muu-dancers*, who had to give "permission" for the burial, have been mentioned above. The implements destined for the comfort of the deceased in future life, which were placed in the burial chamber, were carried in a solemn procession, followed by priests and wailing women. In the chamber itself there were replicas of musical performances, including certain instruments, considered "sacred," which were buried with their owners. These were wrapped in cloth and "entombed" in special small coffins.[29] To such sacred instruments belonged the sistra, which even had a special goddess, the youthful *Ihi*.[30] Originally, the sistrum was the priestly rattle, used in the cult; only in later times was it used merely as an instrument to make noise.

Although this does not belong strictly to the practice of music in Egypt, we should not pass in silence a curiosity of music history about which HICKMANN informs us.[31] DEMETRIOS of PHALERON was a politician, writer, and archivist in Athens; he seems to have been involved in some political intrigue and had to leave Athens (either voluntarily, or because he was banned). He made his appearance in Egypt under the reign of PTOLEMAIOS II PHILADELPHOS (285–247 B.C.E.). The immediate reason for this might have been that he was selected to be in charge of bringing Aristotle's library, bought by PTOLEMAIOS, to Alexandria. There he soon became a favorite of the court and was commissioned to write the liturgy of the new Greek-Egyptian mixed religion of Serapis, propagated by the king. Since he was versed in musical art, he also composed the necessary music; this is the first "commissioned music" in the recorded history of tonal art.

According to their conception of music, the Egyptians believed in the interrelation of music and the cosmos. This developed into the idea of the Harmony of the Spheres, conceived as a mutual influence of the sun, the moon, the earth, and the planets. It is probable that the Harmony of the Spheres, born of earlier cosmological speculations, was developed by the Babylonians and transmitted by them to the Hebrews and Greeks. PHILO, too, ascribed the Harmony of the Spheres to the Chaldaeans (i.e., Babylonians). We come across this notion first in Greek documents in the period of the PTOLEMIES; however, it must have been much older, since we find traces of it in ancient texts found in burial chambers of the pyramids. This becomes evident from a hymn to the goddess Ḥatḥor, found in the temple of Dandera:

> To thee, the heaven and its stars make music,
> Sun and moon sing praises to thee,
> The whole earth is making music for thee.[32]

We find the same idea later with the Hebrews (Job 38:7 and Isa. 49:13). The Greek philosophers developed the idea of the Harmony of the Spheres into a complicated cosmological system. ARISTEIDES QUINTILIANUS says, for instance, about the "music of the planets":

> The poets call it the "dance of the stars," the philosophers, on the other hand, maintain that every solid body creates in flight a certain sound. Thus, also the stars make the ether vibrate, although our ears are too incomplete to hear these sounds.[33]

Due to the overwhelming use of stringed instruments in Egyptian music, we must consider its character solemn and sedate; from this we may conclude that their sacred music must have been rigid and formal, similar to the ceremonies of their ritual. This is in conformity with the strong mathematical trend of the Egyptian mind, whose principal administrators were the priestly class. According to ancient conceptions, mathematics and music were related sciences, and it may be assumed that the interrelation of both in Egypt was so close that the emotional side of music, especially of ritual music, was reduced to a minimum.

As SACHS states, Egyptian music in its later phases oscillates manifestly between these two poles: on one side, there is the artificial clinging in temple and school to the strict norms of autochthonous music, avoiding all foreign influences; on the other, the continuous influx of Asiatic instruments and foreign musical elements, until, during the Greek and Roman period, the last remnants of Egyptian music are lost under the all-covering stratum of Greek musical art.[34]

And yet, it seems that a trace of old-Egyptian music has survived. The Copts, indigenous Egyptian Christians, have preserved not only the racial characteristics of the pre-Islamic Egyptians, but use in their liturgy their old language, the Greek, Roman, Arabic, and Turkish domination having left it almost untouched. In view of this racial perseverance, it can be assumed that the Egyptian music of the late period survived, to a certain extent, in the Coptic liturgy.[35] This is a mere surmise which, however, has a strong probability.

When after the Middle Empire the Egyptian culture started to decline and the institutions of the state and also the ritual of their religion deteriorated gradually, the reigning classes, especially the priesthood, attempted to salvage their privileged status and assure their control of public life. Under these circumstances, the priesthood was faced with the necessity of placing the ritual institutions on a new, more up-to-date basis, especially, since, along with the priestly musicians, a secular class of musicians gradually emerged who, at least in a general way, made successful inroads into the heretofore exclusive art of the privileged temple musicians. The musical and literary product of this guild (according to all appearances it was a guild) was deposited in a *Songbook*, which was inaccessible to the uninitiated.

The main feature of the musical practice of the secular musicians was external display, showing off by means of virtuosity. PYTHAGORAS, who lived in Egypt in the sixth century B.C.E. and, according to DIOGENES LAERTIUS, even studied there, reports that the temple musicians were violently opposed to this abuse of musical art. Their objections had no effect—indeed, could not have any—since the people enjoyed this *ars nova* of the new era.

Our knowledge of Egyptian music is complemented by the utterances of Greek philosophers, describing its character and ethos. These opinions may be used, of course, only with some precaution, since they obviously bear the imprint of the Hellenistic spirit. It is probable that, applied retrospectively, they represent a Greek interpretation rather than a real picture of Egyptian musical practice.

Beginning with the period of Ptolemaic Egypt, the literary sources become increasingly abundant. The love of music of the indigenous population and the joy in singing and music are parallel in Egypt and Greece. This positive attitude toward music did not change considerably during the first centuries of the Common Era, when after CLEOPATRA's death Egypt became a part of the Roman Empire.[36]

PLATO, who traveled in Egypt as a merchant of oil between 398 and 385, reports that the Egyptians attribute their sacred temple melodies to the goddess ISIS. These melodies were supposed to govern human emotions and to purify the spirit of men. "This is divine work," says PLATO. The Egyptians considered their temple melodies sacred and they strictly adhered to their immutability.[37]

PLATO gives high praises to the melody and rhythm of the strictly organized choir-singing at certain festivals.[38] He reports that the youth of Egypt were instructed in choral singing. Among the twenty-four books, dealing with astronomy, the doctrine of the sacred measures and rites, there were "two books of the singer," containing hymns, exclamations, and doxologies, that is, songs of praise to the gods and kings.[39]

Owing to its divine origin, ritual music enjoyed high esteem. It was performed by a special class of temple singers, whose offices were hereditary.[40]

HERODOTUS, who traveled in Egypt around 450 B.C.E., mentions that the Egyptians shunned foreign melodies. He was therefore quite surprised to hear a song well known in Phoenicia, Cyprus, and Greece, namely the *Lament over Linos*, called *Maneros* by the Egyptians.[41] He reports furthermore that women carrying pictures of gods used to sing praises in honor of Osiris. At the festival of Diana in Bubastis, choir groups of men and women were used to perform songs with the accompaniment of flutes and tabrets.[42]

In the last centuries B.C.E., the Mediterranean basin was the theatre of a vigorous exchange of commerce, which was gradually extended to the cultural sphere. SACHS gives a pertinent characteristic of this mutual exchange:

> The Egyptians borrowed from Mesopotamia and Syria; the Jews from the Phoenicians; the Greeks from Crete and Asia Minor and again Phoenicia; the harp, the lyre, the double-oboe, the hand-beaten frame drum were played in Egypt, Palestine, Phoenicia, Syria, Babylonia, Asia Minor, Greece and Italy. The Egyptians called lyres and drums by their Semitic names, and the harp by a term related to the Sumerian word for bow; the Greeks used the same Sumerian noun to designate the long-necked lute and adopted a Phoenician word for the harp; they gave epithets Lydian, Phrygian, Phoenician to the various types of pipes; indeed, they had not a single Hellenic term for their instruments and repeatedly attributed them to either Crete or Asia. Israel had Phoenician and Egyptian instruments.[43]

These comparisons could be extended even further.

Besides musical instruments, which constituted in Antiquity objects of luxury, dancers and female musicians were imported into Egypt from Asia Minor, especially from Syria. As in other countries of the Mediterranean, we find them also in increasing numbers in Egypt. Furthermore, ritual male and female singers who accompanied foreign gods were tolerated in large numbers by the Egyptians.

Beginning with the last centuries of the New Empire and continuing during the Asiatic and Greek inroads into Egyptian life, the mores and customs of the people underwent radical changes. The internal struggle between priestly and secular musicians, together with the external influx of foreign musical elements, created a situation in which artificiality won higher recognition than the intrinsic quality of musical art. This foreign florescence transformed the erstwhile dignified and sacred character of the music of the Old and Middle Empires. Especially after the conquest of Syria, the ritual ceremonies of the religion of this people infused the Egyptian sacred rites with the same orgiastic character, changing thoroughly the ethos of Egyptian sacred music.[44]

In the secular life, virtuosity in musical performances was not only favored but frankly requested. Slowly the sublime art of a great epoch degenerated and became the servant of a society addicted exclusively to luxury and the pleasures of an easy and carefree life.

NOTES

1. *HickMus,* p. 142.
2. *Ibid.,* p. 11.
3. *Ibid.*
4. *Ibid.,* p. 142.
5. Strabo *Geōgraphikōn.*
6. Tonality is used here in its widest sense. The ancient Orient did not know of tonality in the Occidental meaning. Even in Western music, tonality is a relatively late development.
7. *HickMus,* p. 130.
8. *SachsHist,* p. 90.
9. *Ibid.,* p. 100.
10. Cf., however, the description of the Roman *cornu* below.
11. *HickMus,* p. 76.
12. Durant, 1:14.
13. From the Greek *cheiros*-hand, *nomos*-sign.
14. The earliest European symbols for musical notation, the neumes, were probably graphic reproductions of cheironomic movements.
15. *HickMus,* pp. 94, 95.
16. Hickmann, *Musicologie pharaonique* (Kehl a.Rh., 1956), p. 97.
17. *Ibid.,* p. 101.
18. *Ibid.,* p. 102.
19. *SachsRise,* p. 72.
20. *HickMus,* p. 80.
21. *Ibid.,* p. 54.
22. The text is published in *HickMus,* p. 54.
23. Adolf Erman, *Die ägyptische Religion* (Berlin, 1903), p. 14.
24. *HickMus,* p. 9.
25. *Ibid.,* p. 10.
26. *Ibid.,* p. 42.
27. Adolf Erman, *Ägypten und ägyptisches Leben im Altertum.* Neu bearb. von Hermann Ranke (Tübingen, 1923), pp. 281 ff.
28. *HickMus,* p. 72.
29. *Ibid.,* pp. 40, 102.
30. *Ibid.,* p. 46.
31. *Ibid.,* p. 17.
32. *Ibid.,* p. 150.
33. H. J. Moser, *Dokumente der Musikgeschichte* (Vienna, 1954), p. 19.
34. Curt Sachs, *Die Musik der Antike* (Potsdam, 1934), pp. 5–6.
35. *SachsHist,* p. 96.
36. *HickMus,* p. 148.
37. Plato, *Laws* II. 657.
38. *Ibid.,* VII. 799–803.
39. A. Wiedemann, *Die Religion der alten Ägypter* (Münster, 1880), p. 100.
40. J. G. Wilkinson, *The Manners and Customs of the Ancient Egyptians* (London, 1878), 1:444.
41. Herodotus *Historia* II. 79.
42. *Ibid.*
43. *SachsRise,* p. 63.
44. Curt Sachs, *Musik der Antike* (Breslau, 1924), pp. 11 ff.

3

Babylonia

It has been reasonable to assume that the Babylonians inherited their civilization from an earlier people. Until recently, however, the nation that might have been the predecessor of the Babylonian empire was unknown. Excavations and lucky discoveries established the fact that this historical role was played by the Sumerians. The reason that the Sumerians were almost completely forgotten is explained by the fact that the Babylonians had taken over *in toto* the civilization of Sumer and Akkad, its northern Semitic region. Together with the Sumerian cities, their economy, their canals, and their way of life were simply annexed by the Babylonians. Generally, the procedure of ancient Oriental rulers was to destroy conquered cities and render subjugated peoples impotent by deporting or enslaving their inhabitants. The rulers of Babylonia acted more wisely. History has all reason to be grateful to them.

Through the recent discoveries an entirely new world of Antiquity has been disclosed which in the past exercised the most far-reaching effects on the history of mankind. Today, no one who visits the former site of Babylon would suppose that this hot and dry land on the shores of the Euphrates had once been the rich and prosperous capital city of a civilization that pioneered in astronomy and medicine and gave the world the first great code of law. The Babylonians taught the Greeks the rudiments of mathematics, physics, and philosophy, and lent the Hebrews their mythology. It is difficult to believe that the Tigris and Euphrates are the same rivers which in ancient times transformed Sumer and Akkad into a blooming garden, and watered the hanging gardens of Semiramis.

Along with the other institutions of the Sumerian state, their religion, their literature, their social structure, and their laws were adopted by the conquerors. Their new masters continued to write in Sumerian cuneiform letters, but the language was no longer Sumerian; it became Babylonian-Semitic.[1] If we assume that Egypt, owing to its geographical isolation, shows—with certain reservations— the characteristics of *one* people and *one* civilization up to ca. 1000 B.C.E., we may apply to Babylonia the formula of a single culture expanded to absorb the ever-changing peoples, reaching far into the social structure of the surrounding nations.[2]

With their other cultural achievements, the Babylonians took over the music of the Sumerians as well, along with their musical terms and the names of the instruments.

When the Babylonians adopted the old Sumerian prayers, they considered them sacred, just as they did the Sumerian language itself.

Their priests took over in their own liturgy the Sumerian hymns, litanies and prayers, and recited or sang them in the old language, just as Hebrew chants are still sung in our days' synagogues in the original language.[3]

We have already surveyed the music of the Sumerians; that of the Babylonians was basically identical. In the Babylonian cult the music was performed by the priest (*kalū*, in Sumerian *gala*), the singer (*zammarū*), and a special vocalist (*lallarū*) for the lamentations.

The hymns and psalms were sung sometimes by the priest alone and sometimes by the congregation. Mostly, however, they were sung by both, responsively, in the form of strophe and antistrophe. The features of these hymns evidently had a decisive influence upon the Hebrew psalm-authors, with the result that they survived as a part of the early Christian liturgy.

In view of the importance of religion in Babylonia, it is natural that the priesthood had not only great influence, but amassed considerable wealth. In addition to large real estate holdings, the clergy employed a great number of temple slaves. Furthermore, the priests had in their service hundreds of workmen of the most various categories, from musicians to brewers, whom they hired out to secular enterprises for appropriate fees. Thus, the priesthood of Babylonia may be considered as an early forerunner of the Western capitalistic system— surely an unusual phenomenon in the ancient Orient.

LANGDON's investigations afford an excellent insight into the structure of the ritual music of the Babylonians. EA, the patron of the mysteries and arts, was at the same time the god of the flutists-psalmists.[4] The official liturgist (*kalū*) was accompanied by professional singers (*narū*).[5] From earliest times on, the instrument for the *kalū*, used for chanting the litanies, was the pipe, either the ordinary (an oboe-type) instrument, or the reed pipe, *tigū*. Singing was mainly accompanied by the lyre or another stringed instrument and was called *kishub*.[6]

We encountered in the Sumerian cult female psalmists (singers), so that we may assume that this was also the case in the Babylonian cult, although references in this regard are lacking.

About funeral lamentations with musical accompaniment we are informed by a letter, in which the burial rites of a king are reported. It states that the *narū* with his daughters (evidently his assistant singers) intoned wailings before the dignitaries of the state.[7]

The instruments of the Babylonians may have been identical with those of the Sumerians, with perhaps slight modifications, due to the improved technique of manufacturing instruments. Pictures found at Telloh show a harp with eleven strings, played at a sacrificial act (Illus. 42), and others with five and seven strings, found at Bismaya, which are even older than the aforementioned[8] (Illus. 43). At Sandchirli, among other Hittite discoveries, the picture of a lutenist has been found, playing a long-necked instrument, showing also a raptured listener[9] (Illus. 44).

A stone-carving found at Eyuk was considered as showing a bagpipe. In reality, it represents a lutenist (perhaps a court-jester) with a monkey. The pendant objects are ribbons of the animal or of the instrument (Illus. 45). Another stone-relief shows a lyre-player and a hand-drum (Illus. 47). Even sportive events had a musico-rhythmical accompaniment, as shown in a stone-carving (Illus. 49).

Unearthed terra-cotta figurines from the time of GUDEA (ca. 2650 B.C.E.)

represent women holding tabrets before their breasts.[10] Since tabrets in Antiquity were the usual instruments for dancing, these figurines must have represented singing and dancing women. Such women were common features in Babylonia as well as in Assyria, where the ritual singers and dancers served also as temple prostitutes.

We have ample information about the secular music practice of the Babylonians by coeval records. These are mainly preserved in a stone slab from the eighth century B.C.E., found in Assur in 1922.[11] This relic contains a veritable catalogue of Sumerian-Akkadian titles of religious and secular songs.[12] In the eight columns of *recto* and *verso* are listed the titles of psalms, liturgies, and popular songs, a real mine of information for our knowledge of Babylonian music.[13]

Like the Sumerians, the Babylonians called their psalms *ershemma*, meaning "songs with the accompaniment of flutes." As mentioned before, the accompaniment for ritual songs was entrusted to the sacred drum, *balag* (in Syriac *pelagga*), and to the kettle-drum, *lilis* (in Babylonian *lilissu*). Other accompanying instruments were the straight flute (*ti-gi*), the four-squared tabret (*a-dap*), the Syrian reed-pipe (*imbubu* or *malilu*), the "curved" pipe (*pitu*), and the "covered" pipe (*kitmu*), the last one preferred by women. Lovesongs were accompanied by the ten-stringed harp (*eshirtu*).

Each one of the "liturgies" contained in the stone-slab represented a "series" (*ish-kar*, in Assyrian *ish-karatu*), and each series had several songs (*zammaru*), some of them only a few, but some up to twenty-five.[14]

Besides the numerous liturgical songs of this catalogue, the songs are particularly revealing and afford us an insight into the secular music of Babylonia. Among them are, for instance, royal hymns: *12 za-mar shaari ak-ka-du-ú* (12 songs of the king in Semitic). Among the other royal hymns there are five solemn songs in honor of Ishtar, the goddess of love and temple prostitution.

Some of the "series" have the indication *maru mara imni*, "the son told it to the son." These are proverbs of wisdom, such as are found in the literature of Egypt, and later in that of the Hebrews. This indication is highly revealing, showing that the literary products of those times were transmitted orally from one generation to the other.

Furthermore, there are "series" for skilled workmen, evidently for artisans who did not work exclusively for the priestly class, also songs for shepherds (*zammaru*), as well as other types of melodies, sung at country festivals, which were supposed to exert a beneficial influence on the crops.[15]

Several of these "series" contain love-songs, *mur-ta-me*. In some of them the girl addresses her beloved one, *maru*. Number 45 of these inscriptions says:

23 *iratu e-shir Akkad[ki]*. 23 songs of the breast [i.e., love-songs] for the instrument [of strings], in Semitic.

Number 47 of the titles indicates: *24 iratu sha ib-bu-bu*, "24 songs of the breast for the flute." Below each of the "sections" is named the instrument that had to accompany the recitation. In the preserved part of the slab only *tegú* (flute) and *adapa* (drum) are mentioned.

The four columns of the *verso* contain titles of prayers for private sacred services, as well as titles of folksongs and ballads.

We have to be thankful that at least the titles of the various songs for the feasts, for the reed-flute, for the youth, and of the other ballads (all in Semitic) have been preserved.

The main importance of this catalogue consists in the fact that, as formerly in Sumeria, so in Babylonia, the difference between public and private worship was distinctly emphasized. We learn also that psalms of repentance in private worship were accompanied by instruments. These psalms and hymns constitute an official canon, so to speak, proving that they were adopted from the sacred temple ritual of the Sumerians.

This catalogue also contains a list of numerous popular ballads in Akkadian (Semitic). Even if none of the texts has been preserved, the mere listing of the titles is of great value for our knowledge of the music of Babylonia.

The epic poems of Babylonian literature express deep sorrow about the fleeting nature and mortality of man. This is evident in the ancient songs of lament, which were performed every year at the festival of Tammuz (the Adonis of the Babylonians) "with flutes of crystal" (*imbubu*) and "heavy" stringed instruments, that is, "with harps" adorned with precious stones.[16]

The Babylonian language had the peculiarity of naming the instruments according to the number of their strings, or, if these were flute-like instruments, according to the number of the fingerholes. An instrument with six strings would accordingly be called the instrument "of the six," one with three tones or three strings would be called *shushan*, the Babylonian term for "a third." LANGDON thinks that this word derives from the Sumerian *shush*, "one sixth," which, together with the Semitic dual ending *an*, would stand for the word *shushan*, "two sixths," or "one third."[17]

After this philological motivation, LANGDON leaves reality to pass over into the domain of surmise. He believes that a wind-instrument with three tones might have been the flute with three holes in form of an ox-head, found in Babylonian excavations, and that this instrument may be identical with the *shushan* (Illus. 46). He sees a further proof of this assumption in the fact that this instrument, if one blows into it, produces the three tones of a C-major triad, and goes so far as to call it "the instrument of the thirds." There is no need to prove that intervals of thirds, in the Occidental sense, much less harmonies in triads, were unknown notions in Antiquity. Thus, LANGDON's hypothesis cannot be maintained.

One thing becomes evident from LANGDON's otherwise highly meritorious scholarly work, namely, that it is not possible to investigate Oriental music using the principles of our Western musical practice. The Orient has its own conceptions and aesthetics of musical art which—just as in Antiquity—are still valid in our days.

The examination of Babylonian music would be incomplete without referring to the Biblical account, found in the Book of Daniel, about the music at NEBUCHADREZZAR's court. The monarch's orchestra is mentioned there four times (verses 3:5, 7, 10, 15), giving even the exact composition of it.[18] We read in Daniel:

> At what time ye hear the sound of the horn, pipe, harp, trigon, psaltery, bagpipe, and all kinds of music, ye fall down and worship the golden image that Nebuchadrezzar the king hath set up.
> [The original words in Daniel are: *karna, mashrokita, kathros, sambyke, pesanterin*, and *sumponyah*].

In scrutinizing these Biblical terms we must refer first to the fact that the Book of Daniel was written about 165 B.C.E., and that it describes events that took place four hundred years earlier; consequently it has a highly legendary character.[19] It would be better to call this book a "romance" or "novel" of the second century. This was the Hellenistic period of Jewish history, therefore the names of the instruments mentioned are strongly influenced by Greek terms. Furthermore, the author of the book reports an occurrence, real or imaginary (the consecration of a pagan deity), which, by its nature, must have been repugnant to the Jews. For this reason the author has evidently chosen instruments that—if they were really used in NEBUCHADREZZAR's orchestra—were foreign to Jewish musical practice and consequently must have appeared "exotic" to Jewish readers.

Biblical exegetes as well as musicologists tried to identify these terms in the most diversified ways and considered them mainly as transformed names of Greek instruments. For some of them (*karna, sumponyah, pesanterin*) this would be possible, for others (*sambyke, mashrokita*) this would not be applicable. Rather it must be assumed that *all* the names represent real or invented *un*-Jewish instruments, thus stressing the foreign character of this court orchestra and the pagan occurrence.

NEBUCHADREZZAR's orchestra is mentioned in another place in the rabbinical literature, this time without mentioning the names of the single instruments. This passage does not say anything that is different from Daniel.[20]

In addition, the Book of Daniel relates the fantastic story about NEBUCHADREZZAR's madness, his acting like a beast, eating grass, and crawling on all fours, during which time the records of the state kept complete silence about him. Allegedly the condition of the king improved after several years, after he had "recognized" the God of the Jews, an obvious pietistic tendency of the book's author. The king's son, BELSHAZZAR, met an early end, and scarcely thirty years after NEBUCHADREZZAR's death (562 B.C.E.) the Babylonian empire fell to pieces. With the ascending star of Assyria, a new chapter in the history of Mesopotamia and the nations that lived there, as well as of their musical culture, starts. It is significant, however, that by these subversions, the music of Sumeria and Babylonia scarcely was subjected to any revolutionary changes, as will be shown presently.

With regard to music instruction in Sumeria, we have precise statements that were just as valid for Babylonia.

As in Sumeria, the neophytes of the priests were educated in special schools. Each of the great temples had such a school affiliated with it. The temples possessed rich libraries, which served as fountainheads of knowledge for the students. The functions of the priests were hereditary; there were entire priestly dynasties, which had a decisive influence not only in the cult, but also in political life.

As in Sumeria, there are no direct records about a musical system in Babylonia. It is not inconceivable, however, that the Babylonians tried to apply a device of notation, at least to guide the intonation of the singers. Where the verse in poetry had such elementary requirements as in Babylonia, where the partition of the verses is so strictly applied, where it is combined so artfully into stanzas, it is possible that there were probably some rules for the performance itself; the instruments might have underscored the rhythm of the declamation, stressed the acclamations, and filled in the pauses.[21]

The music of Babylonia might have strongly influenced that of the Hebrews, especially in the Second Commonwealth. For half a century, the Jews were captives in Babylonia (585–538 B.C.E.). When NEBUCHADREZZAR conquered Judaea and destroyed Solomon's temple, he carried the flower of the nation, all working men with their wives and children, to Babylonia. There, the exiled lived at the beginning—according to Oriental custom—as slaves. Their situation improved, however, gradually, so that they could adapt themselves to the Babylonian civilization and could even acquire some wealth. The complaint of the psalmist (Ps. 137) expresses the feelings of the old generation, for whom the remembrance of the lost homeland was too immediate and too acute.

It was a lucky circumstance for the exiled Jews that they were not hindered in the exercise of their religion (they had a powerful moral help in the prophet Ezekiel). They were allowed to settle in a specially selected territory, so they were able to preserve not only their religion, but also their ethnic unity. They multiplied, and their economic situation improved to such a degree that, when they returned to their homeland after half a century, their number was 42,360 and, in addition, 7,337 male and female servants. If their fate had been really as hard as the psalmist suggests, it would not have been possible for them to keep so many servants. Also, these returning immigrants represented only one part of Babylonian Jewry.

The people of Israel, deported by NEBUCHADREZZAR, carried with them for the long journey many useful utensils, such as tents, water-bottles, agronomical implements, and probably also music instruments. Thus, the practice of music, perhaps after only a short interruption, continued vigorously in captivity, as we gather from the biblical report (Neh. 7:67). The Hebrews must have used either Babylonian instruments, or must have built, using old or newer models, their own instruments. These may have been brought to Israel after their return. No doubt, the first instruments used in the newly built sanctuary were those which the Jews used in Babylonia. In this way, and not through Abraham and his clan, the Sumerian-Babylonian music came to the Hebrews, at least in its external features, which included responsorial singing, singing of psalms and lamentations, and so on.

Partly the dialogue form, and partly the strophic structure of the Babylonian-Assyrian psalms of repentance and religious hymns strongly suggest that they were performed by one or by several half-choirs, or by a priest (precentor) and the responding choir antiphonally.

A specific feature of Babylonian poetry was the *parallelismus membrorum,* evidently taken over by the Hebrew poets. This parallelism is manifest in Babylonia among others in the magic chants of the seven spirits, "which bring all possible misfortune to humanity."[22]

I have discussed above the drama-like presentations in Egypt. In Babylonia there are records of similar performances. At the annual festivals, especially on New Year's day, there were solemn processions coupled with scenic presentations. In the temples, such events of the sacred legends were represented as the goat feeding the child TAMMUZ and the infant KINGIRSU. The deeds and the battles of the gods against the powers of chaos, as they were presented in the epics, took place in scenic form in daylight performances in the courts of the temples.

Similarly, the nuptial celebration of TAMMUZ, as well as his death and resurrection, were presented with pantomimic evolutions of the participating choirs.

Besides the New Year's play, Nippur and Babylon staged the fight of TIAMAT; Babylon furthermore staged the archetype of the Esther legend (see below), in the focus of which stood the figures of TAMMUZ and ISHTAR, and perhaps also a play dealing with the birth of the god (a veritable "Christmas-play"). In all these performances the leading motive was the life story of the local deity.[23] Each one of the extant epical poems engenderd a mystery-play.

These religious plays, however, were not dramatic representations in the proper sense, although the Babylonian plays were far superior to the Sumerian with regard to dialogue treatment and characterization by the acting persons.[24] For the most part, they can be regarded as the forerunners of the medieval mystery-plays or moralities.

Both the psalms of repentance and the religious hymns, as well as the lamentations at the death of TAMMUZ, were sung antiphonally, a practice taken over by the Hebrews after their return from Babylonia.

In addition, the Hebrews brought back with them from Babylon the Purim festival. Originally, Purim was the perpetuation of the ancient Persian *Farwardīgān* festival, which was celebrated every year in Babylonia. The legend of Esther with its moralizing background, describing the oppression and the eventual deliverance of a freedom-loving people, must have had a strong impact upon the imagination of the Jews, languishing for liberty so intensely that they carried the foreign festival with them to their old homeland.

The generally accepted justification for the incorporation of the Purim legend into the Jewish canon and calendar as the Book of Esther is the fact that the tale, despite its purely legendary character, was earnestly believed by the Jews to be a historical narrative.

The sources of the Esther story are derived unquestionably from the Babylonian mythology, as the names of the principal characters prove. Mordechai is Marduk, Esther is Ishtar, both being the names of the supreme god and goddess of the Babylonian pantheon. Haman is identical with Hamman (or Humman), the supreme god of the Elamites, whose capital city Susa (or Shushan) is the scene of the Esther story. Even Vashti is the slightly misspelled name of an Elamite deity, originally called Mashti.

Mordechai is not even a proper name, but a term denoting worshippers of Marduk, as evidenced by the Greek term in 2 Macc. 15:36: "the day of the worshippers of Marduk."[25]

About the Purim festival more will be said later. Here it was indicated only to refer to one of the permanent influences of the Babylonian sojourn upon the music practice of the Israelites.

PLUTARCH mentions the interrelation between the music of the Babylonians and their conception of nature. He states that the Babylonians equated the relation between spring and fall with the interval of a fourth, between spring and winter with the fifth, and between spring and summer with the octave. It is well known that the Greeks were the first to establish precise terms for the musical intervals. It is highly questionable, however, that the Babylonians used the intervallic names according to the Greek music theory, and even less that they characterized the relationship of the seasons by using the names of Greek intervals. PLUTARCH's statement might be due to the tendency to attribute the Greek conception of nature retrospectively to other peoples.

It might be a mere coincidence that the Chinese used the same system of interrelation for the seasons. It is difficult to establish beyond doubt who borrowed from whom. Certainly the Chinese culture is much older than that of the Greeks or the Babylonians. It is conceivable that the Babylonians, in the usual cultural exchange between the peoples of the Orient, may have taken over this notion from the Chinese and thus it passed in this way to the Hellenes.

Viewed in a historical perspective, the musical practice of the Babylonians was the almost literal continuation of that of Sumeria. History shows that it is sometimes the weaker and conquered land whose culture is taken over by the conqueror. Rarely, however, have the victors adopted the civilization of a conquered nation so completely as the Babylonians did. The fate of Sumeria was sealed when easy life, luxury, and debauchery undermined the power of resistance of the people. The civilization of Sumeria dropped like a ripe fruit into the lap of a powerful adversary. It must have been relatively easy for the belligerent Chaldaeans to conquer and subdue the weakened country of Sumeria.

Although the erstwhile mighty Babylonian empire itself fell into pieces, its civilization continued almost intact through its adoption by the Assyrians. In this roundabout way, the Greeks, and after them the Romans, took over the organization of city life, the basic knowledge of mathematics, of astronomy, of medicine, of archaeology, of historiography. The Greek terms for metals, for constellations, for weights and measures, and for musical instruments, are translations, sometimes simply phonetic adaptations, of Babylonian words. In Babylonia are found the origins of those fascinating legends which, passing through Jewish spirituality, became the basis of Christianity and, eventually, of European civilization.

NOTES

1. C. W. Harris, *The Hebrew Heritage* (New York, 1935), p. 71.
2. *SchneidKult*, p. 6.
3. Carl Bezold, *Ninive und Babylon* (Bielefeld and Leipzig, 1926), p. 148.
4. *LangdLit*, p. XXXI.
5. *Ibid.*, p. IX.
6. *Ibid.*, p. XIX
7. *Ibid.*, p. XXXI.
8. Alfred Jeremias, *Handbuch der altorientalischen Geisteskultur* (Leipzig, 1913), p. 285.
9. *Ibid.*
10. *Ibid.*, p. 286.
11. The texts are published in Erich Ebeling, *Religiöse Keilinschriften aus Assur* (Leipzig, 1918), no. 158.
12. *LangdLit*, p. 169.
13. *Ibid.*, p. 187 ff.
14. *Ibid.*, p. 170.
15. Konrad Neefe, "Die Tomkunst der Babylonier und Assyrer," in *Monatshefte für Musikgeschichte* 22 (1890):9.
16. *Ibid.*, p. 10.
17. *LangdLit*, p. 180 ff.
18. Nebuchadrezzar's orchestra has been examined in several musicological works, but interpreted in a biased way.

19. The original language of one part of the Book of Daniel is Aramaic (2:4 to 7:28). This part was later translated into Biblical Hebrew.

20. Midrash, *Canticum* VII:9.

21. See Galpin's and Sachs's attempts to decipher certain "musical signs" in a Babylonian hymn (p. 22).

22. K. Neefe, p. 6.

23. *SchneidKult*, p. 653.

24. *SchneidHistory*, p. 167.

25. Julius Lewy, "The Feast of the 14th Day of Adar," HUCA, 14 (1939): 150.

Illus. 41 A terra-cotta figurine, from the last century B.C.E., showing a Syrian piper singing and playing. In the manner of itinerant minstrels he combines several activities. An inch under his singing mouth he is holding a pan-pipe; its long canes are connected with a bag that communicates by a flexible tube with a bellows worked by the man's right foot and compressed by his arm. The singer obviously plays his pan-pipe only between the verses, as singing excludes blowing. While singing, he seems to work the bellows and produce a drone on one of the bass canes. Another man, seemingly a dwarf (or a child), plays the cymbals. (After Hans Hickmann, *Musikgeschichte in Bildern*, Leipzig, 1961. Illus. 58.)

Illus. 42 Musicians from Gudea's epoch (2050–1950 B.C.E.). Sacrificial act with musical accompaniment, showing a harp with eleven strings. Old-Babylonian fragment found at Lagash. Musée du Louvre. (After Fritz Hommel, *Geschichte Babyloniens und Assyriens,* Berlin, 1885–1888.)

Illus. 43 Babylonian harp. (After Julius Wellhausen, *The Book of Psalms,* New York, 1898.)

Illus. 44 Babylonian minstrel playing a long-necked lute, with a raptured listener. Found at Sandchirli. Time of the Mitanni. Musée du Louvre. (After Alfred Jeremias, *Handbuch der altorientalischen Geisteskultur,* Leipzig, 1913.)

Illus. 45 Hittite lutanist from Eyuk. The carving represents a lute-player with a monkey. The pendant objects are ribbons of the animal, or of the instrument. (After *Zeitschrift für Musikwissenschaft,* I, 1918.)

Illus. 46 Instrument in the shape of an ox-head. Found at Birs Nimrud, Babylonia. In the Royal Asiatic Society, London. (After Carl Engel, *The Music of the Most Ancient Nations,* London, 1864.)

Illus. 47 Babylonian lyre (ca. 1700 B.C.E.). Im Vorderasiatischen Museum, Berlin. (After Friedrich Behn, *Musikleben im Altertum. . . ,* Stuttgart, 1954.)

Illus. 48 Rock-relief found at Kul-i-Fira, representing an Elamite orchestra. (After G. Hüsing, *Der Zagros und seine Völker. Der Alte Orient,* vol. IX, 1908.)

Illus. 49 Boxing match in Babylonia, accompanied by a kettledrum and by cymbals. (After *Revue d'Assyriologie,* IX, 1912.)

Illus. 50 Big drum on a stone relief from Gudea's times. (After *Revue d'Assyriologie*, IX, 1912.)

Illus. 51 Hittite bronze figurines, showing musicians playing the pipe and hand-drum. Im Vorderasiatisches Museum in Berlin, and Römisch-Germanisches Museum in Mainz. (After Friedrich Behn, *Musikleben im Altertum . . . ,* Stuttgart, 1954.)

Illus. 52 Woman lute-player on a Babylonian stone-relief. Museum of Arts, Philadelphia. (After *Zeitschrift für Musikwissenschaft*, I, 1918.)

4

Assyria

It was the fate of Babylonia that, while the prosperity of the country increased, the morals of the population declined more and more. To the north of the state a new, aggressive people, the Assyrians, had risen. Perpetually menaced by hostile tribes, the Assyrians had developed a warlike existence and an austere form of living. With their power, their covetousness increased, until they conquered city after city in Elam, Akkad, and Babylonia.

To their capital city, and later to their entire realm, they gave the name of the god ASHUR. In time they founded a second capital city in the cooler regions of the country and called it Nineveh, after NINA, the goddess of fertility, who replaced ISHTAR of the Babylonians. In the bloom of its existence, Nineveh had 300,000 inhabitants. From there, the Assyrians ruled the numerous provinces and peoples that they had conquered and enslaved.

The nations that comprised Assyria were thus a conglomerate consisting of the civilized South (Babylonia and Akkad) as well as non-Semitic tribes (the Hittites and Mitannians), and Kurdic mountain-dwellers from the Caucasus. The Assyrians adopted the language and the spiritual achievements of the Babylonians, but repudiated the effeminate mores of the conquered country. They were a rapacious warrior-people and retained this character until subdued by an even more powerful adversary.

It is not surprising that such a mixture of heterogeneous ethnic elements did not develop a musical culture of its own. The Assyrians simply adopted the music of the conquered Babylonia, as Babylonia had previously the music of Sumeria. DURANT describes aptly this mutual give-and-take of the civilizations in the Mesopotamian basin:

> Sumeria was to Babylonia, and Babylonia to Assyria, what Crete was to Greece, and Greece to Rome; the first created a civilization, the second developed it to its height, the third inherited it, and transmitted it as a dying gift to encompassing and victorious barbarians.[1]

The Assyrians were greatly feared because of the cruelty with which they treated the subjugated peoples, their war prisoners, and especially the rulers of the conquered countries. Human life was cheap, and cruel treatment of defeated enemies was customary in the entire Orient of Antiquity. They considered harshness and brutality necessary to put down rebellions and firmly hold together the heterogeneous peoples, from Ethiopia to Armenia, from Syria to Media.

Under such circumstances, it was a small miracle that the Assyrians could develop a civilization of their own. Their building activity was rightly famous in Antiquity. The recently discovered aqueduct of about fifty kilometers built by SENNAHERIB to bring water to the city of Nineveh is the most ancient of known artificial means of supplying and storing water. One of the cruelest rulers of Assyria, ASHUR-IDANNI-PAL (known to the Greeks as SARDANAPALUS), was an avid sponsor of sciences and arts. He invited architects and sculptors from all parts of his realm to build and adorn new temples and palaces. He employed hosts of scribes to copy books for his library in Nineveh, which contained the most important literary works of Sumeria and Babylonia. These were recently discovered almost undamaged after two and a half millennia. Among these treasures was the outstanding literary product of Mesopotamian culture, the Gilgamesh epics, notated on twelve clay tablets.

It is therefore not surprising that despite the rough warrior-like life of the Assyrians, the music of Sumeria and Babylonia was saved and flourished as before. The preserved pictorial documents show the same types of instruments as were found in Babylonia: the horizontal and vertical angular harp, various species of lyres, the double-oboe (an instrument common to all peoples of the Near East), as well as drums, cymbals, sistra, and other shaking and percussive instruments (Illus. 51–63). "Love songs" (there were some even in this rough warrior country!) were accompanied by an instrument with "ten strings."

Everything else that we know about the music of Babylonia applies, with perhaps some minor changes, to Assyria.

The musico-archaeological discoveries relating to Babylonia's music have been dealt with in the preceding chapter. The Assyrians also left us numerous pictorial documents, affording a good insight into the music practice of this nation. They show representations of semi-ritual or secular festivities, for instance, sacrifices with musical accompaniment after hunting,[2] especially after lion-hunts[3] (Illus. 64). Such musical scenes are presented mostly as using harp-like instruments. In a picture from the palace of ASHUR-IDANNI-PAL, we see masked dancers and lutanists, playing long-necked lutes. In an Assyrian war-camp the soldiers are entertained with music.[4] A picture shows prisoners of war (probably Semites) playing identical harp-like instruments, guarded by an Assyrian warrior (Illus. 65).[5]

A beautiful bas-relief from the royal palace at Nineveh depicts an idyllic "garden party." It shows King ASHUR-IDANNI-PAL with his Queen and with his retinue at a merry banquet, free from the duties of the state. The illustrious party is entertained by a harp-player (Illus. 67).

Even if we take into consideration the morals and the mentality of the ancient Orient, in which barbarism and cruelty were common features of war and conquest, it is difficult for us today to understand that in the midst of this peaceful garden entertainment the head of the king of defeated Elam was brought in and put on a high pole, to the general delight of the king's entourage, and that the party continued with music as though nothing uncommon had happened.[6]

The most important pictures illustrating musical practices are those in which the triumphal receptions with music of victorious kings are represented. In SENNAHERIB's palace, excavated in the vicinity of today's Kuyundchik, there are well-preserved bas-reliefs showing musicians and singers extolling the returning monarch. In one of these pictures, SENNAHERIB is shown on his war-chariot reviewing the prisoners after the conquest of a people characterized by an inverted Phrygian cap. In front of him there are harp-players, praising the victor. Still another bas-relief of the palace depicts the end of a victorious campaign. In the conquered capital city palm trees are cut down; this activity is accompanied by musicians playing drums and perhaps cymbals. Singing women, clapping their hands, present a welcome to the victor.

Even more pompous is the reception accorded SENNAHERIB's son, ASHUR-IDANNI-PAL (668–626 B.C.E.) by the population of Susiana, the capital city of conquered Elam (Illus. 66). This picture affords us excellent insight into the composition of an Elamite music group. Three men play harps having sixteen or more strings; two of them are marching, evidently with dance steps; one man plays the double-oboe, another plays, also with dance steps, a kind of dulcimer, an instrument consisting of a hollow box (evidently the resonance body) over which strings are applied. His right hand carries a plectrum, the left either plucks the strings or shortens them to produce different pitches. Four women play large harps, another plays the double-oboe, and another a small hand-drum fastened to her waist. The singing group shows nine boys and four women; one of them exerts with her hand a pressure to her throat, a device in the ancient, as well as today's Orient, to produce a shrill tone (Illus. 66).

The composition of this musical group, which might have been, perhaps with some modifications, the same as an Assyrian musical ensemble, affords us a picture of the general character of the music in Assyria. It shows that the instruments of percussion were of only minor importance in music, and that the main stress was on singing. The use of nine singing boys and six female voices, accompanied by seven stringed instruments, permits the conclusion that this group utilized predominantly softer tone colors. Two double-oboes complete the "orchestra." A small hand-drum and a pair of cymbals is a rather modest use of percussion instruments, in view of the fact that the group was welcoming the triumphal reception of a victorious conqueror. It can be assumed that the basic aspect of the Assyrian music, at least at its height, was of a subdued and sedate character, and revealed the same tendency that is seen similarly at the advanced stage of Egyptian and Babylonian music.

In general, Assyrian music was not much different from that of the Babylonians. In both cultures we found similar types of instruments, the horizontal as well as the vertical angular harp, various types of lyres, the double-oboe and the double-clarinet, metal trumpets, and so on. The percussion instruments of almost all the ancient Oriental peoples are basically the same: hand-drums, cymbals, sistra, and other noise-making implements.

Probably the Jewish *shofar* had its origin in the similar Assyrian instrument, made of the horn of the mountain-goat and called by them *shapparu*. The responsive singing, too, which we have already encountered in Egypt and Babylonia, survived in Assyria and was evidently taken over by the Hebrews.[7]

If we glance at the destinies of the civilizations of the Near East, it becomes evident that mighty empires rise suddenly and disappear just as suddenly, to be either continued by their successors or annihilated by them. Names of nations and their rulers succeed each other in kaleidoscopic rapidity.

There is SARGON I (2872–2817 B.C.E.), who united Sumeria and Akkad, but, after a reign of fifty-five years, left his empire in open revolt. After him, GUDEA's reign (around 2650) was distinguished less by warlike events than by its cultural achievements, such as sponsoring literature, the arts, and useful public works, a rarity in an epoch when brutal force, cruelty, and the mania for conquest reigned supreme.

For two centuries the Elamites and Amorites were masters of former Sumeria. Then, from the North, advanced HAMMURABI (2123–1081 B.C.E.), who created an empire of a type never seen before. Between 2117 and 1094 he conquered the entire Sumeria and Elam. Sumer disappeared, but its civilization survived.

After a "short" episode, lasting only six centuries (1764–1169 B.C.E.), in which the wild mountain tribe of the Kassites ruled Babylonia, SHALMANESER I succeeded, in 1276, in again uniting Assyria.

The greatest name, however, in the history of Assyria was that of TIGLATH-PILESER I (1115–1102), who proceeded with uncommon energy and cruelty in order to procure for Assyria the leading role in the Near East. All that happened after him, under his son SENNAHERIB (705–681) and his grandson, ASHUR-IDANNI-PAL (669–626 B.C.E.), was more or less of an anticlimax.

Fourteen years after ASHUR-IDANNI-PAL's death, the Babylonian king NABO-PALASSAR (ca. 625–584 B.C.E.), together with an army of Media, led by CYAXARES (650–584), and with the help of wild Scythian warriors from the Caucasus, invaded Assyria, and conquered with surprisingly little resistance all the citadels of the country. Nineveh was destroyed and went up in flames; the inhabitants were either slain or carried away as slaves. The palace of ASHUR-IDANNI-PAL was sacked and annihilated. With one mighty stroke, Assyria disappeared from world history.[8]

It is a miracle that in all these convulsions the music, created by the talented people of the Sumerians, has been kept alive. This lucky circumstance is less the merit of the great powers who continued the music practice of the Sumerians, than that of the Hebrews who, in due time, took over the most essential elements of the Sumerian music, and transmitted them to posterity.

In the music of the Hebrews, the last vestiges of Babylonian-Assyrian music have survived, but strongly modified by the spirit of the Hebrew civilization, which became manifest soon after the conquest of Cana'an. In their new home, the Hebrews succeeded in giving their music its own character, its specific ethos.

From this stage of history on, we cannot speak of Babylonian-Assyrian music. It perished, never again to be revived, just as the once-mighty empires of Babylonia and Assyria disappeared from the annals of human civilization.

NOTES

1. Durant, 1:265.
2. A. Jeremias, p. 103.
3. *Ibid.*
4. *Ibid.*
5. *Ibid.*
6. Durant, 1:269. For further edifying details about the treatment of conquered peoples by the victors, see Jeremias, pp. 271–73.
7. *SachsRise*, p. 95.
8. Durant, 1:283.

Illus. 53 Assyrian lyre. (After Julius Wellhausen, *The Book of Psalms*, New York, 1898.)

Illus. 54 Assyrian harpist. (After Julius Wellhausen, *The Book of Psalms*, New York, 1898.)

Illus. 55 Assyrian long-necked lute. (After Julius Wellhausen, *The Book of Psalms*, New York, 1898.)

Illus. 56 Assyrian double-oboe in conical form. (After Julius Wellhausen, *The Book of Psalms,* New York, 1898.)

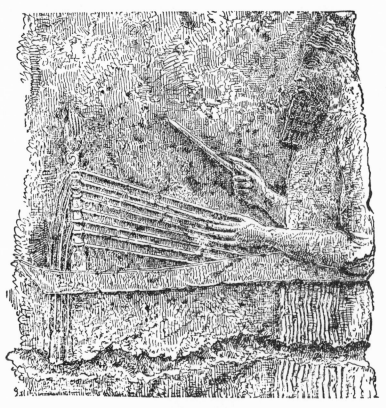

Illus. 57 Assyrian dulcimer-player. Stone-relief (ca. seventh century B.C.E.). British Museum. (After Sir John Stainer, *The Music of the Bible,* London, 1914.)

Illus. 58 Assyrian cymbal-player. (After Carl Engel, *The Music of the Most Ancient Nations*, London, 1864.)

Illus. 59 Assyrian hand-drum. (After Sir John Stainer, *The Music of the Bible*, London, 1914.)

Illus. 60 Assyrian musicians playing dulcimers with sticks. Bas-relief found in Kuyundchik. (After Carl Bezold, *Ninive und Babylon*, Bielefeld and Leipzig, 1926.)

Illus. 61 Assyrian quartet. Bas-relief found at Kuyundchik. Two musicians play lyres of different shapes, a third beats a hand-drum, a fourth cymbals. (After Julius Wellhausen, *The Book of Psalms,* New York, 1898.)

Illus. 62 Assyrian musicians on a stone-relief found at Sandchirli. (After Luschan, *Sendchirli,* 1893–1911.)

Illus. 63 Assyrian quartet. Two harps, a double-oboe, and a dulcimer. The players are apparently dancing. (After F. W. Galpin, *The Music of the Sumerians . . . ,* Cambridge, 1937.)

Illus. 64 Sacrifices after hunting, with musical accompaniment. (After Alfred Jeremias, *Handbuch der altorientalischen Geisteskultur,* Leipzig, 1913.)

Illus. 65 Semitic captives (probably Israelites) playing lyres under the eye of an Assyrian guard. (After Julius Wellhausen, *The Book of Psalms*, New York, 1898.)

Illus. 66 Reception of the victorious Ashur-Idanni-Pal by an Elamite group of musicians and singers. (After Carl Engel, *The Music of the Most Ancient Nations*, London, 1864.)

Illus. 67 "Garden party." Ashur-Idanni-Pal with his Queen at a joyous feast with musical entertainment. Marble relief found at Kuyundchik. British Museum. (After Carl Bezold, *Ninive und Babylon*, Bielefeld and Leipzig, 1926.)

5

Chaldaea

A country mentioned repeatedly in the Bible is that of the Chaldaeans (')erez kasdim). It is necessary to correct a misconception about this country, which has generally been identified with Babylonia. This is, however, erroneous, historically, geographically, and ethnographically. The Chaldaeans were of Indo-European origin, whereas the Babylonians were Semites.[1] The Chaldaeans were bellicose and eager for conquest; they first captured certain parts of Sumeria and subsequently adopted the civilization of the conquered nation. They spread out over the entire southern part of Mesopotamia bordering the Persian Gulf; their ancient capital city was Bit Yakin. From there they first subdued Babylonia (ca. 1300 B.C.E.), and later, after the collapse of Syria, established the Greater Babylonian Empire, *mat kaldu*, which included Babylonia, Assyria, and several other smaller countries, such as Pekod, Sho'a, and Ko'a (Ezek. 23:23).

Other historians think, however, that the *kaldi* were Aramaeans, i.e., Semites.[2] Against this, the view may be cited that the Babylonian king SENNAḤERIB (705–681 B.C.E.) always made a clear distinction between the *kaldi* on the one hand, and the Arabians and Aramaeans on the other.[3] This seems to indicate that the *kaldi* must have belonged to another race. The Bible, too, for the most part, uses different terms for the Babylonians (*benē Babel*) and the Chaldaeans (*kasdim*), an indication that they were considered different peoples (*cf.* Ezek. 23:23; 50:8; 50:24,25; 50:35; 51:24; 51:33, and other places.)

With regard to the history of Jewish music, the land of the Chaldaeans has only a secondary and accessory significance. The obvious resemblances between the music of Sumeria and that of the Hebrews seem to have created the impression that the Israelites might have taken over their music from the Sumerians. This assumption overlooks, however, the considerable time difference between the decline of the Sumerian empire and the beginning of Jewish national existence. In spite of all the similarities, there is scarcely any room for such a hypothesis.

How did this idea originate?

The Bible tells us that Abraham's home town was the Sumerian-Chaldaean city of 'Ur. From there, his father Terah planned to emigrate to Cana'an with his sons and grandson Lot, whose father died at an early age. Terah, however, settled at Haran in the northwest of Mesopotamia, so that henceforth this town was regarded as the domicile of his tribe (Gen. 11:31). Abraham, his wife Sarah, and his nephew Lot continued the journey to Cana'an. Soon after they settled in the already heavily populated country, Abraham and Lot separated by mutual agreement, because there was not sufficient pasturage for their numerous flocks. Abraham took residence at Hebron, where he led a nomadic life. According to the Biblical chronicler, he had all in all 318 servants, "born in his house, all trained men" (Gen. 14:14).

Even if we were to assume that some of these "trained men" sang or played instruments, it is unlikely that a single, relatively small, group of men could have transplanted from one country to another all the ramifications of a complex musical practice. This would scarcely have been possible for a clan, or even an entire tribe. It is rather safe to assume that the music of the Sumerians entered Israel in a roundabout way, namely by the continuous cultural intercourse that took place between the nations of the Near East.

The similarities in musical practice of the Sumerians and the Israelites, so widely separated in point of time, can be explained for the most part by the fact that the ethos of their music, in its "emotional connotation," was very similar.

In the historical period of the Babylonian–Assyrian empire, the Chaldaean dynasty had a rather short existence, lasting scarcely one century. It was preceded by the mighty Assyrian hegemony (ca. 1270–606 B.C.E.), and succeeded by the reign of the Achmenides (538–331 B.C.E.). In the Chaldaean period one of the most fateful events of Jewish history took place, the destruction of Solomon's temple by NEBUCHADREZZAR, and the deportation of the Jewish people to Babylonia. The Biblical authors have ascribed this tragedy to the Chaldaean dynasty and, consequently, identified Chaldaea with Babylonia.

)Erez kasdim is mentioned frequently in the Bible (Gen. 11:28,31; Jer. 24:5; 25:12; 50:8,10; 51:24; Ezek. 23:23, etc.). The term, in the Biblical text mostly refers to Babylonia. This is correct only insofar as the Chaldaeans lived in a territory that later belonged to Greater-Babylonia.

After the conquest of the Sumerian empire by the *kaldi*, the bellicose customs of the new masters were softened by the higher civilization of the conquered. Apart from the general culture, the Chaldaeans also adopted the musical tradition of Sumeria which, in due course, was transmitted to the Babylonians. In this way, the music of Sumeria, in a roundabout way, might have reached Judaea.

NOTES

1. *RiehmHandw,* 1:223.
2. Hastings, *A Dictionary of the Bible* (New York, 1890–1904) 1:368.
3. *Ibid.*

Illus. 68 Musicians on a Phoenician bowl from Cyprus. British Museum. (After Cesnola, *Cypern*, 1881.)

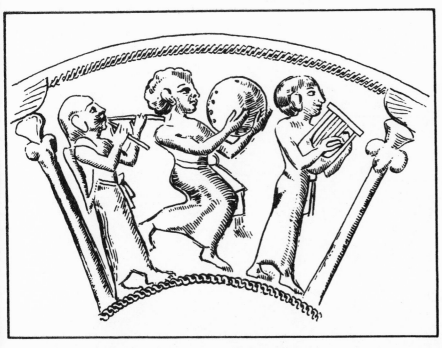

Illus. 69 Musicians on a Phoenician bowl from Olympia. British Museum. (After Curtius-Adler, *Olympia*, vol. IV.)

Illus. 70 Fragment of a Phoenician ivory found at Preneste, showing musicians playing a xylophone, hand-drum, and double-oboe. (After Poulson, *Der Orient und die frühgeschichtliche Kunst,* 1912.)

Illus. 71 Probably Hittite musicians, playing a long-necked lute, double-oboe, and clappers. (After Max Wegner, *Musikinstrumente des Alten Orients,* Münster i.W., 1950.)

6

Phoenicia

The geographic location of Phoenicia and the cultural intercourse carried on for centuries with its neighboring nations determined the civilization of this people, famous in Antiquity for its trading and colonizing activities.

The evaluation of the civilizing role the Phoenicians played in Antiquity has recently undergone some changes. While formerly historiography attributed to them a paramount importance in the civilization of the Mediterranean basin, modern science is challenging this opinion. The pendulum now swings to the other extreme, denying them creative capacities in almost all domains of intellectual life, maintaining that their cultural achievements had been taken over exclusively from other peoples. To a certain extent this would be understandable, considering the centuries-old commercial ties the Phoenicians entertained with the entire civilized world of the Antiquity. The truth seems to lie between these two extremes, since in certain fields (e.g., architecture, sculpture, handicrafts, etc.), the Phoenicians proved to be such accomplished masters that their creative talents cannot be questioned. This is particularly true in the domain of architecture.

We know from the Bible that, toward the end of David's reign, HIRAM I, King of Tyre (980–947 B.C.E.) built for the Jewish monarch a splendid palace of precious cedar-wood (2 Sam. 5:11). Furthermore, David planned to erect, with the assistance of HIRAM, a magnificent temple that would replace the modest tabernacle built by Jewish hands (2 Sam. 7:1–2).

David's project did not materialize before Solomon's accession to the throne (1 Kings 5:15 ff). HIRAM sent to his friend, "to the tyrant of Jerusalem," as the historian DIO calls him,[1] his most skilled carpenters and craftsmen, together with all the necessary material, and thus one of the marvels of Antiquity, the temple of Solomon, was erected by Phoenician artisans,

> skilful to work in gold, and in silver, in brass, in iron, in stone, and in timber, in purple, in blue, and in fine linen, and in crimson; also to grave any manner of graving, and to devise any device; to do whatever may be set before him (2 Chron. 2:13).

The Second Temple, too, was built, after the return from the Babylonian exile, by stone-masons, carpenters, and craftsmen from Sidon and Tyre (Ezra 3:7).

Thus, Biblical, and other sources attest to the proficiency in architecture and to the skill in arts and crafts of the Phoenicians. As to their music, however, we have no more than conjectures, because historical records in this field are few and highly contradictory.

In view of the close cultural intercourse with the Egyptians, and especially owing to the fact that for several centuries Phoenicia was occupied by Egyptian rulers, we might assume that the Phoenicians derived their musical culture mainly from Egypt. The Egyptian civilization was much older than that of the Phoenicians; this alone would presuppose the influence of Egyptian music upon that of the Phoenicians. Even the statement of the priests of Baal-Melkart, patron of Tyre, according to which their temple had existed for 2300 years,[2] would not contradict this assumption. Yet, the music of the Phoenicians might also have been influenced by their immediate neighbors, the Assyrians.

As for their instruments, the lyre (*kinnor*), considered by many to have been a Phoenician "invention," was likely to have had as its model a similar Egyptian instrument (*k•nn•r*). Much more credit is due to the statement of SOPATROS,[3] that the *nabla*, another much used stringed instrument of the Phoenicians, had been invented by the Sidonians and was called, therefore, *sidonion nabla*. Among other popular instruments in Phoenicia, IOUBA mentions the *lyrophonikos* and the small triangular harp, the *trigōnon* (called also *epigoneion*).[4] JULIUS POLLUX, in enumerating the instruments of his time, mentions two stringed instruments, the names of which are indications of their Phoenician origin: the *phoinix* and the *lyrophoinikos*. He gives, however, no further description of them.[5]

Especially relevant is the predominance of musical elements in the mythology of the Phoenicians. The mythical hero and king Kinnyras and his daughters the Kinnyrades, who ministered at the temple of the Phoenician Ashera (called Mylitta) in Cyprus, received their names, by hypostasis, from the *kinnor*. According to the legend, Kinnyras built the temple in Aphaca at the Lebanon, in which the orgiastic spring fire-festival of Astarte was held (see below).[6]

Kinnyras was identical with Adonis, whose early death was mourned by yearly celebrations called "*Adonies*." The lamentations performed at these festivals were accompanied by the playing of the Phoenician-Syrian funeral instrument, the *abobas*, a kind of double-oboe. Therefore, Adonis was also called Abobas in Syria. Besides, the Phoenicians used another pipe, the span-long *gingras*, the sound of which was plaintive and penetrating. Thus, Gingras became, by hypostasis, another name for Adonis.

A being, common in the Phoenician, Egyptian, and Greek mythologies, and closely related to Adonis and the "*Adonies*," was the mysterious LINOS, whom HERODOTUS, to his amazement, discovered in the rites of Cyprus.[7] A song was named after this LINOS which, as already mentioned, was sung under different names in Egypt, Babylonia, and also in Greece. While the Egyptians named this song "*Maneros*," the Bythinians, who adopted it from Phoenician colonists, named it *adonhymaiōdos*.[8] According to Egyptian myth, LINOS (or MANEROS) was the son of the first king of Egypt, whose premature death was mourned with dirges by the people.[9] In Phoenician mythology, the same LINOS was the son of MALCANDER, king of Byblos, and the goddess ASTARTE. Thus, the mythologies of these two peoples with regard to music show some common traits.

The ethnographic, economic, and cultural interrelationships between Phoenicia and Israel might give a support to the assumption that the music of both peoples had many affinities. Such conclusions would be logical, were it not for one serious but completely insurmountable obstacle: the gap between the religious ethics of the two neighboring peoples.

The Phoenician religion was based upon the cult of Ishtar (or Astarte) and indulged in the cruel service of Moloch, in which human sacrifices had to be offered to the gods. According to ancient sources, an immaculate virgin had to be sacrificed at every important event, such as the establishment of a new colony, the founding of a new city, and the like.[10] In times of epidemics, drought, and other natural disasters

> the most cherished child of a family had to be offered to Chronos (=Moloch), after a public vote has taken place. The history of Phoenicia is filled with reports to that effect.[11]

Every year, boys of the noblest families had to be sacrificed to Moloch; later, children bought and specially fattened for this purpose were offered.[12] Once, when several parents managed to conceal their children, three hundred boys of the noblest families were sacrificed simultaneously as expiation to the gods; furthermore, three hundred others (it is not clear whether children or parents), who were under suspicion, offered themselves voluntarily in atonement.[13] PLUTARCH reports that such sacrifices took place to the accompaniment of flutes and drums,

> so that the cries of the wailing should not reach the ears of the people.[14]

One of the sacred institutions of the ASHERA cult was the innumerable hierodules maintained in the temples. These were the *kedeshot* (sing. *kedeshah*) (lit. "dedicated ones"), practicing religious prostitution in the temples. The money so earned was delivered as offerings to the goddess. The *kedeshah* also had to take care of the music and singing in the regular morning and evening sacrificial rites.[15] At the big temples, their number was 3000 to 6000 and even more. Their favorite instrument was the *ʾabub* and the *trigōnon*. Phoenician Syria provided the Near East and the Mediterranean basin with large groups of such *ʾabub*-playing girls, called in Rome *ambubajae*, who populated the streets and places of the great cities, and whose playing and singing was but the cloak for their less honorable trade.[16]

In springtime, at Hieropolis in Syria, the great fire-festival of Astarte was celebrated. At this festival, the orgiastic music of double-oboes, cymbals, and drums created among the onlookers such a delirious frenzy that young men emasculated themselves with their own hands.[17] These were the *Galles*, the servants of Astarte who, dressed in women's attire, marched in processions in the streets of the cities; they cut themselves with swords, flagellated themselves mutually until the blood gushed forth, all this in order to beg alms for the temples of the goddess. This barbarous custom of self-mutilation sometimes assumed such proportions that—according to a report of BARDESANES—the Syrian king ABGARUS had to proclaim a law that anyone who castrated himself would have his hands cut off.[18]

The comparison of these savage customs with the enlightened conceptions of the Jewish religion speaks for itself. The Israelites declared human sacrifices an "abomination" (Deut. 12:31; 18:10; 2 Kings 16:3; 17:17; 21:6; 23:10; 2 Chron. 18:3; 33:6; Jer. 7:31; 19:5; 32:35; Ezek. 16:21; Lev. 8:21; 20:2–5; 1 Kings 15:12), and severely condemned religious prostitution (Deut. 23:18,19; cf. 1 Sam. 2:22). The Mosaic law also established the strong prohibition of harlotry as a means to increase the Temple's treasury (Deut. 23:19).

Strangely enough, the music of the Phoenicians was characterized by the writers of Antiquity in a peculiar way; they based their reports solely upon the orgiastic rites of the Phoenician religion, without the silghtest hint that the

Phoenicians might have had another kind of musical art as well. Among the ancient reports, one is particularly significant, insofar as it gave rise to an entirely biased conception of the music of this people, a conception that lasted almost up to our time.

ARISTEIDES QUINTILIANUS (first to second century C.E.), in his book *De Musica*, (see below) investigated the musical practice of the peoples of the Near East of his time, and arrived at the following conclusion:

> In the realm of [musical] education there are two degenerate trends: one is the entire lack (*amousia*), and the other the wrong practice of art (*kakomousia*).

He gave examples of both phenomena among the peoples of this region; according to his statement, the second category included, among others,

> those who cultivate the sensuous instincts, who are too enervated psychically and not hardened enough physically, such as the Phoenicians and their descendants [the colonists living] along the northern coast of Lybia.[19]

LUCIAN (120–200 C.E.) gives a detailed account of the above-mentioned spring festival at Hieropolis and says:

> But the greatest of all feasts is kept in the first summer season, some call it Fire-Feast, and some Torch-Feast. . . . They cut their own arms and beat each other upon their backs and many that stand there play flutes and many beat timbrels and others sing sacred songs.[20]

This report is generally considered a confirmation of ARISTEIDES' opinion about the music of the Phoenicians. Actually, LUCIAN states merely the facts, without giving any evaluation of the music itself. Thus, the only contemporary judgment about the music of the Phoenicians is that of ARISTEIDES.

His opinion might be authentic, perhaps, for the epoch in which he lived. At that period, the mores and the art of the Phoenicians must already have shown a marked decline. Furthermore, it must be remembered that the report of ARISTEIDES concerns only a special aspect of Phoenician music. He did not elaborate upon other possible musical manifestations of this people, who gave so many irrefutable proofs of their outstanding artistic qualities in other fields, such as painting, sculpture, architecture, and handicrafts.

There are several indications that the Phoenicians, at least at the height of their civilization, might have had a nobler and more refined tonal art, than the *kakomousia* intimated by ARISTEIDES. The Phoenicians had probably taken over part of their music from the Egyptians. As we already know, Egyptian music in its classical period was solemn, sedate, and full of dignity. The music of the Assyrians, apart from its orgiastic features at religious festivals, also showed a nobler aspect on other occasions. We know, moreover, that the Lydians, whose religion contained orgiastic rites similar to those of the Phoenicians, had a more dignified music in addition to the sensuous type (see below). If we recall the cultural relationship that existed among the nations of the ancient Near East, we may assume that the artistic quality of the music of the neighboring civilizations might have exercised a definite influence upon the musical practice of the Phoenicians, a nation so obviously gifted in the arts.

There is an indirect proof for this assumption. The principal stringed instruments, *kinnor* and *nebel*, were identical among the Phoenicians and the Israelites.

We know of the highly artistic use the Hebrews made of these "sacred" instruments. It would not be unreasonable, therefore, to conclude that the Phoenicians also used these instruments in an artistic manner.

In addition, we may point out another fact, considered by CURT SACHS as a definite sign of aesthetic trends in the complex character of the Phoenicians. SACHS proved that the Spanish dance, the basic aspect of which is dignity and beauty of form, originated in Phoenicia.[21] A people that possessed such dances could not have been barbarous without some discernment in its art, but must have had nobler, aesthetically and ethically loftier spheres of artistic activity.

Finally, history provides us with clear indications that the Phoenicians were not lacking in the more refined artistic virtues. Historical records prove beyond doubt that

> the merit belongs to the Phoenicians not only for having reached even in high Antiquity a remarkable degree of civilization, but also for having preserved it longer than all the other nations with whom they had come into contact.[22]

When mighty Nineveh was a heap of ruins, and the mountain-high monument of SARDANAPALUS served merely as a finger-post for passing caravans in the desert,[23] when "Babylon the big city was but a solitude,"[24]

> Phoenicians still vied for five centuries with other civilized nations not only in sciences, but also in art.[25]

The musical culture of such a nation could not have been wholly savage or barbarous, without possessing nobler features, despite its peculiar religious rites which, incidentally, it shared with many peoples of the Near East. Somewhere, and somehow, the finer instincts must have come to the fore of their musical culture, in spite of the total lack of coeval records in this respect.

For want of direct and authentic source material about the music of the Phoenicians, the conclusions as expressed above are conjectures, to be sure, but they possess a high degree of probability. The analogies with the musical civilization of their immediate neighbors, especially of Israel, are the strongest supports for this assumption.

NOTES

1. Preserved in *JosApio*, I, 17, 18 ("*tôn tē tyrannounta Hierosolymon Salomona*").
2. Herodotus *Historia* II. 44.
3. *Athen*, IV, 175 c.
4. *Ibid.*, IV, 183, d,e.
5. Pollux, *Onomasticon*, IV, 59, 76. Also *Athen*, IV, 182 f.
6. Lucian, *De Syria Dea*, 9.
7. Herodotus, *Historia*, II, 79.
8. Pollux, IV, 53.
9. Herodotus, II, 79.
10. Clitarchos, *Scholia in Platonis Minoem*, in Siebenkees, *Anecdota graeca*, p. 46.
11. Porphyrius, *De Abstinentia*, II, chap. 56.
12. Diodorus, *Historia Bibliotheca*, XX, 14.
13. *Ibid.*
14. Plutarch, *De superstitione*, chap. 12, 171 d. See also J. Quasten, *Musik und Gesang in den Kulten der heidnischen Antike* (Münster, 1930), pp. 26 ff.

15. Lucian, 43.
16. For the *ambubajae* of the Roman circus see below.
17. Lucian, 51. Ovid, *Fasti*, IV, 221, 342.
18. Preserved in Eusebius, *Praeparatio evangelica*, lib. VI, chap. 10, in *PG* 13:886.
19. Aristeides, *De Musica*, lib. II, chap. 7 (ed Marcus Meibohm, Amsterdam, 1652), p. 72. See also Rudolf Schäfke, *Aristeides Quintilianus* (Berlin, 1937), pp. 262–63.
20. Lucian, 27, 50.
21. *SachsDance*, p. 98.
22. Franz Karl Movers, *Die Phönizier* (Bonn, 1841–1856), 1:6.
23. *Athen*, XII, 530 b.
24. Strabo, XVI, 1:5
25. Movers; *ibid.*

7

Phrygia and Lydia

Among the peoples of Near Eastern Antiquity, two more must be mentioned, the Phrygians and the Lydians, whose music enjoyed not only wide dissemination, but had a decisive influence upon the neighboring regions, especially on Greece.

The origin of both peoples is uncertain. We possess some legendary tales and rather unreliable historical information provided by the Hellenes. Both peoples inhabited the peninsula of Asia Minor, where, from the most ancient times on, tribes and larger groups of peoples alternated and vied for the possession of the available space. When the region became halfway consolidated, the Phrygians inhabited the northern section plus the entire southern part of the peninsula, while the Lydians settled on the Aegean coast and expanded their living space toward Anatolia in the East.

Ethnologically, the Phrygians seem to have been related to the Armenians. Both were of Indo-European origin; like the language of the Armenians, that of the Phrygians showed Iranian influence.

They were called by the Greeks *"Phrygos,"* that is, "free men," and eventually the entire nation was known by this name. As Greek tradition maintains, they migrated from Thracia and Macedonia to Asia Minor; this might explain their Indo-European idiom.

According to legendary tradition, Gordius, father of Midas (reign 738–695 b.c.e.), was the founder of the kingdom (ca. 800 b.c.e.). His capital city was Ancyra (today's Ankara). The rule of the Phrygians did not last long; soon (between 680 and 670 b.c.e.) a large part of the kingdom was invaded by the Cimbers, who held it until about 620, when the Lydians conquered the country and ruled it until the Persians subjugated them (546 b.c.e.).

Contrary to the Greek tradition, the Phrygians came from Asia, a theory that is probably closer to fact. They were bellicose and powerful enough to challenge for some time even such mighty neighbors as Egypt and Assyria for the possession of the Near East.

Their influence upon Greece manifests itself mainly in two domains: those of religion and music. Originally, they were nature-worshippers, like most of the primitive tribes of that region. After conquering Asia Minor, they adopted the religion of the ancient inhabitants, that of the cult of the "Big Mother" Ma. The residence of this goddess was supposed to be upon a mountain called Cybela; accordingly, the Phrygians named their goddess Cybele. She was worshipped with orgiastic rites and ceremonies and with a specific musical display, exerting a fascinating influence upon the neighboring peoples. She was regarded as the deity of the reproductive and rejuvenating forces of nature, and her religion was soon adopted by the surrounding nations. The Greeks had worshipped her as early as the sixth century B.C.E., and called her Demeter. Like Isis in Egypt, Ishtar in Babylonia, Demeter in Greece, and Ceres in Rome, Cybele was the goddess of fertility. The rites of all these deities were celebrated with similar orgiastic ceremonies, accompanied by a stirring musical background.

The supremacy of the Phrygians ended with the ascending new kingdom of Lydia. The Lydians were of Indo–Pelasgian origin; they owe, however, their cultural achievements to the ancient Cretic–Mycaenic civilization. Their kingdom began with the half-mythological ruler GYGES (ca. 716 B.C.E.) and ended with CROESUS (546 B.C.E.), who, in his turn, was defeated by the Persian ruler CYRUS (558–529 B.C.E.).

Because the origin of the Greek civilization goes back also to the Cretic–Mycaenic culture, the aspects of general life of Greece and Lydia must have been rather similar. When HERODOTUS traveled in Lydia, he observed customs and mores parallel to those of the mother country. At the time of STRABO (b. ca. 63 B.C.E.), the ancient language of the Lydians was completely replaced by Greek.[1]

Their prospering capital city, Sardis, was founded by King GYGES and soon developed into an important trading center, from which caravans went through Carchemish into the regions of the Euphrates as far as Susa.

Statements of Greek philosophers and historians repeatedly carry indications that the Phrygians and Lydians were the instructors of the Hellenes in the art of music. The reports suggest even the approximate time (seventh century B.C.E.) in which this musical fertilization might have occurred. According to these sources, the Greeks took over from these two nations some specific modes. This is proven by the later highly developed musical system of the Hellenes, in which (besides the more ancient Doric mode), the Phrygian and Lydian modes had a dominant role. However, it is highly questionable, as the sources intimate, that the Greeks were instructed in the playing of instruments by these two peoples. This would discard the influence of the Egyptian and Phoenician music upon Greece, two nations with which the Hellenes entertained close commercial and cultural ties. The last-named country, especially, which had an advanced musical culture, might have exerted a strong influence upon the music of the Greeks, proof of which is found in the names of the Phoenician stringed instruments, *kinnor* and *nabla*, taken over by the Hellenes. The same cross-fertilization might have occurred in the fine arts of these nations.[2]

The Lydians are credited with the "invention" of certain musical instruments. This word can be used only with caution, because the musical practice of Near-Eastern Antiquity used basically the same instruments, which were either identical or very similar to each other. SACHS has shown the mutual interrelation of the cultural trends in the Mediterranean basin (see above). The commercial and cultural exchange between the peoples living in this area showed its influence in all the domains of political and social life. Thus, the musical art, too, was determined by the cross-fertilization of the cultural trends. This would mean that the musical art in this area was, so to speak, the common property of all the peoples involved.[3] Applied to musical instruments, this included the frequent exchange of musical tools. A people who took over an instrument from another people would experiment with it and attempt more or less essential changes. Even if the basic form was left intact, something would be added here or taken away there, so that ultimately a different treatment of the instrument became necessary. The change in technique possibly transformed the character of its sound. This should be borne in mind if, as ancient records testify, we sometimes come across instruments having the same name, but serving entirely opposite purposes and being used at completely different occasions.

For instance, the pipe (oboe) was blown strongly by the Lydians; its tone, therefore, had an exciting character. This is how the instrument was used at the feast of the slain and resurrected ADONIS. The Phrygians, on the other hand, accompanied a specific dirge, the *lytiersēs*, with similar pipes which, however, were blown softly. The pipes used for such funeral dirges were called *monauloi thrēnētikoi*, "lamenting pipes."[4] Yet, among the Israelites, the pipe (*ḥalil*) was the instrument of joyous popular festivals, as well as the typical instrument for mourning, used at every funeral.[5]

Returned to their country of origin, after some more or less incisive modifications, these instruments were considered "imported" from a foreign country and called by another name. This explains the multitude of terms that the nations applied to basically the same instruments.

The music of the Lydians, too, might have come to Greece through the general cultural exchange indicated above. The "Lydian mode" encountered less enmity from the Greek philosophers and teachers, but nevertheless was not considered apt for the education of youth. It is not quite clear why such an antagonism existed, since—according to our knowledge of the Greek *modoi*—there is not much difference between the Phrygian and Lydian modes. The question has to be asked: why did the Greeks adopt these modoi, treating them as the strongest pillars of their music system, together with the Dorian mode, if they did not consider them apt for educational purposes? The answer might be that the Hellenes had originally no music system of their own and took them over from the neighboring nations. Later these modes became so popular that it was no longer possible to exclude them from their own music.

The Phrygian mode seems to have been "joyous" to the musical perception of the Hellenes; this may have been the reason for its popularity. From Asia Minor it crossed the Hellespont and landed in Thracia, where it was used mainly for the rites of DIONYSOS. From there it passed over to Greece and became the favorite mode of all the legendary creators of Greek musical art, such as ORPHEUS, MUSAEUS, and THAMIRIS, who were all, according to the tradition, Thracian singers and folkbards.

The character of the Lydians showed qualities that might appear contradictory: a propensity toward licentiousness and debauchery on the one hand, and fierce warrior virtues on the other. HERODOTUS states that he knew no people more valiant and virile. Like other peoples of the area, the Lydians worshipped Cybele, whose rites used orgiastic ceremonies and a noisy music that created a state of sensuous frenzy among the worshippers. It seems, however, that they also cultivated another type of music, which was serious and dignified, for ARISTOTLE considered it particularly appropriate for the education of the young.

If we summarize the characteristics of musical civilization of the ancient peoples in the Near East, we find a rather homogeneous pattern. This music, for the most part, had a sensuous, orgiastic quality that very often turned into mournful lament. Every joyous excitement of the emotions comes, at its climax, to a mysterious turning point where it touches the other extreme and is transformed into sorrow. Thus, the music of Babylonia, Phrygia, Lydia, and, with some restrictions, also of Assyria, primarily designed to stir the emotions and to excite the senses, could just as well be used, at the proper place, to subdue them.

Though it was a common practice among all these peoples to use the instruments capable of sustaining a melodic line according to their intrinsic qualities, and to double, as far as possible, the melody sung by the human voice, this practice was not too typical of the music of high Antiquity. Its character was rather determined by the use of blaring trumpets, of harsh-sounding horns, of noisy cymbals, and of an arsenal of instruments of percussion, which created a mood and a tone color considered orgiastic by their contemporaries. Sedate and dignified music, the noble outlines of its melodic aspect, as we witnessed among the Sumerians, the Egyptians, and partly also among the Assyrians, did not come into its own prior to the Hebrews and Greeks. It was these two latter nations of Antiquity who treated music as an art and who pursued through their musical culture a higher, ethical and educational level.

NOTES

1. Strabo, XIII, 631.
2. Rudolf Westphal, *Geschichte der alten und mittelalterlichen Musik* (Breslau, 1865), p. 3.
3. H. M. Schletterer, *Geschichte der geistlichen Dichtung und kirchlichen Tonkunst* (Hannover, 1869), pp. 10–11.
4. Pollux, IV, 75.
5. In many translations of the Bible, ancient and recent, as well as in numerous literary works about the music of Antiquity, the ancient pipes are incorrectly called "flutes." In their construction and sound, they were in fact oboe-like instruments. The peoples of Antiquity possessed numerous, often dozens of kinds, of oboes, having different tone production, different sonority, and various applications.

8

Judaea

THE ARCHAIC PERIOD

The origin of the Jews lies in complete obscurity. While the precursors of most of the peoples and ethnic groups of the Near East, both Semites and non-Semites, can be traced, at least in broader outlines, to earliest Antiquity, the roots and the country of origin of the Jews are entirely unknown. The only hint as to their early existence is found etymologically in the word "Hebrews." The term applied to the people *Ibriim ha-Nahar*, meaning those "from the other side" (i.e., of the river Euphrates). The "other side" is called in Hebrew *ewer;* those from the other side (of the river) were the *Ibriim*, the Hebrews.

The earliest history of the Jews shows that they belonged to the Semitic race that emerged from the Arabian peninsula; what their country of origin might have been, we do not know. It is assumed, however, that the inbreeding of the Semites might have taken place in prehistoric times in the seclusion of Arabia.[1]

Like other peoples and tribes living a nomadic existence, the Hebrews were worshippers of nature and of idols. Little is known about the period of their pagan religion, for on this matter the Biblical chroniclers are discreetly silent. Nevertheless, the Biblical text contains several allusions to the fact that house-gods and idols were part of every household. The Book of Genesis contains the well-known story of Laban's idol, stolen by Rachel and hidden under the saddle of the camel she was sitting on, so that nobody could find it (Gen.31:34). Less known is the reason why she did this: she was afraid that her father would separate her from her husband, but without the help of his house-god Laban had no power to do so. We must not forget that this episode supposedly took place in "historic" times, in which Jewish monotheism, forbidding idols, must already have existed. Even in the home of the god-fearing David, the Bible mentions *teraphim*, house-idols (1 Sam. 19:13); one of them even served to save his life.

The Bible condenses 800 years of the early history of the Jews in a few short sentences. Anything that is not myth or legend in this narration might have been freely invented by Biblical chroniclers. The history of the Jews actually starts with their sojourn in Egypt. How they arrived there and when they first settled in Cana⟨an are quite unclear in the Bible. Similarly unclear is information about their conquest of Cana⟨an after their exodus from Egypt. While we can reconstruct the historical facts of this early period merely by using Biblical information, its authenticity is highly doubtful.

It is probable that long before the invasion of Palestine, by other Hebrew groups, e.g., the tribe of *Asher* had settled in the north of Palestine, entertaining close economic relations with the Phoenicians. This tribe is mentioned in records that go back to the time of RAMESES II (1298–1232 B.C.E.), who, according to one tradition, is supposed to be the Pharaoh of the Exodus. The powerful tribes of *Joseph*, to which *Ephraim*, *Manasseh* and *Benjamin* belonged, came from the East. Around 1200 B.C.E., we witness the emergence of *Judah*[2] and the related tribes of *Levi* and *Simon*, who penetrated Cana'an from the South. These tribes may have brought with them the God Yahveh and the remembrance of a mighty leader, named Moses.[3]

Our most important source for the history of Palestine in the sixteenth and fifteenth centuries B.C.E., one that allows us to cast some light upon the situation of the Hebrews during this epoch, is the annals and a list of the Palestinian cities of the Pharaoh THUT-MOSES II (1520–1461 B.C.E.). This list of cities mentions the places *Jacob-el* and *Joshep-el*, which are names of two patriarchs of the Jewish tradition. "*El*" stands for the city-gods, and the names are those of the tribes who built the places and dwelt there. Furthermore, Jacob's "divinity" is attested by the name of one of the rulers of the Hyksos dynasty, *Jacob-her*, which means "Jacob is satisfied."[4]

The tribe of *Israel* also bears a name connected with *El*, which was applied at the same time to the tribe and its god. Other tribes, too, which came from Arabia, have similar names, such as *Jacob-el*, "El outwits"; *Joshep-el*, "The seat of El"; *Jishma-el*, "El grants a favorable hearing"; *Jiphtach-el*, "El opens"; *Jizchak-el*, "El laughs"; *Jerachme-el*, "El is merciful." *El*, of course, is not the image of a lofty deity, but merely the mark of a tribal fetish. The purpose of giving a deity such names was to influence the local god to respond to specific requests; the spoken name was thought to insure the fulfillment of the wishes of the individual or a group.[5]

According to the very scant records about the early history of the Jews, it is believed that they entered world history late and in an inconspicuous manner. We have no knowledge of their Stone-Age existence, or of their Bronze period, or of their Iron Age. We know only that during the eight hundred years of their historic existence they shuttled back and forth between the great surrounding civilizations.

Even the great Jewish historian HEINRICH GRAETZ eschews the question as to the origin of the Jews. He identifies the earliest history of the Hebrews with the immigration of Abraham to Palestine and the later occupation of the "Promised Land." These events, however, had already taken place in an earlier period. About the aborigines of Palestine, he mentions a place held by the 'Anakim, a tribe near Hebron and Gaza, called after 'Anak ("long necked", Num. 13.22, Deut. 1:28, etc.), and by the *Rephaim* (Gen. 14:5); both seem to have been a race of giants. They were called by the ancient nations, among them the Hebrews, ⁾emim ("terrible men," Gen. 14:5) and filled the Israelite spies, sent out by Moses to reconnoitre the land, with such abject terror that they said:

"We were in our own eyes as grasshoppers unto them" (Num. 13:33). These giants were eventually overcome and utterly destroyed by the Israelite dwarfs (Josh. 11:12).

As for the origin of the Jewish people, GRAETZ goes no farther back in history than the Egyptian sojourn.

The origin of this people bore but very slight resemblance to the origin of other nations. Israel as a people arose amidst peculiar surroundings in the land of Goshen, a territory situated in the extreme north of Egypt, near the border of Palestine.[6]

When and how they came into this fertile land is not even hinted at by GRAETZ. He states only that the Israelites consisted of twelve tribes, which led a simple life in the land of Goshen. They evidently had no common chieftain before Moses. The elders (*zekenim*) of the families, who acted as their chiefs, were consulted on all important occasions.[7] This was common usage in Antiquity, where the oldest member of a clan or a tribe had the authority and wisdom to decide on all questions relative to the welfare of the community.

In the light of today's Bible criticism, the Hebrews, or the tribes which unified under this designation, had no common history prior to their settlement in Palestine. They were a mixture of diverse ethnic groups, kept together by a common (or similar) language and a common Semitic stock. Each one of these groups probably had its own history and folklore, its own tribal fetishes and customs. At a relatively late period, and not before they were united by external pressure, they made their appearance in the history of humanity.[8]

The newcomers were unprepared for the achievements of a sedentary life. But they learned quickly, and soon were able to make full use of the blessings of an agricultural existence, whether they were driven by fate to Egypt or to Palestine.

How does this concise survey of the early history of the Hebrews fit in with an essay on the use of music by the Jews?

The musical practice of the Jews may be taken for granted from the moment when the Bible mentions Jubal as "the father of all such as handle the harp and pipe" (Gen. 4:21). The legend of Jubal presupposes, however, an advanced stage of human civilization. The instruments mentioned in this Biblical passage (the *kinnor* and the *'ugab*) represent types of highly developed musical tools and are generic terms for two species: stringed and woodwind instruments. The Bible does not give any hint of what might have taken place *prior* to Jubal, nor does it state whether the Hebrews in their nomadic existence had their own instruments or had borrowed those of the surrounding peoples. Just as the Bible chroniclers do not divulge anything about the early life of the Jews (longwinded and manifestly invented genealogies are not history!), they similarly do not use earlier legends or discuss oral traditions that might inform us about the pristine music of the Hebrews.

Yet, we are concerned with what might have happened *prior* to Jubal, and how Jewish music might have developed *before* it reached a stage of civilization in which the existence of the two classes of highly evolved instruments mentioned is attested to.

The answer to this question of origin lies in the religious history of the Hebrews.

Like the wandering tribes of the Bedouins, the Jews were nature-worshippers. The sun, moon, stars, wind, and other natural phenomena were their "gods", who governed their welfare and insured the prosperity of their herds. To these gods they offered sacrifices and invoked their help and assistance. A trace of the old-time sun-worship of the Jews is preserved in the rabbinic literature:

Our fathers turned with their backs toward the temple of the Lord and their faces toward the east, and they worshipped the sun toward the east; but for us, our eyes are turned toward the Lord.[9]

Even the purifiers of the Bible, so eager to eliminate everything which might suggest an early heathen religion of the Jews, have not succeeded in erasing all traces of the ancient sun-worship, which seems to have survived archaic times:

And he brought me into the inner court of the Lord's house, and, and, behold, at the door of the temple of the Lord, between the porch and the altar, were about five and twenty men, with their backs toward the temple of the Lord, and their faces toward the east; and they worshipped the sun toward the east (Ezek.8:16).

In their primitive rites, the Hebrews invoked their gods by offering, as was the custom of nomadic peoples, the firstlings of their flocks to their gods or fetishes, and thus sought to draw the attention of their protective deities to themselves. These invocations were made in a manner differing from ordinary speech. A loud voice was required, stressing certain words or syllables.

These *invocations* are not only the forerunners of the later ritual chanting, but were the initial germ of slowly developing complex religious rites.

It is a scientifically established fact that the origin of music goes back to singing.[10] Joy, grief, love, triumph, and the other inexhaustible elements of human emotions manifested themselves in primitive civilizations in a form of raised speech, punctuated by specific stresses. This may be considered the archetype of singing. With developing human civilization other motives arise for singing: magic rites, exorcism of evil spirits, religious ritual, healing, the daily functions of the working people, and festive events in the life of the individual and the community.

In general, at the primitive stage of civilization, "singing" is far from "art," for it serves merely practical purposes. According to the conception of primitive man, ordinary speech is not effective enough in intercourse with the supernatural beings who govern his fate. This is especially true where religious feelings are being expressed. In reciting the ritual formula, utilized to invoke the deity, and by offering fervent prayers, the ordinary language is changed and transformed involuntarily into that utilizing accentuated declamation. This creates a multiple melodic and rhythmic shaping of the voice, giving rise by this to the first elements of singing.[11] Gradually, certain formulae of speech crystallize and become primitive melodic patterns, which may be considered the first "tunes." From this point to that of "song" as an art form, there is a long but clear path of development, which can easily be traced.

Nomadic existence, such as the archaic living form of the Hebrews, does not favor the creation of a viable art or culture. One aspect of music, however, can be assumed among the Hebrews even in their primitive existence—that is singing, or prayerful chanting.

Like the wandering Bedouins, the nomadic Hebrews probably had many songs to alleviate the monotony of their daily life. These must have been simple shepherd tunes, such as are found among all nomadic peoples at all times and in all countries. The Hebrews of primitive times must have had other songs for special occasions, such as weddings, funerals, and the like. There is, however, no evidence for this assumption.

The next step in the development of the tonal art of the Hebrews deals with the transition from singing to instrumental music, but not in the manner that the Biblical tale about Jubal suggests.

In archaic times, the motive for using instruments was completely different from that which produced singing. Even the most primitive vocal music was conditioned by human speech, and was the immediate outgrowth of emotions and passions. Instrumental music, on the other hand, may have been quite independent of such emotional motivation. It may have started as a reaction to the motor impulses of the body. Its first appearance was the form of clapping of the hands, beating the thighs, and stamping on the floor with the feet. Contrary to vocal music, instrumental music in its lowest stage was exclusively of rhythmic nature.[12]

Out of these first rhythmical impulses the early instruments gradually developed, transforming rhythmical sounds into the mechanized form, represented by drums and the other noise-making instruments.

Primitive man first clapped his hands and stamped his feet in order to create noise. (The "listening" to such noises was a separate phenomenon and became evident much later.) A long period, however, elapsed before man created noises for the purpose of bringing forth special sounds.

This prehistoric development must be taken into consideration if we take for granted the use of certain instruments among the nomadic Hebrews. The drum, either the hand-drum for supporting the dance or a larger species for signal purposes, might have been used by them, in the manner found among all peoples of primitive civilizations. The hunting bow of mankind (whose livelihood depended on such a weapon) is considered unanimously as the archetype of the later harp-like instruments; it is therefore not inconceivable that the Israelites of archaic times may have "invented" the primitive harp or lyre, and that this fact has found an echo in the Biblical narrative.

It can also be assumed that the pipe might have existed in some form in the early existence of the Jews. It does not require much inventiveness to bore a few holes in a pipe of reed, or bone, or wood. Such a simple instrument might have brought forth a primitive "melodic" strain; therefore there is some vague historical justification for the *ʿugab* of the Bible.

However, in the Biblical narrative an instrument is lacking, which the Jews, described as a people of shepherds, must certainly have had: the horn. Whether this may already have been the later *shofar* cannot be ascertained. In all probability, the *shofar* originated in Assyria. Etymologically, the word is derived from the Assyrian *shapparu* (wild mountain goat), although there are still other etymological explanations for it.[13] In the primitive existence of the Jewish shepherds, it is logical to assume that this essential signal instrument was made of the neat horn.

If we compare the customs of the wandering Arabic tribes with those of the nomadic Hebrews, we find a significant amount of supporting information concerning the latter's musical activities. This information is to be found in the writings of the Greek sophist ZENOBIUS, who taught rhetoric in Rome during the reign of the emperor HADRIAN (117–138 C.E.). The literary activity of ZENOBIUS was mainly centered in his hobby of collecting Greek proverbs;

three books of them are partially preserved. These proverbs, clad in metaphors, and occasionally in facetious similes, give us an insight into the thinking and feeling of the Greeks. One of these proverbs characterizes a man too much addicted to music, who played the *aulos* the whole day and thus became a plague to his neighbors; he was called by the nickname *arabios aulětēs* ("Arabian flute-player"). The origin of this term derives from the fact that the Arabs, tending their flocks at night, whiled away their time by sitting around the camp-fire, playing the flute until sunrise.[14] Although the simile is rather vague, it probably parallels the analogous customs of the nomadic Jews.

Let us leave the area of myths and legends about the archaic time of the Jews and turn to chronicled history. First of all, early Jewish historiography is by no means "history" in the proper sense of the term, but consists mostly of imaginary records invented by priestly scribes in honor of a universal Jewish God. It is an artificial medley of myths, either transmitted orally or borrowed from other peoples (e.g., the Flood-saga from the Babylonians), but mostly freely invented in order to prove the reality and uniqueness of Yahveh's power. Such historical "sources" must be used only with utmost caution.

According to modern Biblical criticism, there never existed

> "children" of Israel, a primitive monotheism, or such a historical person as Moses, the passage through the Red Sea, the giving of the Law at Sinai, nor the ark of the Covenant.[15]

Bible history is rather a work of propaganda on a large scale, invented or compiled by priestly scribes during the reign of king JOSIAH (626 B.C.E.). The authors were not historians but writers of fiction, whose imagination created the marvelous book that we call the "Holy Writ." Despite all its weaknesses and exaggerations, it is the most beautiful and the most important product of human civilization. It contains all the wisdom and the ethics bestowed by Judaism on humanity and represents, as such, the first important philosophy of the history of mankind.

All the ancient peoples start their history by describing the creation of the universe and the origin of the human race. Thus, the Biblical novel likewise presents the earliest history of the Jewish people; the imagination of the Jewish "historians" was not handicapped by any restrictions.

The earliest history of the Jews is not connected directly with our subject, but the stirring tale of the patriarchs requires close examination since it is in this period that the first patterns of Jewish musical practices become apparent.

The Biblical writers of novels invented the beautiful story of Abraham in order to give the Jewish people a tangible "ancestor," and they represent Jewish monotheism as the "revelation" made by this ancestor. They used old myths and interpreted them according to their needs. They invented lengthy dialogues between God and Abraham (just as later between God and Moses). Only a god-intoxicated people could believe such supernatural occurrences.

How does modern Biblical criticism evaluate the Abraham-saga? If Abraham was a historical figure (and many doubt even this), he was by no means the ancestor of the Jews, but merely one of the chieftains of the isolated tribes who settled in Palestine in prehistoric times, known as the *Habiru* or *Ibriim*. Isaac and Jacob must have been semi-symbolic figures, or actual tribal chiefs. The twelve sons of Jacob, symbolizing the twelve Jewish tribes, were merely names of the totems of their tribes.[16] Not all of them emigrated from Palestine to Egypt, but perhaps only the tribes of Joseph, Manasseh, and Ephraim. Joseph might have been a historical person, holding an office during the Hyksos Dynasty, who might have facilitated the immigration of his fellow Jews.

The story of the patriarchs has been treated with little reverence by Biblical criticism. Some maintain that these venerable persons were merely tribal gods, brought down from their heaven and, through metamorphosis, usual in folklore, became the forefathers of the Jews. Others believe that with the lapse of time the experiences of the nomadic tribes were transformed into an early common history, from which the saga of the patriarchs emerged.[17]

It is a historical fact, as evidenced by the Amarna-letters,[18] that simultaneously Hebrews lived in Palestine as well as in Egypt, and that the two groups united centuries later and thus became the Jewish people.

In contradistinction to Biblical criticism, let us examine the Abraham saga, as presented in the Bible.

The Scriptures state that Abraham originated from the Chaldaean city of ʾUr. The story of his emigration and his settling in Canaʿan have already been related. The Bible states explicitly that Abraham led the life of a nomadic tent-dweller, who wandered with his herds from pasturage to pasturage and from well to well. At that time, ʾUr was a large, civilized, and almost luxurious city. Such places were not very favorable to the housing of cattle-breeders on a large scale. It is therefore highly questionable whether ʾUr was in reality Abraham's home town. The Bible itself furnishes no proof of it.

After Abraham settled in Canaʿan, and after his son Isaac reached manhood, Abraham sent a kinsman to the city of Nahor in Mesopotamia, situated in the kingdom of Mari, instructing him:

> thou shalt go unto my country, and to my kindred, and take a wife for my son, even for Isaac (Gen. 24:3–10).[19]

In this manner Rebekkah, the daughter of Bethuel, came to Canaʿan. The city of Nahor was indeed "on the other side" (*ewer*) of the river. Obviously, the Biblical chroniclers must have confounded ʾUr with Nahor. It was probably this provincial city rather than ʾUr that was the home town of a nomadic tent-dweller.

The Bible speaks of Abraham's profession as that of a successful cattle-breeder. He must have been one, since he paid four hundred shekels of silver for the burial place of Sarah, and eventually his own and that of his son Isaac, in the field of Machpelah (meaning "Double Cave") before Mamre in Hebron, together with the adjoining field and trees (Gen. 23:16). To his future daughter-in-law he sent a golden ring of half-a-shekel weight, and two bracelets for her hands of ten shekels' weight of gold (Gen. 24:22). His emissary says of him:

> And the Lord hath blessed my master greatly; and he is become great; and He hath given him flocks and herds, and silver and gold, and men-servants and maid-servants, and camels and asses (Gen. 24:35).

As the Bible presents it, Abraham gives the impression of having been a wealthy Oriental sheikh.

After the Biblical writers invented the beautiful story of an ancestor of the Jewish people, they further gave it religious, philosophic significance, and so Abraham became not only the forefather of the Jews, but the man to whom God first revealed Himself, bequeathing to him monotheism, the true religion given solely to Abraham and his people.

The Bible deals with the four-and-a-half centuries of the Egyptian sojourn in a few sentences. The most important questions remain unanswered in the Biblical story: were the Hebrews who left 'Ur (or Nahor) with Abraham in 2000 B.C.E. and the Hebrews who entered Egypt under (or invited by) Joseph in 1600, the same people as the Israelites who were led out of Egypt by Moses in 1200 B.C.E?[20] How much of the Egyptian sojourn was spent in freedom and how much in slavery? Since Moses was brought up as an Egyptian prince, where did he learn Hebrew? Since he had no difficulty conversing with the Midianites, what language did he speak to them?[21] How could the Israelites have preserved, in bondage, their ethnic identity? Who were their leaders before Moses? Why did Moses identify himself with the Jewish slaves instead of with Egyptian royalty?[22] Moses was not circumcised; why had his parents not circumcised him when he was eight days old? Had the covenant requiring this ceremony been made *after* Moses' "encounter" with God?

The Biblical narrative of Exodus is suspiciously reminiscent of Abraham's parallel experience, for it commands Moses to lead the Israelites out of Egypt and take them to the land of Cana'an, the same place that He "promised" to Abraham. However, there are other pertinent questions. Before we come to them, the musical practices of the Hebrews in ancient times deserve to be scrutinized, in order to understand and appreciate the role music played in their existence in Egypt and after the Exodus in the wilderness.

After the initial mention of "music" in the legend of Jubal, we find in the Biblical text the first mention of a secular "song." It appears in the Scriptures almost at the same time as the Jubal story. The same Biblical verse that tells us about the first professions and arts mentions also the first "song" of Jewish history: Lamech's "Song of vengeance" (Gen. 4:23, 24).[23] It is not evident whether the text of this "song" is merely a fragment of a larger bardic poem, as some scholars think, but apparently it is the most ancient Jewish specimen of a song—primitive and coarse, it is true, but nevertheless having an unmistakeably poetic form.

> (And Lamech said unto his wives):
> Adah and Zillah, hear my voice;
> Ye wives of Lamech, hearken unto my speech;
> For I have slain a man for wounding me,
> and a young man for bruising me;
> If Cain shall be avenged sevenfold,
> Truly Lamech seventy and sevenfold.

This wild and brutal song might be the result of a legend. But soon reality appears in the Biblical text. The reproachful admonition of Laban, when he overtakes Jacob in his flight, offers an example of a secular song in its proper sense:

Wherefore didst thou flee secretly, and outwit me; and didst not tell me, that I might have sent thee away with mirth and with songs, with tabret and with harp? (Gen. 31:27)

To understand the abyss between the coarse song of vengeance of Lamech and the song of joy intimated by Laban, we must consider the incomparably higher civilization of the time of the patriarchs. In Lamech's wild and brutal song, there is little in common with "art"; but Laban's speech suggests the existence of an already clearly recognizable artistic set of practices requiring ethical deportment in the form of the beautiful custom of patriarchal times: escorting a departing friend with music and singing.

It is true that Laban was not a Hebrew but a Syrian. But the musical customs of these peoples were so closely related that they must have been almost identical during this period.

From this Biblical passage BUDDE infers that in heroic times Israel might have had a guild of folkbards who, in addition to possessing creative gifts, might have been compilers of many folksongs and ballads, which they performed on suitable occasions. To support his assumption, BUDDE refers to Gen. 4:21 (the Jubal legend) and, as a definite, though later "referential" proof of it, to Num. 21:27:

"Wherefore they that speak in parables [i.e., the poets] say . . ."

From this, BUDDE draws the conclusion that

in ancient times music and poetry have been closely interlinked, one without the other cannot be conceived. . . . Such songs and ballads of unknown poets have been sung by itinerant bards all around the country. No doubt, these bards represented a spiritual power and were considered the strongest levers of public opinion, especially in times of great national decisions.[24]

THE SOJOURN IN EGYPT

Long before their stay in Egypt, the Hebrews, or some of their tribes, had settled in Palestine. The Tel el-Amarna letters, discovered in 1893, addressed by the governors of Palestinian cities to the Pharaoh AMENOPHIS IV (IKHNATON) and his father, contain the earliest mention of the *Habiru* (the Hebrews):

The king, my Lord, must know that the Habiru revolted in the lands, which the king, my Lord has given me, and that I have beaten them; and the king, my Lord, should know that all my brethren [i.e., the other governors of the region] forsook me; and that I and Abdu-Kheba are the only ones, who fight against the chief of the Habiru.

The writer of this letter was SUWARDATA, governor of Hebron, who, according to his name, was no Semite but an Indo-Aryan.

Shortly after this letter, another report went to the Pharaoh, this time with an urgent appeal for help:

The Habiru conquer one city after another,

and if no help is forthcoming, the land of Palestine will be lost for Egypt.

IKHNATON's reign lasted from 1370 to 1352, more than a century prior to the assumed time of the Exodus under Moses' leadership. This is the time period during which the Israelites are believed to have sojourned in Egypt. How did they come into the country? Several hypotheses have been presented. According to one of them, the Hebrews living in Cana'an were forced by a famine to seek asylum in Egypt. Another asserts that the Hyksos, the "shepherd-kings," who were Semites (they reigned from 1730 to 1580), facilitated the immigration of the Hebrews and assigned to them a place for settling in Goshen, in the Nile Delta. Following the downfall of the Hyksos-Dynasty, the Hebrews, being foreigners, were subjected to bondage.

Biblical chronology does not always parallel history, because if the Exodus took place around 1200 B.C.E., as is generally accepted, the sojourn of the Jews in Egypt must have begun in 1650 B.C.E. How much of this period was spent in relative liberty and how much in slavery cannot be ascertained, even approximately. The figures 1580 (the end of the Hyksos), which would indicate the loss of the liberty of the Jews, and 1650 (for their entrance in Egypt) show a wide discrepancy that cannot be dismissed.

Irrespective of this historical disparity, we are here interested only in the question as to what kind of music existed among the Hebrews in Cana'an before they emigrated to Egypt.

During their nomadic life, the Hebrews must have adapted their music to that of their immediate surroundings. If we assume that they had no music of their own during their nomadic times, they must have adopted, or imitated, the musical practice of the peoples of their environment after their first settlement in Palestine (during the IKHNATON-period), and even more so after the conquest of Cana'an as the "land of promise."

At this time, Palestine was a conglomerate of small and even miniature principalities, the limits of which did not go beyond the boundaries of the cities, and which warred constantly with each other and kept the country in permanent turmoil. Each one of these city-states had its own *ba'alim* and its own ritual. Accordingly, their cultic music might have shown certain differences. No wonder, then, that the Hebrews could not develop a music of their own in this period but were compelled to adjust their musical practice to that of their surroundings.

The situation changed radically with their immigration to Egypt. The Jews, whether they came from the nomadic life of the desert or from Palestine, a more civilized surrounding, suddenly found themselves in a country with a significant musical culture. They were permitted to participate in the religious services of their hosts as well as in the popular festivals, and could listen to the songs of the people. It did not take long before they learned to play Egyptian instruments and sing Egyptian melodies. Thus, Egyptian music left indelible traces on the Israelites, which continued in effect even after the fall of the Hyksos, when they were enslaved.

It has been justly said that the sojourn in Egypt was the "music-lesson" of the Hebrews. After their loss of freedom, the Jews continued their "lesson" in oppression, under bondage, but with undiminished fervor. Just as they were able to maintain their ethnic identity despite all hardships, they similarly preserved their acquired musical skill. What practical purpose did this serve?

A parallel with the later Babylonian captivity can be drawn. In Egypt, as later in Babylon, the love of music manifests itself among a people oppressed and afflicted but not broken. Without hope of liberation, they used music to support their visions of deliverance.

The Hebrews were assiduous students. The song of thanksgiving uttered by Moses after the crossing of the Red Sea, in which the entire people took part, and the responsive singing of the women of Israel on the same occasion, were the "final examinations" of the music studies in Egypt. The people of Israel passed this examination with flying colors. At the same time, this occasion held evident promise for the future of Jewish music.

Despite the forty years of existence in the desert, despite fights with inimical tribes, despite the hardships in conquering their promised land, the Jews were able to save intact their musical knowledge acquired in Egypt and transplant it to their new homeland. It would not have been possible that a flourishing musical culture could have risen in an unbelievably short time without such preceding preparation and fertilization.

At this point the question arises as to how the Israelites made use of their musical knowledge acquired in Egypt. And here the name of Moses, the most outstanding among the Hebrew leaders, enters the history of Jewish music.

It is still an unsettled issue whether Moses was a historic person, or merely an "idea" projected back by the priestly scribes for giving to the Law of the Jewish people an "intermediary," as was the case with HAMMURABI and other Oriental potentates.

The answer to this question is indeed important, since in it may be discovered the early roots of the music of the Jews.

Between the Scylla and Charybdis of the fundamentalists, for whom every word of the Scriptures is a divine revelation, and the unbelieving heretics, who apply criticism to everything the Bible says, we shall try to navigate by applying the Socratic method.

Question: Did Moses ever live, or is he a mere legend?

Answer: Biblical exegesis is at variance about this. There is no historical evidence of his existence, no papyrus, no rock-inscription, no stele, no authentic record. The prophets Amos and Isaiah, who lived and preached at least a century before the Pentateuch received its written form, do not mention his name, nor do they refer to the ark of the Covenant. Moses is mentioned once in a later passage of Micah (Mic. 6:4). Jeremiah, too, knows Moses only as a righteous man, and mentions him together with Samuel (15:1), but not as a founder of a religion.[25] Even when Jeremiah refers to the Exodus, Moses' name is not alluded to (Jer. 2:6; 11:4, 7).

Furthermore, much uncertainty surrounds Moses' ancestry. According to the Bible, his father was Amram, of the tribe of Levi, his mother Jochebed, "his father's sister" (Exod. 6:20). A new theory maintains, however, that Moses belonged to the tribe of Ephraim, which would cast shadow upon his Levitical ancestry. Another hypothesis tries to substitute him for Levi, in making Levi's son Gershom the first-born of Moses issue from his Midianite wife, Zipporah.[26] (The name Gershom means in Hebrew "a stranger in a strange land" (Exod. 2:22). Another son of Moses, born also in Midian, was Eliezer ("God is help")

(Exod. 18:4; 1 Chron. 23:15). When Moses returned to Egypt, he took with him Zipporah and his sons (Exod. 4:20), but must have sent them back to Midian, because he evidently considered it dangerous for these "strangers" to stay in Egypt. Only after the Exodus were Zipporah and her sons reunited with Moses in the wilderness (Exod. 18:5).

The Bible leaves us in the dark as to where Moses learned the language of the Hebrews, since he was raised as an Egyptian prince. He had no difficulty communicating with the Midianites. But how did he deal with the Israelites?

Just as we know nothing about his birthplace, so there is no record of where he was buried. A legendary tradition maintains that he was quietly entombed in the land of Moab, in a valley facing Mount Peor, which was held sacred by the population of that district. But no one knew the exact spot where he was buried.[27]

According to another legend, Joshua was the scion of the Joseph-clan, which would upset the whole timetable of Biblical chronology (see n. 3).

It is not strange, therefore, in the face of lack of evidence, that one of our leading Jewish historians states that Moses was the greatest Hebrew who never lived.[28]

Question: If, however, Moses was not a mere legend, was he a Hebrew or an Egyptian?

Answer: The name Moses (possibly the abbreviation of Ahmoses) is quite common in Egypt, especially among the Egyptian Pharaohs. The meaning of the word is "child." THUTMOSES was called the child of (the god) THUT, RAHMOSES the child of RAH, and so on. As a Hebrew, he should have been circumcised, but he was not. When later God finds this out and Moses' life is endangered by His wrath, his wife Zipporah, the daughter of a Midianite priest—was he Jethro (Exod. 3:1; 18:2, 5, 12 ff), or Reuel (Exod. 2:18)?—hurriedly performs the necessary operation with a sharp stone (Exod. 4:25).

Question: Was Moses in reality the "liberator" of the Jewish people?

Answer: JOSEPHUS quotes a report of the Egyptian historian MANETHO (third century B.C.E.), who asserts that the liberation of the Jews was due to an epidemic among them, from which the Egyptians wanted to save themselves. Moses, an Egyptian priest, went voluntarily as a missionary to the settlement of the Jews, in order to impose on them the rules of cleanliness prescribed by the Egyptian priesthood.[29] Greek and Roman writers have given this as the reason for the Exodus,[30] but manifestly they simply took over JOSEPHUS's version, since no real proof was available.

Another hypothesis given to the cause of the Exodus is attributed to their "working-strike" (Exod. 4:4,5). This is a very questionable assumption.[31] In high Antiquity there were sufficient means to force reluctant slaves to resume working. The time was not ripe for a Spartacus.

Question: Is the discovery of Moses by the daughter of a Pharaoh a reality or a fairy-tale?

Answer: A Sumerian legend about the life of the King SARGON I (2872–2817 B.C.E.) suspiciously resembles Moses' early youth. It is said in this story:

> My humble mother conceived me; she brought me forth in secret. She placed me in a basket-boat of rushes; with pitch she closed my door.

According to the legend, SARGON I was found by a workman, who shortly after brought him to the court, where he became the cup-bearer of the king.[32]

To all appearances, the Jewish priestly scribes of the Pentateuch applied this legend to Moses.

Question: Did Moses discover the one and true God independently of Abraham?

Answer: Whether Moses had heard of Abraham's "revelation" cannot be ascertained. However, monotheism was known in Egypt long before Moses. The young idealist AMENOPHIS IV (IKHNATON, 1370–1352 B.C.E.) had imposed the monotheistic worship of the sun on his people with fire and sword, and raised it to a state religion. After his short reign, priestly reaction set in and the old religion with its multitude of animal-headed deities reinstated. Perhaps IKHNATON's innovation continued to live on secretly, carried out by a limited number of his adherents, just as was the case of the Marranos in medieval Spain. It is conceivable that through this secret religious group Moses became acquainted with monotheism.

Question: Why did Moses flee from Egypt after he had killed an overseer? Human life was cheap at that time, and for an Egyptian prince the killing of a subaltern was not regarded as a serious enough crime to cause him to leave the country in a hurry.

Answer: The killing of an overseer was a very incongruous motivation for Moses' flight, doubtless invented by the Biblical chroniclers. The real reason for it must have been quite different. We are obliged to assume that Moses' adherence to the precepts of IKHNATON came to the fore somehow and that his life was endangered by this discovery.

Question: Why did he return to Egypt after all?

Answer: Evidently through a change of government and the amnesty resulting from it ("for all the men are dead that sought thy life," Exod. 4:19).

And now we arrive at a question that interests us directly.

Question: How is Moses' fate connected with Jewish music?

Answer: According to the tradition, Moses was educated by Egyptian priests. As MANETHO reports, Moses functioned for some time as a priest in the Temple at Heliopolis. As an Egyptian priest, his name was OSARSIPH, called after OSIRIS, the protecting deity of this city. He must have been familiar with all the wisdom of the Egyptians, including poetry and music.[33] PHILO particularly stresses Moses' knowledge in theoretical and practical music.[34] It is evident that PHILO speaks from hearsay, since he could not have had authentic information about Moses' education. PHILO probably transposed retroactively into Egypt the manner in which the youth in the time of Moses might have been educated. Another, still later, report about Moses' education in Egypt is furnished by the Church-father JUSTIN MARTYR,[35] similarly without historical basis, unless it refers to JUSTIN's own period.

No doubt, Moses had a thorough knowledge of Egyptian ritual music and must have been a creative artist as well, since only such a gifted individual could have composed and "sung" the "Song at the Red Sea" (Exod. 15), as well as the Hymn of Praise (Deut. 32), which he "sang" shortly before his death.

While all of the above does not prove that Moses might have been more than a legendary figure, we believe that an *indirect* proof indicates that he was probably a living person. This can be inferred from his sister Miriam's mastery in singing.

We have seen that both the sacred dance and the secular dance in Egyptian temples were performed mainly by women. As the Bible indicates, after Moses finished his "Song at the Red Sea," Miriam continued her own song and dance (Exod. 15:20.21). She could easily have acquired her facility in dancing in Egypt.

Things are different with the "singing" Miriam. Any Oriental of a high status, be he an Egyptian, Arab, or Syrian, never, or only on rare occasions, performed music, and then only for ritual purposes (see the *Amon*-singers of Egypt above). To satisfy his personal musical needs, there were professional musicians, who were usually slaves.

According to the Bible, Moses, as well as his older brother Aaron and his sister Miriam, descended from a Levitical family (Exod. 2:1)[36] Moses could not have acquired the levitical musical tradition from his family (even supposing that such a tradition already existed), since from infancy he had been raised in an Egyptian palace by the daughter of the Pharaoh. The Bible makes no reference to the musical ability of Aaron. But the Scriptural text makes it clear that Miriam must have had considerable musical knowledge, since it is stated: "and Miriam sang unto them," and that she led the Hebrew women in singing.

Miriam is called a "prophetess" by the Biblical chroniclers. What does *prophet* (or *prophetess*) mean in the early history of the Jewish people? This distinction is applied to a man (or woman) who feels, suffers, and speaks for the masses as an eloquent interpreter of the beliefs and sentiments of the people and who, in addition, possesses all the qualities of a national leader. These qualities embrace oratorical talent as well as mastery in music, or at least in singing. In Biblical parlance, *prophet* or *seer*, often has the same meaning as *musician* or *singer*.[37] The early history of Israel refers to chosen men who were masters in the musical art. They are nearly always called *prophets* by the biblical chroniclers. No wonder, therefore, that the same epithet is applied to Miriam. It indicates her mastery in music and singing, which in all probability she owed to none other than to her brother Moses.

And just as he taught music to his sister Miriam, he probably taught other individuals among his people in a similar manner. The evidence is contained in the Biblical report:

So Moses wrote this song the same day, and taught to the children of Israel (Deut. 31:22).

Still another Biblical passage furnishes tangible proof that, during the wandering in the desert, a kind of musical instruction must have taken place:

Write this for a memorial in the book and rehearse (*v'sim*) it in the ears of Joshua (Exod. 17:14).[38]

These words are particularly significant, since they are ascribed to God himself. The instruction "to rehearse," therefore, stems directly from God's commandment. It is easy to discover in this primitive statement a distinct method of maintaining oral tradition. This is even more explicitly stated in Deut. 31:19, 22. In fact, not only in heroic times but during the entire existence of music culture in Ancient Israel, oral teaching was the exclusive method of instruction. It consisted in constant repetition ("rehearsing") of text and music, until both were rooted indelibly in the memory.

One may safely assume that even in the desert the Israelites continued to practice music despite all their incredible hardships.

Thus, they were able to keep alive all the musical knowledge acquired in Egypt, as well as maintain in good condition all the musical instruments they might have brought with them from Egypt. This explains why their musical culture in the new homeland came to such rapid fruition in a relatively short time.

It may further be taken for granted that the man who gave the Law to his people had also seen to it that his people should not give up, or neglect their intellectual possessions. "During the forty years of wandering in the desert, Moses instructed the people."[39] Moses, past master in the musical art of his period, was well qualified, as was no one else, to become the music instructor of his people. Thus Moses, the liberator of his people, as well as their first lawgiver, must be considered as probably the first music educator of the Hebrews and, furthermore, the originator of Jewish music culture in general.

While there is no historical proof for this assertion, there is little doubt that Moses was indirectly responsible for what the Jews accomplished in Cana'an in scarcely two centuries. This can only be explained by assuming that they brought with them all the musical knowledge acquired in Egypt.

The priestly scribes who compiled the Pentateuch in the period between 623 and 458 B.C.E., using old legends and bardic songs, until then transmitted orally, have completely overlooked Moses' merits as the earliest musical educator of the Hebrews.

If we assume, however, that Moses was merely a legendary figure, the merit of having transplanted into the new homeland the muscial knowledge gained in Egypt must be attributed to the *entire people of Israel*. This would have been an even greater accomplishment than if a single person had achieved this by his own initiative.

As we see, the Israelites had the good fortune to move into their new homeland with considerable musical knowledge and the results were soon evident.

CANA'AN

Before turning to an examination of the music of Ancient Israel, let us briefly consider the geographical position of the country that became the homeland of the Israelites and the manner in which it provided them with the material basis for the development of their national and spiritual life according to their own ethnic character.

Cana'an, the new homeland of the Hebrews, was situated between the civilizations of the Nile and the Euphrates valleys. This brought the small country trade and wealth, as well as permanent dangers, for it lay between the powerful millstones of two rival empires. Only a hardy people, conscious of its own destiny, could survive under such precarious conditions, and be able to create its own civilization as well as its own music.

Historical research has proven that the land of Cana'an possessed no civilization of its own prior to its conquest by the Israelites. This is best explained by its geographical location, which for thousands of years provided the surrounding empires and their peoples with a corridor that permitted easy and continuous communication. The route between the peoples of the Nile and Euphrates always passed through Cana⟨an. Armies, ambassadors, and trading caravans maintained a steady flow from one country to the other, with letters, reports, and gifts being exchanged between the rulers. All cultural, political, and commercial barter centered on Cana⟨an.

The other reason why Cana⟨an did not develop a culture of its own lies in its political make-up. The entire coast of the Mediterranean north of Cana⟨an was a string of minuscule principalities, mostly resembling the suburbs of a larger city. The most important of these were the Phoenician cities Arvad, Byblos (Gebal), Beirut, Sidon, the island-city of Tyre, and the cities on the coast, Usu and Akko.

The territory of Cana⟨an, too consisted of small city-states, which constantly rivaled each other, and had their own *ba⟨alim* as well as their own ritual customs. The langauage of the land was similar to that of the Hebrews.

There were three civilizations that influenced Palestinian life since the dawn of history: the Hittite, the old Egyptian, and the much younger Babylonian. In addition, upon entering Cana⟨an, the Israelites had found elements of a Philistine-Cretic culture. It is evident through historical research that all three great civilizations had a common origin: that of the ancient Oriental cultural trend, embracing all the nations of this geographical entity. This trend became divided very early in history into two different branches, one on the Euphrates, the other on the Nile. But their basic characteristics are identical and easily recognizable.

Whether the music of the Cana⟨anite religious rites was similar to that of the Phoenicians, or whether it had its own features, can only be surmised. Yet, it is highly probable that the music of the ancient inhabitants of the country exerted its influence upon the newcomers. At the beginning, there might have been a certain blending of the religions of Yahveh with the cult of the Cana⟨anite deities; at this stage, the rites of both must have been similar.[40] Yahveh was worshipped with pagan ceremonies, consequently with pagan songs. The "high places" mentioned in numerous passages of the Scriptures were the sites of such ceremonies.[41]

After the death of the judge YAïR, we find, among the Israelites, Syrian, Phoenician, Moabite, Ammonite, and Philistine rites, the worship of *ba⟨alim* and *asherim,* as practiced by the Cana⟨anites (Judg. 10:6, 10). The Hebrews called these deities by their Cana⟨anite names (1 Kings 18:24), praised (Josh. 23:7) and worshipped them with the same types of ritual songs as were used in the heathen religions.

Soon, however, the spiritually higher religion of Israel prevailed over the temptations of the sensuous worship of pagan deities. These Jewish qualities were victorious in the struggle of the Yahveh religion over the established crude forms of the heathern cults. As a result, a transformation of the music of the pagan Cana⟨anite rites into the spiritually loftier music of the Jewish cult took place.

Yet, the Jewish people alone could never have created its own musical art, had it not been gifted by nature in musical matters. From Egypt and the desert, Israel brought to Cana⟨an the joy of singing, as well as a wealth of old songs.[42] Its natural gifts must have been stronger than the musical influences found in Cana⟨an. This explains why Jewish music prevailed, despite its still undeveloped form. The Hebrews succeeded rapidly in overcoming the pagan practices and finding their own form of musical expression, a development leading within a remarkably short period to the highly organized musical institutions of David and Solomon.

After the conquest of the Promised Land, the Bible, temporarily, makes no mention of the steadily developing form of Jewish music. This development was evidently interrupted by the war of Judah against the Cana῾anites and against the northern tribes of the Israelites, who still were addicted to pagan rites. Led by the general Barak, the Cana῾anites were vanquished; at the victory celebration, Deborah, the elected judge of the land, sang, together with the victorious Barak, a triumphal paean, which, in its poetical beauty, rivals the intensity of Moses' and Miriam's songs at the Red Sea (Judg. 5).

GRAETZ, the classical historian of the Jewish people, does not refer in any way, to the music of the Hebrews prior to Barak's victory. At this point, he mentions for the first time, belatedly and hesitatingly, the musical aptitude of the Jews:

> There was now witnessed a significant change in Israel. The unexpected and eventful victories had aroused amongst them the melodious power of song, the first indication of that talent without which no nation can attain to a superior degree of culture. The first songs of the Hebrew muse were those of war and victory. The authors (*moshelim*) of warlike hymns rose at once in public estimation, and their productions were preserved in special collections, as for example in the "Book of the Wars of the Lord."[43]

Barak's victory brought peace to the country for forty years. This restless land was, however, in a constant state of turbulence, and soon Judah had to fight another war against the Midianites and the Amalekites. This time, the leader of the campaign was Gideon, who had in his army 300 *shofar*-blowers.

There is to be found in the Book of Judges another musical episode, related to the tragic story of Jephtha's daughter, who—according to the custom of the time—went out to meet her father "with timbrels and with dances," a fact that cost her her young life.

Further temporary impediments to the development of Jewish music were the quarrels of the Jewish tribes among themselves, as well as the idolatry of the clans of Dan and Benjamin. But with the Book of Samuel the first authentic reports about the musical practice of the Jews emerge, never again to disappear from the Bible.

In this period fall two important events of Jewish history, both of which have had an immediate impact upon the development of the music of the Hebrews. One of them was the election of a king over Israel, which exerted a powerful influence for the further musical culture of the land; the other was the calling of the young shepherd-boy David to the court. The artistic as well as the sociological implications of both events will be examined later. At this stage, however, we must deal with an unusual phase of the Jewish musical practice, which must be considered the strongest propulsive force responsible for the emerging and flourishing musical culture of Israel, and which deserves more attention than has been its share up to now.

This aspect, often misunderstood and misrepresented, deals with the "Schools of the Prophets," created by Samuel.

THE SCHOOLS OF THE PROPHETS*

That there must have existed during the entire national existence of Israel a widespread and systematic music instruction, becomes evident from the ultimate results: a musical culture, justly famous in Antiquity. There are only scanty reports as to how this instruction took place, who the teachers were, and what the social implications of Jewish musical education were. However, in scrutinizing closely even these brief data, we may arrive at quite a number of pertinent facts.

There are no indications in the Pentateuch (except the two passages in Exod. 17:14 and Deut. 31:19, 22), in the books of Joshua, Judges, and Ruth, how music was taught in Ancient Israel. The initial reference to it, still rather veiled, may be found in the first Book of Samuel. There we learn about

> a band of prophets coming down from the high place with a psaltery, and a timbrel, and a pipe, and a harp, before them; and they will be prophesying (1 Sam. 10:5).

But what does this procession of prophets, "prophesying" with musical instruments, actually imply? Israel's history gives the answer to this question.

After Samuel's political goal was fulfilled, he solemnly laid down his office as the judge of the nation, and devoted himself to the intellectual education of the nation. In his solemn appeal addressed to the entire people on the occasion of his retirement, he stated:

> I will instruct you in the good and the right way (1 Sam. 12:23).

The idea is not new. Samuel merely continued the tradition, established by Moses, that the leaders of the people, the prophets, those privileged by the Lord, had to serve as intellectual educators of the nation. Yet, the manner in which Samuel carried out this duty is as new as it is unique in the cultural history of Israel.

Samuel realized that the education of the people could be safeguarded only if a staff of enthusiastic and capable disciples were to be brought up for the continuation of the work begun by him. In order to create this staff, Samuel founded a special school, with the aim of preparing men not belonging to the priestly class for this important educational task. Samuel alone possessed the necessary popularity and authority to embark on such a venture. After he retired from public affairs, Samuel remained the spiritual leader of his nation. Around him assembled a group of dedicated men of various ages, who understood him and were prepared to place themselves unreservedly in the service of this great project.

HERDER was the first who plainly recognized and appreciated the great design of the schools of the prophets. In pertinent observations he described Samuel's educational goals.[44]

One cannot help assuming the existence of one or several such "schools" when one finds in the Biblical text a sudden and unexplained upsurge of large choirs and orchestras, consisting of thoroughly organized and trained musical

---

* This section and several other portions of chapter 8, Judaea, are based mainly on a previous work of the author, *Music in Ancient Israel*. He is greatly indebted to its publishers, The Philosophical Library, New York, for their permission to use certain portions of that book for the present work.

groups, which would be virtually inconceivable without lengthy, methodical preparation. Similar schools of music are known to have existed among other nations of Antiquity, far back in times of Sumeria.[45]

In the light of ample historical evidence, it is somewhat strange to find, among certain Biblical exegetes, a tendency to deny flatly the existence of such schools of prophets.[46]

Whether we call these institutions "societies," "guilds," or "schools," or whether we use for them the later term "sons of the prophets" (2 Kings 2:3, 5; 4:1; 6:1), is irrelevant. RIEHM calls attention to

the relationship between these mature, in part married, companions and the prophets [namely their "teachers"] themselves as a relation of a spiritual communion based upon piety,

by which the correct approach to understanding the whole institution is established.[47]

Following the model of Samuel's school, institutions of the same order were soon organized in other places. The principals of these schools were "holy men," who were called "fathers." The first of these was Samuel himself (1 Sam. 19:20); later, one finds among them such great prophets as Elijah (2 Kings 2:12) and Elisha (2 Kings 6:1).[48] The pupils were called "sons of Prophets" (2 Kings 6:1). They lived together with their teachers (2 Kings 4:38) and led a frugal life. They built themselves primitive wooden huts (2 Kings 6:1, 2), which in time grew into small villages. There were among these pupils more mature men, sometimes married and with children; others were young and unmarried. They came from all strata of the people, from every tribe of Israel. The sole prerequisite for admission was the wish and the aptitude for learning, plus voluntary submission to the common discipline, and devotion to the religious and national ideals of Israel.

The pupils of the schools were instructed in the Law, in the Scriptures, and in psalm-singing. At the same time, stress was laid upon learning to play an instrument for the accompaniment of singing (*kle shir;* see 1 Chron. 25:1, 7).

Specific care was devoted to instruction in music. Not all the pupils learned to play an instrument, only those who showed some aptitude for it. Singing, however, seems to have been taught to all of them, since common participation in vocal ensembles was a regular feature in the gatherings and processions of the prophet-pupils. Such choral singing with instrumental accompaniment, called "prophesying" in the Bible, must have exercised a fascinating, even hypnotic effect upon the people of those times, as evidenced by the experiences of Saul and his messengers (1 Sam. 19:20–24).

Samuel's association of prophets is without doubt the first *public music school* in human history. Music education in the liturgical schools of Sumeria and Egypt cannot be considered as *public* instruction, since it was restricted to the members of the priestly class, whereas in Israel anyone who so desired was accepted in these associations, or schools.

The locality where the first school of this order was established, was Nayoth in Ramah, a settlement in the neighborhood of Ramah which, in the course of time, increased considerably. From *Nayoth,* meaning "huts," "dwellings," the "sons of the prophets" would march every morning and evening in a solemn procession to a high place (*bamah*), where an altar was erected and sacred ceremonies were performed. This "hill of God" (1 Sam. 10:5) was a ritual institution created by Samuel, a place of devotion and prayer, maintained by the "sons of the prophets," but it was also used by the people as a place of pilgrimage (1 Sam. 10:3).

From the high place at Ramah came the solemn procession described by Samuel in his "prophecy" on the occasion of the anointing of Saul as king of Israel (1 Sam. 10:5). This portion of Samuel's prophecy is not a prediction in the proper sense, for Samuel knew the daily "routine" of his disciples, so that whatever he "foretold" to Saul was nothing but the events taking place daily at the same hour.[49]

But Samuel's prophecy is important for us for another reason. It lists the instruments being taught in this "Conservatory of Music": the *nebel* (harp), the *kinnor* (lyre), the *halil* (oboe, or pipe), and the *tof* (timbrel). All these are instruments known to the Hebrews from Egypt; the long period of life in the desert had not impaired their skill in handling them, as evidenced by the historical facts.

The main subjects in the schools were poetry and music. For this purpose, various collections of poems, bardic songs, popular folklore, fairy-tales, and legends may have been used, as they still existed in heroic times. Unfortunately, these collections, probably assembled in book form in later days, have been lost; we know of them merely from a few incidental remarks in Biblical texts. It almost seems as if these old folk-books had been destroyed purposely, in order that they might be replaced by a single, authoritative book written by priestly functionaries.

While Samuel was alive, his famous school must surely have served as a powerful center of attraction for the entire nation within and without its geographical boundaries. From far and wide the disciples came in great numbers, so that in due course the colony at Ramah could not possibly admit all the neophytes. As a result, similar schools sprang up in Gibeah, Beth-el, Gilgal, Mizpah, Jericho, perhaps also in Carmel, and probably in many other places.

Whereas the intellectual repercussions of Samuel's educational activity in general made themselves felt to the full extent only after a certain lapse of time, his influence in the field of music brought forth immediate and important consequences.

As we know from Biblical history, David escaped from Saul's persecutions by taking refuge in Nayoth at Ramah, where he was in hiding for a certain period (1 Sam. 19:18). When he came to Nayoth he had already established for himself considerable fame as a *kinnor*-player. His enforced sojourn in Nayoth, however, had another beneficial significance for Jewish music. There seem to have originated and matured the plans that eventually led to the creation of Temple music as a permanent ritual institution.

It does not require much imagination to visualize both men, the older one, wise with knowledge, and the younger one, full of ardent initiative, holding long discussions about bringing to life a new important element of the ritual action—organized sacred music. Henceforth music was to be not merely a subordinate element in the ritual, functioning as a stereotyped tonal background for sacred ceremonies. It was elevated and treated as an integral part of the divine cult and coordinated with the other sacred actions, associated inseparably with the sacrifice, in effect becoming itself a sort of tonal sacrifice.

The institution of *organized* sacred music represents a revolutionary innovation. The creation of liturgical music as an equal partner with all other ritual ceremonies is the most important turning point in the history of Jewish music. We do not know whether the plan for this decisive reform originated with Samuel. But it is not unlikely that this promoter, full of ideas, cherished for a long time such plans and that these came to full bloom only when David sojourned at Ramah. At any rate, David, with the energy peculiar to him, was the right man to put such ideas into action. David could hardly do better than to avail himself of a system that had undergone its crucial test at Ramah. All he had to do was apply it, on a larger scale, to the future sacred musical organization he envisioned.

In a short time there developed in Israel a flourishing ritual music of the sanctuary, an innovation that, artistically, ethically, and from the angle of internal and external organization, was exemplary.

The first historical account about such widespreal popular musical practice is contained in the sumptuous description of David's bringing of the ark of the Covenant to Jerusalem (2 Sam. 6:5) (historians date this event 1002 B.C.E.). A significant point concerning this solemn cortège is that the people marched in it "even with songs" (1 Chron. 13:8). The whole description promptly suggests a broad musical culture, which would scarcely have been conceivable without adequate preparatory work by a score of musical educators. And who would have been more qualified for such a task than the "sons of the prophets"? Thus, it stands to reason that the prophet-students, apart from the instruction of professional musicians (all the "students" of these schools must be in fact considered as such), also took zealous care of the musical education of the people itself. About the success of their endeavors the above Biblical passages offer substantial evidence.

These passages cite most of the instruments played by the "sons of the prophets" in their daily processions and which, consequently, were taught in the schools. The omission of the *halilim* (pipes) on this occasion might be explained by somewhat summary reporting, since another passage of the Bible points to this instrument as being widely used in those days (1 Kings 1:40).

THE BEGINNING OF JEWISH MUSICAL CULTURE

As long as the schools of the prophets flourished, they exerted a powerful incentive for music-making in the public and private life of the Israelites. After these schools disbanded, a new organization of professional musicians probably developed to take care of the ever-expanding music instruction. This would explain the sudden resurgence, seemingly without previous preparation, of large choirs and orchestral groups (2 Sam. 6:5; 6:10). How did they come into being?

Saul's court in Gilgal was modest and unostentatious. As soon, however, as David transferred the royal residence to Jerusalem, the attraction and the atmosphere of courtly life drew the choice musicians to David's city. From then on, the musical culture radiated to all the provinces and fertilized the music practice of large segments of the population. In David's court, groups of male and female singers were formed (2 Sam. 19:36), and permanent instrumental ensembles were developed to entertain the courtly retinue. To appreciate this sudden resurgence of music, we must consider the general attitude toward music at the beginning of Israel's kingdom, reflected in the well-known Biblical story of Saul's melancholy. To dissipate the king's depression, his couriers had advised him

> to seek out a man who is a skillful player on the harp. . . . . Then answered one of the young men and said: "Behold, I have seen a son of Jesse the Beth-lehemite, that is skillful in playing". . . . Therefore Saul sent messengers unto Jesse, and said: "Send me David thy son, who is with the sheep" (1 Sam. 16:16 ff).

Thus came David, the simple shepherd boy, to the royal court. His artistry in playing the *kinnor* became the starting-point of his rise to power.

For a simple shepherd boy to be so extraordinarily gifted in playing the *kinnor* that even the members of the royal court took cognizance of his talent must be regarded as unusual for that period. A different view is possible, however, if we consider that the *kinnor*-playing shepherd boy actually represented a cross section of the music culture of that epoch. One may well surmise that there existed quite a number of other players of the *kinnor*, among whom David stood out as being especially gifted. But the great number of minstrels alive at that time indicates the presence not only of a certain order and stability of musical practice but its inevitable corollaries: building of instruments and music instruction.

Apart from its artistic significance, David's musicianship has also a deep sociological implication. His ability to play the *kinnor* was the immediate cause for his invitation to become a court musician and, consequently, was the first step to his future career.

An indirect allusion to the existing music organization is contained in the answer of old Barzillai to David, when the king has invited him to go with him to Jerusalem:

> I am this day four-score years old; can I discern between good and bad? can thy servant taste what I eat or what I drink? can I hear any more the voice of singing men and singing women? wherefore then should thy servant be yet a burden unto my lord the king? (2 Sam. 19:36).

The male and female singers alluded to by Barzillai presuppose logically the existence of some kind of organization that was likely to control the supply of qualified performers for the royal court and for aristocratic homes.

THE CREATION OF THE SACRED MUSICAL SERVICE

David's fame as a conqueror and a statesman is eclipsed by the greatest of his accomplishments, the creation of the sacred musical service as an integral part of the Jewish ritual (we leave aside for the time being David's alleged authorship of the Psalms).

It was shown earlier how Samuel and David discussed the plans for the creation of the Temple music, also that at Rahma the future organization of the sacred musical service was already extant in its germ. All David had to do was to apply things seen at Ramah to the new requirements. How he accomplished this shows a rare ability for organization.

Prior to the final form of the sacred music, there must have been groups of professional musicians similar to those of the later Levitical service. When the ark of the Covenant was transferred to Jerusalem, a large, evidently well-schooled choral group and also a well trained orchestra of numerous players accompanied it. The pioneering work of the "sons of the prophets" is clearly recognizable, for the seeds sown by the inmates of Samuel's schools had ripened very quickly.

According to the Biblical narration of the memorable event, David

gathered together all the chosen men of Israel, thirty thousand (2 Sam. 6:1).

What is here suggested is that a group of thirty thousand singing and playing musicians (not counting the women and children) added immensely to this festive occasion. In evaluating the accomplishments of this huge group, it must be taken into consideration that most of them, with the possible exception of the "sons of the prophets," were amateurs. Professional musicians, i.e., those making a living exclusively or mainly by music, probably existed in those days only in restricted numbers. The numerous singers and instrumentalists in David's procession were dilettanti, lovers of music, from all strata of the people, practicing music for the sheer delight of it. These also included a great number of the prophet-pupils, who had a musical education but did not enter music as a profession.

The first musical organization (in the proper sense of the word) described in the Bible, arose in connection with the sacred musical service created by David. This organization, the outcome of a lengthy development, crystallized into the form of regular Temple services. This is substantiated by the report dealing with the second phase of transferring the ark of the Covenant to Jerusalem (1 Chron. 14:1; 15:1; 15:3; 15:15).

According to David's command, the Levites appointed the leaders of song and the other singer-musicians, all of whom are quoted by name in the Biblical text (1 Chron. 15:17–22).

This detailed account proves that the Levitical organization must have passed a previous extended stage of development, enabling David to select the most qualified men out of the multitude of trained singers. Judging from the previous musical indications of this report, the chronicler himself evidently belonged to the Levitical guild.

First, he mentions the soloists: Heman, Asaph, and Jedithun-Ethan. These were the three outstanding singer-virtuosi of their day. They were appointed precentors and, furthermore, were vested with the privilege of striking the brass cymbals, a function endowed with a high distinction.

Then the chronicler speaks of a group "of the second degree," in which a certain number of musicians played instruments while leading the melody. Still another group of singers played instruments that had certain accompanying functions. This ensemble of singers and instrumentalists was trained and rehearsed by the chief of the Levitical musicians, Chenanjah, "the master of the singers in the song" (1 Chron. 15:27), who also acted as conductor of the performances.

Besides the Levitical singers, a number of priests also were assigned, to sound the sacred silver trumpets (*hazozerot*). These did not belong to the orchestra proper, but had other liturgical duties (1 Chron. 15:24).

At a superficial glance, the Biblical report may leave the impression that the accompaniment of these huge choral masses in an outdoor procession was entrusted merely to fourteen weak-sounding stringed instruments; but such an assumption would grossly underestimate the practical musical sense of the Levites. For, after all, it is a matter of the most elementary knowledge that choral masses, referred to above, have to be accompanied by an adequate number of instrumentalists in order to intone correctly and also to stay together melodically and rhythmically.

In the light of this reasoning, one may well realize that the Biblical report does not deal here with a modest instrumental body of fourteen musicians. It is therefore safe to assume that the eight *nebel*-players and the six *kinnor*-players were merely respective leaders of similar instrumental groups, just as they were the precentors of a choral group.

The assumption that a large choral body was used on this solemn occasion is, in fact, confirmed by the chronicler himself. David appears to have made his final preparations following the selection of the most qualified singers for the sacred service. The number of all the Levitical singers is given as four thousand (1 Chron. 23:5) all of whom probably participated on this memorable occasion.

From the above-mentioned seventeen singer-musicians, David made a scrupulous choice and put the very best of them before the ark when it was finally brought to Jerusalem (1 Chron. 16:5,6).

Then follows the most significant indication of the chronicler, that of the announcement of the starting point of the organized musical service:

Then on that day did David first ordain to give thanks unto the Lord, by the hand of Asaph and his brethren (1 Chron. 16:7).

Thus, the transfer of the ark of the Covenant to Jerusalem was at the same time coincident with the birthday of organized Temple music.

In this manner, the principle of daily musical performances in the sacred service was firmly established and the functions of the temporary office-holders assigned. Now King David could turn his attention to the final organization of the Temple music in accordance with a carefully prepared plan. Until then, he had "appointed" the singers and musicians; but from now on, they were "elected" for the permanent service by means of a procedure that was carried out by the representatives of the musicians themselves. With this act, the corporate spirit of the musicians is revealed for the first time.

The chronicler describes the election itself in all its details. The number of the Levites of thirty years and upwards was thirty and eight thousand (1 Chron. 23:2,3). From this number were selected the Levites trained in music:

four thousand to praise the Lord with instruments (1 Chron. 23:5).

If there were four thousand singers and musicians merely among the Levites, that is, in a single tribe of Israel, it is logical to assume that in the entire nation the number of those well-versed in musical matters must have been proportionately higher.

From these four thousand singers David selected, after careful scrutiny, and obviously in agreement with the musicians themselves, those

> that were instructed in singing unto the Lord, even all that were skillful; and the number of them was two hundred four score and eight (1 Chron. 25:7).

This good-sized choir was divided into twenty-four "wards," forming groups of twelve singers each, under the leadership of a precentor for each one. All these twenty-four group leaders are mentioned by name in the chronicles, a sign of the importance of their office.

Following this arrangement, all those concerned

> cast lots ward against ward, as well the small as the great, the teacher and the scholar (1 Chron. 25:8).

Thus, the order of sequence of the groups was determined by lot, a procedure that quickly eliminated all disputes for precedence and all personal or professional sensibilities from the very outset.

From this time on, the two hundred and eighty-eight singers referred to constituted a closed corporation or class-conscious guild, which had its own rules, its own precepts, and special privileges that were guarded with jealous zeal from possible intruders.

The Temple musicians had their own dwellings and lived in settlements in and around Jerusalem (Ezra 2:70; Neh. 7:73; 13:10). As befitted their sacred office, they represented a prominent and privileged class.

This first election showed that the guild of singers was organized in a manner similar to that of a modern trade union. By casting lots, the young as well as the old, teachers as well as pupils, enjoyed equal rights. Within the corporation, or guild, there were no preferences, no priorities of the older and more experienced ones. The singers admitted to the guild were "all masters" (*meibin*); all had the same privileges and the same duties. Jealousies or disputes of precedence were eliminated by the voluntary submission of all members to the decision drawn by the lot. Thus, the Temple musicians were, from the very start, a select professional group who strictly guarded their prerogatives, and enjoyed great esteem and considerable power.

At the first election, the group leaders were chosen exclusively from among the sons of Asaph, Heman, and Jedithun (Ethan), not merely because they were evidently best qualified for the sacred service, but probably also to honor the fathers through their sons.

According to the chronicler, the sons of the three most famous singers were twenty-four in number (1 Chron. 25:2–5). It would appear, therefore, as if the twenty-four "wards" owed their existence to the fortuitous circumstance that the three singers happened to have twenty-four sons.

Yet, whether Heman had fourteen sons, as stated in verse 4, is highly doubtful. It seems that the chronicler, in order to arrive at the given number of group leaders (24), had invented some of the names. It is evident that he used some liturgical text, possibly a fragment of a discarded psalm, to construct from it the required number of names. Indeed, if we read consecutively the last nine names of verse 4, starting with Hananiah, and interpret the inherent meaning of the words, we find that the text thus obtained represents a little poem:

> Be gracious unto me, O God,
> be gracious unto me.
> Thou are my God.
> Thou hast increased
> and raised up help for him
> that sat in distress.
> Do thou make the [prophetic]
> visions abundant.

According to EWALD,[50] this was part of an ancient famous oracle, while HAUPT[51] is of the opinion that it was a fragment of a post-exilic psalm. It is therefore evident that the names of some of the twenty-four group leaders have been artificially created.

It would be more logical to assume that the number of the groups coincided with some practical necessities of the sacred service.

The central point of the divine service was the sacrifice. The sacrificial act was always accompanied by the singing of the Levites.[52] There were three daily regular services, at morning, *shaharit*, at noon, *minha*, and *maʿarib* in the evening. The daily regular sacrifices were offered in the morning and evening services. Besides, there were numerous additional sacrifices, voluntary or expiatory offerings, the volume and nature of which were most diversified. These were offered in the noon service and required priestly as well as Levitical assistance. Thus, the Levitical singers led three regular services a day.

Each "ward" consisted of twelve singer-musicians; the three daily sacrificial rites required that one of these groups always provide the musical background. On the Sabbath, in accordance with the increased solemnity of the day, two groups might have participated in each service. The three daily services of one group on weekdays, and the three services of two groups on the Sabbath, add up to twenty-four services a week, just as many as there were "wards." On the three great yearly festivals, Passah, Weeks, and Tabernacles, the number of the groups may have been increased considerably—probably eight for every service—so that at these festivals all twenty-four groups performed on the same day.[53]

The coincidence of the number of groups and of the normal weekly services would lead to the assumption that the groups alternated for each service, so that every group had to provide music for one service a week. This alone would have been a rather easy duty for the singers. In reality, the working conditions of the Levitical singers were even more comfortable.

According to the vague indications of the chronicler (1 Chron. 9:25), the groups of singers, like those of the priests and porters, alternated weekly. The weekly alternation is confirmed by JOSEPHUS[54] and also reported by the Mishnah.[55] This would have amounted to an unusual situation, namely, that each group, after a week's continuous service, would have been unoccupied for twenty-three consecutive weeks, almost half a year, except when they were needed for the High Holidays. However, there are weighty artistic and musico-technical reasons against this assumption.

The performances of the Temple singers were justly famous in Antiquity for their artistic perfection. It would have been scarcely possible to attain and maintain this perfection if the singers had had so rare an opportunity to present themselves in the sacred service. A more frequent schedule was indispensable for them to become familiarized not only with the complicated ritual, but also

with performing *in public*. To be sure, they could be taught during the rehearsals how to master their singing and playing; but it is common knowledge
that the criterion of an artistic accomplishment cannot be reached in rehearsals
alone, however assiduous they may be, but in the performance itself. For artistic
reasons, therefore, the assumption that each group had a continuous service a
week, followed by such a long interruption, is highly improbable.

On the other hand, the alternation of the groups after each service would
have involved other disadvantages. Each of the three daily services was different,
not only in the prayers and lections, but also with regard to the other ceremonies
requiring music. Furthermore, on the different days of the week, the Levites
sang different psalms.[56] In the additional sacrifices of the noon service, the
accompanying music had to be adapted to the number and nature of the
multitude of offerings. All these differences were of such nature that alternating
groups would have had difficulties in accommodating themselves to the ever-
changing requirements. This would certainly have influenced unfavorably the
quality of the musical rendition.

Therefore, for practical reasons, the assumption that the groups alternated
after each service must likewise be discarded.

The truth might be found midway. A simple solution to satisfying both the
principle of artistry and that of organization could be reached by assuming
that the groups changed every day, with the effect that the three daily services
were provided by the same group. For weekdays one, and for Sabbath two,
groups would have amounted to a three-weeks' turn for each group. After
three weeks, the turn would have started with a different group, so that every
group would gradually participate in all of the week-day services, thus becoming thoroughly familiar with performing all of the ritual. The increased
number of services on the High Holidays would have somewhat shortened the
alternation every three weeks, but this would not have affected the principle
involved in the rotation of the groups.

The advantages of this schedule are obvious. The singers thus had ample
opportunity to prepare themselves for the services, i.e., to attend the necessary
rehearsals, as well as to learn new psalms and also to teach the younger generation liturgical singing. Furthermore, this would have given them the possibility
of tilling their fields and gardens, a prime economic necessity for the Levitical
singers for the assurance of their subsistence.

Through the assumption of the daily alternating groups is not corroborated
by any coeval sources, it is highly probable, for artistic and organizational,
as well as for economic reasons, that this might have been the case.

LEVITICAL MUSIC INSTRUCTION

The schools of prophets may have flourished for some time after Samuel's
death, although we no longer come across any direct Biblical references either
to their existence or their permanent disbanding. But judging from certain
Biblical allusions, their activity may have been sustained for a certain period
of time. However, their influence gradually decreased, with regard to professional music instruction and general music practice in daily life. The schools
of the prophets ceased to be regarded as the privileged institutions of musical
education. They were replaced—to use a modern term—by the "Academy of

Music," a regular school for liturgical education, with religious music as the main subject of its curriculum, in which hundreds of students were continuously trained for a professional career.

Contrary to the all-embracing musical instruction to be found in the schools of the prophets, Levitical music instruction was one-sided throughout. It was restricted, in fact, to liturgical music alone, and excluded anything of a secular nature.

Thus, the beautiful ancient bardic songs, cultivated with so much zeal by the sons of the prophets, gradually fell into oblivion. Soon, only a faint memory of the earlier treasures of heroic poetry remained, and had not the Biblical text occasionally mentioned the title of one of the old books, we would have no knowledge whatever that such collections had existed in Israel's heroic times.

Levitical music instruction aimed at practical performance, and in this field, the teachers were eminently successful. Men, women, and boys were prepared meticulously as practitioners of sacred music.

There is no doubt that women, too, participated in the Levitical music, at least in its early period. Later editors of the Biblical books, manifestly biased by anti-feminine tendencies, have suppressed most of the data pertaining to this point. Nevertheless, certain clues lead to the definite conclusions that the role women played in Temple music was an important one (see below).

A peculiar opinion has been advanced to the effect that a special music school for women existed in Ancient Israel. GALPIN claims to have found certain indications for this assumption in Biblical passages and especially in some headings of the psalms.[57] Doubtless, women and girls must have received instruction in musical art as long as they took part in Levitical singing. However, the existence of a special school for them is not supported by historical evidence. It is logical to assume that the musical education of both sexes proceeded jointly, even though there might have been on occasion separate rehearsals for the training of women's voices, as is considered practical even today.

The participation of boy singers in the Temple choir is not attested to in the Bible itself. The Mishnah, however, furnishes the information that boys belonging to Levitical families were admitted into the choir. Their participation, already possible in the First Temple, was inevitable, for a Levitical singer had to be brought up under a special system of musical education, and this in early youth if he was to achieve professional efficiency.

The singers were admitted into the Levitical choir when thirty years of age (1 Chron. 23:3). This meant that only when they reached this period of maturity could they become full-fledged members of the Levitical guild of singers. The mere fact that they were admitted at this relatively late age proves that their years of schooling must have been long and arduous. Otherwise they could have started their professional career at the age of twenty-five or even sooner.

They were required to serve for a period of twenty years, until they reached the age of fifty, when the vocal qualities of a singer generally start to decline. Prior to their admittance, they had to pass a five-years apprenticeship.[58] Such a relatively short period of preparation (beginning supposedly at the age of twenty-five) appears inadequate in view of the fact that the Israelites did not have a musical notation, at least in the Occidental sense. The Levitical singers were obliged to memorize the entire voluminous and complex musical ritual in order to master all its details. To achieve this goal, the actual training must have been considerably longer, and thus it was bound to start at an earlier age, most probably in childhood. This is clearly stated in the Mishnah:

None that was not of age could enter the Temple court to take part in the [Temple-] service save only when the Levites stood up to sing; and they [the children] did not join the singing with harp and lyre, but with the mouth alone to add spice to the music. R. Eliezer b. Jacob says: They did not help to make up the required number [i.e., twelve Levites standing on the Platform], nor did they stand on the platform but they used to stand on the ground so that their heads were between the legs of the Levites; and they used to be called the Levites' tormentors (zo'are).[59]

Zo'are is a play upon words, originated by Rashi and Bertinoro. The assonance with so'ade, "helper," had given rise to the interpretation that the little singers, owing to their vocal quality ("to add spice to the music"), may have annoyed the adult singers, to wit, made them jealous. Thus the Levitical singers might have considered "the little ones" as dangerous competitors.

While the Levitical singers accompanied themselves on lyres and harps, the boys sang "with the mouth alone"; by implication, this seems to indicate that they had the lead in singing, or at least that they doubled up the melody in the upper octave. In this tessitura, the pitch level of the boys was identical with that of the female voice; so it came to pass that after the women had been eliminated owing to a growing anti-feminine tendency of the priesthood, boys took over their functions.

To be sure, the rabbinical references to the use of boy singers in the Levitical choir imply the practice of the Second Temple. It is safe to assume, however, that the usage had already been instituted in the First Temple. Without an appropriately long training, the high artistic level and famous musical precision of the Levitical performances, repeatedly attested in the Scriptures, could not have been achieved.

The singing of boys in artistic ensembles warrants the assumption, if only by implication, that children in general might have had their own songs. This is corroborated by two parallel allusions to children's songs in the New Testament (Matt. 11:7 and Luke 7:32), from which we may infer, retrospectively, the existence of similar customs among the Jews during the Old Testament era. For cradle songs we have a direct, even if non-Jewish evidence: the "work-song" for nurses, mentioned by John Chrysostom.[60] Although this item, too, refers to post-Biblical times, we may assume, *per analogiam*, that cradle songs were familiar in Ancient Israel, this being, in fact, a universal practice the world over, and at all times.

Levitical music instruction took place within the enclosure of the Temple itself:

And within the inner gate were the chambers of the singers (*sharim*) in the inner court (Ezek. 40:44).

The Mishnah is even more explicit:

And there were chambers beneath the Court of the Israelites which opened into the Court of the Women, and here the Levites played upon harps and lyres and the cymbals and all instruments of music.[61]

"Played" implies here the act of rehearsing, which evidently was so assiduous that even one of the Temple gates was named after the music resounding there all the time:

> And opposite them on the north, counting from the west [were]: the Gate of Jeconiah, the Gate of Offering, the Gate of the Women, and the Gate of Singing.[62]

The Mishnaic "Gate Tadi" (sometimes spelled "Gate Tari") has been called the "Gate of the Poets," because the authors of the psalms, who were the composers at the same time, used to teach their newly created melodies to the singers in a separate chamber.[63]

SOCIOLOGY OF THE MUSICAL PROFESSION

In addition to artistic considerations, the sociological aspect of the musical profession in Ancient Israel, dealing primarily with the economic situation in this particular field, calls for a brief examination.

Similarly to what takes place in any other profession, the economic factor in the musical profession was regulated by the natural interplay between demand and supply. An intensive cultivation of music opened automatically a large field, for music teachers as well as performers. And their dependence on earnings from their professional practice was operative to the full extent, even in such a relatively uncomplicated economic structure as that of Ancient Israel.

How did the performing musician and the music teacher make a living in Israel? What sources of income did he have? With regard to the Levitical musicians the answer is self-evident, for from the very beginning they were taken care of by the population itself. The singers received their "portion" out of the contributions of the people designed for the priests and Levites (2 Chron. 31:4). As an essential part of their income, they received farming land, by which the sustaining basis of their economic existence was assured. After the return from the Babylonian exile, the provision of foreign kings procured them additional income and other economic advantages. Among these, the most important was the edict, issued by CYRUS and confirmed by DARIUS, stipulating that

> let it be given them day by day without fail . . . that which they have need of (Ezra 6:8,9).

This represented practically a regular "salary." Thus, throughout the entire existence of the State of Israel, the Levitical musicians were free from any concern regarding their economic necessities. The education of the young generation, like their Temple service, was considered an integral part of public duties.

With regard to the secular musicians, a considerable difference in status is to be noted. In general, they were dependent on the income earned through their professional services. But very few could have lived merely by their activity as teachers. They were mainly performing musicians, playing at popular or private festivities, at weddings, banquets, funerals, and the like. Another source of their income might have been the manufacturing and repairing of musical instruments. Among the multiple trades and professions mentioned in the Bible and in the rabbinical literature, that of builders of instruments is lacking. Nevertheless, this profession must have existed, for, with a few possible exceptions, the multitude of instruments used in the ritual services as well as in secular life could hardly have been imported from foreign lands.

The assumption is not far-fetched that the Biblical chroniclers considered it to be self-evident for a musician to build and to repair his own instrument. Only in a few isolated instances was the repair of damaged Temple instruments entrusted to foreign craftsmen.

The early rabbinical literature refers repeatedly to the repairing of instruments,[64] without mentioning, however, the profession of builders of instruments. Thus we are driven to the only possible conclusion that many secular musicians also manufactured instruments for their own and public use. This, in fact, might well have served them as an additional, and perhaps even substantial, source of income. The Levitical musicians, on the other hand, had to build their instruments and maintain them in good shape as part of their service, and without an additional remuneration, of course.

It is largely a matter of conjecture whether the "wages" that the secular musician received for playing at public or private festivities, as well as the "fee" for lessons, were paid to him in money or natural products. There are good reasons to believe that the latter form was prevalent in Ancient Israel, for it is the customary practice in all human societies based on primitive economics. The Bible does not contain any data pertaining to payment for music instruction, but the early rabbinical literature refers to it on several occasions. We are informed, for instance, that the office of the schoolmaster (who was also the music teacher) was a full time job, keeping him busy on week days as well as on the Sabbath:

A school master (*ḥazzan*) may look where the children are reading but he himself may not read [on the Sabbath].[65]

It is certain, therefore, that he received payment for his services.

"Practicing" an instrument is clearly distinguished in the Talmud from "playing" it. Thus, anyone blowing the *shofar* merely for the sake of practice does not fulfill his religious duties.[66]

Among the subjects taught to children was cantillation of the Scriptures. The opinions of the rabbis were divided on whether the teacher was allowed to accept payment for this particular task. Some rabbis opined that the teacher was prohibited from accepting payment for teaching to read the Torah but could receive payment for teaching the rules of punctuation and phrase structure of the Biblical text, both of which also included automatically their perennial musical companion—the Scriptural cantillation. Others insisted that the fee for teaching the punctuation of the Torah, though not of other portions of the Scriptures, be excluded. Still others maintained that the fee was justified in any case, since it did not constitute a payment for the teaching itself but merely for supervising the children in the school. From this discussion, carried on rather extensively in the Talmud, we may gather that there even existed a regular weekly or monthly payment for teaching the punctuation, which also included cantillation.

The following talmudic passage, too, refers to teaching cantillation (or perhaps some kind of regulated psalmody):

[They sing the Hallel] like a school teacher [whose class was usually in the synagogue, where he acted as a precentor], who recites the *Shem'ā* in the Synagogue, viz., he begins and they respond after him.[67]

Apart from cantillation, the Talmud repeatedly refers indirectly to teaching the blowing of the *shofar*.[68]

A special feature of music instruction might have been the art of mournful wailing, performed exclusively by women. That they were actually taught it is evident from the Biblical passage:

Teach your daughter wailing, and every one her neighbour lamentation (Jer. 9:19).

It is obvious that in this case the teachers were the wailing women themselves, having already acquired the necessary experience.

The Levites were duty-bound to teach their art to others. A refusal to fulfill this obligation was considered a flagrant breach of professional ethics. In the long recorded history of Temple music there is only one incident related in which a singer refused to teach his art to anybody. This was the case of the singer-virtuoso HYGROS ben LEVI, discussed in another part of this study.[69]

THE BOOK OF PSALMS

The Book of Psalms (Hebrew: *Sefer Tehillim*, Greek: *Psaltērion*, Latin: *Psalterium*) is a collection of 150 lyric poems,[70] in five sections or books. The Hebrew title refers to the *internal contents* of the book, as praises in honor of God, whereas the Greek and Latin titles define the *external pattern* of the book, as hymns sung to the sounds of the psaltery, one of the principal instruments for the accompaniment of singing in Ancient Israel.

The psalms contain, mainly in their headings, musical terms that are supposedly indications and instructions referring to the music of the psalms or to their musical performance. This attaches to the Psalter a particular importance for our study.

Originally, the Psalter contained probably more than the present number of poems. Some might have been lost, others deleted from the main body by later editors. Whatever remained after the final editing is a unique anthology of lyrico-religious poetry. It is surely not accidental that the Psalter became, and has remained until today, the fundamental liturgical song book of the Israelites.

The Book of Psalms is generally considered the summit of Hebrew poetry. Millennia have passed since its creation without diminishing its lofty beauties. Today, as in the times of yore, the psalms cast an irresistable spell upon the spirit of man; their poetic qualities are virtually timeless; their ethos, their religious and moral power, is bound up with eternal human values.

The voluminous and basically diverging opinions of Biblical exegetes about the origin and the final order of the Psalter can be only slightly touched in this survey. Biblical commentators disagree upon even such elementary questions as whether the Psalter, or certain portions of it, originated before or after the Babylonian exile. On the other hand, there is almost complete unanimity among the commentators that the Psalter received its final form around 200 B.C.E.

The majority of the commentators place the origin of the Psalter in the period of the early kingdom (eleventh to twelfth century B.C.E.). Some of its parts might conceivably have been added in Hezekiah's time (eighth century B.C.E.). The fourth book was presumably written in the time of the Babylonian exile or shortly thereafter (sixth century B.C.E.), and the remaining portion during the three following centuries.

Considering the many analogies between the civilizations of Babylonia and Israel, it is not surprising to discover certain similarities in the poetical output of each nation. Scholars have established some striking parallels in form, language, and ideas between the Hebrew psalms and certain Babylonian poems.[71] On the other hand, there are substantial differences between them, mainly because of the higher religious ethics of the Israelites.

Beside the Babylonian influence, a few Egyptian traits likewise penetrated the Hebrew psalms. Best known is the resemblance between IKHNATON's (AMENOPHIS IV, 1370–1352 B.C.E.) "Hymn to the Sun" and Psalm 104. Another similarity may be observed between the "Precepts of Amenophis" (AMENEMHET I, ca. 2000–ca. 1970 B.C.E.) and the "Proverbs of Solomon" of the Old Testament (Prov. 22:17–23:14). Psalm 29 is believed to be of Cana'anite origin.[72]

In spite of these occasional foreign infiltrations, however, modern exegesis of the psalms has convincingly proved that, on the whole, the Psalter is a genuine creation of the Jews.

The majority of the psalms include in their headings the supposed author's name. Out of the one hundred and fifty psalms, seventy-three are ascribed to David, twelve to Asaph, eleven to the children (the progeny) of Korah, two to Solomon, one each to Moses, Heman, and Ethan. According to the tradition, David was the most prolific author of psalms, for which reason his name has been attached to the entire collection, which is often called "The Book of Psalms of David." In view of the fame of King Solomon and of his recognized talent as a poet, it is rather surprising that no more than two psalms are ascribed to him, the more so since the Bible reports elsewhere that

he spoke three thousand proverbs; and his songs were a thousand and five (1 Kings 5:12).

It might well be that a number of these were actually incorporated into the Psalter, although it would be difficult to understand, in such a case, why the name of the famous author was not mentioned. The most probable assumption is that in the turbulent centuries following Solomon's reign the majority of his proverbs and songs (=psalms) were lost.

About the alleged authorship of the psalms more will be said later.

Fifty-one psalms carry no author's name. In the talmudic literature these are called, characteristically, "orphaned psalms"[73]

At all times, the headings, as well as the various indications, directions, and names contained in them, intrigued Biblical exegetes. It is generally agreed that they are important allusions to the origin, character, purpose, and, most of all, the musical rendition of the psalms.

They fall into two main categories:

They either are general terms referring to the species or the character of the psalm, having only a loose relationship, if any, to music, or they are terms of the musical practice itself, pointing to some particular feature, such as the melody to be used as a pattern for the music of the psalm, the choice of the accompanying instruments, the way of actual performance, and the like.

Both categories contain terms the meaning of which is clear from their etymology or other unmistakable characteristics; they also include terms that are obscure, and even patently incomprehensible. Commentators of all times have exerted their utmost efforts and ingenuity to unravel the secrets of those mysterious terms. Thus, countless opinions, interpretations, and hypotheses have arisen, often diametrically opposed to each other, creating a confusion that largely continues to this day, although recent exegesis has removed many a doubt and straightened out a number of errors in this respect.

Before discussing the various terms found in the headings of the psalms, let us review briefly some of the multitudinous translations, old and new, of the Bible, restricting ourselves to Greek, Latin, English, and German, the principal languages used in our study.

The worldwide diffusion of the Hebrew Bible began when it was first translated from its original language into Greek. About this a venerated legend is preserved, which differs remarkably from historical fact.

With the clash of two civilizations, the Jewish and the Greek, there resulted a peculiar situation, in which many Jews, mainly those residing in the large cities, spoke Greek and studied Greek literature, thus becoming more and more estranged from their own national idiom. To enable these Hellenized Jews to read their own Scriptures, as well as to acquaint the Greeks with Jewish religious traditions, morals, and ethics, it became necessary to translate "God's word" into the Greek language. Here, legend and the historical facts go their separate ways.

King PTOLEMY PHILADELPHOS II (283–246 B.C.E.) favored a translation, not so much for literary reasons as for political expediency, hoping that it would cause the Jews of Egypt to untie their bonds with Jerusalem, thus lessening their contributions to the treasury of the Temple. PTOLEMY heard about the famous Book of the Hebrews and, at the suggestion of DEMETRIOS of PHALERON, invited, about 250 B.C.E., some seventy (according to another tradition, seventy-two) Jewish scholars from Judaea to undertake the translation into Greek. As the legend unfolds, the king assigned to each of the scholars a separate room on the Island of Pharos, keeping them without communication in order that they should work independently of each other. When they finished, each of the seventy translations conformed word for word, thus "proving" the divine inspiration of the Hebrew text as well as its translation into the Greek language.

The Greek version of the Bible came to be known as the *hermēneia kata tous hebdomekonta*, "the Interpretation according to the Seventy." However, a Latin translation that followed soon after called it "Interpretatio Septuaginta (*sc.* Seniorum)." Thus, the Latin word *Septuaginta* was adopted as the term for the Greek translation, which was finished in the third century B.C.E.

The growth and expansion of the Roman Empire gave Latin a prominent place among the Mediterranean languages, and it soon became mandatory that a Latin translation of the Bible be made. For this undertaking, several unknown authors worked separately, or perhaps collectively, producing the first Latin translation, called the "*Old Latin Version.*" At the close of the fourth century, St. JEROME (340–420 C.E.) made a thorough revision of the "*Old Latin*

Version." His work was called the *Vulgata* (the "popular one"), which the Latin Church recognized as the Authorized Version of the Bible. The *Psalterium Vetus*, the "Old Latin Psalter," was the first book revised by St. JEROME. In the course of his life, St. JEROME made three further revisions of the Psalter, the first called the *Roman Psalter*, which was published in Rome in 383. The second, the so-called *Gallic Psalter*, was issued in Bethlehem in 387. His best translation is considered to be the third, the *Hebrew Psalter*, (published about 392), which he made directly from the original Hebrew.

After the unprecedented success of the SEPTUAGINT, several other translators attempted to improve upon its text, among them AQUILA (second century C.E.), who was evidently a Greek convert to Judaism. He made his translation under the supervision of R. AKIBA or, according to another tradition, under R. ELIEZER and R. JOSHUA. Another Greek convert, SYMMACHOS, who lived under the reign of the Emperor SEVERUS (193–211 C.E.), tried to improve upon the previous translations. His version is preserved in mere fragments. Another early translator, THEODOTION, also a Greek convert (in the second century C.E.), tried to emulate the text of AQUILA, without adequate results.

Furthermore, among the early translations those of the Targumim should be mentioned. These were transformations of the original Hebrew into Aramaic, a dialect that was then much in vogue among the populace. While these translations are preserved only in incoherent fragments, they nevertheless shed useful sidelights upon some of the seemingly enigmatic terms employed in the Hebrew original.

After these "classical" translations, many others followed suit in practically all the languages of the civilized world, the most numerous, perhaps, in English. British and American translators vied with each other to establish an "authoritative" text of the Holy Scriptures. One of the earliest English translations was that made from the *Vulgate* by JOHN WYCLIFFE (about 1380), revised by his followers JOHN PURVEY and NICHOLAS of HEREFORD.

The most important of all English versions is that initiated by King JAMES (1611), which has since remained the *Authorized Version* of the Protestant Church. The beauty and force of its language exerted a strong and lasting influence upon the English tongue itself, just as did the translation of MARTIN LUTHER (1483–1546) upon the German language.

All subsequent English translators followed the *King James Version* quite closely by restricting themselves to "modernizing" in various passages some obsolete terms, for the most part keeping the inherent beauty of this epoch-making translation intact. Not to be outdone by the Protestants, the Catholic Church brought out its own translation, called after the place of its publication the *Douai Version* (the New Testament published in 1582, the Old Testament in 1609–1610). It closely followed the original Hebrew, as well as the Greek and other early translations. It was revised in 1750 by Bishop CHALLONER, and is now accepted as the *Authorized Catholic Bible*.

Jewish attempts to establish their own authoritative translation scrupulously followed the Masoretic text. The first Jewish translation was published in Philadelphia in 1917. Since then, several new Jewish versions have been printed, with no discernible improvement.

There is a multitude of other English translations, among them the *Re-*

vised Version (1885), the *Revised Standard Version* (1952), *Moulton** (1895), and *Moffat* (1922).

As for the Psalter, all of the English versions translate the headings, also some other terms of the psalms, in various, and in some cases highly contradictory, ways. We cannot deal with these incongruencies in the present study, because they are not directly connected with the main subject, namely, the "social" implications of the music in Ancient Israel. I therefore refer readers to my *"Music In Ancient Israel,"* (New York, Philosophical Library, 1969), which explores this matter in greater depth.

GENERAL TERMS

The canonical text of the Bible has no general designation for the Book of Psalms as a whole, only special terms for individual psalms in their headings. In the Jewish liturgical use, however, the Psalter has long been called *Sefer Tehillim*, "Book of Songs of Praise." This colloquial title of unknown historical date is an indication of the purpose of the collection.

Tehillah, "Song of Praise," is derived from *hallel*, "to praise." Curiously enough, this specific term is used only once in the subtitles of the psalms, in the heading of Psalm 145. It appears frequently, however, in the psalmodic text itself, and also in other portions of the Scriptures. The general term seems to have been omitted from other headings. Probably all psalms were primitively called *tehillim,* as they are called conventionally in our days.

Tefillah is the common term for "prayer." It is to be found at the head of four psalms only, and again in Hab. 3. In the postscript to Psalm 72:20, all psalms up to and including this number are called *tefillot.*

The headings of fifty-seven psalms carry the subtitle *mizmor,* a term not to be found elsewhere in the Bible. The etymology of the word (from the root *zmr*) indicates a song accompanied by instruments. A frequently used stringed instrument to accompany singing was the *nebel* (Gr. *psaltērion,* Lat. *psalterium*), rendered in the English translations as "psaltery." Eventually, the Greek (or Latin) name of this instrument was affixed to the collection of songs themselves, hence the name "Psalter."

Another of the several subtitles is *shir,* signifying "song." This must have been the earliest term for the psalms. Originally the word designated a lyric poem, intended for singing, especially at joyous occasions. Eventually the name was given primarily to songs of praise used in the cult, particularly to songs performed by the Levitical choir.

Shir is usually coupled with *mizmor,* five times immediately before, and eight times after this latter term.

The Midrash interprets *mizmor* as a psalm accompanied by instruments, and *shir mizmor* as a psalm sung by a choral group alone.[74]

Another subtitle appears in fifteen psalms following consecutively, 120 to 134, namely *shire ha-maʿalot,* with the variant in Psalm 121, *shir la-maʿalot.* The ancient translations (Septuagint, Vulgate, and Jerome), render the term

---

* To indicate how arbitrarily some of these versions treat the Scriptural text, it may suffice to give one example: Moulton's translation omits *all* the superscriptions of the psalms, which contain our most valuable source of information concerning their musical rendering. They also constitute the essential elements for our understanding of the musical practice of Ancient Israel.

as "Songs of Degrees." Josephus mentions the fifteen steps leading from the Court of the Women up to the Court of the Israelites.[75] The oldest rabbinical tradition connects these fifteen steps with the fifteen psalms, saying that the Levites used to stand on each of the steps while singing one of the psalms at the Feast of Tabernacles during the ceremony of the water-libation.

The Church Fathers, while maintaining the ancient Jewish tradition of the fifteen steps, attribute to them, in addition, a mystico-religious allegorical meaning:

Just as there are fifteen songs in the Psalter, there are fifteen steps on which [the faithful] could rise to God [by means of] singing[76]

The later translators, Aquila, Theodotion, and Symmachus, abandoned the idea of the "degrees" or "steps," and translated the term as "Songs of the Ascent." The explanation was that these were the psalms sung by the repatriates from the Babylonian captivity when they "ascended" to Jerusalem. Indeed, Ezra called the return from Babylonia *ha-ma'alah mi-Babel* (Ezra 7:9). As for the plural, the expounders try to elucidate this particularity by referring to the historical fact that the return from Babylonia took place in successive groups, as if "by degrees," first under Zerubbabel in 537 (Ezra 2:2 ff), then under Ezra in 458 (Erza 7:6–8). Against this interpretation, however, stands the fact that Psalms 122 and 134 intimate the existence of a newly built temple, a well-organized cult, and the completion of the walls of Jerusalem. All this could have been accomplished only after the return from the exile.

The third, and most probable, traditional interpretation maintains that these fifteen psalms were sung by the pilgrims going annually to Jerusalem for the three great agricultural festivals, when they offered to the Temple the first fruits and the products of their harvest. Thus, *shir ha-ma'alah* would imply "Song of the Ascending Pilgrims," or "Songs of Pilgrimage." The contents of these short popular songs are indeed appropriate for the occasion, some of them even containing direct allusions to pilgrimage, like Psalms 121, 122, 132, 133. Jerusalem had an elevated geographical location, the Temple itself being situated on a high ground; it was therefore logical to term the pilgrimage to the sanctuary an "ascent."

The yearly pilgrimage to Jerusalem was a ritual ordinance prescribed by the Law (Exod. 34:24), and it was carried out in the form of a solemn procession. Several authentic and detailed descriptions of this religious custom are preserved. According to Philo,[77] and the rabbinical scribes,[78] this offering of the first fruits was always a joyous popular feast. The husbandmen gathered in the larger places and marched to Zion with singing and piping. By the time the procession arrived at the outer court of the Temple, the Levites would intone the 30th Psalm.

In spite of all the historical and liturgical evidence to the contrary, Thirtle gives to these psalms an entirely different interpretation. In basing his theory on a passage in Isaiah 38:20, in which Hezekiah offers the Lord his thanksgiving for his miraculous recovery from mortal sickness, Thirtle ventures a new and rather problematic hypothesis. He maintains that

the Songs of the Degrees were specifically compiled and in a definite manner associated with King Hezekiah and his experiences on the throne of Judah.[79]

The historical events during Hezekiah's reign, mostly the Assyrian invasion, but also the king's sickness and recovery, his service in the Lord's House, and his Passover celebration, are considered by THIRTLE as "underlying motives" for the psalms. The "Songs of the Degrees," some originally written in Hezekiah's time, some selected from ancient poems, supposedly constitute a commentary upon these events. Thus, THIRTLE views these fifteen psalms as being simply commemorative of Hezekiah, that is, written or adapted for the purpose of underscoring the most important occurrences of his reign.[80] The coincidence between the years that were miraculously added to the king's life and the number of songs (fifteen), especially, are taken by THIRTLE as validating his theory.[81]

THIRTLE's assumptions are in sharp contradiction to the findings of a host of Biblical exegetes, traditional and modern, proving with great probability that the Psalter as a whole (but not necessarily the fifteen "Songs of Ascents" as an independent unit), in its final shape, is the result of an organic development during at least eight centuries.

Most of the Biblical scholars agree that the fifteen psalms formerly constituted a small independent collection. And the title of this minuscule song book may well have been *Shire ha-ma(alot*. When this collection was eventually incorporated into the complete Book of Psalms, the former plural title might have been superimposed in the singular over each one of those fifteen psalms.

Another hypothesis is advanced by the classical interpreter of the Hebrew language, WILHELM GESENIUS, and after him, by a number of other expositors.[82] They suppose that the term in question refers to a specific rhythm in poetry, the so-called rhythm of degrees (Gr. *anadiplosis*). This theory is based on a particularity found in several of these psalms, namely the poetical formula according to which a certain phrase or expression at the end of a verse is transferred to the beginning of a new, similar or contrasting, idea. If this procedure is applied repeatedly within a poem, the verses of it are linked like "degrees."

This principle indeed prevails in some of the Psalms of the Degrees, most distinctly perhaps in Ps. 121. In other psalms, however (e.g., 120, 127, 129, 131), it is only sporadic, and in Psalms 128 and 132 it is entirely lacking. On the other hand, the "rhythm of degrees" can be found in other psalms not belonging to the group (e.g., in Ps. 29), and also in other portions of the Bible (Judg. 5:3–6; Isa. 5:6, etc.). It is, therefore, highly questionable whether *ma(alah* in reality refers to this particular technique of poetry.

In a comprehensive study of the psalms, SIGMUND MOWINCKEL established an entirely new theory concerning the origin and purpose of the Psalter.[83] His unusual approach was highly commended by some and rejected by others. His findings interest us only insofar as they have any bearing upon the music of the psalms.

The main tendency of his study, the leitmotif of his entire approach to the Psalter, is to show that after David's reign the Judaeans adopted the Cana(anitic annual festival of the enthronement of Ba(al, which was based upon a similar festival held in the temple of MARDUK at Babylon. According to MOWINCKEL, this pagan festival was subsequently celebrated in honor of Yahveh at the Feast of Tabernacles, an assumption which, in the light of history, is unacceptable.

MOWINCKEL interprets the terms appearing in the headings of the psalms either as indications for certain ritual actions, or as directives how to perform specific religious ceremonies.

According to him, *ma'alah* means neither degrees, nor ascent, nor even pilgrimage, but the solemn procession that took place on New Year's day at the festival of Yahveh's ascension to the throne.

As he maintains, there is a weighty argument against the traditional interpretation, namely, the fact that several *ma'alah*-psalms were not meant to be sung in the procession, but in the Temple itself. He points out, for instance, that Psalm 134 was sung at the nocturnal feast in the court of the sanctuary; Psalms 124 and 129 are liturgical chants in antiphonal form, consequently songs of the cult in the proper sense of the word. Psalm 128 is a priestly benediction, Psalm 121 a liturgical antiphonal chant with a priestly blessing. All this seems to indicate that these psalms were performed in the Temple proper.[84]

From all these allegedly "clear" explanations, MOWINCKEL draws the amazing conclusion that *ma'alah* cannot be interpreted in any musical sense whatsoever.

The headings of thirteen psalms contain the term *maskil*, which is also to be found in the text of Psalm 47:8. The word is probably derived from the verb *sakal*, "to have insight" or "comprehension"; about its meaning, however, as a designation for a poem or song, the opinions of the commentators are divided.

Some think it means a "didactic poem" (GESENIUS, HENGSTENBERG, *et al.*), some others a specific form of poetry (ROSENMÜLLER), still others "meditation," while LUTHER translates it as *Unterweisung*, ("instruction").

MOWINCKEL's interpretation differs substantially from all these.[85] He does not deny that *maskil* refers to a poem of a specific kind or for a specific use. But he maintains that the heterogeneous contents of these psalms preclude their definition as "didactic poems." According to him, these psalms must be considered as songs intended for the cult alone. He refers to the fact that, according to the conception of Ancient Israel,

> there existed a close relationship between the composition of psalms and acts of prophecy; both were considered as manifestations of a specific endowment, which in later times was identified with rapture or inspiration.[86]

He quotes examples from the Scriptures that reveal that the authors of psalms as well as the sacred singers had a firm belief that their respective poetic and musical talents stemmed from prophetic inspiration.

From all this, MOWINCKEL concludes that *maskil* must have been a song for the cult, performed with musical instruments, and induced by a particular "insight" or "intelligence," or by a specific power of inspiration.

The question arises, however, why only thirteen psalms out of one hundred and fifty carry the term *maskil*. If poetry was a matter of divine inspiration, all the psalms, not only a limited number of them, should be called *maskilim*. The fact that only a handful of them were thus termed leaves doubts as to whether *maskil* may not have had, after all, a somewhat different meaning.

In my opinion, of all the different interpretations of *maskil*, the most probable is that of a penitential song. All the *maskil*-psalms, with the exception of the wedding ode (Psalm 45) and of the lengthy Psalm 78, could—at least according to their contents—be considered as belonging to the category of penitential songs.

The headings of six psalms contain the term *miktam*, the meaning of which created considerable controversy. Etymologically, the term could be derived from *katab,* or *katam*—"scripture," "poem," or "riddle," "maxim"—while some commentators trace it back to *ketem,* "gold," and, accordingly, invest the term with the meaning of "golden [Psalm]."

LUTHER's translation, "ein gülden Kleinod" ("a gilded gem"), comes rather close to the same idea. Probably following up this meaning, some commentators (HORNE and d'HERBELOT) have advanced the hypothesis that, on special occasions at the Jerusalem Temple, the psalms termed *miktam* were written in gilded letters and suspended in the sanctuary.

All the six psalms have the character of lamentations or supplications which, in the light of the above-presented idea, would suggest that *miktam* indicates a species of supplication that was presented to God in a written form.

LANGDON submits an entirely different reasoning and interprets *miktam* as a musical instrument.[87] According to this theory, the word is connected with the Babylonian noun *naktamu,* "metal cover [for a vessel]," and is—as LANGDON thinks—the name of a percussion instrument, possibly the tambourine or cymbal. Peculiarly, in an earlier passage of the same essay he says that *miktam* "probably means a flute."[88]

MOWINCKEL tries to find his own solution on the basis of the concordant contents of the respective psalms. He suggests as an appropriate translation "a psalm for atonement," which seems to correspond, as he thinks, to the contents of the psalms.

The *Vulgate* translation, *tituli inscriptio,* points to still another conception. Some commentators suppose that *miktam* was a musical indication the meaning of which fell into oblivion with the passing of time. Should one try to find an indication for this assertion from the musical point of view, one would immediately discover that the word *miktam* is practically always connected with certain titles in the headings that seemingly have no relationship whatever to the contents of the psalms (Psalms 56, 57, 58, 59, 60). Many exegetes of the Bible consider these indications to be the titles of well-known songs or tunes, serving as melodic pattern for the respective psalms. From this, they conclude that *miktam* might have signified an instruction to employ a borrowed melody, the title of which appears in the heading of the psalm.

This assumption is corroborated by the fact that ancient Syrian hymn-writers used to place at the head of their poems certain musical indications, such as

to the melody (*'al kālāh dh'* . . .) "I will open my mouth with knowledge."[89]

Assyrian excavations have yielded a slab of stone containing a veritable catalogue of Sumerian and Assyrian songs, such as psalms, hymns, liturgies, and popular and love songs (see p. 54). This catalogue comprises numerous titles of songs, whose melodies were supposed to be applied to a number of different psalmodic and liturgical texts.[90] It is evident, therefore, that the indications of widely familiar melodies by means of textual titles belonging to various psalms or hymns, so that they could easily be sung with changed lyrics, must have been a persistent practice in the music of Antiquity.

The objections could be raised that *miktam* is used once in the superscriptions (Psalm 16) without being connected with a song-title, and furthermore, that a certain number of headings contain song-titles without the word *miktam.*

Yet, all this is not conclusive proof against the assumption that *miktam* implied the use of some current popular melody for the psalm. It is an established fact, first noticed by THEODORE of MOPSUESTIA, a theologian of the school of Antioch (d. ca. 428 C.E.), that the headings and superscriptions were a later addition to the psalm texts; in the Christian versions they do not even belong to the canonical text. The original *Septuagint* lacked the historical titles of Psalms 51, 52, 54, 57, 63, and 142. On the other hand, the *Septuagint* contains liturgical and historical data in the psalm headings that are not included in the Masoretic Hebrew text. Moreover, the Syriac version of the Bible has entirely different titles.[91]

These headings might well originally have been some marginal notes for the choir-leaders or precentors. The Biblical scribes of earlier times may have been aware of the fact that the headings had no relationship to the psalm text proper. Therefore, they probably did not transfer these headings into later copies as scrupulously as they handled the text itself. This explains the various readings in the preserved ancient manuscripts, the frequent inversions of letters, and other inconsistencies, such as, for instance, the fact that some manuscripts contain words that are left out in others. This alone would explain why a term may occasionally be lacking in certain headings.

Yet, another circumstance has to be taken into account with regard to these musical instructions. As long as the primary tradition of the Temple music was alive and the meaning of the musical terms was familiar to anyone connected with the sacred music, a great many indications, however important, could be omitted from the superscriptions without endangering their correct understanding. This could serve as a further explanation of why *miktam* has been left out in some of the headings, where—by analogy—we would expect to find it. On the other hand, *miktam* stands alone at least on one occasion (Psalm 16). This must have been an instance when, because of the practical necessity to change sometimes the musical material of the sacred service, the choice of a song was left to the discretion of the Levitical choir-master. A situation like this would naturally preclude the specific mention of the song in the heading of the psalm. This, of course, is but a surmise, having, nevertheless, some probability.

Later scribes copied the headings with all these simplifications and abbreviations; in the end, they were taken rather naïvely as representing the "authentic" version and, since the establishment of the Jewish canon, accepted as a sacred and unimpeachable text. Thus, the musical terminology of the psalm headings has been preserved with all its "mysteries" and apparent inconsistencies.

In the superscription of Psalm 60 there is, in addition to *miktam le-David,* the term *le-lammed.* All the ancient translations, including those of the Targumim, give the term the meaning of "to teach," and all the modern Bible versions follow this interpretation.

The question arises, however, whether this should have been the only psalm to be taught to the young. The practice of singing psalms was preserved from generation to generation by oral tradition. Therefore, it may well be taken for granted that numerous other psalms, texts as well as melodies, were taught, i.e., rehearsed and continually repeated until they were indelibly engraved in the memory of the young generation. It is difficult to explain why this psalm alone contains the instruction *le-lammed,* or why the author of this psalm should have considered it necessary to specially indicate an accepted procedure for this particular psalm.

It is rather safe to assume that all or most of the psalms headed by *miktam* were poems to be taught to the youth. The term *le-lammed* may very well have withered away gradually and, intentionally or by oversight, have been preserved in this one heading. It might also be that all the psalms superscribed with *miktam* originally constituted a small independent collection. This is corroborated by the fact that in the final order of the Psalter they are grouped together, immediately following each other, with the exception of Ps. 16. Perhaps Ps. 60 was originally the initial poem of this small collection and contained in its heading the underlying purpose of the entire set, *le-lammed*, that is "to be taught to the youth." When the Psalter took its final shape, the first piece might have been transferred for some reason to the end, and so *le-lammed* lost its meaning as a generic term and was retained merely in a single psalm.

All these are no more than conjectures, to be sure, but they furnish at least a plausible explanation for the fact that the indication *le-lammed* appears only once in the Psalter.

The superscriptions of two psalms contain the indication *le-hazkir;* all ancient translations express the idea of "in remembrance," as a term of the psalmist or the singer of it, as the expressed desire to be remembered by God.[92]

The translation of the Targum, however, implies another idea; it points to a certain sacrificial ceremony at which, with a handful of flour and a drop of oil, incense was thrown into the sacrificial fire. If the interpretation of the Targum is correct, both psalms were parts of this sacrificial rite, called ʾaskara ("memorial"; *cf.* Lev. 2:2,9,16).

The translation in the *Septuagint* of Ps. 38, *eis anamnēsin,* with the additional remark *peri sabbatou,* seems to be an indication that both psalms were not sung at the regular daily ʾaskara, but only at that of the Sabbath.[93]

Finally, there is in the headings of the psalms the subtitle *shiggayon* (Ps 7). The same word, in a somewhat altered form, ʿal shiggionot, appears in Habakkuk 3:1.

All the early Greek and Latin translators interpreted *shiggayon* as a synonym for shegiʾot, "error," "fault." The Midrash and RASHI follow the same idea while speaking of "David's transgressions." According to modern exegesis, however, *shiggayon* would mean a poem with a changing meter or a changing melody, according to the etymology of the word, connected with the verb *shagah,* "to reel," "to go astray."

Another meaning of the verb *shagah* is "to be large." From this and the original meaning of the word, modern commentators derive the most diverse interpretations, such as a "plaintive song" or an "elegy," "song of wanderings" (PARKHURST), and *"chant mixte"* (HOUBIGANT), that is, "a song set for several parts." This, however, is an obvious anachronism, for the music of Antiquity did not know part-setting in the Occidental sense.

As for the interpretation of the term as "song of wanderings," the commentators explain this by assuming that David wrote the psalm during his years of wandering when, as a fugitive, he tried to escape from Saul's pursuits.

A more appropriate explanation of the term can be obtained by examining its equivalents and parallel uses in other ancient religions. The word seems to be connected with the Assyrian liturgical term *shigū,* meaning a plaintive song of several stanzas. In Babylonia, such poems were performed with musical accompaniment and with special rites.[94] In the Assyrian language, the verbal form of *shigū* means "to rave," "to lament vehemently." From this GESENIUS derives the meaning of an "ode," or a "dithyramb," i.e., "a wild, passionate song, with rapid changes of rhythm."[95]

Mowinckel likewise views the word as related to the Assyrian *shigū,* "plaintive psalm." He surmises furthermore that this term came anciently to Cana'an, being first introduced into the rites of the local tribes and then, in a roundabout way, into the Hebrew cult. Accordingly, he interprets *shiggayon* as a "psalm of lamentation (of a sick man)."[96]

TERMS OF MUSICAL PRACTICE

The Levitical singer-musicians must have indicated in writing the important guiding marks pertaining to their performances. This practice may have accounted for those indications inserted in the headings of the psalms which, no doubt, represent instructions for their musical rendering, and are of special importance at a time when notation in the Occidental sense was unknown. These instructions were useful to contemporaries of the psalmists as well as to their immediate successors, because their meaning was understood by everyone connected with sacred music.

Eventually, however, their meaning fell gradually into oblivion, which is not surprising if we consider how vague these terms are. In the fourth and fifth books of the Psalter, which are later additions to the collection, scarcely any of these indications can be found, a proof that their meaning must have become rather obscure even in the relatively short time after the first three books were compiled. Thus, the translators of the *Septuagint* (completed in the third century B.C.E.) no longer understood these terms and were compelled to take some of them over phonetically from the original Hebrew (the same method having been applied by the later Old Latin translators). Owing to the unintelligibility of these terms, whose meaning was entirely lost by subsequent desuetude, the early Fathers of the Church completely refrained from giving them any rational interpretation and, in accordance with the general tendency of early Christianity, attributed to them all sorts of moral, allegorical, and mystical implications.

Since no musical notation was known at that period, the Levites were confronted with the problem of perpetuating in some other way the music of the psalms, both the melody and the accompaniment. They solved this problem by establishing a musical terminology which, in a nutshell, would contain all that the Levitical singer-musicians had to know. The proper application of these indications was supposed to furnish future generations with the key to the correct rendering of the psalms.

The only place where such indications could be inserted was the heading of the psalms. It goes without saying, therefore, that such indications, pointing merely to the performance of the music, did not belong to the text proper and that their corresponding words were *not* sung in ancient times.

Here we must refer to an entirely new interpretation of the musical instructions of the psalms, which heretofore were unanimously considered as headings, i.e., superscriptions of the individual psalms.

Greek, Latin, Hebrew, and other ancient manuscripts used to be written in such a way that the text ran without any break or division between words and without the indication of chapters or paragraphs. The Biblical verses themselves were divided, not by their authors or the scribes who wrote them down initially, but by subsequent editors, priestly and Levitical functionaries, and mainly by the Masoretes, who were chiefly responsible for the actual form of the Holy Writ.

This situation is of special significance for the Book of Psalms. Similarly to other ancient manuscripts, the psalms followed one another without divisions, leaving the door open to all kinds of individual interpretations as to where a psalm had to begin or to end. It is well known that this incertitude resulted in a different arrangement of psalms in each of the various Bible versions (Hebrew, Greek, Latin, Syriac, Arabic, etc.).

THIRTLE, after closely examining the textual relationship between the psalms and the terms contained in the headings, has made the important discovery that some of these terms apply not to the following, but to the preceding psalm.[97]

THIRTLE also found two Scriptural instances outside the Psalter that undeniably corroborate his contention and that must be considered as typical examples of what the psalms of Israel were in point of external form. One is the "Song of Thanksgiving of Habakkuk" (Hab.3), which opens with "A prayer of Habakkuk upon Shiggionoth," and ends with "To the Chief Singer on my Stringed Instruments." The other is Hezekiah's Thanksgiving, "when he had been sick, and was recovered of his sickness" (Isa. 38:10–20), ending with "Therefore we will sing songs to the stringed instruments all the days of our life in the house of the Lord." These two poems are looked upon by THIRTLE as the normal, or standard, procedure for all psalms. He concludes that words of instruction, which today stand in the *Septuagint* and all subsequent versions, belong in reality not to the psalm that follows them but as *sub*scriptions to the psalm that precedes them.

It is surprising that none of the innumerable Biblical scholars ever sensed even the remotest possibility of the headings belonging as subscriptions to the preceding psalm. If nothing else, a striking analogy from Antiquity should have pointed to it. Sumerian and Babylonian psalms always have in subscription that which Hebrew psalms have in their headings: the name of an author, the musical instrument to be used as accompaniment, the tune to which it was to be sung, the kind of musical composition, the purpose of the psalm, and sometimes even the collection to which it belonged.

THIRTLE's discovery establishes indeed a closer relation between the contents of certain psalms and their musical rendition. Though in some isolated cases (e.g., Psalms 49, 140 etc.) the musical instructions would be more appropriate as headings than as subscriptions to the preceding psalm, there is, in general, all reason to accept THIRTLE's arrangement as representing the true meaning of most of the musical instructions.

Most of the terminological "enigmas" in the psalm headings yield an instant solution by viewing them mainly in the light of our day's rudimentary musical necessities. Some of these indeed include terms the meaning of which is often so obvious that, contrary to what has actually taken place in many instances, their interpretation should not have ever raised any doubt. Such is especially the case with the term *la-menazzeah*, used frequently in the Psalter.

The word is derived from the verb *nazzah*, "to shine," "to triumph," "to lead." Apart from other Biblical passages, 1 Chron. 15:21 gives the correct meaning of the word, where it indicates a definite function in the Temple music, "to lead" or "to direct" the song.

It is surprising that, having at hand such an unmistakable meaning of the word, all the early translators of the Bible, including the Targumim, failed to do justice to its real implication.

Outside of the psalms, *la-menazzeah* is to be found only in Habakkuk 3:19, where it appears at the end. It has been surmised that Habakkuk's poem represents a displaced psalm which, for some reason, was not incorporated into the Psalter, or was removed from it in later times. This assumption is supported by the fact that this song of thanksgiving contains three times the term *selah*. Outside the Psalter, this is the only place in the Scriptures where this term is employed.

Out of one hundred and fifty psalms, fifty five contain the indication *la-menazzeah*. In the fourth book it is entirely lacking, in the fifth book it appears three times.

Menazzeah was the singer chosen to lead the music or to officiate as precentor, who probably also instructed the choir, or at least supervised the rehearsals. He must have been an especially qualified artist with a superior musical knowledge. Furthermore, he must have been entrusted with the occasional solo passages in psalm singing. Thus, he may be considered the precursor of later days' *hazzan*, the precentor of the synagogue's sacred service.

At all times and in all places, the performing artist was subjected to human vanity. Whether he was a sacred or a secular musician, a singer or an instrumentalist, his aim was to put his artistry into the brightest possible light (cf. the original meaning of the verb *nazzah*, "to shine."). The Levitical singers

that were instructed in singing unto the Lord, were all skillful

in their craft, as the Scriptures tell us most explicitly (1 Chron. 25:7). The precentor, however, was *primus inter pares*, the singing virtuoso *par excellence* of those days, and as such, without doubt, the artistic "attraction" of the sacred service. With all the solemnity of the Jewish religious ceremonies, the effect that the singing virtuoso of yore used to exercise upon his audience must have been considerable. This fact was bound to procure for him great popularity among the congregants and increased authority in his relations with the priests.

In actual practice, this may have resulted in the demand of the precentor for an opportunity of displaying his virtuosity during the sacred services. This, of course, could be effected only while singing psalms. It is reasonable to assume that the psalms in which the precentor was granted this much-desired opportunity were specifically designated in advance.

The singer-virtuoso might not have been satisfied with the given verbal assurance that certain psalms would be permanently assigned as his "show-pieces." He might have asked, in addition, that his privilege should be stipulated in writing. The priests had to consent to this demand. And so their pledge found its expression in the headings (or at the end) of the psalms. This is, in my opinion, the real significance of the term *la-menazzeah*.

If our assumption is correct, then the sacred musical practice of Biblical times divulges the same phenomena of artists' vanity, the urge to show off, and other traits of spoiled virtuosi, of which the *hazzanim* of the later synagogue were so frequently accused.

MOWINCKEL, who tries to interpret most of the terms in the headings as marks for ritual procedures, offers a corresponding explanation also for *la-menazzeah*.[98] He rejects the very idea of "leading," especially "to conduct a band" or "a choral group," as "impossible to prove." Accordingly, he declares both passages (1 Chron. 15:21 and 2 Chron. 34:12,13), generally quoted as supporting the notion of "leading," as untenable. He concludes that *le-hashmi(a* and *la-menazzeah* indicate the main purpose for sacred music: first, to draw, by clashing cymbals, the attention of Yahveh to the worshippers, then, to please Him and obtain His mercy through singing and playing.

Another term in the headings is *neginah* (*pl. neginot*). The meaning of the word is unmistakeably expressed by its origin from the verb *naggen,* "to touch the strings." Its vocal parallel is the verb *zammer,* "to sing with musical accompaniment."

The procedure of accompanying singing with instruments is indicated in the Hebrew by the prepositions *be* or *bi,* "with," and *(al,* "upon," both having the same musical implication and connected with *neginah.* The heading use is always *bineginot,* except in Psalm 61, which has *(al-neginot.* The term always appears jointly with *la-menazzeah,* their combined meaning being, therefore,

to the master of song (or precentor), (to be accompanied) on stringed instruments.

It is worthy of note that none of the many instruments mentioned frequently in other portions of the Old Testament appears in the headings, whereas they are repeatedly quoted in the text proper of the psalms. This is by no means a lack of reportorial precision, but rather a corroborative evidence that common knowledge needs no minute description. *Neginot* was a collective term for the family of stringed instruments, so that those adding the headings considered it superfluous to mention a particular species.

In later times *neginah* obtained still another meaning. The signs of the accents for Biblical cantillation were called *neginot, ta(ame ha-neginah,* or, briefly, *ta(amim.* These signs were added to the text of the Scriptures, and their primary function was syntactic-punctuating. As time passed, they became a sort of rudimentary musical notation, indicating groups of tones and, in some respect, differences of pitch of the cantillation. Gradually, the *ta(amim* developed into a complex pattern of notation, designating ascending and descending figures, scale patterns, slurs, and other devices, thus constituting an elaborate system for traditional cantillation. In this stage of evolution, *neginah* implied the entire method of accentual signs, as well as the rules of their application.

The term *(al (alamot,* which appears in the heading of Psalm 46, and in a single other passage of the Scriptures (1 Chron. 15:20), has given rise to the most diverse interpretations.

The Hebrew noun *(almah* means "maiden"; the majority of the translators implement this meaning in various ways. There is, however, a second meaning of the word, implying "secret." The early translators of the Bible used sometimes one, sometimes the other sense. Most of the modern English Bibles avoided these difficultuies by taking over the term phonetically from the Hebrew.

In spite of the glaring discrepancies in the interpretation of the word, a logical solution presents itself naturally if we apply to it the considerations of normal musical practice.

We know that since the earliest times women were employed in the rites of Yahveh. The passages referring to this fact were intentionally obscured in, or eliminated from, the Scriptures for purposes of textual "purification." About the role of women in Jewish rites, especially as singers, more will be said later. Here I refer only to the most weighty evidence for the participation of women in the music of the Temple, the term *'al-'alamot*. Some commentators interpret the word as the title of a well-known song, others attach to it the meaning of a musical instrument (see below). Yet, it refers most logically to the *range of the female singing voice*. This becomes evident if we assume, with THIRTLE, that this heading represents in reality a subscription to Ps. 45, surnamed "A Song of Loves,"—a nuptial ode,—which is, more than any other, suited for female voices.

Even more obvious is the meaning of this term in 1 Chron. 15:20. "Psalteries set to *'alamot*" indicated here a psaltery (*nebel*) in the range of women's voices, i.e., in the "higher tessitura" ("high" according to Western conception; see below), namely a smaller, therefore high-pitched type of *nebalim*, which must have played an essential role in the music of the Temple, leading (i.e., doubling) the melody in the soprano range.

The contrasting term to *'al 'alamot* is *'al ha-sheminit* (Psalms 6, 12, and in 1 Chron. 15:21). Its literal meaning in Hebrew is "on the eighth," or, if the linguistic vocalization is correct, "over the eighth." In spite of innumerable beliefs, assumptions, and hypotheses about the meaning of this last term, the most logical explanation of *'alamot* and *sheminit* presents itself automatically, if we assume that they refer to the two vocal ranges of the human singing voice, the treble and the bass, the latter being usually an "octave" lower.

But the Oriental (and also the Greek) conception of vocal ranges is quite different from our theory of "high" and "low" sounds. In our acoustic system, we determine and measure the differences of pitch by the number of vibrations per second produced by sounding bodies. The higher the number of vibrations, the higher the sound.

This is different in the Orient, and especially in Semitic usage. There, "high" and "low" of the tone and, accordingly, the "raising" or "falling" of the voice is not determined by the number of vibrations but by the manner in which the sound was produced. A "large" pipe or a "long" string has a "high" tone, while a "small" pipe or a "short" string produces a "low" sound.[99] On the Greek *kithara* the longest string was called *hypatē*, "the highest," and with the diminishing length of the strings the tone became gradually "lower."

The same principle prevails in Hebrew phonetics. Hebrew grammarians consider the vowels *u* and *o* "high" sounds; accordingly, the punctuation in written texts is *above* the consonants. The vowels *a, e,* and *i* are "low" sounds, consequently the punctuation is *below* the consonants.

All this would, seemingly, undo the theory that *'alamot* represented the range of the high voice, whereas *sheminit* would be the opposite, low range. In reality, however, the two conceptions are not incompatible.

The interpretation of *'alamot* in the sense of the "range of women's voices" should not necessarily be excluded, if we abandon the idea that the Hebrews were thinking of this range in terms of either "high" or "low." In the conception of the Israelites, *'alamot* might simply have represented the sound whose pitch corresponded generally to that of women's voices, regardless of whether it was actually designated as "high" or "low." The opposite was *sheminit*, indicating, as it were, the sound whose pitch was characteristic of male voices. It does not interfere with the Oriental conception of "high" and "low", and does not exclude the assumption that the Hebrews considered women's voices as "low," and men's voices as "high."

Thus, we are led to the logical conclusion that the women's and the men's voices doubled the same melody, that is—according to our Western conception—singing in the interval of an octave.

The question now arises whether one would be justified to assume that the ancient Hebrews knew the notion of the "octave" in the intervallic sense, being the higher or lower repetition of the same tone.

About the music system of Ancient Israel no direct information has been preserved. Especially, we have no knowledge whether the Israelites considered the "octave" as the eighth tone in an established scale. Among the string instruments of the Greeks there existed a larger species, the *magadis,* with twenty strings but only ten different tones, which were duplicated in the interval of an octave, called by the Greeks *diapasōn* It is conceivable that some of the Levitical musicians of the Second Temple may have been familiar with the music theory of the Hellenes. However, between the possibility of the knowledge of the Greek music system and its actual application in the practice of the Temple there is an abysmal gap. The guardians of the sacred tradition, the priests, would scarcely have tolerated the incursion of Hellenistic notions into the sacred precincts of their liturgical hymnal. The sound effect of *sheminit* might in fact have been recognized by some Levitical singers as that of doubling the voice in the octave; the terminology in the intervallic sense of "eightness" was certainly not applied in this meaning.

The simplest interpretation of the two contrasting terms is found in 1 Chron. 15:21. There we read of *binebalim ʿal ʿalamot* and *bekinnorot ʿal ha-sheminit.* *Nebalim* and *kinnorot,* as names of musical instruments, are generally used by the chroniclers without any specific epithets or other qualifications. Why is this different here, as well as in the three psalm headings? Everything points to the possibility that different species of instruments are meant for both categories: a smaller, therefore higher pitched type of *nebalim* which—in this case—could very well lead (i.e., double) the melody in the upper register, and a larger, consequently lower sounding species of *kinnorot,* for doubling the melody in the subjacent register.

Among the countless interpretations of *sheminit,* I refer merely to that of MOWINCKEL, who thinks that the term refers neither to an instrument nor to the musical practice in the sense of the octave-interval, but maintains that Psalms 6 and 12 were "doubtless" designed to serve as the climax of purifying rites, and concludes that they evidently belonged to the final, the "eighth act of purification." Consequently, according to MOWINCKEL, the logical interpretation of *ʿal ha-sheminit* would be "the eighth time," or "the eighth (act) of purification," intimating that the psalm was performed at this particular rite.

The headings of Psalms 53 and 88 contain the indication *ʿal maḥalat.* The meaning of this term was not clear even to the early translators of the Bible, for which reason they did not attempt to render it in their respective languages, but took over the word phonetically from the original Hebrew.

The extant interpretations of the word are again most contradictory. Some commentators derive it from the Hebrew *maḥaleh* or *maḥalah,* "sickness," while others follow the idea of *maḥol,* "dance."

Songs as a musical background for dancing are frequently mentioned in the Scriptures. Consequently, it would by no means be unexpected to find dance songs mentioned in the headings of the psalms, possibly connected with sacred dances, or with the ceremony of a processional encompassing the altar. On the other hand, the textual examination of both psalms (53 and 88) in no way justifies the assumption that these psalms were employed to accompany dances.

From the other numerous interpretations, I wish to quote two, those of MOWINCKEL and RASHI. MOWINCKEL tries to establish a relation between *mahalat* and some kind of ritual action.[100] In his opinion, the performance of the two psalms was a feature at the rites of the New Year's festival, intended as magic against diseases. Therefore, he suggests as translation "against sickness," or "above the sickness," or "above the sick (spot of the) body."

We have, however, one, a musically satisfactory, explanation, that suggested by RASHI: "(accompanied) by pipes." Unquestionably, the contents of both psalms, one in a pensive, the other in a joyous mood, favor the idea of accompanying the singing at times softly, and at other times by vigorously blown *halilim*. Should the term *mahalat* have any relation to music (and all evidence seems to support this assumption), then RASHI's interpretation is to be given the preference.

There was until now no clear-cut explanation for the term *ʾel ha-nehilot* in the superscription of Psalm 5. The origin of the word has been explained in various ways, e.g., from the verb *nahal*, "to possess," or from *halal*, "to pierce," attaching to the last interpretation the meaning of a "pierced" instrument, the flute or the pipe.[101] Among the English Bibles, some translate "for flutes," while others have taken over the term phonetically from the Hebrew as "upon the Nehiloth." Again, MOWINCKEL tries to establish a relation between the term and some kind of ritual action. He maintains that the psalm was used specifically to heal diseases (cf. verse 4) and, consequently attributes to *ʾel ha-nehilot* the same meaning, "against sickness," as to *mahalat* of Psalms 53 and 88.[102]

The superscriptions of Psalms 8, 81, and 84 contain the indication *ʿal ha-gittit*, which also has given rise to the most diversified explanations. Since the majority of the expounders hold that the term signifies a musical instrument, it will be examined in the section dealing with the instruments of the Hebrews.

Among other musical indications in the psalm headings, *shir hannukat ha-bayit*, "Song at the Dedication of the House" (Psalm 30), should be mentioned. The title intimates that the psalm was sung at either the dedication of Solomon's Temple or of the Second Temple, but most probably at the rededication of the sanctuary, desecrated by ANTIOCHUS EPIPHANES in 165 B.C.E., as related in the Book of Maccabees (1 Macc. 4:54).

OESTERLEY maintains that the psalm originated in the time of the Maccabees, or at least the superscription was added at this period.[103] This assumption does not exclude, of course, the possibility that the psalm is much older and had been used at former dedications or rededications.

The superscription of Ps. 40 contains the expression *shir yedidot*, translated as "A Song of Loves" (LUTHER: "A Bridal Song"). Apparently this psalm was sung in ancient Israel at wedding ceremonies.

Several psalm headings include terms the meaning of which has no bearing upon the contents of the psalms; their implication, therefore, is obscure, at least at first sight. These terms are:

'al mut labben (Psalm 9),
'al 'ayyelet ha-shaḥar (Psalm 22),
'al shoshannim (Psalms 45, 69, 80),
'al shushan 'edut (Psalm 60),
'al yonat 'elem reḥokim (Psalm 56), and
'al tashḥet (Psalms 57, 58, 59, 75).

The simplest, and musically the most logical, explanation of these terms would be that they represent either the names or the first words of the lyrics of certain secular songs that were popular in the epoch when the Psalter was compiled, and the melodies (but not the text) served as the pattern for singing the psalms. Thus, the musical practice of the Temple would foreshadow a similar procedure in synagogue-singing during medieval times, when some *hazzanim* adapted popular melodies to liturgical texts for use in synagogue worship.

A direct analogy to this procedure can be found in the catalogue of Sumerian and Assyrian liturgies and hymns, referred to earlier in this study. Line 44 of this catalogue is Semitic and represents the title of a religious hymn. Other items in this catalogue are titles of secular songs.[104]

In spite of the fact that the interpretation of the above-mentioned Biblical terms as song-titles or lyrics of songs appears logical and is corroborated by historical records, it did not seem to satisfy the classical Biblical exegetes. More than once, these titles were suspected of having hidden meanings, and expounders tried hard to solve these alleged mysteries. Instead of dilating upon the numerous and highly contradictory linguistic, historical, and musicological arguments for and against their alleged meanings, I present a succinct summary below, which will show the most logical and most probable interpretations of these terms in the light of our present knowledge. My preference is for the explanations that conform to the general character of the Psalter as the musical song-book of Ancient Israel.

General Terms

1) *Tehillah,* the liturgical name for psalms. It appears only once in the Psalter.

2) *Tefillah,* signifies the prayer in liturgy. It is used in four superscriptions.

3) *Mizmor,* indicates an accompanied psalm to be sung by the precentor, or in which the precentor and chorus sang in responsorial form. Fifty-seven headings contain this term.

4) *Shir* is the specific name for a song of praise, mostly performed by the choir alone. Fifteen psalms are thus termed.

5) *Shir ha-ma'alot* is a popular type of song used by pilgrims on their way to Jerusalem to attend the yearly festivals of the agricultural cycle. Psalms 120 to 134 carry this term.

6) *Shir yedidot,* "a love song" which probably was sung at wedding ceremonies. One psalm has this distinction.

7) *Shir ḥanukkat ha-bayit,* used for the dedication, or rededication of the house of God. It appears in one psalm.

8) *Maskil* stands for a song of praise of a special kind, possibly sung by a soloist with occasional participation of the chorus. It appears in thirteen psalms.

9) *Miktam* means, in all probability, that a certain type of popular song is to be selected as a melodic pattern for the psalm. If divested of a musical meaning, it may be explained as a personal or private prayer or meditation. Six headings carry this term.

10) *Le-lammed* indicates that the psalm had to be taught to young people. It is prescribed for only a single psalm, though there can be no doubt that numerous other psalms had to be taught.

11) *Le-hazkir* implies that the psalm was sung at the sacrificial rites of the *)askara.* It heads two psalms.

12) *Shiggayon* is a penitential or lamenting song. A single psalm is thus termed.

Terms Referring to the Musical Performance

1) *La-menazzeah,* "for the precentor," an indication that in such a psalm substantial solo passages, with or without the participation of the chorus, were assigned to the leader in song. Fifty-five titles carry this label.

2) *(Al-neginot* and *bineginot* are instructions to accompany the singing with stringed instruments, to be found in eight psalms.

3) *(Al ha-gittit,* another collective term for stringed instruments, indicating that these are prescribed for the accompaniment of the psalm. More probably, however, the psalms were destined to be sung at the Festival of Tabernacles. Three psalms contain it.

4) *(Al (alamot* is a specific instruction for the accompaniment of the song with high-pitched instruments; the psalms might have been sung by a women's or boys' choir. It applied to one psalm.

5) *(Al ha-sheminit* is, in a sense, the opposite indication for the accompaniment with larger, low-pitched instruments, or probably used for a male choir. Two psalms are thus termed.

6) *(Al mahalat* signifies accompaniment with pipes. If read as *meholot,* it would refer to victory celebrations with dancing. To be found in two headings.

7) *)El ha-nehilot* has the same implication as *(al mahalat,* indicating woodwinds for accompaniment. If read as *nehalot* ("inheritance"), it would signify the commemoration of taking possession of the Land of Promise. One heading carries this instruction.

8) *(Al mut labben, (al (ayyelet ha-shahar, (al shoshannim, (al shushan (edut, (al yonat)elem rehokim,* and *(al-tashhet* are the titles or the catchwords of popular songs serving as melodic patterns for psalms. Six such titles appear in eleven superscriptions.

If we divest the above titles of their musical connotation, they could be interpreted as historical or seasonal psalms, and would probably mean:

mut labbeyn, "the death of the Champion" (i.e., Goliath),
(ayyelet ha-shahar, "the Hind of the Dawn,"
yonat)elem rehokim, "the Dove of the Distant Terebinths,"
shoshannim, psalms destined for the Passover Feast,
shushan (edut, psalms destined for the Second Passover,
(al-tashhet. "Destroy not," as a motto for penitential psalms.

The Proper Names in the Headings

These names are traditionally supposed to have been those of the authors of the respective psalms. This is inferred mainly from the preposition *le,* appearing immediately before the names. Many commentators, however, do not consider this preposition to be the *lamed auctoris,* but interpret it in the sense of "for." Accordingly, the heading would not mean "A Psalm of David," but "A Psalm for David." This, of course, would invalidate the assumption of David's authorship.

The preposition "of" would even be less appropriate in connection with the names of Asaph, Heman, Ethan (Jedithun), and the Sons of Korah. In the last case, particularly, it is quite unlikely that entire families would figure as collective authors of certain psalms. It is more probable that the names refer to certain groups of Levitical singers and that the *lamed* is either an indication that the respective psalm belonged to the choice repertoire of a given choral group, or that it has been taken from a hymnal originally compiled (not created) by this family or choral group.

There is another valid argument against considering the *lamed* as an indication for authorship, namely, the fact that in some headings more than one individual is mentioned. Thus, the names of David and Jedithun appear in Psalms 39 and 62, and those of Asaph and Jedithun in Psalm 77. The *Septuagint* attributes Psalm 137 to David and Jeremiah despite the fact that this psalm originated in the Babylonian exile. Psalm 138 even names three authors, David, Haggai, and Zechariah.

Biblical criticism has gradually abandoned the assumption that the proper names in the heading represent the author of the psalms. The opinion prevails that they rather refer to previous collections from which they were taken over.

As for the period, or periods, in which the psalms were created, the opinions of the expounders are sharply divided. Some maintain that the origin of various types of psalms goes as far back as the period of the early monarchy (GUNKEL), the time of David, Moses, and even of Jacob (WILSON). Others (CHEYNE and DUHM) doubt the existence of any Davidic psalms and maintain that all the psalms were written in the post-exilic period. OESTERLEY, on the contrary, opines that a considerable portion of the Psalter, at least in its primitive shape, must have originated in pre-exilic times.[105] Historical evidences are in favor of this assertion. The Sumerians, Babylonians, and Egyptians used hymns and psalms in their liturgy even in primeval times.[106] Considering the close cultural interrelation of the nations of the Near East, it may be assumed that this liturgical custom was in early times adopted by the Hebrews.

Yet, it is well-nigh impossible to determine the time of origin of a collection such as the Psalter, into which items from a period extending over almost nine centuries have been incorporated. Since it is an established fact that

> compiling the Psalter was not motivated by a literary urge, but by a practical religious need, it may be assumed that this justified radical changes of the text, in order to adapt the songs to the actual requirements of the worship,[107]

rendering even more difficult the determination of their original dates.

In the light of all historical evidence, it is difficult, if not impossible, to accept THIRTLE's statement, which asserts in all seriousness that the text of the Psalter comes into history, not as so many fugitive poems, but rather as a single document continuously written,[108]

an assertion that is in glaring contradiction to the generally accepted findings of Biblical exegesis.

The expounders are almost unanimous in assuming that the major Psalter was gradually assembled from several smaller collections that existed from the early kingdom until the times of the Maccabees. Even a century later, at the time of POMPEY's reign (67–48 B.C.E.), the urge to compose psalms had not subsided, as proven by the apocryphal *Psalterium Salomonis*, which originated at this time and which, of course, has nothing to do with Solomon except the name.

After the destruction of the Temple by the Romans, devout and poetically gifted writers continued to compose psalms, imitating the style and form of the canonical psalms. Sometimes these "new songs" were nothing but a mosaic of Biblical quotations. In some instances, however, they give testimony to real inspiration which, had they been composed in Biblical times, would probably have warranted their inclusion in the canonical Psalter. Their number must have been considerable. THIMOTEUS, Nestorian Patriarch of Seleucia (726–819 C.E.), reports in a letter to SERGIUS, Metropolitan of Elam, that in a cave near the Dead Sea, about 800 C.E., ancient Hebrew manuscripts have been discovered, adding:

we have found more than two-hundred psalms of David among our books.[109]

Of course, these were all noncanonical psalms, the name of David being attached to them but pseudepigraphically. But if this number was found in a single cave, the chances are that other places, such as libraries of sects, monasteries, early churches, and the like, also held a great number of post-Biblical psalms. This assumption is borne out by the recently discovered Dead Sea Scrolls, which contain a considerable number of post-Biblical "Psalms (or Hymns) of Thanksgiving," which will be discussed in another section of this study.

As to authorship by David and the other persons and families named in the headings, there are historical and philological arguments against this assumption.

It is common knowledge that the literary production of Antiquity was mostly anonymous. No stress was laid in those times upon the preservation of an author's name for posterity. The great Egyptian, Persian, Indian, Babylonian, and Assyrian poems were created by the concerted work of numerous and anonymous authors during long periods of time. The same holds true for the Bible. With the exception of the Prophets and the books of Ezra and Nehemiah, the authors of the Biblical books are not known by their names.

Even the prophetic books, though they carry the name of an "author," were apparently not written by the prophets themselves. These books do not represent "literature" in the proper sense of the word, but are rather pamphlets for fight and propaganda. Their aim was to preserve the true religion and its institutions, and they also comprised exhortations and commandments for a life that would be pleasing to God. The names of the prophets have been put at the head of these writings not for the mere attestation to their authorship, but because it was indispensable for the prompt success of these books to know whose teaching they contained. The Book of Isaiah is a collection of "prophecies" (i.e., sermons) by two, or possibly more authors, ranging from 710 to 300 B.C.E. Chapters 1–39 are usually ascribed to the "First Isaiah," the rest to a writer (or writers) generally designated "Deutero [i.e., "Second"]-Isaiah."

The Books of Ezra and Nehemiah are the documentary evidence of one of the most important national events in the history of the Jewish people: the return from the Babylonian exile. Again, the authority of the two famous scribes had to attest to the authenticity of the reports, whether they wrote them or not. This is the reason why their chronicles carry their names.

All the other portions of the Scriptures are anonymous, despite the fact that some of them are attributed to an "author." Moses, for instance, is supposed to be the author of the Pentateuch, as the tradition maintains.

> In reality, the work was handed down to posterity without any name of an author, like all other historical literature of the Hebrews; wherever Moses appears, the Pentateuch not only speaks of him in the third person, but it makes a clear and impartial distinction between the narrator on the one hand, and Moses on the other.[110]

True, the "Song of Songs," "Proverbs," and "Ecclesiastes" are ascribed to Solomon, yet Biblical exegesis is extremely doubtful about his authorship. The Psalter is certainly no exception to the general rule.

The Jewish inner direction for establishing national symbols built, in later times, a "Davidic tradition," by creating, as it were, an idealized figure of the king, which deviates considerably from the historical person. It was in keeping with this tradition to represent David, apart from his other virtues, as the famous author of psalms. This is the reason why seventy-three psalms have been ascribed to him. The Greek version of the Psalter contains even additional Davidic psalms, and the Syriac version attributes almost all the psalms to him.

One should remember that posterity often identifies the name of a compiler with the material of his collection. We speak of Gregorian and Ambrosian chants, although Pope GREGORY and Bishop AMBROSE of Milan were merely compilers and editors, not the authors of these chants. We may therefore use the term "David's Psalter" without necessarily considering him the author of the poems ascribed to him.

The authorship of Moses for Psalm 90 is highly doubtful, if for no other reason than that this psalm appears in the fourth book of the Psalter, which originated at a much later time than the first three books. Should a psalm composed by Moses ever have existed, it would most certainly be incorporated into an early, even the earliest, psalmodic collection.

Solomon's authorship, too, meets with serious doubts, although, insofar as the time factor is concerned, the first of the two psalms ascribed to him (Psalm 72) and incorporated in the second book, could have been written by him (for his alleged authorship of the "Song of Songs" see below).

The same doubts are valid for the family names of the Korahites and Asaphites. They all seem to have belonged to a special hymnal of these singer-guilds, from which they were transplanted into the major Psalters.[111]

The name of Jeduthun (or Jedithun) gave rise to all sorts of speculation. Some modern expositors see a connection between *le-Yedithun* (or *ʿal-Yedithun*) and the preceding *la-menazzeah*, and arrive at the conclusion that the heading should signify:

To the leader (or to the chief-musician) of the family of Temple singers named after Jedithun.

EWALD completely disqualifies the assumption that Jedithun is a proper name and interprets it as a term referring to a key (or mode, "Tonart").[112] LAGARDE thinks that it is a corrupt spelling of ('al) yede 'ethan, "(upon) the hands of Ethan," i.e., in charge of the guild led by Ethan.[113]

Inasmuch as most of the psalms were either composed or adapted for liturgical use, it is not too difficult to determine at least the circle from which they have emanated. Everything intimates that the authors of the psalms are to be traced back to the ranks of the functionaries of the Temple, especially the Levitical singers.

It is obvious that, individually or collectively, the singers also took care of the musical adaptation of the psalms by selecting and arranging the melodies that served as patterns for the psalms. This is the living testimony of the paramount role of the Levitical singers as authors, composers, and performers of psalms.

In conclusion, we should briefly consider Psalm 151, incorporated into the *Septuagint,* which has been rejected by the Jewish canon. All councils of the Apostolic Christian Church have likewise opposed its admission into the Psalter. On the other hand, it was incorporated into the Syriac, Arabic, and Coptic versions of the Scriptures.[114] Its heading reads:

A Psalm, in the hand-writing of David, composed by David, when he fought in single combat with Goliath.[115]

It is evident that the psalm is much older than the Codex Alexandrinus of the Bible (sixth century C.E.), in which it is preserved. Because of its linguistic features, quite different from those of the canonical psalms, Biblical criticism unanimously brands it as spurious.

The psalm contains a couple of musical terms:

Verse 2. My hands made the organ,
        and my fingers jointed the psaltery.

The original words are *organon* and *psaltērion,* the Greek equivalents for *'ugab* (cf. Ps. 150:4) and *nebel,* unless we assume that these are collective terms, *organon* for wind, and *psaltērion* for stringed instruments. I may mention in passing that this is the only psalm in which David is portrayed as a builder of musical instruments (but cf. 1 Chron. 23:5, translated by the *Septuagint* as "he made," instead of the Hebrew "I made").

Selah

More than any other technical term of the Psalter, the mysterious word *selah* has excited the imagination of scholars of all times. In fact, no other term of the Scriptures has created such a plethora of divergent opinions.

It appears in the Psalter 71 times, in the psalmodic text 67 times, and 4 times at the end of a psalm. Out of 39 psalms that contain *selah,* 31 also have the indication *la-menazzeah* in their headings. Since psalm-exegesis agrees upon the musical connotation of the last-mentioned term, it was concluded that *selah*, too, refers, in one way or another, to music. This conclusion is corroborated by another Biblical passage, the only one outside the Psalter, in which *selah* is employed (Hab. 3), and where the word has unmistakeably a musical implication.

Habbakuk's "prayer," more precisely "song of praise," seems originally to have belonged to the canonical Psalter, from which it was subsequently removed for reasons unknown to us.[116] That this song is in reality an abrogated psalm is proven by the fact that *selah* appears in it three times, and furthermore by the musical instruction *la-menazzeah bi-neginotai*, "For the leader, with my string-music." The only difference between this song of praise and the regular psalms is that the latter carry the musical instruction exclusively in their headings, while in Habakkuk it stands as a postscript.

Outside of the Bible, *selah* is used only in the *Shemoneh ʿEsreh* (the Eighteen Prayers), where it appears after the third and the eighteenth blessing. This series of prayers has many affinities with the psalms, so that *selah* in them does not represent a special characteristic. It demonstrates, at any rate, that in the time when the *Shemoneh ʿEsreh* originated, the term *selah* was well known in the liturgy.

The early translators of the Bible attributed to *selah* the most diversified meanings. The *Septuagint* translates it *diapsalma*, "a pause in singing", i.e., "an instrumental interlude," but the *Vulgate*, AQUILA, ᴏYMMACHUS, and THEODOTION give different interpretations. JOHN CHRYSOSTOM has his own definition. In referring to David as the author of the psalms, he says that David used to assign different parts of a psalm to alternating choral groups. Such a change from one group to another was indicated by the interpolated word *diapsalma*.[117] The Mishnah reports a similar custom in later times: the psalms, in this period, were sung in several sections, the breaks between these being filled with blasts of trumpets.[118] Hence commentators concluded that *selah* stood at the places where interruptions occurred.

The majority of classical and modern commentators are inclined to accept the *Septuagint's* translation of *diapsalma*, "a pause in singing." Yet, the specific meaning and implementation of this pause are by no means clarified, either by the *Septuagint* or by the expounders. It would lead too far to quote the most relevant of the dozens of interpretations that cropped up in the vast literature about the subject. The simplest explanation of the term, generally considered authentic, is hinted by the talmudic tradition:

> Ben Arza clashed the cymbal and the Levites broke forth into singing. When they reached a break in the singing, they [the priests] blew upon the trumpets and the people prostrated themselves; at every break there was a blowing of the trumpets and at every blowing of the trumpet a prostration.[119]

The division of the psalm-text by the *selah*-interludes (or whatever these may have been) is quite irregular and does not allow any conjecture as to the rules of their application. There are only a few instances where the psalms are broken up by such interludes into more or less equal sections. Seldom do psalmodic contents themselves justify any preceding or following instrumental intermezzo. Sometimes *selah* enhances markedly the impact of a dramatic phrase; sometimes it is difficult, or even impossible, to discover why the term stands at a place where there does not seem to be the slightest inducement for an interlude. Therefore, unless we assume that *selah* has been distributed indiscriminately or erroneously between the psalmodic verses, we must admit that the reason for its insertion in the Masoretic text represents an insoluble riddle.

It is possible, and even probable, that the word does not stand in every place where an interlude of some kind would actually be called for, The preserved old manuscripts are quite inconsistent with regard to *selah*. The chances are that this word, which originally did not belong to the text and had no bearing upon the contents of the psalm, was not handled by the *soferim* (the scribes) with the same care as the text itself, at least prior to the fixed Hebrew canon. Also, there are some obvious errors by the copyists, for in various Bible versions the word has changed places. For instance, in the Masoretic text *selah* stands after Psalm 57:4; in the *Septuagint* after 57:3; the Hebrew text has *selah* after Psalm 61:5; the *Septuagint* after 61:4. Sometimes the word appears manifestly at a wrong place, as in Psalm 68:8; according to the logic of the text, 68:9 would be more appropriate; also, *selah* would stand better after Psalm 88:11 than after 88:10. In Psalm 55:20, *selah* even stands in the middle of a phrase, disrupting the whole sentence. Almost contrary to the sense of the phrase is the location of *selah* in Psalm 57:4.

In various codices and manuscripts a number of *selahs* have been found that apparently are correct but are missing from the Masoretic text. The canonical arrangement, therefore, does not furnish a definite clue as to where and how often a break in psalmodic singing might actually have occurred in the ritual.

According to R. Kimhi's interpretation, *selah* would be an instruction for the instrumentalists, who until then accompanied the singing softly, to start forcefully, in using trumpets and percussion instruments. During this loud music the singing was supposed to stop.

This interpretation seems to be quite logical if we take into account a simple practical necessity that arises from the physical limitations of the average human voice. The main burden of music in the Temple service, rather extensive as a rule, rested upon the shoulders of the Levitical singers. Even with the greatest devotion of the singers to their service, there would be a natural limit to the endurance of their vocal cords. In lengthy performances, solo as well as choir singers needed a short repose for recuperation. The breaks in singing might have caused the resorting to instrumental interludes indicated by *selah*. However logical the above explanations may appear, they have never been considered as conclusive.

Quite a number of sophisticated theories cropped up, the most incongruous perhaps propounded by Stainer:

> *Selah* is always a musical interlude, but not always what is known to modern critic as "pure music." . . . More often it represents what we should call "programme music," and is consciously and deliberately descriptive of the text which it accompanies.[120]

To be sure, program-music is by no means a modern or Occidental achievement. Its beginnings may be traced as far back as the sixth century B.C.E. At the artistic festivals at Delphi, the aulētes used to illustrate musically Apollo's fight with the dragon. Sakadas, a famous aulos virtuoso, had obtained the prize with such a composition, the *nomos pythikos*, at the first Pythian competition (586 B.C.E.). Centuries later, this melody still was highly praised. Timosthenes, admiral of Ptolemy II (285–247 B.C.E.), gave a detailed description of it, which is preserved by Strabo. Two other writers of Antiquity, Pausanias and JULIUS POLLUX, also mention this famous melody. Other historical records, originating in the fourth century B.C.E., furnish additional evidence about the accomplishments of Greek virtuoso performers of dithyrambs, depicting with instrumental or vocal means storm, gale, the singing of birds, and so forth, of which the rendering of a sea storm by the instrumental virtuoso TIMOTHEUS is a prominent example.

Attempts of the same kind have been attested throughout the Middle Ages, continuing uninterruptedly until modern times. Composers of all epochs tried to stimulate the imagination of their audiences by using associative means, such as titles, descriptions, and sometimes by underscoring their lyrics with characteristic rhythms.

Between such tonal pictures and a hypothetical program-music in the Jewish Temple there is an impassable abyss. The Greek and also the medieval attempts at depicting physical events and actions with musical means have been performed at secular occasions and aimed to amuse the audiences at festivals and, in the Middle Ages, at popular feasts and fairs. Such musical displays have always been caused by, or associated with, material motives. The Greek dithyramb-virtuosi did not play out of enthusiasm for art, but for awards offered, the amount of which was sometimes quite considerable. The musical images produced by the jugglers have been, as regards their aim, mere musical tricks designed to stimulate the generosity of their audiences. It is obvious, therefore, that the nature of such Greek and medieval productions of program-music was entirely different from that of Jewish sacred music.

The hypothesis that program-music was performed in the Temple would presuppose a tonal art aiming at the presentation of picturesque musical effects, something wholly extraneous to the cult. However, the principal, if not exclusive goal of Hebrew sacred music consisted in praising the Lord with singing and playing. Program-music in the sanctuary would represent a procedure entirely opposite to the religious conception of the Jews, to their ritual, and also to the character of Temple music itself. Therefore, the assumption of program-music within the Temple service, and as a part of the ritual, cannot be justified historically, religiously, or least of all, ethically.

The confusion of ideas that prevailed in assuming that program-music in Jewish cult was possible, or even probable, created some further eccentric offspring. E. CAPEL CURE,[121] and after him W. W. LONGFORD,[122] are not satisfied with merely postulating that *selah* is program-music. They go as far as to describe exactly its specific features. They speak of "flight motives," of "storm motives," of "sacrifice-" and "war-*selahs*," terms taken over directly from RICHARD WAGNER's technique of applying leading motives in his music dramas.

In order to lend force to his program-music hypothesis, CAPEL CURE appends a musical description of a *selah*, which reads as an analytical review of a modern symphonic poem:

> It is a most vivid picture of a tropical storm, . . . the wild melody being sustained and reinforced . . . receives a thrilling intensification from the Death *selah*, which immediately follows.[123]

The comparison between the Biblical *selah* and WAGNER's music dramas shows the twisted ways followed by some modern expounders of the Bible in order to make plausible their peculiar ideologies.

Not all modern interpretations of *selah* go such befuddled ways as those mentioned above. Some of them are guided by the spirit of music; among them has appeared a new theory, based upon well-established musical principles.

In a remarkable essay, K. J. ZENNER[124] refers to a graphic illustration in the CODEX of KOSMAS INDIKOPLEUSTES (first half of the sixth century C.E.), preserved in the Vatican. In this illustration various groups of Temple singers are portrayed performing songs antiphonally. (Illus. 72).

As mentioned earlier, the *Septuagint* translates *selah* as *diapsalma*. The usual, and somewhat free explanation of the Greek term is *dia* in *psallein*, that is a "break in singing," while the modern expounders are rather bent upon the conception of *psallein dia*, i.e., "to play between (the singing)," hence the idea of "interlude."

Following ZENNER's theory, the logical interpretation is contained in JOHN CHRYSOSTOM's phrase:

autē hē diadochē tou psalmou ekaleito diapsalma.

such a division of the psalm was called *diapsalma.*[125]

As ZENNER maintains, as *dialogos* is the kind of *legein*, "to speak," done between two persons, so is *diapsalma* the kind of *psallein*, "to play (with singing)," which takes place alternately between two groups.

According to KOSMAS, *selah*, or *diapsalma*, stands always *kata tōn mesōn tou psalmou*, "within the psalm." But we have already pointed out that in the canonical text as well as in the various translations, several *selahs* stand at the end (Psalms 3, 9, 24, 45). This would suggest that prior to the canon the psalms were assembled in different groups. Even the *Septuagint* shows, in many instances, divergences from the Masoretic text. Should we consider KOSMAS's indications authentic, we would be bound to assume that in the original setup, *selah* always stood within the psalmodic text.

KOSMAS avers that there were six groups of singers to alternate. In the Holy Writ, as we know, there is not the slightest indication to that effect. ZENNER claims, however, that the very construction of Psalm 1 yields certain internal evidences supporting the assumption that it was performed by six alternating choral groups.[126]

Wherever *selah* makes its appearance, the alternation of the choral groups would be logical; but *selah* is not applied to all the places where the text seems to be appropriate for changing the groups. Following ZENNER's idea, *selah* should have been used much more frequently. Indeed, in the *Codex Vaticanus* there are several *selahs* (e.g., Psalms 34:11; 80:8) that seem to stand in conformity with ZENNER's principle but are missing in the Hebrew text. In Greek minuscule manuscripts JAKOB discovered twelve additional *selahs*, which have not been preserved in other manuscripts.[127] Furthermore, the *Psalterium Vetus*, the first, Old Latin, translation of the Psalter, preserved in the *Codex St. Germani*, contains some additional *selahs*.[128]

With these arguments, ZENNER thinks to have proven that *selah* indicated the change of the performing groups in antiphonal singing. KOSMAS's illustration and CHRYSOSTOM's allusion to a similar procedure offer strong supports for this assumption.

Selah is the only term that the English versions, old and recent, did not even attempt to translate. Those which do not take it over phonetically, leave it out altogether in the psalms as well as in Habakkuk.

Higgayon

The examination of the term *higgayon* (Psalm 9:17) has been assigned to this place because its meaning is closely connected with that of *selah*.

The root of the word is *hagah*, meaning "to murmur," "to growl," in general "to produce a low sound." Applied to music, the verb is believed to be an instruction for the musicians to keep the accompaniment in subdued and solemn tone colors.

Besides this basic meaning, the verb has another implication, "to meditate," "to muse." According to ancient philosophical conceptions, thought mutters in the heart and talks in undertones. Thus, the affinity of both meanings becomes obvious. In Ps. 15:19, the differently punctuated word is translated as "meditation." The interpretations of the term by Biblical exegetes oscillate between these two imports.

The fact that *higgayon* appears in the Psalter conjointly with *selah* led to the almost unanimous belief that both represent certain musical instructions, which either belong together or complement each other. There are three possible explanations:

1) *Higgayon selah* is the term in its complete form, and *selah* would merely be an abbreviation of it

2) *Higgayon* is a gloss to, or synonym of, *selah*, and both terms are basically identical, so that the shortened form would not alter their meaning

3) Perhaps an earlier order of the Psalter had Psalm 9 put in a place where the complete expression *higgayon selah* appeared for the first time. Since its correct meaning was thus established, the psalm editors used only the abbreviated form in subsequent passages, and so *selah* remained alone.

Psalm commentators attach various implications to the dual term; some interpret it as an instruction for the singers to immerse themselves in meditation, during which the music would be silent.

As a contrasting opinion, MOWINCKEL interprets *higgayon* as an instruction for exclamations such as "for ever," or "in all eternity," which, with the rustling of harps and together with the "interlude" (*selah*) represented a single and unified ritual action.

Just as the early translators of the Old Testament failed to disclose the exact meaning of the word, the English versions, too, refrained from looking for equivalents and, as with *selah*, took over the expression phonetically from the Hebrew, unless leaving it out entirely. LUTHER alone tried to reproduce in German the hypothetical meaning of the term by translating it as *"Zwischenspiel,"* "interlude."

In contrast to the "Book of Psalms," the "Song of Songs" has only minor importance for our subject. This jewel of lyric poetry is completely devoid of any indication as to how it was sung in Ancient Israel. The Canticle is ascribed to King Solomon, the poet and musician, therefore it has been surmised that, like the psalms, it was sung with instrumental accompaniment. There is, however, not the slightest allusion to it, either in the text itself, or in contemporary or later sources.

The only reference to music in the "Song of Songs"—if we disregard its very title and two amorous allusions in it (2:14; 5:2)—is the passage where spring is called "the time of singing" (2:12). Furthermore, there is a reference to the "Dance of Maḥanaim" (7:1), which will be discussed in a later part of this study.

But few passages found in "Ecclesiastes" reveal any relationship of its author to music (2:8; 3:4; 7:5); likewise, the book of "Proverbs" contains little that relates to our subject. We can therefore dispense with examining these books closely.

SINGING IN ANCIENT ISRAEL

SINGING IN HEROIC TIMES

Music in Ancient Israel had a central aim: the glorification of God, served by the threefold art of singing, playing instruments, and dancing.

Contrary to the alleged "ancestor" in the Bible of instrumental music (Gen. 4:21), singing is as old as humanity itself According to post-Biblical Jewish legends, singing existed even prior to the creation of man; the song of angels praising God after the act of creating the world constitutes a celestial parallel to the terrestrial song of praise exalting the Lord.[1]

According to the naïve belief of primitive man, ordinary speech is not sufficient for the intercourse with supernatural beings, on whom, supposedly, his fate depends. Thus, in reciting the ritual formulae, in addressing the deity, in prayers and supplications, ordinary speech would undergo transformation by overflowing instinctively into accentuated declamation. This engendered a manifold melodic and rhythmic remodeling of the worshipper's voice, and thus created the first element of "singing."[2] Gradually, some specific formulae of speech-melody emerged and primitive melodic patterns crystallized, which may be considered as forerunners of "tunes." Between this stage and the "song" as a form of art, there is still a long but more or less straight development, which can easily be followed up.

In the early life of every people acts of worship and religious ceremonies are the primary sources of organized singing. The musical sentiment of the deeply religious Jewish people likewise manifested itself in singing far back in their history.

> This natural tendency of men to singing is conspicuous among the Semitic race and espe-
> cially among the Hebrews, the more so as their life and actions have their roots in the
> depths of subjectivity and in their intrinsic feelings.[3]

Since the written records about the primeval existence of the Jewish people are more replete with myth than history, we are informed at a relatively late period about the purely cultural manifestations of the Hebrews, including their singing. As in their poetry, so also in their music the early evolutionary phases are concealed from our observation, and when any tangible products in these domains suddenly emerge, they already show forms of art that are advanced stages of a long and organic development.

The earliest poems of ancient peoples were all sung. "Song and Tale"

(*Singen und Sagen*) is the external form of early poetry of all nations. All had their folkbards, who have been the preservers of the art-form of sung poetry.

Modern Biblical exegesis favors the theory that, although there is no positive evidence sustaining this belief,

> one must not overlook the possibility that considerable portions of the stories of Genesis were sung in verse by minstrels before they were retold in prose by biblical authors.[4]

This would be in conformity with the view of modern literary historians that "poetry," as an artistic expression of elated human sentiments, constitutes a preliminary stage to "prose," the narrative style of common speech; at best, the two are considered as "sisters of equal rights."[5] For our subject, this implies that "poetry" was sung, "prose" recited. However, there might have been only a slight difference between the singing of poetry and the recitation of a narrative, as carried out in the exalted speech of the ancient folkbards.

Ritual prayers offered up with singing, or rather with chanting, have been used in all ancient religions. The Sumerians enunciated longer and shorter formulae of prayers with singing; some of their texts have been preserved. The sacred services of the Babylonians and Assyrians contained numerous hymn-like songs.[6] For the well-being of the king and for temple dedications, the Babylonians recited litanies, which unmistakeably show a responsorial form.[7]

Even assuming that these and similar evidences furnished by the history of religions are to be considered, in some measure, as precursors of the liturgical singing of the Hebrews, the influence of heathen rites upon Jewish musical practice should not be overestimated. The religious institutions of other ancient peoples have been so different from the patriarchal cult of the Israelites that this fact alone must have greatly diminished the penetration of pagan musico-liturgical elements into Jewish worship.

In early times the heads of the families have been the qualified stewards of the priestly functions. The rites of this epoch must have been simple, rudimentary, and without elaborate ceremonies. Accordingly, the singing in those patriarchal times, too, must have been rather primitive. There are allusions to singing liturgical formulae of these rites in the indications *kara shem 'Adonay*, or *kara b'shem 'Adonay*, "to call the name of God," or "to call upon the name of the Lord," which might have constituted the essential musical part of the simplest organized worship (Gen. 12:8; 13:4; 26:25; 33:20).

As we know, the rhythmic shaping of speech requires a stressed diction, an increased intensity of expression, a richer deployment of the accent inherent in the word and sentence. Eventually, the stretching of the vowels served as the last link toward the establishment of a declamatory artifice, which was already close to real singing, because the vowels of human speech and the musical sounds are of a kindred origin.

This artifice is the norm that we have to take into account when facing the earliest testimony of the Bible concerning secular singing. It goes as far back as the Jubal legend. The same Biblical passage that informs us about the three primeval professions and crafts, including music, contains the first secular "song" of Jewish history, known as "Lamech's song" (Gen. 4:23,24).[8] Whether the text of this poem, as quoted by the chronicler, is in reality a fragment of a more extensive bardic ballad, as surmised by some historians,[9] is a matter of conjecture. At any rate, it is the oldest Jewish specimen of a secular song, primitive and crude, to be sure, but already presented unmistakably in a poetic form:

> (And Lamech said to his wives:)
> Adah and Zillah, hear my voice;
> Ye wives of Lamech, hearken unto my speech;
> For I have slain a man for wounding me,
> And a young man for bruising me;
> If Cain shall be avenged sevenfold,
> Truly Lamech seventy and sevenfold.

If this savage and brutal "song" still has more or less a legendary tint, historical reality soon presents itself in the Biblical text. Laban's reproachful speech when he overtakes Jacob in his flight contains a reference to a secular song already in its proper sense:

> Wherefore didst thou flee secretly and outwit me; and did not tell me, that I might have sent thee away with mirth and with songs, with tabret and with harp? (Gen. 31:27).

To understand the abyss gaping between Lamech's uncouth song of hatred and Laban's song of mirth, we must compare the mental stage of a primitive man with the markedly higher civilization at the time of the patriarchs Laban and Jacob. The first is a crude and barbarous song that has little to do with art; in the second, singing accompanied by instrumental music suggests a clearly recognizable artistic manifestation against an ethical background: that of sending a friend on his journey with music and singing.

From this Biblical passage BUDDE draws the conclusion that as early as heroic times the Hebrews might have had a group of singers, by which he evidently means folkbards. These were poets and singer-musicians who, besides possessing creative gifts, were compilers of many folksongs and ballads, which they performed on suitable occasions.[10]

One of the most beautiful, and artistically the most relevant, songs of the Old Testament is the one offered as a thanksgiving to the Lord by Moses and the people of Israel after their miraculous escape at the Red Sea (Exod. 15:1–21). It is surmised that originally it must have been shorter and that it acquired its final form only after the Israelites settled in Cana'an.[11] It is the first religious national song in the Bible, and as such, it is the starting point of a development that culminated in latter-day musical achievements of the people of Israel.

As for its musical rendering, it is safe to assume that the *Shirah* was sung by Moses and the people responsorially. There is no direct reference to this in the Biblical text, to be sure, although later rabbinical sources confirm explicitly this kind of rendition.[12] According to the prophetic vision, the seraphim, too, sang responsorially:

> And one called unto another, and said: "Holy, holy, holy, is the Lord of the hosts; the whole earth is full of His glory (Isa. 6:3).

The songs of praise and triumph of Moses, as well as the one sung by his sister Miriam, were spontaneous religious outbursts but not yet ritual songs in the proper sense. Liturgical song, as such, came into being when Israel, through the covenant on Sinai, became the "chosen" people and, through this, met its ultimate destiny. From then on, Israel possessed not only its own religion, but also its own form of cult, the dignity of which transfigured all former ritual actions, and its liturgical music as well.

The subsequent heroic age of Israel brought forth numerous war- , triumph- , and other bardic songs, in which happiness about the conquest of a new home-land and enthusiasm about the deeds of famous national heroes found their crystallization in poetic form. Ancient songs of minstrels, interspersed with occasional historic reports, used to be compiled in books, most of which, unfortunately, have been lost. But the Scriptures preserved some vestigial fragments from them in the form of quotations by Biblical chroniclers; also, the titles of some of these books indicate that they have actually existed.

One such compilation may have been *Sefer milḥamot ꜣAdonay*, "The Book of the Wars of the Lord," from which the chronicler quotes two passages (Num. 21:14,15 and 21:27–30). Another collection of minstrels' songs has apparently been *Sefer ha-yashar*, "The Book of the Righteous," mentioned in two places in the Old Testament (Josh. 10:13 and 2 Sam. 1:18).[13] Still another vestige pertaining to a lost historical document may be traced in the Lord's com-mandment to Moses to perpetuate in a book the victory over the Amalekites (Exod. 17:14). It is not evident from the Biblical text whether this book was ever written. Possibly it is identical with the afore-mentioned "Book of the Wars of the Lord."

Generally, folkbards would recite ancient tales at banquets and sing heroic ballads. The vivid prose description by Biblical chroniclers of the Exodus from Egypt and other outstanding national events seem to reflect the spirit of such ancient bardic songs.

Primitive marching songs are mentioned soon after the Exodus from Egypt, during the wandering in the desert. At breaking camp and at putting up a new one, the people would dash into vigorous songs:

> And it came to pass, when the ark set forward, that Moses said: "Rise up, O Lord, and let Thine enemies be scattered; and let them that hate Thee flee before Thee."

And when it rested, they said:

> Return, O Lord, unto the ten thousands of the families of Israel (Num. 10:35,36).

Analogy with the general practice of those times warrants the conclusion that Moses did not sing this by himself. The ark of the Covenant was carried like a banner in front of the marching crowd, and at such solemn processions the people would intone the first song; the second song might have been rendered responsorially. Both songs, owing to their popular character, have partially been incorporated into the Psalter (Psalm 68:2).

Marching songs pertaining to the later epoch of Israel's history are likewise mentioned in the Bible (2 Chron. 20:21; 20:27,28).

Another category of secular songs, mentioned frequently in the Scriptures, is the one connected with work. Such songs can be found among all peoples, in all epochs, and on all levels of civilization. The Hebrews, too, have known the enlivening effect of common worksongs, and the Bible contains numerous examples of their use; in some instances, even their textual fragments are pre-served in the Scriptures. There are numerous references in the Bible to joyous singing at the harvest and vintage (Exod. 23:16; Isa. 9:2; 16:10; 24:7–9; Judg. 9:27; Jer. 25:30). Traces of a vintage song are preserved in Isa. 65:8:

As, when wine is found in the cluster, one saith: "Destroy it not, for a blessing is in it."

The Bible mentions, or alludes to, several other worksongs, one of these being the song of the masons laying the corner-stone (Job 38:7), or the top stone (Zech. 4:7; cf. Ezra 3:10,11). Some Biblical exegetes believe that the prophetic answer of the guard,

the morning cometh, and also the night—if ye will inquire, inquire ye; come (Isa. 21:12).

represents a sort of song of the night-watchman.[14]

Another species of Jewish vocal art was the song of triumph. It was intoned mostly by women, receiving with songs and dances the returning victor and his army. Deborah's paean (Judg. 5) is such a spontaneous manifestation. Even though, as the Bible indicates, the victorious general Barak participated in this song, Deborah was, in reality, the leader of the singing, as evidenced unmistakably by two passages (verses 3 and 12).

Judith's song of triumph (Judith 16) is not inferior to that of Deborah, either in inspiration or in poetic loftiness. The fact that the Book of Judith is a late product and lies outside the Old Testament canon does not detract from the importance of this song. The poem is enlivened by the same power of expression, figurative speech, and heroic impulsion, as Deborah's song. Their musical rendering may have been akin to that of simple, unsophisticated folk-songs, as was usual among ancient peoples. Judging from certain analogies (cf. Exod. 15:20,21), it may be conjectured that both paeans were sung with instrumental accompaniment.

On the occasion of great national events, the participation of the individual in the singing gave him a vivid notion and experience of active cooperation and kindled his feeling of belonging to the same ethnic community. The social moment is even more conspicuous when antiphonal singing is artistically synchronized with the dance of women. The "Song at the Red Sea," mentioned above, may serve as a case in point.

At secular occasions, for instance, at the return of King Saul and David from the victorious battle against the Philistines (1 Sam. 18:6,7), antiphonal singing was a frequent occurrence. This solemn reception with antiphonal singing is reported by the chronicler in two other passages of the same book (21:12 and 29:5).

With the institution of a regular musical service in the cult by David and Solomon, antiphonal singing—although not mentioned directly—was introduced into the liturgy and became, from the outset, an essential feature of sacred musical performances. Quite a number of Biblical passages, especially in the Psalter, refer to it repeatedly, directly and indirectly.

The musical service held at the solemn laying of the foundation of the Second Temple took place with antiphonal singing (Ezra 3:10,11). In the big procession, which was the feature at the dedication of the newly erected walls around Jerusalem, two choral groups sang antiphonally (Neh. 12:31–42).

Antiphonal singing retained its full liturgical significance far into talmudic times, proof of which is the frequent reference to it in the early rabbinical literature.[15]

Apart from joyful occasions, antiphonal singing is also referred to at funeral services, which were minutely regulated in Ancient Israel. At private funerals the women of the house were assisted by professional wailing women, which constituted a special profession of female musicians. They were called in the various English Bibles "wise women," "skillful women," or "women well-versed in dirges." The lamentations have always been performed responsorially or antiphonally, as evidenced by the Scriptures (Zech. 12:12–14).

MUSIC IN THE LITURGY

In the pre-Davidic era, singing originated partly from certain ritual necessities and partly from the common national consciousness. With the institution of the organized Temple music by David and its further development by Solomon, the ethos of singing changed fundamentally. It ceased to be merely the sounding upshot of the common experience. It was elevated to an art and became coordinated with poetry, another artistic manifestation permitted, and even encouraged, among the Jews by their religious laws. In Solomon's Temple, with its sumptuous ritual appeal to all the senses of the worshippers, singing became the focus of musical attraction.

The central feature of Jewish Temple ceremonies was the sacrifice. From the very inception of the organized sacred service, sacrifice was closely connected with music. Singing was considered an integral and indispensable part of the sacrifice; lack of singing even invalidated the sacrificial action.[16]

Owing to the paramount importance of singing in the sacred service, it is natural that the Bible should refer to it quite frequently. The reports of the chroniclers about singing in the ritual, and also about the Levites, the chief representatives of the sacred vocal art, belong to the most momentous information about the music practice of Ancient Israel.

Besides religious songs of all categories, the Scriptures mention practically all the current species of secular songs. Among them, two species are virtually lacking and, curiously, just those which have a particular significance in the family life: the cradle song and the children's song. The latter has certain points of contact with Levitical singing; therefore, it may be appropriate to examine this apparent Biblical omission in connection with singing in the sacred service.

It should be surprising if a people whose entire tradition was centered in the family did not have the species of songs that are most intimately connected with family life. Though the Scriptural text does not mention children's songs specifically, there is ample evidence that such songs were a current feature in Biblical times (see Zech. 8:5; 1 Chron. 13:8, and 1 Sam. 18:7). Some commentators refer also to Job 21:11,12 as a proof for children's song in the Bible. The original Hebrew word in this passage, *y'rakkedun*, "dancing," has the meaning of "dancing *and* singing," an assumption based upon the *Septuagint's* translation, "to rejoice at the sound of a *song*."

The Old Testament refers to children's songs only indirectly. However, the early rabbinical literature contains definite references to them, and thus we may infer quite legitimately that boys participated in the Levitical choir. We do not know why the Biblical chroniclers omitted mentioning this important feature of the Levitical music organization. The assumption, however, that boys participated in the Levitical choir at an early epoch, possibly even in the

First Temple, is inevitable if we consider the manner in which a Levitical singer was brought up to achieve professional mastery.

The long preparation described earlier warrants the assumption, if only by implication, that children in general might have had their own songs, other than those learned in the sacred service. This is corroborated by two allusions to children's songs in the New Testament (Matt. 11:17 and Luke 7:32), from which we may infer, retrospectively, the existence of similar customs among the Jews during the Old Testament era. For cradle songs, on the other hand, we have a direct, even if non-Jewish evidence: the "work-song" for nurses, mentioned by JOHN CHRYSOSTOM.[17] Although this item, too, refers to post-biblical times, we may assume *per analogiam* that cradle songs had been used in Ancient Israel, this being, in fact, a universal practice the world over, and at all times.

The most momentous feature of sacred singing in Israel, the summit of Jewish musical culture, was psalm-singing. The inward poetic and musical inspiration of the Jewish people centered wholly in the creation of psalms. The fact that other Oriental peoples had also written and sung psalms does not alter the truth that the Israelites were the first to impart to this vocal form the artistic and ethical loftiness that, even now, after millennia, exercises an irresistible sway upon the human mind.

In the early period of Temple music, psalm-singing had been the exclusive prerogative of professional Levitical singers, in the capacity both of soloists and choristers. The Psalter had originally been designed for their use. Yet, as time went by, the mere passive participation of the worshippers in the divine service might not have satisfied the inner craving for a more rapturous communion with the ritual. This brought forth the desire to join the Levites in the songs of praise, which became reality when the worshippers began first to interject single words (acclamations) and then to repeat entire verses (refrains). This is the origin of the active participation of the congregation in liturgical singing, and from this primitive popular usage responsorial and antiphonal singing gradually developed in the sacred service.

The Babylonian exile was a period of suffering for the people, but this tribulation prepared them for a deeper understanding of the religious and ethical values contained in the Psalter. In the ordeal of collective fate, the individual was bound to realize the import of the liberating and comforting song; only then could the psalms become real folksongs. After the return from the exile the Psalter ceased to be used exclusively in the sanctuary; it served the entire community for devotion and consolation. Thus, the psalms have gradually become the common property of all Jews wherever they lived.

Some commentators maintain that the Psalter did not represent for the Jews a hymnal in the modern sense, but was merely a collection of poetry serving as prayers.[18] It is reasoned that the common people could hardly have been able to sing such songs properly, because the psalms had an irregular metrical setup and were not partitioned into easily grouped symmetrical strophes like, for instance, the hymns of later Christian congregations; therefore, the reasoning goes, they had to be performed more or less in a recitative manner. This amounts to cantillation, a style and technique that allegedly conflicts with the principle of popular singing.

This, however, is but partly correct. For there are good reasons to believe that the people could actually participate in the Levitical singing routine even beyond acclamations and refrains. One must recall that the basis of Oriental music is the *makamat* (about which more presently), "tunes" or "melodicles," which constituted the melodic skeleton of psalm-singing. The principal "tunes" must have been known to practically everybody; this is a foregone conclusion in view of the high standard of music education in Ancient Israel. It is therefore not too far-fetched to suppose that the people, or at least large sections of them, were able to follow the conventional melodic patterns.[19]

The musical rendition of certain psalms actually requires, and even demands, the participation of the congregation, as one may well judge from the poetic setup of some psalm-texts. Thus, Psalms 44, 47, 80, 99, 144 (verses 1–11) contain responses after each verse (cf. also Psalms 103, 104, 106, 107, 118, etc.). To ensure a uniform response, the congregation received—at least in the Second Temple—a signal by winking a piece of cloth.[20]

Religious singing was not restricted to ritual occasions or to official public festivities. The intrinsic urge of the Jewish people to express its religious sentiment with singing soon created the custom of embellishing private feasts with songs. According to ancient beliefs, people eating and drinking together in company were united spiritually in close friendship, and this feeling of solidarity was bound to manifest itself in singing jointly. The common sacrificial meals especially, connected with religious festivals, in which rich and poor participated with their families and friends, took place in high spirits and were always accompanied by singing.

Among the festive celebrations, the historically and nationally significant Passover meal was outstanding in its embellishment with singing. The Pesah-Haggadah, though fully developed only in the Midrashic era, might still contain remnants of certain songs that had been sung at the Passover meal in ancient times.[21]

As mentioned earlier, the culminating point of the sacred ceremony at the Temple was the sacrifice. Each sacrificial action had its own musical setting and specifically selected psalms. Gradually a tradition developed requiring the performance of particular psalms for the various sacrifices. Thus, the daily burnt, expiatory, laudatory offerings and libations had all a different musical layout, which was strictly regulated like any other part of the ritual.

There was a different psalm assigned for each day. The Mishnah contains detailed indications as to the psalms designed for the weekdays as well as for the Sabbath and the High Holidays.[22]

In the morning and evening services of the Sabbath, the sacrificial offerings were more numerous than on weekdays; they amounted for each of these services to as much as for the daily morning and evening services together.[23] All these were public offerings and their volume alone was considerable. Yet, it was dwarfed by the abundance of private offerings. With the approach of the High Holidays the volume of private offerings became so huge that even the increased number of the officiating priests could hardly attend to the sacrifices with all the required ritualistic formalities. The minute observation of the sacrificial rites was, according to the conception of Israel, the principal means of securing God's favor, and therefore the Levites, even Levitical singers, were frequently obliged to assist the overburdened priests in the preparation of the sacrificial victims (cf. 2 Chron. 29:34). Since the offerings have always been accompanied by the singing of the Levites, the normal daily task of the Levitical choir alone must have been considerable. On High Holidays, the Levites must have had an uninterrupted musical service.

Among the psalms sung at the High Holidays, the group of the *Hallel*-psalms occupied the most prominent place. To this group belonged the Egyptian *Hallel* (Psalms 113–118), the Great *Hallel* (Psalms 120–136), and Psalms 146–148, specifically called the *Hallel*-psalms.

At the Feast of Tabernacles, Psalm 118:25 was sung at every morning service. While the Levitical choir was singing, the worshippers surrounded the altar. Subsequently the priests sounded the trumpets and on this signal the congregation retreated from the altar with the repeated exclamation "Homage [lit., "Beauty"] to thee, O Altar!"[24]

At this festival three symbolic ceremonies, richly adorned with music, gained a paramount importance, although they were not directly connected with the Temple worship. To these belonged the ceremony of carrying wood for the burnt offerings, the rite of the water libation and, finally, the popular festivity of *Bet ha-She'ubah* (or *Sho'eba*), which took place at night in the Court of Women, with an abundant display of singing, playing instruments, and dancing (see below).

THE SYNAGOGUE

While the Temple existed, psalm-singing provided the ritual background and, at the same time, the artistic adornment of the principal section of the cult, the sacrifice. Unlike the Temple, the Synagogue had no altar, therefore it could not perform sacrificial rites. This, however, could not possibly prevent the transplantation of psalm-singing from the Temple to the Synagogue.

The origin of the Synagogue is shrouded in obscurity. And even though it must have been an age-old institution,[25] we possess historical records about the Synagogue only from a relative late period immediately preceding the Christian era, when it already represented the central form of Jewish worship.[26]

The original aim of Sabbath meetings was not divine service, but rather study of the Law. This explains why, even in later times, a mere subordinate role has been assigned to the worship and praise of Yahveh in the Synagogue, as compared with religious instruction. The Mishnah contains detailed indications with regard to the reading of the Torah and the Prophets in the Sabbath meetings, whereas psalm-singing is not mentioned at all.

The earliest historical reference to the Synagogue worship by a coeval witness is to be found in PHILO's writings:

Moses commanded the people to gather on the seventh day in a meeting place and to listen with awe and reverence to the lecture of the law, so that everybody could understand its meaning.[27]

Pertinent information concerning the purpose of the Synagogue—and, incidentally, the nature of its musical manifestations—is contained in another statement of PHILO, which testifies to the fact that the Sabbath meeting of his time was not restricted to the instruction of the Law. In this reference, he characterizes the Synagogue as a place of worship and prayer, adding that the participants perform "hymns and songs and canticles (*hymnoi, paianēs, ōdais*)."[28]

Psalm-singing, the tonal aspect of religious expression, was always considered an indispensable stimulant for adoration, and therefore it must have been introduced without much delay into Synagogue worship. Although the singing of psalms did not constitute here the musical background to sacrificial cere- monies—for these were lacking in the Synagogue—it served an essentially sim- ilar purpose: to praise God in a form arising directly from the soul with the aid of songs.[29]

With the destruction of the sanctuary by the Romans, the Jewish religion and its established customs, including singing, would have been in extreme danger of being dissipated, had not the Synagogue become that institution which succeeded in maintaining the tradition.

> Unlike the Temple, a synagogue could not be destroyed by an enemy. With the burning of the Temple, its entire sacrificial system was obliterated. The destruction of any number of synagogue buildings entailed no change in the established liturgy or mode of worship. The Jews assembled anywhere in public or private were the real *synagōgē* which could conduct regular service like that held in the largest and most gorgeous structure.[30]

From the time of the Second Temple, there are no direct contemporary records about the sacred service and psalm-singing in the Synagogue. Our knowledge of the early synagogue ritual is based on talmudic sources. These inform us that to lections, benedictions, and short prayers, first mere portions of psalms and, eventually, entire psalms have been added.

Except for the fact that it was not accompanied by musical instruments, the singing in the early Synagogue was not essentially different from that of the Temple. The tonal system of the songs and the manner of their rendition were certainly identical; this is a foregone conclusion in view of the fact that, at the inception of the Synagogue in Jerusalem, the Levitical singers provided also for the musical part of the Synagogue service, which was held in the confines of the Temple itself. This service took place in the court of squared stones (*lishkat ha-gasit*), where worshippers prayed and received daily instruction. Its head was called *Rosh ha-keneset* and its chief functionary *hazzan ha-keneset*.[31]

The instrumental part of the Temple music consisted mainly in accompanying the vocal numbers; therefore, the lack or reduction of instrumental music in the Synagogue after the destruction of the Temple would have had no influence upon the fundamental character of the sacred songs. The talmudic statement that "the song may be sung even without the [attending] sacrifice"[32] applies, no doubt, to the extensive practice of the Synagogue. To be sure, psalm-singing in the Synagogue may have been reduced in quantity, but it served the same purpose: to enhance the religious devotion of the worshippers. Even when instrumental music was eventually abolished in the Synagogue, singing survived unchanged, at least temporarily.

It is generally assumed that in the early Synagogues outside of Jerusalem singing was unaccompanied from the very outset. This, however, is only partly true. Certainly, in smaller communities, musicians able to accompany the com- plex Temple songs in a satisfactory fashion were lacking. But in larger cities there might have been musicians sufficient in number and quality to meet the artistic requirements of sacred music. This assumption is corroborated by an

unmistakable reference in the Mishnah. Among other instructions pertaining
to music, the rabbinical writer indicates how to handle broken strings of the
kinnorot and *nebalim*:

> They might tie up a string [of a musical instrument] in the Temple, but not in the
> province.[33]

This instruction proves that "in the province," i.e., in Synagogues outside of
Jerusalem, singing must have been accompanied by the traditional Temple
instruments. Moreover, the second part of the instruction,

> and *in either place* it is forbidden to tie it up for the first time [i.e., before the singing
> started][34]

confirms the fact that whenever musicians were available outside of Jerusalem,
instrumental music was a regular feature in Synagogue worship.

In spite of its official banishment after the national catastrophe in 70 c.e.,
instrumental music in the Synagogue was never completely abandoned, at least
in some larger communities, as some well-attested documents stemming from
the Middle Ages, and even from much later times, unmistakably prove. Thus,
BENJAMIN of TUDELA from Navarra, who in 1160–1173 made extensive travels
in the Orient, reports in his diary about the musical practice in the Synagogue
of Bagdad.[35] He refers to the learned Rabbi ELEAZAR ben ẒEMACH,

> the master of one of the ten Hebrew colleges in Bagdad of that time, who was a descendant
> of the prophet Samuel and a man who knows the melodies that were sung in the Temple
> of Jerusalem during its time of existence.[36]

A man with such claims was probably bent on rendering the ancient melodies
in the traditional manner of the Temple, that is, with accompaniment. And, in
fact, there exists historical evidence to the effect that during the intermediate
days of the Feast of Tabernacles, singing in the Synagogue of Bagdad was
accompanied by instruments.[37]

Rabbi PETAHYAH of REGENSBURG [Ratisbon] was another traveler who toured
the Orient in the twelfth century. He furnished a valuable description of the
customs of the Jews whom he visited in Babylonia, Ashur, Media, and Persia.[38]
His observations contain various details concerning synagogal music in the places
referred to, among them the statement that psalm-singing was accompanied
by instruments.[39]

Preserved historical records state that as late as the fifteenth century, on the
island of Corfu, the *Shem'ā* was accompanied by music (*b'niggun ha-musika*).[40]
And in the *Sidur Amsterdam*[41] there is an indication that in the Meisel-Synagogue
of Prague

> they used to play [in the Friday evening service] before *Lekah Dodi* a lovely melody by
> R. Solomon Singer with organ (*b''ugab*) and string instruments (*u-binebalim*).[42]

The importance of the musical practice in the Synagogue cannot be overlooked
if we consider the multitude of such houses of prayer and devotion, called in
those times *didaskaleia*, or *proseuktēria*, meaning "houses of study," or *sabbateion*,
"house of Sabbath." In most cities with a large Jewish population there were
several of these, and in some places even numerous Synagogues. According to

the rabbinical tradition, Jerusalem had, at the time of its destruction by the Romans, 394,[43] and following another tradition, 480 Synagogues.[44] Every trade and profession had its own Synagogues in Jerusalem, where the members met for services.[45] The Jews from other cities, especially those whose vernacular was Greek—for instance, those from Cyrene, Alexandria, Cilicia, Tarsus, and so on—possessed their own houses of prayer in Jerusalem,[46] as well as in other larger cities of Palestine. Tiberias had 13 Synagogues;[47] Alexandria had numerous Synagogues in various districts of the city.[48] At the time of AUGUSTUS, there were quite a number of Synagogues in Rome.[49] The inscriptions of six of these Synagogues of Rome are preserved.[50] In his travels through Asia Minor and Greece, the Apostle Paul found Jewish Synagogues everywhere, even several of them, in larger cities like Damascus, and Salamis on Cyprus.[51]

According to rabbinical tradition, every Synagogue in Jerusalem was provided with a grammar school and also a school for higher learning,[52] in which young people were instructed in the Law and the poetical books of the Scriptures. The same may have been true, even if to a lesser degree, for the numerous Synagogues in the provinces. The instruction of sacred texts always proceeded with the aid of singing, as stated explicitly by the Talmud:

> If one reads the Scripture without a melody or repeats the Mishnah without a tune, of him the Scriptures says: "Therefore I gave them also statutes that were not good."[53]

This method was based upon two practical considerations. On the one hand, chanting of the Scriptural text was looked upon as essential for clarity, for syntactic intelligibility, and, last but not least, for the solemnity of the lection; on the other, the living experience showed that studying with chanting was infinitely more effective than the spoken word alone in memorizing the text. Because the tradition was transmitted exclusively by oral means, chanting became an indispensable mnemonic aid in learning lengthy passages from the Scriptures.

One can therefore readily realize how much the numerous houses of study, affiliated with the Synagogues, were bound to contribute toward the preservation and dissemination of Jewish singing.

From all that has been said above, it is obvious that the tradition of Temple singing was largely adhered to in the Synagogues of Jerusalem and its immediate neighborhood. How was this tradition carried, however, to distant communities, and how was it kept alive in such localities? This question is answered by the Mishnah.

It tells us about the institution of the *ʾAnshe Maʿamad,* an organization of laymen, delegates of the people, established mainly for the purpose of transplanting to distant places the routine of the Temple liturgy in its authentic form. *ʾAnshe Maʿamad* means literally "man at the place of standing" (or, as one translator puts it, "stand-up-men"). It was a term to designate a group of representatives from remote districts. Matching the twenty-four courses of priests and Levites (1 Chron. 23:6; 25:7), the country was divided into twenty-four sections. Each section had to delegate twice a year, always for a week, a representative to Jerusalem, who had to attend the Temple services and to participate in the sacrificial rites. What was the purpose of this participation? Doubtless, to make the *Maʿamad* thoroughly familiar with the details of liturgic usage. Back in their home towns, they would see to it that in their own places of worship, i.e., the Synagogues, the rites, customs, and songs should be performed according to the tradition of the Temple. The *Ma'amad* participated in regular refresher courses, so to speak, and received twice-a-year practical instruction in the liturgical ceremonial. They brought back with them the knowledge of the sacred routine and so they helped to safeguard the tradition. To be sure, our sources do not reveal anything about the *Ma'amad* having received direct instruction in liturgical singing. It may be reasonably assumed, however, that this important phase of the ritual has not been neglected. An indirect evidence of this is the indication of the Mishnah that the *Ma'amad* were bound to assist at the sacrificial ceremonies. The Synagogue, as we know, had no sacrifices. What then was the purpose of this ruling? Evidently, the purpose was to give those *Ma'amad* who had a previous musical knowledge some insight into the substance and the technique of Levitical singing.

It could be rightly argued that "instruction" twice a year for only a week each time would hardly be sufficient to obtain even a smattering of the complex art of Levitical singing. It must be stressed, however, that the basic melodic style of Jewish sacred singing was in no way different from Oriental singing in general. Anyone familiar to some extent with the rudiments of Oriental song could, without much difficulty, grasp the most evident characteristics of Temple singing. Furthermore, it may well be surmised that the *Ma'amad* had been selected mostly from among such men as already had some preliminary notions about singing. However short the time allotted to such refresher courses may have been, the intense and regular coaching might have accomplished its purpose, at least to a certain extent.

The institution of the *'Anshe Ma'amad* cannot be overestimated in the matter of dissemination and preservation of the Jewish sacred song. Through it, the knowledge of Temple melodies was carried into the farthest Jewish communities, and even if these melodies might not have been transmitted everywhere in their spotless purity, the *Ma'amad*, while they flourished, stood as the legitimate guardians of the musical tradition of the Temple.

JEWISH SECTS

In the concluding centuries of Israel's national existence, singing, sacred as well as secular, attained a towering significance among the artistic manifestations of Jewish life. It is not surprising, therefore, that it penetrated the hard core of the Jewish religious sects which, despite the fact that their forms of living were so different from those of the average population, adhered strictly to the traditional musical practice as handed down by the forefathers.

Among the Jewish sects there were two, the Essenes and the Therapeutae, about which coeval historical records are preserved. Of these, the extant reports concerning the singing of the Essenes are rather scanty, but they afford nevertheless some insight into their world of music and the spiritual background connected with it.

The Essenes were a community of men,[54] mostly of mature age, who led a self-denying and godly life, in which they renounced all mundane possessions and maintained a frugal existence based upon strict observance of the rigid Mosaic laws. Their day started with prayers and singing hymns:

Before sun-rising they speak not a word about profane matters, but offer certain prayers, which they have received from their forefathers, as if they supplicated it to rise.[55]

HIPPOLYTUS (d. 230 C.E.) even gives some indications about the character of these hymns, quoting the content of one of them:

From thee [comes] father, and through thee [comes] mother, two names immortal, progenitors of Aeons, O denizen of heaven thou illustrious man[56]

PORPHYRY (233–ca.304 C.E.) who, in his statements about the Essenes, follows in general JOSEPHUS's indications, adds to them a significant remark, saying that

they devote the Sabbath to singing praises to God and to rest.[57]

The other Jewish sect which, like the Essenes, distinguished itself by a pious and God-fearing life, was that of the Therapeutae, meaning "Healers of the Soul." They lived in the Egyptian desert at the Lake Mareotis, near Alexandria, male and female, occupying solitary cells and avoiding sexual relations. They met on the Sabbath for common prayer and for the *agapē*, the friendship- and love-feast, which had a particularly important role in their life, replacing, as it were, the Jewish religious service. PHILO, whose home-town was Alexandria, visited the sect repeatedly and left us a substantial report about their mores and customs.

The feast started with prayers, after which one of the participants expounded upon a passage from the Scriptures or a religious topic that was submitted to him. The didactic exercises were followed by singing, after which a frugal supper was offered. Then the nocturnal celebration started. The participants rose simultaneously, forming two choruses, one of men and one of women, and intoned hymns in honor of God, which were enlivened with round-dances. Finally, seized by the purest love of God, they united into a single chorus,

a copy of the choir set up of old beside the Red Sea in honor of the wonders there wrought.[58]

The singing and dancing of the Therapeutae at their *agapē* were not merely the imitation of the manifestation at the Red Sea, but the conscious *return* to the ancient tradition of the Temple, to the epoch when in the musical portion of the divine service men and women had their equal share. This constitutes the particular significance of PHILO's report.

Finally, we have scant records about the music practice of another Jewish sect, the Samaritans. In their sacred services psalm-singing alternated with readings from the Law.[59]

Love of music and the practice of it were similar among the early Christians, who in those days were generally looked upon as mere Jewish sectarians. And because they considered themselves as full-fledged members of the Jewish faith, it was only natural that the early Christians continued using the songs of the Jewish liturgy.

The first Judaeo-Christians held their services in the Temple (Acts 2:46,47; 3:1; 5:42; 21:26; 22:17; 24:17,18), or in the Synagogue (Acts 22:19; 25:11).

At the conclusion of the Sabbath, the Christians would gather together in their houses for the *agapē*. Throughout the night they would keep watch, reading the Scriptures, praying, singing psalms. In the early hours of dawn the Mass would be celebrated, after which the faithful resort to the Temple in order to assist at the offering of the Jewish sacrifice.[60]

As at the *agapē* of the Therapeutae, singing among the Judaeo-Christians represented that element of worship that was best suited to create and enhance the feeling of close communion among the congregants. The songs were simple and unaffected, like popular melodies. The simplicity of singing in the Synagogue, in which everyone was able to participate, was imitated by the early Christians.

Besides community singing, in which all took part, some of the particularly inspired individuals would give vent to the collective emotions of the worshippers in improvised chants. Such "new songs," kindled by the stirring enthusiasm of the people, passed from mouth to mouth, to become eventually the common property of the congregation. As a matter of fact, the first Christian songs were either ancient synagogal chants, or were based upon Jewish "tunes" that were familiar to everybody in those times. Owing to the changed spiritual approach of the worshippers and to the uncommon manner of creating these outpourings, they were considered to be "inspired songs," somewhat different from those of the ancient tradition. Some of their texts were actually written down by the devout brethren,[61] and served as the basis for the primitive Christian liturgy.

THE SCROLLS DISCOVERED AT THE DEAD SEA

I referred above to a letter written by the Nestorian Patriarch of Seleucia, THIMOTEUS I, to SERGIUS, Metropolitan of Elam, informing him that, about 800 C.E., Jewish manuscripts were found in a cave near the Dead Sea. These manuscripts contained more than 200 "psalms," attributed pseudepigraphically to David, the "classical" author of psalms.

It is amazing that this exact information as to the precise location of the discovery was not followed up by archaeology, and that it needed a haphazard event, the search of a Bedouin shepherd boy for a lost sheep, to rediscover a rich repository of ancient Jewish manuscripts at the very spot THIMOTEUS indicated in his letter. They were found in 1947 in several caves, seven and a half miles south of Jericho, in a place called Khirbet Qumrān.

On this site a monastic Jewish community seems to have flourished from about 100 B.C.E. to 60 C.E. Extensive excavations have unearthed a city of ruins and the remnants of a large cemetery, testifying to a highly developed communal organization. The community thus discovered is generally called the "Qumrān Sect," after the name of the site of these ruins.

The discovered scrolls raised a considerable stir among biblical scholars, both Jewish and non-Jewish, mainly because of the still unsettled question about their origin and the time their authors are supposed to have lived. One group of scholars places them in the pre-Christian era, by which the musical references contained in them would rightfully belong to the scope of these investigations. Another group, however, maintains that the scrolls could not have been composed at that time because, judging from a number of evidences, they represent typical Karaitic literature. The Karaites were a Jewish sect that seems to have arisen around the seventh century of our era. According to

Solomon Zeitlin, the chief advocate of this belief, the scrolls originated sometime between the seventh and twelfth centuries c.e. This, naturally, would place the musical references in the scrolls outside of our investigation, unless we would project them back, historically, that is, and try to tie them up with the musical usage of the ancient Hebrews and consider them, possibly, as late remnants of similar practices of the Jewry of the Second Commonwealth.

In the present stage of the clashing opinions it is difficult to take sides. Inasmuch, however, as the musical references in the scrolls are contained in genuine Jewish writings and, furthermore, as they might reflect, even if retrospectively, the Jewish musical culture of the era presented in our study, I feel justified in incorporating them here.

Among the discovered scrolls there is an elaborate treatise in which the rules and laws of the Qumrān brotherhood are laid down in all their minutest details and which, therefore, is called by modern scholars the *Manual of Discipline.* Its eleven columns regulate every phase of the communal life of the members of this pious group, who lived strictly according to what they believed to be the divine ordinances. It was a priestly community inasmuch as it was directed by priest-like superiors, who called themselves "the Sons of Zadok," the descendants of David's high priest. Hence, the Qumrān Sect is also called "the Zadokites."

This sect shows such distinct affinities with the Essenes that modern scholars consider the Zadokites and the Essenes to be of the same Jewish sect.

The assumption of the latter opinion would lead us to conclude that the musical practice of the Zadokites was identical with that of the Essenes. The question arises, however, whether the discovered documents justify such an assumption from the musical point of view. Unfortunately, the scrolls contain only scattered references to music, and do not enrich our knowledge of the musical practice of this Jewish sect.

On the other hand, there are indications that appear to minimize considerably the value of even the few musical references found in the scrolls. Zeitlin expressed serious doubts as to the authenticity of the discovered documents. In a number of essays, he endeavored to show that the scrolls are erroneously identified with the pre-Christian era. He assumes that they were placed at a much later date in the caves where they were recently found.[62]

Regardless of the outcome of this controversy between two opposite factions of Biblical scholarship, we cannot shun the necessity of discussing the musical references found in the scrolls, be it only for the sake of completeness. We have to leave it to further investigations to determine whether these references are likely to shed any new light upon the practice of the pre-Christian Jewish sects. It is possible that they have merely historical value in fortifying the widely accepted view that the ancient musical culture of the Jews continued into the medieval karaitic period.

Among the musical references found in the scrolls the most numerous and the most significant are those belonging to two treatises, the *Psalms* (or *Hymns*) *of Thanksgiving* and *The War Between the Sons of Light and the Sons of Darkness.*

It is not too far-fetched to assume that these religious poems were written at a later date and performed more or less similarly to those of the canonical Psalter, either with or without accompanying instruments.

The musical terminology in these new "psalms" is easily enumerated. We find several times the word *neginah* ("song," Ps. II. column 2:11; Ps. X, 5:30), or its verbal forms *rinnah* and *zammer* (Ps. IX, 5:13; Ps. XVII, 11:5; Ps. XVII, 11:14; Ps. XVIII, 11:22–27; *Manual,* stanza 10, a.o.). Furthermore, there are references to some of the Biblical instruments, e.g., to *kinnor* ("lyre," Ps. X, 5:30; Ps. XVIII, 11:22–27; *Manual,* stanza 10), *nebel* ("harp", Ps. XVIII, 11:22–27; *Manual,* stanza 10), *halil* ("pipe," Ps. XVIII, 11:22–27; *Manual,* stanza 10). In the context, in which these biblical terms are used, they do not reveal anything we do not find in the Scriptures themselves.

In the *War between the Sons of Light and the Sons of Darkness* it is stated that before battle the priest intones a warlike song, the text of which consists mostly of Biblical quotations (X:11 ff). After the battle the entire army shall

intone the hymn of return . . . and they shall extol His Name in joyful unison (*y'rannenu kulam,* XIV:2).

All in all, neither the *Psalms of Thanksgiving,* the *Manual of Discipline,* nor the other tractates reveal anything that cannot be found either in the Scriptures or in the early rabbinical literature. Thus, except the rather hypothetical use of trumpet signals as reflected in an imaginary battle (see below), the musical implications of this newly discovered literature have largely a corroborative value in the description of the ancient musical culture of Biblical and post-biblical Jewry.

CHRISTIAN PSALM-SINGING IN TALMUDIC TIMES

We have followed the development of Jewish singing up to the point where it emerges with the liturgy of the new Christian community and becomes the assistant of the new religion. From here on the original Jewish song is gradually modified to become the tonal symbol of the new Church. At first, its ethos remained unchanged, its substance and its form free of essential modification. The development of music was slow and hesitant in those days. Even the different languages (Greek, Latin, Syriac, etc.) could not substantially alter the character of the Jewish song. Inasmuch as psalms did not have a quantitative metric structure, the melodic pattern of Jewish singing adapted itself easily to the rhythm of other languages.

Only in the course of several centuries was Jewish singing transformed. It gradually lost more and more of its Oriental-Jewish characteristics and, through a slow metamorphosis, became assimilated to the new liturgical use, eventually merging completely with Christian sacred singing. The affinity of the Temple song of Ancient Israel with the liturgical song of the early Christian Church has only recently been rediscovered by musicology. For a long period of time it had remained hidden from the eyes of the historical observer.

However, prior to its complete transformation, the Temple song of Ancient Israel exercised for a long period of time a beneficial influence upon the liturgical music of the new Church. The writings of the early Church Fathers, who were reliable chroniclers of the new faith, express appreciation of the religious, moral, and ethical qualities of Jewish Temple singing. Their chronicles are full of praise for psalm-singing in the ancient Davidic style, in accordance with the tradition of the Temple.

Numerous utterances of St. Augustine (354–430), Eusebius Pamphilius of Caesarea (ca.260–ca.340), St. Jerome (ca.340–420). St. John Chrysostom (ca.347–407), Isidore of Seville (ca. 560–636), and many others, testify to the significance in the ritual of the new faith to psalm-singing. Singing of psalms has been for the new Christians one of the strongest stimulants for religious exaltation and furnished all the participants with an emotional experience that is reflected again and again in the writings of the Church Fathers.

Singing of psalms by laymen has always been a matter of heart and sentiment; with the clergy and other servants of the new faith, it became a religious duty. In addition to the Davidic psalms, new hymns and psalms for the new faith were soon created, born out of the inspiration of individually gifted members of the congregations. These have been described by Clement of Alexandria (b. ca. 215), as

> the new songs, the songs of the Levites, with their eternal strain that bears the name of God and which gave order and harmony to the universe. . . .

This and other utterances provide only some general idea about the character of psalm-singing in that epoch. The Church Fathers, however, offer many valuable hints about the melodies of these songs. Clement calls them "at the same time psalmodic and prophetic"; other writers characterize them as "angelic." Well known is the famous passage in Augustine's *Confessions*, in which he says:

> How abundantly did I weep to hear those hymns and canticles of thine, being touched to the very quick by the voice of the sweet church song (X:33).

The emotional power of psalm-singing has become at times so overwhelming that words to the melody were considered to be superfluous. Solo singers, in a sort of religious rapture, dropped the consonants, so that their singing acquired a mystic implication that suited very well the intentions of the early Church. These are the songs of which Augustine says:

> He who rejoices needs no words; for the song of delight is without words.

Most usual in these wordless hymns was the singing of *Alleluiah*. This consisted in leaving out the consonants and pronouncing only the vowels A E U I A; later, these vowels were replaced by those of the doxology, *Seculorum amen*, E U O U A E. Such wordless ecstatic songs were called *jubilus*, gushing forth from the most exalted religious emotions.

But in general, high significance has been attributed to the Hebrew words of the psalmodic text. The Hebrew tongue, the language of David, was venerated and cherished in early Christian times, and there are instances where people learned Hebrew with the specific purpose of singing psalms in the original tongue and thus enjoyed them all the more.

At an early period of Church history psalms were sung not only for religious purposes, but also on various secular occasions. Both sexes, of all ages, participated in psalm-singing; men, women, maidens, "even little girls were obliged to sing psalms," says JEROME. Thus it is highly probable that psalm-singing may have had the same significance in the life of the Christians as the popular song in later centuries. Accordingly, the melodies of the psalms must have been simple, so that anybody could sing them without difficulty. JOHN CHRYSOSTOM states that certain psalms were so popular that they

> were known to nearly everyone by heart, and were sung daily in the evening assembly by old and young.

In daily life, psalm-singing appears to have had widespread usage among working people. Its aim was mainly to alleviate manual work, or render more pleasant the working drudgery of certain professions. JOHN CHRYSOSTOM mentions some of the professions in which singing was customary. The professions referred to by him are without exception of the kind in which singing would facilitate the work by its rhythmic regularity: nurses rocking babies, wagoners driving animals, vintagers treading grapes, sailors pulling the oars, weavers tossing the shuttle. Psalm-singing in all these cases has only a slight religious motivation; in reality, it simply represents work songs.

The early rabbinical literature, too, mentions work songs, without specifying them, however, as psalms. As a talmudic report states:

> The singing of sailors and ploughmen is permitted, but that of the weavers is prohibited.[63]

To this passage, RASHI adds the comment:

> Sailors and ploughmen sing to facilitate their work, whereas weavers sing out of frivolity.[64]

In Christian usage, the terms *hymn* and *psalm* have not been too clearly distinguished, and the Church Fathers used them rather indiscriminately. One species, however, the "spiritual songs," *ōdai pneumatikai,* has been used exclusively on religious occasions. They constitute in the writings of the Church Fathers a third category of songs, in addition to the hymns and psalms.

Finally, there is mention in the patristic writings of the practice of psalm-singing at funeral ceremonies. The melodies were probably of a simple and popular character. They were generally rendered in a responsorial form, one singer taking up the psalm, with the assembled congregation answering him.

These brief statements selected from the multitude of references in the patristic literature about early Christian psalm-singing, however, present a very incomplete picture of the early Christian musical practice despite the abundance of historical records.[65] It is surprising that it took two millennia to discover the true sources of Christian singing. Not until our time, through the assiduous research of a few scholars, has the affinity between Jewish and Christian psalmody been firmly established. Fortunately, musical discoveries in recent decades have brought forth factual proof as to how closely both were interrelated.

Moreover, diligent comparison between the preserved Biblical chants of the Jews and the earliest Christian melodies handed down to us in the Ambrosian and Gregorian collections illuminates one of the darkest historical domains of ancient music. Through these discoveries, the musical world of Ancient Israel, long considered extinct, has experienced a resurgence, a veritable rebirth, such as we would not have dared to imagine a few decades ago.

ATTEMPTS AT RECONSTRUCTING THE ANCIENT JEWISH SONG

Attempts have not been lacking to revive, by speculation, or by artificial devices, this relatively unknown area of the world of music. For the mystery which enshrouded it was too intriguing to be left unsolved for ever. Many refused to believe that with the destruction of the Jerusalem Temple, Jewish song had been irretrievably lost. It seemed improbable that such an extensive musical culture as that of the Hebrews could survive without any musical notation. As a result, scholars, and even amateurs, searched eagerly to discover some indications of a system of notation that—if deciphered—might bring ancient Jewish music back to life. Some of the attempts in this respect should be briefly mentioned, at least for the sake of curiosity, if for no other reason.

In this survey, we can easily dispense with discussing the first such known attempt, made in the eighteenth century by JOHANN CHRISTOPH SPEIDEL, who tried to prove, merely theoretically, that the Hebrews were acquainted with part-singing and that they identified notes by the names of their vowels.

Toward the end of the same century, CONRAD GOTTLOB ANTON endeavored to bring about the resurgence, in modern notation, of ancient Jewish melodies. ANTON discussed ancient Jewish music mainly in terms of harmonic structures, in accordance with the style of his own time. The musical examples of his pamphlet, that is, the Jewish melodies "reconstructed" by him, appear exactly like Protestant chorales in a four-part setting, an evident anachronism.

About half a century later, LEOPOLD HAUPT tried to reconstruct melodies of six Old Testament psalms by availing himself of the Hebraic accentual signs (ta'amim). He, too, invested his reconstructed melodies with a stiffly conventional harmonic setup, typical for his period, a plainly abortive attempt at reconstructing "ancient Oriental" songs.

A short time later, LEOPOLD ARENDS sought to prove the possibility of reviving the music of Ancient Israel. He approached the problem from another angle, first by interpreting the Hebrew letters, consonants and vowels, as musical notes. He further erred in assuming that Oriental music used major and minor keys, in accordance with Occidental practice, revealing a glaring misunderstanding of the intrinsic character of Oriental music. Furthermore, the "accompaniments" supplied by ARENDS for his melodies—patterns of broken chords in the style of piano exercises for beginners—are curious examples of how the basic characteristics of Oriental music in general, and Jewish music in particular, could be so grossly misinterpreted.

In more recent times, HEINRICH BERL scrutinized the problem of reviving vocal music of the Biblical past. His argument is that such attempts have to start with linguistic considerations. His definitions deal mainly with theoretical premises. However, the crucial practical question as to *how* such a reconstruction could be effectuated is not answered by theorizing of this kind.

Lately, OTTO GLASER tried to clarify somewhat the situation and to answer the question whether or not ancient Jewish song can be revived. Like other "reconstructors," he failed to suggest anything practical toward the solution of the problem under consideration.

This problem has been now more practically defined by Joseph Yasser. As he points out, it is centered not so much in an outright discovery of some supposedly preserved melodies, but rather in becoming aware of

the changes perpetrated—consciously or not—by individual performers at different historical stages.

His method comes close, at least theoretically, to making possible the reconstruction of the ancient form of Biblical melodies:

As one moves back into the historical past, one finds, *first*, that the number of notes used in any given type of this melody grows smaller; *second*, that its range becomes narrower; and, *third*, that semitones are encountered in it less frequently.

Yasser considers this merely as a general norm. He thinks, however, that it is a practical way of procedure, and he supports his theory with some pertinent musical examples.[66]

THE NATURE OF ORIENTAL SONG—MAḲAMAT

Nearly all the scholars who have ever indulged in attempts at reconstruction, or who plumbed theoretically its possibilities, ignored the aesthetic standards of Oriental music. Ancient Jewish song differs quite appreciably from Occidental song. This being so, the true approach to Oriental music in general has to be established before the innate characteristics of Jewish music in particular can be investigated. As the first step along this path, the Bible itself furnishes the most relevant data.

As noted earlier, the headings of the psalms contain a number of specific terms that apparently have no bearing whatever on the text of the psalms. The majority of the psalm-commentators consider these terms to be the names, or the initial words, of certain popular songs, and the preposition *le* or *'al* before them would represent, according to this widely accepted interpretation, the instruction to sing the psalm in question to the melody of these songs.

From the musical standpoint, this would be a highly satisfactory solution of what has long been considered the psalm-heading enigma. However, it has been frequently argued that many difficulties lie in the path of this explanation. How did our forefathers manage, for instance, to adapt a specific melody to the text of a psalm, considering the fact that certain psalms are very extensive; that most of the psalms have no strophic structure; and, moreover, that the verses of the psalms display great differences as to the number of their syllables and their meter? All these questions are easily answered if one examines Oriental music on the proper grounds.

First of all, such terms as *song* or *melody* in the accepted Occidental sense cannot be applied to the musical rendition of the psalms. Oriental music does not know the regularly articulated melodic structure characterized in Western music by motives, phrases, measures, groups of measures, half-periods, periods, sequences, and all the other paraphernalia of our musical system. Oriental music is determined by the principle of standard motifs, or thematic kernels, within some basic scale-forms. These are stereotyped musical patterns, melodic formulae ("melodicles"), sometimes comprising only a few notes. Owing to the specific musical ear of the Orientals, such "tunes" are considered as independent melodic units, easily recognized by the audiences.

This principle of using such "tunes" as the foundation of the entire musical conception of the Orient has been preserved to this day in the *makam*, a song-type of the Arabian-Persian cultural sphere.

Makam signifies, strictly speaking, a "tone," and in a wider sense a "musical tune." *Makamat* is an organized melodic system showing how the single *makams* are put together, and it constitutes the basis of Oriental music theory. Each *makam* is an independent melodic unit, composed of some specifically built motivic elements, the basic form of which is invariable. The artistry of the Oriental musician consists in his ability to embellish a *makam* with constantly changing variations and to create, by this device, a new, artful, musical product.

With all his inspiration and imagination, the performer is never allowed to deviate from the original *makam*. The indivisible union of the specific scale-form and the tune represents an entity that the trained ear recognizes infallibly as this or that *makam*. The Oriental ear considers any musical piece as strange and inartistic if it does not display the characteristic motives and phrases of some pre-selected *makam*.

Ancient Jewish music is a product of the general Oriental musical culture, and is therefore subject to the same laws. Thus, the principle of the *makamat* must also be applied to Jewish music.

The Book of the Psalms furnishes tangible evidence of the actual use of the principle in question. The above-mentioned "enigmatic" terms in their headings must have been largely the names of certain *makams* to be applied in the musical elaboration of those psalms. In the light of this interpretation, there is nothing mysterious about these terms. It is quite obvious that the Levitical singers used specific *makams* for different psalms, and through their skill in variation they were able to adopt without difficulty these "melodic kernels" to verses, whether short or long.

The main prerequisite for this procedure would be the people's familiarity with such *makams*, so that they could be used not merely by the actual performers, but also by future generations. The tunes mentioned in the Psalter seem to have been such generally known *makam*-types, which were popular during a relatively long period, and which fell into oblivion only after several centuries, owing to external circumstances, such as wars, political unrest, apostasy from Yahveh's religion, and perhaps also the Babylonian exile.

Biblical commentators agree that the latter portions of the Psalter originated, or were compiled, several centuries after the initial books. It is indeed striking that all the specific names for the melody-types referred to above appear in the first three books of the Psalter. This is a clear indication that the *makams* that had primitively been used for the psalms fell into oblivion in the lapse of centuries, so that the later writers and singers of psalms could no longer use them.

Another reason might have been that, as time passed, other *makam*-types cropped up and became popular. The fact, however, that the older *makams* had been forgotten would reasonably deter the writers and singers of psalms from prescribing for the later books any specific *makams*. It might rather have been left to the judgment of the performers to select the appropriate *makam* for a psalm. (In fact, no such names are found in the headings after Ps. 88).

In spite of the fact that the last books of the Psalter contain no indications of *makams*, we have positive knowledge that quite a number of psalms had been sung in the Temple as well as in religious feasts outside the Sanctuary. Consequently, there must have actually existed appropriate "tunes" for their musical rendition, and these were the "oral" *makams*, so to speak, widely used at that time.

It would not even be too far-fetched to assume that most of the vocal music that has been preserved since the destruction of the Jewish national existence and subsequently taken over by the new Christian liturgy, represented such *makam*-types.

Makam is by no means identical with the tropal motif (*ta'am*) of the cantillation. The latter, generally permanent in its appearance, is strictly connected with the syntactical order of the Biblical sentence, whereas the former, even though always retaining a distinctly recognizable melodic pattern, is more or less freely varied and freely applied to a given text by the performer.

The variation principle of Oriental music, and especially of Oriental singing, affords a full disclosure of many features that concern the character of ancient Jewish singing.

For the Orientals, the interpretation of their music is of paramount importance. According to our Western conception of music, the main thing is the art product, that is, the musical texture worked out in the most minute details and put down in written form, which is considered as final and immutable. Consequently, any unmotivated infringement upon the finished product, that is, any arbitrary alteration of the musical substance, is considered an unlawful trespassing on the creator's rights. The interpretation of the art product assumes, in the Western world, only a secondary importance, however indispensable it may be in actual practice.

In Oriental music, however, its interpretation is the primary factor, the principal thing, almost more important than the original musical idea.

The manner in which the performer interprets it, tells the Oriental listener that a musical idea has been awakened to a real, flourishing life; the interpretation infuses his idea with flesh and blood; without it, it is merely an empty, barren skeleton, a rigid, dead structure of bones.[67]

This "flourishing life," this "flesh and blood" is identical, for the Oriental feeling, with the artistry of the performer who adorns a melodic kernel with all kinds of embellishments: coloraturas, gruppetti, runs, trills, repetitions of tones, portamenti, and glissandi. Particularly the portamento and glissando are, as with all primitive peoples, the outstanding feature of artistic Oriental performances, which are loaded, especially at the beginning and the end, with all kinds of ornaments, so that the melodic kernel is sometimes overgrown beyond immediate recognition.

The Oriental listener is capable of separating entirely the rendition of the song from the melody itself. About this, RABINDRANATH TAGORE makes some pertinent observations:

In our country the understanding portion of the audience think no harm in keeping the performance up to standard by dint of their own imagination. For the same reason they do not mind any harshness of voice or uncouthness of gesture in the exponent of a perfectly formed melody; on the contrary, they seem sometimes to be of opinion that such minor external defects serve better to set off the internal perfection of the composition.[68]

This approach of Oriental man to his own music is stressed and complemented by the observations of the German philosopher HERMANN KEYSERLING, after listening to Hindu *ragas:*

Nothing intentional, no definite shape, no beginning, no end; a surge and undulation of the eternally flowing stream of life. Therefore, always the same effect upon the listener: it is not wearisome, could last forever, since nobody ever gets tired of life.[69]

And yet, a *raga,* the Hindu parallel to a *makam,* consists of only a few tones compared with an an Occidental piece of music.

Both descriptions throw light upon the essence of Hindu music. The same principle, however, may be applied to all of Mid-Eastern music and similarly holds true for the character of music in Ancient Israel.

Aesthetic pleasure in listening to music can be discovered early among the Israelites. The concept of "beautiful singing," however, with its psychological effect upon the soul, came to full bloom much later. This attitude is clearly discernible in talmudic writings, despite some scruples of the latter-day rabbis who raised their voices against the indiscriminate musical enjoyment that had spread throughout certain social strata of that period.

Beautiful singing was produced by a fine voice, and, according to rabbinical conceptions, the possession of a fine voice involved the duty to serve God with it. Considering the paramount importance of a fine voice for the sacred service, and also its appreciation as a phenomenon of art, it is surprising that the sages seemed to be undecided whether in the Temple service instrumental music or singing should have preeminence. On this subject numerous and lengthy rabbinical discussions have taken place. There was even a difference of opinion whether singing on the Sabbath should be prohibited or not. Finally, a middle-of-the-road decision was adopted, which apparently satisfied everyone:

Vocal music is dominant, and the instrument [is used] to sweeten the sound [by accompaniment].[70]

SECULAR SINGING

Both the Bible and the Talmud provide us with ample information concerning the nature of religious singing; but we have only a modest knowledge of the character of secular singing as transmitted through the somewhat general references found in the Biblical and post-Biblical sources.

Contrary to sacred music at a more advanced stage, secular music in Ancient Israel was employed exclusively for "utilitarian purposes" (*Gebrauchsmusik*). Its essence was largely characterized by the cooperation, and participation, of the individual in collective music-making. In spite of the pleasure it dispensed to all concerned, secular music could not be granted the privilege of passive enjoyment which, in its more highly developed phase, was characteristic of sacred music. The highly artistic structure of Levitical singing excluded *a priori* the extensive participation of a non-Levite. Therefore, the role of the people at large was confined to passive listening, which they gradually learned to enjoy. As a consequence, religious singing possessed all the criteria of an autonomous art, while secular singing was and remained heteronomous.

Singing played an all-important role at the most joyful event in the life of the individual, the wedding. At no other festive occasion was there more abundant singing than at weddings. At all times there existed wedding songs, as may be gleaned from all sorts of allusions in the Scriptures (Jer. 7:34; 26:9; 25:10; 33:11, and in Rev. 18:23).

Wise and virtuous rabbis did not consider it below their dignity to adorn the wedding ceremonies with their songs; they sang alone or in groups in honor of the bridal couple, and sometimes topped off the songs with dances.

When the political situation deteriorated, joyous singing at weddings had to be curtailed. In spite of this restriction, however, the merriment at weddings seems to have continued unabated, for it was necessary to issue a new interdiction.[71]

Considering the paramount importance of singing at weddings, it is surprising that the Bible mentions this primeval custom only in passing. And yet the Bible contains a rich assortment of wedding songs, when one grasps the true meaning of a document that has been almost generally misunderstood and misinterpreted. I refer to the "Song of Songs," or using the implication of the Hebrew title, *Shir ha-Shirim,* "The most beautiful Song (of Solomon)". A complete reexamination and reevaluation of its contents leaves no doubt as to the fact that the book has been accepted into the canon merely because of its later allegorical interpretation.

This book deals exclusively with love between the two sexes, and this in an incredibly earthly, even sensuous manner. It certainly must have been a formidably difficult task to attribute an allegorical meaning to erotic folksongs of this kind.

But the book carries the name of Solomon, which made it a venerable remnant from the times of divine inspiration. These were the times from which no other but sacred writings have been preserved. . . . Thus, there was nothing left except resorting to allegorical interpretation, and this naturally construed the whole contents of the book as Yahveh's love for Israel and His matrimony to His people, a favorite idea of the prophets since Hosea's times.[72]

Solomon is only nominally the author of the "Song of Songs." In reality, the author is the people itself. Just as popular poetry generally comes into being, so the "Song of Songs" might have originated and developed gradually from the life and feeling of unsophisticated people. It may first have been crystallized into single little songs, which were subsequently collected by scribes and embodied into a book. It follows the general rule of Antiquity in that the name of a compiler or editor was not preserved. Instead of the real compiler, the name of the patron of the arts and sciences, King Solomon, was attached to the book. It is also possible that Solomon himself ordered the compilation of these scattered wedding songs, for which reason the book carries his name. It is quite certain that the question of whether or not the "Song of Songs" belongs to the canon would never have arisen if Solomon's name were not in the title.

Neither Solomon's name nor the adoption of the book into the canon can alter the fact that we are confronted here with wedding songs, now loaded with facetious, and now with erotic, contents. They are genuine folksongs, composed by unknown, naïve popular poets, and as such, they constitute the pure type of "utilitarian music."

In this connection it is revealing to find an indication in the rabbinical literature to the effect that its contemporaries considered the "Song of Songs" as a purely secular book. Young men were accustomed to singing some stanzas of this poem as love ditties in public taverns, which aroused the ire of some zealous rabbis.[73]

In modern times the "Song of Songs" has repeatedly been interpreted as a dramatic play with accompaniment by music, song and dance. About these attempts more will be said in a later chapter.

For the ordinary people, singing constituted a necessity of daily life, and their spiritual leaders, the sages and rabbis, fully appreciated the moral values of singing. Later, however, particularly in the Hellenistic period, some rigorously austere rabbis showed a more severe, even hostile attitude toward secular singing. Under Greek influence, the universal joy of singing had been degraded to a level where it became a servant of sybaritic epicurianism and a constant companion of drinking-bouts. For moral reasons, therefore, the rabbis felt justified in vigorously opposing this kind of licentious singing. It is evident that the hostility of the sages was not addressed against singing as such, but only against the pagan influences that brought about such revelries.

The rabbinical attitude toward Greek song manifested itself most conspicuously in the case of the notorious talmudic teacher ELISHA BEN ABUYA, whose apostasy was attributed to the fact that "Greek song did not cease from his mouth."[74] Rabbinical contempt for this singer went so far that subsequently he was referred to only as "AḤER" (the "other one"), like someone whose very name was sinful to pronounce. The anathema against AḤER went so far that another talmudic sage, R. MEÏR, "who learned tradition at the mouth of AḤER," was also subjected to the ban. After AḤER's death, even his daughter was deprived of the safeguard of religion.[75]

In general, however, the rabbis were sensible enough not to hinder too rigorously the people's pleasure in singing. An opposite policy in this respect has even brought forth evil consequences on one occasion, as recounted in the rabbinical literature. For some reason, which is not divulged by the Talmud, R. HUNA forbade secular singing. As a result, all mundane feasts ceased, for singing was an indispensable part of such festivities. Thereupon a social calamity ensued and, together with an economic crisis, took such proportions that the prices of the most essential commodities fell to a bottomless low.

> A hundred geese were priced at a *zuz* and a hundred *se'ahs* of wheat at a *zuz* and there were no demand for them [even at that price].

R. ḤISDA, successor to R. HUNA, was more understanding and abolished his predecessor's prohibition of singing. Immediately prices rose again:

> A goose was required [even at the high price of] a *zuz* but was not to be found.[76]

This talmudic tale, however spurious it may appear, points up the cheerful conception of life among the Israelites, with its invariable "leitmotif" of merry singing.

In the religious conception of the Jews, singing was not only a mundane, but also a celestial institution. According to a talmudic legend, three groups of angels sang daily songs of praise in honor of the Most High.[77] And the same talmudic passage attributes to the angel who wrestled with Jacob (Gen. 32:26) the words:

> I am an angel, and from the day that I was created my time to sing praises [to the Lord] has not come until now.[78]

This passage would point indirectly to the existence of a multitude of singing angels, according to Jewish belief. Curiously enough, God prefers the mundane singing to that of the angels, for

> the ministering angels sing praises but once a day, whereas Israel sings praises to the Lord every hour.[79]

According to the legend, the Lord himself indulges in singing, which corroborates most strongly the rabbinical contention that singing is of divine origin.[80]

Thus closes the great cycle which, in the conception of Ancient Israel, had been assigned to singing: even before the creation of the world there was singing in heaven. In mundane life, singing is inseparable from man, whose joys and sorrows it reflects. As a symbol of its inherent divine nature, singing returns eventually to the source of everything that is lofty and sublime, into the celestial regions.

Celestial singing is connected with the mystic idea of the exultant song of stars and other celestial bodies and may be found in Biblical poetry (e.g., Job 38:7; Isa. 49:13). This reflects the teaching of the Ancient Orient about the "Harmony of the Spheres." According to it, the seven planets, in passing the zodiac, produce the seven tones of the basic musical scale as discovered independently and expounded by ancient theorists. The early translators of the Bible assumed the poets of the Old Testament to have been familiar with the ancient Oriental teaching of the harmony of the spheres. Several Biblical passages explicitly mention the sounding world of the celestial bodies (Ezek. 1:24; Ps. 19:1–5; Ps. 148:3).

Talmudic writers adopted the Biblical conception that the movements of celestial bodies produce certain sounds. According to the theory of the Israelites, the sound is like a flash of fire which, emanating from the producing body, travels directly to the ear of the listener.[81]

Aside from the stars and planets, the Talmud attributes to the sun the production of its own sounds, which to be sure, are interpreted less in a musical than in a realistic sense. The rabbinical writer expresses his astonishment that this phenomenon could be heard in the daytime, since a sound is less audible in the day than in the silence of the night:

> Why is the voice of a man not heard by day as it is heard by night? Because of the revolution [*lit.* "the wheel"] of the sun which saws in the sky like a carpenter sawing cedars.[82]

PERFORMER AND AUDIENCE

Considering the comprehensive character and the minute precision that prevail in the early rabbinical writings with regard to reporting and expounding the Law and the Jewish customs, it is surprising that this vast literature does not contain a description of such an important religious institution as sacred music, vocal and instrumental. True enough, musical details of varying importance are frequently discussed in the Mishnah and the Talmud; but the essence of Jewish music, its system and its tonalities (if any), are passed by in complete silence. Likewise, we have no information whatever about the ethical side of Jewish musical practice, especially the highly important psychological and aesthetic approach of Jewish audiences to tonal art. We find, here and there, a few casual references, sometimes in the form of anecdotes, which afford insight into the cultural relation between music and other aspects of the intellectual life in Ancient Israel.

The musical leaders of the Second Temple, as we know, were determined to keep the form and expression of singing as plain and dignified as possible. Nevertheless, certain bad habits infiltrated liturgical singing, and on occasion even endangered its sacred character. Among these, one may mention the nasal tone production and vibrato of the voice which, though generally recognized in the Orient as accepted features of art-singing, got out of hand in the long run. The dignified character of Temple music, however, was mainly imperiled by a gradually evolving and highly stressed predilection for virtuosity of certain singers. This becomes evident from a report of the Mishnah.[83] There, mention is made of a curious new technique of singing, "invented" by the principal of the Levitical singers, HYGROS ben LEVI, apparently a famous singer-virtuoso of his time. He guarded his "invention" so jealously that he refused to teach it to others. The Talmud ventures to characterize this singing technique, but gives only a very superficial and incomplete description of it.[84] According to this report,

> when he [HYGROS ben LEVI] tuned his voice to a trill, he would put his thumb into his mouth and place his fingers [on the division line] between the two parts of the moustache, so that his brethren, the priests, staggered backward with a sudden movement.[85]

It is not said, however, whether this happened because the priests were either enchanted with the beauty of the singing, or startled by the power of his voice. Talmud Yerushalmi gives a somewhat different description:

> HYGROS ben LEVI was famous for the beauty of his voice. He would put his thumb in his mouth and would produce varied tunes, to the extent that the priests reeled with joy.[86]

Maybe this singer-virtuoso used still other tricks, which escaped the rabbis' observation and which the "inventor" kept secret in order to protect himself from imitation. The fact that he refused to divulge his secret, enraged the sages so that "his memory was kept in dishonor."[87] The stubborn refusal of this singer was incompatible with the most elementary duty of the Levites to teach their art to the coming generation. Consequently, the Talmud might have been right in assuming that HYGROS's refusal was motivated by selfish reasons.

This was only a single but by no means unique example of the gradual growth of all sorts of expressions of personal vanity in the sacred musical service. As a result of the exaggerated importance attributed by the singers to their own accomplishments and of the admiration bestowed upon them by the worshippers, each sought to put his own person into the limelight at the expense of the sacred service. This became possible only because the community had manifested by that time an unmistakable aesthetic attitude toward, and one of pleasure in, the performances of the Levitical singers. For what period can the existence of this particular attitude in Jewish musical practice be proven for the first time?

At the primitive stage, any music is "utilitarian music," or "music for practical use," the production of which is necessitated by factors of environment or social conditions. There ensues a lengthy evolutionary process from this stage to that in which music represents for the listener a product of art involving the element of artistic enjoyment. The importance of tonal art in the life of the Jewish people, the impregnation of the individual as well as the community with music in all its aspects, was responsible for the fact that Israel passed relatively soon the phases of development from the heteronomous to the autonomous "music as art phenomenon." We find the proof for this in the Bible itself.

We discover the attitude toward the enjoyment of music in the words of old Barzillai when he speaks of the temporal and spiritual goods of life to be aspired to:

Can I discern between good and bad? can thy servant taste what I eat or what I drink? can I hear any more the voice of the singing men and singing women? (2 Sam. 19:36)

Even more emphatically is this attitude exposed in the book of Ecclesiastes, where music is declared to be indispensable to enhancement of the pleasure of life:

I got me men-singers and women-singers, and the delights of the sons of men, as musical instruments, and that of all sorts. (Eccles. 2:8).

And when the prophet speaks of the chosen one of the Lord who should be "as a love song of one that hath a pleasant voice, and can play well on an instrument" (Ezek. 33:32), this metaphor is an unmistakable sign that for the Israelites of those times listening to fine singing and to alluring music definitely included the element of enjoyment.

We read in the Talmud that

the Exilarch MAR 'UKBA in Babylonia would retire and rise with music [with songs of Israel which they used to play before him].[88]

The meaning of this ceremony seems to be the honoring of a highly placed person. However, it also shows clearly that the sages considered music to be indispensable for the enjoyment of life. Here, too, the attitude of pleasure toward music is obvious.

These Biblical and talmudic passages show that the function of music in Ancient Israel gradually underwent a complete transformation. At first it served religion, helped in the daily work, was an indispensable attribute of popular merriment; then, it liberated itself more and more from this servitude and developed into an independent art phenomenon. But even as such, it remained imbedded in the consciousness of the nation and never lost its intimate bond with the life of the people.

With the destruction of the Jerusalem sanctuary by the Romans, the fate of the instrumental music of the Hebrews was sealed forever, since no artistic activity that depends entirely on perpetuity of practice has a chance to survive after a few decades of forced cessation.

But if the instrumental music of the Jews could never be retrieved, vocal music, fortunately, was spared the same bitter fate. Singing happened to be an inborn urge of the Jews; its roots penetrated so deeply into the soul of the people that the cruel fate of the nation could not prevent the individual from expressing in singing his natural sentiments, his sorrow, longing, hope, and trust in God.

Besides, religious singing—in contrast to secular singing—has never ceased. To be sure, the rabbinical prohibition of music embraced all kinds of musical manifestation. Singing in the sacred service, however, as a spontaneous expression of Jewish piety, had withstood the most rigorous ban. Furthermore, the rabbinical authorities themselves were at variance as to whether singing was to be radically abolished or not. Some advocated a complete prohibition;[89] others maintained that only instrumental music, not singing, had to be banned.[90] The result of all this controversy turned out to be that singing in the cult, and also in intimate religious celebrations, was never seriously menaced.

In spite of this historical evidence, an almost unanimous belief prevailed until recent decades that the song of the Biblical era was irremediably lost.

This belief was completely shattered by the tremendous research work done by ABRAHAM ZEVI IDELSOHN (1882–1936). It is his distinctive merit to have proven that remnants of ancient Hebrew music still exist in our days, practically untouched by time and circumstances.

On his extended journeys in the Orient, IDELSOHN has found in Yemen, Babylonia, Persia, Buchara, Daghestan, and in other places, Jewish tribes that had seceded from the mother country mostly during the times of the Kings, and had established for themselves a new home in these foreign countries. They lived there in complete religious and cultural isolation and succeeded in preserving through all the millennia their national and religious characteristics, and also their songs.

IDELSOHN has collected these songs and, besides fixing them in modern musical notation, has also recorded them on discs. His publications[91] constitute an unexpected wealth of information about ancient Jewish singing and have created a real sensation in the world of comparative musicology. The results of IDELSOHN's research, despite some debatable points with regard to his methodology, are recognized today as the foundation of our knowledge of ancient Jewish song. They have actually opened entirely new vistas for further research in the field of Jewish music.

IDELSOHN was one of the first to prove that there are striking parallels between ancient Hebrew songs and those of the early Christian Church. Some of the melodies of the Yemenite and Babylonian Jews, which he notated for the first time, show the closest conformity with Gregorian chants. As a result, there remains today not a shadow of a doubt that the early Christian liturgy took over a great many of its songs from the melodic repertoire of the Temple, or the Synagogue, or both.

THE ETHOS OF SINGING IN ANCIENT ISRAEL

The interpretation of songs in Ancient Israel was not outwardly different from that of other peoples of Antiquity in the Near East, or—except for some un-avoidable changes—from that of present-day practice in the same area.

However, with all the similarity between Jewish singing and that of their neighbors, there was a deep-seated difference. This difference has been nurtured by the particular ethos of the Jewish song. Music and singing have been considered by certain peoples as a useful and practical form of art, constituting in part an external adornment of life, and in part an essential element for the education of the youth. Their importance with the Jews lies in an entirely different field.

In spite of the fact that music among the Hebrews did represent essentially "utilitarian music" (though in a higher sense), it is not wholly expressed by "activity" and "cooperation." Nor, even though explicitly manifest, are the principles of "enjoyment" and "aesthetic pleasure" the decisive criteria in Jewish music. The roots of the Jewish musical art go deeper; its ultimate meaning can rather be found in the spiritual, ethical sphere.

In Ancient Israel, music—especially singing—meant: to serve God, to exalt God with sounds. Singing, in whatever form, is for the Jew the religious creed expressed in sounds, the palpable affirmation of his close connection with the Eternal, the union in harmonious sounds of the Creator with his creation.

This ethical conception of music and singing appeared for the first time in Antiquity with the Jewish people and represents one of the greatest accomplishments of the human spirit. Opinions are sometimes expressed to the effect that Jewish music was not an original creation, that all its elements were taken over from other peoples, or at least were influenced by foreign civilizations. However, it is not so much the vessel, the external form, that has to be taken into consideration, as what the Jews have been able to achieve by filling this vessel with the fruits of their own spiritual endeavors.

They have attached to their music the imprint of a mysterious, almost super-natural art, which is ultimately rooted in God, which can be explained neither by the intellect nor by sentiment, but which has its justification in the divine pleasure that human singing offers to the Creator Himself. This pleasure was refracted to mankind through God's grace, giving to human life splendor, bliss, and spiritual rapture.

No other people of Antiquity shows in its song more thoroughly than do the Jews, the fundamental forces that rise from the depths of the soul. The mysterious emanations of psychic impulsion are exposed in the Jewish song with elementary power.

Through the power of music the Jew merged with his God and became united with the Universe. This constitutes the high ethics of the Jewish conception of art, and because of it, Jewish musical genius proved to be worthy of being counted among the greatest spiritual achievements of Antiquity.

THE MUSICAL INSTRUMENTS OF THE HEBREWS

Despite the prominence of music in the popular life of the ancient Hebrews, the Biblical chroniclers have not revealed to posterity anything about the nature of their musical instruments. Their reports do not contain any indications as to the form and technique of these instruments, and scarcely any allusions to their sound qualities. Here and there an adjective, such as "sweet," "pleasant," and "solemn," is all we learn about their sonorities.

The chroniclers restricted themselves mainly to mentioning the names of the instruments. But with the lapse of time even this primary knowledge was dimmed to such an extent that already the early rabbinical writers were in doubt as to whether some of the terms referred to a stringed or a wind instrument. In some cases the differences of opinion were even more conspicuous, some rabbinical authorities defining, for instance, a given term as the name of a musical instrument, while others understood it to be something of an extra-musical nature.

The extant authentic illustrations of instruments of Ancient Israel are few and scarcely appropriate for conveying a clear idea about their shape and musical qualities (Illus. 73 to 84). Therefore, our sole reliable, though incomplete, source in this respect is the abundant pictorial material preserved in the antiquities of the peoples with whom the Israelites were closely associated and whose musical practice they have in no small measure absorbed.

The pictorial representations in Egyptian, Babylonian, Assyrian, and partly also in Greek and Roman antiquities, furnish us with a working basis for drawing reasonable conclusions about the instruments of the ancient Hebrews. The etymology of the Hebrew names of instruments affords valuable information as to their origins, and sometimes also their sound quality.

The names of the "first" instruments mentioned in the Bible should not be understood literally. Jubal's two instruments, *kinnor* and *'ugab*, do not represent single species of instruments, but are general terms for stringed and wind instruments. Percussion instruments, such as drums, hollow tree-trunks, concussion instruments, as well as horns of animals, hollow reeds, and sea-shells, producing primitive sounds, must have already existed when the instruments with distinct pitch had allegedly been invented.

All in all, the Bible mentions sixteen musical instruments as having been used in Ancient Israel. The Book of Daniel refers furthermore to six instruments, which were played at King NEBUCHADREZZAR's court; their names, however, characterize them as non-Jewish instruments. In the Targumim and in the talmudic literature we find sixteen additional names of instruments not mentioned in the Scriptures. It must be assumed that these were instruments of the Gaonic centuries, whose use the rabbinical scribes have partly projected back into the Biblical period. However, since they were actually used by the Israelites, it is in order to examine them in this study. Finally, it should be mentioned that ABRAHAM da PORTALEONE, in his treatise *Shilṭe ha-Gibborim* (Mantua, 1612), names thirty-four instruments that were allegedly known and used in Ancient Israel. It is obvious that the majority of these terms represent instruments of PORTALEONE's own time, which he arbitrarily placed back into the Biblical period.

Illus. 72 Levitical singing groups in the First Temple. (After Codex Kosmas Indikopleustes, Cod. Vat. Graec. 699.) Frontispiece of K. J. Zenner, *Die Chorgesänge im Buche der Psalmen,* Freiburg i.B., 1896.)

Illus. 73   A Semitic lyre player entering Egypt with his clan, asking for asylum, as pictured on the Beni-Hassan Monument (ca. 1900 B.C.E.). (After *The Biblical Archaeologist,* New York, 1941.)

Illus. 74   The Jewish *kinnor.* (After Maria Rita Brondi, *Il liuto e la Chitarra,* Torino, 1926.)

Illus. 75   The Jewish *nebel.* (After Maria Rita Brondi, *Il liuto e la Chitarra,* Torino, 1926.)

Illus. 76 Vase found at Megiddo, showing a lyre (ca. 1025 B.C.E.). (After *The Biblical Archaeologist,* New York, 1941.)

Illus. 77 Bronze-figure found at Megiddo, representing a Jewish flute girl (ca. 1300–1200 B.C.E.). (After Gottlieb Schumacher, *Tell el-Muteselim,* Leipzig, 1908.)

Illus. 78 Ivory found at Megiddo, showing a lyre-player (ca. 1200 B.C.E.).
(After E. W. Heaton, *Everyday Life in Old Testament Times,* New York, 1956.)

Illus. 79 Enlargement of the lyre-player in Illus. 78.

Illus. 80 The captured vessels of the Jerusalem Temple, with the sacred trumpets. Relief from the Arch of Triumph of Titus in Rome.

Illus. 81   The sacred Temple instruments (*kinnor* and *ḥazozerot*) on Bar-Kokba's coins (132–136 C.E.)

Illus. 82   The sacred Temple instruments (*kinnor* and *ḥazozerot*) on Jewish coins.

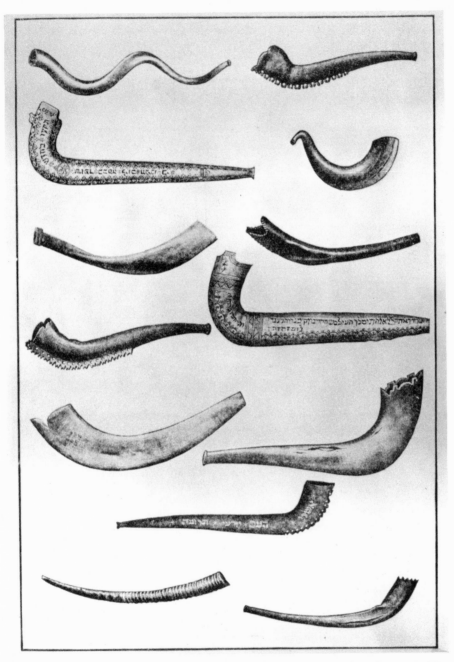

Illus. 83 Different shapes of the *shofar*. (After *Jewish Encyclopedia*, vol. **XI**.)

Illus. 84 Yemenite *shofar* richly carved with Biblical quotations (about 54″ long). Courtesy of Mount Sinai Memorial Park, Los Angeles.

למלאכתקעו בחצט שופר · ויבארך
באי אמרה אשר קדשנו במצותיו
נעוט לשמוע קול שופר·· באי אמר
שהחייט וקיימנו והגעונו לזמן הזה

ויתקע [ ]זין [ ]שין [ ]

יי שפתי תפתח ופי יגיד תהלתך באי
אלהינו ואלהי אבותינו אלהי אברהם
אלהי יצחק ואלהי יעקב האל הגדול ·
הגבור והנורא אל עליון גומל חסדי
טובים וקונה הכל וזוכר חסדי אבו
ומביא גואל לבני בניהם למען שמו
באהבה·· זכרנו לחיים מלך
מלך חפץ בחיים וכתב·
בספר חיים טובים למענך אלהים
חיים אלהי מלך עוזר ומושיע ומגן
באי

Illus. 85 Probably the oldest known signs for *shofar*-tones in a Hebrew manuscript of the thirteenth century (*Codex Adler* 932, fol. 21b). Courtesy of the
Jewish Theological Seminary of America in New York.

Illus. 86 Claus Sluter (d. 1406). Moses. Museum Dijon.

Illus. 87 Michelangelo (1457–1564). Moses. In the Church San Pietro di Vincoli, Rome.

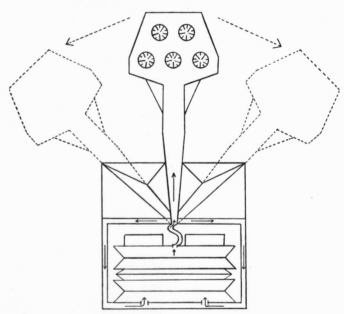

Illus. 88 The *Magrephah.* (After Joseph Yasser, *The Magrephah of the Herodian Temple: A Fivefold Hypothesis,* in *Journal of the American Musicological Society,* vol. XIII, 1960.)

INSTRUMENTS MENTIONED IN THE BIBLE

(a) Stringed Instruments

1. Kinnor. The *kinnor* is one of the two instruments, the "invention" or the "practice" of which is ascribed to Jubal. It was "David's harp," the preferred instrument for accompanying singing in Israel's music practice. The word has two plural forms, one masculine, *kinnorim,* and one feminine, *kinnorot,* an unexplainable peculiarity not to be found with any other name of instruments.

The instrument of the Phoenicians, played by their legendary hero, KINNYRAS, was called *kinnor.* From Phoenicia the word might have come to the Greeks who used it first in the substantive form *kinnyra.* The Hebrews have taken over the word from the Phoenicians; thus, the Hebrew *kinnor* and the Greek *kinnyra* are both of Oriental origin.

In Ancient Israel, a town on the Lake Genezaret was called *Kinnorot;* the lake's ancient name was *Yam Kinnorot.* The tradition explains that the lake had the shape of a lyre (*kinnor*), which allegedly was the reason for the lake's name. However, the lake has not the slightest resemblance to a lyre; it rather resembles a harp. In later times other explanations cropped up, among them those that the inhabitants of the town excelled in playing the *kinnor,* or else that they have been experts in building such instruments. The latter assumption is more likely, since Antiquity knew several cities the names of which indicated the principal trade of their inhabitants.

The rabbinical authorities, too, tried to establish some sort of relationship between the word *kinnor* and the town Kinnorot on Lake Genezaret. Their interpretations are, however, extremely far-fetched. One of them is:

Why is its name Kinneret? Because its fruits are sweet as the sound of the *kinnor.*[1]

The Bible mentions *kinnor* in forty-two places. In the early translations the word is rendered in most different ways. Some commentators take it for a lute- or guitar-like instrument; others believe it had the form of a harp. Some identify it with the Syrian four-stringed *trigōnon.* PORTALEONE maintains that it was a large harp with forty-seven strings, a description evidently suggested by the rather developed harp of his own time, which cannot be applied to a Biblical instrument.

Modern research holds that the *kinnor* was neither a harp-like instrument, nor a type of lute with a long-necked fingerboard, as is sometimes asserted, but an instrument similar to the Greek *kithara.* Probably the earliest known picture of a Semitic *kithara* has been found in a sepulchral grotto at Beni-Hassan (Illus. 73).

In Assyrian antiquities, too, the *kithara* is frequently depicted. Its simplest type appears in a picture that shows three Semitic captives playing instruments, while guarded by an Assyrian warrior (Illus. 65).

It is generally assumed that the *kithara* originated from Asiatic countries. Pictorial representatives of it from archaic times were found at Nineveh and Babylon (Illus. 47). In addition, the Asiatic origin of the *kithara* is hinted by the fact that the Greek writers have frequently substituted the term *asias,* "Asiatic lyre," or "Asiatic harp," for the *kithara.*[2]

Finally, on Jewish coins of the epoch of the high priest Simeon (132–135 c.e.) are shown pictures of the *kinnor,* which are quite similar to the Greek *kitharas* (Illus. 81, 82). Since these coins were made during the second Maccabaean revolt, it might be questionable whether the instruments depicted on them still represent the authentic form of the ancient Biblical *kinnor.* However, we may take into consideration the fact that the Orientals are very conservative in their customs and implements. We might assume, therefore, with reasonable probability, that the Biblical *kinnor* is reproduced on these coins, at least in its basic form.

SACHS, after scrupulous examination of all involved factors, comes to the conclusion that the Biblical *kinnor* was a *kithara* or *lyra.*

The last doubt is silenced by the fact that *k•nn•r* designated the same *lyra* in Egypt.[3]

Etymology and history corroborates this opinion.

Kithara and *lyra* represent essentially the same type of instrument; the difference lies mainly in their size. The *kithara* was the larger of the two, the *lyra* the smaller, more delicate type. On Bar Kokba's coins both types are reproduced (Illus. 81, 82).

Minnim (sing. *men*) and *yeter,* in post-Biblical literature *nimin,* are terms designating strings, but they refer, figuratively, to stringed instruments in general (cf. Ps. 150:4). They were made of sheep's guts, sometimes also of plant-fibers.[4] According to a rabbinical source, the strings of the *nebalim* (see following chapter) were made of the "entrails" (*meyav*) and those of the *kinnorot* of the "chitterlings" (*b'ne meyav, lit.* the "sons of the sheep gut").[5] By the latter term tripe is meant, the portions of the entrails lying directly below the stomach of the animals which, in sheep, are particularly thin. Strings of metal were unknown in Antiquity.

The pins or pegs, on which the strings were fastened, were called *niktimon.*[6] The same word was also used to indicate the pegs of drums, which held the skin stretched. The frame or arm of harp-like instruments, on which the pegs were fastened, was called *markof.*[7] Neither of the two words appears in the Old Testament, therefore they must have been introduced initially in the post-Biblical era.

We find in the Talmud precise instructions as to how a broken string could be tied up. It was considered important that the instruments accompanying the singing during the sacrifices be in perfect order, because any irregularity, like a broken string, for instance, would invalidate the sacrifice. Therefore the Talmud says:

If a *nima* (string) broke, they retied it three times on the peg properly.[8]

The opinions of the commentators are widely divided with regard to the number of strings on the *kinnor.* Between the statement of JEROME (six strings) and that of PORTALEONE (forty-seven strings), there seems to be no possible compromise. It is self-evident, however, that PORTALEONE described the harp of his own epoch, which in the Middle Ages was already a markedly developed instrument.

On the Jewish coins mentioned above, mostly three, sometimes five or six

strings are visible. Because the coins of that epoch were rather crudely executed, the number of strings depicted on them can hardly be considered conclusive. The same doubt exists with regard to the statement of a spurious
letter written by JEROME to DARDANUS,[9] according to which the *kithara* had
twenty-four strings. On the other hand, JEROME's assertion that the ordinary
kithara had six strings, might come closer to the truth.[10] JOSEPHUS submits
again a different number: "The *kinyra* is an instrument provided with ten
strings."[11] It is probable that several types of *kinnorot*, different in size and
in the number of strings, were used by the ancient Hebrews. This might explain the divergences in the existing descriptions.

The early rabbinical sages, too, are far from unanimous with regard to the
number of strings used for the *kinnor* (and also for the *nebel*), the reason being
that they were not sufficiently familiar with the described instruments. They
frequently confound the *kinnor* with the *nebel*, and vice versa, so that it is
never too clear which one of the two instruments is referred to in their writings.

To play a stringed instrument was called *naggen* (1 Sam. 16:16 ff; 18:10;
Isa. 23:18, etc.), which indicated the plucking of the strings with the fingers,
but sometimes also with the plectrum, made of quill, wood, bone, or metal.
It was reported about David that he "played with his hand" (*niggen b'yado*)
the *kinnor* before the ailing King Saul, and also on other occasions (1 Sam.
16:16; 16:23; 18:10; 19:9). This specifically repeated indication intimates that
it might have been something uncommon, at variance with general usage.
Accordingly, this passage is frequently commented on as representing a performance "without a plectrum," which furthermore is corroborated by the fact
that, on these occasions, David did not sing but merely played. David's playing
"with his hand" might have represented a special skill in those days, a fact that is
suggested by the chronicler's stressing it four times.

In Ancient Israel the *kinnor* was largely the instrument of joy and gaiety
(Job. 21:12). As early as in the time of the patriarchs it was the customary
instrument at family festivities (Gen. 31:27); it was played by shepherds
(1 Sam. 16:16), and by women (by "harlots" Isa. 23:16); it was the dispenser
of joy at merry banquets, at popular feasts, and at celebrations of victories
and coronations.

The *kinnor* becomes silent when the joy ceases (Ps. 137:2). As punishment
for the people's transgressions, the prophets threaten that the sound of the
kinnor would no longer be heard. (Isa. 24:8; Ezek. 26:13).

King David was the most famous *kinnor*-player in Israel's history; only
Jedithun-Ethan came close to him as a virtuoso on the instrument. It is understandable, therefore, that David and his "harp" became the subjects of many
legendary tales. As the Mishnah and the Talmud relate, a *kinnor* was suspended
above his bed; at midnight, the north wind used to sweep over the strings,
which started to sound by themselves. Or, as another version has it, David
would rise at midnight to play his instrument.[12]

The *kinnor's* frequent use at the carousals of wealthy revelers was considered by the prophets as a defilement of an instrument designed for sacred
use. When the prophets raised their voices against the abuses of wealth, against
debauchery and sybaritic life, they thundered also against singing and music

as media for carnal pleasures. As a concomitant phenomenon of the voluptuous revelries, the *kinnor* was also a target of their disapproval. This attitude, however, did not impair its significance in the sacred service. As one of the principal instruments of the cult, supplying the accompaniment for Levitical singing, the *kinnor* retained an unchallenged esteem throughout the entire existence of the Temple.

2. *Nebel.* The other stringed instrument for the accompaniment of singing, mentioned frequently (twenty-seven times) in the Scriptures, is the *nebel* (pl. *nebalim*). In its original meaning, the word signifies "to inflate," "to bulge," therefore in the Hebrew language *nebel* is also the term for the leather bottle and other bulky vessels holding water, milk, wine, and also pots made of clay.[13]

The Semitic word *nebel* passed into Greek and Latin as *nabla, nablion,* and *nablium,* and served, as among the Hebrews, as the term for a stringed instrument of a bulky shape. In the Greek version, the *b* has been transformed into a *v,* and so eventually the instrument was called *navla* or *naula.*

POTALEONE identifies the *nebel* with the Italian lute of his time. He describes minutely the fingerboard, the sounding box, the arrangement of the strings, and gives in general a portrayal of an instrument which is manifestly an image of the coeval *Chitarrone* or *liuto chitarronato.* It goes without saying that this description is without any foundation.[14]

In the writings of the early Church Fathers the *nebel* is generally called *psaltērion;* however, their descriptions are hardly elucidative with regard to the shape and nature of the instrument. Only in one detail do the Church Fathers agree, namely that the *nebel* had its sounding-box on the upper part, while the *kinnor* had it at the bottom. In Greek music, the term *psaltērion* applied apparently to an entire family of more or less similar instruments and, in a wider sense, to stringed instruments in general. All the numerous testimonies in the Greek as well as in the patristic literature indicate that the instruments played with both hands without a plectrum bore the generic term of *psaltērion,* and have been variously shaped harps. They might have been different with regard to size, number of strings, volume, sonority, and tuning. However, their construction and technique of playing must have followed the same pattern.

The word *psaltērion* has a double meaning, as it appears from ancient sources:

> In the strict sense, it signified a particular stringed instrument that was played by the fingers of both hands, therefore it was easily accessible from both sides, had several strings, and a harp-like shape (Illus. 75). In a wider sense, instruments were also called psalteries, the strings of which were stretched above a sounding body, and which, therefore, could be played only from one side, and with a plectrum [or small sticks].[15]

The Arabian *santir,* a kind of dulcimer, depicted in several Assyrian antiquities, might have been such an instrument (Illus. 59, 60). This, however, could not have been identical with the Biblical *nebel,* since all the sources indicate that the *nebel* was played with the fingers and thus must have belonged to the family of harps.

Nevertheless, the idea has been persistently maintained that the *nebel* was not a harp but a dulcimer, an offshoot of which is preserved in the modern cymbal (*cimbalom*) of the Hungarian gypsy-music. This opinion rests upon the assumption that dulcimer-like instruments already existed in Antiquity, as evidenced by numerous pictorial documents. The most revealing of these is the bas-relief found in ASHUR-IDANNI-PAL's palace at Kuyundchik, on which eleven instrumentalists and fifteen singers are portrayed (Illus. 66). Among these instruments one resembles a dulcimer, which some modern scholars consider the Biblical *nebel*.[16]

The spurious Dardanus-letter mentions the *nebel* as having *forma quadrata*. The dulcimer had indeed a square sounding-box. This gave additional support to the assumption that the *psaltērion*, and therefore also the *nebel*, was identical with the *santir*.

This opinion, however, is strictly contradicted by the explicit statements of the Church Fathers, according to which the sounding-box of the psaltery was placed above. This flat shape would also be in conflict with the etymology of the Hebrew word, which indicates manifestly something bulging.

As the rabbinical writers assert, the *nebel* was larger than the *kinnor*; it must have been, therefore, the lower pitched type. However, the Hebrew collective term for string instruments, *kle shir*, ("tools [instruments] for the song") opens the possibility that, besides the instruments mentioned in the Scriptures, other species of the same family may have existed. Two of these might have been a small *nebel* and a larger *kinnor*.

The spurious Dardanus-letter further states that the psaltery had the form of the Greek letter $\triangle$, *delta*. This statement has been taken over by a number of medieval ecclesiastical writers, who draw on the alleged authority of JEROME.[17] This indication, however, is contrary to the description given by the early Church Fathers, according to which the *psaltērion* had its sounding-box above. The Greek letter *delta*, or a similar geometric figure, would exclude a bulky sounding body on the upper part. Matters are different, however, if we take into account the fact that the initial mention of the *nebel* takes place at a relatively late period (1 Sam. 10:5). This might suggest that the Israelites did not bring this particular instrument from Egypt, but became acquainted with it through their intercourse with Asiatic peoples. Indeed, the Assyrian angular harps have a form similar to that of a *delta*. A certain oblique position of this instrument when played, could suggest that its sounding-box was placed above.

The Bible furnishes three indications as to the number of strings on the instruments: in Psalm 92:4, *'ale 'asor v''ale nebel*, "with an instrument of ten strings, and with the psaltery;" in Psalms 33:2 and 144:9, *nebel 'asor*, "psaltery of ten strings." The first passage refers to two different instruments, one having ten strings *and* the *nebel*, whereas the two other passages suggest that there also existed a *nebel* with ten strings. JEROME translates *in decachordo et in psalterio*, a definite indication that there are two different instruments involved.

In the rabbinical literature, there are only isolated references to the number of strings of the *nebel*. In general, it is said

that the difference between *nebel* and *kinnor* is that one (*nebel*) has more strings than the other.[18]

The Bible informs us about the use of the *nebel* in the cult. From the Mishnah we learn that *nebalim* were used for secular purposes as well, and that they were also played by women. A significant statement says:

The harps (*nebalim*) of the female singer (*ha-sharah*) [i.e., for secular use] are unclean; the harps of the sons of Levi [i.e., for liturgical use] are clean.[19]

In view of the numerous descriptions of the *nebel,* and more so of the abundant pictorial representations concerning harp-like instruments in Egyptian and Assyrian archaeological discoveries, it is astonishing that the opinions of scholars with regard to the Biblical *nebel* show great discrepancies. Some think it was a lyre; others consider it to have been a harp; again others that it was a dulcimer, or the small Greek triangular harp, the *trigōnon.* All these opinions have at least one thing in common, namely, that they understand *nebel* to be a stringed instrument.

Yet, some commentators believe that the *nebel* was a wind instrument. This opinion stems from a misunderstood statement of JOSEPHUS, in which the difference between the *kinnor* and *nebel* is reduced to the fact that the former instrument has

ten strings (*chordai*), and the latter "twelve sounds" (*phthongoi*).[20]

The Greek expression *phthongos,* generally a sound distinguished from the "voice" (*phonē*), seemed to be for some exegetes an indication that it referred to pipes "with reeds," similar to those of an organ. This assumption is invalidated by the simple fact that Antiquity did not have organ pipes with reeds (or vibrating tongues).

What could have been the reason for JOSEPHUS's differentiation between *chordai* and *phthongos,* since both terms applied to stringed instruments? It is probable that he thereby intended to characterize the difference between their basic sonorities. For strings plucked with the fingers certainly have a more muffled sound than the sharp tones of the *kinnor* produced by the plectrum.

Some commentators, of ancient and more recent times, assume that the *nebel* was a wind instrument, due to an ancient report that it had ten openings, which could only be the holes of a flutelike instrument.[21] If the *nebel* indeed had ten openings, these must have been the holes of the resonating box.

The seventeenth-century writer MICHAEL PRÄTORIUS declared that the *nebel* was a sort of bagpipe.[22] The same opinion was shared by the eighteenth-century explorer of Egyptian antiquities, GUILLAUME ANDRÉ VILLOTEAU.[23] As late as in our time, IDELSOHN considered the *nebel* to be a wind-instrument. He states that the term used in 1 Chron. 15:20, *nebel ʿal ʿalamot,* refers to a kind of bagpipe. *Nebel* would be the bag on which the pipes were fastened. Thus, IDELSOHN considers the ʿalamot to be a double-flute, and derives it from the Assyrian word ʿalamu, "usually employed to two bodies close together and yet parted", and is of the opinion that this "precisely fits the structure of the double-pipe."[24]

Thus, we see that in ancient as in modern times there has been a wide divergence of opinions about the basic question, whether the *nebel* was a stringed or a wind instrument.

Yet, apart from the numerous descriptions of the early Church Fathers, there are two classical testimonies that eliminate any doubt that the *nebel* was a stringed instrument. OVID says that the player of the *nabla* sweeps with both hands over the strings,[25] and JOSEPHUS states explicitly that the *nabla* was played not with the plectrum, but with the fingers.[26]

All the factors considered, there can hardly be any doubt that the *nebel* was the upright, portable, angular harp. It might have existed in various sizes with tunings involving different intervallic arrangements, but its basic form has been modified only in some minor details throughout the centuries.

3. *'Asor.* The word *'asor* appears three times in the Old Testament (Psalms 33:2; 92:4, and 144:9). It is considered generally as a derivative from a root meaning "ten." Since *'asor* is always mentioned in connection with some stringed instrument, the early translators of the Bible have considered the notion of "ten" as referring to the number of strings of this instrument.

The correct definition of the term is rendered difficult by the fact that in all three Biblical passages *'asor* is connected with another instrument. Psalms 33 and 144 have *nebel 'asor;* from this the early translators concluded that *'asor* is an adjective modifying *nebel,* and accordingly translated "*nebel* of ten strings." JEROME was the first to recognize that this might have referred to two different instruments, and accordingly translated "in the 'ten-stringed' *and* the *nebel.*"

SACHS's opinion about the characteristics of the instrument differs considerably from the traditional interpretation. In examining the possibilities as to which category of instruments the *'asor* might belong, he arrives at the conclusion that it must have been a sort of zither.[27]

SACHS's opinion contradicts that of GALPIN.[28] The latter examines the word philologically and claims that *'asor* is a misspelled and misunderstood, or else a dialectical form of, *'ashor,* "Assyrian." He concludes that *'asor* was the name of the Assyrian harp, which was taken over by the Hebrews. In spite of some good points in GALPIN's theory, SACHS's interpretation must be credited with the greater probability, since the Biblical text in Psalm 92 indicates clearly that *nebel* and *'asor* were two different instruments, which would not apply conclusively to instruments of the same type with the only difference in the number of their strings.

4. *Gittit.* The term *gittit,* found in the headings of Psalms 8, 81, and 84, has for the most part been taken as referring to a musical instrument. The literary meaning of the word is "that from Geth." Thus, *'al ha-gittit* would represent an instruction for accompanying the psalms in question with an instrument originating from Geth. As we know, David stayed for some time in the Philistinian city of Geth (or Gath; cf. 1 Sam. 27:2; 29:3), and he might well have brought this indigenous instrument (a sort of lute) to his own country.

Another interpretation also uses the name of that city, but explains *gittit* not as an instrument, but as the name of a song, or a joyous tune, "perhaps a march of the Gittite guard."[29] It is, however, inconceivable that the priests, bent on preserving the purity of the cult, would ever have permitted any psalm—a portion of the sacred service—to be sung to a Philistine, heathen melody.

There exists yet another and even more implausible interpretation connected with the city of Geth. It assumes the word *gittit* to imply "a choir of female singers from Geth," which David is supposed to have brought with him on his return from this city. In other words, the three psalms were

given to the class of young women, or songstresses of Gath, to be sung by them.[30]

An analogy in the Bible itself is invoked as furnishing historical evidence for this assumption. As the chronicler reports, David held in his army six hundred warriors from Geth (2 Sam. 15:18), who had been faithfully devoted to him in luck and adversity (2 Sam. 15:21). There is, however, an abysmal difference between foreign mercenaries in the army and non-Jewish songstresses in the cult. The very idea of employing Philistine songstresses in the Temple would certainly have been considered by the priests as a sacrilege and would have been opposed violently. This hypothesis must therefore be rejected as wholly untenable.

The Hebrew word *gat* has still another meaning, "a press," "a vine press," or rather "a trough," "a vat," in which the grapes were trodden with the feet.[31] The early translators follow this meaning and render the term "upon the wine-pressers," or "for the vine-treaders," which—according to this idea—could be paraphrased as "for the Feast of Tabernacles."[32] This interpretation would imply that the three psalms were sung at Tabernacles during the procedure of treading the new wine, a conception justifiable perhaps for Psalm 81 if we take into account its contents, while the texts of the two other psalms do not contain anything suggestive of their performance at the harvest thanksgiving festival, or, specifically, while treading the grapes.

There are a number of other hypotheses for the explanation of *gittit:* "an instrument played at the treading out of the grapes" (Jahn,[33]), "a *piyyut,* the initial word of which was *gittit* (Ibn Ezra,[34]), "a vintage song" (Oesterley,[35]), and that of Thirtle, who also considers them as belonging to the Festival of Tabernacles. However, in his renumbering of the three psalms, they fail to bear out his explanation.[36] Mowinckel scrutinizes several possibilities with regard to *gittit,* adding some ideas of his own. He finally admits frankly that none of them represents a usable solution.[37]

Luther's translation follows the idea of an accompanying instrument:

on the *gittit,* to lead the song (auf der Gittith vorzusingen),

leaving open the question of what kind of instrument the *gittit* might have been.

In view of these divergent opinions, I favor the hypothesis that the word referred to some kind of stringed instrument, about the character of which, however, we are completely in the dark.

5. *Sabbeka.* The Book of Daniel mentions repeatedly the *sabbeka* as one of the instruments played at King Nebuchadrezzar's court (Dan. 3:5, 7, 10, 15). It is almost generally agreed that this instrument is identical with the Greek *sambykē* and the Roman *sambuca.* The Hellenes as well as the Romans used the instrument mainly to enhance the exuberance of their banquets.[38]

The word *sabbeka* is derived from *sambucus,* "elder," the wood of which, when dried, was durable and hence appropriate for musical instruments. Naming an instrument after the material that served for its construction was a frequent practice in Antiquity.

The very name of the instrument seems to indicate its Asiatic, or better, Semitic origin. The double *b* in the Semitic form has been transformed in Greek and Latin into the diphthong *mb,* as with the word *ambubajae,* the Syrian flute-girls, the name of which is derived from the Semitic term *ᵓabbub,* "pipe."

Even if we accept a Semitic origin of the word, it may be assumed with certainty that such an instrument was not used by the ancient Israelites. This is evidenced first by the fact that, except in the Book of Daniel, it is not mentioned elsewhere in the Bible. The Book of Daniel was originally written partly in Aramaic,[39] and it relates events that occurred four centuries earlier. Furthermore, Daniel mentions *sabbeka* among foreign instruments of a pagan country and on an occasion that, by its very nature, must have appeared repugnant to the Jews: the erection and worship of an idol set up by NEBUCHADREZZAR. It may be taken for granted, therefore, that the *sabbeka* had no part in Israel's musical practice. Merely the fact that it is mentioned in one of the canonical books is the reason why it has been examined at all by Biblical commentators.

Despite the multitude of Greek and Roman descriptions, the expounders are not in agreement on the real nature of the *sabbeka*. Some define it as a bagpipe[40], others as *mahol*, an instrument of the family of pipes.[41] Some others declare that it was the *ʿugab*, a kind of oboe,[42] or that it was similar to the *nebel*, a harp-like instrument.[43] Others maintain that it was a kind of guitar, or a lyre,[44] or else a "triangular" instrument, or possibly the Assyrian dulcimer,[45] even identifying it with the *lyrophoininx*, the Phoenician lyre.[46]

Yet, all the classical evidence, which in this case is more abundant and more detailed than for any other instrument, drives one strongly to the conclusion that the *sabbeka* was a horizontal, angular harp, similar to the triangular, four-stringed, and high-pitched *sambykē* of the Hellenes.

In English medieval literature *sambuca* represents a woodwind instrument with reeds, like the "shawm," hence a species of oboe. In the *Psalter of Boulogne* (ninth century) there is an illustration of the *sambuca*, depicting it correctly as a stringed instrument.

6. Pesanterin. Another instrument played at the court of NEBUCHADREZZAR and mentioned in the same verses of the Book of Daniel (3:5,7,10,15) was the *pesanterin.* Owing to its phonetic affinity with the Greek *psaltērion*, it has been widely assumed that both instruments were identical. Since the majority of the Biblical expounders define the *psaltērion* as the Biblical *nebel*, the belief has long been entertained that the Babylonian *pesanterin* was the same instrument as the Hebrew *nebel*.

In opposition to this belief, it must again be emphasized that the Book of Daniel enumerates foreign, heathen instruments, which were not in use in Israel's music practice. The instruments of the Jews of Biblical times also had similar names in the Aramaean language, at least in their basic form; hence, if both instruments were identical, it would not have been necessary for the chronicler to use the unknown word *pesanterin* for the well-known *nebel*. It is obvious, therefore, that the chronicler has intentionally mentioned here exotic instruments, in order to stress the alien character of the idolatrous ceremony.

If Daniel's *pesanterin* were identical with the Greek *psaltērion*, it must have been a harp-like instrument. There are, however, weighty arguments against this assumption. Despite the phonetic similarity to *psaltērion*, its etymology points to a quite different root, namely the Arabian *santir*, the name of a kind of dulcimer. *Pi-santir* means in Arabian "small *santir*," and this is the term taken over by the Aramaean language.

Corroborative evidence is to be found in the picture of a group of musicians found in the ruins of Nineveh. This picture shows, among other instrumentalists, a musician playing a seemingly square instrument, which he holds horizontally before him; its eight strings are stretched above a slightly arched sound box. The player strikes the strings with a rather large stick, whereas in Oriental pictures the plectrum is considerably smaller (Illus. 57).

From this picture, and from the etymology of the word *pesanterin*, it becomes evident that the Semitic peoples of Antiquity knew a dulcimer-like instrument. The doubt is, therefore, amply justified about the assumption of several expounders that Daniel's *pesanterin* and the Biblical *nebel* were identical.

7. *Kathros.* Still another instrument played at NEBUCHADREZZAR's court and mentioned in Daniel (3:5,7,10,15) is the *kathros* (or *kithros*). It seems easy, at first sight, to explain this term as the Greek *kithara*. Consequently, Biblical exegesis unanimously considers the word as the transformed name of the Greek *kithara*.

Yet, this assumption, though basically correct, does not provide us with any indication of either the form or the character of the instrument. Almost no other instrument of the ancients has had so many varieties as the *kithara*. Its name was identical, or similar, among the different peoples. But already in Antiquity, and more so in subsequent times, the name indicated instruments of the most varied types.

The Arabian *kuitra* was a species of lute; the Persian *kitar* a long-necked guitar; the Nubian *kissar* a lyre; furthermore, the Egyptians called the *kissar* also *gytarah barbaryeh*, "Berber's guitar." However, the Greek *kithara*, as also the Roman *cithara*, was a lyre.

The origin of the word points to the Far East. In Sanskrit *katur* means "four," in Persian *chutara* means "four-stringed," and the Hindus have a popular instrument called *si-tar*, the "three-stringed instrument," a kind of long-necked lute, invented allegedly in the twelfth century C.E., but which is manifestly of ancient Asiatic origin.

After the instrument had been taken over by the music practice of the Occident, its name and its shape were subjected to the most incisive transformations. *Guitern* (Old French), *gythorn* (Old English), *gittern, cithern, cither, ghiterra,* or *chiterra* (Italian), and *Zither* (German), are all transformed varieties (in name or substance, or both) of the ancient *kithara*. One has only to recall the Italian *chiterra* or *chitarrone* and the German *Zither*, which, as time passed, developed into entirely different types of instruments.

As mentioned earlier, the Hellenes frequently took over many inventions from the Orientals, including musical instruments; they improved them by their higher artisanship, and then brought the developed products back to their country of origin, mostly with their Greek names. The Israelites similarly adapted Oriental instruments and practices to their own use. There is a significant passage in the Old Testament pertinently characterizing the mutual exchange of goods, the intensive trade of the Mediterranean peoples with one another (Ezek. 27:12–24). There can be no doubt that musical instruments of the various trading peoples, representing part and parcel of the luxury of Orientals, likewise belonged to the "riches," "wares," and "merchandise" (Ezek. 27:27).

It would not be too far-fetched to assume that the Assyrian *kathros* (or *kithros*), named in Daniel, was such an "exchanged" instrument, akin to the Greek *kithara* but perhaps a more developed form.

8. *Neginot.* The word neginot, frequently mentioned in the Bible, has been subjected to the most contradictory interpretations of ancient and modern

expositors. The general meaning of the term is "to sing to the accompaniment of stringed instruments," but also simply "song". However, since *neginot* is frequently interpreted as a music instrument, or a family of such, it is indicated to examine it anew in this light.

The various renditions of the early Bible translators created a confusion that has not been dissipated even in our time. Nevertheless, the root of the word refers unmistakably to its real meaning; etymologically, *neginot* is derived from the verb *naggen*, "to touch," "to strike," indicating clearly the manner of playing a stringed instrument.

There is no doubt about the meaning of *neginot* as "string instruments," or "music with the accompaniment of strings." This meaning is unmistakably conveyed by the headings of the psalms, as well as by a few other Biblical passages, where the harp-player is called *menaggen* (1 Sam. 16:16; 2 Kings 3:15; Ps. 68:26.)

In post-Biblical times *neginot* acquired a different meaning. It was applied to Biblical accents (grammatical as well as tropal), whose graphical signs probably developed from cheironomical practice.[47] Subsequently, *neginah* (pl. *neginot*) was adopted for the whole system of Biblical cantillation.

It is strange that PORTALEONE still commits the error of considering the *neginot* to be an ancient Jewish instrument,[48] particularly so, because in PORTALEONE's time (sixteenth to seventeenth century) the meaning of *neginot* as referring to the system of accents and their application for Biblical cantillation must already have been quite widely known.

9. *Shushan*. The headings of Psalms 45, 60, 69, and 80 contain the word *shushan* (or *shoshan*), explained by almost all Biblical exegetes as the initial word of a popular song whose melody was utilized for these psalms. This song might have started with the verse "A lily is the testimony," or "Lilies are the testimonies."[49]

Some expounders, however, define *shushan* as an instrument, basing their opinions upon RASHI, who attaches to the word a double meaning: 1) he derives it from *shesh*, "six," which points allegedly to an instrument of six strings, and 2) he considers this instrument to have been in the shape of a lily.

GESENIUS, ROMANOFF, and others follow RASHI's arguments more or less closely. LANGDON also considers *shushan* as an instrument, but on an entirely different basis.[50] First, he points to a particularity of the Babylonian language, which uses ordinals for naming an instrument according to the number of its strings. Thus, an instrument of six strings, or six tones, would be called the instrument "of the sixths"; one with three strings, or three tones, would be called *shushan*, this being the Babylonian word for "one third." As LANGDON reasons, the word is derived from the Sumerian *shush*, "one sixth," which, together with the Semitic ending *an*, would constitute the word *shushan*, meaning "two-sixths," that is "one-third."

After this, however, LANGDON enters the domain of surmise. He concludes that this instrument with three tones might have been a "flute" having three holes, and supposes that an instrument in the shape of an ox-head, found in Babylonian excavations, might have been the *shushan* (Illus. 46). As a further "proof" of his hypothesis, he claims that this ancient instrument, when blown into, produces the three tones of a C major triad, and he concludes from this that it may be called an "instrument of thirds." But intervals named as thirds, and even more so diatonic triads, were unknown notions in Antiquity, which alone invalidates LANGDON's theory. In addition, he maintains that the Babylonian term *shushan* (together with the instrument) was taken over by the Hebrews, an assumption without any foundation.

By analogy with other psalm-headings containing terms that have no connection with the contents of the psalms, the simplest and musically the most plausible explanation of the term *shushan* is that which interprets it as the title or the initial word of a popular song.

10. *Kle Shir*. The general term for musical instruments used in the Old Testament is *kle* (lit. "tool"; pl. *kelim*). *Kle ʿoz* means "loud instrument" (2 Chron. 30:21), *kle David* an "instrument (ordained) by (or for) David" (2 Chron. 29:26).

The most important combinations of words in which *kle* is used is *kle shir*, or *kle ha-shir* (2 Chron. 5:13; 7:6; 23:13), "instruments of (or for) the song," and *kle shir David* (Neh. 12:36). All these terms designate an entire group, or family, of stringed instruments, considered as the most appropriate to accompany singing.

Another combination with *kle*, also applied to stringed instruments, is *kle nebel* (Ps. 71:22), with the variant *kle nebalim* (1 Chron. 16:5). Some commentators consider another variant, *kle minnim*, from the extra-canonical book of Ecclesiasticus (39:20), as belonging to this category.

Further collective names for instruments accompanying singing were *neginot* (see preceding chapter) and *minnim*, "strings" (Ps. 150:4), the latter having also the meaning of *minni* or *minne* (lit. "my strings") in Ps. 45:9.

Finally, the stringed instruments are also paraphrased as *le-sharim*, "for the singers" (1 Kings 10:12; 2 Chron. 9:11), clearly indicating their accompanying functions.

The rabbinical literature calls these instruments *kle zemer*,[51] with the variants *mine zemer*,[52] and *mine kle zemer*.[53]

In a few instances the psalm-headings contain indications that imply that sometimes other than stringed instruments were used to accompany singing. But these were exceptions. The character of singing in the sacred service required soft and smooth instruments for the accompaniment, in contradistinction to the practice of other Oriental peoples, whose liturgical singing had an orgiastic character and therefore was preferably accompanied by noisy instruments.

From this point of view, the term *kle shir* and other expressions referring to the same category of instruments have a particular significance for the music practice of Ancient Israel. They serve as unmistakable evidence of the ethos of Jewish singing and particularly of the high esteem the Israelites showed from the very outset for the most beautiful of all music instruments, the human voice.

(b) Wind Instruments

11. *ʿUgab*. The *ʿugab* is one of the two instruments mentioned in the earliest musical reference of the Bible, their initial use having been attributed to Jubal, the "father," or patron of the musical profession (Gen. 4:21). The word is used furthermore in Job 21:12, 30:31, and in Psalm 150:4.

The diversity of renderings of the word *ʿugab* in the ancient and modern translations brought about glaring discrepancies in interpreting the nature of the instrument. To mention only a few of such translations: a double or multiple pipe,[54] the Greek *syrinx*,[55] the ancient organ,[56] a vertical flute,[57] a bagpipe,[58] and even the *hydraulis*, the water-organ of the Greeks, as the Talmud maintains.

SACHS rejects the supposed identity between the 'ugab and the *syrinx*, since the initial trace of a Pan's pipe in the Near East can be found only two millennia after the epoch indicated by the story of Genesis. And as for the bagpipe, no such instrument was known in the earliest history of Israel, with which the initial mention of the 'ugab is associated. According to available evidence, the bagpipe was unknown in Israel prior to the Greek and Roman epoch.[59]

The ancient Bible versions, but also some modern ones, render 'ugab as "organ." This, of course, is manifestly an anachronism. In Greek and Latin, instruments are called generally *organon mousikōn* and *organum musicum*, the term *organon* having been in those days the generic term for all kinds of musical instruments. The narrower use of the term "organ" for the instrument with rows of pipes of a different pitch, activated by a specific mechanism, came into being in a later period.[60]

In all probability, the word 'ugab did not refer to a specific instrument at all, but to a whole family of wind instruments. This is clearly indicated in Psalm 150:4, which reads:

Praise Him with stringed instruments (*minnim*) and the pipe ('ugab).

"Stringed instruments" is here manifestly a collective term. The parallelistic construction of Biblical poetry makes it certain that 'ugab refers here to the family of wind instruments, usage similar to that of the Egyptians, where *ma•t* first signified the vertical flute, and later all pipes, including oboes and clarinets.[61]

12. *Halil*. The word *halil* (pl. *halilim*), generally but erroneously translated as "flute," or "flute-like instruments," occurs six times in the Old Testament (1 Sam. 10:5; 1 Kings 1:40; Isa. 5:12; 30:29; and Jer. 48:36), twice in the last-mentioned passage.

Etymologically it derived from the verb *halal*, "to pierce," hence the original meaning of the word is "hollow tube." This is a clear indication of the material from which the first flute-like instruments were made: bulrush and other reed-like plants, and animal bones. Judging from its described nature and sonority, the *halil* was akin to the Greek *aulos*; each had a double-reed mouthpiece, hence they did not belong to the family of flutes, but to that of the shawm, the precursor of the oboe of later times.

The *halil*, as well as the *aulos*, is of Asiatic origin. The Babylonians had known it under the name of *malilu*; the Assyrian name for it was *halhalattu* and *halalu*, the player being called *mutta-halalu*.[62]

Even in Antiquity the flute had an extended history, having been developed from simple to rather elaborated forms. In Egyptian and Assyrian pictorial representations we see simple longitudinal flutes of various lengths, also transversal flutes, also nose-flutes, and double-flutes of two types, either with parallel tubes, or with pipes set at an angle but blown simultaneously. Besides, as remarked above, the Syrians, or more precisely the Phoenicians, knew a small, span-long pipe, called *gingras*, the tone of which was shrill and lamenting; it was used mainly in wailings for ADONIS, who was therefore also called GINGRAS by the Phoenicians.[63]

Whether one or the other of these instruments corresponded to the Hebrew *ḥalil,* we do not know exactly. Perhaps *ḥalil* included several of them, or possibly covered an entire family of pipes.

The *ḥalil* is one of the few Jewish instruments of which we possess a coeval pictorial reproduction. A small bronze figure found at Megiddo, a city of Ancient Israel, represents a flute-girl (Illus. 77). It originates from 1300 to 1200 B.C.E. and it is therefore assumed that it depicts a Jewish instrument. It was evidently the lower part of a lamp (the upper part is missing), but the instrument blown by the girl does not afford a precise idea about the nature of the *ḥalil.*

The Mishnah mentions *ḥalilim* of solid metal as well as of wood covered with metal.[64] Another Mishnaic passage states that "flutes made of reed were preferred to metal flutes."[65] According to a rabbinical tradition,

> there was a flute (*'abub*) in the sanctuary, which was smooth, made of reed, and dated from the times of Moses. At the king's command it was overlaid with gold, but its sound was no longer sweet. They removed the overlay and its sound became sweet as it was before.[66]

Contrary to this rabbinical statement, many commentators assert that there were no *ḥalilim* (or flute-like instruments) in the First Temple, since in the counting of the Temple instruments *ḥalil* is not mentioned. This assertion, however, is disproved not only by the rabbinical tradition, but also by some Biblical passages, which confirm explicitly the use of *ḥalilim* in the early ritual. One of them is 1 Sam. 10:5, in which *ḥalil* is mentioned as one of the instruments played by "a band of prophets." To prophesy with the accompaniment of music was in a way a ritual action, and the "band of the prophets" were the pupils in Samuel's schools of prophets. The musical organization of these schools served as prototype for the forthcoming Davidic and Solomonic sacred musical institutions. It is unlikely that an instrument such as the *ḥalil,* having been used in the ritual in times of Samuel and Saul, would have been abandoned in David's sacred music, which was established soon afterwards.

Furthermore, the use of the *ḥalil* in religious ceremonies is directly referred to in Isa. 30:29:

> Ye shall have a song as in the night when a feast is hallowed; and gladness of heart, as when one goeth with the pipe (*ḥalil*) to come into the mountain of the Lord, to the Rock of Israel.

In addition, the talmudic tradition states that

> the *ḥalil* was played at the sacrificial altar twelve times during the year.[67]

And the Mishnah contains precise indications as to the ceremonies in which this took place.[68]

Ḥalil, 'ugab and *'abub* are the three words found in the Bible and in rabbinical writings that indicate woodwind instruments, individually as well as collectively. Judging from the fact that the Israelites used to clearly separate sacred and secular objects, we may assume that *ḥalil* and *'ugab* were the pipes used in the ritual, whereas *'abub* was the name of similar instruments in popular usage.

The sanctuary used the single pipe of oboe-type. It cannot be stated unequivocally whether or not the Israelites used double-oboes, despite some vague hints to this effect in the rabbinical literature. We come across, for instance the Mishnaic term *kanafayim,* "wings," which is interpreted by some commentators as pointing to the two pipes of a double-oboe.[69] Accordingly, some modern translators identify the instrument *sumponyah,* having allegedly had such *kanafayim,* as "double-flute." It will be shown later that *sumponyah* could not possibly have been such an instrument.

However, the assumption that the Israelites might have known the double-oboe is somewhat supported by another controversial Mishnaic passage. In the instructions with regard to playing the pipe at sacred services, it is said:

They ended [the music] only with a single flute (*be'abub yehidi*), since this made the better close, or, according to another translation: to make the end agreable [*sic*].[70]

Some expounders interpret this passage to mean that Oriental musicians considered solo playing as the most beautiful means of ending a piece, an idea not corroborated by historical evidence. SACHS gives a more plausible explanation, based upon the nature of the instrument.[71] He considers this Mishnaic text as proving that the instrument was a double-oboe; when playing one of its pipes, certain tonal interferences, caused by slight differences of pitch, could be avoided, which probably was not the case, as a rule, when both pipes played simultaneously. Therefore, the end sounded "more agreeable."

There is, however, an even more logical explanation for *'abub yehidi.* A talmudic passage indicates the allowable number of players for each category of instruments.[72] The respective regulation for *halilim* was: no less than two, and no more than twelve in each service. The reed instruments had evidently some unevenness in their tuning, created either by slight differences of their dimensions, or by minute deviations in the boring of the fingerholes. These differences of pitch were not too disturbing as long as the *halilim* played together with the Levitical singing. However, in instrumental endings that must have taken place mostly after the choir finished singing, these differences came clearly to the fore. Therefore, as a remedy, the solo-playing with only one instrument was preferred.

R. MEÏR says about the players of *halilim* that

they were slaves (*nethinim*).[73]
R. JOSE says: They were from the families of Bet ha-Pegarim and Bet Zipporya and from Emmaus, and they were eligible to give [their daughters] in marriage to the priestly stock.
R. ḤANINA ben ANTIGONUS said: They were Levites.[74]

From the fact that the *nethinim* were originally slaves, attending to the menial work connected with the sacrifices, the conclusion was sometimes drawn that the Levites had performed only the vocal part of the sacred service, while the instrumental accompaniment, as a subordinate function, has been entrusted to slaves. But numerous Biblical passages attest that the Levites were at once singers and instrumentalists. The above rabbinical discussion, moreover, reverses any assumption that the instrumental accompaniment would have had merely an accessory character, and therefore be assigned to other than Levites.

As shown above, the talmudic scribes stated that the *halil* was played twelve times on different days in the sanctuary.[75] Another tradition, however, has it that the *halil* was used twice daily in the Temple, namely for the accompaniment to the psalms of the day at the libation in the morning and evening services. One of the Tannaites considers even the "flute" as an integral part of these sacrifices.[76]

On the Sabbath, it was prohibited to play the *halil* in the Temple, since it was not considered as belonging to the same category of "sacred" instruments as the *kinnor* and *nebel*.[77]

In Ancient Israel the *halil* was preeminently the instrument of joy and gaiety; it was played at all merry occasions, such as festivals, banquets, popular entertainments, coronations, and the like. The Bible does not refer to it as having been employed at weddings, but there is an indication to this effect in the Mishnah: "If a man hired . . . pipers for a bride (*halilim l'kallah*)."[78] Since this usage certainly did not originate in Mishnaic times, we may retrospectively assume the use of *halilim* at weddings in the Biblical period.

In spite of its basically joyful character, its tone was frequently turned into wailing and thus became the appropriate musical accompaniment for funeral services. Even the poorest man in Israel had to hire for the funeral of his wife at least two *halil*-players and a wailing woman.[79] If there were no Jewish players for this purpose, even Gentiles could be hired.[80]

In later Biblical times, the *halil* was considered by the spiritual leaders of the Israelites an emotionally exciting instrument, just as the Hellenes termed the *aulos* as *orgiastikos* and *pathētikos*. The attitude of the rabbis against the *halil* might have been similar. The hostility against the orgiastic *aulos* and the similar-sounding *halil* is still reflected in the writings of the early Church Fathers.

13. *Nekeb*. Ezekiel 28:13 uses the word *nekeb*, which is interpreted by many Biblical expounders as a "flute," or a "flute-like instrument."

The earliest translations of the Bible, however, do not attach any musical connotation to the word. The etymology of *nekeb* points to a root signifying something "hollow." This could mean a hollow tube (hence the interpretation as "flute"), or else the hollow cavity in which precious stones were set. Thus, even JEROME translated the word as *pala gemmarum*, "the setting of thy precious stones." Following this interpretation, STAINER suggested replacing the usual musical meaning of the word ("of thy tabrets and of thy pipes"), as it is expressed in the English Bibles, with another meaning, corresponding to JEROME's idea:

The workmanship of the jewels, and the setting of the stones . . .[81]

Most of the English translations doubt whether *nekeb* refers to a musical instrument at all. When the Old Testament mentions the tabret and pipe, this instrumental combination is usually expressed as *tof v'halil* (1 Sam. 10:5; Isa. 5:12). The interpretation of *nekeb* as "flute" does not fit the context in which the word is used by Ezekiel. This Biblical passage tells about the abundant wealth of the king of Tyre, his precious stones and splendid jewels.

Nor does the word *tof* (hand-drum) here refer to the Biblical tabret. In the Latin language, *tympanum* (drum) sometimes indicates objects having some similarity to the hand-drum.[82] The same holds true for the Hebrew *tof*. The frame in which precious stones were set could have suggested a similarity to the cavity of a drum.

In spite of the fact that the majority of the Biblical exegetes agree that *nekeb* does not refer to music, the idea of a musical instrument has been persistently maintained by some scholars. The reason for this is probably LUTHER's translation (*"dein Paukenwerk und Pfeifen"*). It is evident, however, that all these interpretations are not borne out by linguistic considerations, in the light of which the word *nekeb* does not seem to carry any musical implication.

14. *Nehilot.* The expression *'el ha-nehilot* is used only once in the Bible, in the heading of Psalm 5. A somewhat related indication, *bineginot*, appearing in the superscriptions of six psalms, is generally explained as an instruction to accompany the respective psalm with stringed instruments. Other expounders, however, are of the opinion that *nehilot*, referring to flutes or pipes, stands for an instruction to accompany this psalm with wind-instruments.

This opinion is based upon the etymology of the word; its root, *halal*, "to pierce," is the same as that from which *halil* is derived. The perforation does not refer to the finger-holes, but to the hollow body of the instrument.

The interpretation of the term in the sense of an instruction for the accompaniment of the psalm (either by stringed or by woodwind instruments) would therefore be acceptable philologically as well as musically. It is consequently the more surprising that the early translators of the Bible attach to *nehilot* entirely nonmusical meanings. In sharp contrast with the extra-musical interpretations of the early translators, the rabbinical explanations, although rather vague, still attach to the word a musical implication.

Among modern commentators, some define *nehilot* as a double-flute; others, on the contrary, consider the interpretation as "flutes" untenable, since—as they maintain—such instruments are "nowhere" mentioned in the sacred music of Ancient Israel. They seem to ignore the several direct and indirect Biblical references attesting the use of woodwind instruments in the rites; moreover, the use of *halilim* in the Second Temple is sufficiently evidenced in the rabbinical literature.[88]

Since the majority of the commentators agree that *nehilot* represents a collective term for wind instruments, we are justified in assuming that the expression *'el ha-nehilot* is an instruction for accompanying Psalm 8 with woodwinds (pipes), in contrast to most other psalms for which stringed instruments were generally used, or expressly prescribed.

15. *'Alamot.* The meaning of this word has already been substantially examined in one of the preceding sections. However, in addition to the opinions of many commentators scrutinized there, one more must be added, namely that which attaches to *'alamot* the meaning of a wind-instrument, notably the double-oboe. It is therefore mandatory to ponder over the term once again.

There is a striking, but apparently fortuitous, assonance between *'alamot* and the Greek *elymos*, a term used by the Hellenes for a type of double-oboe with pipes of different length, the *aulos elymos*. The word *elymos* is of Assyrian origin, derived, it seems, from the verb *'elamu*, "to stay opposite." In Assyrian, this verb signifies two similar objects that are close, yet separated from one another. This would apply to the form of a double-oboe with a single mouthpiece and two pipes. The Assyrian word has an etymological parallel in Arabic, where *'alama* means "open lips," or "separated lips."

The double-oboe has played an important role in the music of the Egyptians, Assyrians, and Hellenes. The Old Testament, however, does not contain any direct reference to such an instrument, though the word *'alamot* appears in several Biblical passages.

For a correct interpretation of the word we must rely on the Biblical context.

And here we find a psalmodic verse that is quite unambiguous:

The singers (*sharim*) go before, the minstrels (*neginim*) follow after, in the midst of the damsels playing upon timbrels (*'alamot tofefot*) (Ps. 68:26).

'Alamot is the plural of *'almah*, "maiden," "damsel," and *'alamot tofefot* are the "dancing girls," accompanying their dances with *tuppim*, the traditional hand-drums of Ancient Israel.

Insofar as we attach a musical meaning to *'alamot*, connected at the same time with the notion of *'almah*, "maiden," the most natural explanation seems to be the one holding that it refers to a stringed instrument in the range of "maidens' voices," i.e., "in the high pitch"—high according to our Occidental concept, of course.

16. *Mahol.* The derivation of the word *mahol* from the verb *hul*, "to dance in a circle," "to whirl," seems to be quite obvious.[84] In spite of the fact that many among the early translators of the Bible have followed this meaning, some ancient and modern Biblical expounders explain the term as a musical, especially a woodwind, instrument.

This interpretation recurs again and again in the commentaries of rabbinical writers. Among them, I mention only RASHI (1040–1180), who derives the word from *halal*, and maintains that it signifies a "pierced," therefore flute-like instrument.

Several Biblical passages do not permit an interpretation of *mahol* in the sense of "flutes" or "pipes." In others, however, this explanation as "flute" would not be conflicting with the meaning of the Scriptural text. For the assumption that *mahol* might refer to the *halil*, there is some probability. The *halil* served in ancient Israel for two wholly opposite purposes. On the one hand, it was a widespread popular instrument, played at all joyous festivities (cf. 1 Kings 1:40); on the other, it was the typical instrument for mourning, never lacking at any funeral. The direct confirmation that *halilim* were used in the sacred service is to be found in the early rabbinical literature.[85]

In the light of these arguments, the assumption seems to be justified that the term *'al mahalat* in the superscriptions of Psalms 53 and 88 refers indeed to the musical rendition of these psalms, indicating their accompaniment with woodwinds. Nothing conflicts with this theory from the musical as well as the poetical points of view, since, owing to the mournful character of both psalms, the special use of the *halil* as a lamenting instrument would be appropriate.

17. *Mashrokita.* Among the instruments played at NEBUCHADREZZAR'S court, the chronicler mentions the *mashrokita* (Dan. 3:5,7,10,15). The word could be derived from the Hebrew *sharak*, "to hiss," "to whistle." Nevertheless, it is generally assumed that *mashrokita* refers to a foreign instrument. I have repeatedly mentioned that, in order to stress the pagan character of this feast, the chronicler intentionally selected names of instruments that were either not used by the Hebrews, or were unknown to them, so that they would be considered "exotic." One of them was the *mashrokita*.

Translators and expounders were in doubt about the real nature of this instrument. The early Greek translations interpreted the word as *syrinx*, thus identifying it with the Pan's pipe of the Hellenes.

Yet, it is questionable whether the name of an instrument not in use in ancient Israel could be derived from a Hebrew root. It seems more probable that a similar onomatopoeic verb may have existed in other Semitic languages, so that *mashroḳita* could conceivably have originated from a non-Hebraic root.

It cannot be said with certainty whether this instrument was in fact identical with the Pan's pipe. Some commentators believe that it was indeed the *syrinx*, others define it as a flute, a double-flute, while SACHS supposes, in a general way, the *mashroḳita* to be a woodwind instrument, probably the double-oboe.

Any attempt to arrive at a working conclusion with regard to the true meaning of the *mashroḳita* is beset by insurmountable difficulties. For want of a more definite solution, we have practically no other choice than to follow the interpretation of the early translators and identify the *mashroḳita* with the *syrinx*.

18. Sumponyah. This instrument appears in the Book of Daniel among those played in NEBUCHADREZZAR's orchestra (3:5,10,15). Whereas all the other instruments are mentioned four times, the *sumponyah* is omitted in verse 7, this being generally taken as an error of a scribe, subsequently perpetuated in the Masoretic text.

Until today the opinions are divided whether or not *sumponyah* represents a mere transliteration of the Greek word *symphōnia*. The doubt has been occasioned mainly by the fact that the Syrian Greeks knew an instrument that they called *samponia*. This name has been preserved until our time in Italy, where the bagpipe is called *sampugna* or *zampugna*. It is difficult to ascertain whether the Syrian *samponia* and the Chaldaean *sumponyah* had been original terms or phonetic adaptations of the Greek word. The instrument might well have been one of those which the Hellenes took over from the Orient, improved technically, and then traded back, with new Greek name, to the country of their origin.

The original meaning of the Greek *symphōnia* is "sounding together," specifically the simultaneous playing of instruments, or voices, producing a concord, or a consonant harmony of two tones, forming the intervals of a fourth (*dia tessarōn*), a fifth (*dia pente*), or an octave (*dia pasōn*).

In the writings of the early Greek philosophers the word did not as yet indicate a musical instrument, especially not the bagpipe. This instrument does not appear before the fourth century B.C.E., and then under the name of *physetēria* ("bellow") and *physallidēs* ("bladder pipes").

The word *symphōnia* as a term referring to a single musical instrument appears first with ATHENAIUS (second century C.E.). He uses the name rather frequently, but the context in which it appears in the different places does not indicate clearly the nature of the instrument. He does not even give us a clue as to whether he alludes to a stringed, wind, or percussion instrument. From all his descriptions one thing at least emerges unmistakably: that it does not refer to the bagpipe, or to any percussion instrument, probably not even the name of an individual instrument at all.

Not until the first century B.C.E. do Roman writers give precise information about the bagpipe, called *tibia utricularis, utricularium,* or *chorus.* For the Romans (first century C.E.), *symphonia* meant something entirely different; it was used in the sense of a "company of musicians," a band.

NERO (Emperor 54–68 C.E.), notorious for having considered himself a great musician, had a predilection for the bagpipe. DIO CHRYSOSTOMOS relates that NERO knew how to play the pipe with his mouth and the bag thrust under his arms.

SUETONIUS, in his *Life of the Roman Caesars,* reports about NERO that

> towards the end of his life he has publicly vowed that if he retained his power he would
> at the games in celebration of his victory give a performance on the water-organ (*hydraulis*),
> the flute (*choraulos*) and the bagpipe (*utricularium*).[87]

In the Latin parlance of the early Middle Ages, *symphonia* meant a single musical instrument, but about its real nature opinions were at wide variance. Some believed it to be a double-oboe, others the bagpipe, while ISIDORE of SEVILLA defined it as a kind of tympanum.[88]

On the Jewish side, the Mishnah contains various details concerning Daniel's *sumponyah* which, however, do not afford a clear idea about its nature. Some of these details would permit this inference in favor of a bagpipe, whereas others would exclude it altogether.

The strongest argument against the interpretation of the *sumponyah* as bagpipe is the historical fact that in the epoch of NEBUCHADREZZAR (first half of the sixth century B.C.E) there existed no such instrument.[89] At first sight, this fact seems to be refuted by a bas-relief found in the excavations of a Hittite palace at Eyuk. In this carving a musician is portrayed, playing what appears to be a bagpipe. On closer scrutiny, however, the picture turns out to be a representation of a court-jester, or a lute-player with a monkey.[90] Two pendant objects of the carving could be indeed taken on the surface as the "pipes" of a bagpipe, but they are, in reality, ribbons of the animal, or of the lute-like instrument (Illus. 41).

In the time of the Roman Emperors, the equivalent in the Latin language for *symphōnia* was *consonare, consonantia,* terms used to indicate the singing of choral groups, or the playing together of instruments, therefore what we call today a group of musicians (orchestra, band, ensemble). This is the most pertinent explanation of *symphōnia,* since neither in Greek nor in Latin is there an equivalent term for our Occidental notion of "orchestra."

A similar interpretation for *sumponyah* in Daniel imposes itself automatically. First, the chronicler enumerates the individual instruments playing alone. Then they all play together, a procedure expressed logically by *sumponyah,* in the Greek meaning of the word. Finally, *v'kol zene zimrah,* "all kinds of instruments," indicates that to those already mentioned, the percussion instruments were added—drums, cymbals, sistra, and so on—which were never lacking at festive celebrations in the Orient.

The controversy as to whether *symphōnia* was a bagpipe or not survived even until recent times.[91] This controversy is the more astonishing in that a passage of St. Luke's Gospel (15:25) excludes not only the idea of the bagpipe, but even the identification of the *symphōnia* with any kind of instrument.

19. *Ḥazozerah.* The word *ḥazozerah* (pl. *ḥazozerot*) "trumpet" is derived etymologically from the verb *ḥazar,* "to be present." In one grammatical form, *ḥazozerah* would signify the "convoker." In Arabic, the same root, *ḥezar* has a similar meaning; in the applied form it refers to "calling a meeting." A similar Arabic root signifies "narrow," also "to howl," by which the trumpet's shape as well as its sound are well characterized.

GESENIUS considers the word to be an onomatopoeic construction, in which the duplication of consonants, especially the sibilants, would imitate some of the characteristic sonority of the instrument.[92]

The *hazozerah* was a long straight trumpet, built by the Israelites after Egyptian models. In Egypt it was a familiar instrument long before the Biblical Exodus, since we find pictorial reproductions of it in the oldest, well-preserved, monuments of the New Kingdom, as early as 1415 B.C.E.

In TUT-ANKH-AMON's tomb two trumpets have been found, one of silver, the other of gilt bronze (Illus. 32). The Musée du Louvre in Paris houses another ancient Egyptian trumpet of gilt bronze, which is dated about 1000 years later. The Pharaoh TUT-ANKH-AMON reigned about the year 1360 B.C.E., a little over a century before the Exodus of the Israelites from Egypt,—ca. 1240 B.C.E., according to many present-day authorities. Thus the Israelites were residents in Egypt before, during, and after the age of TUT-ANKH-AMON, which makes it logical to assume that they took over their trumpets from the Egyptians.

Trumpets were also used by the Assyrians, as is evidenced by bas-reliefs found in excavated monuments.

JOSEPHUS gives a detailed description of the instrument, which agrees essentially with the pictorial representations on Egyptian antiquities.[93] All the available pictures reveal that the form of the ancient instrument was identical with today's signal trumpet, which we call "herald's trumpet."

The *hazozerah* is the only Jewish instrument of which we possess at least one coeval picture and some others not too far removed historically. The Arch of Triumph of the Emperor TITUS in Rome, erected after the victory over the Jews and the destruction of the sanctuary in Jerusalem, shows the captured implements of the Temple, carried in a triumphal procession. Among them, the two sacred silver trumpets are depicted, which the sculptor must have copied from the originals. Several coins issued during the Maccabaean revolt (132–136 C.E.) show two trumpets on their faces, designed rather clumsily and shortened considerably, evidently to fit into the face of a small coin. It is characteristic, in these reproductions, that right below the mouthpiece the tube is widened like a bell, serving obviously to reinforce the tone.[94] On the Arch of Triumph of TITUS, the mouthpieces of the sacred trumpets are hidden, which makes it impossible to ascertain iconographically whether these instruments had a similar device.

According to Greek and Roman sources, the trumpet was invented by the Etruscans, the first bronze-casters of the Mediterranean.[95] The Egyptians must have become familiar with the instrument through their cultural intercourse with the Etruscans. From Egypt, the trumpet was taken over by the Tyrrhennian peoples and thence by the Greeks and Romans.[96]

Like the Egyptian trumpet, the Jewish *hazozerah* was made of metal, either of bronze or, for the sacred trumpets, of beaten silver. The form of the trumpet was known to Moses and the Jewish people from Egypt. Therefore, when— according to the scriptures—God commanded Moses to make two trumpets (Num. 10:2), only the material was indicated together with instructions how to use the instrument on different occasions, but the shape of it was not mentioned at all. The fact that God commanded two trumpets is the reason that the Bible uses the word, with one exception,[97] in the plural form as *hazozerot*.

The sounding of the *hazozerot* was the exclusive privilege of Aaron's descendants, the priests (Num. 10:8). They adhered strictly to this privilege

(2 Chron. 5:12 ff; 7:6; 13:12,14; Ezra 3:10; Neh. 12:35,41). The prerogatives of the Aaronites applied only to the sacred trumpets of the ritual, for on secular occasions trumpets were also blown by others than priests, as, for instance, by royal heralds (2 Kings, 11:14; 2 Chron. 23:13). The Bible does not reveal whether these were the same trumpets of silver or of some other metal. Since the silver trumpets belonged to the *kle ha-kodesh,* "the holy vessels" (Num. 31:6; 2 Kings 12:14), it would be logical to assume that the trumpets used on secular occasions were made of bronze, like the Egyptian instruments. The players of trumpets were called *hazozerim* (2 Chron. 5:13; 29:28).

As with the loud instruments of other ancient Oriental peoples, the original purpose of the Jewish trumpets may have been to draw the attention of the deity to the ritual action and to the worshippers. Thus, the sound of the *hazozerot* served as a means for a persistent invocation of God. Although with the subsequent maturing of the Jewish religious concept the loud invocation of God was gradually abandoned, we still find the custom of the loud call in the relatively late epoch of the Maccabaean revolt (middle of the second century). On that occasion, the sacred trumpets were blown and the people called, reportedly, with loud voice to implore God's assistance (1 Macc. 4:40; 5:33; 16:8).

A spiritually higher purpose of the trumpets emerges from the command that their blowing should be undertaken *leziharon,* "for a memorial before your God" (Num. 10:10), that is, as a symbolic reminder of God's presence amidst the people.

The manner of blowing the trumpets is described in the Bible in all its essentials for various occasions (Num. 10:2–10): to gather the congregation to the tent of meeting, to cause the camps to set forward, to invite the princes for a gathering, to sound alarm in danger, to give a signal when going to war. All this refers to the secular use of the instrument.

As to their sacred functions, the trumpets were blown at all religious feasts, the New Moon, the daily burnt and peace offerings, as well as at all important ritual ceremonies.

In the daily sacred service the trumpets had the essential function of indicating the prostration of the worshippers. To be sure, references to this effect are lacking in the Scriptures. But the rabbinic scribes mention explicitly that this was a ritual action in the Second Temple:

Ben Arza clashed the cymbal and the Levites broke forth into singing. When they reached a break in the singing they [the priests] blew upon the trumpets and all the people prostrated themselves; at every break there was a blowing of the trumpet and at every blowing of the trumpet a prostration. This was the rite of the daily Whole-offering in the service of the House of God.[98]

Since we have good reasons to believe that the routine of the Second Temple's daily service was merely the continuation of that of Solomon's Temple, we may safely assume that the functions of the *hazozerot* were identical in both sanctuaries.

A talmudic passage indicates that the two sacred trumpets were of exactly the same dimensions.[99] This was an obvious necessity, because the trumpets were blown mostly in pairs, producing powerful unisons.

At first, the trumpet-players may not have exceeded the three or four easily producible tones of the natural harmonic series, beginning with the octave of the fundamental, the upper fifth, the upper octave and, possibly, the tenth (c'-g'-c''-e''). At this primitive stage, the *ḥazoẓerot* must have been used primarily for signal purposes, both within and without the sanctuary.

However, as the priestly trumpeters gradually developed their technique and learned how to produce additional partials, the *ḥazoẓerot* might well have surmounted the initial stage as a mere signal instrument and risen into the sphere of more artistic playing.

The number of trumpets in the daily sacred service was at least two; at High Holidays and other important religious festivals their number could be increased without restriction. Whether or not one hundred and twenty trumpeters actually participated at the dedication of Solomon's Temple cannot be positively ascertained. Still, it is quite likely that all the trumpet-playing priests had been summoned to this important event; and their number must have been considerable, even if we make certain allowances for the well-meant exaggerations of Biblical chroniclers.

For the trumpet blasts, the Biblical text uses mostly two terms, *tekiʿah* and *teruʿah* (Num. 10:2 ff.). The root *ruʿah* has the meaning "to be agitated," "to make noise." Consequently, *teruʿah* would indicate a series of acute, staccato-like blasts. The opposite, *tekiʿah*, implies the use of sustained, long-drawn tones. With the passing of time, however, the two terms have been interpreted in a different way.

The use of the trumpets in the First and Second Temple is attested by quite a number of Biblical passages. Furthermore, a number of references in the early rabbinical literature give us a clear picture about the functions of the trumpets in the ritual. The Mishnah, especially, furnishes precise indications as to the exact number of blasts that had to be drawn at the various ritual ceremonies.[100]

Besides the indications of the trumpet calls found in the Scriptures and in the rabbinical literature, there are some fanciful descriptions of war-signals contained in the recently discovered Dead Sea Scrolls.

One of these scrolls found in a cave at Qumrān contains a detailed strategic plan for an apocalyptic war to be fought between *The Sons of Light and the Sons of Darkness*. Notwithstanding its manifestly imaginary character, this description is considered by some Biblical scholars as "largely conforming to standard Roman patterns of military organization, procedure and strategy."[101] It is not impossible that some of these trumpet calls might have been imitations of actual Roman military signals, such as, for instance, the "trumpets of assembly," which reminds us of the analogous Roman *tuba concionis*. This, however, is merely a surmise.

This *Rule of Battle* intimates that the priests and Levites have been assigned quite an important role in the battle, namely, to direct the operations of the troops in the midst of the combatants. In giving appropriate signals with trumpet and *shofar* blasts, they marked the different phases of the battle.

Looking into the purely musical (i.e., rhythmical) aspect of this detailed order of battle, we realize that the priest-strategists had at their disposal seven different kinds of blasts: for the assembly, the advance, the attack, the ambush, the pursuit, the reassembly, and the recall. Such blasts must have had some conspicuous rhythmic or other characteristics, without which their specific purpose could not have been recognized by fighting men.

The imaginary character of this war becomes even more manifest through further detailed indications about the inscriptions, evidently symbolic, that were allegedly applied to the trumpets of war. None of our Biblical or post-Biblical sources ever mentions inscriptions on musical instruments, and such a custom is not known to have existed in the ancient Near East. The only allusion to an inscription on an object belonging to the family of musical instruments is to be found in Zech. 14:20, where it is said that the *mezillot,* hung on horses, carried the inscription *ḳodesh le-YHVH,* evidently a superstitious practice for the protection of useful animals against evil spirits. It would be more difficult to apply inscriptions on trumpets, especially in view of the fact that some of these alleged inscriptions are rather lengthy. Nevertheless, the passage in Zechariah may be considered as an indication that such a custom might have existed, even if historically unrecorded.

Not only the trumpets but also the standards to be used in this imaginary war are said to have had appropriate inscriptions. There were such mottos for the entire army, as well as for all categories of combatants and all sizes of groups,—different inscriptions for the camp commander, for squadrons of a thousand, of one hundred, of fifty, and

> on the standard of [the group of] ten they shall write: *Songs* [or *Hymns*] (*rinnot*) *of God on the stringed harp* (*nebel 'asor*), together with the names of the commander of the ten, and of the nine men under his command.

Of all the numerous standards, only that of this group has an inscription with a musical implication. It may have had certain numerological reasons, establishing an esoteric relation between the smallest group of combatants and the number of strings on the *'asor,* and thus vesting such a small group with a sort of supernatural power for subduing the enemy.

After the collapse of the Jewish national existence and in the subsequent general abasement, some musical notions disappeared from people's minds, others became confused owing to lack of familiarity with them. So we find a talmudic statement reflecting this chaotic state with reference to the nomenclature of certain instruments:

> The following three groups of words are changed in meaning after the destruction of the Temple. . . . What was formerly called *ḥazozarta* [*ḥazozerah* in the Aramaic dialect] was called *shifurta* [*shofar* in Aramaic], and what was called *shifurta* became *ḥazozarta.*[102]

The Talmud recounts a peculiar and manifestly fictitious story that, at the time of Ezra, priests with golden trumpets stood on the walls and on the broken ramparts of Jerusalem, fanning the zeal of the people with *teḳi'ah* and *teru'ah* blasts for building the new wall. A priest who had no trumpet in his hand was considered to be no priest at all, and the inhabitants of Jerusalem made a good profit by renting trumpets to the priests for a gold denarius apiece.[103] A legend of this sort could have originated only in the mind of someone completely unfamiliar with the religious and musical tradition. For trumpets made of noble metal were judiciously kept inaccessible to anyone but the priests. No ordinary citizen was likely to have a trumpet in his possession even by chance, since this has never been a popular instrument, not to mention the fact that the expression "golden trumpets" belongs quite obviously to those naïve exaggerations found so often in the rabbinical literature.

20. *Shofar.* The *shofar* is the only instrument of ancient Israel that survived in its original form and which is still used in the Jewish liturgy, although with greatly curtailed functions.

The Hebrews took over the *shofar* from the Assyrians. The word itself is derived from the Assyrian *shapparu,* *"wild goat"* (of the ibex family). More often, however, the Jewish *shofar* (pl. *shofarot*) is made of a ram's horn; as in other instances, the instrument received its name from the material from which it was made.[104] The ancient Hebrews did not recognize the ritual validity of *shofarot* made of cattle horn,[105] only those made of ram's horn and that of the wild goat.

The original form of the *shofar* was a curved one like that of the natural ram's horn. Later, a special mechanical procedure was to change the shape of the natural horn, producing straight *shorafot* with a distinct bend close to the bell. In the Second Temple both species, curved and straight, were used (Illus. 83).

After the destruction of the Temple by the Romans the embellishment of *shofarot* with gold and silver or with other showy ornaments was prohibited, and in its plain form the instrument still exists and functions.

Primitively, the Israelites connected the blowing of the *shofar* with magic and sorcery; similar customs prevail among practically every other primitive people and at all periods. At a later historical stage the blowing of the *shofar* on New Year's Day was supposed to remind God symbolically of His promise given to Abraham, Isaac, and Jacob. The blowing on other days was also in the nature of a symbolic action: the faithful were to remember the ram sacrificed by Abraham instead of his son (Gen. 22:13).

After the destruction of the sanctuary in Jerusalem, all music was prohibited as a sign of mourning. Only the blowing of the *shofar* was permitted, but this practice now had a messianic significance and was connected with the providential hope that at some future time the prophet Elijah will sound the *"shofar* of deliverance," thereby announcing the advent of the Messiah.

The primitive *shofarot* were made by cutting off the tip of the natural horn, or boring a hole in it. The instrument made in this way had no mouthpiece and could produce only crude sustained tones. The *shofar* with a mouthpiece (*ḳos,* "cup") represents a more developed form of the instrument. But even in this improved form, the *shofar* tones were limited usually to two in number (sometimes to three), these being the second, third, and fourth partials, i.e., the octave, the upper fifth, and the second octave of the fundamental (c′, g′, c″, for instance). It is evident that the *shofar* could not carry out any musical assignment in the artistic sense; its function was restricted to two simple but important roles: a signal instrument in war, and, later, use in the religious services of the Temple and Synagogue.

A rather obscure passage of the Mishnah refers to a peculiar ritual custom:

to blow the *shofar* in a cistern or in a cellar or in a large jar [better barrel; Aramaic *pithos*][106]

Even the chronologically close commentary of the Gemara betrays ignorance about the true meaning of this custom. To all appearances, it was a remnant of some primitive Hebrew ritual connected with magic and sorcery. The superstitious belief populated such dark places with all kinds of malevolent demons, who were to be frightened and chased away by sounding the horn, or even killed by the magic power of the *shofar*-blasts.

As with the *hazozerot,* there were precise instructions for blowing the *shofar*. Their correct meaning, however, was not always interpreted in like manner. Originally, the sustained tone was called *mashah* (Exod. 19:12; Josh. 6:5) and, inferentially, the short blast *teki'ah*. But the Mishnah interprets *teki'ah* as the sustained tone, and this meaning remained uncontested until after the third century.

For a long time rabbinical opinions were divided about the manner of blowing *teru'ah*. Some claimed that it implies short (staccato-like) blasts; others maintained that the term refers to a sort of tremolo or vibrato on a sustained tone. Finally R. Abbahu of Caesarea in Palestine (fourth century) found a way out: he called the short staccato-blasts with alternating tones *shebarim,* and the tremolo on the same note *teru'ah*. After some dissenting rabbinical opinions, Abbahu's regulation was eventually adopted,[107] and this meaning of the two terms prevails to this day.

There is a significant talmudic discussion about the question why a series of *shofar*-blasts is first sounded while sitting, then sounded twice while standing. The rabbis say: "It is to confuse the Accuser (in Hebrew "Satan")."[108] The meaning of this statement is somewhat obscure, despite Rashi's commentary on the passage:

> The devotion of the Jews to the precepts nullifies Satan's accusations against them.

In the rabbinical thinking, the second and third series of *shofar*-blasts were intended to bewilder and stagger Satan who, considering the first series as a mere compliance with the Law, is surprised by the second series, assuming that it announces the advent of the Messiah. Listening to the third series, Satan becomes afraid that the Resurrection is going to take place, with which his power over the Jews will cease. Thus, it is obvious that the repeated series of *shofar*-blasts were caused originally by the superstitious belief that the sound of the *shofar* has the power of bewildering and chasing away evil spirits, in this instance the Accuser.

On *Rosh ha-Shanah* the *shofar* was originally blown in the early part (*Shaharit*) of the morning service, but subsequently was transferred to a later hour in the *Musaf* portion.[109] The reason for this was a tragic occurrence, which is related in the Talmud. It seems that the Jewish *shofar*-blasts resembled the military signals of the Roman army stationed in Palestine. As a result, the Roman authorities suspected that the Jews were preparing an attack on them and that the *shofar*-blasts served to call the men together. So, in order to prevent an armed revolt, troops were unexpectedly dispatched in the early morning to the synagogues, where real carnage was committed among the worshipping Jews before an explanation could be given. Therefore, in the succeeding years the *shofar*-blasts were omitted in the *Shaharit* and deferred to the *Musaf*, where it was obvious that they served merely for ritual use.[110] In his commentary to this passage, RASHI adds:

> The Romans issued an ordinance that the *shofar* should not be blown at all, and in order to enforce this prohibition, they sent out spies every six hours.

It seems, however, that the Jewish religious leaders gradually succeeded in persuading the occupation authorities that the *shofar*-blasts had merely a ritual significance, because in subsequent years the *shofar* was again allowed to sound in the *Shaḥarit*. But even after the original order was eventually restored, the sounding of the *shofar* in the *Musaf* was retained as a supplement to the early morning blowing.

As with the *ḥazozerot*, the daily number of blasts on the *shofarot* was strictly regulated: "Never less than twenty-one, and never more than forty-eight."[111] However, this regulation of the *shofar*-blasts engendered all kinds of interpretation, owing to the fact that some rabbis, poorly versed in musical matters, considered the group of *teḳi'ah*, *tern'ah*, and *teḳi'ah* as *one* sound, while others held that each blast represented a *separate* sound. This resulted in protracted differences in the meaning of the groups.

The Mishnah contains detailed indications as to the metric value of the *shofar*-blasts. Commenting upon these indications, the Gemara establishes the relationship of the duration of the various *shofar*-calls in the following way:

> The length of the *teḳi'ah* is equal to three *teru'ahs* . . . The length of the *teru'ah* is equal to the length of three *yebaboth* . . . But it has been taught, "the length of the *teru'ah* is equal to three *shebarim* [lit. "breaks"]."[112]

In this Mishnaic passage the Aramaic word for *teru'ah*, "alarm blast," is *yebabah* (pl. *yebaboth*). Targum Onkelos to Lev. 23:24 also uses this word as translation for *teru'ah*.

Today's synagogue ritual uses four different kinds of sounding the *shofar*:

1) *teḳi'ah* ("blast"), a relatively short pick-up note on the tonic, leading to a sustained note on the fifth, and ending, on some *shofarot*, with the higher octave of the tonic;

2) *shebarim* ("breaks"), alternating rapidly the tonic and fifth, ending with a sustained note on the fifth;

3) *teru'ah* ("din"), a rapid staccato-like repetition of short notes on the tonic, ending with a long note on the fifth;

4) *teḳi'ah gedolah* ("great blast"), basically identical with the *teḳi'ah*, but using longer note values, and ending with a long sustained note on the fifth or, on some *shofarot*, on the higher octave.

The *shofar* used in today's Jewish ritual is normally a straight tube, about fourteen to fifteen inches in length, with the widened bell bent slightly sidewise. Since its interior is rather rough and the instrument is usually blown through a mouthpiece of irregular shape, its pitch is highly variable and not always distinct. The *shofarot* vary also as to the number of their available harmonics. Some can produce only two, possibly three, and rarely four sounds of their respective natural series.

Here follow, in musical notation, the basic patterns of *shofar*-calls as heard in modern synagogues. These calls show, however, many variants in the Ashkenazic as well as in the Sephardic services, and mainly according to the origin and background of the *ba'ale toḳe'ah*, as the *shofar*-players are called.

Example 1 **ASHKENAZIM** after Francis Lyon Cohen
(in *JE*, XI, p. 306)

(x) This note is quite irregular and could have been produced only as a distortion of the tonic by means of some extra lip pressure. It is a foreign note in the natural series of harmonics and certainly not typical for *shofar* tones. F. L. Cohen must have heard it played by some local performer on a particular instrument, and should not have quoted it among traditional *shofar*-calls.

Example 2 **SEPHARDIM** after Francis Lyon Cohen
(*ibid.*)

In this example there is no difference between *teru*(ah and *teki*(ah gedolah, except for more staccato notes on the tonic of the latter. Sephardic *ba*(ale toke(ah doubt the authenticity of this call, since the *teki*(ah gedolah is supposed to be a prolongated *teki*(ah.

Example 3 **SEPHARDIM**

as heard on an ancient *shofar* without mouthpiece, blown by a *ba*(al toke(ah from Israel. The fundamental tone of this instrument was

and the following example was transposed a minor third down.

Example 4 after Solomon Sulzer, *Schir Zion*
(Vienna, 1838, 1865), vol. II, p. 257.

Tekiʿah gedolah

The Parma notation of *shofar*-calls is interpreted by Sulzer
in the following way:

Tekiʿah   *Shebarim*   *tr*   *Teruʿah*

While explaining this notation, Sulzer says that the ancient *Quilisma*-
sign   in reality represents a *trill*, not a rapid tone-repetition, as used
generally. In his compositions for the *shofar* ceremony, Sulzer notates
the *shofar*-calls in accordance with this interpretation.

Example 5   *First Version*   after Abraham Beer, *Baal Tefillah*
(Gothenburg, 1877), p. 254.

Tekiʿah   *Shebarim*   *Teruʿah*   *tr*

Tekiʿah gedolah

Second Version

Tekiʿah   *Shebarim*   *Teruʿah*   *tr*

Tekiʿah gedolah

Example 6   after E. J. Stark, *Shofar-Service*
(San Francisco, 1905), pp. 6 ff.

Tekiʿah   *Shebarim*   *Teruʿah*

Tekiʿah gedolah

The *shofar*-calls of Stark's Service are written for a *trombone,* which is contrary to the spirit of the Jewish tradition. In Stark's notation these calls sound an octave lower than quoted above:

Example 7   *LITHUANIAN VERSION*

as heard in the Fairfax Synagogue at Los Angeles, on a centuries-old *shofar,* blown by a former choir singer and *ba⁽al toke⁽ah* of the Great Synagogue at Vilna. The fundamental tone of this instrument was:

 the following example was transposed a minor third up.

This example is acoustically enigmatic. The three initial notes might be explained as harmonics 4-6-9. Or else the uppermost note may be due to an unusual shape of the instrument (see Kirby's statement on p. 626). However, the outward appearance of the instrument did not reveal any particularity accounting for the uppermost note.

Example 8

In Appendix V to Stainer's *The Music of the Bible* (London, 1914, p. 225), F. W. Galpin gives the following *shofar*-calls, which he "copied down from those sounded by the *shofar*-player in the London Western Synagogue." The persistent fourth throughout, without any other interval, is certainly unusual.

Example 9

For the sake of curiosity, I add a strange type of *shofar*-calls, as used in Edward Elgar's oratorio *The Apostles* (pp. 19–20). They are rhythmically the same as the ordinary *teki⁽ah, shebarim,* and *teru⁽ah* blasts, but the interval is consistently a major sixth, quite unusual on regular *shofarot.* It must be assumed, however, that the composer had heard this *shofar*-call played somewhere.

The Yemenite Jews have huge *shofarot,* sometimes a yard long, straight or twisted. Their calls are basically identical with those of the Ashkenazim (Illus. 84).

Of all Israelitic instruments the *shofar* is mentioned most frequently in the Bible (seventy-two times), thus indicating its paramount importance in the religious as well as secular life of the Jewish people.

The religious use of the *shofar* is attested at the transfer of the ark of the Covenant by David (2 Sam. 6:15; 1 Chron. 15:28), the renewal of the Covenant by King Asa (2 Chron. 15:14), announcing the New Moon (Ps. 81:4), thanksgiving to God for His miraculous deeds (Psalms 98:6, 150:3), and many other places.

Among secular events at which the *shofar* was sounded, I mention only a few: Absalom's accession to the throne (2 Sam. 15:10), Solomon's ointment as king (1 Kings 1:34), Yehu's accession to the throne (2 Kings 9:13), and others.

In times of war the *shofar* was the regular signal instrument—for assembling the warriors, attacking the enemy, pursuing the vanquished, or announcing the victory.

The well-known episode of the siege of Jericho (Josh. 6), in which the *shofarot* played a decisive role, is left out in the present synopsis because these "trumpets" belonged to a different category of instruments, as will be shown in the following chapter.

The secular use of the *shofar* demonstrates its two basic groups of practical functions, one of these being connected with ancient magic customs, which have survived incognizantly with the people, and the other symbolizing fateful and heroic events of tragic nature, such as wars, national disasters, but also some important political events.

In post-Biblical times the use of the *shofar* has been even more diverse. To begin with, the *shofar*-blasts kept on announcing the approach of the Sabbath.[113] Besides the *ḥalil,* the *shofar* was used at funerals. According to ancient Jewish conception,

at the death of a person, spirits and demons are supposed to be present; either they wish to get back into the body, or to take the body with them as a prey.[114]

The sound of the *shofar* was invested with the magic power to frighten off the evil spirits. The Talmud mentions even a specific kind of *shofar,* the *shipura deshikta,* "funerary bugle."[115] However, the Sages do not reveal whether this kind of instrument was a changed form of the Biblical *shofar,* or what were its characteristics.

Furthermore, the *shofar* was used at procedures of excommunication. The blowing announced the anathema or its abrogation.[116] The faculty of preventing natural catastrophes was also attributed to the *shofar.*[117] This again is connected with the belief in magic and sorcery, but in the long run their original meaning was lost and survived only subconsciously in the minds of the Israelites.

The blowing of the *shofar* at droughts, disasters, and natural catastrophes had, as stated above, besides its original meaning, a partly religious, partly secular significance. On such occasions the rabbis ordered special fast days; the ordinances issued by them contain detailed instructions as to the use of the *shofar.*[118]

Finally, the Talmud refers to a peculiar custom, also partly religious and partly secular. It was usual to hold public prayers with blowing the *shofar* in times of impending calamity, such as the decline in trade or decrease of money's buying power. Thus we read

that linen garments in Babylon and wine and oil in Palestine have become so cheap that ten are sold [at the price of] six.[119]

This amounted to a drop of forty percent of the commercial values which, even in a relatively primitive economy affected both the public affairs and the interests of the individual producers. Public prayers were, therefore, in order, and the part the *shofar* played in these manifestations was akin to that of the magic *shofar*-calls: to draw the attention to the deity to the sacred ceremony, or the worshippers, or both.

Toward the end of Israel's national existence a latent struggle developed between the priestly and secular forces with regard to the elimination of the *hazozerot* in the sacred service in favor of the *shofar*.[120] This struggle was automatically decided with the destruction of the Temple by the Romans. Since the *hazozerot* were the instruments associated with the daily sacrifices, permissible only in the Jerusalem sanctuary, their complete cessation also terminated the use of the *hazozerot*. The *shofar*, on the other hand, continued to perform its normal functions as heretofore, that is, to announce the New Year, to carry out certain rites on the Day of Atonement, to usher in the New Moon, to introduce the Sabbath. In addition, it took over all the functions fulfilled by the *hazozerot* outside the sanctuary. Thus the *shofar* became, and remains to this day, the only ancient musical instrument in the Jewish sacred ritual.

One may ask how it actually came about that of all Jewish instruments used in the sacred service, the *shofar* alone has survived. During all the centuries, and often under the most adverse circumstances, the Jews maintained not only their religious institutions, but also their musical tradition, including the actual music practices. The period of the Babylonian exile may serve as the most striking example in this instance. Would it then not be expected that, after the annihilation of their national existence in the year 70 C.E., the Jews would also have succeeded in preserving their musical culture in the dispersion? Not merely their songs, but also their instrumental music has always been an integral part of their religious institutions. If it was possible to keep the musical tradition alive in the Babylonian captivity, why not in the Diaspora?

First, it must be remembered that, as a sign of mourning for the lost sanctuary, the rabbinic authorities abolished "loud singing," meaning the public practice of music. In spite of this prohibition, the private practice of secular music would probably still have been preserved under average conditions, since love of music was too deeply ingrained in the Jewish soul to be easily extinguished. However, a pernicious combination of factors brought about a situation that not even the strictest rabbinical measures would have achieved.

To understand the intrinsic reasons for this, it suffices to examine, if but briefly, the specific difference between the situation in the captivity and the Diaspora.

In the Babylonian exile, despite all oppression, the Jews lived as a compact religious and cultural group; they were able, therefore, to preserve at least their spiritual life intact; despite all the hardships of their precarious existence, they were never menaced with the extinction of their religion. Subsequently, they gradually gained more freedom to pursue their civic activities; their human dignity was restored; their religious institutions (with the exception of the sacrifice) were reestablished. Their musical practice similarly suffered no radical changes. Thus, their music survived the captivity almost intact.

Following their defeat by the Romans, the Jews were dispersed all over the known part of the globe, mostly in small, incohesive groups, a circumstance that does not favor a homogeneous musical culture. Not only were they social outcasts living mostly under economic duress, but their religious institutions were menaced by an unprecedented sectarian factionalism, and mainly by the rising Christianity. To be sure, immediately after the downfall of the Jewish national state, JOHANAN ben ZAKKAI and his adepts united their efforts to create in Jabneh a central institution for the preservation and continuation of Jewish life under the changed circumstances. Their aim was no less than to substitute for the lost Jewish state a sort of supra-national leadership by creating a supreme authority with the purpose of concentrating all Jewish energies toward one goal: religious and spiritual survival, with the exclusion of all social implications that did not directly serve their higher end. To what extent they succeeded is evidenced by the subsequent destiny of Jewry, showing to the world the complete religious unity of a people torn nationally to shreds, but unbroken in spirit.

History shows us also where Jabneh failed: namely, in the preservation of the ancient musical heritage of the Jewish people. We understand, of course, that the solicitude of the new spiritual leaders of Judaism was focused on a great many and, in their opinion, much more important elements of Jewish life than music, despite all the love the Jews showed for their tonal art during all the centuries of their independent national life.

The odds were simply against those, among the dispersed Jews, who might have succeeded in saving their beloved instruments—*kinnor, nebel, halil*—and taking these along with them into exile. Soon the fragile instruments must have largely deteriorated, the strings broken, and the reed-mouthpieces worn out. Cracks, splits, and other damage of the wooden parts could no longer be repaired. The making of instruments, a necessary handicraft, had rapidly disappeared, for who indeed would have asked for a musical instrument in the misery and abasement of the Diaspora?

The same was true of music instruction, both religious and secular, once a flourishing profession in Ancient Israel. When "loud singing" was abolished, the urge for instrumental music-making decreased more and more. Even the Jews' normally strong longing for musical activity could not remedy the situation. The *kle shir*, the instruments that accompanied the singing in the Temple and in secular life, could no longer be used, hence the necessity of learning and teaching them became extinct. The knowledge of technique waned more and more until eventually it fell into complete oblivion. And this, in turn, still further aggravated the decline of the entire culture of practical music.

What remained was solely a rather primitive instrument of religious import, easy to make from the horn of certain domestic animals, and able to be handled by anybody without much study. Furthermore, there remained in the subconscious of the Jews certain residues of ancient magic and sorcery, long connected with the use of the *shofar*, which in the national tragedy were felt even more keenly. To these was added the messianic significance attributed in the Diaspora to the sounding of the *shofar*. Thus it came about that of all Biblical instruments the *shofar* alone survived.

21. Keren. The literal meaning of the word *keren* is "firm," "solid," originating from the verb *keren*, "to be firm." It refers to the hard horn of the neat, in contrast to the soft flesh of this bovine cattle. Thus, logically, the meaning of the word was derived from the material of which it was made, the neat's horn.

Besides, *keren* is used in the Biblical text in more than one extra-musical sense. The most important use of the term is that which appears in Jer. 48:25 and Psalm 89:18, where the word stands symbolically for power and dignity. This meaning inspired two medieval artists to represent Moses, as an exalted person of Jewish history, with two horns on his forehead (Illus. 86 and 87).

The implication of *keren* as an instrument made from animal horn, and one being "powerful," i.e., "loud," is thus self-evident. Nevertheless, its translations, ancient and modern, were handled with little or no care at all. It was considered mostly a synonym for *shofar* and, consequently the translators almost constantly confound both instruments.

It is surprising that the difference between the varieties of horns is not sufficiently understood, since the rabbinical literature contains both direct and indirect references to their true nature. From the numerous references to both instruments, I mention only one, which gives an unmistakable proof of their difference:

All *shofarot* are called both *shofar* and *keren,* whereas neat horns are called *keren* but are not called *shofar*.[121]

A passage of the Mishnah states that there existed certain types of horns, put together from several pieces. These pieces could be of either horn or metal, so that the same instrument could have parts of both materials. The importance of this statement will be clear in the following chapter.

As did the *shofar,* the *keren* served as a signal instrument; it was made exclusively of neat horn and apparently had no metal parts. Because the Biblical text never connects the word *keren* with the sacred service, it may be safely assumed that it was exclusively a secular instrument.

Since the word *keren* is generally considered to be synonymous with *shofar,* the English (and other) versions do not make any distinction between the two and translate indiscriminately "trumpe," "trumpet," "clarioun," "horn," "cornet," "ram's horn," and "bugle," all of them erroneous.

22. Yobel. The term *yobel,* alone and with *shanat,* as "*Shanat ha-yobel*", appears in Lev. 25:9–54 for the first time in the Bible. There, it signifies the termination of forty-nine years, that is of seven Sabbatical years. The fiftieth year was called *Shanat ha-yobel,* the Year of the Jubilee (or the *yobel*), the holy year, in which all inhabitants of the country had to be freed and all property restored to the original owner.

On the first day of the seventh month, the Year of the Jubilee was ushered in with blasts of horns in the whole country.

LUTHER calls *Shanat ha-yobel* appropriately "*Halljahr,*" the "Year of Sounding." The translation of the *Vulgate, annus jubilei,* or *jubilus,* is responsible for the generally accepted term of Jubilee, which is merely phonetically associated with the Hebrew *yobel,* implying the meaning of "Jubilee" as a festive occasion, which originally was lacking in the Hebrew term.[122]

It is generally assumed that the *shofar* that would announce the Year of the Jubilee was the ordinary instrument used for other solemn occasions. This belief, however, is erroneous, as is obvious from the specific name of the instrument, *shofar teru(ah*, a word combination not found elsewhere in the Biblical text. The coupling of *shofar* with *teru(ah* must therefore have had a particular reason.

The word *teru(ah* in itself means "alarm" (Jer. 4:19; Zeph. 1:16). Therefore, it would be quite appropriate to render *shofar teru(ah* in Lev. 25:9 as "horn of alarm." This instrument has been correctly defined by some commentators to be a "horn with the big blast," that is, an instrument with a far greater sound volume than produced by ordinary *shofarot*, apparently a specific type of horn.[123]

And indeed, the siege of Jericho and the magic action used at this occurrence, testify to the fact that the horns used there belonged to a specific type. The proof of it may be found in the text of Joshua 6.

It is striking that in verses 4, 5, 6, 8, and 13, in which the horn is mentioned repeatedly, the name of the instrument, be it *shofar* or *keren*, always appears, first, together with *yobel*, and later alone. This is by no means fortuitous, but rather a clear indication that the Biblical chronicler, using the epithet *yobel* five times, wanted to stress again and again the fact that a specific type of horn, supposedly much louder than the ordinary *shofar* or *keren* was meant. Such an intensely powerful instrument, however, was bound to have a larger shape.

That this is not a mere surmise becomes evident from a Mishnaic statement, in which such a larger type of horn is explicitly mentioned.[124] The solution of the enigma resides in the wide resounding bell of metal, referred to in this Mishnaic passage. For this part of the horn could be put on and taken off and, functioning like a megaphone, not only increased considerably the sound of the instrument, but imparted to it the hollow, gruesome, tone quality, thus investing the magic occurrence at Jericho with its specific flavor.

The dramatic description of Moses' ascension of Mount Sinai (Exod. 19:13, 16,19) contains a further indication that such a larger horn with a resounding bell might have been meant which, together with lightning and thunder, would create the mystic tonal background for God's revelation.

It is important to clarify the obvious difference between the meaning of the three varieties of horns mentioned in the Scriptures. Inasmuch as the word *shofar* has been widely adopted in the English language, it would be most practical to use it phonetically in all the passages where it stands in the Hebrew text, or to render it uniformly as "ram's horn." The equivalent of *keren* ought to be "horn," or more precisely "neat's horn." The adequate translation of *yobel* would be "horn of the Jubilee," or "high-sounding horn." This rendition would refer to the special occasion on which this instrument was blown and also indicate unequivocally its difference from the other species of horn.

(c) Percussion, Shaking and Rattling Instruments

The linguistic form for the names of this category of instruments is predominantly onomatopoeic, not merely in Ancient Israel, but in practically the entire Oriental Antiquity and, in part, among the Greeks and Romans. Quite a number of words formed in Antiquity have been adopted by the

Western world and even today can be traced in almost all European languages.

23. *Tof.* Tof (pl. *tuppim*), is a collective term for all kinds of hand-drums of the ancient Hebrews. The word is evidently of Assyrian origin (*tuppu*); the precursors of the Assyrians, the Sumerians, also called the hand-drum *dup* or *tup*, and one species of it *adapa.*[125] In the Arabian, too, the hand-drum is called *duff.*

Since the Scriptures do not contain any indications as to the form of the instrument, we have to rely on analogies with similar instruments of other ancient Oriental peoples and on the pictorial reproductions provided by Egyptian and Assyrian antiquities.

Percussion instruments constitute one of the most characteristic features of ancient Oriental music, both sacred and secular.

> Some tablets of clay engraved with cuneiform writing . . . give information of drums, on their outstanding role and importance—indeed, on the ritual veneration that they were granted.[126]

The Egyptians and Assyrians had many varieties of drum, such as the small circular hand-drum, the square-shaped species with lightly arched bays on the four sides, also the long cylindrical form that hung on ribbons from the necks of the performers and was played either with both palms or with two slightly curved sticks (Illus. 24 and 59).

If we apply the forms reproduced in Oriental antiquities to the Jewish usage, we may assume that the *tof* consisted of a wooden or metal hoop covered with animal skin on one or both sides, and that it was played either with the fingers or with the clenched fist. In Israel it was played mostly by girls and women, though there are some Biblical indications that men, too, might have played the instrument occasionally (1 Sam. 10:5; 2 Sam. 6:5; 1 Chron. 13:8).

Dancing was an important element at many performances of Jewish music. The joy and merriment of individual and community were usually released in rhythmical motions of the participants, and the leadership in the orderly dancing routine was entrusted to girls and women as a rule. The rhythmical background to dances was furnished by hand-drums, and this explains why in Ancient Israel the instrument was played mostly by girls and women.

Early in the history of the Jews the *tof* was used in religious ceremonies. At the primitive stage of the Jewish religion we witness dancing as one of the three elements (along with singing and playing) that served to glorify God. As in Egypt, the ritual dance was performed exclusively by women who, of course, accompanied themselves with *tuppim.* Later, priestly purificators of the Biblical text have tried to eliminate anything that could remind one of this primitive ritual. This zealous expurgation went hand-in-hand with the elimination of women dancers from ritual ceremonies.

The word in the meaning of hand-drum appears fifteen times in the Bible. In another place where it is used, it has no musical connotation (Ezek. 28:13).[127]

In his treatise *Shilṭe ha-Gibborim,* PORTALEONE gives shorter and longer descriptions of the Jewish instruments mentioned in the Bible.[128] These descriptions, apart from being manifestly influenced by the musical practice of his own time, are full of glaring mistakes, as, for instance, when he calls the *shofar* "a kind of flute," the *magrephah* a "clapper," or when he identifies the *mashriḳuta* (*sic*) with a "reed flute." Actually startling, however, is his description of the hand-drum, the use of which in Ancient Israel he completely misunderstood. PORTALEONE, who certainly was thoroughly familiar with the Scriptures, completely missed the relationship between the *tof* and the dance in ancient Israel. At least, his treatise does not contain anything referring to it.

24. *Meẓiltayim, Ẓelẓelim.* The only percussion instruments admitted in the sacred service were bronze cymbals, which—owing to their duality—were named in the plural form as *meẓiltayim* or *ẓelẓelim.* Both words originate from the verb *ẓalal,* "to resound," "to tingle,"[129] and are manifestly onomatopoeic constructions.

The fact that in numerous Assyrian bas-reliefs cymbals are depicted gave rise to the opinion that these instruments originated in Assyria. But practically all peoples of early Antiquity knew cymbals made of metal. The instruments on Assyrian pictures show two different forms: the flat, saucer-like shape, held upright and played by striking them sideways, and the bulging, bell-like shape with long handles, played vertically (Illus. 34 and 58). The Jewish *ẓelẓelim* might have been similar; according to JOSEPHUS, they were large bronze plates played with both hands.[130] This corroborates the Biblical statement that the cymbals of the Temple were made of brass "to sound aloud" (1 Chron. 15:19).

Psalm 150, itemizing all the instruments used in the sacred service, mentions two different kinds of cymbals, the *ẓilẓele shem'ā,* and the *ẓilẓele teru'ah.* Their difference might have been in their size, perhaps also in their material. The *ẓilẓele shem'ā* may have been the smaller brass instruments, having a brighter sound and played by vertical motion. The *ẓilẓele teru'ah* were probably the larger instruments, made of bronze (a heavier metal), held in an upright position when played, their sound being more penetrating.

In the New Testament the Apostle PAUL distinguishes between *chalkos ēchōn,* "sounding brass," and *kymbalon alalazon,* "tinkling cymbal" (1 Corinth. 13:1). The first term is usually interpreted as "a brazen instrument, a trumpet," whereas the second seems to imply the Greek cymbals of those days. It is more probable, however, that the Apostle's metaphor refers to the Jewish cymbals and that his opposition of the two terms is an intentional parallel, if not a direct quotation, of the two kinds of Jewish cymbals.

In David's musical organization the three precentors Asaph, Heman, and Jedithun-Ethan, each heading a group of singers, had the privilege of beating the cymbals as a signal for beginning the singing. Many Biblical commentators interpreted this as "leading," i.e., "conducting" the Levitical singing by beating the cymbals. In other words, according to this interpretation,

the cymbals apparently served the purpose of a baton in the hand of a modern orchestra leader marking the rhythm with their sharp penetrating tone and so holding together the whole.[131]

This, however, represents a complete misunderstanding of the nature of Oriental music.

To be sure, the music practice of the Occident furnishes many examples for the loud marking of the musical beats, such as hitting the floor with a thick staff, beating the measure with a music scroll or with the violin bow, and so on. Nevertheless, it is erroneous to assume that beating the cymbals might have served the same purpose. Jewish, and in general Oriental, song was not strictly metrical like our Western music; the musical phrase and the melodic structure were not governed by ironclad measures or groups of measures (a system unknown to Orientals), therefore the marking of "beats," as we understand it, could not be applied in the music of the Temple. In Jewish rites, as in those of the ancient Orient in general, the clashing of cymbals originally aimed at drawing the attention of the deity to the worshippers. Only in later Jewish ceremonies was this aim combined with the signal for starting the choir-singing.

The Israelites did not seem to know how to prepare the proper alloy for cymbals. When once the cymbals of the Temple were damaged, artisans from Alexandria had to be called to repair them. The repair work obviously changed the sound of the cymbals, because

> its sound was not pleasant any more. Thereupon they removed the improvement and its sound became as pleasant as it was before.[132]

Other Temple instruments, too, after they were repaired, had to be restored to their original condition, since their sound qualities had been impaired.

In the chapter "Temple Music on New Moon" of his *Shilte ha-Gibborim*, PORTALEONE ventures to reconstruct minutely the musical procedure the way he imagined it to have taken place on that occasion. In his lengthy elaboration of this ceremony, PORTALEONE mingles indiscriminately fancy and reality, absurdity and truth. The manner of explaining the blowing of ancient Jewish trumpets is just as abstruse as his assertion of attributing to castanets (i.e., cymbals) the faculty of "carrying over the tone" to singers from one group to the other.

In the enumeration of the various functionaries of the Second Temple, Ben Arza's name is specifically mentioned, indicating that "he was over the cymbal."[133] This is repeated in another Mishnaic passage,[134] a sign that in the Second Temple, too, striking the cymbals was considered such an important ritual function that the rabbinical scribes even perpetuated the name of the player.

Zelzelim are mentioned three times in the Old Testament. The other term, *meziltayim* occurs thirteen times in the Bible. Although the cymbals were mainly ritual instruments, their use outside the Temple on semi-religious, or secular, occasions is attested several times in the Bible and once in the Talmud.

25. *Shalishim.* This word appears only once in the Bible (1 Sam. 18:6). At the reception of King Saul and David, after their victorious campaign against the Philistines,

> the women came out of all the cities of Israel, singing and dancing, to meet King Saul, with timbrels (*betuppim*), with joy and with three-stringed instruments (*beshalishim*).

It has long been accepted that the word is somehow connected with the Hebrew *shalosh*, "three," or *shlosha*, "three times." Yet, how this concept should be associated with a musical instrument is still a matter of vague speculation. In fact, this very vagueness challenges in no small measure the validity of the concept itself.

Biblical commentators base their interpretations on the number "three," but otherwise their opinions are widely divided. They oscillate between castanets, a triangle, cymbals, a small triangular harp, the *trigōnon* of the Greeks, and a long-necked lute or guitar with three strings.[135]

SACHS has his own hypothesis concerning *shalishim*. He thinks that the word does not refer to a musical instrument, but possibly

> to some form of a dance, as dance names composed with "three" are not unusual, such as the Roman *tripudium* of the priests of Mars, the old German *Treialtrei* and the Austrian *Dreysteyrer*.[136]

WEISS, however, offers a solution that does justice to the etymology of the word (*shalosh*=three), and at the same time sustains an idea of a *sistrum*, as interpreted by other expounders.[137] He interprets *shalishim* as a *sistrum* with three rods, or a rod with three rings. Since SACHS likewise points out several kinds of *sistra*,[138] among them some with three rods, WEISS's assumption seems to be plausible.

Some Biblical commentators doubt that the word *shalishim* has really been derived from *shalosh*.[139] The chances are, in fact, that the assonance between the two words is of purely fortuitous nature, though instruments with names of double derivation are not uncommon in the Hebrew language. A bit of evidence in the matter of defining the instrument in question is furnished by its very name, strongly imitative of its sound. This being so, it would seem more reasonable to assume that, owing to its onomatopoeic characteristics, the word *shalishim* refers to a shaking or rattling instrument. Such point of view would naturally give a definite credence to the interpretation of WEISS, in preference to all others.

26. *Mena'an'im*. This word appears in the Biblical text only in 2 Sam. 6:5. It originates from the verb *nu'a*, "to shake," "to move about," and it signifies a shaking instrument, like the Egyptian *sistrum*, though it may not be so richly adorned. It consisted of a metal frame, in which rods were inserted, carrying loose rings. The frame had a handle, which was held while shaking the instrument, thereby creating a tinkling sound (Illus. 9 and 36).

Some years ago *sistra* were excavated from Sumerian tombs; consequently the instrument must have been known to the Babylonians and Assyrians as well. The Israelites might have taken it over from Egypt or Babylonia.

The *Septuagint* mistranslates *mena'an'im* as *kymbala* (cymbals), whereas the translation of the *Vulgate*, *sistra*, gives the correct meaning of the word. With occasional deviations, all the other translations, ancient and modern, follow this meaning.

27. *Pa'amonim*. The word *pa'amonim*, derived from the verb *pa'am*, "to strike," signifies the little bells attached to the lower seam of the High priest's purple garment, in order that

> the sound thereof shall be heard when he goeth in unto the holy place before the Lord, and when he cometh out, that he die not (Exod.28:33–35; 39:25, 26).

The bells were made of gold and they had a bright, yet unobtrusive sound, just loud enough to indicate the whereabouts of the High priest, but not to interfere with the sacred ceremony itself.

The Biblical indication "that he die not" is, like some other elements of the

Jewish ritual, a remnant from pristine times, when superstition and magic were closely linked with the crude religion of the Hebrews.

SACHS interprets it as a remnant of primitive magic:

> Here, as everywhere, the bell is used as a defense against evil spirits. The demons like to frequent sanctuaries and thresholds. Therefore, the High priest does not have to be protected when he is *in* the holy place, but when he *goeth in* and *cometh out*.[139]

My interpretation differs from that of SACHS and is based upon the Jewish religious law, emphatically debarring any human from seeing God. Whoever ventures to do so must die (Exod. 19:21). Even direct listening to God's voice brings immediate death to a common mortal (Deut. 18:16). Only someone exceptional, like Moses, was privileged to communicate eye to eye with the Creator. Any other human being, even one in such exalted position as that of the High Priest, was strictly subject to this law. However, during his ministration, the High Priest had once a year to enter the Holy of Holies, God's own dwelling. Thus, he might have chanced inadvertently upon the sight of God, on these occasions; but this would have instantaneously cause his death, as actually happened to the men of Beth-shemesh, who were smitten by God, "because they had gazed upon the ark of the Lord," i.e., they had made an attempt to look inside the ark (1 Sam. 6:19). The bells on the High priest's garment had primitively the purpose of forewarning the deity, supposed to be present in some form in its earthly dwelling, so that no entering human being could see it.

PHILO refers to another device designed to avoid the unexpected possibility of seeing God in the sanctuary:

> All inside is unseen except by the High priest alone, and indeed he, though charged with the duty of entering once a year, gets no view of anything. For he takes with him a brazier full of lighted coals and incense, and the great quantity of vapour which this naturally gives forth covers everything around it, beclouds the eyesight and prevents it from being able to penetrate to any distance.[140]

In the later development of the Jewish ritual, the primitive aim of the bells had evidently disappeared, and they were regarded as merely ornament on the High priest's attire. It is manifest, however, that they did not originate from an aesthetic need, but from a superstitious belief.

The Hellenistic age, with its philosophy so different from that of the Bible, attributes a transcendent meaning to the purpose of the *pa'amonim*, as well as to other liturgical customs:

> The bells represent the harmonious alliance of these two [the earth and water], since life cannot be produced by earth without water or by water without the substance of earth, but only by the union and combination of both.[141]

Yet, this statement of PHILO does not reveal how these two elements of the Greek conception of nature, earth and water, are causally connected with the Biblical *pa'amonim*.

28. *Mezillot. Mezillot* is mentioned in Zech. 14:20 and is rendered generally as "bells," which were hung upon horses. It is derived from the same root as *meziltayim* and *zelzelim* and, like these two terms, is of an onomatopoeic nature. Similarly to all noise-making instruments of pristine ages, these bells had the

purpose of keeping away evil spirits and demons from their bearers, in this case from useful domestic animals.

Contrary to the dainty *pa'amonim* on the High priest's garment, the Jewish *mezillot* must have been larger and more compact, since they were supposed to carry an inscription according to the Biblical text:

In that day shall there be upon the bells of the horses: HOLY UNTO THE LORD.

It is indeed difficult to imagine how an inscription could have been put upon little round bells. Judging from the entire chapter 14 of Zechariah, the allusion of the prophet must have had only a symbolic meaning.

However, according to WEISS, the inscription upon the *mezillot* should be interpreted literally. As he thinks, *mezillot* were not bells but small plates, akin to the one on the High priest's tiara. These might have very well carried the inscription *kodesh le-YHVH*.[142] We possess ancient pictorial reproductions showing harnesses of horses adorned not only with bells, but also with buckles, which look like small cymbals. It was surely much easier to put an inscription of this length on such plates, or buckles, than on bells.

The *pa'amonim* and *mezillot* were not musical instruments in the proper sense of the word. They did not serve musical or artistic aims; their purpose was to exert by their sound an extra-musical, in this instance, magical effect. In the primitive stages of music, the borderline between noise and music is often hazy. Especially when musical elements are introduced into the cult, it is sometimes difficult to establish where noise ends and music commences.

Originally, *pa'amonim* as well as *mezillot* had some music-like functions in the service of magic; therefore, in this primitive stage, they represent musical instruments to a certain extent. Consequently, they are generally classified as belonging to the instruments of the ancient Israelites.

INSTRUMENTS MENTIONED IN POST-BIBLICAL LITERATURE

In addition to the instruments mentioned in the Biblical books, quite a number of instruments appear in the rabbinical writings. But only in isolated instances do the Sages give information about the nature of these instruments. Sometimes these are identified with Biblical instruments. In other instances it is possible to grasp their character by comparing them with ancient Jewish instruments of the same, or similar categories. For the most part, however, the descriptions of the rabbis are not factual but frequently misleading, so that it is rarely possible to draw any conclusions as to their true nature.

To be sure, the rabbinical scribes were not supposed to possess a thorough knowledge of music in general, or of instruments in particular. Yet, in view of the care and precision, even pedantry, frequently observed by them in describing the minutest items of the daily life, this sheer ignorance in musical matters, and especially with regard to musical instruments, is simply astounding.

This being so, the rabbinical indications about music and musical instruments can be used only with extreme caution. A highly critical approach to them will therefore be the guiding principle in the following scrutiny. Even so, it is sometimes difficult, if not impossible, to determine with reasonable probability the nature of instruments mentioned in the Mishnah, the Talmud, and other rabbinical writings.

To what extent the Hebrews in the first centuries after the destruction of their national existence still used the instruments of Biblical times cannot be ascertained. One may assume that a considerable number of these instruments could have been preserved. But in the troubled times, music teaching and music practice in general slowly fell into desuetude, which brought about their unavoidable neglect, leading to the gradual deterioration, and eventually to the abandonment of Biblical instruments.

The rabbinical prohibition of music-making after the national tragedy— though not abolishing entirely the practice of music, especially singing— certainly discouraged the making of new instruments, and the surviving Biblical *kinnorot, nebalim,* as well as the *halilim* and the other delicate species of stringed and woodwind instruments were condemned to a slow but inexorable death.

However, in the course of the centuries the never-ceasing need of the Jewish people for music and, by implication, for musical instruments, created new types and new species. Jewish musicians either modeled them after the Biblical prototypes, or improved and developed them into new variants, or, finally, imported from the surrounding nations entirely different instruments. How they acquired the new arsenal of musical instruments is not divulged by the rabbinical writers. We learn only the names of the instruments, and sometimes are given scant information about their external characteristics. For the rest, we must rely upon analogies and deductions in order to compare them with similar instruments of those nations among whom the Jews lived.

(a) Stringed Instruments

29. *Pandura.* According to talmudic statements, the *pandura* had a double function in the life of the shepherds: first, to alleviate the monotony of the profession, and second, to rally the flocks by musical sounds. It might have been a three-stringed lute, having a small body and a long neck, as we see it depicted in Assyrian, but mainly in Egyptian antiquities. The word seems to have been derived from the Sumerian *pan-tur,* meaning "bow-small," or "small bow." Since such an instrument does not resemble a bow, its Sumerian origin is doubtful.

It is more probable that it originated in Western Asia, where a stringed instrument named *fandur* or *fandir* had been used. It had three or four strings that were played with the fingers or with a plectrum.

The Talmud does not furnish any explanation why Jewish shepherds did not use any of the ancient Hebrew stringed instruments for their pastime, such as the *kinnor, nebel,* or *'asor.* The reasons appear obvious: Biblical instruments might have fallen into obsolescence after the national disaster; they were not made any more, and the surviving ones may have deteriorated to a point where they were no longer usable. Furthermore, the *pandura,* with its smaller size and reduced number of strings, was more convenient to carry and easier to learn, while the *kinnor* and *nebel,* with more strings, required greater skill in playing and maintenance, evidently beyond the ability of simple shepherds. Therefore, despite the *pandura's* reduced sonority in the open air, the talmudic report about it as the favorite instrument of shepherds has a definite credibility.

30. Ḥinga. The *ḥinga* is mentioned in a fantastic tale of the Talmud, which narrates a fight between mortals and demons.[143] To exorcise these demons (60 of them), a *ḥinga* was suspended on a tree, to the accompaniment of which some magic formulae were sung to chase away the demons. Thus, the word *ḥinga* is here used in the meaning of a musical instrument, but of what particular kind can only be surmised.

The term, however, has two other meanings:[144] 1) A circle, dancing, chorus, feast, and 2) the dancing place in the vineyards. Since none of these meanings can be applied to the talmudic story, we have to assume that the word *ḥinga* in this case indeed signifies a musical instrument.

This conjecture is corroborated by the fact that Targum Onkelos to Gen. 31:27 renders *kinnor* as *ḥinga*. Some confusion is created, however, by other Targumim, which translate *ḥinga* as the Biblical *ḥalil*, or the Biblical *meḥolot*, "dances."

It is well known how arbitrarily the Targumim handled the names of music instruments. In this case, however, where the fight of humans with demons is described, there appears little doubt that—notwithstanding the other meanings —the term denotes some kind of a stringed instrument, perhaps a lute or possibly the *baton*.

31. Baton (Baṭnon). The term *baton* (or *baṭnon*), mentioned in the Mishnah,[145] may be derived from the Hebrew noun *beṭen*, meaning "belly," or an "empty" or "hollow" object. It is probable, therefore that *baton* refers either to the bulging form of the instrument, or to the indication that it had to be played at waist level, in contrast to other stringed instruments, which were held in front of the breast.

Our only knowledge about this instrument stems from a late commentator of the Mishnah, OBADIAH of BERTINORO (fifteenth century), who declares that the *baton* was a large guitar (which he calls *zithra* in his commentary), hung over the player's body or carried in front of it.

Neither the Egyptians nor the Assyrians had zithers or zither-like instruments. Israel's neighbors, the Phoenicians, however, knew such a type. Two of them are depicted on a carved ivory pyxis of the eighth century B.C.E. On this relief the backs of the zithers cannot be seen, so it is not possible to verify whether they are flat or bulging.[146]

Whether such an instrument was used by the ancient Hebrews cannot be ascertained; there is no mention of it in the Bible, the Apocrypha, or in the early rabbinical literature. It is also doubtful whether the Mishnaic reference means a zither or a somewhat similar instrument. According to the etymology of the word, it more probably denotes a belly-shaped guitar or lute.

In modern Hebrew, *baṭnon* is the name of a very large *kinnor*, with a heavy sound, consequently a double-bass.

32. ʾAdrabolin (ʾArdabalis or ʾArdablis). Much confusion remains about two Aramaic names of instruments mentioned in the Midrash. As a commentary to Gen. 4:21, the Midrash interprets the Biblical *kinnor* as *ʾadrabolin*, "organ-players," and the *ʿugab* as *barbolin* (spelled also *korablin*, or *karkalin*) "flautists" (the English rendition belongs to the translator of the Soncino Press). In another passage of the Midrash both words are mentioned together, but in a completely different meaning.[147] Here, *ʾadrabolin* is again translated as "organs" (or "organ-players"), but *korablin* as "cymbals." Neither "organs" nor "organ-players" is the correct translation for the Biblical *kinnor*, just as "cymbals" cannot be considered as the exact rendering of the instrument named *korablin.* This latter term is obviously the Aramaic adaptation (or corruption) of the Greek *choraulēs*, "flute-player"; the English interpretation would at least render justice to the original meaning of the word, as well as of the Biblical *ʿugab.*

But how about *ʾadrabolin* which, in the Aramaic text, stands for *kinnor?* In the rabbinical writings *ʾadrabolin* has many other spellings, such as *ʾardabalis, ʾadrikolin,* and *hardulis.* This last variant, in particular, strongly suggests that it was the Aramaic corruption of the Greek *hydraulis,* the water-organ.

The existing confusion is further aggravated by RASHI's commentary to Midrash, Genesis 50:9, in which he defines both words as *mine zemer,* "instruments for the song." If it could be assumed that the *korablin,* the *ʿugab,* might have been used on certain occasions as accompanying the song, the same cannot be valid for the *hydraulis,* a rather clumsy and loud instrument at that epoch.

A further controversy with regard to the interpretation of both names of instruments was even increased by the statement of one of the early Amoraim, R. SIMEON ben LAKISH (d. 275 C.E.), who declared that "the *ʿugab* was the *ʾirdablis* (or *ʾidrablis*)," meaning, of course, the *hydraulis.*[148] It was repeatedly pointed out that the statements of the rabbinical writers about instruments have to be taken with utmost caution. Yet, SIMEON ben LAKISH was certainly qualified to know the *hydraulis* better. For in his early youth he used to be a gladiator in the Roman circus, where he must have had the opportunity of seeing and hearing the *hydraulis,* a characteristic musical instrument at such popular shows of those days.[149] The fact that he confounds the *ʿugab,* a small and delicate instrument, with the voluminous and noisy *hydraulis,* is not only an obvious error, but a further proof that relatively soon after the destruction of the sanctuary the knowledge of Biblical instruments has been lost or was completely eclipsed by the different musical practice of the talmudic age.

In contradistinction to the erroneous interpretation of R. SIMEON ben LAKISH, the logical meaning of the two instruments, *ʾadrabolin* and *korablin,* corresponding to the Biblical text of Gen. 4:21, comes clearly to the fore. In the Midrashic concept, *ʾadrabolin* referred to some stringed instrument, or to a generic term for such, while *korablin* signified the pipe, or a pipe-player, or was also a collective term for woodwinds, as will be shown later.

As for the other Midrashic passage where the two terms appear together, the only explanation that presents itself is that this comment had been written by a different scribe, who seems to have been ignorant of how his predecessor interpreted in Aramaic the two instruments in Gen. 4:21. For the latter passage (on Gen. 19:14) we must therefore accept *ʾadrabolin* at its face value, as referring to the *hydraulis* of the talmudic age.

(b) Wind Instruments.

33. *ʾAbub.* The term *ʾabub* (pl. *ʾabubim*) is used by rabbinical writers as a synonym of *halil* and *ʿugab.* According to R. PAPPA, the three words designate the same instrument, the pipe, (or oboe).[150] *ʾAbub* is related to the name of the Akkadian (Semitic) *ʾimbubu,* an instrument of the pipe family brought to

Syria, where eventually it became one of the domestic instruments. From there, the Israelites might have taken it over.

A rabbinical legend states that

> there was an *'abub* in the sanctuary, which was smooth [i.e., it had a pleasant sound], made of reed and dated from the time of Moses. At the king's command it was overlaid with gold, but its sound was no longer sweet. They removed the overlay and its sound became sweet as it was before.[151]

If there really was among the instruments of the cult one dating back to Moses' times, the Biblical chroniclers would hardly have failed to mention this venerable item. It is clearly one of those legendary tales so frequently encountered in the talmudic literature.

The Mishnah states that there were *'abubim* entirely of metal, differing in their sonority from those of reed by their stronger sound.[152] In his commentary to this passage, MAIMONIDES says that the *'abub* was a pipe of reed with a mouthpiece of metal or reed. It is difficult to figure out how a reed instrument could have had a mouthpiece of metal.

In the later period of the Second Temple the soft *'ugab* might have been permanently supplanted by the more vigorous sound of the Syrian *'abub*.

Of widespread notoriety in Antiquity were the Syrian *'abub*-playing girls, who were renowned not so much for their artistry as for their immoral life. Roman poets refer to them as *ambubajae*, flute-girls, who lived in the basement of the Roman circus which, accordingly, was surnamed *ambubajarum collegia*. Here, their pipe-playing was used merely as a pretense for their ignoble trade. It is highly probable that such Syrian flute-girls had found their way to Israel as well. It is understandable, therefore, that the anathema of the rabbinical Sages against immoral life in general applied also against the musical instruments themselves, implements of this kind of life.

34. Magrephah. No instrument supposedly known to the Israelites has created so many contradictory reports, opinions, and hypotheses as the *magrephah*. The various statements and descriptions of it in rabbinical writings are so fragmentary and confusing that it is nearly impossible to gain a clear idea about this instrument from them.

It is not even evident that the *magrephah* existed as a musical instrument in the Temple. Some Sages are affirmative, others deny this explicitly. Furthermore, the terminology of the rabbinical writers varies greatly about the character, shape, and size of the *magrephah*. Some identify it as the Greek *hydraulis,* the water-organ; others hold that it was quite a different instrument, or implement, of the Temple. None of the rabbinical Sages who discuss in the Talmud the existence or nonexistence of such an instrument in the Temple lived in the time when the sanctuary still stood; consequently, their testimony is based not on their own observations but on hearsay.

Some of the rabbinical statements and descriptions of the instrument would conform with the assumption that the *magrephah* and the *hydraulis* were one and the same instrument. Others are contradictory. They invoke liturgical and musical arguments against the assumption that held that such a clumsy and loud instrument was used in the Temple. This, as the rabbinical opinions go, would certainly have "interfered unfavorably with the sweetness of the singing."[153]

It is striking that neither the Apocrypha, nor the writings of Josephus and Philo, or their contemporaries, contain the slightest allusion to such an instrument. It would seem that the implements of the sacred service, and especially its musical part, should have been well known to at least the two Jewish historians, both of whom lived during the last decades of the Third (Herod's) Temple. Their complete silence on this point is all the more significant since we learn from the Talmud that the sound of the instrument was extremely powerful, and this could have hardly remained unnoticed by the Jewish writers.

A further complication arises from the fact that in two different tractates of the rabbinical literature, the word *magrephah* refers to completely different objects. Apart from its meaning as a musical instrument, the Talmud says that it was a shovel made of brass that was used for removing the ashes and cinders from the altar. Rashi suggests that

there are possibly two sorts of *magrephot*, one for the ashes and one for music.[154]

Furthermore, he has a third explanation of the term, identifying the *magrephah* with "a set of bells."

According to a rabbinical description, the *magrephah* had "ten holes, and every hole emitted ten different sounds."[155] The Palestinian Talmud contains a *verbatim* discussion about the *magrephah* by two learned rabbis, Rab and Samuel, one of whom said that the instrument had ten holes, each producing one hundred different sounds, the other that it had one hundred holes, each emitting ten sounds, amounting in both cases to one thousand different sounds.[156] A famous rabbi, Nahman bar Isaac, felt induced to utter a warning that this was an obvious exaggeration. It is commonly known that the rabbinical writers, in retrospect, frequently attributed grandiose and exalted qualities to the institutions of the Temple. This might have been such a case.

The Talmud says that the *magrephah* was cast or thrown (to the floor?), thereby producing a sound that was so loud that, according to one rabbinical statement,

no one could hear the voice of his neighbor in Jerusalem because of the sound of the *magrephah*,

and it was added in the same passage that

from Jericho they could hear the sound of the *magrephah*.[157]

Here are two irreconcilable statements. Should the *magrephah* have been a musical instrument, it would have been unthinkable to throw or cast it without inflicting serious damage to its many delicate parts. If, on the other hand, it was a shovel to clean the altar from the slags, it could not have produced a sound so powerful as is claimed in the Mishnah.

There is one point on which the rabbinical descriptions concur, namely, that the instrument (or whatever it might have been) had a handle. This was probably the main reason why the *magrephah* has been identified with a shovel.

Modern commentators are inclined to interpret the *magrephah* as a kind of signal instrument, a drum, a gong, a tympanum, or something similar. Among the contemporary explanations, that of Joseph Yasser deserves particular consideration.[158] According to his theory, the *magrephah* was a pipe-work, not an organ of any kind serving musical purposes, but a noise-making signal instrument, consisting of a great number of small shrill pipes, activated pneumatically and sounding simultaneously. YASSER thinks that the "throwing" or "casting" of the instrument might have involved the back-and-forth swinging of the handle that pumped the air for the pipes and which, incidentally, may conceivably have been shaped like a shovel (Illus. 88).

From such a mass of contradictory statements it is difficult to pick a kernel of historical truth or even a remote probability. Nevertheless, a few facts emerge as explanations for the radically divided opinions of the rabbis about the *magrephah*.

Manifestly, Hellenistic Jewry must have known the Greek *hydraulis*, the water-organ, or its equivalent, the primitive pneumatic organ. If we follow YASSER's theory, the *magrephah*, having been a sheer noise-making contrivance, might have been more acceptable to the Temple authorities than an instrument for the accompaniment of song. Furthermore, nothing opposes the assumption that the *magrephah*, in the meaning of a shovel, was one of the cleaning implements in the Temple service.

This assumption is apt to be reconciled with the rabbinical statement that there never existed a *magrephah*, i.e., a Greek water-organ, in the sanctuary. As for its powerful sound, this may be one of the frequent exaggerations of rabbinical scribes, which is even shattered by the Mishnaic text itself.

As for the use of the *hydraulis* by the Jews outside the sanctuary, there are reasons to believe that this may have occurred at secular occasions. There are a few references in the Midrashim to the effect that players of water-organ (*ʾadrablin-hydraulis*) had been employed at festivities.[159] To be sure, the Midrash does not make clear whether such itinerant organ-players were Jewish or non Jewish. But probably the latter was the case, since it is known that Gentile musicians were frequently employed at Jewish weddings, especially on the Sabbath, when playing of instruments was forbidden to the Jews.

35. *Barbolin (Korablin, Korbalin, or Karkalin).* As shown above, two Midrashic passages mention *barbolin* (or its numerous variants) together with *ʾadrabolin*.[160] Their juxtaposition suggests that these two terms imply two different types of instruments.

The etymology of the word is obvious. In one of these passages (Gen. 50:9) *barbolin* appears merely as a corruption of the word *korablin*, which can easily be identified with the Greek *choraulēs* (or *chorablēs*), the term for "flute-player." In a further metamorphosis, *korablin* might have changed to *sorbalin*, *borbalin*, and was eventually incorporated as *barbolin* into the Aramaean language.

Another, even simpler, explanation as to how *korablin* might have mutated into *barbolin* is that by an understandable inaccuracy of a rabbinical scribe the initial letter *kaf* may have been taken for a *bet*, so that the word *korablin* could easily be read as *barbolin*.

For the Midrashic passage

there are organs and cymbals (*ʾadrabolin u-barbolin*) in the land . . . ,[161]

JASTROW suggests as a translation:

There are *hydraules*-players and flute-players in the land . . .[162]

JASTROW's suggested translation may be correct for 50:9, but does not take into consideration the meaning of the other passage (23:3), referring to Gen. 4:21, in which the juxtaposition of the two categories of Biblical instruments, *kinnor* and *ʿugab,* should be expressed also in Aramaic. It should also be recalled that in his commentary to this passage, RASHI characterized *ʾadrabolin* as well as *barbolin* (this latter word in a different spelling) as *mine zemer,* "instruments for the song,"[163] only one of them referring, by inference, to a stringed instrument. Thus, neither the extant translations of the Midrashim, nor JASTROW's suggestion, nor RASHI's commentary does justice to the unmistakable and radical difference in the meaning of the two terms.

36. *Kalameyles.* The name of a medieval instrument, *kalameyles,* serves RASHI as an explanation of the Biblical *halil.* It is evident that the two instruments, one of the Biblical epoch and the other in France of RASHI's time (1040–1105), could not have been identical. The medieval French word is derived from the Greek *kalamos,* or from its Latin equivalent *calamus* ("reed"). Both denote in Antiquity, besides the plant itself, an oboe-like instrument made of reed. RASHI's term is merely the medieval French *chalamele* (the later *chalumeau*), the instrument mentioned in the Talmud in a Hebraized form.

(c) Percussion, Shaking, and Rattling Instruments

37. *Niktimon (Nikatmon).* In several Mishnaic passages we come across the word *niktimon* which—judging from the context—seems to indicate the pegs on which the strings were fastened. Yet, several talmudic writers and commentators interpret the word as the name of a musical instrument, resembling the protruding arm of an object or a "wooden leg."[164]

In discussing the prescriptions for cleanliness, the Mishnah mentions *niktimon* repeatedly, without giving any indication about its specific characteristics. On these contradictory explanations SACHS sheds some light by his interpretation of the seemingly enigmatic word:

> If this term does mean an instrument, it might refer to those Egyptian clappers of wood or ivory which were carved to form a human arm with the hand and which were exclusively played by women; or the boot-shaped clappers of the Greeks.[165]

Cautiously SACHS adds: "But this is nothing more than a suggestion." It is probable, however, that the word refers indeed to a kind of clapper, since such an instrument is mentioned also at another place in the rabbinical literature.[166]

RASHI's commentary may be mentioned merely for the sake of curiosity. He defines *nikatmon* as a

> sort of instrument for the song (*niggun*), made in the form of a wooden foot (or an artificial leg).[167]

A stringed instrument in this shape was not known in Antiquity. A clapper, on the other hand, cannot be considered "an instrument for the song."

SACHS's interpretation comes closest to a satisfactory solution, and therefore it may be assumed with a certain probability that, if a musical instrument is meant by it, the term indicates clappers made of wood or bone.

38. *Tabla.* An instrument *tabla* is mentioned in several rabbinical writings.

About its nature and character there are only vague and largely contradictory opinions.

In the Assyrian language there is a word, *tabalu*, implying a drum. This word seems to have been taken over by the Greeks as *tabala* (or *tabla*), generally meaning "something square."[168]

In several rabbinical writings, however, *tabla* is the generic word for musical instruments.[169] RASHI's commentary to the word gives some clues as to the form and purpose of it. He explains it as a set of "wedding bells" to be shaken. The belief of the Orientals that the tinkling of bells would chase away evil spirits, makes it very probable that the use of such an instrument at weddings was based upon this superstition.

The majority of the commentators take the *tabla* for a hand-drum (possibly square-shaped), with the same functions as those of the Biblical *tof*. In later times, the instrument may have been bedecked with all sorts of ornaments, among them also little bells. This might have been the reason that the *tabla* was considered a bell or a bell-like instrument.

In a fantastic tale of the Talmud, the *tabla* was invested with the magical power of bringing the dead back to life. To confirm the "authenticity" of such an occurrence, even a rabbinical Sage such as RAB is quoted as an eye-witness. The statement reads:

> Rab said to R. Hiyya: "I myself saw an Arabian traveller take a sword and cut up a camel; then he rang (*taraf*) a bell (*tabla*), at which the camel arose.[170]

It is obvious that RAB was deceived by some trick hatched by an Oriental magician. Here, we are mainly interested in the fact that the sounding of the *tabla* was brought about by an action characterized by the word *taraf*, i.e., "to hit," which evidently refers to a percussion instrument.

The real form of the *tabla* is easily discovered once we realize the purpose of the instrument. It was doubtless played at weddings to enhance general rejoicing, which manifested itself mainly in dances. To these, *tabla* might have been the appropriate instrument of accompaniment. The little bells hung upon it might have been responsible for the opinion that *tabla* was a bell or a bell-like instrument.

39. *)Erus ()Irus)*. The word *)erus* (or *)irus*) is found in two passages of the Mishnah, indicating in both places a drum-like instrument.[171] Nevertheless, talmudic commentators give the word distinctly different meanings. RASHI says that it was "a bell with a single clapper." MAIMONIDES believes it to be a round tambourine. Several commentators have ventured the supposition that the *)erus* must have been a rather voluminous drum since, according to a rabbinical statement, the wailing women would sit on it at funerals.[172] This, however, is an obvious mistake, because the drum referred to was not the *)erus* but the *rebi(it* (see below).

We probably will come closest to the truth by assuming that the *)erus* (like the *tabla*) was a small, brightly adorned hand-drum, used at weddings for the accompaniment of the dancing and for enhancing the general rejoicing.

40. *Tanbura (Tanburi)*. The instrument *tanbura* is used in the Talmud in a connection that gave rise to all kinds of misinterpretations. As an indirect illustration of the various types of hand-drums, I quote a talmudic passage, in which a rabbinical scribe relates a supposedly authentic occurrence:

RABBAH ben R. HUNA made a drum (*ṭanbura*) for [the wedding of] his son; his father [i.e., the bridegroom's grandfather] came and broke it, saying to him "It might be substituted for a drum (*ṭabla*) with a single bell. Go, make for him [an instrument by stretching the skin] over the mouth of a pitcher or over the mouth of a *kefiẓ* [a vessel of the capacity of three log]."[173]

The meaning of this tale is somewhat difficult to unravel. It may have intended to show that the head of the family (the grandfather) faithfully observed the prohibition according to which

during the war of Vespasian they forbade the crowns of the bridegroom and the [wedding] drum (*'erus*).[174]

But, on the other hand, the rejoicing at the wedding should not be curtailed by eliminating the dancing. Thus, R. HUNA's father (R. JOSHUA) applied a sort of talmudic casuistry by stretching the skin of a drum over the mouth of a pitcher of clay or a large measuring vessel. By this, the "instrument" could not be considered a drum in the proper sense, so that the prohibition was not violated and, at the same time, an instrument for the accompaniment of the dances was not lacking either.

In the above rabbinical passage three different terms are used for a specific category of hand-drum, *'erus*, *ṭabla*, and *ṭanbura*. The last-named instrument, which was broken by R. HUNA's father, was apparently the *'erus*, even though it is called here *ṭanbura*. This opinion is also held by RASHI.[175]

41. Rebi'it. A larger type of drum was the *rebi'it*, used at funerals by the wailing women who, during the funeral oration, used to sit upon it. There is an obvious assonance between this word and two other terms of the Targumim and the Peshitta (the Syriac version of the Bible). They are *rebi'in* of the former, and *rebiy'a* of the latter. Both are renditions (in Aramaic and Syriac) of the Biblical *mena'an'im* (2 Sam. 6:5), all unanimously interpreted as *sistra*.[176]

According to MAIMONIDES, the *rebi'in* were two wooden sticks struck together rhythmically, thus representing a clapper instrument. For such sticks there is an analogy in Egypt; in a mural painting harvesters are portrayed using "concussion sticks" (Illus. 11), the striking of which had the purpose of expediting the work of the reapers by offering them uniform rhythmical support.

However, the passage of the Mishnah in which *rebi'it* is mentioned, does not agree with the idea of concussion sticks. *Sistrum* would be a more appropriate interpretation; but to the use of *sistra* at Jewish funerals there are no references in rabbinical writings.

The *rebi'it* might have been a rather large, oblong drum with a deep tone. The hollow sound quality of such a drum may have blended better with the gloomy mood of the funeral ceremony than the lively tone of the *'erus*, or the shrill rattling of the *sistrum*.

The rabbinical writers indiscriminately employ the terms *'erus*, *ṭabla*, *ṭanbura*, *rebuba*, *dekoba* (or *koba*), *rebi'it*, to which the Aramaic and Syriac *rebiy'a* (*rebi'in*), *pelaga*, and *tuppa* could be added. All these terms designate hand-drums which, in all probability, could be distinguished merely by some differences in shape, size, and construction.

42. Zog. An instrument frequently mentioned in rabbinical literature is the *zog*. It is essentially similar to the Biblical *pa'amonim*, the little golden bells on the High priest's garment, which in talmudic times served various purposes. They were widely used on doors, garments, even on the locks of the bearers, and hung on domestic animals. They were the magical means of protecting persons and animals against the harmful influence of evil spirits and demons. The *Gemara* discusses extensively the prescriptions compulsory for men, women, and children for their protection when leaving the house on the Sabbath. Since all active precautions exercised on weekdays were forbidden on the Sabbath, the hanging of bells upon oneself remained the only measure that automatically safeguarded the individual against evil influences. The same belief applied to the use of bells on doors, which was to prevent a malevolent demon from sneaking into the house with the entering person.

The *zog* of talmudic times was a metal sphere of various sizes, with several holes or slits, like our sleigh-bells. For wealthy people *zogin* were sometimes made of gold, as were their clappers also, or these were at least gold plated.[177] A rabbinic writer uses the word *zog* for children's clappers.[178] Yet, it is more probable that *zogin* meant "bells," not "clappers."

Apart from the Biblical *pa'amonim*, the talmudic term *zogin* was applied also to the *mezillot* (Zech. 14:20), which indicated the bells hung upon horses and other domestic animals.

A talmudic passage contains the peculiar statement that a bell (*zog*) with a clapper ('*anbol* or '*inbol*) is unclean; without a clapper, however, it is clean, and this despite the explicit indication that both parts belong together. It is difficult to find a reason for such a strange regulation.

The widespread use of *zogin* on doors, garments, and domestic animals as preventive means against disaster, sickness, and evil influences in general, shows how ancient heathen superstitions survived in both religious and secular customs, even far into post-Biblical times.

43. *Karkash (Kashkash)*. The Aramaic verb *karkash* means "to strike," "to knock." The substantive built from it (with the variants *kashkash*, or *kishkush*) designates an instrument the sound of which is produced by striking it. The word is obviously an onomatopoeic construction, for there are many others among the Hebrew sound-producing instruments.

In spite of its clear etymology, which refers to a clapper, only the rabbinical commentator RASHI gives a different interpretation of it.

In commenting on the talmudic saying:

At sixty as at six, the sound of a timbrel (*tabla*) makes her nimble [lit. "run" to see a wedding ceremony],[179]

he says that the *tabla* was a *kishkush ha-zog*, i.e., "wedding bells"; that it was like the tambourine.

This explanation is obviously erroneous for historical as well as for reasons inherent to the nature of the instrument itself. Historically, it constitutes an anachronism, because instruments of the tambourine type (hand-drums with small metal plates fastened to their frame) are not attested to prior to the thirteenth century.[180] As to the tone production of the instrument, there is quite a difference, depending on whether the sound is achieved by striking or shaking. Among the Biblical instruments, the *tof*, *meziltayim* and *zelzelim* were percussion instruments, the *shalishim*, *mena'an'im*, *pa'amonim* and *mezillot* shaking or rattling instruments. The inherent meaning of the word *karkash* conflicts therefore with RASHI's interpretation.

The functional meaning of the word *karkash* (as well as of its variants) is strongly onomatopoeic; the letter *k* used twice in each term points clearly to clappers, whereas the names of shaking instruments usually contain sibilants, like the Greek *seistron,* the Latin *sistrum,* and the Hebrew *shalishim* and *mezillot.*

44. *Sharkukita.* According to a talmudic indication, the lead goat had around its neck a "bell," called in Aramaic *sharkukita.*[181] With the Hebrew *mezillot* and *pa'amonim,* and with the Aramaic *zog,* we have altogether four different terms referring to the same kind of object, namely, to bells hung on the neck of domestic animals.

The word *sharkukita* is derived from the Hebrew verb *sharak,* "to hiss," "to pipe," "to whistle," which is also the original word for the instrument *mashrokita,* named four times in the Book of Daniel. The peculiar thing about these two Aramaic words, however, is that *mashrokita* indicates a wind instrument, whereas *sharkukita,* if the talmudic indication is correct, seems to refer to a shaking instrument. It is difficult to understand how both actions, the whistling of a pipe and the tinkling of a bell, could be expressed imitatively with the same sibilant sounds.

The Talmud declares that the *mashkokit* (evidently a corrupted spelling of *mashrokit*) is the same as *sharkukita,* and gives a rather vague explanation of the instrument by stating that "you hang a *zog* around the neck of a big sheep."[182] However, another explanation in the same paragraph says explicitly that it was a wind instrument:

[it is] a hollow instrument like the horn of a steer which the shepherds use to call together the animals.[183]

These contradictory statements, made almost in the same breath, render it difficult to determine which definition is the correct one.

JASTROW's explanation is also rather vague, leaving open the possibility of both talmudic versions. Disregarding the above-indicated misspelling, he says that the *mashkokita* were the

shepherds' principal implements, such as the staff, the bell, the pipe, etc.[184]

On the other hand, KRAUSS is more inclined to the belief that the *sharkukita* was a flute, "or something alike,"[185] or else, more precisely, "the Pan's pipe."[186] For this assumption there is even a vague corroboration in the Bible itself. In Judg. 5:16 we find the expression *sherikot 'adarim,* "the piping for the flock;" *sherikot* has the same Hebrew root as the Aramaic *sharkukita.*

From all this only one thing emerges as certain, namely, that *sharkukita* refers to an implement (or instrument) having had some function in the life of shepherds. But whether this was the pipe, the Pan's pipe, the horn, or bells, cannot be positively determined from the rabbinical indications. We must always be aware that the rabbinical scribes had little if any familiarity with musical matters, and thus their reports abound in inaccuracies and contradictions.

How long the instruments of talmudic times remained in use of the dispersed Jews cannot be said with certainty. The Biblical instruments must have changed under the influence of the times, being either transformed into newer variants, or abandoned as obsolete and replaced by more advanced types. Thus, the instruments used by the Hebrews in the first centuries of the Diaspora may have been superseded by better-constructed and more effective-sounding instruments of the ascending Middle Ages.

We have documentary evidence that the Jews living in Germanic countries adopted the instruments of their host nations. In Latin countries, particularly in the Islamic portion of the Iberian peninsula, there are abundant records in this regard. Moreover, it is in the Moorish world, that the instrumentarium of the Jews became completely assimilated by the conquering Moslems and, still further, at a later date, yielded to the more developed instruments of the Christian world.

THE DANCE IN ANCIENT ISRAEL

The dance is as old as music itself. It originated from the need of primitive man to express his emotions in the form of bodily movement. If these emotions accumulate and reach a high degree of intensity, the body starts moving involuntarily, as it were.

> The dance, all important in primitive life as a magic, musical, social, indeed a gymnastic, athletic phenomenon, presents itself to the mind as the most vital link between the flowing melodic impulse of singing and the regulating rhythmic impulse from bodies in motion.[1]

Among primitive peoples, dance is generally induced by acoustic means. The clapping of hands, the stamping of feet, the rhythmic beat of noise-making instruments evoke almost unfailingly some sort of bodily movement that may be considered the archaic type of dancing. There is a vast distance between this initial stage and dancing as a civilized art form in its various manifestations. But in principle there is no radical difference between primitive dancing and the dance of a higher artistic order.

Like all religious, cultural, and social institutions of the Hebrews, their dance reveals certain features that had their origin in similar customs of neighboring nations, the Assyrians and the Phoenicians, but mainly the Egyptians.

As for Assyria, we have positive historical evidence about the role of dancing. In Assyrian excavations, numerous pictorial representations of dancing men and women have been found. In the palace of ASHUR-IDANNI-PAL a procession is depicted, led by men playing harps; some of them have their feet raised, manifestly executing dancing steps. They are followed by a group of women whose raised arms seem to indicate dancing and mimic evolutions. The subsequent groups of children are clapping their hands, a customary means in the Orient for the rhythmical accompaniment of dancing. The entire group represents a band of musicians, singers, and dancers in their characteristic "triple" manifestation at an ancient Oriental court (Illus. 66).

Religious dancing must have been most spectacularly developed among the Phoenicians, since they had a special deity for the dance, *Ba'al Markod,* "Baal (or Lord) of Dancing."[2] He was called so either because the Phoenicians believed that he was the creator of the dance, or because—contrary to other deities—he was mostly worshipped by dancing,[3] particularly in bacchantic dances that were performed in his honor.[4]

The Egyptians allotted an important role to the dance in their religious rites. The large temples maintained a special class of male and female dancers. Numerous Egyptian pictures show ritual dancers performing either in a solemn manner, with rolling steps and raised arms, or in a state of wild ecstasy, with their contorted bodies in acrobatic displays (Illus. 38).

The dance in Egypt, as in Phoenicia, was considered of divine origin. Hathor, the mother of Horus, was the goddess of heavens, of trees, and of love.[5] She was also the goddess of music and dancing, and is frequently depicted with a small boy shaking a sistrum in front of her. The priests of Hathor are represented "dancing and clattering castanets."[6] Dance and music also characterized the joyous goddess Bastet (or Bubastis, as the Hellenes called her). She is generally depicted holding a sistrum, the attribute of dancing girls in Egypt[7] (Illus. 5).

Apart from religious festivals celebrated in the temples, there were in Egypt abundant secular feasts at which the dance was ever-present. After the ingathering of the harvest, the husbandmen, marching in a solemn procession, would offer to the deity the first fruits of the land and perform dances of fertility in honor of the gods.[8] In gratitude for the yearly overflow of the Nile, the Egyptians offered their thanks to the god Ptah with dance ceremonies. During this ritual, the dancers held small sticks in their hands, which they struck together, thus providing the harvesters with rhythmic support[9] (Illus. 11). Many of these dance performances, needless to say, must have been witnessed repeatedly by the Jewish people, who lived for more than four centuries under Egyptian rule.

It is no wonder therefore that the Egyptian dances left a strong imprint upon the Israelites, except that the frankly acrobatic abuses of the former have never been imitated by the latter. All the other characteristics of the sacred as well as secular dances of the Egyptians can be found almost without modification in Jewish customs. Like their close neighbors, the Israelites honored their God with dances as well. David's ecstatic dance before the ark of the Covenant is akin to that of the sacrificial dance of the Egyptian Pharaohs[10] (Illus. 37). The ritual dance of the Hebrews was similar to that of the classical period of the Egyptian religion, sedate and dignified. In both religions, processional forms of dance were used in ritual ceremonies. Joyous national festivals were always adorned with popular dancing. The thanksgiving festival at the ingathering of the harvest was celebrated by both peoples with rites aimed at fertility. Its main feature consisted of complex dance patterns. At harvest time the husbandmen in Israel would celebrate the Feast of the Lord, as the Egyptians did, with dances, using

branches of palmtrees, and boughs of thick trees, and willows of the brooks (Lev. 23:40).

In both Egypt and Israel dance was never absent from any festivity of the nobility or the wealthy. Even the belief of the Egyptians that their gods themselves indulged in dancing had its parallel in the conception of the Jews. All these common traits inspire the belief that the dance of the Israelites was not just decisively influenced by that of the Egyptians, but was perhaps taken over from them entirely.

(a) The Terminology of Dance

Dance is mentioned in countless passages of Biblical and post-Biblical literature. This alone would prove its outstanding importance in Jewish religious and secular life. Even more light is thrown upon the significance of dance in ancient Israel by the fact that the Biblical Hebrews had no fewer than twelve verbs to express the act of dancing. Should we add to this the numerous terms found in the rabbinical literature pertaining to this occupation, it could properly be stated that no other ancient language possessed this wealth of expression describing the various aspects of dancing.

The most frequently used word is *hul* or *hil*, "to whirl." From this root the noun *mahol*, "dance," is derived. The word also signifies the "writhing" or "twisting" of a woman in childbirth, or the "writhing" of a person in great pain (Isa. 13:8). When the word is used in the sense of dancing, it refers to a brisk dancing motion.

Sahak and *zahak* mean literally "to laugh," "to play," "to make merry," "to make sport" (in Greek *paixein*, in Latin *ludere*). In a figurative sense, however, they mean "to dance." Because dance has been an ever-present entertainment at any joyous occasion, "to make merry" and "to dance" are synonymous terms in Hebrew.

Hagag, in the strict sense, means "to celebrate a *hag*, a festival." Primitively, *hag* was the term for a feast combined with a solemn procession, or with a devout dance in the sanctuary. Ancient Jewish colloquial usage considered the words *festival* and *dance* as belonging together, and thus, *hagag* automatically acquired the meaning of dance.

Karar, "to whirl about," "to rotate," occurs in the Bible only once in the sense of dancing (2 Sam. 6:14).

As a synonym of *karar*, the same Biblical passage uses the verb *pazzaz*, in its strict sense "leaping," and, applied to dancing, "to dance hopping" (2 Sam. 6:16).

Another verb, *rakad*, means "to skip about"; it is found applied to dancing in several Biblical passages. In the Midrash it is said that

when a man plans a sin, Satan dances encouragingly before him.[11]

The Aramaic word for dancing is here *rikkudin*, derived from *rakad*.

Dalag has the same meaning as *rakad*. In one Biblical passage the word signifies a sort of skipping step of a pagan ritualistic character (Zeph. 1:9). This step must have been connected with some heathen superstition, as one may infer from 1 Sam. 5:5, where a similar custom is mentioned at the entering of Dagon's temple in Ashdod. The custom was evidently a remnant of the ancient pagan religion of the Hebrews and was therefore prohibited, even subjected to punishment.

Kafaz is synonymous with *dalag* and is used as its parallel expression. It occurs only in one Biblical passage (Cant. 2:8).

The word *zal'a* is likewise used but once in the Bible (Gen. 32:32). It indicates some sort of limping ritual dance. As the burial place of Kish, Saul, and Jonathan, *Zel'a* may have been an ancient sanctuary where this peculiar limping dance was performed. This dance used to take place at the rise of the sun (cf. verse 31), which suggests that in primeval times it might have been some kind of ritual action in the religion of sun worshippers.

Duẓ is used in the Biblical text in the sense of "to leap" (Job 41:41).

Pasaḥ is derived from a root the proper meaning of which is "to pass over," "to spare," "to save" (Exod. 12:11, 23, 27; Isa. 31:5). In connection with the Passover-festival, the word is used in many other passages of the Bible. A second meaning of the word *pasaḥ* is "to limp," consequently "to dance in a limping fashion," which suggests a religious ceremony, possibly a limping ritual dance from the early stage of the Jewish religion (cf. the limping dance of the priests of Baʿal at Mount Carmel (1 Kings, 18:26). Some Biblical commentators therefore maintain that *Pesaḥ*, the Passover-festival, owes its name to the peculiar limping dance usually performed on this festival.[12]

Sabab means "to move round" [a sacred object], "to encircle" [the altar]; it is a solemn procession, or a pantomimic evolution, rather than a dance in the strict sense (Psalm 26:6). Encircling sacred places like the altar, sacred trees, and cities seems to have been an ancient ritual custom based upon the idea of the "magic circle." The psalm-verse "Walk about Zion, and go around her" (Psalm 48:13) intimates the consecration of the city by way of ritual encircling, whereas the repeated encircling of Jericho (Josh. 6) seems to indicate belief in the power of an ancient magic custom, as is evident from verse 17.

The custom of ritual processions around a holy place or a sacred object has survived since before Biblical times. This is manifest from a talmudic statement that on the Feast of Tabernacles, following the sacrifices, the priests walked in a procession around the altar, while the Levites sang Psalm 118:25. The first six days of the feast they encompassed the altar once daily, on the seventh day seven times.[13] This must surely have been a primeval ritual institution, like all the other similar customs mentioned in the Old Testament. Their origin goes back to magic and sorcery.

In the Midrash we come across a non-Biblical word, *ḥolah*. The term might be a transmuted form of *maḥol* or *meḥolah* (i.e., "round dance"), a linguistic procedure for which there are many analogous instances in the Hebrew. All these variants are derived from the same root, *ḥul*.

In the Targumim we find an additional term for dance, *ṭafaẓ* or *ṭafas*. Its meaning is "to leap," and it corresponds to the Biblical *ḳafaẓ*.

The word *rakʿa* seems to allude to an ancient ritual at funerals. It is used in 2 Sam. 22:43 and Ezek. 6:11 in the sense of "stamping with the feet," but has, in these Biblical passages, no connotation of dancing. In the talmudic literature, however, this connotation emerges unmistakably. In post-Biblical times it was an exequial custom on the part of the mourners to accompany the funeral oration with rhythmic stamping the ground. There are certain indications that at primeval burials it was customary for the survivors, men as well as women, to honor the deceased with dances.[14] This ancient custom was eventually confined to merely stamping the floor. The word *rakʿa* is derived from the verb *raḳad*.

Further terms in the rabbinical literature, having a more or less obvious connection with the dance, are:

Kartʿa, meaning boundless skipping and hopping, such as, according to the imagination of the Hebrews, Satan would do in dancing.[15] Originating from the Greek verb *skirtaō*, "to spring, leap, bound," the word was transplanted in a phonetically modified form into the Aramaic.

Haddes or *haddes,* means "to dance on tiptoe," as used for dancing before a bridal couple.[16]

Shavar signifies "to leap." In a broader sense, the word is interpreted as "leaper on [or with] a rope."[17]

Hanag is a kind of round-dance and is used as a synonym of *holah.* *Hanag* has always been accompanied by instrumental music; its musical background called *hanagnay⁽a* or *hanagt⁽a* in Aramaean.[18] From this word the Aramaic term *hinga* might have derived, its different meanings being "a circle, dancing, chorus, feast."[19]

Sanat means literally "to tease," but it is closely associated with the idea of dancing, signifying a saltatorial entertainment in which all the participants would engage in mutual teasing.[20]

⁾Afaz might be a variant of *tafaz;* there seems to be no indication for any other derivation, and it is used in the same sense.[21]

For the sake of completeness it should be mentioned that the part of the Jewish population influenced by Hellenistic culture, i.e., mainly the inhabitants of the great cities, called the refined dancer, especially professionals, by the term *⁾arkestes.*[22] This is merely the transliteration into Aramaic of the Greek word for dancer, *orchēstēs.*

The Talmud contains no minute description of the various species of dance, with the possible exception of the word *rikkud,* mentioned probably because it occurs most frequently in rabbinical texts. The rabbinical authors explain the difference between *kipuz* (from *kafaz*), "to leap," and *rakad,* "to dance."[23] In the former, both feet are lifted, or pulled simultaneously from the ground (*⁽akar*); in the latter, the feet are placed alternately one before the other (*heniah*).

Nothing testifies more emphatically to the paramount importance of dance in the life and mind of the Jewish people than this overabundance of terms designating the various forms and phases of dancing.

(b) The Forms of the Sacred Dance

The somewhat sparse mention of the religious dance in the Old Testament might suggest at first that this institution was assigned only a minor role in the ritual. This, however, was by no means the case. The fact alone that, of the twelve terms in Biblical Hebrew, enumerated above, eleven refer to sacred dance and only one to secular dance, proves eloquently that the former of the two categories must have played an essential part in the cult.

Religious dance is mentioned quite early in Biblical tales. After the miraculous passage of the Red Sea, immediately following Moses' song of praise,

Miriam, the prophetess, the sister of Aaron, took a timbrel in her hand; and all the women went out after her with timbrels and with dances (Exod. 15:20).

Here, dance is the solemn conclusion of thanksgiving to God and undoubtedly represents a ritual action, although not in the strict sense of a sacred ceremony, because in those heroic times a thoroughly organized sacred service did not as yet exist. But the dance in honor of God had in the early stage of Jewish religion already assumed a definite ritual connotation; it had certainly originated in similar sacred ceremonies belonging to the Egyptian religion. In the eventual elaborate development of the Jewish sacred service, other ritual actions (sacrifices, benedictions, songs of praise, etc.) took precedence, without, however, completely obscuring dancing.

There can be no doubt that Miriam's sacred dance was performed in a solemn and dignified manner, especially when compared with an event reported shortly afterwards in the Bible, namely, the notorious pagan dance performed around the golden calf (Exod. 32:6). A later description of a heathen dance by the priests of Ba'al, who "limped about the altar" on Mount Carmel (1 Kings 18:26), likewise characterizes an un-Jewish, pagan, custom.

On the Feast of the Lord, the daughters of Shiloh used "to come out to dance in the dances" (Judg. 21:21). Though the Scriptures do not characterize these dances as expressly belonging to the ritual, there can hardly be any doubt that they were sacred dances, since the occasion, that of the annual Feast of the Lord, was one of the most important religious festivals in the Jewish calendar.

The best-known example of sacred dance in Jewish history is that performed by David on the occasion of bringing the ark of the Covenant into Jerusalem. Representing one of the most outstanding events in Israel's religious and national existence, it is mentioned no less than three times in the Bible (2 Sam. 6:14; 1 Chron. 15:8 and 15:28).

The first two of these descriptions contain the expression "with all his might," pointing to a degree of rapture that probably reached religious ecstasy. David's dance is a ritual action *kat' exochēn*, that manifests his sublime adoration of God. At this moment, David the king represents the concentrated religious feeling of the entire Jewish People.

In other passages of the Old Testament, dance as an element of the sacred ceremonial is mentioned but cursorily and in a rather veiled fashion. It seems almost as though the overzealous purifiers of the Biblical text have considered dance to be incompatible with the sacred character of the Scriptures, or looked upon dance as a preeminently secular occupation. No wonder that they sought to eliminate anything that would refer directly to it. Nevertheless, a few allusions remained, proving unequivocally the survival of dancing in the sacred service. The allusions remain especially in the Psalter, which underwent only minor changes by purgers, and contains repeated references to sacred dance.

The dance of worshippers around the altar is mentioned in Psalm 26:6. A counterpart to it is the solemn procession to the altar (Psalm 118:27). Other psalm-verses refer directly to the sacred dance (Psalm 81:2,3). "Sound the timbrel" in this verse points unmistakably to the ritual dance as a complement to singing praises. In the two following quotations from the Psalter, the sacred dance is explicitly stated:

The singers go before, the minstrels follow after, in the midst of damsels playing upon timbrels (Psalm 68:26),

And whether they sing or dance, all my thoughts are in Thee [my Lord] (Psalm 87:7).

Furthermore, the two concluding psalms contain direct proof of the recourse to dancing in sacred ceremonies:

Let them praise His name in the dance, let them sing praises unto Him with the timbrel and harp (Psalm 149:3).

Praise Him with the timbrel and dance (Psalm 150:4).

The dance in the ritual ceremony might have been confined to some sym- bolically suggestive dancing configurations. One has to imagine it as in the manner of a solemn display, using rhythmical gestures and pantomimic motions of the arms and the body, as reproduced in numerous Egyptian pictures. The Jewish sacred dance, as an element of the ritual, must have been radically different from David's ecstatic dance before the ark. In the latter, the rapture was justified by the extraordinary event; in the regular service the sacred dance might have well taken place in a quiet, sedate way, adapting itself to the solemn character of the Temple ritual.

In Israel, dancing was incorporated into the *musical* portions of the sacred service. Therefore there must have been a close interrelation between sacred music and sacred dance. In a remarkable study, K. J. ZENNER investigated this relationship.[24]

According to his findings, dance played in the sacred service a much more significant role than the allusions in the Psalter suggest. He refers to the Christian *Codex Kosmas Indikapleustes* (first half of the sixth century), pre- served in the Vatican, where it is stated that the Psalms were

sung, played and danced (*adontes kai psallontes kai orchoumenoi*).

ZENNER sees a positive proof for this in the psalm-heading *)al maḥalot* (Psalms 53:1; 88:1), rendered by the *Septuagint* phonetically *hyper Maeleth*, which is without an exact translation. But AQUILA actually translates it as *epi choreia*, SYMMACHUS as *dia chorou*, THEODOTION and QUINTILIANUS as *hyper choreias*, JEROME as *pro choro* (53:1) and *per chorum* (88:1). In all these translations dancing is unmistakably indicated. Furthermore, there is conclusive evidence for performing psalms with accompanying dances in JOHN CHRYSOSTOM's writings.

As ZENNER maintains, Psalms 26:6, 118:27, and 43:4 have unmistakable indi- cations for sacred dance. Moreover, verse 26 of Psalm 68 is, in ZENNER's opinion, the conclusive proof that the psalms were not merely sung, but also danced, *ēdon meta orchēseōs*, as the *Codex Kosmas* states. From this, ZENNER concludes that the psalms, or at least many of them, are qualified as "lyric dances" (*"Reigenlyrik"*) in the Old Testament. As in classical Greece, these lyric dances in Israel represent

the result of the co-operation of three arts, poetry, music and mimic.

These were performed by choirs, accompanied by instruments, and enlivened pantomimically by dancing evolutions and appropriate motions of the arms, called by the Hellenes *orchestics*.

Religion was the factor that created these single arts and succeded to unite them in a beautiful alliance.

SACHS also stresses the numerous facets of the Greek complex art of *orchestics*,

in which words, music, dancing, marching, and gestures combined the expression of the mind and the body.[25]

Yet conservative Biblical exegetes look upon the mutual influence of the three arts as merely an occasional, fortuitous phenomenon. In their opinion, nothing proves that the lyric dance brought forth a specific art form that would owe its existence exclusively to the combination of the three arts in question.

Nevertheless, ZENNER maintains emphatically that the Hebrews, especially gifted by nature for lyric arts, knew and practiced lyric dances. His strongest argument is the frontispiece of the *Codex Kosmas,* which shows a pictorial reproduction of the *orchēsis,* the performance of choral songs with pantomimic evolutions (Illus. 72). Thus, lyric dances of Antiquity, in general, are preserved in even pictorial form.

In this connection, certain analogies may be invoked with the Egyptians, who used "dance tours," that is, various positions and evolutions employed when two or more people danced together, as was mentioned above. ZENNER asks the question (without answering it, however) whether certain expressions in the headings of the psalms, such as *'al 'ayyelet ha-shaḥar* (Psalm 22), or *'al shosh-annim* (Psalms 45, 69, 81), do not actually represent instructions for a specific "dance tour" in the performance of these psalms. He finds an analogy with the Hellenes, who knew a special kind of dance that they called *krinon* ("lily"). Would it not be possible that the psalm-heading *'al shoshannim* suggested a similar instruction?

The time when lyric dances allegedly flourished in Ancient Israel is placed by ZENNER in the pre-exilic period of Jewish history. Among other indications to this effect, he cites the magnificent religious festivities of David and Solomon. The Babylonian exile might have caused the discontinuation of the lyric dances along with other institutions not directly connected with the ritual. The sacred dance itself, however, was not touched by this interruption and survived for a while—perhaps in a changed form—as proven by post-Biblical sources.

It may safely be assumed that at least some of the psalms were sung *and* danced. For this, the evidence furnished by KOSMAS INDIKOPLEUSTES constitutes the strongest support. Another reasoning for this fact may be based upon the possibility that certain psalms were used for the purpose of expiation, purification, and healing.[26] It might also be that dancing evolutions of the participants, coupled with corresponding pantomimic gestures, were considered appropriate for enhancing the effectiveness of such supplications. OESTERLEY points out the commonly known fact that, in primitive religions, the sacred dance

is an appeal to the pity of the god. Not far removed from this is the idea of compulsion upon the god; . . . and it is quite possible that in some cases the sacred dance was believed to have the effect of coercing the god to do what was required of him.[27]

Among the ancient sacred dances that used to be performed around some devoted objects, the one connected with well-springs is occasionally implied in the Old Testament, without however, being directly described or even specifically mentioned. The reason for this peculiar situation is that

the priestly historians and legislators resolutely excluded, as far as possible, everything that could infer any similarity between the worship of Yahveh and that of heathen deities.[28]

Nevertheless, the custom in question must have been so deeply rooted in the religious consciousness of the Israelites that dancing around particularly venerated objects was cultivated as much after this "editorial exclusion" as before it. When nomadic Arabs found a well, this important event was celebrated with songs and dances.[29] A similar celebration must have taken place when

Moses led the people to a well in the desert (Num. 21:16-18). As a proof of the importance of the occasion, the Biblical chronicler quoted the "Song of the Well" textually. However, the sacred dance appertaining to it, as self-evident, was not mentioned specifically, because as it occurs so often in the Biblical text. Another form of sacred dance of the Israelites is revealed in 1 Sam. 10:5:

> Thou shalt meet a band (*hebel*) of prophets coming down from the high place (*bamah*) with a psaltery, and a timbrel, and a pipe, and a harp, before them; and they will be prophesying.

The translation of *hebel* as "band" or "company" is not accurate, because the proper meaning of the word is "rope," "cord," or "string." The same word used in Josh. 2:15 gives the correct meaning: "then she let them down by a cord (*hebel*) through the window." If we apply this meaning to the prophets coming down from the sanctuary, it would indicate that they marched in single file. Such a procession in a single row, accompanied by singing and playing, especially using the *tof* (hand-drum), suggests unmistakably that this procedure must have taken place in some form of dancing.

The dancing of the early Jewish prophets assumed the form of ecstatic bodily movements. They whirled themselves into a state of frenzy; in this mood they pronounced their prophecies, and even inspired the onlookers with their rapturous dancing (1 Sam. 19:20–24).

Singing as accompaniment to dancing was self-evident in Ancient Israel, so that Biblical chroniclers mention but cursorily the combination of the two. Examples of this are Miriam's dance with the women of Israel after the passage through the Red Sea (Exod. 15:20,21), the dancing and singing of the women welcoming Saul and David after their victory against the Philistines (1 Sam. 18:6,7; 21:12; 29:5), and others. On all these occasions the people danced in groups, just as the singing was performed by choirs.

As in other ritualistic acts, men and women were generally separated at religious dances. Only one Biblical report indicates that both sexes danced together in the dance around the golden calf (Exod. 32:6,19). This, however, is not an Israelitic dance in the proper sense, since it occurs at an idolatrous feast; hence it provides the exception to the rule.

After the destruction of the Jerusalem sanctuary by the Romans, music, and apparently dancing also, ceased to exist as part of the religious rites, and even in secular life. But a custom as deeply rooted in the popular consciousness of the Jews as the dance, could not be completely eradicated from the ritual, even less so from secular usage. The early rabbinical literature furnishes proof that, after the religious and national catastrophe that befell Judaism, the dance still survived in religious as well as in secular life.

(c) The Dance at Religious Festivals

As long as the Israelites were nomadic shepherds and were not compelled to rely on agriculture for their principal means of existence, they did not have any festivals connected with the harvest. It is supposed that they took over such festivals from the residents of Cana'an after the conquest of the new homeland; subsequently, they celebrated these festivals in honor of their own God.

The Jewish festival cycle was governed by the seasonal changes of the soil's productivity and aimed at the religious consecration of these changes. Thus, the three great events in the life of the husbandmen, all celebrated with profuse festivities, were the offering of the first fruits, the end of the harvesting, and the ingathering of the entire harvest. Each of these feasts was called *hag*, a term indicating that the essential feature of these festivals was the religious dance around the sanctuary.

The names of the three principal agricultural festivals were:

(1) *Hag ha-mazzot*, the feast of the unleavened bread, the spring festival, the feast of the newly awakened nature, "when the sickle was first put to the standing corn," and when the first fruits were offered to God (Deuter. 16:9). The *hag-hapassah*, "the Feast of Passover," was originally the spring festival of nomadic Jews, at which the first-born animals of the flocks were sacrificed (Exod. 34:19). In the latter-day agricultural existence of Israel, both festivals were combined, in which only the Exodus from Egypt was celebrated (cf. Ezek. 45:21).

(2) *Hag shabuot*, "the Feast of Weeks" (Exod. 34:22; Deut. 16:10), or *hag ha-kazir*, "the Feast of Harvest" (Exod. 23:16), which took place seven weeks after the *hag-hapassah*, as the harvest was completed.

(3) *Sukkot*, "the Feast of Tabernacles," called also *hag ha^asif*, "the Feast of Ingathering," the festival of thanksgiving,

at the end of the year, when thou gatherest in thy labours out of the field (Exod. 23:16).

Prior to the centralization of the national-religious cult at Jerusalem (620 B.C.E.), the festivals of the nomadic Jews were not held on specific days of the year. After they settled in Cana'an, however, they adopted the dates of the agricultural festivals of the residents of the land.

Originally, the three festivals had the same religious importance. The Mosaic law prescribed that all men visit the sanctuary on each one of them (Exod. 23:17; 34:23). As time passed, the Feast of Tabernacles gained precedence, becoming the outstanding festival in Israel, called "the Feast of the Lord," or simply "the Feast" (Lev. 23:39,41; Judg. 21:19; 1 Kings 8:2; 12:32, etc.).

As already mentioned, in all these *hagim*, dance was an essential element of the religious celebration. When the daughters of Shiloh "came out into the vineyards to dance the dances," this event took place

"on the feast of the Lord," which was held "from year to year in Shiloh" (Judg. 21:19)[30]

The Biblical scribe reports this custom in a cursory way, but the rabbinical literature describes it more extensively. According to Rabban SIMEON ben GAMALIEL,

there were no happier days for Israel than the 15th of Ab and the Day of Atonement, for on them daughters of Jerusalem used to go forth in white raiments; and these were borrowed, that none should be abashed which had them not; [hence] all the raiments required immersion [i.e., they were newly washed]. And the daughters of Jerusalem went forth to dance in the vineyards. And what did they say? "Young man, lift up thine eyes and see what thou would'st choose for thyself; set not thine eyes on beauty, but set thine eyes on family."[31]

Dancing at the vintage was instituted in early times and, judging from Biblical accounts, must have been a widespread practice. The birth place of the prophet Elisha, *'Abel Meḥolah* ("the field of dancing," 1 Kings 9:16), may have been a locality where such feasts with sacred dances took place regularly. When the Day of Atonement was transformed into mourning for the destroyed sanctuary, the dancing, connected with the former, was abolished altogether.

Rabbi ELIEZER ben HYRCANUS (first century C.E.) expounds upon the feast of the 15th of Ab.[32] According to his testimony, the worshippers brought wood for the altar in quantity sufficient for the burnt-offerings through the whole coming year. JOSEPHUS also mentions this feast, which he calls in Greek *xylophoria*, "the Feast of carrying wood."[33] Besides its practical purpose, this was a ritualistic practice, one performed in a solemn procession, possibly with some pantomimic evolutions. It may be counted, therefore, among the religious ceremonies interspersed with dance elements.

Among the other festivals in which dance had an essential part, the Sukkot-Feast deserves particular mention. As mentioned earlier, on this day, immediately following the sacrifices, the altar was encompassed in a solemn dancing evolution,[34] during which the Levites sang Psalm 118:25.[35] On the seventh day, called *Hosh'ana Rabba*, the altar was encompassed seven times.[36] The procession was concluded in directly addressing the altar: "Homage [lit. "Beauty"] to thee, O Altar!, or "To Thee O Lord and to thee, O Altar!"[37]

At the most outstanding national-religious festival of the Maccabaean period, the rededication of the Sanctuary, a dance-like procession was part of the sacred ritual (2 Macc. 10:7).[38]

Curiously enough, the Bible does not mention a religious ceremony that—judging from rabbinical tales—must have been the crowning event at the Feast of Tabernacles. This was the rite of the *Bet ha-She'ubah* (or *Ha-Sho'eba*), observed in the night between the first and second day of the festival, at which torch-dances were performed in the Court of the Women. The court was illuminated by chandeliers of four arms, and

> countless Levites [played] upon harps, lyres, cymbals and trumpets and instruments of music.

Before a large audience

> men of piety and good works[39] [i.e., rabbis and distinguished laymen] used to dance with burning torches in their hands, singing songs and praises.[40]

Dancing and singing at the Feast of Tabernacles seem to have served the sole purpose of celebrating joyfully the ingathering of the harvest and thanking God with music and dance. It may be surmised, however, that this festival, or at least some of its ritual actions, originated in earlier magic customs. This is corroborated by the rabbinical description of the water libation, which represented an important ceremony of the *Bet ha-She'ubah*.[41]

On this occasion water was drawn from the pond Shiloam (or Shiloah) and carried in a solemn procession to the Temple. When the cortege arrived at one of the Temple gates (called "Water Gate"), several priests blew a trumpet blast in unison. In the Temple, the water was poured out on the altar, with the priests again sounding the trumpets. This ceremony was performed similarly on all seven days of the festival. The analogy with the technique of imitative magic is unmistakable in the procedure of water libation. The purpose of any magical act is to achieve the desired effect by reproducing it on a smaller scale. The rabbinical writers themselves admit that the aim of the ceremony was to secure rain for the coming year:

> The Holy One . . . said: "Pour out water before Me at the Feast, in order that the rains of the year may be blessed to you."[42]

Judging from this rabbinical statement, the custom of water libation was established in obedience to God's own commandment. It is, however, easy to discover that this is merely giving a modified interpretation to the ancient rain magic incorporated into the ritual customs of the Jewish religion at a more developed stage.

The "men of good works,"[43] who performed the torch-dance at the *Bet ha-She'ubah* were apparently considered capable of exercising, through their prayers, songs, and dances, the "Power of Rain," thus putting into effect the sympathetic rain magic. The term "men of good works" is also interpreted as "men of might," or "workers of miracles." R. HANINA ben DOSA was supposed to be such a man. When called to a sick person, he was reputedly able to foretell who should live and who should die.[44] Whoever could perform such miracles was credited with the faculty of obtaining the most auspicious result from the rain magic through the religious power inherent in his dance.

Singing, instrumental music, and dancing, combined with the specific spell of the nocturnal scenery, must have created such a rapturous state of mind among all the participants, performers as well as onlookers, that one may well understand why one of the rabbinical writers was induced to exclaim:

> He that has never seen the joy of *Bet ha-She'ubah* has never in his life seen joy.[45]

The general sentiment at this feast must have been a sort of religious ecstasy, a familiar phenomenon at nocturnal ritualistic feasts in the ancient and present-day Orient, as well as in primitive religions in general.

At the Festival of Purim, dancing was again the outstanding feature. Originally, Purim was the perpetuation of the ancient Persian *Farwardīgān* festival, in which dance played an essential part, and which was transmitted to the Jews by the Babylonians. The Hebrew name of the festival was explained by two different folk-etymologies, one derived from the Akkadian *purruru*, "to destroy," and the other from the Babylonian *pūru*, "lot."[46] The word Purim is the Hebrew plural of the Babylonian *pūru*.[47] The generally accepted justification for the incorporation of this feast into the calendar of the Jewish festivals was the Purim tale which, despite its foreign origin and its thoroughly legendary character, was earnestly taken by the Jews for a historical narrative.

The sources of the Esther story may be found in Babylonian mythology, as the names of the principal characters indubitably prove. Mordechai is *Marduk* and Esther is *Ishtar*, both names of the supreme god and goddess of the Babylonian pantheon. Haman is identical with *Hamman* (or *Humman*), the supreme god of the Elamites, whose capital city Susa (or Shushan) is the scene of the Esther story. Even Vashti is supposed to be the name of an Elamite deity, slightly misspelled as *Mashti*.[48]

The Purim festival was evidently brought back to the homeland by the repatriates from the Babylonian exile and continued to be celebrated by the Jews after their return. It was likely to exercise an irresistible influence upon the minds of a people, living under conditions of austerity and in dire need of psychological stimulants such as were able to kindle the imagination and the patriotic sentiments of the nation. The story certainly circulated among the Israelites long before the book was written. Along with the celebration of the feast in Israel, it became deeply rooted in the national consciousness of the Jews. The written form might have constituted but the last step toward general acceptance by the Jews of the Esther legend as historical fact. The story of the canonization of this wholly secular book corroborates this assumption.

The outstanding feature of the Purim festival was its frolicking and boisterous mood, with participants masquerading in all kinds of disguises, human as well as animal, forming joyous corteges and with a good deal of dancing taking place. On this day everybody danced, rich and poor, men and women, young and old. The casual saying "On Purim everything is allowed" became in the long run a general Jewish custom, even to the point of transgressing the Mosaic laws. Thus, at the popular Purim masquerading, men would disguise as women and vice versa, which is strictly prohibited by religious laws (Deut. 22:5).[49]

Judging from a talmudic report, a pagan custom, common to many primitive religions, survived in one of the ceremonies of Purim. This was "leaping through fire."[50] In Babylonian countries there existed a custom, called in Aramaean *meshavarta depuriy'a*, the "jumping place of Purim." According to a Gaonic explanation, this involved the following procedure: Four or five days before Purim, young men would make an effigy of Haman and hang it on the roof. On Purim itself, they would set a bonfire and cast the effigy into it, while standing around, joking and singing. Thereafter, they would jump over the fire above a hoop placed upon the burning stake.[51] This hoop was called the "place of jumping," *dereh ha-'abarah*. The custom itself was a remnant of an ancient fire-dance, practiced in many primitive religions.[52] Its magic meaning was the destruction of the demon by fire. The existence of this custom may have been widespread, because in 408 C.E. the Emperor THEODOSIUS II issued a decree forbidding the Jews of the Byzantine Empire to practice it. In spite of this prohibition, the fire-dance survived in many countries. R. NATHAN ben YEHIEL of Rome (d. 1106) mentioned that the custom continued among the Italian Jews in the same manner as among the Byzantine Jews.[53]

(d) Dance in Popular Usage

In primitive religions the deity was not only the originator of human existence, but the sole being who determined and guided the fate of the people as well as that of the individual. Joyous and sorrowful events of life were caused by the deity, and therefore blessings as well as supplications for absolution had to be offered to him in strictly prescribed ritual ceremonies, which included dance as one of their major elements.[54]

Originally, the sacrificial dance, the expiatory dance, the dance at celebrations of victory, at weddings, at funerals, at the harvest festival were all of sacred character. However, with the gradual development of religion, only those dances which were incorporated directly or indirectly into ritual ceremonies preserved this character. The others lost their liturgical implications and became part and parcel of popular customs. At this stage, they were but loosely connected with religion and may therefore be classified as secular dances, constituting the essential element of all popular festivities. On these occasions, joy and gladness, and sometimes the sorrow of the individual and of the masses, manifest themselves most conspicuously.

The frequent derivation of Biblical female names from the dance constitutes a parallel to the numerous Hebrew terms expressing the dancing action itself. We find repeatedly, for instance, the names *Maḥelah* and *Maḥalat* in the Biblical text. *Maḥelah* was the daughter of Zelophehad (Num. 26:33), *Maḥalat*, Esau's wife, the granddaughter of Abraham (Gen. 28:9). Rehoboam's wife, David's granddaughter, had the same name (2 Chron. 11:18). A similar name for males, *Maḥelon*, appears in Ruth 1:2. Whether the Levitical family of the *Maḥelites* (Num. 26:58) likewise derived its name from dance cannot be said with certainty. Yet, it is possible that in the early history of Israel this family distinguished itself particularly in dancing, hence this name was given to the clan.

Among all the secular festivities, it was the wedding at which, because of its joyful character, dance fulfilled the most pertinent function. Rabbinic writers state repeatedly that

they dance before her [i.e., the bride], they play before her,[55]

and the scribes furnish all kinds of information as to how the dances and the appropriate songs and recitations were performed on such occasions.

The participants in the bridal street-procession danced all the way until they arrived at the house of the wedding. Only in times of a national catastrophe, such as during the war of VESPASIAN (69 C.E.), did it happen that "the crown of the bridegroom and the [wedding] drum (ʾerus)," implying dancing at weddings, were prohibited.[56]

Respected rabbis did not consider it beneath their dignity to dance before the bridal couple, and several were so famous for their artful dancing that the rabbinical writers gave them special praise. One of them was "R. JEREMIAH of the BRANCH," so called because he used to dance at weddings with a crown of olive-tree branches braided on his head.[57] Another was

R. SAMUEL ben R. ISAAC, the man who used to dance on [or "with"] three branches [before bridal couples].[58]

Still another was R. JUDAH ben ILAʿI who

used to take a myrtle twig and dance before the bride and say [i.e., sing]: "Beautiful and graceful bride."[59]

The most distinguished rabbi of his time, Rabban SIMEON ben GAMALIEL, must have been a virtuoso in dancing. At the Feast of *Bet ha-Sheʾubah* he performed a torch dance with eight burning torches, throwing them alternately in the air and catching them, and none of them touched the ground when he prostrated himself, touched the floor with his fingers, kissed the ground, and leaped up again.[60]

The wedding customs among Babylonian Jews differed from those of Jews living in Israel, because the Talmud discusses the question "how does one dance before the bride?" A distinguished visitor,

R. DIMI came [to Babylonia] and said: Thus they sing before the bride in the East [i.e. in Israel]: "No powder and no paint, and no waving [of the hair], and still a graceful gazelle."[61]

Famous rabbis used to dance before the bridal couple not merely for the sake of rejoicing, but in order to honor the bride. The dance before a person or object had the ancient ritual meaning of honoring this person or object. One danced in honor of God, or the people, or the bride, or also the deceased (see below). One danced before people of standing, just as one sang or played for them.

There is not the slightest allusion either in Biblical or post-Biblical sources that ancient Israel cultivated dramatic plays with singing and dancing. Nevertheless, numerous attempts have been made to interpret one of the Biblical books, the "Song of Songs," in this sense. According to this concept, the Canticles represent a dramatic play, with acting persons and groups of singers and dancers, which—as was asserted in all seriousness—was actually performed on the stage in ancient Israel. Since in this alleged play the dance was supposed to have had a leading role, it may be proper to describe these attempts here.

We know that in the ancient Near East it was a religious custom to usher in the New Year with a sort of dramatic play representing the combat of the New against the Old.

In Egypt, such "mystery plays" were based upon the Osiris myth, but these were expanded liturgical ceremonies rather than dramatic presentations in the strict sense.[62] In ancient Babylon, the New Year festival comprised the recital, possibly also with some kind of staging, of the primordial myth relating how Marduk, the supreme deity and patron of the city, defeated Tiamat, who challenged the authority of the gods. A similar myth existed in Cana'an, as recorded in the *Ras Shamra* tablets, originating in the fourteenth century B.C.E. and discovered in Syria in 1920. The tablets preserve a tale in which the Cana'anite supreme god, Ba'al, lord of fertility, defeats Yam, the god of waters, and Mot, the god of death. The tablets do not reveal, however, whether this rite was only recited or was also enacted at the New Year celebration in Cana'an. In Assyria one may find historical records of pantomimic representations with choirs and acting persons, played by priests and laymen.[63]

All these plays, however, have been not so much *theatrical* dramas as personified representations of the mythology of these peoples, rites in histrionic disguise, somewhat akin to the medieval Easter plays of the Christian Church. Not before Hellenic times did the dramatic idea develop to its full bloom.

By analogy, one would be inclined to assume that the ancient Israelites also had dramatic plays, at least in some primitive form.[64] There are, however, important arguments against such an assumption.

The literary achievements of the Israelites manifested themselves mainly in the domain of lyricism. Dramatic art was not in the least appropriate to their innate nature. Even apart from this psychological factor, one has to consider the all-round lack of historical evidence with regard to the existence of dramatic plays in Ancient Israel. Had there been plays of this order, they would have constituted such outstanding events in Israel's existence that they could not possibly have been passed by in silence by Biblical and post-Biblical chroniclers. JOSEPHUS and PHILO, too, make no mention whatever of Jewish theatrical performances.

The weightiest argument against dramatic plays, however, may be found in Israel's religious laws, for the Mosaic law expressly prohibits the imitation (pictorial as well as corporeal) of persons and objects, which is the very essence of any scenic representation. To be sure, the letter of the law says only

> thou shalt not *make* unto thee a graven image, nor any manner of likeness, of any thing that is in heaven above, or that is in the earth beneath (Exod. 20:4; Lev. 26:1).

But in the strictly religious sense the *making* of an image was extended to all kinds of reproduction, or imitation, of persons and objects. The priesthood, as the traditional authority for the enforcement of the law, would certainly have opposed with all its might any such attempts in which the personification, i.e., imitation of other individuals, is the essence of the play.

The idea of the dramatic character of the Canticles goes back to ORIGEN (ca. 185–ca. 254 C.E.), whose followers gave the book an intermediate position between the dramatic and lyric creations. They called it "a nuptial poem composed in dramatic form" and "regarded it as a dramatic epithalamium celebrating Solomon's marriage with Pharaoh's daughter."[65] However, the most obvious historical considerations invalidate this assumption. According to modern Biblical expositors, the time of origin of the Canticles is about 250 B.C.E., which in itself disproves Solomon's authorship as well as the use of the poem at his wedding.

Nevertheless, the idea was kept alive for centuries. The first attempt in modern times at dramatization of the "Song of Songs" was that of an Englishman, JOHN BLAND (d. 1788), a teacher of Hebrew, as he indicated. He wrote a play in seven scenes, and it was printed in 1750. Since then, there has been an uninterrupted string of dramatizations throughout the late eighteenth and early nineteenth centuries, continuing up to our day. Among these, ERNEST RENAN's attempt attracted the greatest attention because of the author's worldwide fame as a scholar and historian.[66] RENAN supplied the text with a multitude of scenic instructions, and also appended a thoroughly elaborated scenario, which reads like the script of a theatrical producer.

In the twentieth century the idea of dramatizing the Canticles has not slackened despite all the numerous earlier attempts that had for the most part an ephemeral life. The latest one of the series is LEROY WATERMAN's "arrangement" as a real play for the theatre, which has actually been performed on the American stage.[67]

In contradistinction to these attempts at dramatization, the fundamental fact cannot be overlooked that the "Song of Songs" is actually an anthology of lyric poems, of a humoristic, roguish, even erotic nature, a series of wedding songs that depict

> with brilliant imagination and consummate art the thrills, delights, torments, and dreams of love between man and woman—love in bud and full bloom—against the background of the charming Palestinian countryside in the springtime.[68]

The contemporaries of those who compiled the Canticles certainly understood the basic character of the poems better than did later generations, whose minds were biased by its manifold allegorical and moralizing interpretations. The early readers of the "Song of Songs" indeed took the love poems in their literal meaning, and young men used to sing them as erotic ditties in wine houses. This attitude, naturally, constituted a "sacrilege" in view of the canonicity of the book—a fact that aroused the raging ire of Rabbi AKIBA (ca. 50–ca. 132 c.e.), as we learn from the rabbinical literature.[69]

The conclusive refutation of the claim that the Canticles represented a dramatic play is furnished by J G. WETZSTEIN who, as a long time resident of Damascus and its vicinities, has studied the customs and manners of the population and has been considered as one of the authorities in the domain of Oriental ethnology.[70] The analogies between the wedding customs of the Syrians, as observed by him, and the allusions to wedding entertainment contained in the "Song of Songs," are so striking that they merit a brief discussion at this point.

The bridegroom and the bride are called "king" and "queen" during the seven days of the wedding festivities, beginning with the morning on which they rise as a young couple. They take their seat on the only available large-sized wooden implement, the thrashing-floor, which serves the "royal" couple as a throne. During the entire seven-day period—carrying the name of "royal week"—dances, jokes, and plays are performed before this throne. In this entertainment, the major role is assigned to the songs describing the young marital bliss of the newlyweds. These songs dealing mostly with the beauty of the young couple and their wedding ornaments, refer to the bride as "the most beautiful of the women." In addition, dances are performed in her honor.

In the "Song of Songs," too, the newlyweds are referred to as the "young royal couple," and the allusions to erotic matters in the Canticles (for instance, to "the Dance of Maḥanaim," see below) represent nothing more than the rude jokes that are customary, as a rule, at all rustic wedding feasts. The expression "daughters of Jerusalem" in the Canticles suggests companions of the bride, with whom she might have performed a group dance, which is quite usual at weddings in general, and those in the countryside in particular. Finally, the "Shulammite" stands for none else than "Abishag the Shunammite," the virgin from Shunem, who—according to 1 Kings 1:3—was considered the most beautiful of the daughters of Israel and was chosen to become King David's last wife. She was proverbial in Israel for her perfect female beauty, and this is the reason why the poet (or poets) of the Canticles have given this name to the heroine, that is, to the bride.[71]

With this, the whole castle in the air of a "dramatic play" falls to pieces. From king and queen, from Solomon and his bride the Shunammite, nothing remains but facetious wedding songs and a dancing entertainment, in which the bride was possibly engaged in a dance similar to that performed on Arabian wedding nights, when the bride, in all her finery, used to burst forth in a sword dance and, later on, in a torch dance.

According to ʾAggadic ideas, even the angels danced in heaven. Hosts of angels performed a round-dance (ḥul) for Jacob on his journey home, and danced (raḳad) before him.[72] In Jacob's vision of the celestial ladder the angels of God (Hananiah, Michael, and Azariah) [danced] ascending and descending on it [the ladder], exalting him and debasing him, dancing (*'afaz*), leaping (*kafaz*) and teasing him (*sanat*).[73]

Dancing was also indulged in by Satan, whom the rabbis call "arch-robber" (*'arkilistes*, the Greek word *archilēstēs* taken over phonetically). At exuberant revelries the main entertainment, aside from eating and drinking, was dancing. The diabolic, demoralizing effect of such carousals is expressed in the rabbinical maxim:

wherever you find eating and drinking, the arch-robber [Satan] cuts his capers [is dancing].[74]

The word used here for dancing, *kart'a* (obviously derived from the Greek *skirtaō*) suggests the unbridled leaping and skipping, as by one who is intoxicated. At the dance around the golden calf, Satan mingles with the circling (*higeg*) and swaying (*gahan*) masses, and he leaps (*tafaz*) and jumps (*shavar*).

Jewish 'Aggadic fancy goes even so far as to assume that sometimes God Himself dances.[75] The same idea is set forth by some rabbinical authorities in a more or less embellished form. According to these descriptions, in the Time to Come, the heavenly hosts will be the dancers, and the people of the righteous the onlookers. The righteous follow rapturously the motions of the divine leader of the dance, point to Him with their fingers, and compare it with the dance of young maidens. In the general rejoicing, they surround the leader of the dance and perform a round-dance around him.[76]

The attitude of the rabbis toward the dance has not always been so favorable as might be assumed from the above quotations. Especially after the eventual intrusion of Greek dance customs into certain areas of the Jewish population, some Sages have quite thoroughly changed their opinion about dancing. The professional dancer in particular aroused the ire of the religious leaders, as may be seen from the contemptuous remark: "The *'arkestes* is the emptiest of the empty."[77] Other talmudic passages express the hostility even more indignantly:

Every scholar who feasts much in every place, eventually destroys his home, widows his wife, orphans his young, forgets his learning. . . . Said Abaye: He is called a heater of ovens. Rabba said: A tavern dancer! R. Pappa said: A plate licker.[78]

R. NAḤMAN's servant, Daru, is characterized in terms of contempt as "a notorious dancer in the wine houses."[79]

Scorn and disdain are contained in the talmudic saying:

Thereupon a voice cried out: "Thou leaper, son of a leaper, leap."[80]

The word used here, *shavar*, means literally "to leap," but in a figurative sense it is interpreted as a "leaper on [or with] a rope"; it refers therefore to the lowest class of dancers and jokers, akin to medieval itinerant dancers and jugglers. Such entertainers roved around in taverns and public places in Babylonia, and, while performing their grotesque dances, indulged in certain "manners" (*gavne* in Aramaic). These are interpreted as some sort of gestures or motions with the head,[81] but actually they might have been certain "dance tours," similar to those mentioned above. Even the Talmud hints at such "tours," for it characterizes such a joker:

Loss of time would be where he was a dancer in wine houses and has to make gestures by moving his head.[82]

In his commentary to this passage, RASHI adds

that these gestures were of a comic sort in order to make people laugh,

and calls such dancers *ha-lezonim,* "merry-makers."

The welcome of the returning victor by dancing and singing women is an ancient custom; with these performances they not only celebrate the victor, but also offer thanksgivings to the deity, to whom the victory is solely ascribed. Even victorious enemies have been welcomed by the citizens of conquered cities with singing and dancing. Thus, HOLOFERNES was received by the subjugated population "with garlands and dances and timbrels" (Judith 3:7).

The round-dance was the most typical and popular one in Israel. It was performed mainly by young maidens, either alone (Exod. 15:20; Judg. 11:34; cf. Matt. 14:6), or in groups (Judg. 21:21; Jer. 31:4,13). Older women, too, participated occasionally in the dances (1 Sam. 18:6,7), and sometimes the round-dance was performed by the entire people (Exod. 32:6,19). Dancing children are mentioned only twice in the Old Testament (Job 21:11; Zech. 8:5, cf. Matt. 11:7; Luke 7:32). Young men would form their own group in dancing, and so also would the elderly men (Jer. 31:13). Toward the end of the Second Temple, however,—evidently under Roman influence—the dancing of men alone was considered indecent.

The orgiastic as well as the grotesque dance was not appropriate to Jewish customs. Early in their history, the Israelites refused to take over such dances from the Babylonians and Assyrians, and also continued in later times to keep their dances dignified and well mannered, even on the most joyous occasions.

In the life of husbandmen, dance played an important role. At the harvest festival, at the vintage and other happy events in the yearly cycle of fertility, dancing was always the crowning part of the celebration (Judg. 9:27; Isa. 16:10; Jer. 25:30). The dance of the maidens of Shiloh in the vineyards on the Feast of the Lord belongs to this category.

Apart from its direct purpose of offering thanksgiving to the Lord for His bounty, dancing at those agricultural festivals had a veiled magical significance. Dances at such feasts were mostly performed with green branches, by which—according to the concepts of the ancients—the carrier of live vegetation became the symbol of fertility. To be sure, the Jewish religion has interpreted this custom as a commandment of God (Lev. 23:40). Nevertheless, this custom was actually a remnant of the ancient superstitious belief in sympathetic magic. The fact that the magical practice aimed at fertility, though in an altered form, was admitted into the Jewish religion, shows how deeply the belief in the power of fertility dances was rooted among the Israelites. A similar act of sympathetic magic was the rite of Water Libation on the *Bet ha-She'ubah,* described above.

The war dances, or the dance preceding the battle, frequently reported by Oriental peoples, had a double aim: first, to create physical excitement and thereby to stir up the courage of the warriors; second, it was a demonstration of power and ferocity, in order to impress the enemy troops and strike terror among them.[83] But originally, the war dance was motivated by magic considerations, namely, to appease the souls of the killed enemies, or ward off the spirits who protected them.

The Old Testament does not mention war dances, but we read in the annals of Israel that the warriors "consecrated themselves" before joining the battle (Isa. 13:3). "To prepare" oneself for the battle (Micah 3:5; Jer. 6:4) has the same significance as "to sanctify, or consecrate" the war.

A veiled mention of a war dance might be contained in Ezek. 6:11:

Smite with thy hand, and stamp with thy foot (*u-raḳ'a b'ragleho*),

which alludes to a dancing ceremony in preparation of the battle. Before the battle "burnt-offerings" and "peace-offerings" have been presented (1 Sam. 13:9,10), and after the battle the booty, or a portion of it, was "consecrated," or "dedicated" to the Lord (1 Sam. 15:21; 2 Sam. 8:11; 1 Chron. 18:11).

In which particular form this "consecration" of the warriors before the battle took place is not related by the Biblical chroniclers, except that the soldiers participated in a sacrificial ceremony, through which God was to be induced to support them in the battle and to secure victory for them. One can hardly doubt that, like other Semitic peoples, the ancient Israelites resorted to dancing during such sacrificial rites.

(e) Dancing at Funerals

As in the case of war dances, there is no mention in the Old Testament of dances at funerals. Indirectly, however, by analogy and by certain allusions in post-Biblical writings, we may assume that the Israelites honored not only the living, but also the dead with dances.

Originally, dancing at funerals had a magic motivation. In primitive cultures the spirit of the deceased was supposed to have a hostile attitude toward the survivors. The funeral ceremony, including the dance, was intended to appease his hostility and, possibly, to transform his anger into benevolence. The dance was also believed to be an effective means of restraining the spirit of the deceased from going astray. Above all, some peoples believed that the deceased was surrounded by all sorts of evil demons who sought to capture him or his spirit. The dance was supposed to possess the power of keeping the evil demons away from the departed one. Significantly, such dances were performed in the form of a circle; the "magic circle" was meant to protect not only the deceased, but also the participants in the funeral from the influence of evil demons.[84]

What might have been the reason for the complete silence of the Biblical chroniclers about this ancient custom? The simplest explanation is that dances at funerals, like many other practices, were self-evident in Ancient Israel, so that the scribes considered their specific mention superfluous. Another reason might have been that such ritual dances evoked the memory of the ancient pagan religion of the Jews, so that the Biblical authors, and later the editors, tried to eliminate any allusion to them in the sacred text. It is a well-established fact that this text was repeatedly, and sometimes even radically, purified of the remnants of ancient pagan and magic customs.

The fact that dances at funerals existed in ancient Israel for many centuries is substantiated by more than a single evidence. The Bible passes over in silence other funeral customs, such as piping the *halilim*, lacerating one's body as sign of mourning (later replaced by the tearing of garments), cutting off one's hair, removing the footwear, and so on. Here again, silence does not necessarily indicate that these customs were unknown.

Rabbinical writers relate that, at funeral ceremonies, the mourners clapped their hands (*safak*) and rhythmically beat their thighs (*tipaḥ*).[85] All these, as we already know, were habitual practices occurring during secular dances, and they were also used in dances honoring the dead. Even when funeral dances were abolished, these earlier aspects of the dance survived.

Another custom at Jewish funerals, one that certainly sprang from dancing, flourished in talmudic and post-talmudic times. It consisted in the mourner's monotonous, rhythmic, stamping of the ground during the entire funeral oration. Originally, this might have been a religious dance in honor of the dead, reduced, as time passed, to this simplified mechanical form, in which the idea of honoring the deceased was retained merely in the subconscious mind of the Jews. The dance act on this occasion is expressed by the Rabbinical scribes with the word *rak'a*, the same word used in the Bible for stamping the feet (2 Sam. 22:43; Ezek. 6:11). The Talmud has yet another term for stamping with the feet:

Tipaḥ is clapping one's hand [to indicate the dance rhythm], and that of ḳillus is [tapping] with the foot [in mourning]![86]

Whereas in dances among the Jews both sexes were commonly separated, at funeral ceremonies men and women performed these veiled dancing steps together, in addition to certain pantomimic gestures with the hands and fingers.[87]

Today's Sephardim (the Spanish and Portuguese Jews) still cling to a peculiar custom at their funeral rites, one that strongly reminds of a processional dance. This is the act of walking seven times around the bier, during which seven short prayers are recited or chanted, each one ending with the words:

And continually may he walk in the land of life, and may his soul rest in the bond of life.[88]

The procession around the bier is apparently a remnant of an ancient dance act. There might be also a bit of imitative magic in *walking* around the bier and in the prayers' wish that the deceased may *walk* in the land of life. Curiously enough, this custom has entirely disappeared among the Ashkenazim (the German, Polish, Russian, Hungarian, and Rumanian Jews), and can be traced only among the Eastern Ḥasidim. But the Sephardic custom is an unmistakable sign that dancing at funerals represents a primeval custom that, in a transmuted form, has survived to our day.

(f) The Metaphoric Use of Dance Terms

Apart from the rich vocabulary, there is still another indication of the paramount importance of the dance in the feeling and thinking of the Jewish people. I refer to their frequent use of dance terms and expressions in similes, parables, and metaphors, both in the poetical and in the daily language. With all these resourceful figures of speech, the Biblical scribes sometimes attain an extraordinary descriptive power, which is particularly noticeable in the prophetic books.

When joy of life disappears,

the joy of our heart is ceased; our dance is turned into mourning (Lament. 5:15).

When God punishes His people,

The mirth of tabrets [i.e., dancing] ceaseth . . . (Isa. 24:8).

After the tribulations of the people are over, the "virgin Israel" will hear God's pronouncement:

Again shalt thou be adorned with thy tabrets, and shalt go forth in the dances of them that make merry (Jer. 31:4).

Then shall the virgin rejoice in the dance . . . (Jer. 31:13).

The dance used in Biblical metaphors is often imbued with an even more descriptive force. The tale about the Leviathan, for instance, contains this highly impressive simile:

In his neck abideth strength, and dismay danceth before him (Job 41:13).

Eternal wisdom is manifest in one of the Proverbs:

To everything there is a season, and a time for every purpose under the heaven. . . . A time to weep, and a time to laugh; a time to mourn, and a time to dance (Eccl. 3:4).

Another of the Proverbs (26:7) contains a simile, which is best expressed in LUTHER's translation:

Wie einem Krüppel das Tanzen, also stehet dem Narren an, won Weisheit zu reden (Like the dancing of a lame one, so is a parable in the mouth of fools).

The "Song of Songs" contains a reference to a seemingly peculiar kind of Jewish dance (7:1; 6:13), the "dance of Maḥanaim," which has been misunderstood and interpreted erroneously by all Biblical expositors, and mistranslated in *all* English Bible editions. Even the generally reliable *Jewish Translation* does not do justice to the passage, rendering it as

What will you see in the Shulammite? As it were a dance of two companies.

Modern Biblical exegesis misses completely the meaning of the term and its application in the Canticles. The interpretations oscillate among

an ancient city celebrated for its bayaderes and for the orgiastic cults which were practiced there (Ernest Renan),
a dance or a round in the camp (Morris Jastrow Jr.),

a traditional war dance between two armies before they joined battle (Leroy Waterman),

each one being more misleading than the others.

Without reference to an earlier Biblical passage, in which the word *mahanayim* is used for the first time, the simile in the "Song of Songs" is bound to be incomprehensible. In the story of Jacob's flight from Laban, the chronicler relates the eventual reconciliation of the two patriarchs. After which

> early in the morning Laban rose up, and kissed his sons and his daughters, and blessed them. And Laban departed, and returned unto his place. And Jacob went on his way, and the angels of God met him. And Jacob said when he saw them: "This is God's camp" (*mahaneh*). And he called that place *Mahanaim* [literally "two camps"] (Gen. 32:1-3).

What Jacob saw in his vision was two groups of angels who—similar to antiphonal singing—performed a sort of "antichoreic" dance ("one to another"), i.e., in two groups which alternately led the dancing. Therefore Jacob called the place *Mahanaim,* "Two Camps."

The true interpretation of the "dance of Mahanaim" becomes simple and natural if this expression is read in close connection with its related context as presented in the Hebrew numeration of the verses:[89]

> 7:1 "Why will ye look upon the Shulammite,
> As upon the *dance of Mahanaim?*

> 7:2 How beautiful are thy feet in sandals,
> O prince's daughter!
> The joints of thy thighs are like jewels,
> The work of the hands of a cunning workman.

> 7:3 Thy navel is like a round goblet,
> Wherein no mingled wine is wanting:
> Thy belly is like a heap of wheat
> Set about with lilies.

> 7:4 Thy *two breasts* are like *two fawns*
> That are *twins* of a roe. . . .

Verse 2, immediately following the "dance of Mahanaim," deals with the dancing Shulammite, and the subsequent verses form a single dithyramb to the beauty and charm of the dancing maiden. Among these, that the pertinent simile of verse 4 harks back to the two dancing groups of angels in Genesis 32:1-3 lends itself logically and irresistibly. The "dance of Mahanaim" is none other than a reference to the breasts of the Shulammite, which are swaying rhythmically in her dance, like the two groups of angels in Jacob's vision.

This explanation fully conforms with the roguishly erotic character of the wedding songs compiled in the Canticles, and at the same time unriddles the hitherto misconstrued and misunderstood expression in the Biblical text.

Should one put together these multitudinous details into a composite picture, one would surely admit that dance played the same significant part in the life of ancient Israel as singing and playing. As a concurrent expression of any popular celebration, dance was always the most effective physical release of psychic tension, especially when a common feeling of happiness pervaded the masses.

Voice, instrument, and body, the natural media for singing, playing, and dancing, were united in the music of Ancient Israel into an indivisible entity. In them, collectively, music in the broader sense became a reality.

THE HEALING POWER OF MUSIC

David's playing the "harp" to chase away Saul's melancholy permits insight into the belief, generally accepted in Antiquity, that music had the specific property of healing mental diseases.

At the time when the Biblical text received its written form, music had already lost its magic connotation. The memory of it, however, was still strong enough in the conviction of the Jewish people to attribute the healing of Saul to the magic sound of music. According to this belief, music was a means of overpowering evil spirits so that they would abandon their victims.

It was an ancient belief that music had not only a sedative, but also a stimulating effect, capable of increasing the morbid impulses and bringing them to a climax. Thus, through a violent discharge, music would bring about the intended relief. Music as a form of therapy may be said to represent a transitional form between magic and medicine. This may be observed even today among primitive peoples, where the priest is at the same time magician and medicine man.

In an attack of madness, and under the exciting effect of music, Saul made an attempt on David's life (1 Sam. 18:10,11). After the attempt failed, the desired relaxation in Saul's state of mind must have been accomplished, for shortly afterwards "he made him his captain over a thousand," an act caused not only by his fear of David (1 Sam. 18:12), but probably also by the remorse highly characteristic of overexcited persons, desiring to make up, through increased zeal, the wrong committed in a state of frenzy.

In connection with the ability of music to heal certain diseases, the Talmud tells of an appliance that caused drops of water to drip continually on a vessel of metal and thereby produce a monotonous buzzing sound, by which the sick person was put to sleep and, eventually, led to recovery.[1] Although this cannot be considered "music" in the proper sense of the word, the rhythmical monotony produced by this device might nevertheless have had a certain music-like effect upon the sick body or the sick soul. At any rate, it shows that primitive superstition, in magic as well as in medicine, used semi-musical procedures for its aims.

SACHS makes pertinent observations concerning the relationship of primitive medicine and music:

> Where the medicine man (*shaman*) performs religious ceremonies, the music approaches the liturgical intonation. And from the chants of the witch doctor it has descended by a long chain of heredity to the liturgy of higher religions; it lives on in the *Saman* of the Hindu as in the *Leinen* of the Jews and the *Lectio* of the Christian Churches.[2]

ATHENAIOS states that music, and especially certain modes (*modoi*), serve as remedy against specific physical diseases:

> The music can also heal diseases as Theophrastus recorded in his work "On Inspiration"

(*Peri Enthousiasmou*): he says that persons subject to sciatica (*ischiakous*) would always be free from its attacks if one played the flute (*aulos*) in the Phrygian mode over the part affected.[3]

There are legends in Antiquity that tell us of other singer-musicians who were efficient in curing diseases by their art. Among them were TERPANDROS and ARION, who healed the Ionians and Lesbians by their singing. HISMENIAS was credited with relieving the Boeotians of their gout by his singing. Of EMPEDOCLES it is reported that by the power of his song he succeeded in calming the rage of one of his guests.[5]

The idea of the healing power of music was particularly widespread among the Jews until late talmudic times. We even find in the Talmud the mention of a song (*shir peg'ayim*) that was allegedly capable of serving as protection in times of epidemic[4]

These are of course but legendary tales, but they show that the belief in the healing power of music was widespread in Antiquity, and continued through the Middle Ages and even into the "enlightened" era of the Renaissance.

PROPHECY AND MUSIC

Among all the peoples of Antiquity music was generally considered a divine gift. This explains its constant association with prophecy which, in many instances, was looked upon as something profoundly akin to music in spiritual substance.

The affinity between prophecy and music is particularly conspicuous among the Hebrews. It can even be said that Jewish prophecy was born out of the spirit of music. The musican belonging to the Levitical fraternity was called a "prophet," a "seer." As a designation for Levitical singing, the chroniclers employ the term *nibba*, using the same word to characterize the enthusiastic attitude of the prophets (1 Chron. 25:1ff.).[5]

The singer-prophet is driven by the spirit of Yahveh (2 Chron. 20:14), therefore he is at the same time *ro'eh*, "seer," or "diviner" [of the future]. Not only were the three precentors of David (Asaph, Heman, and Jedithun-Ethan) such prophets or seers, but the chroniclers also mention Gad and Nathan (2 Chron. 29:25).

There is no radical difference between the great national prophets such as Isaiah and Amos, and the singer-prophets. The latter pour out their enthusiasm in harmonious sounds; the former clothe their visions in the spoken form of language heightened by ecstasy and having a specific melodious undercurrent. In this extraordinary state of mind, the rapturous "seer" does not use daily language, but employs a form of "poetry" or "song." His utterance is called *masa*, a Hebrew word that appears in 1 Chron. 15:22, 2 Chron. 24:27, Isa. 13:1, Prov. 31:1, and Lam. 2:14, and that was given in our English translations the most diversified and seemingly contradictory meaning: song [of the Levites], oracle, prophecy, visions, dreams, revelations, warnings, sayings—but mostly "burden."

These different interpretations, however, are not so incompatible as may appear on first sight. They all refer to the various forms of prophetic message (or pronouncement), which weighs like a burden upon the prophet's soul, a burden imposed upon him by the Lord's commandment and which he transmits to the people in a tangible form akin to a solemn song of the Levitical singers.

In the primitive meaning of the word, *nabi*, the prophet (pl. *nebi'im*) had no relationship to music. It implied "speaker," i.e., a person who could render eloquently the exalted sentiments of the people. This is what the term originally signified when it was used for the first time in the Bible. When Moses, entrusted by the Lord with the formidable task of liberating his people, pointed to his inability to speak fluently (he was probably a stutterer), God Himself advised him that

> Aaron thy brother shall be thy prophet (*nabi*), . . . and Aaron thy brother shall speak unto Pharaoh (Exod. 7:1, 2).

In a former passage, the Lord says about Aaron:

> And he shall be thy spokesman (*dibber*) unto the people; and it shall come to pass, that he shall be to thee a mouth (*lepeh*) (Exod. 4:15).

In particular, *nabi* is the man who speaks in the name of God, whom the Lord has chosen as his spokesman in order to proclaim His will to the people. The root *naba*, "to announce," is identical with the verb *naba*, "to gush" (like a well) and, in a figurative sense, "to speak easily, with enthusiasm," for the gift was generally bestowed upon men enlightened by God .

The Septuagint always translates *nabi* as *prophētēs*. This word is derived from *prophanai*, "to speak in the name of someone" and, in a wider sense, it originally had the meaning of "spokesman," and "interpreter." PLATO called the poets the "prophets of the Muses," that is, their interpreters.[6] The interpreter and expounder of ARISTOTLE's works was called his "prophet." Apollo was said to be Jupiter's "prophet," since he was able to render most precisely the thoughts of the supreme god. Following this idea, PHILO says about Moses:

> Of the divine utterances, some are spoken by God in His own Person with His prophet for interpreter.[7]

The Church Fathers also used the word in this sense. JOHN CHRYSOSTOM stated repeatedly that the prophets were spokesmen of God.

Thus, in accordance with its etymology as well as its general use, the term *nabi* stands for a man enlightened by God and serving as His mediator. He is not necessarily a foreteller of things to come, but it is essential that his word be imbued with a divine revelation. As a rule, however, all the Jewish prophets have predicted the future, or at least warned about future consequences, since God infused their speeches with terrifying or hopeful prophecies, depending on whether He wanted to punish or console His people. Thus, the prophets were called by all sorts of significant terms, such as *ro'eh*, "seer," *hozeh*, "diviner" [of the future], *'ish ha-ru'ah*, "man of the (divine) spirit," and *'ish 'elohim*, "man of God."

The difference between "prophet" and "seer" is clearly defined by the Biblical chroniclers:

> Beforetime in Israel, when a man went to inquire of God, thus he said: "Come and let us

go to the seer"; for he that is now called a prophet (*nabi*) was beforetime called a seer (*ro'eh*) (1 Sam. 9:9).

Consequently, the function of the *ro'eh* was mainly that of predicting the future, while the later *nabi* was rather the "spokesman of God." At the time of Amos the stress was again laid more upon the visionary qualities of the prophet, who was supposed to possess the gift of "second sight"; he then was called *hozeh*. Soon, however, the term was tainted with a bad flavor; *hozim* were the false prophets who fraudulently attributed to themselves certain qualities in order to satisfy their greed (Micah 5:7,11).

The different meanings of the term *nabi*, as exposed in the Biblical text, can be summarized as follows:

1) The confidant of God (Gen. 20:7; cf. Isa. 48:1 ff; Ps. 105:15).

2) The interpreter of God's thoughts, a spokesman of God (Exod. 7:1; Deut. 18:18; Jer. 15:19).

3) A singer, musician, poet (Exod. 15:1–20; Judg. 4:4; 5:2 ff; 1 Sam. 10:5 ff; 1 Chron. 25:1 ff; etc.).

4) A seer who predicts and reveals the hidden events of the future and who has visions of God (Deut. 13:2; 2 Sam. 9:9; 1 Kings 22:7,8; 2 Kings 3:11; etc.).

5) A madman, possessed by the evil spirit, or pseudo-prophet, in a state of frenzy (1 Sam. 12:10; 1 Kings 18:29).

6) A worker of miracles (Deut. 13:1; Ecclus. 48:14,15; cf. 2 Kings 13:21).

According to the fundamental interpretation, however, the prophet was God's spokesman, a mediator between the Lord and His people. This is beautifully expressed by PHILO in a musical metaphor:

Under the prophet's words I recognized the voice of the invisible Master whose invisible hand plays on the instrument of human speech.[8]

At another place he says also:

For prophets are the interpreters of God, who make full use of their organs of speech to set forth what He wills.[9]

Moses was the first of the great prophets (Deut. 18:18). God revealed himself to Samuel (1 Sam. 3:10). David had at his court the "seer" (*hozeh*) Gad and the "prophet" (*nabi*) Nathan, who told him the past and the future (2 Sam. 7:2; 7:17; 12:1; 12:25; 24:18,19; 1 Kings 1:10; 1:22; 1:32 ff; 2 Chron. 29:23). David himself used to prophesy; in the song of praise, called by the chronicler "the last words of David," he said himself:

the spirit of the Lord spoke by me, and His word was upon my tongue (2 Sam. 23:2).

Besides prophets, there were prophetesses in Israel. The first of them mentioned in the Bible was Moses' sister Miriam (Exod. 15:20). The meaning of "prophecy" here is still that of the heroic age, when the prophet was identical with the singer-musician, that is, the folkbard, not the divinely inspired intermediary of God, as outlined above.

Deborah was a judge in Israel,[10] but was also called by the chronicler a "prophetess" (Judg. 4:4). As did Miriam, she owed this distinction to her attributes as a minstrel. Again, there are no indications of Deborah's ability to foretell the future, which goes to show that the term "prophetess" as applied to her was due to her gift as a singer.

After Deborah, there was a centuries-long dearth of information about prophetesses. This certainly was due not to their actual absence, but probably to the fact that in the opinion of the chroniclers their importance was eclipsed by that of Miriam and Deborah.

The next woman mentioned as *nebiy)ah* was Isaiah's wife (Isa. 8:3). Many exegetes, both Jewish and non-Jewish, consider her to have been a real prophetess, "even if we know nothing of the prophecies pronounced by her."[11] There are good reasons to assume, however, that Isaiah's wife belonged to the category of folkbards, just as did Miriam and Deborah.

A real prophetess, Huldah, is mentioned in the days of King Josiah (2 Kings 22:14). The king sent messengers to her to ask for an oracle; she proclaimed the Lord's forgiveness to the king because of his remorse and repentance (2 Kings 22:19,20).

After this, prophetesses are mentioned by Ezekiel (Ezek. 13:17–23). But they apparently belonged to the class of unethical sorceresses and diviners against whom other prophets besides Ezekiel poured out their wrath.

Finally, we come across the prophetess Noadiah of the post-Babylonian period (Neh. 6:14). We know nothing about her except her name, and there are no indications whether she belonged to the category of minstrels, or else possessed—like Huldah—a gift for true prophecy.

The announcement of the prophet Joel that "your sons and your daughters shall prophesy" (Joel 3:1) has only a symbolic meaning; it is unlikely that prophetesses who could foretell future things were referred to here.[12]

The Old Testament even mentions a prophet who did not belong to the Jewish faith: Bala(am, the author of several exquisite poetic parables. To be sure, the Biblical text does not apply the term of prophet to him directly. But the Lord revealed Himself to him, he spoke in the name of God, and his language is very similar to that of the great Jewish prophets (Num. 22:3,8,12). No wonder that the early rabbinical writers attributed to him a rank akin to that of Moses.[13]

During the early history of Israel, wandering prophets roamed about in groups and excited themselves mutually by music and dance until they arrived at a state of ecstasy. Their fanatic songs, their violent gestures combined with bewitching and probably wordless incantations, the rhythmic beating of drums, and the continuous invocation of the deity all produced upon the onlookers such a fascinating effect that, by way of mass-suggestion, the state of rapture was evidently transferred to them as well. At times, this actually reached such enormous proportions that the persons so influenced lost all awareness of their surroundings (1 Sam. 19:20–24; Num. 11:25; 11:26–29).

A most conspicuous collective prophecy directly associated with music is related in the speech of Samuel held at the anointment of Saul as king of Israel (1 Sam. 10:5,6).

The Fathers of the Church compared the prophets either to instruments of music that, in the hands of the Holy Spirit, produce harmonious sounds, or to brilliant mirrors of crystal that reflect faithfully the divine thought.

God's communications with the prophets came about in three different ways: through the word, through visions, and through dreams. In general, the divine verbal utterance was not given in an articulate language, heard by mortal ears; it was perceived only by the "inner hearing" of the chosen ones. Only on very rare occasions did God reveal Himself in a manner that could be heard by outsiders, as at the invocation of Moses from the bush (Exod. 3:4), at the addressing of Samuel in the Sanctuary (1 Sam. 3:4 ff), and a few other instances. God's messages received by the prophets in this manner were then transmitted to the people either in the form of exalted oracles,[14] or else they were put into writing in the prophetic books and thus preserved for posterity.

Numerous Biblical and post-Biblical passages testify to the religious ecstasy induced by music. David's enraptured dance at the occasion of bringing home the ark of the Covenant belongs to this category (1 Chron. 13:8). Elisha needed music for his prophecy (2 Kings 3:15). The chroniclers firmly believed that religious ecstasy would exert an influence upon the events themselves, which otherwise would not occur. Once, when the Levites had put themselves into a state of prophetic rapture by singing hymns, a surprising miracle happened: Israel's enemies, the Moabites, Ammonites, and Edomites mutually annihilated themselves (2 Chron. 20:21 ff).

In a later source, the gnostic acts of St. Thomas, there is a passage giving an eloquent description of the ecstatic rapture created by music:

> The flute girl, holding the flute in her hand, went round them all; and when she came to the place where the apostle was, she stood over him, playing the flute over his head a long time. . . . And the apostle began to sing and to repeat this song . . . and what had been said by him they did not understand. . . . But the flute-girl alone heard all, for she was Hebrew by race.[15]

Besides the *halilim*, the prophets also used other instruments for evoking ecstasy, such as the psaltery (*nebel*), the lyre (*kinnor*) and the timbrel (*tof*), the last one used as rhythmical support for dancing. For music was always served as the strongest stimulus to men endowed with ecstatic dispositions. The most striking example of this phenomenon is the enraptured King Saul. His prophetic outpourings reached such a degree of ecstasy that he stripped off his clothes and stayed naked for a whole day and a whole night (1 Sam. 19:24).[16] To be sure, the excitement of Saul may be explained to a certain extent by his abnormal psychic disposition, which manifested itself in recurrent fits of melancholy and raving madness (1 Sam. 16:14 ff; 18:10). Nevertheless, he undoubtedly belonged to the category of ecstatic *nebi'im*.

The state of unconscious and musically stimulated ecstasy, primitively the concomitant phenomenon of prophecy, receded more and more into the background among the later great prophets. There remained merely the innermost and rather unobtrusive possession by the spirit of God, in which state the prophet announced the Lord's message orally.

As a general rule, the authors of the Biblical books were not intent on preserving their names for posterity. Anonymity was a common characteristic of literature and poetry in the ancient Orient. As for the prophetic books in particular, these were in reality not so much the products of the prophets themselves as of their disciples, who were anxious to preserve in writing, for future generations, the teachings of their masters—the true heralds of national consciousness. It will probably never be possible to find out how many of the prophetic books were written by those prophets whose names they bear. This circumstance, however, does not diminish their poetic beauty or their intrinsic message, both of which represent eternal and priceless spiritual treasures.

The Oriental poets have always been considered as possessing supernatural gifts. Ancient Israel shared this belief and thus, in the imagination of the people, the poet and the prophet were blended into a single individual. The Jewish *nebi⁽im* were at the same time poets, even though not all of their utterances were presented in the form of regular poetry. At any rate, the oracles of the prophets distinguished themselves by a literary language palpably different from ordinary prose. Furthermore, it may safely be assumed that these oracular statements were musically intoned and presented in a chanting manner, the necessary prerequisite for exerting a stirring effect upon the masses listening to them. All this contributed to the belief, widely shared in the ancient Semitic world, that both prophecy and poetry originate from a supernatural inspiration and must be cast, therefore, into a poetic form.

Just as the prophet was inspired by music, so was the poet. The prophet conveyed his sacred message to the sounds of the harps:

> Hear this, all ye peoples; give ear, all ye inhabitants of the world, both low and high, rich and poor together. My mouth shall speak wisdom, and the meditation of my heart shall be understanding. I will incline my ear to a parable; I will open my dark saying upon the harp (Psalm 48:2,3).

As may be learned from this and other Biblical passages, the poet-prophets proclaimed their messages in the form of a rhythmic, metrical prose, different from the style of ordinary recitation, different inasmuch as it had an enhanced ardor and a specific speech-melody. This may be the reason why the liturgical functions of the Levitical singers were associated with the verb *nibba,* "to prophesy." (1 Chron. 25:2,3).

The divine power of poetic inspiration applies to all art forms created by the agitation of the soul, and it also constitutes the psychological background for prophecy. Thus, the innermost association between music, poetry, and prophecy becomes invested with an inherent mysterious force in which music has the ability to stir the human soul to such an extent that those who are susceptible to it "speak with tongues," meaning that they enter a state of rapture displaying the presence of divine revelation. The Arabs believe that the inspiration of the poet and musician derives from a specific demon of poetry and music.[17] In ancient Israel it was not a demon who brought about the prophetic ecstasy, but the hand of God reposing on the prophet. God's breath permeated the prophet's whole being. His commandment served as an inducement to perform the holy ministry.

Thus, prophecy in Israel, especially in its higher stages, was the manifestation of the religious power ingrained in the human soul; it was a valve through which the religious feeling of the people, often reaching its highest level, strove to escape; it was the visible embodiment of the word, the will, and the omnipotence of God, which revealed themselves through His chosen spokesmen.

In all this, music played an essential aiding role. Primitively a subordinate element of magic and later in healing ceremonies, music at the highest stage of Jewish religion had the amazing ability to stir the innermost sentiments of the soul, to awaken the supernatural powers of God's chosen men. Thus, music was considered one of the most important factors that enabled humans to participate in the divine revelation.

WOMEN IN THE MUSIC OF ANCIENT ISRAEL

The history of civilization of the ancient Orient contains ample documentation about the role women played in the sacred and secular life of that time. Written records as well as pictorial displays testify to the various activities of women as dancers, singers, and instrumentalists.

Judging from Biblical sources, the role of women in the musical practice of the Hebrews was uncontested only in the dance. As singers, their role appears to have been of subordinate importance. As instrumentalists, their activity is so veiled, even blurred by the Biblical scribes, that at a superficial glance women seem to have been kept aloof artificially from instrumental music or, worse, were shown to have little if any aptitude for it.

One of the reasons why the role of women in the musical practice of Ancient Israel is rather obscurely documented is that, as time passed, the Biblical text underwent repeated, and rather incisive, editorial changes. In their purificatory zeal, the priestly chroniclers tried particularly to eliminate anything that might have alluded to, or recalled, the primitive pagan, pre-Yahvistic rites of the Hebrews, when women participated regularly in them. With the suppression of the Biblical allusions to such practices, references to women as ritual singers and instrumentalists were also deleted. Only scattered references to their participation appear here and there in the Scriptures.

The other reason might have been due to the gradually developing anti-feminine tendency of the priestly caste, to the extent that women were gradually displaced from practically all ritual functions. Consequently, the indications in the Biblical text that they ever had a share in the sacred service had also to be erased, or so transformed as to become almost irrecognizable.

The priestly scribes seem to have taken no offence at the role of women in secular music, therefore most records of their activity remain unchanged in the Bible. To this category belonged primarily the part women played as dancers and singers outside the sanctuary.

A reason for the underestimation of women's ability as instrumentalists might have been the self-conceit and narrow attitude of the Levitical music guild.[18] Possibly also the elementary instinct of self-preservation might have induced the Levites to eliminate women-musicians, as dangerous competitors, from the Temple ritual. There is no doubt, however, that in olden times, prior to the establishment of the organized Temple service, and even in the First Temple, women regularly participated in the ritual as singers and instrumentalists.

The activity of women as dancers has been examined in an earlier section of this study. Also their role as singers has been treated previously in a general way. It will be necessary, however, to discuss the activity of women as singers from a more specific angle.

The Bible contains no direct references to the participation of female singers in the Temple choir. Nevertheless, there are indirect allusions to singing women in the sacred service, among these the statement that in the pre-Davidic sanctuary the women, like the Levites, had to make their appearance at the east side of the tent and perform certain ritual functions (Exod. 38:8). Is it to be supposed that these were merely subordinate functions, consisting of some menial work? This is rather improbable, because such menial services were assigned to a special class, the *Nethinim,* who originally had been slaves of the Levites.

The "Court of Women,"[19] with its metal mirrors and probably other implements, testifies expressly to the role of women as performers of dances in religious ceremonies. This must have been the place in the sanctuary where the dancers for the divine service could put on special attire, adorn themselves with a specific headdress, and apply the makeup customary in the Orient, and so forth.

Apart from dancing, the women's part in the cult might have been identical with that of the Levitical musicians. Up to the time of David, women were the predominant performers of singing and dancing.[20] Miriam is the prototype of these women in early Jewish rites (Exod. 15:20). In olden times women seem to have served merely part time in the sanctuary. Subsequently, the custom developed that young maidens, but mostly widows, devoted themselves permanently to the sacred service.[21] These women were recruited generally from among the wives and daughters of the Levitical singers.[22] However, there were members of the priestly families among them as well.

In scrutinizing the role of women in the Temple and the Synagogue, SCHECHTER refers to an ancient rabbinical book in which he had professedly discovered some indications for the participation of women in the Levitical choir. He says that

> if we were to trust a certain passage in the "Chapters of R. Eliezer," we might perhaps conclude that during the First Temple the wives of the Levites formed a part of the choir.[23]

However, he restricts his statement to saying that

> the meaning of the passage is too obscure and doubtful for us to be justified in basing on it so important a reference.[24]

It is surprising to find such an extremely cautious statement with regard to the participation of women in the sacred service, especially when PHILO's writings furnish indisputable evidence to this effect.

The Biblical story of the Jews returning from the Babylonian captivity contains definite proof that the Levitical choir employed female singers even in the First Temple. This story has been treated in another part of this study; nevertheless, we have to come back to it once more in order to fully clarify the subject.

When the Israelites were carried into the Babylonian captivity in 586 B.C.E., following the destruction of Solomon's temple, the sacerd service, the sacrifices, the entire ritual ceremonial, and also its musical background, ceased to exist. Temple music became devoid of its purpose, but popular music also suffered, for the joyful expression of the people's soul was condemned to silence in oppression and sorrow.

Nevertheless, when in 538 B.C.E., after an exile of forty-eight years, the first group of repatriates started their march home, there were among them "a hundred twenty and eight singers: the children of Asaph," that is, the descendants of Asaph, and also of the other Levitical singers, for whom the chronicler uses the name of the most famous precentor of Solomon's Temple (Ezra 2:41). Furthermore, there were in the procession of the repatriates "two hundred singing men and singing women" (Ezra 2:65). The figures in the Book of Nehemiah are slightly different; here, the number of the Levitical singers, "the children of Asaph," is one hundred forty-eight (Neh. 7:44), and that of the "singing men and singing women" two hundred and forty-five" (Neh. 7:67). For the total number of repatriates (42,360 and 7,337 servants), the number of the returning male and female singers is proportionately considerable. Moreover, we have to bear in mind that not all the Jews living in Babylonia returned to Zion with the first group. A relatively large number remained in exile voluntarily, among them male and female singers.

A second group returned to Israel in 458 B.C.E. And still there must have remained in Babylonia, with other parts of the Jewish population, male and female musicians. For we possess documentary evidence that the Jews who settled permanently in Babylon continued to cultivate the ancient musical tradition. The fortunate musical discoveries made in Babylonia by IDELSOHN in our own time would not have been possible without the Jewish splinter group's clinging to the ancient musical heritage.

The relatively large number of singers returning with the first repatriates constitutes definite proof that the cultivation of music was continued in the exile, regardless of all hardships. In spite of the fact that Jewish liturgical music had been for half a century without its ritual meaning and purpose, the Levites managed to preserve the ancient tradition, thus nursing the faint hope of an eventual return to the homeland.

But how about the "singing men and singing women" mentioned specifically by Ezra and Nehemiah? Following RASHI's interpretation, many Biblical expositors consider them to have been secular singers who merely accompanied those returning home and, through the medium of their art, alleviated the hardships of the wandering. No doubt joyous singing had the power to lift the spirit and kindle anew the courage of the repatriates. This, however, would hardly explain the disproportionately large number of "secular" male and female singers in Babylonia.

> It is not a happy suggestion that the function of these singers was secular. Is it likely that this company of religious enthusiasts, returning to a desolate home, had carried with them this number of singers for secular amusement?,

asks PERITZ.[25]

This objection, however correct in itself, is only partially justified. To understand and fully appreciate the relatively large number of the returning secular singers, we have to examine the aim and purpose of musical culture during the exile. The intense cultivation of liturgical music among the Babylonian captives did not stem exclusively from the urge to preserve the Levitical tradition, however desirable this goal might have been. It had still another, deeper meaning: music in the exile represented, as it were, a substitute for the divine service of the Temple. In keeping alive liturgical music, the Levitical singers became the legitimate guardians of the religious tradition. Music became a spiritual substitute for the animal sacrifice, for which it formerly furnished the tonal background in the sanctuary. In the exile, music substituted for the sacrifice, symbolically, and no longer physically.

Would it not then be logical to assume that the returning "secular" male and female singers had also been prepared in the exile, at least partially, for the future sacred service? The number of the Levitical progeny must have undergone certain fluctuations in Babylonia. The Levitical tradition, however, had to be preserved under all circumstances. With this in view, is it too far-fetched to suppose that many non-Levitical singers have been trained ahead of time as prospective substitutes for the Levites in case the latter should not survive the exile in sufficient numbers? It is indeed highly probable that the "male singers and female singers" mentioned by Ezra and Nehemiah must have been in part non-Levitical singers, whose functions did not terminate with the repatriation, but were supposed to start just after the return to Jerusalem.

PERITZ is right insofar as he assumes that the returning non-Levitical singers did not accompany the repatriates "for secular amusement" alone. In reality, they represent extra-Levitical reserves for the sacred service, the restitution of which was planned for as soon as possible after the return, and for which "women singers" were just as necessary as "men singers."

This is the main significance of Ezra's and Nehemiah's statements which, besides their authenticity as historical records, furnish the irrefutable proof that women participated in the Levitical choir from the very beginning, and even after the Babylonian exile, at least for a certain time, in the Second Temple.

Apart from the above-quoted Biblical references, PHILO's writings contain further indications pertaining to the role of women in sacred singing. This Judaeo-Hellenistic writer and philosopher lived during the last decades of the Third (Herod's) Temple, in a period in which the ancient Jewish tradition was still alive. His historical statements have, therefore, a high credibility. His enlightened education protected him from orthodox literal belief in the Biblical text as well as from bias with regard to the priestly tradition, insofar as these contradicted the philosophy and advanced knowledge of natural phenomena accepted by the coeval Hellenistic civilization.

The participation of women in the cult as dancers and also, possibly, as singers, is mentioned several times in his writings.[26] However, his works do not contain any hint as to whether in his day women were still employed in the sanctuary. Probably this was no longer the case, as indicated by his remark that women were

> resolved to win the prize of high excellence [and] not to be outstripped by the men in holiness.[27]

This might have constituted for the Levitical musicians too dangerous a competition, so that women were gradually eliminated from ritual ceremonies.

It is beyond doubt, however, that women and maidens participated as singers in the Davidic and Solomonic music organization. Even after the return from the Babylonian exile, at least in the first period of the Second Temple, they might have retained the same functions, until they were removed and replaced by singing boys.[28]

In addition to their participation in the Temple choir, women had another important function, one not mentioned in the Bible, to be sure, but constituting an indispensable requirement for certain ritual ceremonies.

On the great religious festivities like Passover, the Feast of the Weeks, the Tabernacles, and even on minor festive occasions, regular pilgrimages to Jerusalem took place on an annual basis, in which men and women participated in large numbers. Following the daytime religious devotions in the Temple, the festivity was brought to a climax by a popular entertainment, in which dances were the main feature. These dances were performed, according to the ancient custom, by the sexes separately, or by women alone.

> If numerous women from each of the tribes always took part in these dances on festivals, there must still have been some constantly at the Sanctuary who should know how to lead the dances, and they may have been the same as those who daily performed the sacred music there.[29]

In other words, in the evening of the religious festival the female singers belonging to the regular staff of the Temple functioned as dance leaders, a role assigned to women in ancient Israel from primeval times, as we know from the Bible (Exod. 15:20; Judith 3:7, a.o.). In addition, EWALD finds it possible to assume with certainty

> that women who sang and played lived there [i.e., in the Temple].[30]

This, however, is very doubtful, because the Temple did not contain any living quarters so far as we know. Even the guardians of the gates had to pass the night in the Sanctuary in the most primitive way, sleeping on mats spread out on the floor, as we learn from rabbinical statements. Such primitive accommodations would certainly not have been adequate for the female members of the Temple personnel.

The role of women as "prophetesses," i.e., as folkbards, has been examined earlier.

Whereas the part women played in sacred singing can be established from the Scriptures but indirectly; their place in secular music is handled by the Biblical chroniclers with much less restraint. Secular female singers (*sharot*) are mentioned in several places in the Bible, e.g., 2 Sam. 19:36; Isa. 23:16; Eccl. 2:8, and so on. They participated in social entertainments, weddings, banquets, and popular festivities, and thus enhanced the joy of living and the pleasures of the festivals.

At all times, male and female singers belonged to the personnel of Oriental royal courts. Even in David's entourage there were "singing men and singing women," as evidenced by Barzillai's appeal to the king (2 Sam. 19:36). "Singing men and singing women" are also mentioned in the Proverbs (Eccl. 2:8), and in King Josiah's court (2 Chron. 35:25).

The role of the royal singers of both sexes was providential at the siege of Jerusalem by SENNAḤERIB in 701 B.C.E. In Assyrian cuneiform inscriptions are preserved the stipulations that the victorious SENNAḤERIB imposed upon King

Hezekiah in exchange for sparing Jerusalem from being pillaged and destroyed:

> Together with thirty talents of gold [and] eight-hundred talents of silver, he sent to me to Nineveh, my chief city, precious stones, cosmetics, . . . pure Uknû stones, couches of ivory, thrones of ivory, elephant skins, ivory, Ushû and Urkarinu wood, all kinds of treasures in quantity, and his daughters and women of the palace, and male and female musicians. He sent his messengers to deliver his tribute and to declare his subjection.[31]

It is not obvious from this text whether the singers mentioned among the other "treasures" of the tribute were Hezekiah's court singers or those of the sacred service. It is rather to be assumed, however, that the latter was the case, because the Jewish Temple singers acquired great fame in the ancient Orient. It is obvious that SENNAHERIB took advantage of the opportunity to enhance the lustre of his own court by demanding the deliverance of these renowned Israelitic singers. At any rate, this is one of the rare cases in which an Oriental monarch renounced the capture and pillage of the capital of a conquered enemy in exchange for its intangible artistic possessions.

Another aspect of the secular singing of women deals with the fact that the singing and playing of certain instruments belonged to the profession of women leading an immoral life (cf. Isa. 23:16; Ecclus. 9:4), since this was the general custom with courtesans of ancient Orient.[32]

There was in ancient Israel a musical profession belonging exclusively to the distaff side, that of the wailing women at funerals (*mekonenot*, or *ʾalit*).

The wailing women were not just any females participating at funerals, but only those who possessed certain prescribed skills, for which they had been specially trained, as is stated explicitly in the Bible:

> Teach your daughters wailing (*nehi*), and every one her neighbour lamentation (*ḳinah*) (Jer. 9:19).

Some of them must have been particularly efficient in this profession, and thus able to impart a highly emotional character to funeral ceremonies. Such women are alluded to in the Biblical passage:

> Consider ye, and call for the mourning women, that they may come, and send for the wise women, that they may come; and let them make haste, and take up a wailing for us (Jer. 9:16,17).

Amos's remark,

> proclaim lamentation to such as are skillful of wailing (Amos, 5:16)

likewise refers to such specially trained women.

To strike up wailing or lament was called *ʿanah*, "to sing," or "to intone." The procedure was either responsorial, when one began and the others responded, or antiphonal, when two groups alternated. The Mishnah gives a precise definition of both species:

> What is lamentation (*ʿinnuy*)? When all sing together. And wailing (*ḳinah*)? When one begins by herself and all respond after her.[33]

For wailing in antiphonal form there is a clear reference in the Bible. According to the prophet Zechariah, at the great lamentation in Jerusalem the houses of David, Nathan, Levi, and of the Shimeites will wail apart,

every family apart, and their wives apart (Zech. 12:12–14).

That wailing was a distinct profession is confirmed by the Talmud:

In Palestine [it is customary that] whenever a professional lamenter comes round people say: "Let those who are sore at heart weep with him."[34]

The Bible expresses the same idea in a somewhat generalized form:

Because man goeth to his long home, and the mourners go about the streets (Eccl. 12:5).

Also in another tractate:

When R. Ishmael died, a professional mourner commenced thus: "Ye daughters of Israel, weep over R. Ishmael."[35]

Wailing women accompanied the funeral procession and used various songs for different ceremonies in the course of it; every ceremony had its specifically prescribed song. The Talmud quotes the texts of eight such song-patterns.[36] Once the corpse was buried, the wailing would stop.[37] On certain days of the month and on other special days of the Jewish calendar, the functions of the wailing women were somewhat modified or limited.[38]

Some Biblical expositors characterize the activity of the wailing women not only as a profession, but also as an "art."[39] Others even consider them as "poetesses,"[40] trying to justify this by Jer. 9:19 ("Yea, hear the word of the Lord, O ye women, And let your ear receive the word of His mouth"). They allude also to the characteristic pattern of the *kinot*, common to most of the wailing songs, which warrants their classification as "poetry."[41] Undoubtedly, the profession of the wailing women required a certain training. However, to consider them as "poetesses" is scarcely justified. Generally, they used traditional threnodies, which any woman could learn easily. They were not necessarily endowed with poetical gifts, because these were not required for this profession.

Besides the wailing songs, the musical background of the funeral ceremony contained the playing of *halilim*, though the latter was not always performed by women. According to a rabbinical statement,

even the poorest in Israel should hire [for his wife's funeral] not less than two flutes (*halilim*) and one wailing woman (*mekonenot*).[42]

It may be inferred from this that whoever had the means could hire more than two instrumentalists and any number of wailing women. This shows that the volume of music at funerals was determined by the wealth and social standing of the deceased. Sometimes, when insufficient numbers of *halil*-players or skilled wailing women were available in a place, they were fetched from other towns.[43]

Another musical function assigned to women is indicated by the psalmist:

The Lord giveth the word; the women that proclaim the tidings are a great host (Psalm 68:12).

The Biblical word used here is *mebasserot* (SEPTUAGINT: *euangelizomenois;* VULGATE: *evangelizantibus*). It alludes to women who used to announce victories and celebrate them with songs, musical instruments, and dances.

Such women extolling victories are frequently mentioned in the Old Testament,[44] even though not always with the specific term of *mebasserot*. These victory celebrations of individuals and groups have one thing in common: they have an unmistakable religious background, a further indication of the participation of women in early religious ceremonies and ritual actions. Several of these Biblical references preserve fragments of songs performed on such occasions, as in Exod. 15:20 (Miriam's song after the passage of the Red Sea), Judg. 5:4 (Deborah's and Barak's triumphal paean), Judith 15:12 ff; 16:1. The term *mebasserot* apparently indicates a semi-religious function assigned to women outside the ritual ceremony, because they were the ones who welcomed the returning warriors and celebrated victory.

The anti-feminine tendency of the later priestly scribes has manifestly influenced some of the rabbinical Sages. In general, the singing of women is appreciated in the talmudic literature as one of the most beautiful divine gifts. Yet, the laxity of morals and customs under Hellenistic-Roman influence, and especially the practices of the courtesans, for whose trade music and singing were widely used requisites, gradually changed the aesthetic and moral attitude of the Sages. The rabbis say, for instance, that the voice of a woman has a sensual charm and is considered dangerous for men:

Listening to a woman's voice stirs his passions.[45]

The same idea is expressed even more emphatically by another teacher:

R. Joseph said: "When men sing and women join in, it is licentiousness; when women sing and men join in, it is like fire in tow."[46]

Still more intolerant are the following rabbinical statements:

Rab said: "The ear which listens to song should be torn off." Raba said: "When there is song in a house there is destruction on its threshold."[47]

The instruments used for the accompaniment of women's songs were considered unclean, contrary to the same instruments played by the Levites:

The harps whereto they [the women] sing (*nible ha-sharah*) are susceptible to uncleanness; but the harps of the sons of Levi (*nible bene Levi*) are not susceptible.[48]

A similar hostility toward singing by women can even be found with MAIMONIDES (1135–1204), who declares that secular music is prohibited, especially if it is performed by singing women.

The rise of Jewish sects restored the singing of women to its original significance in the religious usage of Jewry. Generally speaking, in their religious customs these sects followed the tradition of the Temple and Synagogue. The religious song of the sacred service, too, was taken over by the sectarians.

The two best-known Jewish sects were the Essenes and the Therapeutae, of which the latter accepted women in their ranks. Whatever formal position women may have occupied within the Therapeutae, their musical participation in the common convocations seems to have been equal to that of men.

While describing a large community of Therapeutae in the neighborhood of Alexandria (PHILO's home town), which he must have visited frequently, PHILO informs us, among other things, that the members of this sect spent six days of the week in isolation in their locked houses, and on the seventh day assembled in the common praying hall in which, following the custom of the early Synagogue, men and women occupied *separate* places.[49] The oldest of them read the Scriptures and gave explanations in a simple, unaffected manner. All listened to his talk in silence and with absorption.

> Then the Speaker rises and sings a hymn composed as an address to God, either a new one of his own composition or an old one by poets of an earlier day who have left behind them hymns in many measures and melodies, hexameters and iambics, lyrics suitable for processions or in libations and at the altars, or for the chorus,[50] whilst standing or dancing, with careful metrical arrangements to fit the various evolutions. . . . When they have to chant the closing lines or refrains, then they all lift up their voices, *men and women alike.*[51] (Italics mine)

A common frugal meal then would follow this hour of edification.

> After the supper they hold the sacred vigil which is conducted in the following way: They rise up all together and standing in the middle of the refectory form themselves first into two choirs, *one of men and one of women,* the leader and precentor chosen from each being the most honoured amongst them and also the most musical. Then they sing hymns to God composed of many measures and set to many melodies, sometimes *chanting together,* sometimes taking up the harmony *antiphonally.* . . . Then when each choir has separately done its own part in the feast . . . they mix and *both together become a single choir,* a copy of the choir set up of old beside the Red Sea in honour of the wonders there wrought. . . .
>
> It is on this model above all that the choir of the Therapeutae of *either sex,* note in response to note and voice to voice, *the bass of the men blending with the treble of the women, create a harmonious concent (symphonia), music in the truest sense!* (Italics mine).[52]

Thus, PHILO compares the choric singing and dancing of the Therapeutae with the "Song at the Red Sea." Yet, the musical practice of the Therapeutae was not merely the imitation of the manifestation at the Red Sea, but the conscious *return* to the ancient tradition of the Temple, namely to the epoch when in the musical part of the divine service men and women had their equal share.

Anti-feminine priestly scribes might have obscured this fact in the Biblical books. PHILO's report, interpreted correctly, brings to the fore once again the participation of women in the cult.

MUSIC AFTER SOLOMON'S DEATH

After Solomon's death (931 B.C.E.) the disruption of the nation into two kingdoms, those of northern Israel and southern Judah, resulted in fateful consequences. The people, weakened internally by frequent disturbances and fratricidal wars between the two halves of the nation, and shattered externally as a result of being wedged between the two rival powers Egypt and Assyria, were no longer able to ward off the cultural and spiritual influences of paganism, including those in the field of music.

Good and bad kings followed each other in rapid succession in both Israel and Judah. The frequent apostasy of the kings, who worshipped pagan deities, caused spasmodic interruptions of the sacred service, sustained sometimes for several decades, and in one case even for more than a century.

These political vicissitudes, plus the recurring apostasy and repentant return of the people to Yahveh's cult, had an immediate repercussive effect upon Temple music. Each time an idolatrous king abandoned the religion of the fathers, the sacred music was condemned to silence and threatened with extinction. Ordinarily a few years, even a few months, of inactivity suffice to jeopardize the stability of a musical tradition. And from this state until complete destruction is relatively a short time. It must be remembered that the ancient Jewish musical art was based exclusively on oral tradition, which could be preserved only if maintained without interruption.

In spite of all such setbacks, the fame of the Jewish singers gradually spread far beyond the boundaries of Israel, so much so, in fact, that when the Assyrian conqueror SENNAḤERIB besieged Jerusalem (701 B.C.E.), he demanded as ransom for sparing the city, and apart from a heavy tribute, the delivery of King Hezekiah's male and female singers. As noted earlier, in order to save David's city from destruction, the king had to comply with the victor's demand. How great must have been the value of these singers if an Oriental ruler, in exchange for them (and other treasures), was ready to refrain from the rudimentary compulsion of a conqueror to capture and pillage the enemy's capital!

In 537 B.C.E. a national disaster struck the Jewish people. NEBUCHADREZZAR conquered Jerusalem, destroyed Solomon's Temple, and carried off the flower of the nation into captivity to Babylonia. On the surface, this constituted the extinction of Jewish music, the sacred as well as the secular. Musical education, instruction in music, seemingly lost its aim and purpose. In Babylonia

> we hanged upon the willows our harps, for . . . how shall we sing the Lord's song in a foreign land? (Psalm 137:2).

In reality, however, the practice of music, and with it musical instruction, continued unabatedly, despite—and probably even because of—all the tragic circumstances.

The accomplishments of the Levitical singers during the Babylonian exile represent the most outstanding page of their history. Although in a foreign country, in suppression, they carried on their musical tradition in secrecy and succeeded not only in preserving the ancient tradition intact, but also in saving Jewish music from total extinction. During the forty-eight years of captivity new generations had to be instructed, the traditional music had to be transmitted from mouth to mouth, from ear to ear. Without foreseeable hope for return to the old homeland, a complex art discipline was kept alive, for which there was apparently no use in the exile and which was virtually meaningless for the Jews deprived of their sanctuary. Without the methodical work of the Levitical musicians, Jewish music would have perished irretrievably.

The Levites were not the only ones who kept the musical art alive during the Babylonian captivity. The secular musicians vied with the Levites in the preservation of the popular music practice, which must have had a sufficient number of teachers as well as pupils for several generations. For when, after forty-eight years of captivity, the first repatriates marched back to their old homesteads, there were among them one hundred and twenty-eight Levitical singers, and in addition two hundred male and female secular singers and musicians (Ezra 2:41,65).

A substantial part of the Israelites remained voluntarily in Babylonia. Freed from the fetters of slavery, living under favorable economic conditions, they were able unrestrictedly to maintain their cherished musical activity. Thus, we may take it for granted that musical instruction, liturgical as well as secular, was greatly stimulated among the Jews remaining in Babylonia.

About eighty years after the first stream of repatriates, a second group of Israelites returned to Zion. Among the immigrants there were again a number of Levitical singers (Ezra 7:7) and also secular musicians, even though the latter are not mentioned specifically this time. Their presence, however, may be inferred indirectly from Neh. 7:73, where the enumeration of the Temple dignitaries (priests, Levites, porters, singers, Nethinim) is followed, after "singers," by the somewhat puzzling interpolation "and some of the people." This would be manifestly superfluous in view of the comprehensive remark "and all Israel" that terminates the entire phrase. However, the correct meaning of the interpolation referred to presents itself logically if it is completed by the qualification "some *singers* of the people," i.e., non-Levitical, secular singers.

Even after this second repatriation, quite a few Israelites still remained in Babylonia. And all extant evidence seems to indicate that a substantial number of musicians also stayed behind to take care of the musical needs of the remaining Jews. Thus, besides the newly awakened musical culture in the Jewish homeland, there was a parallel phenomenon flourishing among the Israelites who chose Babylonia as their permanent domicile. The music of the homeland was irretrievably lost after the destruction of the Jewish national state; that of the Babylonian splinter group has been preserved until our own day, as proven by fortunate discoveries of recent times.[53]

The prominent position of the Temple singers has already been noted in connection with their activity of the First Temple. After the return from the exile it rose to an even higher level. The exercises in singing and playing, never neglected in the exile, were resumed with increased zeal. And so we see that at the laying of the foundation of the new Temple, shortly after the return, the Levitical singers, as before, provided the music for the ceremony (Ezra 3:10,11).

The artistic status of the Levitical singers was not affected by the Babylonian exile. Socially and economically, their situation improved compared with their ancient place in the Temple's hierarchy. The Kings DARIUS and ARTAXERXES instituted comprehensive reforms for the position of the Temple musicians, thereby creating an entirely new basis for their existence. Both Kings generously ordered that the Temple singers, supported until then by voluntary contributions of the people, be elevated to the status of employed functionaries, their subsistence henceforth provided by the royal treasury.

Already King CYRUS, after approving the construction of the new sanctuary with the restitution of the ancient divine service, decreed that the ministers of the cult, including the singers, should receive regular dues, that is a kind of "salary." These dues were mainly food produce taken from the king's estates:

> That of the king's goods, even the tribute beyond the River, expenses be given with all diligence unto these men, that they not be hindered (Ezra 6:8,9).

CYRUS ordered that such dues "be given them day by day without fail" (*Ibid.*), and DARIUS explicitly confirmed his predecessor's edict.

Soon the Temple singers became beneficiaries of even more far-reaching privileges. About eighty years after the first colony of captives returned under Zerubbabel, a second followed in 458 B.C.E., under Ezra's leadership (Ezra 7:7). Ezra, the Scribe, must have enjoyed special favors with King ARTAXERXES, because not only was he given permission for the second group to return, but "the king granted him all his requests," and these were by no means few in number (Ezra 7:6). The King's edict, which Ezra carried with him in a copy, enumerates all the things the repatriates were allowed to carry with them, which included practically everything they possessed in Babylonia, as well as what they needed after their return for the perpetuation of their cult. (Ezra 7:19,20).

For the Temple musicians, Ezra demonstrated special solicitude. He received from ARTAXERXES repeated confirmation of the daily salary for the singers, as guaranteed by his predecessor (Neh. 11:23). In addition to this salary furnished by the king's treasury, the Temple singers had still another source of income. Out of gratitude

> all Israel in the days of Zerubbabel, and in the days of Nehemiah, gave the portions of the singers and the porters, as every day required (Neh. 12:47).

The economic welfare of the singers was thus secured from two sides. Their wealth, and with it their influence and social standing, increased accordingly.

Apart from economic advantages, Ezra received from his royal benefactor further rights and privileges. The above-quoted edict of ARTAXERXES stipulates:

> Also we announce to you, that touching any of the priests, and Levites, the singers, porters, Nethinim, or servants of this house of God, it shall not be lawful to impose tribute, impost, or toll, upon them (Ezra 7:24).

This constituted the exemption of the musicians from all taxes, a privilege surpassing even that which King CYRUS granted to the corporation of the Temple singers. From now on, they were not only state functionaries, but were elevated to the rank of tax-exempt ministers to the sanctuary.

After the repatriates had settled in their ancient dwellings, they started to rebuild what was destroyed and, having secured their material existence, proceeded to reestablish their religious and national institutions. Surmounting many obstacles, and despite all kinds of intrigues, they succeeded in building strong walls around Jerusalem, thus insuring the new sanctuary with efficient protection.

After thus safeguarding Jerusalem against hostile attacks, Nehemiah ordered a census of the people, based upon the book of genealogy of the repatriates. The number of the Temple singers, "the children of Asaph," which had been one hundred and twenty-eight at the first return (Ezra 2:41), had risen to one hundred and forty-eight. (Neh. 7:44), while the number of secular male and female singers increased from two hundred (Ezra 2:65) to two hundred and forty-five (Neh. 7:67). This increase, considered numerically, does not seem to be very substantial for a lapse of more than half a century. The picture changes, however, if we take into account the economic situation prevailing at the period.

The first decades following the return were filled with securing a bare existence and attending to reconstruction. Rebuilding the national institutions demanded the undivided energies of the repatriates. We should not lose sight of the fact, furthermore, that about fifty thousand persons returned to the old home with Zerubbabel, and not more than two thousand with Ezra. For this relatively small population, a hundred and forty-eight liturgical, and two hundred and forty-five secular, musicians represent a high proportional number. It is due merely to the pressing need of the Jewish people for musical activity that all the musicians referred to could make a living. As a proof of the artistic disposition of the Israelites, the fact is significant that in these difficult times of national reconstruction, and despite the natural reduction by death, there was even an increase in both categories of musicians, liturgical as well as secular. This increase clearly shows that the musical culture was never abandoned by the Jews, not even during the most difficult period of the struggle for survival. At the same time, this also explains why, after the return, such a relatively large number of musicians found means of livelihood and that their number continued to increase.

Up to this point, we have mainly examined the economic and social situation of the liturgical musicians. Let us now scrutinize briefly the same subject with regard to the secular musicians after the return from Babylonia.

Members in this category must be considered free-lance artists, working for remuneration. Their number certainly could not have been very large without the constant presence of sufficient and remunerating work for them. There was bound to exist a ceaseless demand for the creators and performers of secular music.

The wages paid to the secular musician, whether in money or in natural produce, provided the basis for his existence. These wages represent, in a somewhat rudimentary form, the "honorarium" of the artist. In the history of civilization, this notion received its full impact at a much later epoch, namely, with the beginning of modern concert institutions (middle of the eighteenth century).[54] But its artistic and social implications already prevailed unmistakably in ancient Israel. In addition to wages, the secular musician of those days might have received income from making and repairing musical instruments.

All indications favor the assumption that, in a manner similar to the musicians of the Temple, the secular musicians organized themselves in a guild. Its purpose, naturally, would be virtually the same, namely, to safeguard the professional interests of its members. As compared with the Levites, the secular musician was, of course, in a less favorable economical position. He was, however, by no means handicapped by this. The secular musician in Israel was not a type of poor and despised wandering minstrel; he never represented the miserable, itinerant profession that in medieval times brought popular musicians into discredit.

In Israel, the secular musician was a free man; he belonged to a respected and well-liked class; he had a remunerative profession; his livelihood was secured by the insatiable craving of the Jewish people for music; he was the recognized representative of popular art, conscious of his mission, and sure of his influence upon his "audience," the people. There existed no musical "proletariat"; the musician was not a "pariah" in Israel. There he was a giver, like the folkbards of heroic times, and on the other side of the "footlights," there was a crowd of enthusiastic and grateful receivers.

Thus, the sociological features of the Jewish secular musician appear in a form well ahead of its time. They show a stage of development for which there is a parallel only in our own epoch. Perhaps, even more than by the institutions of Temple musicians, the artistic sense of the Jewish people is evidenced by the sociological aspect of the secular musical profession.

As employees of the state, exempt from all concern for their livelihood, the post-Babylonian Temple musicians gained not only prosperity, but high authority and increased influence.

The outstanding position of the Temple singers in Jewish life gradually led to rivalry between the priests and singers. On one recorded occasion of an economic conflict, the rivalry brought forth a trial of strength in which the singers obtained full victory. This was the "strike" of the musicians, a stoppage of work due to "nonpayment" of their salaries. The chronicler Nehemiah reports it in detail; his description is so vivid, and he deals so clearly with the causes and consequences of this economic struggle, that it would be almost superfluous to add anything to his account.

It was mentioned above that the Temple musicians received from the royal treasury a regular daily salary; also that

> all Israel in the days of Zerubbabel, and in the days of Nehemiah, gave the portions of the singers and the porters, as every day required (Neh. 12:47).

As time passed, these voluntary contributions, together with the regular emoluments, became so voluminous that the storage rooms for all sorts of products became insufficient and new chambers had to be built for them. The administration of these chambers was assigned to the priest Eliashib, who had a relative named Tobiah. The latter was

> the servant, the Ammonite, [who]was) grieved exceedingly for that there was come a man to seek the welfare of the children of Israel (Neh. 2:10).

Through intrigues and subterfuges he tried to thwart the construction of the new city walls (Neh. 3:55; 4:2), and even sought to take Nehemiah's life, by luring him into a pitfall (Neh. 6:10).

This priest Eliashib turned out to be an unfaithful steward of his office. As the chronicler reports,

> Eliashib the priest, who was appointed over the chambers of the house of God, being allied unto Tobiah, had prepared for him a great chamber, where aforetime they laid the meal-offering, the frankincense, and the vessels, and the tithes of the corn, the wine, and the oil, which were given by commandment to the Levites, and the singers, and the porters (Neh. 13:4,5).

Eliashib not only granted his relative unlawful advantages but, in addition, withheld the "salary" due to the Levites and singers.

The complaints against these abuses apparently remained unanswered and so, as a last resort, the musicians proceeded to a stoppage of work "for non-payment of their salary," to use today's legal term.

At that time Nehemiah happened to be in Babylonia. After his return, he saw

> the evil that Eliashib had done for Tobiah, in preparing him a chamber in the courts of the house of God (Neh. 13:7).

He learned

> that the portions of the Levites had not been given them; so that the Levites and the singers, that did the work, were fled every one to his field (Neh. 13:10).

> And it grieved me sore; therefore I cast forth all the household stuff of Tobiah out of the chamber . . . and thither brought I again the vessels of the house of God, with the meal-offerings and the frankincense (Neh. 13:8,9).

Nehemiah's main concern was to restore the interrupted sacred service. He took measures not against the striking singers, but against the priests who tolerated such abuses:

> Then contended I with the rulers, and said: "Why is the house of God forsaken?" And I gathered them together, and set them [i.e., the Levites and singers] in their places (Neh. 13:11).

Through the abusive practices the provisions designed for the Levites and singers must have shrunken badly, so that it was necessary to appeal for renewed voluntary contributions. The people, happy that the divine service was restored, brought the tithe and all necessary provisions to the treasuries (Neh. 13:12).

Then, Nehemiah turned to sanctions. The unfaithful Eliashib, and probably his accomplices also, were deposed (Neh. 13:13), and he appointed new trustees for the proper distribution of the provisions and to insure the avoidance of such abuses in the future.

The quoted analogies with the contemporary struggle of the working classes are by no means fortuitous, nor do they represent an artificial interpretation of the Biblical text. Their existence is as real as could be: strike for nonpayment of wages; solidarity of the strikers; avoidance of penalization of the strikers; and, finally, appointment of trustees in order to avoid further abuses. The incident, described so vividly by the chronicler, represent the very first recorded struggle of workmen in the history of mankind. The fact that the musicians of Israel succeeded in emerging victoriously is the proof of the external and internal strength of their professional organization.

Toward the end of the sanctuary's existence the Levitical singers once again ran the risk of a trial of power with the priestly class. Temporarily, they again obtained complete victory. Eventually, however, this success turned against the victors themselves and became instrumental in the total crushing of the musicians' organization.

The ever-growing esteem their congregation bestowed upon them, and the increased consciousness of themselves as a specially privileged class, caused Temple musicians to consider themselves a sort of professional aristocracy. They aspired to more external honors and wanted to be equal in attire with the immediate ministers of God, the priests. So they demanded of King AGRIPPA II (reign 53–100 C.E.) the privilege to wear, while in function, the white linen garment of the priests.

This request must at first have encountered considerable resistance, for JOSEPHUS reports this presumptuous demand with deep moral indignation.[55] This is understandable, since JOSEPHUS was himself the offspring of a priestly family, and the Aaronites represented the highest class in Israel, the nobility of the nation, as it were. He therefore considered the singers insolent for seeking to become the equals of the nobles.

The understandable opposition that the unusual request of the Levitical musicians encountered among the priests induced the former to proceed more cautiously this time than in the earlier case of the strike. They knew how to flatter the king's vanity, persuading him

> that this would be a work worthy the times of his government, that he might have a memorial of such novelty, as being his doing.[56]

To be sure, the demand of the Levites had to be submitted to a vote of the Sanhedrin. But the authority of this law-giving assembly had already been considerably reduced by that time. Furthermore, the king might have exercised the necessary pressure upon the members of this assembly, so that the demands of the Levites were eventually granted.

Encouraged by the success of the singers, other functionaries of the Temple likewise ventured to attack the traditional order. The Levitical helpers in the sacrifices, the liturgs (*leitourgountos*), belonging to the lowest class of the Levites, asked permission to learn psalm-singing at the Temple service. In actual practice, this meant that they asked to be instructed in the art of singing by the Levites, so as to be accepted eventually into the ranks of the Temple singers. This request, too, was granted by the king, with the result that these lower Levites not only could ascend into the higher class, but were also privileged to wear the white garment on a par with the priests.[57]

The priests, the Aaronites, immediately affected by this change, were deeply hurt in their pride, but were helpless for the moment against the royal decree, legally approved by the Sanhedrin. JOSEPHUS, however, foresaw and announced almost prophetically, that

> all this was contrary to the laws of our country, which, whenever they have been transgressed, we have never been able to avoid the punishment of such transgression.[58]

Retaliation did not fail to come soon. Since the royal decree could not be annulled, the priests tried to hurt the singers where they were most vulnerable. The priests had always been the stewards of the tithes offered by the people, serving as subsistence for all the officers of the divine service, tithes that were evenly distributed among all the Temple functionaries. As a retaliatory measure against the Levites, the Aaronites simply withheld from the singers the portion of the tithes due them.[59] The singers filed a complaint with the Sanhedrin, but apparently the lawgiving assembly was unable to do anything about it.

With the impending national catastrophe, that of the destruction of the sanctuary by the Romans (70 c.e.), the significance of the Levitical singers lessened considerably, whereas the priests retained their authority even after the Temple services ceased. The Levites made strenuous efforts to win back their ancient privilege of the tithes. However, despite the fact that their claim was sustained by distinguished rabbinical authorities, such as R. Joshua and R. Akiba, they could not obtain any concession from the stubborn priests. Thus, they were left until the third century without their share of the people's contributions.

With the annihilation of the Jewish national state, music as a *profession* of ancient Israel apparently disappeared. Yet, its spirit, its enduring power, remained intact in a latent form, and during the centuries of the Dispersion it emerged time and again, never failing to infuse new breath into what remained of Jewish musical practice. It stood the test in peaceful as in stormy periods, always awakening new energies and kindling new flames throughout the long history of the Diaspora.

NOTES

1. *SchneidKult,* p. 10.
2. "The tribe Juda, Jehuda, originally probably Jahuda, seems to have been an Aramaean wandering clan. It brought with it from the desert a fetish of the same name, Yahud, later abbreviated as Yahuh , Yahu, or Yah." The name has later been transformed into Yehovah, or Yahweh. (*Ibid.,* p. 269).
3. Should this interpretation be correct, Moses came later, in point of time, than Joshua, whom tradition associates with the Joseph clan (*SacharHistory,* p. 24, n. 1).
4. This is not uncommon with the names of Egyptian rulers. Amenophis IV, after having introduced in Egypt the monotheistic religion of Aton, changed his name to Ikhnaton, meaning "Aton is satisfied."
5. *SchneidKult,* p. 285.
6. *GraetzHist,* p. 7.
7. *Ibid.*
8. *RothHistory,* pp. 7–8.
9. Mishnah, *Sukkah* V:4.
10. *SachsWellsprings,* p. 91.
11. *Ibid.,* p. 92.
12. *Ibid.*
13. *GesThes,* 1469 b.
14. August Wilhelm Ambros, *Geschichte der Musik* (Breslau, 1862), 1:82.
15. *SchneidKult,* p. 226.
16. *RothHistory,* p. 8.
17. *SacharHistory,* p. 13.
18. The Tell-el-Amarna letters, discovered by Sir William Flinders Petrie in 1893, consist of over 350 clay-tablets in cuneiform writing, addressed to the Pharaoh Ikhnaton by his governors in the East. They carry on the general picture of Palestinian and Syrian life almost to the entrance of the Jews into the valley of the Nile. It is probable, though not certain, that the "Habiru" spoken of in this correspondence were the Hebrews (*CAH*[2] [1924]:719 n.).
19. Isaac, before he died, gave to his son Jacob similar advice: "Thou shalt not take a wife of the daughters of Cana'an. Arise, go to Paddan-aram, to the house of Bethuel thy mother's father; and take thee a wife from thence of the daughters of Laban thy mother's brother." (Gen. 28:1–2).
20. Max Dimont, *Jews, God and History* (New York, 1962), p. 41.
21. *Ibid.,* p. 40.
22. *Ibid.*

23. It is called "Lamech's song" in all the historical essays in which ancient Hebrew literature is treated (e.g., *RiehmHandw*, I, p. 805; *BuddeGesch*, I, p. 14; C. W. Harris, p. 59).

24. *BuddeGesch*, p. 9. Some English Bibles are even more explicit in characterizing those "that speak in parables" or "in proverbs" as folkbards. Thus, *Moffat* renders it "Hence the song and satire of the bards," and the *Revised Standard Version* "Therefore the ballad singers say."

25. *SchneidHistory*, p. 286.

26. *Ibid.*, p. 285. A legendary tradition maintains that Moses was quietly entombed in the land of Moab, in the valley facing Mount Peor, which was held sacred by the population of that district. To this day, no one knows the spot where he was buried.

27. *Ibid.*

28. *SacharHistory*, p. 18.

29. *JosAnt*, II, 466; *JosApio*, I.

30. Strabo, XVI, II. 35; Tacitus, *Historia* V. 3.

31. C. O. Ward, *The Ancient Lowly* (Chicago, 1907), 2:78.

32. R. F. Harper, ed., *Assyrian and Babylonian Literature* (New York, 1904), p. 1.

33. *JosApio*, I, 26. 9; 28. 12; 31. 1. *Cf. Acts* 7:32.

34. *PhiloMos*, I, 5. 23.

35. Justin Martyr, "Cohortatio ad Graecos," chaps. VII and X, in *PGL* VI, col. 251–52.

36. According to a new theory, Moses belonged to the tribe of Ephraim.

37. A. A. Wolf, *Der Prophet Habakkuk* (Darmstadt, 1822), p. 41.

38. Translation of the *Jewish, Authorized,* and *American* version, and *Moulton. Douai* has: "and read it aloud to Joshua," the *Revised Standard Version,* "and recite it in the ears of Joshua."

39. *GraezHist*, p. 25.

40. P. Scholz, *Götzendienst und Zauberwesen bei den alten Hebräern* (Regensburg, 1877), pp. 54 ff.

41. Friedrich Baethgen, *Beiträge zur semitischen Religionsgeschichte* (Berlin, 1888), pp. 20 ff. See also P. Scholz, p. 162.

42. *BuddeGesch*, p. 23.

43. *GraetzHist.*, I, p. 29.

44. Johann Gottfried Herder, *The Spirit of Hebrew Poetry*, trans. James March (Burlington, 1833), 2:217 ff.

45. See p. 14. *Cf. SachsRise*, pp. 58–59; *LangdLit*, pp. xii, xix.

46. *RiehmHandw*, p. 826. *Cf.* W. Robertson Smith, *The Prophets in Israel* . . . (New York, 1882), p. 85.

47. *Ibid.*, p. 1233. *Cf.* 2 Kings 2:3, 5; 4:1 ff.; 4:38; 5:22; 6:1.

48. Subsequently, the leaders of the Levitical singers were likewise called "fathers," and their schools termed as "Fathers' houses of the Levites" (1 Chron. 9:33, 34). In Sumeria, the headmaster of the school was called "school father," while the pupil was called "school son." (Samuel Noah Kramer, *"From the Tablets of Sumer"* [Indian Hills, Col., 1956], p. 5).

49. In recent times the character of these fraternities of prophets has still been greatly misinterpreted. See Solomon Reinach, *Orpheus* (New York, 1941), p. 205. *Moffat* also completely misunderstood the character of this educational institution in calling, in his Bible translation, the "sons of the prophets" a "band of derwishes."

50. Keil, *Kommentar zur Chronik* (1870), p. 200.

51. *ZAW* 34 (1914):142 ff.

52. Tal. Bab., *'Arakin* 11a.

53. Mishnah, *Sukkah* V:6–8, and Obadiah of Bertinoro to *Sukkah* V:5.

54. *JosAnt*, VII, 14, 7.

55. Mishnah, *Sukkah* V:6; *Ta'anit* IV:2.

56. *Ibid., Tamid* VII:4.

57. *StainMus*, p. 90.

58. Tal. Bab., *Ḥullin* 24a.

59. A variant reads *ze'irim*, "the little ones" [of the Levites], instead of *zo'are*, "tormentors."

60. Chrysostom, *"Eis tōn Psalmōn XLI," PGL*, LV, col. 156.

61. Mishnah, *Middot* II:6.

62. *Ibid., Shekalim* VI:3.

63. *Ibid., Middot*, I:3.

64. Tal. Bab., *Beẓah* 36b; *'Arakin* 10b; Tal. Yer., *Sukkah* V:6 (55c).

65. Mishnah, *Shabbat* I:3.

66. Tal. Bab., *Rosh ha-Shanah* 33b.

67. *Ibid., Soṭah* 30b.
68. *Ibid., Rosh ha-Shanah* 29b; *Sukkah* 42b, 43a; *Megillah* 4b.
69. See p. 000.
70. The Greek version of the Bible contains an additional, noncanonical psalm, which has the number 151.
71. *SchneidKult,* 1:114.
72. Th. Gaster, Psalm 29, in *JQR* 37 (1946–7):55 ff.
73. Tal. Bab., *'Abodah Zarah* 24b.
74. Midrash, *Tehillim,* ed. Buber (1891), XXIV:7, p. 204.
75. *JosWars,* V, 5:3.
76. Jerome, *Commentarium in Epistolam ad Galatas,* I, cap. 1, in *PL,* col. 354.
77. *PhiloLaws,* Book I, XIV:76–78.
78. Mishnah, *Sukkah* V:4; *Middot* II:5; Tal. Bab., *Sukkah* 51a, b.
79. *ThirProblems,* p. 52.
80. *Ibid.,* p. 67.
81. *Ibid.,* p. 31.
82. GesHandw, p. 446. Fr. Delitzsch, *Biblical Commentary on the Psalms* (Edinburgh, 1892), 2:276, a.o.
83. Sigmund Mowinckel, *Psalmenstudien,* 6 vols. (Kristiania (Oslo), 1923–1928).
84. *Ibid.,* 4:3–4.
85. *Ibid.,* 4:5–7.
86. *Ibid.*
87. *LangdTerms,* p. 184.
88. *Ibid.*
89. W. Robertson Smith, *The Old Testament in the Jewish Church* (London, 1926), p. 209. The same usage can be found in the Palestinian Hymnology. See S.I.N.P. Land, *Anecdota Syriaca* (Leiden, 1870), 4:111 ff.
90. Published in *LangdTerms,* pp. 170 ff.
91. *PfeifferIntro,* p. 644.
92. Friedrich Baethgen, *Die Psalmen übersetzt und erklärt* (Göttingen, 1897), p. x.
93. *Ibid.*
94. *LangdTerms,* p. 175.
95. *GesLex,* p. 993.
96. *MowPsalm,* IV, p. 7.
97. *ThirTitles,* pp. 13 ff.
98. *MowPsalm,* IV, pp. 17–22.
99. *SachsRise,* pp. 69–70.
100. *MowPsalm,* IV, p. 34.
101. J. A. Alexander, *The Psalms Translated and Explained* (New York, 1855), 1:36; *BaethPsalm,* p. ix.
102. *MowPsalm,* IV, p. 34.
103. W. O. E. Oesterley, *The Psalms in the Jewish Church* (London, 1910), p. 125.
104. *LangdTerms,* pp. 169–91. Also *GalpSum,* p. 61.
105. Oesterley, p. 86.
106. *LangdTerms,* p. 169.
107. Baethgen, p. xxxix.
108. *ThirProblems,* p. 146.
109. O. Braun, "Ein Brief des Katholikos Timotheus I über biblische Studien des 9. Jahrhunderts," in *Oriens Christianus* 1 (1901):304.
110. *BuddeGesch,* p. 43.
111. *RiehmHandw,* p. 849.
112. *EwDicht,* I, pt. 1, p. 215.
113. Anton Paul Lagarde, *Übersicht über die im Aramäischen, Arabischen und Hebräischen übliche Bildung der Nomina* (Göttingen, 1889), p. 121.
114. Syriac sources reveal four other apocryphal psalms, two of them ascribed to David, and one to Hezekiah (W. Wright, in *Proceedings of the Society of Biblical Archaeology,* June 1887).
115. The Septuagint also associates Psalm 144 with Goliath.
116. *BuddeGesch,* p. 91.
117. John Chrysostom, *Prooimia tōn Psalmōn,* in *PGL,* LV, col. 533.
118. Mishnah, *Tamid* VII:3.

119. *Ibid.;* Tal. Bab., '*Erubin* 54a.
120. *StainMus,* p. 92.
121. Quoted in *ibid.,* pp. 90 ff.
122. W. W. Longford, *Music and Religion* (London, 1916), p. 42.
123. *StainMus,* p. 93.
124. K. J. Zenner, *Die Chorgesänge im Buche der Psalmen* (Freiburg, 1896). The picture is reproduced as the frontispiece of his book.
125. John Chrysostom, *Prooimia tōn Psalmōn,* in *PGL,* LX, cols. 531–33.
126. See his notes to the translation of Psalm 1.
127. B. Jakob, *Beiträge zu einer Einleitung in die Psalmen,* in *Zeitschrift für die alttestamentliche Wissenschaft,* (1896) 16:134.
128. Published by Sabatier. See Jakob, pp. 134–35.

Singing in Ancient Israel

1. Tal. Bab., *Ḥullin* 91b. Cf. *Isa.* 6:3.
2. *LeitGes,* pp. 1 ff.
3. *EwDicht,* I, pt. 1, pp. 209–10.
4. *PfeifferIntro,* p. 272.
5. *SieversMetr,* p. 376.
6. Carl Bezold, *Ninive und Babylon* (Bielefeld and Leipzig, 1926), pp. 147 ff.
7. C. A. Reisner, *Sumerisch-babylonische Hymnen nach Tontafeln griechischer Zeit* (Berlin, 1896), p. xv.
8. *RiehmHandw,* I, p. 805; *BuddeGesch,* pp. 14 ff.
9. *LeitGes,* p. 26.
10. *BuddeGesch,* p. 9.
11. *EwDicht,* I, pt. 1, p. 175.
12. Mishnah, *Soṭah* V:4; *Sukkah* III:10; Tosefta, *Soṭah* VI:2; Midrash, *Exodus* XXII:3; XXIII:2–12; Tal. Bab., *Soṭah* 30b; Tal. Yer., *Soṭah* V:4 (20a).
13. Modern exegesis surmises that the word *y–sh–r* (without vowels) is misspelled and should rather be read *sh–y–r,* "song." This is based upon an interpolation in the Septuagint, after 1 Kings 8:55, lacking in the Hebrew original and also in other translations, "as it is written in the Book of Songs." (See *PfeifferIntro,* p. 272.)
14. A. Bertholet, *A History of Hebrew Civilization* (London, 1928), pp. 324–25.
15. Mishnah, *Soṭah* V:4; *Sukkah* III:1; Tosefta, *Soṭah* VI:2 (ed. Zuckermandel, p. 303); Midrash, *Exodus* XXII:3; XXIII:2–12; Tal. Bab., *Sukkah* 38a,b; *Soṭah* 30b; Tal. Yer., *Soṭah* V:4, etc.
16. Tal. Bab., '*Arakin* 11a.
17. John Chrysostom, "Eis tōn Psalmōn XLI," in *PGL,* LV, col. 156.
18. Hubert Grimme, *Psalmenprobleme* (Freiburg, Switzerland, 1902), p. 146.
19. The strophic structure of many a psalm certainly facilitated the common singing. See especially Pss. 120–34, the "Songs of the Ascent."
20. Mishnah, *Tamid* VII:3.
21. David Cassel, *Die Pesachhaggada* (Berlin, 1895) pp. i, ii. Leopold Zunz, *Die gottesdienstlichen Vorträge der Juden* (Berlin, 1832), p. 126.
22. Mishnah, *Tamid* VII:4.
23. *Cf.* Num. 29:9, 10; *JosAnt* III, 10:1.
24. Mishnah, *Sukkah* IV:5.
25. This is indicated by a Biblical passage and its translation by the Targumim. The Pentateuch reads: "The tent of the meeting afar off from the camp" (Exod. 33:7). Targum Onkelos renders the term as "Home of Instruction," the Palestinian Talmud as "Place of Instruction."
26. For the various theories concerning the origin of the Synagogue, see *KraussSynAlt,* chap. 10, pp. 52 ff.
27. *PhiloMos,* II, 214–16.
28. Philo, *In Flaccum,* XIV.
29. *Jew. Encycl.,* II:620.
30. Salo W. Baron, *A Social and Religious History of the Jews* (New York, 1937), 1:290.
31. Tosefta, *Sukkah* (ed. Zuckermandel, p. 199). The Talmud uses the term "the little sanctuary of God" (Tal. Bab., *Megillah* 29a), which is frequently identified with the Synagogue in the Temple court.

32. Tal. Bab., *'Arakin* 11b.
33. Mishnah, *'Erubin* X:13; Tosefta to *'Erubin* 11:19 (p. 154).
34. *Ibid.*
35. First published 1543 in Constantinople.
36. For a modern publication of his writings, see Manuel Komroff, *The Contemporaries of Marco Polo* . . . (New York, 1928).
37. Leopold Zunz, *Die Ritus des synagogalen Gottesdienstes geschichtlich entwickelt* (Berlin, 1859), p. 57.
38. His diary was first published in 1595 in Prague.
39. For a modern publication of these travel notes, see Lazar Grünhut, *Die Rundreise des R. Petachjah aus Regensburg* (Frankfurt, a. M., 1904), sec. 18.
40. *KraussTA*, III, p. 88.
41. Published by Shabbetai Bass together with *Sifte Yeshenim* (Amsterdam, 1680).
42. *Ibid.*
43. Tal. Bab., *Ketubot* 105a.
44. Tal. Yer., *Megillah* III:1 (73d). These figures, of course, are greatly exaggerated. It is certain, however, that Jerusalem must have had a considerable number of Synagogues, because, in view of the ever-increasing population of the city and its suburbs, the capacity of the Temple must have been completely insufficient for the multitude of worshippers. Moreover, when the pilgrimages for the annual festivals took place, the Temple had to be reserved mainly for the pilgrims, so that the native population had to worship in their Synagogues.
45. *Ibid., Megillah* III:1.
46. Acts 6:9. *Cf.* Tal. Bab., *Megillah* 16a; Tosefta, *Megillah,* chap. II.
47. Tal. Bab., *Berakot* 8a.
48. Philo, *De Legatione ad Caium,* chap. 20.
49. *Ibid.*
50. About the Synagogues in Rome at the time of the Emperors, see E. Schürer, *Gemeindeverfassung der Juden in Rom* (Leipzig, 1879), pp. 15 ff.
51. Acts 13:14; 14:1; 17:2, 3; 15:19, etc. For the Synagogues authenticated in the Near East (all in all 138), see *KraussSynAlt*, chaps. 21–28, pp. 200–207.
52. Tal. Bab., *Ketubot* 105a; Tal. Yer., *Megillah* III:1 (73d).
53. *Ibid., Megillah* 32a; *Sopherim,* ed. Higger, (1939), III:13, p. 129; *cf.* Tal. Bab., *Shabbat* 105b. See Rashi's commentary to the passage.
54. *JosWars,* II, 8:13. He mentions also another sect of Essenes, which admitted women.
55. *Ibid.*, II, 8:5.
56. Hippolytus, *Tractatus contra omnes haereses,* IX, 15. This invocation refers to Adam, whom the Essenes venerated particularly.
57. Prophyry, *On the Abstinence of Animal Food,* IV, 13.
58. *PhiloTher,* XI, 83–89.
59. J. K. Joost, *Geschichte des Judentums und seiner Sekten* (Leipzig, 1857), p. 58.
60. Richard B. Rackham, *The Acts of the Apostles* (London, 1912), p. 378.
61. Eusebius, "Historia ecclesiastica, V, 28:5," in *PGL*, XX, col. 514.
62. Before Zeitlin, A. Büchler had already shown that the *Zadokite Fragments,* discovered in 1900 by Solomon Schechter in a Genizah at Cairo, and which are very similar to the contents of the recently found *Manual of Discipline,* was a Karaitic work, composed in the Middle Ages. (See *JQR* (1913), pp. 422–85.)
63. Tal. Bab., *Sotah* 48a.
64. *Ibid.*
65. For a thorough investigation of the subject see the author's *Music In Ancient Israel* (New York, 1968), pp. 196 ff.
66. Joseph Yasser, *Restoration of Ancient Hebrew Music* (New York, 1946). Abstract published in *First Ten Years of the Annual Three Choir Festival* (New York, 1948), p. 47.
67. Robert Lach, *Die Musik der Natur- und der orientalischen Kulturvölker,* in Adler's *Handbuch der Musikgeschichte* (Berlin, 1929), 1:28 ff.
69. Rabindranath Tagore, *My Reminiscences* (New York, 1917), p. 189.
69. Hermann Keyserling, *Das Reisetagebuch eines Philosophen* (Darmstadt, 1921), 1:399.
70. Tal. Bab., *Sukkah* 51a.
71. Mishnah, *Sotah* IX:14; see also Tal. Bab., *Gittin* 7a.
72. *BuddeGesch,* p. 188.
73. Tosefta, *Sanhedrin* 12.
74. Tal. Bab., *Hagigah* 15b.

75. *Ibid.*
76. Tal. Bab., *Soṭah* 48a.
77. *Ibid.*, *Ḥullin* 91b.
78. *Ibid.*
79. *Ibid.*
80. Tal. Yer., *Soṭah* VII:2 (21c).
81. Midrash, *Numeri* XIV:21.
82. Tal. Bab., *Yoma* 20b.
83. Mishnah, *Yoma* III:11; *cf.* Tal. Yer., *Yoma* III:7 (40d).
84. Tal. Bab., *Yoma* 38b.
85. Tal. Yer., *Shekalim* V:2 (48d).
86. *Ibid.*
87. Mishnah, *Yoma* III:11.
88. Tal. Yer., *Megillah* III:2 (74a).
89. Tal. Bab., *Soṭah* 48a.
90. *Ibid.*, *Giṭṭin* 7a; *cf.* *'Arakin* 11a; *Sukkah* 51b; *Ta'anit* 17a.
91. Abraham Zevi Idelsohn, *Hebräisch-Orientalischer Melodieschatz* (Jerusalem, Vienna, Berlin, 1914–1932), 10 vols. Also in an English and a Hebrew edition.

The Musical Instruments of the Hebrews

1. Tal. Bab., *Megillah* 6a.
2. Euripides, *Cyclops* V, 442 (in *The Complete Greek Drama*, [New York, 1938], 2:408). Aristophanes, *Thesmophoriazusae* (in *Eleven Comedies* [New York, 1943], 2:285).
3. *SachsHist*, p. 107.
4. *Ibid.*, p. 131.
5. Tal. Bab., *Kinnim* 25a.
6. Mishnah, *Shabbat* VI:8; *Kelim* XV:6.
7. *Ibid.*, *Kelim* XV:6; XVI:7.
8. Tal. Yer., *'Erubin* X:1 (25c).
9. Jerome, "Ad Dardanum de diversis generibus musicorum instrumentis Epistola XXVIII," in *PL*, XXX, col. 215.
10. Jerome, "Breviarium in Psalmum XXXII," in *PL* XXVI, col. 969.
11. *JosAnt*, VII, 12:3.
12. Midrash, *Numeri* X:16; *Lamentations* II:19; *Ruth* VI:1; Tal. Bab., *Berakot* 3b; *Sanhedrin* 16a; Tal. Yer., *Berakot* I:1 (2b); *cf.* Ps. 119:62.
13. *GesHandw*, p. 481.
14. *PortShilṭe*, chap. V.
15. *WeissInstr*, p. 54.
16. Ambros, 1:206–7, and others.
17. Cassiodorus, Isidore of Sevilla, Beda Venerabilis, *et al.*
18. Tal. Yer., *Sukkah* V:6 (55c).
19. Mishnah, *Kelim* XV:6.
20. JosAnt, VII, 12:3.
21. Ibn Ezra, *Commentary to Isaiah*, V:12.
22. Michael Prätorius, *Syntagma musicum* (Wolfenbüttel, 1614–1619), p. 110.
23. Guillaume A. Villoteau, *Description de l'Égypte* (Paris, 1809), 13:477.
24. *IdelJewMus*, pp. 13–14.
25. Ovid, *Ars amatoria*, III, 325.
26. *JosAnt*, VII, 12:3.
27. *SachsHist*, p. 118.
28. *StainMus*, p. 42.
29. *DelPsalms*, I, p. 149.
30. Augustin Calmet, *A Dictionary of the Bible*, English ed., (London, 1732), 1:619.
31. *GesLex*, p. 387.
32. *BaethPsalms*, p. xvi.
33. Johann Jahn, *Biblical Archaeology* (New York, 1853), p. 103.
34. Ibn Ezra, *Commentary to Psalm* 8.
35. E. O. W. Oesterley, *The Psalms in the Jewish Church* (London, 1910), p. 55.
36. *Thirtitles*, p. 30.
37. *MowPsalm*, IV, p. 46.

38. *Athen,* IV, 129a; XIV, 634b.
39. Verses 2:4 to 7:28. These have since been translated into Biblical Hebrew.
40. Isidore of Sevilla, *Etymologiae,* III, 21:7, in *PL* LXXXII, col. 167.
41. A. F. Gallé, *Daniel avec Commentaires* (Paris, 1900), p. 32.
42. Sa'adia, *Commentary on Daniel* 3:5.
44. *EngMus,* p. 186.
45. In *Cyclopedia of Biblical Literature* (New York, 1883), s. v. *Musical Instruments,* 6:767.
46 A. Gevaert, *Histoire et théorie de la musique de l'Antiquité* (Gand, 1881), 2:245.

47. Oscar Fleischer, *Neumen-Studien* (Leipzig, 1895), 1:31.
48. *PortShilṭe,* chap. II.
49. *DelPsalms,* II, p. 77.
50. *LangdTerms,* pp. 180 ff.
51. Midrash, *Genesis* XXIII:3.
52. *Ibid.,* L:9.
53. *Ibid.*
54. *GesThes,* 988 b.
55. Pfeiffer, Jahn, Forkel, Engel, *et al.*
56. A. Calmet, 3:334, 336.
57. *SachsHist.,* p. 106.
58. *PortShilṭe.*
59. *SachsHist.,* p. 64.
60. Willi Apel, *Early History of the Organ,* in *Speculum* 23, no. 2 (April 1948): 191 ff. Also *FarOrg,* pp. 9 ff.
61. *SachsHist,* p. 106.
62. Morris Jastrow, Jr., *Die Religion Babyloniens und Assyriens* (Giessen, 1905–1912), 2:4.
63. *Athen,* IV, 174 f, 175 a.
64. Mishnah, *Kelim* XI:6.
65. *Ibid.,* '*Arakin* II:3.
66. Tal. Bab., '*Arakin* 10b. An analogous statement, in a shorter form, in Tal. Yer., *Sukkah* V:6 (55c).
67. Tal. Yer., *Sukkah* V:1 (55a).
68. Mishnah, '*Arakin* II:3.
69. *Ibid.,* *Kelim* XI:5.
70. *Ibid.,* '*Arakin* II:3.
71. *SachsHist,* p. 120.
72. Tal. Bab., '*Arakin* 10b ff.
73. *Nathin,* pl. *nethinim,* lit. "given," were descendants of the Gibeonites, whom Joshua made into Temple slaves. *Cf.* Joshua 9:27.
74. Mishnah, '*Arakin* II:4.
75. Tal. Bab., '*Arakin* 10a.
76. *Ibid.,* *Sukkah* 50b; Tal. Yer. *Sukkah* V:1 (55a), *cf.* Mishnah, *Sukkah* V:1.
77. *Ibid.,* *Sukkah* 50b.
78. Mishnah, *Baba Meẓiah* VI:1.
79. *Ibid.,* *Ketubot* IV:4; *cf.* Matt., 9:23.
80. Tal. Bab., *Shabbat* 151a.
81. *StainMus,* p. 101.
82. Pliny the Elder, *Historia naturalis,* XXXIII, 52. 146.
83. Tal. Bab., '*Arakin* 10a.
84. *GesThes, s. v. ḥul.* See also the section "The Dance."
85. Mishnah, *Sukkah* IV:1; V:1; Tal. Bab., *Sukkah* 50b; '*Arakin* 10b; Tosefta, *Sukkah* IV (p. 198); Tal. Yer., *Sukkah* V:I (55a).
86. *SachsHist,* p. 83.
87. Suetonius, *Nero* 54.
88. Isidore of Sevilla, *Etymologiae,* 3:14, in *PL,* LXXXII, col. 169.
89. *SachsHist.,* pp. 84, 141.
90. *Ibid.,* p. 141.
91. See the articles of Phillips Barry and George Moore in *JBL* 23 (1904) and 24 (1905).
92. *GesHandw,* p. 253.
93. *JosAnt,* III, 12:6.

94. Sachs claims that this picture represents an oboe-like instrument (*SachsHist*, p. 120). For a different opinion see above.

95. *SachsHist.*, p. 145.

96. Clement of Alexandria, *Paidagōgos*, II, 4, in *PG*, VI, col. 244.

97. Hosea 5:8. Here, however, the gemination is expressed by the juxtaposition of *shofar* and *hazozerah*.

98. Mishnah, *Tamid* VII:3; Tal. Bab., *'Erubin* 54a.

99. Tal. Yer., *Yoma* VI:1 (43b).

100. Mishnah, *Sukkah* V:4; V:5.

101. Th. Gaster, p. 277.

102. Tal. Bab., *Shabbat* 36a; *Rosh ha-Shanah* 36a; *Sukkah* 34a.

103. Tosefta, *Soṭah* VII:15 (p. 308).

104. For other etymological derivations see *GesThes*, 1469 b.

105. Mishnah, *Rosh ha-Shanah* III:2.

106. *Ibid.*, III:7.

107. Tal. Bab., *Rosh ha-Shanah* 34a.

108. *Ibid.*, 16b.

109. Tal. Yer., *Rosh ha-Shanah* IV:8 (p. 40).

110. Tal. Bab., *Rosh ha-Shanah* 32b.

111. Mishnah, *Sukkah* V:4.

112. *Ibid.*, IV:9.

113. *Ibid.*, V:5; *'Arakin* II:3; Tal. Bab., *Sukkah* 53a; *'Abodah Zarah* 70a; Tosefta, *Sukkah* IV:11 (p. 199).

114. *FineShof*, p. 114.

115. Tal. Bab., *Mo'ed Katan* 27b; *cf.* Tal. Bab., *Megillah* 19a.

116. *Ibid.*, *Mo'ed Katan* 16a.

117. *FineShof*, pp. 210 ff.

118. Mishnah, *Ta'anit* III:1–8.

119. Tal. Bab., *Baba Batra* 91a.

120. *FineShof*, p. 228.

121. Tal. Bab., *Rosh ha-Shanah* 26a.

122. *RiehmHandw*, I, p. 733.

123. *Ibid.*

124. Mishnah, *Kelim* XI:7.

125. *LangdTerms*, p. 171.

126. *SachsHist.*, pp. 73–78.

127. See p. 313.

128. Chap. V.

129. *GesLex*, p. 595.

130. *JosAnt*, VII, 12:3.

131. *RiehmHandw*, p. 1043, a.o.

132. Tal. Bab., *'Arakin* 10b; Tal. Yer., *Sukkah* V:6 (55c).

133. Mishnah, *Shekalim* V:1.

134. *Ibid.*, *Tamid* VII:3.

135. Galpin, in *StainMus* p. 46.

136. *SachsHist.*, p. 123.

137. *WeissInstr.*, p. 104.

138. *GressMus*, p. 32, a.o.

139. *SachsHist.*, p. 109.

140. *PhiloLaws*, XIII:72.

141. *PhiloMos*, II, 24:119.

142. *WeissInstr.*, p. 101.

143. Tal. Bab., *Pesaḥim* 111b.

144. *JastrDict.*, I, p. 458.

145. Mishnah, *Kelim* XV:6.

146. *SachsHist.*, pp. 117–18.

147. Midrash, *Genesis* XXIII:3.

148. Tal. Yer., *Sukkah* V:6 (55c).

149. C. Daremberg and E. Saglio, *Dictionnaire des antiquités grecques et romaines* (Paris, 1877), 2:1594. M. Mielziner, *Introduction to the Talmud* (New York, 1925), p. 48.

150. Tal. Bab., *'Arakin* 10b.

151. *Ibid.;* Tal. Yer., *Sukkah* V:5 (55c).
152. Mishnah, *'Arakin* II:3.
153. Tal. Yer., *Sukkah* V:6 (55c, d); Tosefta, *'Arakin* I:13.
154. Tal. Bab., *'Arakin* 10b, 11a.
155. *Ibid.*
156. *Ibid.*, 11a.
157. Mishnah, *Tamid* V:6.
158. Joseph Yasser, "The Magrephah of the Herodian Temple: a Fivefold Hypothesis," in *Journal of the American Musicological Society* 13 nos. 1–3 (196):24–42.
159. Midrash, *Genesis* L:9.
160. Midrash, *Genesis* XXIII:3 and L:9.
161. "Cymbals" is an erroneous translation of the Soncino Press.
162. *JastrDict*, I, p. 625.
163. *Ibid.*, L:9.
164. *JastrDict*. I, p. 78; II, p. 908.
165. *SachsHist.*, p. 109.
166. Tosefta, *Shabbat* XIII, ed. Zuckermandel (1937), p. 130.
167. Mishnah, *Kelim* XV:6.
168. *LangdLit.*, p. LII.
169. Tal. Bab., *'Arakin* 10b; Tosefta to Tal. Bab., *'Arakin* 11a.
170. *Ibid.*, *Sanhedrin* 67b.
171. Mishnah, *Soṭah* IX:14.
172. *Ibid.*, *Kelim* XV:6.
173. Tal. Bab., *Soṭah* 49b.
174. Mishnah, *Soṭah* IX:14; Tal. Bab., *Giṭṭin* 7a.
175. Tal. Bab., *Soṭah* 49b.
176. *JastrDict*, II, p. 1443.
177. Midrash, *Song of Songs* VII:9.
178. Tal. Yer., *Shabbat* VI:1 (7d).
179. Tal. Bab., *Mo'ed Katan* 9b.
180. *SachsHist.*, p. 289.
181. Tal. Yer., *Kiddushin* I:4 (65b).
182. *Ibid.*
183. *Ibid.*
184. *JastrDict*, II, p. 854.
185. *KraussTA*, II, p. 527, n. 984.
186. *Ibid.*, III, p. 88.

The Dance in Ancient Israel

1. *SachsRhythm*, p. 38.
2. Ernest Renan, *Mission de Phénice* (Paris, 1864), pp. 355 ff.
3. W. Robertson Smith, *Religion of the Semites* (New York, 1894), p. 93.
4. P. D. Chantepie de la Saussaye, *Lehrbuch der Religionsgeschichte* (Tübingen, 1925), 1:637, 645.
5. Kurt Heinrich Sethe, "Urgeschichte und älteste Religionen der Ägypter" (Leipzig, 1930), in *Abhandlungen für die Kunde des Morgenlandes* 18, no. 4.
6. Hastings, *ERE*, 10:294b.
7. Adolf Erman, *Die ägyptische Religion* (Berlin, 1905), p. 14.
8. *Ibid.*, p. 280.
9. *Ibid.*
10. H. Kees, *Der Opfertanz des ägyptischen Königs* (Leipzig, 1912), pp. 105 ff. For Egyptian dance rituals combined with music see Lucius Apuleius, *Metamorphoses* (*The Golden Ass*) English ed. (New York, 1927), pp. 253 ff., also Herodotus, *History*, II, pp. 58–60, English ed., (New York, 1939), pp. 101–2.
11. Midrash, *Numeri* XX:11.
12. *SachsDance*, p. 130.
13. Mishnah, *Sukkah* IV:2.
14. *KraussTA*, III, pp. 67 ff, 483.
15. Midrash, *Genesis* XXXVIII:7.
16. Tal. Yer., *Pe'ah* I (15d). The word occurs only in the Vilna edition (1922), p. 4.

The Krotoschin edition has for it *mekales; kalas* means "to be done honor by a song" (*JastrDict.*, II, p. 1379).

17. J. Gur (Grasowsky), *Milon Ibri*, 2nd ed. (Tel-Aviv, 1947), p. 1007.

18. Tal. Bab., *Pesaḥim* 111b; Targum Yer. to *Exodus* 15:20; 32:19. See *JastrDict*, Vol. 1, p. 481.

19. *JastrDict.*, I, p. 458.

20. Midrash, *Genesis* LXVIII:13.

21. *Ibid.*

22. Tal. Yer., *Sukkah* V:4 (55c); Tal. Yer. *Sanhedrin* II:4 (20b).

23. *Ibid..*, *Beẓah* V:2 (63a).

24. K. J. Zenner, *Die Chorgesänge im Buche der Psalmen* (Freiburg, 1893).

25. *SachsRhythm*, p. 29.

26. *MowPsalm*, IV, pp. 22 ff.

27. W. O. E. Oesterley, *The Sacred Dance* (New York, 1923), p. 37.

28. J. Hastings, *A Dictionary of the Bible* (New York, 1902), 1: 550b.

29. Neilos (Nilus), *Narratio V*, in *PG* LXXIX, col. 650.

30. Not only Shiloh, but practically every vineyard in Ancient Israel had a "dancing place," used exclusively by women. The ditty sung on this occasion has been paraphrased and versified by Edersheim, in Hastings, *A Dictionary of the Bible*, 1:550b.

31. Mishnah, *Ta'anit* IV:8; Tal. Bab., *Ta'anit* 31a.

32. *Megillat Ta'anit* V.

33. *JosWar*, II, 17:6.

34. For the encompassing of the altar, see Pss. 26:6; 32:7; 68:26; 81:3; 118:27; also Mishnah, *Sukkah* IV:5.

35. Mishnah, *Sukkah* IV:1.

36. *Ibid.*, also Midrash *Leviticus* XXX:5; *cf.* Psalm 119:164.

37. Mishnah, *Sukkah* IV:5.

38. Also *JosAnt* XII 7:7; XIII 13:5.

39. Interpreted as "men of might" or "workers of miracles."

40. Mishnah, *Sukkah* V:4.

41. *Ibid.*, IV:9; *Berakot* V:2; Tal. Bab., *Rosh ha-Shanah* 16a.

42. Tal. Bab., *Rosh ha-Shanah* 16a.

43. Mishnah, *Sukkah* V:2.

44. *Ibid.*, *Berakot* V:5.

45. *Ibid.*, *Sukkah* V:1.

46. Julius Lewy, *The Feast of the 14th Day of Adar*, in *HUCA* 14 (1939):127–51.

47. *Ibid.*, p. 144. According to Lewy, Mordechai is not even a proper name, but a term denoting worshippers of Marduk, as evidenced by the Greek term in Macc. 15:36: *hē Mardochaikē hēmera*, "the day of the worshippers of Marduk." (Lewy, p. 131).

48. *Ibid.*, p. 146.

49. This laxity in observing the law at Purim was partly responsible for the origin of latter days' Purim plays, the only kind of dramatic productions tolerated by the religious leaders of the Jews.

50. Tal. Bab., *Sanhedrin* 64b. See also *KraussTA*, III, p. 102.

51. Louis Ginzberg, *Genizah-Studies*, in *JQR* 16 (1903–1904): 650.

52. About this custom among the Hebrews and other peoples, see *SachsDance*, pp. 71 ff.

53. *U.J.E.*, 3:458.

54. For other motivations pertaining to ritual dances, see Oesterley, pp. 22 ff.

55. Tal. Bab., *Ketubot* 16a.

56. Mishnah, *Soṭah* IX:14.

57. Midrash, *Lamentations* V:16; *Ecclesiastes* X:5.

58. *Ibid.*, *Genesis* LIX:4; Tal. Bab., *Ketubot* 17a.

59. Tal. Bab., *Ketubot* 17a.

60. Mishnah, *Sukkah* 5:4; Tosefta, *Sukkah* IV:4. A somewhat different description of this dance is given in Tal. Bab., *Sukkah* 53a.

61. Tal. Bab., *Ketubot* 17a.

62. *SchneidKult*, p. 56.

63. *Ibid.*, p. 125.

64. Latter-day Purim plays would seem to lend a certain justification for this hypothesis. "In Gaonic times the dramatization of the story of Esther was a well-established custom among the Jews of the Orient." (*Jew. Encycl.*, 10:279). Similar plays are reported to have been performed by Jews of other countries in the Middle Ages.

65. *PfeifferIntro*, p. 715.

66. Ernest Renan, *The Song of Songs*, English trans. William M. Thomson (London, 1860).

67. Leroy Waterman, *The Song of Songs*, trans. and interpreted as a dramatic poem (Ann Arbor, Mich., 1948).

68. *PfeifferIntro*, p. 713.

69. Tosefta, *Sanhedrin* XII.

70. J. G. Wetzstein, "Die syrische Dreschtafel," in Bastian's *Zeitschrift für Ethnologie* (1873), 5:270–302.

71. Another interpretation explains "Shulammite" as the feminine of Solomon, namely "Shelomith," "Solomoness." See Edgar J. Goddspeed, The Shulammite, in *American Journal of Semitic Language and Literature* 50 (1933–34): 102–4.

72. Midrash, *Genesis* LXXIV:17; *Canticum* VII:2.

73. *Ibid., Genesis* LXVIII:7.

74. *Ibid.,* XXXVIII:7.

75. *Ibid., Leviticus* XI:9. For the same dance the Talmud uses the word *maḥol* (Tal. Bab., *Ta'anit* 31a).

76. Tal. Yer., *Megillah* II:3 (73b); *Mo'ed Katan* III:7 (83b). Midrash, *Canticum* I:3, par. 2.

77. *Ibid., Sanhedrin* II:4 (20b).

78. Tal. Bab., *Pesaḥim* 49a.

79. *Ibid., Baba Kamma* 97a.

80. *Ibid., Sanhedrin* 96b.

81. *KraussTA*, III, p. 100.

82. Tal. Bab., *Baba Kamma* 86a.

83. Hastings, *ERE* 10:359 b.

84. *SachsDance*, p. 74.

85. Mishnah, *Mo'ed Katan* III:9.

86. Tal. Bab., *Mo'ed Katan* 27b.

87. *KraussTA*, II, pp. 67 ff.

88. This ceremony is described in Moses Gaster, *Daily and Occasional Prayers* (London, 1901), 1:197.

89. I here use Moulton's translation.

The Healing Power of Music

1. Tal. Bab., *'Erubin* 104a. See also Leopold Löw, *Beiträge zur jüdischen Altertumskunde* (Szegedin, 1875), 2:304.

2. *SachsDance*, pp. 201–2.

3. *Athen*, XIV, 624 a,b.

4. Tal. Yer., *'Erubin* X:1 (26c).

Prophecy and Music

5. Unlike other translations, that of Harkavy always renders *nibba* as "played," instead of "prophesied."

6. Plato, *Phaedrus* 262.

7. *PhiloMos*, II, 35:188.

8. Philo, *Peri tōn metonomazōmenōn* (*On the Change of Names*), XXIV:139.

9. *PhiloLaws*, Book I, XI:65.

10. The translation of the Hebrew *shofetim* as "judges" does not represent its conventional meaning. The *shofetim* of Israel have not been officers of a court of justice, but the elected leaders and the chief magistrates of the nation. Their functions corresponded to those of the *shupetim*, the regents, of Phoenicia, and to the *sufetes* of Carthago, whose office was similar to that of the Roman consuls.

11. K. W. E. Nägelsbach, *The Prophet Isaiah* (New York, 1906); see commentary on 8:3.

12. The four hundred and fifty priests of Ba'al on Mount Carmel are considered by the chronicler as heathen, i.e., false prophets (1 Kings, 18:22 ff.).

13. Midrash, *Siphre*, Commentary to Num. 24:10.

14. Isa. 7:3 ff.; 36:21; Jer. 21:1 ff.; 18:5; Ezek. 16:1; Amos 7:10, etc.

15. M. R. James, *The Apocryphal New Testament* (Oxford, 1924), pp. 367–68. Cf. *ZNTW*, II, pp. 287 ff. Translation of the *Ante-Nicean Library* 16:390 ff.

16. A parallel to this is the story of the Arabic prince *Abu Said Kukuburi*, Lord of Arbella, . . . who "would pass nights in listening to religious music to which he was so sensible that,

when excited by its influence, he used to pull off part of his clothes." (See the *Biographical Dictionary* of Ibn Khallikan [Thirteenth Century] 2:538 in the English ed.)

17. J. Goldziher, *Abhandlungen zur arabischen Philologie* (Leiden, 1898–1899), 1:3 ff, 15 ff.

Women in the Music of Ancient Israel

18. Primitively, women also belonged to this guild, as is apparent from 2 Chron. 35:25.
19. Mishnah, *Middot* II:6.
20. *EwAnt*, pp. 285 ff.
21. P. Scholz, *Die heiligen Altertümer des Volkes Israel* (Regensburg, 1858), 1:36.
22. *RiehmHandw*, I, p. 447.
23. Solomon Schechter, *Studies in Judaism*, 1st ser. (Philadelphia, 1898), p. 316.
24. *Ibid.*, p. 317.
25. Ismar Peritz, *Women in the Ancient Hebrew Cult*, in *JBL* (Syracuse, 1898), p. 148.
26. Philo, *Peri Apoikias* (*On the Migration of Abraham*), XVII, 97.
27. *PhiloMos*, Book II, XXVII:136.
28. Mishnah, *'Arakin* II:6.
29. G. H. A. Ewald, *The Antiquities of Israel* (London, 1878), pp. 285–86.
30. *Ibid.*, p. 286.
31. H. Winckler, *Keilinschriftliches Textbuch zum A.T.* (Leipzig, 1909), 2:45. E. Schrader, *Die Keilinschriften und das Alte Testament* (Giessen, 1882), pp. 45 ff. Alfred Jeremias, *The Old Testament in the Light of the Ancient East*, English ed. (London, 1911), 2:234.
32. *Cf.* the *ambubajae* of ancient Rome and the *aulētridēs* of the Greeks. See also *Philo-Ther*, VII, 58.
33. Mishnah, *Mo'ed Katan* III:9; Tal. Bab., *Mo'ed Katan* 28b.
34. Tal. Bab., *Mo'ed Katan* 8a.
35. *Ibid.*, *Nedarim* 66b.
36. *Ibid.*, *Mo'ed Katan* 28b (to Mishnah, *Mo'ed Katan* III:9).
37. *Ibid.*, *Mo'ed Katan* III:9.
38. K. Budde, *Das Hebräische Klagelied*, in ZAW (1882), pp. 24 ff.
39. *BuddeGesch*, p. 21.
40. *Ibid.*
41. *Ibid.*, pp. 24 ff.
42. Mishnah, *Ketubot* IV:6; Tal. Bab., *Ketubot* 48a.
43. Tal. Yer., *Berakot* III:1 (5d).
44. Exod. 15:20; Judg. 5:1; 11:34; 1 Sam. 18:6; 21:12; Ps. 68:28; applied to non-Jewish women, 2 Sam. 1:20.
45. Tal. Bab., *Berakot* 24a.
46. *Ibid.*, *Soṭah* 48a.
47. *Ibid.*
48. Mishnah, *Kelim* XV:6. This might already have been the later usage, when women were eliminated from the Temple choir.
49. *PhiloTher*, X, 79–80.
50. The Greek word here is *chorikōn*, meaning a "danced hymn," in general "dance song."
51. *PhiloTher*, X, 79–80.
52. *Ibid.*, XI, 83–89.

Music after Solomon's Death

53. See Idelsohn's publications, pp. 274 ff.
54. See the author's *Rundfunk und Musikpflege* (Leipzig, 1931), p. 54.
55. *JosAnt*, XX, 9:6.
56. *Ibid.*
57. *Ibid.*
58. *Ibid.*
59. Heinrich H. Graetz, *Eine Stafmassnahme gegen die Leviten*, in *MGWJ* 35 (1876):97–108.

9

Homer and the Bible

Finally, a new scholarly development of considerable significance was made possible by the discovery of the Ugaritic culture, until recently believed lost. This requires a short examination.

Ugarit was a city-state at the Mediterranean north of Phoenicia, situated between the Hittite empire and Cana'an. The existence of Ugarit was known for a long time from the Amarna-letters (1400–1200 B.C.E.), but its exact location was unknown until 1928, when it was discovered by pure chance. Assiduous excavations have brought to light objects and texts in increasing number, by which our knowledge of Ugarit has been considerably increased.

The settlement may be rightly considered as Semitic, since the Ugaritic language, used in official business, belonged to the Semitic language-group. Furthermore, there was in Ugarit an influential enclave of Aegean people, as proven by Cypro-Minaean texts and Mycenean art objects. Ugarit also had in its pantheon a god from Caphtor.[1]

From the discoveries and the deciphered Ugaritic texts, published since 1930 in increasing numbers, CYRUS H. GORDON of Brandeis University has made the significant discovery[2] that the Greek, and also the Hebraic, civilizations are parallel phenomena, having had their common origin in the currents of the eastern Mediterranean world. The connecting link between the two cultures was the settlement of Ugarit.

I cannot dwell *in extenso* upon GORDON's discoveries; I cannot quote the numerous analogies found by this scholar between Hebraic and Ugaritic poetry on the one hand, and Greek and Ugaritic poetry on the other hand, in order to prove that Ugarit constitutes indeed a bridge between Greek and Hebraic civilizations.

I can refer only to a singularly significant disclosure of GORDON, namely, that the poetry of Ugarit and that of the Hebrews were closely interrelated. This clears up a long-existing enigma. It was held generally that the classical Hebrew language was the creation of "primitive" Hebrew men and it was considered almost a miracle that such primitive tribes could have devised by themselves such a remarkable literature. As it turns out now, the Hebrews found in Cana'an a highly cultivated literary medium, proven by Ugaritic myths and epics, which must have been known in Cana'an long before the conquest of the country by the Hebrews. The proof of this is furnished by the Bible itself; the Biblical authors never speak of the "Hebrew" or "Israelitic" language, but always of the "language of Cana'an."[3]

Furthermore, GORDON establishes undeniable similarities between HOMER

279

and Ugaritic epic poetry, and furnishes proof that there are affinities between HOMER and the Bible. Among the numerous proofs of this, I want to pick out only one: the similarity between the description of the Jewish conception of the world, as presented by the Pentateuch, and the long narrative by HOMER in which he describes the shield of ACHILLES, made for him by the divine forger HEPHAESTOS (*Iliad*, XVIII:483–560).

The Pentateuch furnishes us with the Jewish conception of the cosmos, the creation of the Universe and mankind. It gives descriptions of the social institutions of the Hebrews, their litigations, wars, agriculture, royalty, sacrifices, and so on. All these cultural aspects are also present in the tale about the shield of ACHILLES. The story starts with the description of the earth, the sea, and the heaven (*Iliad*, XVIII:483–89), and ends with describing the cosmic river Oceanos (*Ibid.*, 607–8). It contains the description of the social institutions, litigations, wars, agriculture, and grazing places, as well as the lives of humans and animals in city and country, and the joyous feasts of mankind. Besides country-dances, there is a ritual dance mentioned, which—in the memory of the homeric poem—goes back to Cnossos of Crete.[4] The similarities in the two descriptions are obvious; both are parts of the same conception of the world as manifest in the culture of the peoples of the eastern Mediterranean.[5]

Only two peoples of Antiquity have left "canonical" writings,[6] the Hebrews and the Greeks—the Hebrews with the Bible, the Greeks with the homeric epics, which for them represent just as normative rules of life as the Torah for the Hebrews.

The bridge between HOMER and the Bible was the great epic poems of Ugarit, which deal with a mystic king of the name of KRET, pointing unmistakably to Crete as the cradle of Greek civilization.[7]

GORDON quotes a good many examples from the pre-homeric and pre-mosaic literature of Mesopotamia, Egypt, and Ugarit in order to prove the common origin of Hebraic and Greek literature.[8] He arrives at the conclusion that Ugarit, as the connecting link between Cana῾an and the Aegean, represents the most important element for the reconstruction of the source of Western civilization.[9]

The mythology of Cana῾an is important in more than one respect for understanding the civilization of the Near East. Its utmost significance lies in its effect upon ancient Israel. The mythology of Cana῾an exerted its immediate impact upon the Bible, and what use the Old Testament made of this mythology was what it objected to. GORDON's final conclusion is that the epic poetry of Ugarit applied a decisive influence on Greek, as well as on Hebrew, literature: it constitutes the connecting link between the early Hellenistic and Hebrew literary achievements.[10]

NOTES

1. Caphtor was the country from which the Philistines immigrated to Palestine. According to another theory, Caphtor was identical with the Aegean world, especially with Crete.
2. Cyrus Herzl Gordon, *Before the Bible: The Common Background of Greek and Hebrew Civilizations* (New York and London, 1962).
3. *Ibid.*, p. 131.
4. *Ibid.*, p. 281.
5. "Canonical" is not the appropriate word for Greek epic literature, and for the Bible it

represents an anachronism, since the Jewish canon was not established prior to the first century C.E.

6. Koller, p. 81.

7. Gordon, p. 300. Gordon considers the Krete-Epic as an "Ur-Iliad" in Semitic dress (p. 13.).

8. Pp. 226 ff.

9. P. 128.

10. P. 205.

Greece

MYTHOLOGY AND MUSIC

No other nation of Antiquity has bequeathed so many written records about their musical culture as the Greeks. Mythology, history, theory, philosophy, and ethics contain superabundant comments about their Arts. A multifarious legacy of highly artistic pictorial representations has given us additional insights into their musical practices as well. And yet, as musicology has been compelled to admit, no other manifestation of Greek culture, neither the visual arts nor poetry, has shared the fate of music, whose documents were almost completely destroyed.

The primeval history of Greek music is so closely interwoven with myth and legend that it is difficult to extricate from this maze a kernel of historical truth. In order to survey the history of music in Greece, we must first approach it from the viewpoint of mythology. Here, music assumed a sort of "leitmotif," a permanent "ritornello" clarifying daily life in relation to the divine. For instance, all Greek instruments are attributed to divine origin, and though there were relatively few instruments in the musical practice of the Greeks, each of them was believed to have been invented by several deities. The nine divine Muses, the female representatives of the aural arts, are those of rhetoric, song, and the playing of instruments. These are the so-called *Mousic* arts, personified by the Muses, from whom our *music* also received its name.

In Greece every artistic skill was called *technē* and preceded by a suffix: *ikē*, such as *rhetorikē, logikē, politikē, technē* and thus also *mousikē technē* i.e., "the art of the Muses," which entered into Western civilization simply as "music."

For thousands of years the Greek people sang, played instruments, and danced. The shepherds blew their syrinx, the priests played their *auloi*, the bards recited their ballads to the accompaniment of the *kithara* or *phorminx*. However, "music" as such did not come into being before the fifth century B.C.E.[1] It is no accident that the Greeks had no Muses of painting, sculpture, or architecture, even though magnificent specimens of these arts were produced and preserved. These were the "practical" arts, while the *Mousic* arts were those which, according to ARISTOTLE's definition, were created by *enthousiasmos*.

To fully understand the nature of the Muses, we must glance at the figures of Greek mythology most closely related to the Muses—the nymphs.

Nymphai are called in Greek principally "maidens in the marriageable age," brides or virgins. It is therefore not always clear which category is meant in the literature, whether the term refers to human or divine beings.[2]

This ambiguity is constantly present in mythology as well as in practical life.

Young girls, worshipping the goddess Artemis in dances, are called nymphs. In their dances, they become, under the guidance of the goddess, nymphs, god-like creatures, elevated to divine status by their enthusiasm. Thus, the action takes place simultaneously in the divine and human sphere.[3]

According to the Greek conception, the ecstasy manifested by the dancing girls elevated them to divine creatures.

The choir of the dancers calls always upon the goddess to take part in the dances, the maidens being transformed, while dancing, into the mythical *Thiasos*, the retinue of the goddess; or, more precisely, the worshipping choir identified as the *Thiasos* itself.[4] *

The divine nymphs were supposed to dwell on the summits of mountains, in caves, springs, trees, rivers, and seas. MARTIANUS CAPELLA called the Muses *fontigenae*, "born in springs," just as the nymphs were termed. Like the gods, the nymphs were worshipped in the dances of young maidens. In numerous localities of Greece, there were places of worship where the maidens of the district assembled for rural festivals to honor the Muses and the nymphs with their dances. Gradually the difference disappeared between the two; the nymphs of mythology were a collective group of anonymous divine, or semi-divine creatures, while the Muses emerged from primitive anonymity to have specific names.

The male counterparts of the nymphs were also divine or semi-divine figures, such as the *Pans, Curetes, Corybants, Silens,* and *Satyrs.* All these were not simply conventional figures of a mythical divine cult but actors of plays, emerging from the religious dance, and belonging to the *Mimēsis* of every play. Like the nymphs, they were anonymous, and during their ecstatic dancing they underwent a transubstantiation and became divine beings.

The close relationship existing between the Muses and the nymphs went so far that the Greeks generally considered them to be identical. The Lydians, i.e. the Greeks living in Asia-Minor, did not differentiate between the Muses and the nymphs, calling both Muses [SUIDAS, *s.v.* "*Nyhphai*"]. The Greeks of the mainland, for whom dancing was also a divine revelation, did not make any attempt to distinguish between the divine and human nymphs.

While the nymphs were supposed to be present everywhere in nature, the Muses were restricted to a specific *locality.* They had their own regions where they were supposed to live: Thrace and Olympus in the north, and the region around the Helicon in Boeotia, central Greece. HESIOD gave us a complete genealogy of the Muses; he even reported their original names.[5] Their mother was MNEMOSYNE, remembrance, memory; their father ZEUS, the omnipotent.

The names mentioned by HESIOD were all meant to indicate the *technē*, the skill, innate to the Muses. This will become evident when we make a literal translation of their names.

Thaleia means "feast," *Melpomēne* "the one who sings and dances," *Terpsichorē* "the one who takes pleasure in the round dances," *Polyhymnia* "rich in

---

* *Thiasos* was the name for a group of dancing worshippers (see below).

hymns," *Kalleiopē* "the one with the beautiful voice." While these names refer to the kitharōdic song, there are others which were also taken from the vocabulary of kitharōdy: *Kleiō* is "the proclaimer of the glory," since the Muses as well as the singers *kleiousin,* i.e., "proclaim the glory." *Euterpē* is "the one who gives pleasure," since playing and dancing should *terpein,* "afford pleasure." *Eratō*'s name is derived from the adjective *eratos,* "lovely" a characteristic of the kitharōdic singing. *Urania* is "the heavenly one."[6]

The Muses bestowed upon the singer the gift of prophecy, thus enabling him to proclaim the present, the past, and the future. HESIOD said that the Muses transformed the thinking man into a seer, capable of expressing himself in parables. In this state of mind, the singer or poet becomes *nympholeptēs,* "possessed by the nymphs," and is at the same time a seer, capable of divinity. (Compare this with the Jewish prophet, the *nabi*—a term of unification in the conception of the Jews, the singer, the poet, and the foreteller of the future.) As with the Israelites, the man in Greece possessed by the Muses did not enunciate his own experience, but was merely a tool of the divine power.

The *enthousiasmos,* the rapture created by the Muses, is the origin of music and poetry, which is the essence of the Greek term *Mousikē.*

The places where the Muses were worshipped were called

> *Mouseion,* which was never a temple in the city, but a sacred precinct outside of the daily activities of the humans, a grotto with a dancing place, or a grove, as remote as possible from human habitation. When there was no such facility available, an artificial imitation of it had to be created.[7]

The garden plots erected for the Muses in Boeotia were especially famous. The statues placed in the groves of the Muses were considered art collections in the open during the epoch of Alexandria, and they maintained their ideological connections with the grotto of the Muses and were called *Mouseia.* With the passage of time, the notion was extended to any art collection, thus leading to the modern *museum.* Thus, it was the locality where the Muses dwelled that gave its name to the art collection, not the originally loose connection of music with the plastic arts.[8]

The most important feature of the classical myth about the Muses concerns their relationship to APOLLO, the leader of their group. He was called *Musagētes,* meaning the one who "starts the dance-song," the *kitharōdos,* who leads the singing and accompanies the choral performance of the dancing Muses.[9]

There was also a very significant relationship between the *Sirens* and the Muses. According to tradition, the Sirens were the daughters of the river-god ACHELOOS and were consequently river-nymphs. Their mother was the Muse, TERPSICHORĒ—already mentioned. They bewitched the mortals who sailed to their island Anthemoessa and cast their anchors. Their sweet song made the sailors forget their homeland along with their wives and children. The best-known adventure of this kind was the one experienced by Odysseus, of the Homeric epics.

But even prior to ODYSSEUS, in an epic about the Argonauts, it is related how ORPHEUS, the famous singer, intoned a song while passing the island of the Sirens. He was accompanied by the phorminx, which drowned out the song of the Sirens, and he thereby proceeded unmolested.[10]

In the ancient epics, the songs of the Sirens were called *Molpē,* meaning "dance with song." This may logically explain the origin of the Sirens, the daughters of TERPSICHORE. Also, it is not quite evident from mythology what the Sirens did with their bewitched victims. ODYSSEUS was forewarned by the nymph CIRCE:

> To the Sirens first shall thou come, who bewitch all men whosoever shall come to them. . . . The Sirens enchant him with their clear song, sitting in the meadow, and all about is a great heap of bones of men, corrupt in death, and round the bones the skin is wasting.
> (Odyssey, XII, 39 ff.)

Nevertheless, ODYSSEUS followed CIRCE's advice. He poured wax into the ears of his companions in order to prevent them from hearing the sweet song of the Sirens, and he ordered them to bind him with open ears to the foremast. Thus he and his companions were safe from their bewitching songs.

According to their nature, the Muses were goddesses addicted to music, singers who also played instruments. The Greeks originally conceived of a single Ur-Muse, the goddess of singing. Later, this *Mousic* idea was extended to encompass the three forms of tonal art: vocal, instrumental, and dance.[11] (Compare this with the similar conception of the ancient Hebrews.) With the passage of time, mythology created a choir of nine Muses, among whom was KALLEIOPE, the Syrinx-blower, considered to be supreme. The Greek called her "the fine-voiced," and she or her immediate successor might have been considered as the Ur-Muse.[12]

The scholium to HESIOD's *Theogony* attributes to the Muses certain domains of knowledge, which, curiously enough, markedly contradicts their original names. It was stated that:

> "The "inventions" of the Muses are the following: *Kleiō* invented rhetoric,—*Euterpē* the music of the auloi,—*Thaleia* the comedy,—*Melpomēne* the tragedy,—*Terpsichorē* the kitharōdy,—*Eratō* poetry,—*Polymnia* geometry [!],—*Urania* astronomy,—but *Kalleiopē,* the most important of all, epic poetry.[13]

By such a classification, the divine group of singing Muses was transformed into a scholarly "College," thus running counter to the original idea of the *Mousikē,* which referred basically to the artful skill of the Muses.

In spite of this scholarly classification, the Muses, according to the conception of the Greeks, maintained their relation to the *Mousikē.* This is evident from numerous pictorial representations, in which the Muses are shown playing instruments. *Kalleiopē* played the syrinx and the lyre; *Melpomēne,* the harp and the double-aulos; *Terpsichorē* likewise the harp and the lyre; *Kleiō* the double-aulos; and *Eratō,* the hand-drum. SOPHOCLES said that the Muses liked the aulos (*Antigonē,* 965), and EURIPIDES stated that the aulos was the servant of the Muses (*Elektra* 717). (See Illus. 104, 106.)

To humanity the Muses gave music, which originally consisted exclusively of singing. Only later was the notion of music extended to the playing of instruments as well. PLATO still considered music, when separated from the *logos* (the word), as:

> sounds of animals, and of men and instruments, and every other sort of noise, as if they were all one.

> For when there are no words, it is very difficult to recognize the meaning of the harmony

and rhythm. And we must acknowledge that all this sort of things, which aims only at swiftness and smoothness and a brutish noise, and uses the aulos and the lyre not as mere accompaniment of the dance and the song, is exceedingly coarse and tasteless.[14]

The choir leader of this divine group of singers was APOLLO. Right after his birth, by LETO, on the island of Delos, APOLLO felt the urge to play an instrument. However, it was after a quarrel arose between him and his brother HERMES that he took possession of the instrument that was to become his artistic emblem. HERMES, through the deceitful looting of APOLLO's cattle, provoked his brother's ire. Both turned to ZEUS for arbitration. To appease his brother for the damage he had done, HERMES consented to give APOLLO the lyre invented by him.[15] Thus APOLLO became known as the lyre-playing god. As a singer, he came to the fore much later. In addition, APOLLO is mentioned occasionally in Greek literature as a player of the syrinx and the aulos, though these are rare exceptions.

The name APOLLO means "moving together." From this, SOCRATES derived the theory that APOLLO, being the god of harmony, made all things move together by his harmonious power. His four attributes were music, prophecy, medicine, and archery, all having harmony as their unifying factor.[16]

APOLLO's musical activities were restricted mainly to Delphoi. Here, after his victory over the dragon PYTHON, he sang his first triumphant song accompanied by the kithara. The pictorial representations usually depict him with a stringed instrument, at first with the kithara, later with the lyre. In one picture he is shown playing the syrinx, particularly when, as an atonement for ADMETOS, he tended his flocks as a shepherd. Since the syrinx was the characteristic instrument of the shepherds, it was logical to depict APOLLO as a player of it.[17] Also, at the banquet of the immortals on Olympus, APOLLO entertained the gods with his playing, and he accompanied the singing of the Muses.

According to Greek mythology, HERMES "invented" the lyre. Among the gods anything was possible, but what this son of ZEUS accomplished right after his birth is fabulous beyond belief.

As HOMER reported, this Stradivarius of mythology, as a young child, found a large turtle. In a flash he was inspired with the idea that this turtle could be transformed into a musical instrument. Where he obtained the necessary tools for this complicated undertaking is not divulged. The turtle had to be eviscerated. From cane he made a yoke and then covered the open shell of the animal with the skin of a cow. After he completed the sound box, he applied two arms to it made from horns of goats and connected these with a cross-bar, from which he stretched across the bridge seven strings made from the guts of the stolen cattle. Unquestionably, this was a highly complex *tour de force*, having been conceived in the mind of a young child. Moreover, the youthful inventor did not tarry to demonstrate his mastery on the instrument before his brother APOLLO. According to the saga, this was the first "kitharōdy."

The Greek word for turtle is *chelys*, and so the instrument was called by the same name. Later it was made of wood, but the back was plated with tortoise-shells so that it would look like a natural turtle casing.

We may imagine the extent of HERMES' annoyance when he was obliged to give his instrument to APOLLO at the decree of ZEUS. However, he soon

Illus. 89 Attic amphora from Dulci. Sacrificial procession, showing two kitharas and two auloi. (Sixth century B.C.E.). State Museum, Berlin.

Illus. 90 Muses with aulos and lute. Marble relief. National Museum, Athens. (After Max Wegner, *Das Musikleben der Griechen,* Berlin, 1949.)

Illus. 91 Contest of Apollo Kitharōdos with the aulos-playing Marsyas. Marble relief. National Museum, Athens. (After Max Wegner, *Das Musikleben der Griechen,* Berlin, 1949.)

Illus. 92 Heracles kills his teacher Linos (vase originated about 480 B.C.E.).
Munich, State Collection of Antiquities. (After Max Wegner, *Musikgeschichte in Bildern,* Leipzig, 1962. Illus. 57.)

Illus. 93 Orpheus playing the lyre to listening Thracians. State Museum, Berlin.
(After Max Wegner, *Musikgeschichte in Bildern,* Leipzig, 1962. Illus. 75.)

Illus. 94 Orpheus attacked by a tattooed Thracian woman. Amphore. State Collection of Antiquities, Munich. (After Max Wegner, *Das Musikleben der Griechen,* Berlin, 1949. Plate 17 b.)

Illus. 95 Terra-cotta lyre-player from Thebes (sixth century B.C.E.). Musée du Louvre, Paris. (After *The Horizon Book of Ancient Greece,* New York, 1965.)

Illus. 96 A small Cycladic statue, showing a seated harpist (ca. 2500 B.C.E.).
Metropolitan Museum of Art, New York. (After *The Horizon Book of Ancient
Greece,* New York, 1965.)

Illus. 97 Bronze statuette of a *phorminx*-player. Probably of Cretic origin.
(End of the eighth century B.C.E.). Iraklion Museum (Crete). (After Max
Wegner, *Musikgeschichte in Bildern,* Leipzig, 1962. Illus. 1.)

Illus. 98 Three satyrs playing kitharas. (After Hermann Koller, *Musik und Dichtung im Alten Griechenland,* Bern and Munich, 1963.)

Illus. 99 Dionysos playing the barbiton, and satyrs. Bibliothèque Nationale, Paris. (After Max Wegner, *Musikgeschichte in Bildern,* Leipzig, 1962. Illus. 25.)

Illus. 100 Kithar̄odos. Museum of Fine Arts, Boston. (After Max Wegner, *Musikgeschichte in Bildern*, Leipzig, 1962. Illus. 73.)

Illus. 101 Music instruction. (After Hermann Koller, *Musik und Dichtung im Alten Griechenland*, Bern and Munich, 1963.)

Illus. 102 Kneading of bread, with accompaniment of the aulos. Terra-cotta sculpture. Musée du Louvre, Paris. (After Karl Bücher, *Arbeit und Ryhthmus*, Leipzig, 1924.)

Illus. 103 Participants in a *komos,* disguised as birds. (After Hermann Koller, *Musik und Dichtung im Alten Griechenland,* Bern and Munich, 1963.)

Illus. 104 The nine Muses, with aulos, harp, cradle-kithara, and lyre. Museum Munich. (After Max Wegner, *Die Musikinstrumente des Alten Orients*, Münster i.W., 1950.)

Illus. 105 Barbiton, aulos, and cradle-kithara in the women's chambers. Museum Würzburg. (After Max Wegner, *Die Musikinstrumente des Alten Orients*, Münster i.W., 1950.)

Illus. 106 Muses and Mousaios, with stringed instruments and double-aulos. British Museum. (After Max Wegner, *Musikgeschichte in Bildern*, Leipzig, 1962. Illus. 22.)

Illus. 107 Girl playing the kithara. She seems to be tuning the instrument. Musée du Louvre, Paris. (After Max Wegner, *Musikgeschichte in Bildern*, Leipzig, 1962. Illus. 4.)

Illus. 108 Lute and kithara. Relief on a tomb. (After Espérandieu, *Recueil général des bas-reliefs de la Gaulle Romaine,* Paris, 1907.)

Illus. 109 Sappho, called the "tenth Muse," with Alcaios, strumming the barbiton. Glyptothek, Munich. (After *The Horizon Book of Ancient Greece,* New York, 1965.)

Illus. 110 Aulos, lyre, xylophone (?), and harp, in the women's chambers. (After Max Wegner, *Die Musikinstrumente des Alten Orients,* Münster i.W., 1950.)

Illus. 111 Aulos-playing courtesan, carved in high relief on the side of an altar. Museo delle Terme, Rome. (After The *Horizon Book of Ancient Greece,* New York, 1965.)

Illus. 112 Athena, goddess of warfare, already dressed for battle, sprang from the head of her father, Zeus, to the sounds of the kithara. Museum of Fine Arts, Boston. (After *The Horizon Book Ancient Greece,* New York, 1965.)

Illus. 113 Aulos at sports. Museum Würzburg. (After Max Wegner, *Die Musikinstrumente des Alten Orients,* Münster i.W., 1950.)

Illus. 114 Aulos-player with the *phorbeia.* British Museum. (After Max Wegner, *Musikgeschichte in Bildern,* Leipzig, 1962. Illus. 11.)

Illus. 115 Kroupezion (scabellum). Part of a sculpture. (After Max Wegner, *Musikgeschichte in Bildern,* Leipzig, 1962. Illus. 27.)

Illus. 116 Cretic sistrum on a vase-relief of Hagia Triada (ca. 1500 B.C.E.). (After Max Wegner, *Die Musikinstrumente des Alten Orients,* Münster i.W., 1950.)

Illus. 117 Cretic dancing girls, accompanying themselves with the lyre. Clay-figurines from Palaicastro. Candia Museum. (After Curt Sachs, *Die Musik der Antike*, in *Handbuch der Musikwissenschaft*, Potsdam, 1934.)

Illus. 118 Instruction in music and poetry. (After Hermann Koller, *Musik und Dichtung im Alten Griechenland*, Bern and Munich, 1963.)

Illus. 119 Instruction in playing the aulos and barbiton. British Museum. (After Max Wegner, *Die Musikintrumente des Alten Orients*, Münster i.W., 1950.)

Illus. 120 Instruction in playing the kithara. (After Furtwängler-Reichhold, *Griechische Vasenmalerei*, vol. II, 1909.)

Illus. 121 Singing lesson, with accompaniment of the aulos. (After Furtwängler-Reichhold, *Griechische Vasenmalerei,* vol. II, 1909.)

Illus. 122 Linos teaching to play the kithara. State Museum, Schwerin. (After
Max Wegner, *Musikgeschichte in Bildern,* Leipzig, 1962. Illus. 56.)

Illus. 123 Two hymns to Apollo, chiseled on a wall of the Athenian treasure house in Delphoi (ca. 138–128 B.C.E.). (After Max Wegner, *Musikgeschichte in Bildern,* Leipzig, 1962. Illus. 76.)

Illus. 124 The "Berlin Papyrus." (After *Musik in Geschichte und Gegenwart,* vol. V, Plate 36.)

consoled himself with the "invention" of another instrument, the syrinx. Since HERMES was also the god of the shepherds, the new instrument was immediately associated with shepherd life. HERMES' son, PAN, took over the syrinx. PAN was also considered as a god of the shepherds, and subsequently the instrument was called the Pan's-pipe.

Another mythological "inventor" of musical instruments was ATHENA, who is credited at the same time with being the inventor of the single- and double-pipe (aulos). There was another tradition which attributed the "invention" of the double-aulos to MARSYAS, a Phrygian "demon." Here mythology becomes somewhat confusing because, according to other sources, MARSYAS was a high-priest of the Phrygian goddess CYBELE, for whom the double-aulos was a main attribute. The Greeks took over the instrument together with the cult of CYBELE in the fifth century B.C.E.

Yet, MARSYAS was connected in another way with the "invention" of the double-aulos. According to the legend, ATHENA saw in her mirror how her beautiful face was disfigured by blowing the instrument. She angrily threw away the pipes and cursed them. The myth went on to state that MARSYAS found the abandoned pipes, restored them, and soon became a master of the instrument. Being presumptuous, MARSYAS challenged APOLLO to a contest. The Muses were chosen as judges and, of course, they declared the lyre-player APOLLO as winner. At this point, ATHENA's curse took effect. According to a prior agreement, the loser was to subject himself completely to the power of the victor. APOLLO was cruel and flayed MARSYAS alive, a drastic and undeserved punishment for the loser in such a *Mousic* contest.

According to another version of mythology, the Muses gave MARSYAS the palm, but APOLLO asked for another bout, which could not be denied to him. In this, he reversed his instrument and played it on the backside, which MARSYAS was unable to do with his pipes. By this trick APOLLO won the contest. In this version the result also brought about the flaying alive of the loser.

This saga symbolically reflects the difference between two kinds of music— the playing of the sweet stringed instruments and the orgiastic sound of the Phrygian auloi.

Despite ATHENA's aversion to the auloi, the Boeotic poetess CORINNA asserted that APOLLO learned to play it from ATHENA. Seemingly, the goddess must have found something attractive about this instrument, since she took the time to teach it to APOLLO. It is probable that the saga of ATHENA and MARSYAS does not belong to the ancient mythology but developed after the Persian wars. In Athens strong opposition arose against the use of this foreign, Asiatic instrument.[18]

Another "invention" of ATHENA was the *salpinx*, the trumpet. Since she was the goddess of war, it is logical to connect her with this specific instrument. At the forum of Argos, she was worshipped as ATHENA SALPINX, the trumpet-blowing ATHENA, and there a sanctuary was erected in her honor.[19] It is probable that the trumpets were invented by the Etruscans, the first bronze-casters in the Mediterranean.

Still another myth, evidently of later origin, asserted that AMPHION, the son of ZEUS and ANTIOPE, invented the lyre. At least this is what PLATO said (*Laws*, 677 d). But another version states that AMPHION received it from

HERMES. This would indicate that HERMES fashioned a second instrument, since he had to give the first one to his brother APOLLO.

Mythology ascribed to AMPHION still another "invention," which in reality was made by TERPANDROS (ca. 675–659 B.C.E.).[20] The myth describes how AMPHION's playing of the lyre was responsible for building the walls of Thebes. Through his singing and playing, the stones moved by themselves to the desired spot. This myth thus has symbolic meaning about the transcendental power of music. Other mythical persons connected with music were THAMYRIS and LINOS. The former, son of the nymph ARGIOPE, was such an expert in singing and playing on the lyre that he presumptuously claimed himself able to outdo the Muses in singing. The angry Muses blinded him and took from him the divine gifts of song and play.[21] His and MARSYAS's example shows how dangerous it was for mortals to challenge the divine beings in the field of music.

The oldest representative among the *Mousic* heroes was LINOS, the son of APOLLO and the Muse URANIA. He was supposed to have been the first to receive the gift of singing and to have taught it. Among others, ORPHEUS was his pupil. He met a violent end through HERACLES, one of his pupils. After his death he was worshipped as the Muses were on the Helicon. His name lives on in the "Song of Linos." It may well be that the song, a lamenting melody, existed formerly and that it was attributed, by hypostasis, to this mythical person.

Another pupil of LINOS was MUSAIOS, with whom the teacher had better luck than with HERACLES. Even his name seems to indicate that he was well versed in all the *Mousic* arts. According to another version, MUSAIOS was only a pallid copy of ORPHEUS, a kind of Attic ORPHEUS.[22]

The original lyre made of the turtle, the *chelys*, was later called *phorminx*, *lyra*, and *kitharis*. All these terms represent more developed forms of the instrument. As a matter of fact, no other instrument of the Greeks had undergone so many and such thorough transformations as the lyre.

The lyre, the symbol of the music-making APOLLO, was called "Apollinic." APOLLO was the prototype of the human singer. Like the divine kitharōdos, his human equivalent was the leader of the choir and he had the honorary function of singing the *Prooimion* or *anabolē*, an improvised musical introduction for the choir-dance that followed.

As in other civilizations of the antique world, in Greece the heroic ballads of ancient times, as well as the tales about the gods, were always recited (or sung) to the accompaniment of stringed instruments.[23] Whenever the singer of epics had to perform, he usually accompanied himself on the kithara. In the epic poem, his song was called *anabolē* or *archē*, which comprised introductory verses called *"prooimion."*

The *Prooimion* closed in general with the invocation of, or the invitation to participation of, the god (or the Muse); then follows a stereotyped formula of taking leave of the divine being, with the transition to the main part of the choir-song, the *nomos*.[24]

Thus, the form of the kitharōdy presented itself in three sections: a prologue in hexametric form (with the accompaniment of the kithara); a danced choir-song, called *agōn;* and an epilogue.[25] The kithara served as an accompaniment, stressing the melodic line but never dominating. In the verses of the *prooimion*, the singer could improvise, but the main part, the choir-song, must have been thoroughly rehearsed in all its details.

According to one tradition, LINOS was the pupil of ORPHEUS; according to another, his teacher. He was supposed to have received the lyre directly from APOLLO. PARIS, the handsome shepherd boy on the mountain of Ida, played the Apollinic lyre while judging the beauty contest among the three goddesses HERA, ATHENA, and APHRODITE.

With the young HERACLES, whom he was supposed to teach the lyre, LINOS was most unfortunate. HERACLES revolted against his teacher and menaced him, so that LINOS had to use his lyre for protective measures; he struck HERACLES with it, causing it to break. Another version says that LINOS reprimanded his pupil for a mistake and, in a rage, was slain by him (Illus. 92). At a later time, HERACLES must have learned to play the kithara, for he is represented in several pictures as a kitharōdos, a player of the kithara. He was depicted in *Mousic* as well as gymnastic agōns, and once was shown playing the aulos between two dancing satyrs.

The oracles in Delphoi were always sung in hexametric form and accompanied by the kithara. These songs were called *thespiaiōdē*, "songs proclaiming oracles." Even without an instrumental accompaniment, they belonged to the *Mousikē*.

The names that have been mentioned up to this point were exclusively mythological figures. However, ORPHEUS was considered to be the bridge between myth and reality. In the Greek saga that emerged around the fifth century B.C.E., the mundane singer ORPHEUS appears as an earthly parallel to the divine kitharōdos APOLLO. Although he was supposed to have lived in the mythical period, his actions, which were exclusively of a musical nature, had made such an impression upon the Greek mind that his achievements were regarded as real. His lyre-playing had a magical effect in bewitching not only men but also wild animals, and in some instances even inanimate objects. His biggest and best-known feat was his conquest of the Underworld, where he almost succeeded in freeing his deceased wife, EURYDICE. This and other achievements of the famous singer represent examples that indicate how *Mousic* art as a Greek conception possessed an irresistible power throughout the whole life of mankind. Through the magic of his song, ORPHEUS was able to soften the hearts of Thracians (Illus. 93). But his influence upon these rough warriors caused their wives to exhibit such outbreaks of frenzy that they mercilessly slew the defenseless singer with their hammers and swords (Illus. 94). The fate of ORPHEUS was similar to that of THAMYRIS, a singer who was not murdered, but was bereft of his divine gifts—a fate tantamount to an artistic death.

It has been necessary to deal thus extensively with Greek mythology and legend because not only did they influence the entire domain of the *Mousic* arts, but they were inextricably bound up with Greek life. Their effect was visible not only in the religious, political, and social life of Greece, but especially in the education of the young.

For an understanding of the musical art of the Greeks, it is important to realize that ORPHEUS and AMPHION, the singers of paeans and hymns, were both credited with the initiation of the musical art as well as with the creation of the entire human culture. And it is significant that they achieved this with

their *singing*. The oracles were proclaimed with *songs;* public and private life
was governed by *singing;* the *song* of the Muses led mankind to a peaceful
existence, whereas it was formerly under the influence of the war-songs of
TYRTAIOS. Thus, the *Mousic* arts were able to transform the earlier wild and
uncivilized men into a moral society.

Besides LINOS and AMPHION, the half-mythical musicians from Phrygia, the
three most ancient aulētes of the legend, HYAGNIS, MARSYAS, and OLYMPOS,
were also mentioned. ARION, an aulēte of Methymna from Lesbos, was also a
half-mythical musician who was supposed to have lived at the beginning of
the sixth century. HERODOTUS's report about ARION evidently had confused his
legendary traits with reality, making it difficult to determine where myth
ends and history begins.

According to the Greeks, every legendary god, god-like creature, and real
or imaginary artist was purported to have created some aspect of music as
well as to have contributed to its gradual development. It should be noted
that one thing is significant in all these sagas: if we should examine more
closely the names of musicians, instruments, and the essence of music itself,
we will find that the actual origins of Greek music stem from places outside
of Greece proper, namely, Thrace, Thessaly, and Asia Minor. In these sagas
the ancient domiciles of the Greek tribes, prior to the great Doric invasion
(ca. 1100 B.C.E.) are revealed. In later times, these tribes were united into
a homogeneous Greek nation that gave succeeding generations their ethnic
imprint and developed a civilization that until then was unmatched in the
history of mankind.

THE HISTORICAL ORIGIN OF THE MUSIC OF THE GREEKS

Before leaving the world of myth and saga to consider the musical practice
of the Greeks, we must first glance at the meagre extant historical records
that deal with the sources of Greek music.

From the seventh to the fifth century B.C.E. a Greek civilization emerged
comparable to a mature state. How did it come about? Where were its roots?
What were its preliminary stages?

It is true that we possess the Homeric epics, which existed long before
the eighth century B.C.E. Yet, despite their homogeneous character, it is almost
generally accepted that these were not created during the alleged time of
HOMER, but were circulated for hundreds of years by oral tradition, to be
unified only at a much later date.

Our knowledge of Greek music in Antiquity does not go back beyond the
times of the Doric migration. We possess some knowledge of Greek music,
allegedly from the eighth century, from a bronze statuette and musical
depictions on vases. These belong to the epoch during which the *Iliad* was
supposed to have been created. However, according to another chronology,
HOMER's life was assigned to about 1400 B.C.E., while the eighth century is
to be regarded as the time during which HOMER's poems were probably
written down after having been circulated by oral tradition for many
centuries.

Historical research maintains that the Greek civilization was a continuation
of the Cretan–Mycaenic culture, either by natural adoption or by violent con-

quest. Prior to the Doric migration (ca. 1100 B.C.E.) the Cretan–Mycaenic culture was the most important civilizing force in the Mediterranean basin. This culture, which contains many affinities with that of Egypt, may be traced back at least to 3800 B.C.E.[26] In addition, the culture of the Phoenicians appears to have its roots in the Cretan–Mycaenic civilization, despite the differences of their religions.

Between the Cretan and the Greek cultures there are more than merely superficial affinities. First of all, there is no sharp dividing line between the Mycaenean culture (especially in its later stage) and the Achaean civilization, as mentioned in the Homeric epics. They seem to have intermingled and become a single society.[27] However, it cannot be ascertained whether Crete or Sparta was the first to have introduced the Doric ways of life. Both states were governed by a Senate and each was administered by ten *kosmoi* ("Prefects"), called in Sparta *Ephores*. It is possible that both civilizations had developed under the pressure of external circumstances, to emerge in the same direction. The visit of LYCOURGOS, who brought to Sparta many institutions from Cretan life, gives some credibility to this theory.

How the ancient flourishing Cretan civilization was destroyed and transformed into that of the Greeks cannot be treated here. Rather, it is my intention to restrict this investigation to those musical aspects which the earlier civilization transmitted to the latter, as documented by the preserved relics. Fortunately, the discoveries from this archaic period have enabled us to formulate some basic ideas about the music practices of those times.

A few small marble idols representing aulos-players and harpists, preserved from the Cycladic culture of the third millennium, were discovered on the isles of Thera and Keros (Illus. 95–97). At Keros a statue was found that depicted a man playing the harp in a sitting position. The harp somewhat resembled the trigōnon-type of a later time (Illus. 96).[28] The auloi of the Cycladic players resembled the shape of the later Greek double-auloi. However, this type of instrument was known throughout the Ancient Orient, Sumeria, Egypt, Babylonia, Phoenicia, and so on.

On a wall-painting in Crete dating back to the Minoan culture, there is preserved, in fragments, a single figure of a lyre-player. The approximate time of this picture is surmised as 1950–1800 B.C.E.[29]

The most important musical discovery from Cretan culture is the painted clay sarcophagus from Hagia Triada. On each of its long sides is illustrated a sacrifice, which is accompanied by music. On one side, an aulos is visible behind the sacrificial animal; on the other, a lyre-player is seen participating in a libation.[30] The lyre bears a certain likeness to the classic kithara, which also had seven strings. It is curious that the classic kithara, which developed from the Homeric phorminx, subsequently carried four strings.

Greek historiography attributes to TERPANDROS the addition of three strings to the kithara, i.e., from four to seven. With this instrument, he was victorious in Sparta in the Karneic plays in 676–673 B.C.E. Furthermore, he was the first folk bard to recite the verses of HOMER accompanied by the kithara. Thus, it is remarkable that the sarcophagus of Hagia Triada depicted a kithara (or lyra) with seven strings a thousand years prior to TERPANDROS! The double-aulos on the sarcophagus displays eight finger-holes, just as in classic times. On a cameo, also found in Crete, a woman is shown blowing a huge conch-trumpet, and on a vase, a sistrum is depicted accompanying the dance.

Another important pictorial representation of the Cretan culture referring to music is the "reapers' vase" from Hagia Triada. Here, marching reapers are shown preceded by three men, before whom a fourth man is swinging a sistrum (Illus. 116). At this time (ca. 1500 B.C.E.) the sistrum was known only in Egypt and must have been imported from that land. When the Cretans adopted this instrument, its function was changed, since in Egypt it was an instrument of the cult. It is possible that in Crete a march of reapers had some cultic connotation, which may explain the use of a sistrum for such occasions. Another discovery dating from Cretan times is a terra cotta group from Palaicastro. It shows a lyre-player with three female figures.[31] The representation of the lyre in this group could be interpreted as an early type of accompaniment for the choral dance, although this is merely an assumption.

From Mycenean culture have been preserved such relics as the ivory fragments found in a tomb at Menidi. In addition, a small metal lyre that resembled the later phorminx was found at Amyclaion.

These sparse discoveries represent quite vaguely the Greek musical culture prior to the Doric migration. After this ethnic regrouping, our information about Greek music comes from the Homeric epics. While instrumental music, as an independent genre, is not mentioned by HOMER, we may still continue to ponder about his excessive allusion to "song and play."[32]

A popular stringed instrument of Homeric times was the phorminx. The technique of playing a stringed instrument was called, by HOMER, kitharis. The differentiation between the kitharis, as action, and the phorminx, as the instrument, ultimately led to a compromise that brought about the change of meaning—for the term *kitharis* to mean instrument and not act of playing. It even took a long time for the primitive phorminx to be transformed into its final (and multi-shaped) kithara, as we see in numerous pictures (see Illus. 136).

The wind-instruments are mentioned only occasionally by HOMER, and seem to have been of lesser importance than the stringed instruments. The salpinx, a trumpet, is mentioned only once in the *Iliad*. Occasional mention is made of the syrinx and the auloi, particularly of their use at the night watchfires of the Trojans which created surprise among the Greek besiegers. Perhaps at this time these instruments were unknown to the Greeks. This seems plausible since historical records indicate that the aulos was not imported earlier than around 700 B.C.E. (according to other sources, 500 B.C.E.) from Phrygia in Asia Minor. The aulos was brought to Greece only after this time, along with the cult of CYBELE.

For a long period the playing of auloi did not belong to the *Mousikē*, because, as ARISTOTLE said, "playing the aulos excludes the words of the poets."[33]

Percussion instruments are not mentioned at all during this period. Rhythmic accompaniments for dancing, supplied by such instruments as the krotala, kymbala, and tympana, as well as the clapping of hands, were subsequently recorded as practices found among all ancient Oriental cultures.

Kitharōdy, singing and dancing accompanied by the kithara, is, in HOMER's works, the only reminiscence of the great Cretan past, which separated the later epic singer of classical Greece by the long and dark centuries of the Doric migration.[34]

HOMER mentions four different genres of song, which were later retained in Greece: the *Song of Linos;* the *Thrēnos,* a dirge; and two kinds of choral songs, the *Paian* to APOLLO, and wedding songs, particularly the *Hymenaios.* There are in HOMER, besides, a number of additional references to choir-dances. These suggest a much richer musical life than that described by the epics themselves.

This brief survey was restricted to the centuries preceding the Doric migration, prior to which we know very little about Greek musical life, other than its having some superficial resemblances to Egyptian music. True, CURT SACHS said that "Greek music has been altogether imported," which is valid only with certain qualifications. The Greek music of Antiquity was completely different from that of the Ancient Orient. The many similarities in the musical practices of the various nations in the Ancient Orient were conditioned by the common cultural currents emanating from Mesopotamian and Egyptian regions, which exerted their influence upon all the neighboring peoples. For Greece, this was only partially the case, since it would be erroneous to assert that the music of Greece "belongs inseparably to the ancient Orient."[35]
The proof becomes evident when we compare the many forms of Oriental music practice with that of the Greeks. There we witness a multitude of irregular music patterns, while the Greeks present a clear aspect of transition in their use of typical and traditional instruments from the archaic to the classical period. No other nation of Antiquity had so few instruments as the Greeks. The two main types were the Apollonian lyre (or kithara) and the Dionysian aulos, both of course with numerous variants. Furthermore, in no other nation of the Ancient Orient had music assumed such an outstanding role in state affairs, as set forth in PLATO's works. Therefore, we must conclude that Greek musical practices are markedly different from those of all other Oriental nations.

MUSIC IN PUBLIC LIFE

Nowhere in the Greek states of ancient and later times was there to be found an independent musical practice similar to that of our modern music. Music was utilized at festivals and in social institutions that reached back into archaic times.[36] In the cult as well as in communal life, music has precisely prescribed functions. The Spartans, whose attitude toward music was somewhat reserved, regarded music of importance only in the education of the youth; while in Athens the tonal art enjoyed a favored position in all phases of life.
The focal point of the public music practice in Athens was the "Dithyrambic Choir." Following a primary education, to which every youth was subjected, every free-born citizen was supposed to participate in this choir if he had a thorough foundation in music from his earliest youth. Slaves and foreigners, i.e., people who were not citizens of Athens, were not admitted into the municipal choir. Every year, each of the Attic *philēs* (districts within the city) had to furnish a choir of fifty men, which vied with the choirs of the other *philēs.* The "Dithyrambos" (as the song of this choir was called) was danced in a circle, therefore it was called *kyklos,* "circle"; the choir itself was called *kyklios choros,* "the choir for the round dance." The rehearsals took a long time, and the man who prepared the participants for their task

was not only the poet of the song, but the composer and dancing master as well; his official title was *chorosdidaskalos,* "dancing master."[37]

Each *philē* had to select from among its members a wealthy citizen, *Choregos,* who had to sponsor the *philē.* During the rehearsals, which took considerable time and effort, the members of the choir lived on the subvention of the *Choregos.* In addition, he had to cover the expenses for the costumes of the festival, the hiring of an aulos-player, the prizes, and in most cases the appropriate publicity for the winner, whose victory was inscribed on a marble plate.[38]

In ancient times the *Choregos* also functioned as the stage-manager, who was responsible for finding, auditioning, selecting, and rehearsing the choir. Later, he had only to carry the financial burden of the performance.

The public instruction of the citizens of Athens took place in the *kyklios choros.* The young Athenian was trained in the movements according to the rhythm of the poem. Here he learned the *baseis,* i.e., the steps for the dance, and became familiar with the music, which was based upon the accent of the Greek language. It was called *prosōdia,* "a song based upon the accent of the poem," not a melody without words. The key (*modos*) of the song was predetermined. To learn a song in the community chorus was therefore a difficult task, especially if the song had several stanzas.[39] It was the pride of every *philē* to perform perfectly the words, songs, and dances of the *kyklios choros.* Much time and effort were devoted to this civic duty, with the result that Greek citizens and musicians excelled at these regularly held performances.

GREEK ATTITUDE TOWARD THE MOUSIC ARTS

As we have seen, the basic attitude toward the *Mousic* arts in classical Greece was the *enkykliō paideia,* the education of the free man "in the circle," providing the skill for the ability to participate in the choir-dance.

Not only in Athens, but in the other Greek city-states, the *Mousic* education and the participation in the choir-dance was a civic duty. PLATO, in a conversation with CLEINIAS, his Cretan friend, quotes him as saying:

we of Crete and Lacedaemon know no strain other than that we have learnt and been accustomed in our chorus.[40]

This is merely a literary reference to the actual practice. Indeed, the songs learned in the *kyklios choros* remained for a long time in the memory of the Choreuts. Even without having been performed in their entirety, these melodies belonged to the repertoire of the participants in the singing contests at banquets. After the food was cleared away, the participants started a sort of song-contest while drinking cups of wine. The singing had always to start "from the right." The *Symposiarch,* the leader of singing, either prescribed the theme of the singing, in which case every participant had to improvise upon it, or left it to everyone's discretion to choose his own theme. Familiarity with the choric songs was generally so widespread that any well-educated man could perform quite a number of them to the accompaniment of the lyre.[41] To "intone the round-singing" meant in Greek usage "to take over" and continue the *skolion,* the drinking-song.

Performances of the *kyklios choros* took place not only in their own city, but quite often the *polis* (the state or the community) delegated whole groups of singers to a sanctuary in a different part of Greece. Such a delegation was called *theory,* "a festive present," and its leader was called the *architheoros,* meaning the "leader of the theory." Every year such a delegation was sent from Athens to Delphoi on a ship of state. (Until this ship returned to Athens, no execution of any prisoner could be carried out.)

As PLUTARCH reports, each year seven pairs of sacrificial youths (male and female) were sent to Delos, to perform the so-called Dance of the Labyrinth. This custom had its origin in a legend described vividly in the seventeenth ode of BACCHYLIDES of Cheos (fifth century B.C.E.). This ode in honor of APOLLO was performed on the island of Delos as a processional song while proceeding from the harbor to the sanctuary of the god.

In rough outline, this legend stated that:

> The Athenians had committed a wrong against the king of Crete. They were vanquished by MINOS and had to pay from then on an annual tribute. They had to send yearly to the monster MINOTAURUS, who dwelled in the Labyrinth of Gnossus, seven maids and seven youths as a sacrifice. When the young hero THESEUS came to Athens, he offered to accompany the victims and try to vanquish the monster, in order to free his home-town from this heavy duty. ARIADNE, the daughter of MINOS, fell in love with THESEUS and with her help he was able to find his way in and out of the Labyrinth by following "the string of ARIADNE." He was able to kill the MINOTAURUS, and return safely to Athens with the youths and maidens. From then on, every year, in thanks for this liberation, a festive delegation was sent to Delos, as PLATO informs us. From the time when the delegation left and until they returned, the city had to be, according to the ancient custom, free from defilement, and no execution could be carried out before the boat sent to Delos returned. Thus, SOCRATES, condemned to die by poison, had to wait in his prison until the boat arrived in 399.

Not only Athens, but all the Greek cities sent choirs to the festival in Delos honoring APOLLO.

In many localities of Greece there existed societies that cultivated music and dance in honor of some divinity. There were ancient institutions, "cultic societies," in many of the cities, which in time developed into guilds and occasionally substituted even for religious functions for the community.[42] They were called *thiasoi,* and represented the retinue or attendance of a particular divinity. Among them were societies of different age groups, also groups of women; the most famous of these was that of Lesbos, with SAPPHO as its leader. The Muses themselves were considered to be such a *thiasos,* which originated in Thrace; they became the creators of the kytharōdy.[43]

Another *thiasos* was that of the Deliades, the maidens of Delos, who were the priestesses of APOLLO. According to the myth, LETO gave birth to her children ARTEMIS and APOLLO on the island of Delos, which was from the oldest times on the sanctuary of all Ionic tribes. The blind singer from Chios, who composed the choir-song for the *Deliades,* was a wandering kitharōdos, and a *Demiourgos* ("Half-god"). His song is specified as a *mimēsis,* meaning that it was performed in dancing.

THUCYDIDES states that from archaic times on, Delos was the cultural center of Ionia. There, regularly, gymnic and *Mousic* contests were held, and all the cities sent choral groups to participate in them.⁴⁴ The Delic choir of the maidens was a permanent institution of the island.

Another *thiasos* was that of the *Couretes* of Crete. HESIOD called them "dancers capable of creating pleasure," and they belonged to the category of nymphs and satyrs. In Crete, the *Couretes*, or *Couroi*, were the young adults, who would be submitted to the rites of initiation. Just as the nymphs were either human maidens or superhuman beings, the young men of Crete were likewise transformed into mythical *Couretes*, or *Couroi*, in their cultic dances.

ZEUS was the greatest *Couros*. Each year he appeared leading the *Couretes*, his *thiasos*, which rejuvenated the world of nature. He was said to bring fertility and prosperity to all living beings. The story of the god and of his retinue was retold every year by the *Couretes*. During this ritual, the singers themselves became the mythical *Couretes*, so that the legend and earthly cultic event merged into one.⁴⁵

Another such *thiasos* was that of the women of Elis. On this island was a group of sixteen women who devoted themselves to the services of the god DIONYSOS. From their cult we possess a hymn that is regarded as the most ancient Greek choral song; its text is preserved in its entirety. It describes how DIONYSOS was invited to participate in the dance of the women. How this "sorority" imagined the participation of the god is not clear, because the women of Elis had expected their god to present himself in the form of a bull. It is evident that in the Greek mythology every *poetica licentia* was permissible.

The most important *thiasos* of DIONYSOS was that of the *satyroi* (satyrs), the half-human, half-animal beings, having tails of horses. They were wild and unruly fellows who, together with the Maenads, lead mischievous lives. Their unbridled pranks are represented on hundreds of vase-pictures. They accompanied themselves on the kithara and their typical dances consisted of specific steps and leaps. In these pictorial representations we must differentiate between those illustrations which refer to a mythical action and those which reproduce a scene from a theatrical satyr-play. An especially fine example of three satyrs playing kitharas is painted on a vase (Illus. 98). Here we have no indication of human representation, but rather superhuman, mythical beings.

The numerous pictures of satrys on vases have given us a clearer understanding of the *Satyr-thiasoi* by illustrating how human actors were represented in satyr-plays as figures honoring DIONYSOS at the feasts devoted to him. On several of these vase-pictures, the loincloth is specifically depicted on which the horse-tail and phallos are shown. In their plays all satyrs wear a typical face-mask with a turned-up nose.

With the passage of time, these satyr-plays developed into regular dramatic plays. In the classical period, every performance of a tragic trilogy had to be concluded by a satyr-play. Although the subject ef every satyr-play was full of comical elements, it had been absolutely unthinkable that a comedy should follow a tragic trilogy. Authors of comedies had never written satyr-plays because this was the domain of the poets of tragedies. Satyr-plays and comedies were entirely distinct literary genres.⁴⁶

Judging from unmerous vase-pictures that depict the satyr-plays dealing with mythological themes, "the return of HEPHAESTOS to Olympus," must have been most popular. This myth can be retold in its broad outlines.

HEPHAESTOS was most angry about his maltreatment by his mother, HERA. To avenge himself for the alleged injustices suffered at her hands, he constructed an artful throne, which he gave her as a present. It was a malicious gift contrived so that anyone sitting on it could not free himself from it. Only the inventor could liberate HERA from her uncomfortable position. But no one could induce him to return to Olympus, even the powerful ARES. Eventually, DIONYSOS succeeded in outwitting the recalcitrant forger. He gave to the thirsty smith enough wine so that he was drunk, and then carried him by mule-pack to Olympus, where he was obliged to free HERA from her pathetic position.

Only a few fragments remain from various satyr-plays. One, the *Cyclops* of EURIPIDES, has been completely preserved. It deals with the saga of the one-eyed Polyphemos, who held the satyrs as slaves and forced them to do slave labor after they were shipwrecked on the rocky coast of Aetna. When ODYSSEUS and his comrades landed on this unknown island, they found the satyrs, who complained bitterly about their fate, especially that on the island there was neither wine nor dancing. From the skin-bottles of his ship, ODYSSEUS gave the satyrs wine to drink, and promptly their real nature broke forth with elemental force. ODYSSEUS devised a plan to free them from their cruel enslaver. He asked them to help him murder Polyphemos and said that their reward would be their return to DIONYSOS. The satyrs, being unreliable and cowards by nature, did not contribute too much to the plan. Eventually, ODYSSEUS succeeded in blinding Polyphemos, and the satyrs were able to leave the unhospitable island with ODYSSEUS.

Another satyr-play, *The Sleuth-Hounds* of SOPHOCLES, dealt with the Homeric hymn of HERMES. As in the aforementioned play of EURIPIDES, the motive again concerns the servitude of the satyrs under foreign lords and their eventual liberation from bondage. Since most of the satyr-plays used this subject, the theme of the cult of DIONYSOS was later rather restricted.

PLATO, with his puritanical attitude, wanted to ban the representation of the wild *satyroi* from his ideal state—not only the plays themselves, but also the *thiasoi* of satyrs, who acted in them. PLATO seems to have had no success, because the populace took pleasure in these plays, and his attempt to reduce the enjoyment of the masses was in vain.

From the periodic feasts, and from the cultural associations of the *satyr-thiasoi*, there developed in certain localities regular dance-plays, satyr-dramas, whose songs were called "kitharōdic dithyrambos." These songs, however, should not be confused with the "aulētic dithyrambos" of the *kyklios choros*, which had to be performed every year in Athens by the *Phylai* (the Tribes) at a contest. This latter dithyrambos did not change, since it was an established cultic choral form. Yet, in the satyr-plays it was always the satyrs themselves who performed these songs, likewise termed in a wider sense *dithyrambos*.

THE VOCAL ARTS OF THE GREEKS

With the exception of the Hebrews, no other people of Antiquity assigned such an important role to singing as did the Greeks. Throughout Antiquity up until the decline of Greek civilization, poets and singers were inextricably connected. The poets were also the composers of their own works. This union of poet-composer is aptly termed *melopoios*, or *melikos poiētēs*, to describe the lyric poet and his poem.

From ancient times on, Greek song was governed by the word. Whether a solo or choral song, a religious or secular melody, the *melos* (melody-line) was determined by the spoken word. A "song without words" (a term emanating from the Romantic period in the Occident) would have been unthinkable and incomprehensible in Greece.

According to PLATO,[47] *melos* comprised such components as *logos* (words), *harmonia* (key, or better, *modos*), and the *rhythmos* (moving order). Only later did a difference exist between *melos* as a melodic line, and *melos* as a lyric poem, yet from the beginning both terms were inseparable. When a lyric poet is represented in pictures, he is always shown holding the lyre, or its later species, the barbiton (see below).

The lyric singer-poet is easily recognizable in pictures, for he is always shown playing the lyre with his head thrown back on his neck, frequently with open lips (Illus. 100). In later pictures, the mouth of the singer is closed, but from it a caption emanates, a sort of banderol, indicating the beginning of a well-known tune, which clearly represents a singer.

Another peculiarity found in the pictorial representations of singers depicts the singer putting his open right palm to his ear, seemingly to hear better. This custom is indigenous throughout the ancient Orient, and still exists in Arabic countries. It is generally overlooked, however, that the singer simultaneously presses his larynx with the thumb of his right hand, in order to produce a shrill tone or an exaggerated tremolo, both highly valued in the Orient. Both customs were already known in Egypt. The most evident pictorial representation of this custom may be found in the Assyrian rock-relief showing the arrival of the victorious ASHUR-IDANNI-PAL in Susa, the conquered capital of the Elamites. There we see an orchestra and a group of female and boy-singers. One of the female singers executes the same double-movement as is seen in the Greek pictures (Illus. 66). This Oriental custom was perpetuated until the nineteenth century by the Jewish cantors; HEINE, in his "Hebraic Melodies," refers to this as an ancient custom.

At banquets and drinking bouts, the participants reclined on the *klinē* (couches on which the participants stretched) and sang "round and round," while they improvised on the barbiton. In artful singing, however, at public performances, at *Mousic* contests (*agōn*), as well as at solemn occasions, the singers are represented standing. The young boys learned this in their early music instruction. In the pictorial representations, the music students are always standing as if at attention (Illus. 118, 120). At public song-recitals, the singer stands for the most part on a higher elevation called the *bēma*. This was a wooden frame or scaffolding, which was intended not only to give the singer a higher place, but also to reinforce the resonance of his voice. In contrast to solo-singing, rendered at the same place, there was the *thiasos*, in which the singers marched or performed songs while moving in circles.

Solo singers accompanied themselves on the kithara or on one of its various species. At their music lesson, the pupils usually sang to the accompaniment of their teacher, a kitharist. Sometimes during their vocal lessons they were accompanied by the aulos or the syrinx.

The artist-painters did not usually represent the singers, but references to them abound in the literary sources. HOMER's epics, in particular, characterize extensively the activities of the *aiōdos*, the poet-singers. HOMER stressed solo-singing and kept choral-singing in the background. However, we find that the *kyklios choros* and the dance-songs of the various *thiasoi* are mentioned frequently in later literary sources.

It must appear odd that HOMER ranked the singer in the same category as the physician and the carpenter.[48] This may be explained by the fact that while the singer and the seer represented the *Mousic* art, the physician and the carpenter were concerned with the practical necessities of life, of which singing was one.

Singing, instrumental playing, and dancing accompanied each banquet. HOMER said that there is no greater joy than when the people were frolicking, and when they listened throughout the house and courtyard to the singer.[49] It was the generally accepted rule that singers performed only after the meal. In order to give ODYSSEUS the opportunity to admire the art of the Phäakes, their King ALKINOOS ordered for his guest a round-dance performed by young men; in the midst of them the blind singer DEMODOKOS accompanied the dance upon his lyre and sang the beautiful ballad about the love of ARES and APHRODITE. This might have been a solo-song without the choir's participation.

PLATO's description of AGATHON's banquet is well known. At the end of the discussion about EROS, ALCIBIADES breaks in with noisy companions and transforms the sophisticated arguments into an uproarious convivium.[50]

In the *Mousic* arts, a threefold parallel is drawn between singing, playing of instruments, and dancing, on the one hand, and *logos, harmonia* and *rhythmos* on the other, and finally between the poem, its performance (*melody*), and the order of the movements (*choreography*).[51] The complete union of all the arts, the ideal conception of the Occidental Romantic period, was already achieved by the Greeks in early times, within the norms of a naïve and unassuming approach to their *Mousikē*.

THE GENRES OF SONG IN GREECE

In order to define and classify the various lyrical song categories of Greek music as well as determine their place within the musical practices of the Greeks, we must start with the notion of the *nomos*.

The original meaning of the *nomos* was "Law," or "Order." Consequently, a song constructed according to a certain rule was called a *nomos*, and like many other facets of the *Mousikē*, it was ascribed to the gods.

Nomos represented the correct *harmonia*, which was inherent in any "well-ordered" melody. Only later the term assumed the meaning of "Law", of the state and of political life. PLATO's *Nomoi* ("Laws") treat both categories extensively. The strict meaning of *nomos* was, however, a "cultic song." In general, any composed melody was called *nomos;* in particular, the notion of *nomos* was extended to other spheres of the Greek *technē*, especially to architecture; for example, a temple in Doric, Ionic, or Corinthian style was called an architectural *nomos*.

Literary sources have recorded famous *nomoi* (songs) of such celebrated aulētes as OLYMPOS (ca. 100 B.C.E.), CLONAS (sixth century), POLYMNESTOS (sixth century), and SAKADAS of Argos. The latter was the victor at the Pythic plays in 586 B.C.E. with his "Nomos Pythikos." This *nomos* was not sung, it was performed as an instrumental solo. Its subject concerned the fight of APOLLO and the dragon, an early, if not the earliest example of program music (see above). Centuries later, this *nomos* was praised by TIMOSTHENES, admiral of PTOLEMY II (283–246 B.C.E.), whose detailed description of it was preserved by STRABO. PAUSANIAS (fifth century B.C.E.) and POLLUX (2nd century C.E.) also mention this famous *nomos*.

Beginning with the fourth century B.C.E., references describing the musical character of the *nomoi* occur more frequently. We learn of *nomoi* describing storms, rain, the singing of birds—all performed by song and instruments—including a "description" of a sea-storm by the kitharistēs TIMOTHEOS.

Little by little, the general term of *nomos* was replaced by genres such as *paian, hymnos, dithyrambos,* but, as PLATO stated, *nomos* remained the generally accepted designation for the "well-ordered" song.

Originally, the *hymnos* was a cultic song in honor of the gods. Later *hymnos* shifted freely from one genre to another such as paians, dithyrambs, prosodies, and the like, eventually becoming identical with the *nomos*.

Hymnos does not appear in the *Odyssey*, nor in the *Iliad*. Yet, the chants in the Homeric poems were called hymnoi at the time when these epics were created. The hymnos to APHRODITE, one of the earliest, dates from the sixth century B.C.E. The first mention of a hymnos appears to be that in the ancient divine poem to the DELIC APOLLO. This hymn was sung on the island of Delos by a choir of maidens in honor of APOLLO, LETO and ARTEMIS. PINDAR mentions that they were sung exclusively in honor of the gods in cultic feasts.

Gradually the strict meaning of the term became relaxed. AESCHYLOS wrote a hymn to the river Nile; the song of the Eumenides to ATE is said to be a hymn; even mortals like AGAMEMNON were honored by hymns.[52]

SOPHOCLES called the wedding-song hymnos, meaning a solemn song, although the proper term for wedding-songs was *hymenaios*. In one instance, ARISTOPHANES called a song of lament a hymn. The widest divergence from the original meaning of the word as a song in the cult occurs in the writings of EURIPIDES. He stated that poets compose hymns for joyous occasions, banquets and the like. Soon, every festive poem with singing was called hymnos; thus the original meaning of the term was completely obscured.

The hymns were accompanied by stringed instruments such as the phorminx, kithara, barbiton, or one of the other variants of the string category. ARISTOPHANES called the kithara the "mother of hymnoi."

The *paian* was originally, like other cultic songs, a variety of song having a single characteristic cry or shout. In the cult of APOLLO, it referred to a specific ritual, the "stamping dance," which dancers performed in an attempt to obtain the favors of the god. This dance was based upon the exclamation *Iē Paian*, that gave the name to the dance. "*Paieon*," "paian," was a combination of singing, exclamations and the stamping of feet on the ground, which describes an intense dance. In HOMER, the paian was sometimes a song of propitiation, at other times a song of victory. ARISTOPHANES used it to celebrate peace. AESCHYLOS in the *Persians* gave to the paian the meaning "a song of hope" for the warriors before the battle.

Mostly, the paian honored APOLLO as its "inventor." But paians were also sung in honor of ARTEMIS and DIONYSOS, and even of the gods of the Netherworld. Sometimes even mortals were honored by paians. In festive banquets such songs occasionally made their appearance (by ALCMAN and XENOPHON). Here, we witness the same confusion in terminology as was the case with the hymnos.

But in the majority of the cases, the paian was a group dance by men; however, in honor of ARTEMIS, maidens were permitted to participate in this dance.

In ancient times the paian was accompanied by the phorminx, later by the kithara. APOLLO is represented in pictures as the lyre-playing and paian-singing kitharōdos. In only one instance (by ARCHILOCHOS), is the paian accompanied by an aulos. This would signify its absorption into the Dionysian custom, since the paian was usually sung in honor of APOLLO.

Just as the paian was devoted to APOLLO, the *dithyramb* became the regular cultic song of DIONYSOS. According to PLATO (*Laws*, 700 b), it was created to commemorate the birth of this god. It is a delirious, enthusiastic song honoring DIONYSOS. During the winter months, when APOLLO dwelled among the Hyperboraeans, DIONYSOS substituted for him in Delphoi. In place of the Apollonic paian, the Dionysian dithyrambos was sung.[53]

The half-mythical singer ARION of Lesbos (ca. 600 B.C.E.) is credited with having elevated the paian to an art form. As HERODOTUS reported, ARION was returning from Tarent to Greece. Along the way he was captured by Corinthian pirates, who stole his money and gave him the choice of either being stabbed to death or thrown into the sea. ARION asked permission to sing for the last time and the pirates consented. The singer then took his lyre, and intoned a "high song," after which he threw himself into the sea. Thereupon a "music-loving" dolphin rescued him and carried him to the Cap Tainaron, where later, in memory of this miraculous escape, a picture of the singer was placed in the temple of POSEIDON.[54]

According to ARISTOTLE, all dithyrambs were composed in the Phrygian *modos*, which indicates that they were akin to the Phrygian and Lydian cultic songs performed in the rites of the "Great Mother CYBELE," who was worshipped in those countries and later transplanted into Greek lands. At the same time, there is a veiled indication of the Phrygian-Lydian (therefore Asiatic) origin of DIONYSOS, which explains the orgiastic character of his cult. Furthermore, this characteristic of the Dionysian dithyrambs is stressed by the usual accompanying instruments, the Phrygian auloi and tympana, to which undoubtedly other percussive instruments were added.

Linos was originally a folk-melody which, through hypostasis, was transformed into a legendary person. In the legend, *Linos* was described as the music teacher of HERACLES. (Concerning HERACLES' experience with LINOS see p. 289 above).

The origin of the *linos* was a lamenting song with the ritornello *Ailinon*, from which the name of the song later derived. HERODOTUS reported that he was most surprised to hear the linos-song in Egypt, for, as he was told, the Egyptians never used foreign melodies. Furthermore, he pointed out that this song was very well known in Phoenicia, Cyprus, and throughout Greece. The Egyptian called it *maneros*. It seems to have been one of those migrating melodies that have been encountered throughout history—in Antiquity, in the Middle-Ages, and even in our day.

Sharing the same importance as the cultic exclamation of the paian was the call (or exclamation) of the *Lament of Adonis,* which occurred in certain songs, particularly those of Aeolian lyric poetry. The worship of the young god of fertility, ADONIS, may have come from the Orient to Greece by way of Cyprus. An idyll of THEOCRITOS describes how the festival of ADONIS was celebrated in Alexandria. Two women, PRAXINOA and EUNOA, the main participants in the ceremony, comment upon these happenings. Before ADONIS descended into the Netherworld, the women implored him:

> Be merciful, Adonis, and bring us
> Joy also for the coming year!
> Now, thou had been gracious to us,
> Be it also if you return![55]

After ADONIS descended into Hades, the women's lament was intoned with the ritornello: *"O tōn Adōnin!"* The rhythm of this cultic lament, called *Adoneion*, became the pattern for many such lamenting songs.

The *hyporchēma* was basically a dance-song, in which the union of dancing with the playing of instruments and singing was so interwoven that it represented a choreographic interpretation of the lyrics, and sometimes even developed into "dances without words." By ATHENAIOS's description of the hyporchēma we learn that "the choir dances, while the participants sing."[56] Sometimes this manifestation was called *pyrrichē* (translated literally, "clothed in red"), although the term refers to war and weapon-dances. In HOMER's description of ACHILLES' shield, there are scenes in which dancing, the playing of the phorminx, and singing are so intertwined that they may be described as hyporchēmata.

Iambos was the generic term for satirical songs, which were usually written in iambic meter. ARISTOTLE said that the iambic meter comes closest to ordinary speech, therefore it was most appropriate for improvisations. The leaders of contesting choirs scoffed at each other, improvising in iambs. Iambos, as the term for improvised satire was called, made such an impact on the ordinary parlance that *iambizein,* "to speak in iambs," carried the meaning "to mock each other."

In the cult of DEMETER, such satirical songs were sung along the sacred way from Athens to Eleusis. At a short distance outside the town, there was a bridge, at which such satirical exchanges between choirs took place as a prescribed part of the ritual itself. The Greek term for bridge was *gephira,* and a song performed on this bridge was called *gephirismos,* "song at the bridge." The iambic scoffing songs were so characteristic of the cult of Demeter, that through hypostasis, *Iambē* became a person in the myth of Demeter.

The improvisation was so closely connected with iambic poetry that the *autokabdaloi,* the "improvisers," were simply called *Iamboi,* like their poems.[57]

In time the iambos developed into a spepific form of lyric poetry whose creation was ascribed to ARCHILOCHOS of Paros (ca. 720 B.C.E.).[58]

One of the most important genres of Greek poetry with musical accompaniment was the *elegy.* Until the fifth century B.C.E. it was always accompanied by auloi. The poetic form of the elegy was the distich, in which the regular alternation of hexameters and pentameters took place. The aulos had the function of enlivening the verses and occasionally filling in the pauses of the pentameter.[59]

While the original function was clearly determined for all categories of Greek songs, the elegy exhibited the greatest variety and even discussed such contradictory subjects as: warfare, meditative contemplations, teachings of wisdom, memorials for the dead, dedications for votive offerings to the gods, and sometimes even erotic poems.

Elegeion was the term employed for the verse-group (hexameter plus pentameter), which was used for the *elegos*. The word *elegos* must have been originally the Oriental term for a wind-instrument, which was later superseded by the aulos. The same word was also used for the lamenting songs for the dead, also accompanied by the aulos.

Curiously, the elegos accompanied by the aulos, which was destined to glorify the dead, became at the same time an invitation to joyous living for the survivors, who participated at the *perideipnon*, the funeral feast.[60]

The *elegeion*, a stanza honoring the deceased, was sometimes engraved upon the sepulchral monument. Its verse-form also applied to the *epigram*, first as an epitaph for the grave, and later it developed into the most popular poetical genre of Antiquity. For a whole millennium the epigram became in the Greek and Latin literature the popular vehicle for expressing wit, satire, mockery, and even graceful and noble sentiments that enticed the poets to express their often trivial ideas in a concise form, manifesting a spirited play on words.[61]

Soon the elegy rid itself of its instrumental accompaniment and became a vocal form. But even then it still belonged the *Mousikē*. At the *Symposion*, the common meal, the elegy was still propagated, for at these convivial gatherings all the motives of the elegy were used to describe the love of women and boys, politics, aphorisms about wisdom, and all the infinite variety of human thought and morals. In the final analysis, the elegy became a comprehensive code of manners for a closed society, of a congenial circle.[62]

In later times, this witty form of entertainment at the Symposion was replaced by an oratorial contest (Plato, *Symposion*, 176 c). From then on, the elegy was no longer considered a form of the Greek *Mousikē*, but instead a literary product.

The *thrēnos* was a lament and at the same time a song of praise for the deceased, a choral song accompanied mostly by the aulos. In HOMER's epics, the funeral lament for HECTOR was performed by a male-choir while the women sighed and groaned. *Thrēnodies*, lamenting songs, were known among all peoples of Antiquity: the Sumerians, Egyptians, Babylonians, Hebrews, and others. The custom of the Hebrews is well known, in which every man had to hire for the funeral of his wife at least two pipers and a wailing woman, who had to wail according to a strictly prescribed ritual. In Greece, the wailing women of Caria were in particular demand because they were experts in all aspects of the funeral ceremony. For the funerals of rich or distinguished persons, such wailing women were brought from far-away places.[63]

The song of praise for living persons was the *enkomion*. It was a eulogy that was intoned during the *komos*, the festive procession honoring a returning victor. In later times this song was also called *epinikos*. In PLATO's time, not only humans but also gods were honored by an enkomion. The instruments that accompanied this song were the phorminx, lyra, and sometimes auloi. The importance of the *komos* will be shown below (see p. 308).

For less solemn occasions than cult and celebrations of victory, there were songs of a special secular character, among them marching songs, called *embatēria*, which were very popular in Lacedemonia. The songs of TYRTAIOS of Sparta (seventh century B.C.E.) were such embatēria. They were accompanied by auloi.[64]

The *skolion*, "drinking song," was performed at joyous banquets either by single persons or all the participants. There are many pictorial representations on vases and bowls of such revelries, showing also such accompanying instruments as the auloi or the barbiton. The lyre seems to have been used only in exceptional cases. In the British Museum there is a bowl from Boeotia which depicts drinking companions from whose mouths banderols are shown with the incipits of the songs performed.[65] The skolion may originally have been a folk-song, even of vulgar character; ANACREON (ca. 560–475 B.C.E.) was the first to give it artistic form.

Among the utilitarian songs of the Greeks, the *hymenaios*, a wedding song, or more often a group of wedding songs, must be mentioned. They were performed during the entire wedding day with dances, accompanied by instruments, or left unaccompanied. HESIOD (ca. 720 B.C.E.) describes such a wedding celebration, at which the bridal procession marched with burning torches and humorous choirs were followed by boys singing to the auloi, while girls performed dances. Everywhere one notes joy and jubilation, and, of course, choral-singing.[66] The numerous fragments of SAPPHO's wedding songs have proven this event.

On the other hand, the wedding feast of PELEUS and THETIS, at which the bridal couple was honored by Apollo's singing and by the syrinx-blowing Calleiopē, belongs to the realm of myth. This is depicted on a vase.[67]

The wedding festivities came to an end with the *epithalamion*, "the song before the bridal chamber." It was sung with dances and with obvious jokes until late at night.[68]

To the Dionysian cultic songs belong the Phallos-song (*phallikon, ithyphallikon*). The phallos, as symbol of fertility, was venerated everywhere in the Ancient Orient and so it is not surprising that the Greeks also gave it a place among their *Mousic* creations. We find in ARISTOPHANES' comedies literary proofs for it; it was performed with dances and with the accompaniment of auloi.[69] According to our Occidental conception, strongly influenced by Christian ethics, such songs would be considered obscene. The mentality of the Greeks, naïve and unspoiled, did not think of them as such, but considered them a form of cultic song just as all others were, and identified them with the forms of expression belonging to the Dionysian *enthousiasmos*.

Finally, the work songs must be mentioned, which were known in Greece as in all other cultures of the Ancient Orient. Each profession based upon regular rhythmic movements had its specific work-songs. In the ancient and classical literature of the Greeks, the following work-songs were referred to.

The song of the vintager (*epilēnion*), sung by a boy with the accompaniment of the phorminx; this was the "beautiful linos-song," reserved for this occasion. Then, as among all other peoples of the ancient world, there were shepherd-songs. In Antiquity, the shepherd-songs were the symbol of a primitive, nature-oriented life. HESIOD, before he received from the Muses the gift of poetry, was a simple shepherd at the Helicon. The Greeks called the shepherd-songs *bucolica*. A scene on the shield of ACHILLES shows two shepherds, one singing, while the other accompanies him on the syrinx. In the comedies of ARISTO-PHANES, old women sing while grinding barley, and the water-bearers lighten their burden with song. Weaving women alleviate the monotony of their occupation with spinning songs, called *iouloi*, and the songs of the weavers are called *elinoi*. Even if we discard the legendary weaving women of the *Odyssey*, CIRCE and the nymph CALYPSO, we may assume that the women, while weaving, had always tried to alleviate their tedious work by singing.

The songs of the reapers were called *lityersēs*. In addition, POLLUX mentions (IV, 52) songs at the vintage to the accompaniment of auloi, songs at the removing of the husks of the corn, songs of the oarsmen, and a curious song of the swineherds.

ATHENAIOS completes the list by adding the following categories: the song of the millers, of the spinners of wool, of the sheaf-binders of the harvested barley; cradle-songs of the nurses and their songs at the rocking of the infant; reapers' songs; songs of the agricultural laborers, of the bathing attendants, and so on (XIV, 10). There were some songs that were not exactly work-songs, such as the *symposiaka*, the songs at the banquets and the following drinking bouts, also the *epinikia*, which were sung at the victory-celebrations of the athletes, and the *erotika*, the love-songs.

Whether we may include in the category of work-songs those of the buffoons in the *Iliad*[71] is a matter of interpretation. The fact is that their singing and dancing was accompanied by the phorminx and that was the "work" by which they had made their living. It is therefore logical to include them among the work-songs.

Just like humans, the legendary Sileni sang a vintage song while treading the grapes. An exquisite terra-cotta group, well preserved, shows four women kneading bread, while a fifth plays the aulos, evidently to promote regular rhythmic movements for the others (Illus. 92). This representation cannot truly belong to the category of work-songs, because it does not convince us that the kneading women are singing at the same time. On the other hand, the song of the oarsmen is a typical example of the work-song, because their singing not only regulates their uniform movements, but also lessens the physical strain. EURIPIDES and ARISTOPHANES in particular alluded to the songs of the oarsmen.

Furthermore, in the patristic literature there is mention of the songs of the wagoners. It is to be assumed that this species existed among the ancient Greeks as well, despite the time difference between the Greek civilization and the epoch when the patristic writings were created (third to fifth century C.E.).

THE GREEK FESTIVAL CYCLE

The Greek calendar did not contain a Sabbath day of rest. Originally, the Hebrews did not treat the Sabbath as a religious institution either, but adopted it from the Babylonian. In Babylon, the 7th, 14th, 21st, and 28th days of the month were considered "unlucky" days. During these days the people refrained as much as possible from normal activities and no new enterprise was begun. With the Hebrews, this day became the "day of rest" which, according to their religious beliefs, God observed after His efforts of Creation. It was a day whose memory had to be celebrated for all eternity. Thus, the observance of the Sabbath day became one of the most important religious institutions of the Jewish religion.

The missing day of rest in Greece was amply compensated by a cycle of festivals celebrated on a year-round basis, which gave the Greeks much more leisure time than either the Jewish Sabbath or the Christian Sunday.

Characteristically, Hellenism did not reckon calendrical time by its wars and victories, or foundations of cities and states. Neither did it count the years following heroic achievements of its rulers, but measured the months according to the *Festivals of Olympia*, to which the harmonious education of the body and the mind was devoted.

These festivals date from 776 B.C.E. in Olympia and were held every fourth year in the month of June. There stood, since about 450 B.C.E., in the magnificent temple of Zeus, the famous statue of this god made by PHEIDIAS. Since the seventh century, the Olympiade became a national holiday, to which Greece and all her colonies sent teams to the contests, as well as numerous delegations of spectators. Invitations to the Olympiade were sent by the priests who ruled this sanctuary, to all the cities and the other districts of Greater-Hellas. The solemn opening of the festivals began with a sacrifice to Zeus accompanied by processions with music and singing. The conferring of the prizes to the victors in the numerous contests was likewise accompanied by singing, playing, and dancing festivities.

Among the national festivals the Pythic plays, devoted to APOLLO and held in Delphoi, were the most outstanding. At the outset they occurred every nine years; from 586 B.C.E. on, every third year of the Olympiade, in the month of September. On the first day of this festival, the *Nomos Pythikos* was performed, in which APOLLO's victory against the dragon was celebrated (see below). As a novelty, in 586, the *psylē aulēsis* "the solo-playing on the aulos," was admitted to the *agōns* ("the contests"). Delphoi was the locality where the *Mousic agōns* were held, the institution which gave its imprint to the intellectual life of Greece. It was always a characteristic feature of Hellenic man to distinguish himself by his individual achievements in the contests. Thus, besides the gymnastic agōns, in which the sports dominated, there were *Mousic* agōns which represented an expression of the highest spiritual aims of the Greeks, the *Mousikē*. In addition, there were agōns comprised of single men, choral-groups, professionals, amateurs; there were also *agōns* in kitharōdy, in kitharistic, aulōdy and aulētic, that is, in solo-playing and singing with accompaniment by the kithara or aulos.

For the festival of the *Panathenaens*, PERICLES created in 442 B.C.E. a *Mousic* agōn, destined as a contest for singers, kitharists and aulētes, that is, for soloists. These took place every four years with great pomp and lasted for six full days.

The Dionysian and Thargelian festivals, instituted after 509 B.C.E., were devoted to agōns of male choirs. Their festival plays, honoring APOLLO and ARTEMIS, were held during the month of *Thargelion* (March). Other festivals were the Nemeic, which took place in the grove of ZEUS NEMEIOS; the Isthmic, called

after the Greek *isthmos;* and contests that took place in Epidauros, in honor of
ASKLEPIOS. Likewise in Athens agōns were held for choirs, which began in
the first half of the fifth century.

Besides the great national festivals of Greek history, numerous festivals were
sponsored by the various states, and were not overshadowed by the national
ones. These included the *Panathenaeans* in Attica, and the *Eleusinies* as well
as the *Dionysies* of the various cities. In addition, a goodly number of harvest
festivals took place each year in Sparta and other cities. Other numerous feasts
took place yearly in Argos, Thebes, Delos, and Rhodos.

Among the various harvest festivals were the feast for "tasting the beans,"
and the feast of the grapes, both of which took place in October. The "feast of
threshing" in honor of DEMETER was held in December. The vintage festival
was celebrated by a specific "feast of the wine-pressers," at which dithyrambic
choral songs were performed. An additional vintage feast was the *Antherestria,*
held in February, which lasted three days. On the first day of the feast the
"opening the cask" took place; the second day was the "day of the jug," and
the third day was devoted to the memory of the dead.

Among the feasts of Sparta, the spring-festival held the foremost rank. It
was adorned with rich musical trimmings. Besides the festival of APOLLO,
Delphoi had a spring-festival, and so did the cities of Delos and Rhodos, where
gymnastic and *Mousic* agōns were held, together with celebrations honoring
DIONYSOS.

From these feasts of DIONYSOS—the smaller rural ones held in December,
and the larger communal *Dionysias* held in March—there developed dramatic
plays accompanied by music and dancing, which eventually evolved into
fully developed dramatic productions.

The national festivals, besides being devoted to the agōns, likewise had
religious motivations: they were to honor the gods. In the *Panathenaeans* at
Athens, the goddess ATHENA was worshipped. Almost the entire population
marched in a splendid sacrificial procession to the sanctuary of the goddess,
with sacrificial gifts of all sorts, among them a bull with a garland in his horns,
accompanied by the sensual sounds of the auloi.

The sacrifice itself was accompanied by auloi. This ritual had both a musical
and a symbolic significance. The music was supposed to substitute for the loud
shouting of the women at the sacrifice, described by HOMER and mentioned
also by AESCHYLOS. According to Oriental conception, loud noises are supposed
to drive away evil spirits, hence the shrill tones of the auloi at the sacrifice
were meant to have the effect of chasing away demons.

The calendar of the Greeks, with its almost continuous series of festival days
and weeks, was interrupted only by the inclement weather of November. All
of these festivals were richly adorned by strings and aulos-music, with or without singing, as well as by dancing and pantomimic displays (*mimēsis*).

Although the auloi were the usual instruments for the huge festive processions, the *Panathenaeans* also employed strings. This might have had a special
significance, probably a manner of expressing consideration to the goddess
ATHENA who, as we have seen earlier, originally repudiated the auloi. The
addition of the kithara to the ensemble was probably meant to mitigate the
use of the auloi.[72]

We possess numerous pictorial representations of the agōns on vases, am-
phoras and bowls. They depict the singers and aulētes standing together on

the *bēma*. In some instances the audience and judges are shown. Oddly enough, the aulōdy (the solo-playing of the instrument) enjoyed only a short existence, probably because of the Athenian aversion to this "foreign" instrument. Only on a single occasion, in Delphoi (586 B.C.E.), was an aulōdic agōn permitted to participate in the festival. This was discontinued with the following Pythic play.

The Greek festival year gave the population ample occasions for rejoicing, with processions, dances, and all kinds of entertainment. At these occasions, groups called *komoi* strolled freely from place to place. Such popular feasts took place mainly at the beginning of the year, also in the spring and at harvest and vintage times. All of these events were primarily agricultural festivals, held by all peoples of Antiquity. The participants often masqueraded as birds, frogs, horses, and other animals (Illus. 103). These practices were common features of the cult of DIONYSOS, and played an important part in popular entertainment. In the countryside, these participating groups moved from village to village; the Greek word for village is *kōmē*, therefore such processions were called *komazein*, meaning "to wander from village to village." In general, every festive, joyous wandering group was called *komos*. Their accompanying instrument was the aulos, and singing on such occasions was known as *komoidia*, "the singing of the *komos*."

From the *komos* celebrating DIONYSOS there developed in Athens a theatrical play called the *komoidia*. It was performed by real actors and contained scenes of dialogue, like the earlier *tragoidia* (*see below*). In time, to this new species of entertainment (the *komoidia*) a singing choir was added. This novelty caused a serious revolt, as mentioned in a satyr-play of PRATINAS (fifth century B.C.E.).[73] In this play, the *komos* and the accompanying aulos were turned away from the *thymēlē*, the altar of DIONYSOS, which was placed in the center of the stage. This prohibition had no lasting effect, since the new genre (the *komoidia*) held the public interest and became one of the mainstays of repertoire in Greek theatre. The instrument accompanying the *komos* as well as its marching and mocking songs was the aulos, which remained, until the end, the characteristic accompanying instrument of the fully developed comedy.

THE MUSICAL INSTRUMENTS OF THE GREEKS

It is odd that despite the highly developed musical culture of the Greeks only a few instruments were employed in their music practice. The two main types of instruments were the kithara and the aulos, of which there were variants or subtypes. This could account feasibly for the lack of other instruments.

The kithara, especially, had a long history. It developed from the primitive chelys and its successor, the four-stringed phorminx, to the lyra and the seven-stringed "cradle-kithara."

HOMER makes a distinction between the kitharis and the phorminx. Originally the kitharis meant the instrument itself; later, however, the term meant the playing on the kithara, *kitharizein*. In Greek parlance there was also a verb *phormixein*, indicating the playing of the *phorminx*.

Besides these principal types, there later evolved an entire family of stringed instruments, including the lyra and the barbiton,[74] which became the most frequently used.

I mentioned earlier the "invention" by HERMES of the first stringed instrument, the chelys, as recounted in mythology. As time passed, this species branched out into about thirty subspecies, most of which were mentioned by ATHENAIOS, although his list is by no means complete.[75] During his time (second century C.E.), the most popular stringed instruments were the magadis, barbiton, baromos, pandura, trigōnon, sambykē, iambikē, pēktis, phoinix, nabla, klepsiambos, skindapsos, pēlex, lyrophoinikos, simikeion, epigoneion, the "nine-stringed," the "seven-stringed," the "three-stringed," the "two-stringed pēktis," the "psaltērion orthion" (the upright psaltērion), and, of course, the kithara and lyra.

According to ATHENAIOS, it is evident that these instruments were not too different from one other, for he quoted various contemporary and ancient writers such as APOLLODOROS, who declared: "What we call today psaltērion, was the magadis.[76] Another writer, EUPHORION, said: "The instrument known as magadis is very old, but its construction has been recently changed and its name transformed into iambikē.[77] ALEXANDER of KYTHERA remarked that the magadis "has been completed by adding a greater number of strings."[78] And IOUBA mentioned the lyrophoinikos and the epigoneion, which were transformed into a psaltērion orthion (upright psaltērion).[79]

Other ancient writers dealt with the Greek stringed instrument as well. HESYCHIOS included the trigōnon and the pandourion among the psaltērion. In the Greek parlance, it was not the term for a single stringed instrument, but of a specific type. In a wider sense it embraced the entire family of strings.

The similarities and differences between the instruments are indicated by other writers, quoted also by ATHENAIOS:

The pēktis and the magadis are the same instrument as ARISTOXENOS declares.[80]

Also MENAICHMOS, in his work on *Artists,* asserts that the pēktis is the same as the magadis.[81]

But DIOGENES, the tragic poet, thinks that the pēktis differed from the magadis.[82]

PHYLLIS of DELOS also maintains that the pēktis is different from the magadis.[83]

The differences become even more obvious if the unequivocal reports about the number of the strings are to be believed. For instance, ANACREON said: "With the magadis in my hands, I sing to its twenty strings."[84] But TELESTES, in his *Hymenaios,* asserts that the magadis has only five strings.[85] According to some descriptions, the pēktis had two strings (if this was correct, it could have been a small lute). However, SOPATROS declared that this small number of strings produced a "barbaric music," which means that music played on only two strings might have sounded so inadequate to the musical tastes of the Greeks that they characterized it as "barbaric." Therefore, the pēktis must have been displaced quickly by the nabla and sambykē which had more strings.

The magadis must have been a Greek harp-like instrument with twenty strings, as ATHENAIOS informed us:

The magadis is an instrument played like the harp (*hē gar magadis organon esti psaltikon*), as ANACREON states.[86]

While it may be true that the magadis had twenty strings, it could play only ten different tones: the seven basic tones of the scale with some chromatic additions duplicated at the octave (*dia pasōn*), so that the melody could be doubled in octaves. Numerous Greek theorists used the term *dia pasōn*, which later was used to describe the principle of our "octave."

The magadis was not originally a Greek instrument, but was probably of Assyrian origin, although there were in Egypt similar harps with many strings. Aristoxenos, the theoretician, and Diogenes, the poet of tragedies,[87] mentioned the magadis among other "foreign" instruments, whereas Euphorion mentioned it among the ancient instruments.[88] Assyrian pictorial representations display a harp, which has indeed the same number of strings as the magadis, mentioned by Anacreon.[89]

In connection with the magadis, a "technique" must be mentioned which, among others, is described in detail by Athenaios. This technique or manner of playing, called *syrigma*, employed the well-known principle applied to all stringed instruments, namely, that of touching lightly the exact midpoint of the string before striking it, so that the octave or first overtone was produced. Athenaios explains this in greater length:

> Philochoros, in the third book of his *History of Attika* declares: Lysander of Sykion was the first harp-player to institute the new art of solo-playing, tuning his strings high and making the tone full and rich, in fact giving that flute-like tone (*tēn enaulon kitharisin*) to the strings which Epigonus and his school were the first to adopt. He abolished the meager simplicity prevailing among the solo-harpists (*psilois kitharisin*), and introduced in his harp-playing highly coloured variations, also iambi, the magadis and the syringmos, as it is called.[91]

Aristoxenos confirmed this:

> Because with the two kinds of instruments the magadis and the barbiton, played together at the interval of an octave (*dia pasōn*) there is perfect unison of men's and boy's voices.[92]

This kind of playing or simultaneous singing in octaves was called *magadizein*, a verb, the etymology and function of which are clearly given in the above quotations. Aristotle also used the verb *magadizein* to describe the musically obtained interval of an octave (*dia pasōn*).

As we know, Greek musical notation employed specific signs to designate low and high tones, as well as to differentiate between the singing of men and boys. Specific symbols were also used to indicate the various sizes of auloi, and even the manner of playing stringed instruments, i.e., the syrigma.

The Greeks did not always exhibit a tolerant attitude toward foreign instruments. The Oriental magadis, with its numerous strings, so different from the traditional, domestic instruments, aroused displeasure among certain conservative-minded politicians. Athenaios reported such an incident:

> Timotheos of Miletos is held by most authorities to have adopted an arrangement of strings with too great a number, namely that of the magadis; wherefore he was even about to be disciplined by the Lacedemonians for trying to corrupt their ancient music, and someone was on the point of cutting away his superfluous strings when he pointed to a small image of Apollo among them holding a lyre with the same number and arrangement of strings as his own, and so was acquitted.[93]

Nevertheless, the artistry of TIMOTHEOS on his multi-stringed instrument continued to be met with marked hostility. With his lyre, he not only broadened the art of kitharōdy in the direction of virtuosity, but also attempted to develop harp contests. Because of his instrumental showmanship, displayed so openly, the texts of the poems were obscured, and this brought about many complaints. PHERECRATES, a contemporary of ARISTOPHANES (450–385 B.C.E.), in one of his plays caused "Poetry" to lament on account of its maltreatment, suffered at the hands of both PHRYNIS and TIMOTHEOS.

The great number of names of stringed instruments was not caused exclusively by variants of the form and the number of strings of the traditional kithara and lyra, but also by new types of instruments, such as the "cradle-kithara," the body of which resembled a cradle, and the "thamiris-kithara," so called because it was depicted on a vase, played by THAMIRIS. It is certain that all, or most, of these instruments were not known in the classical period of the Greek musical practice, but developed from earlier forms or were imported from foreign countries. This might be the explanation for the multitude of names mentioned by ATHENAIOS.

Women never played the kithara. This instrument might have been too massive and heavy for the hands of frail maidens. The stringed instrument for women was the less unwieldy lyre or the more delicate barbiton. We see the kithara only in the hands of NIKE, the goddess of victory, at agōns, when she extolled the accomplishments of the winners. For the announcement of victory, NIKE also blew the salpinx, the trumpet (see below).

Besides the "official" instrument for the kitharōdic or kitharistic agōns, the barbiton (or barbitos) was the most popular stringed instrument for the accompaniment of singing. It was more slender than the massive kithara; it was easier to carry and to handle, and it replaced almost all the accompanying stringed instruments. The difference between the kithara and the barbiton was not only in construction and tonal character but in diversity with regard to use. The kithara and lyra were the Apollinian instruments, while the barbiton served more or less in the Dionysian rites. Therefore, at solemn occasions the former was employed while the barbiton was used at social entertainments.

The barbiton was also the preferred instrument of the lyric poets. SAPPHO, ALCAIOS, and ANACREON are shown with it on vase-paintings. According to tradition, ANACREON was even credited with having "invented" the instrument. It was also the instrument used by ORPHEUS. When the famous singer was attacked by the furious Thracian women, his only weapon was his barbiton (see Illus. 94). It was also frequently used in the komos, because it was easy to carry. In the women's chambers it was almost the exclusive instrument for accompanying singing. For ensemble playing, the barbiton also was preferred.

The harp was never popular in Greece. This is all the more astonishing since we know that the harp assumed a leading role in the musical practice of Egypt and Babylonia-Assyria. Nevertheless, the harp must have been known to the Greeks in archaic times, having been part of the island culture of the Cyclades, as is proven by archaeological discoveries that date it at the end of the third millennium (Illus. 95, 96, 97).

The harp (or some of its variants) appears in Greek literature no earlier than the fifth century. The Greek harp had no characteristic form of its own, yet, unlike the Egyptian bow-shaped harps, those of the Greeks were closer to the angular type. The harps were called *polychordon,* "many-stringed" instruments. Illustration 106 shows thirteen strings, whereas the magadis, as mentioned above, had twenty. Other species of harps were the trigōnon, the sambykē, and the pēktis. Nonetheless, the opinions of the ancient writers are somewhat divided and not very conclusive in this regard. As mentioned earlier, the pēktis had allegedly only two strings, which excluded it from the family of harps.

Oddly enough, harps or harp-like instruments were not admitted to the agōns, nor were they considered useful for the education of youth.

The phorminx, kithara, and lyra were related instruments; their names were used quite indiscriminately. Only with the creation of the kitharōdic-school in Lesbos by TERPANDROS was a distinction made between them: the kithara introduced by the pupils of TERPANDROS was the concert-instrument that was admitted to the kitharōdic agōn.

As mentioned above, kitharis was originally the term for a song accompanied by stringed instruments; later, in the verbal form of kithara, it was extended to the instrument itself. It was a rather bulky instrument, used by professionals. Even APOLLO gave up the kithara and—as depicted on vase-paintings—preferred the more practical lyra. As long as the phorminx had only four strings, there was not much chance for its employment in the agōns. Only when the number of strings of the phorminx, or the kithara, was increased to seven did they become kitharōdy and kitharistically full-fledged instruments of *Mousic* agōns.

The seven strings of the kithara correspond to the seven tones of the Greek diatonic scale. The relatively restricted compass of Greek instruments (strings as well as woodwinds) was determined by that of the human voice, as stated by PROTAGORAS (ca. 490–ca. 421 B.C.E.) who held that "man is the measure of all things." The strings of Greek instruments were all of the same length. Differences in pitch were obtained by using thinner or thicker strings, or by their different tensions.

The harp-like playing with the bare fingers was called *psallein;* to play with the plectrum, *plēktein.* This latter manner of playing must have been introduced in later times; HOMER did not mention it.

The term trigōnon might have alluded to the triangular shape of the harp, called "angular" harp. Another species was the "curved" harp, which, however, was only rarely depicted. We see it in Illustration 104, where one of the Muses, TERPSICHORE, plays it for APOLLO.

The many-stringed harp-like instruments were the given media for the development of instrumental virtuosity, which in time became highly popular and brought fame and wealth to their players.

The *nabla* (or *naula*) was also a harp-like instrument which the Greeks probably adopted from Phoenicia. The Hebrews, too, employed it. They called it *nebel* (or *nevel*) and for them it became one of the most popular instruments for accompanying singing. We do not know its precise form among the Greeks. It may be assumed that it was a variant of the trigōnon, that it had numerous strings, and that it was played with the fingers, like the harps. Pictorial representations of it are completely lacking.

Despite their evident usefulness, harps are rarely depicted in ensembles. We see them together with other instruments, mainly in Lower-Italic vase-paintings.

On a volute-crater, three Muses are shown playing the harp, the cradle-kithara, the lyra, and auloi; this represents a rather "full" orchestra, at least according to the Greek conception (Illus. 104).

There may have been some interrelation between the harp and CYPRIS, the goddess of carnal love, since we find it represented mostly in the women's chambers, especially the bridal chamber, while the specific bridal song, the hymenaios, sung by women, was generally accompanied by auloi. The harp was also the favorite instrument of the *hetairai*, the courtesans, at the symposia. ARISTOTLE condemned the music of the harps because of its sensuous character. This is stressed by several pictures, in which the youthful god EROS is represented in the company of harp-players. Yet, owing to its many strings and the artistic use of it, the harp was considered the point of departure for the later and more refined musical practice. The epithet *eroessa*, "sweet," "charming," given by ANACREON to the harp, is an appropriate characterization of its tonal quality.

Finally, among the stringed instruments, the lute known under the name of *pandura* must be mentioned. The word comes from the Sumerian term *pan tur*, which means a "small bow." The Greeks could not have taken over the instrument from the Sumerians, since the Sumerians were long extinct at the start of Greek civilization. The word, like the instrument itself, seems to have survived through the Cappadocians; from them the Greeks may have taken over the term as well as the instrument—a long-necked lute with a small resonating body. Supposedly, it had only three strings, for which reason it was also called trigōnon (although trigōnon was a species of harps). It was rarely depicted and those paintings which were preserved do not indicate whether it was fretted like the similar Egyptian instruments.

The finest pictorial document of a lute can be found on a relief from Mantinea (fourth century B.C.E.), where it is shown in the hand of a Muse. Because of its excellence, this sculpture is generally attributed to the school of PRAXITELES.

The lute, the only stringed instrument of the Greeks that required greater artistic skill on account of its string-stopping technique, entered Greek musical practice only after the zenith of the classical period.

Another stringed instrument that the Greeks might have known was the *kinyra*, possibly introduced from Phoenicia. It was used only occasionally. It is not mentioned at all in the classical literature. But in view of the close cultural and economic ties existing between Phoenicia and Greece, it can be assumed that this instrument, very popular in Phoenicia, was not unknown in Greece (the Hebrews took over the *kinyra* as their *kinnor*).

The main difference between the families of the kitharas and harps was that the latter instruments not only had a larger number of strings, but also had strings of different lengths. This must have brought about tuning problems. From the extant literature it is not evident what implements they might have used for this purpose. Possibly the tuning was done with the aid of a small cross-shaped gadget, which is shown in several paintings notably in the upper margin. Its function is not explained by the literature (Illus. 101, 105, 122), so we have to rely merely on conjecture.

APOLLO mainly used the kithara and lyra, thus the latter instrument was termed the Apollinian lyra. In the fifth century popular esteem for the rather bulky and clumsy kithara dwindled and in its place came the lighter and easy-to-manipulate lyra, the barbiton.

However, before this substitution took place, the kithara had developed into certain types favored by the virtuosi (the "cradle-kithara," and the "thamiris-kithara," as mentioned earlier). On a clay vessel, a twelve-stringed kithara is depicted, and on a tombstone of Krissa in Delphoi, there is an upright kithara with nineteen strings, having an unusual width (Illus. 105). Such instruments were exceptions. They were made for specific purposes or occasions.

In view of APOLLO's predilection for stringed instruments, it is strange to find one example where he is depicted as an aulos-player. We may surmise that he acquired the mastery of this instrument from his sister ATHENA, who, as the legend goes, originally repudiated and cursed the aulos, although such contradictions are numerous in the mythological world.

The player of the kithara is usually depicted in a standing position, while that of the lute (or lyra) player is seated.

Occasionally, the Apollinian lyra was employed to honor the dead at funeral ceremonies. In pictorial representations, the deceased is shown playing the instrument, or it is presented to him by a survivor. The symbolic meaning of such representations is that the deceased desired to console himself with music in the solitude of the Nether-World. A saying of PINDAR corroborates this:

> Some [of the deceased] enjoy horses and wrestling, others like games played on boards, others playing the phorminx.[94]

Along with the funeral ceremonies, we see players on vase paintings, as well as spear-throwers and war dancers honoring the deceased. Such plays and athletic contests were accompanied by the aulos. It is uncommon to find the lyra as an accompanying instrument for funeral ceremonies, although it may also have had a symbolic meaning.

Generally speaking, it can be said that the stringed instruments represented the *Mousic* arts in Greek life. Whether we call them Apollinian or Dionysian, it is merely a question of semantics. Their function was the accompaniment of singing, either for solo or choral. This function is best compared with that of the Hebrew stringed instruments, for which the Israelites used the term *kle shir* ("tools for the song"), since they were considered the exclusive accompanying media for singing.

CURT SACHS posed the question: "Did the Greeks have zithers?" While there exist no pictorial representations for this type of instrument in Greek musical practice, SACHS sought out clues in the writings of ARISTOTLE and IOUBA (d. 24 C.E.). These authors mentioned an instrument, the *simikeion*, which supposedly had thirty-five strings, and the *epigoneion*, with forty strings. Both were described as "ancient" and "foreign" instruments. A zither could not be played in an upright position, nor while marching, although an Assyrian bas-relief shows musicians playing the dulcimer, a zither-like instrument that was fastened to their bodies (Illus. 60, 63). The Greek zither—if such an instrument existed at all—could be played only in a horizontal position, either on a table, or—as the literal translation of epigoneion indicates—on the knees of the player (*epi-* upon, *gony-*the knee).The assumption that the instrument was "invented" by a certain EPIGONOS and had been imported from Alexandria or from Ambrakia to Epirus, is obviously fictitious. The indication of JULIUS POLLUX, according to whom a man named SIMOS "invented" the simikion, similarly had no basis.

SACHS found three Roman sarcophagi on which pictorial representations of instruments could possibly be zithers. Unfortunately the pictures are too fuzzy to interpret as valid conclusions. Furthermore, these pictures originated from Roman times, and therefore cannot be applied to Greek musical practice. Consequently, if we assume that the epigoneion was an instrument played "on the knees," the term can be understood only as applying to a harp or a specific instrument of the harp family.

The aulos, an oboe-like instrument, generally and erroneously translated as "flute," did not originally belong to the *Mousikē*. A more appropriate translation would be "pipe" or "shawm," although the latter term refers to a medieval instrument, derived from the Greek *calamos*, "reed," from which the aulos was initially made. Around the lake of Copais in Boeotia, situated in the neighborhood of Orchomenos, there grew a special kind of reed, considered by the ancients to be the best material for manufacturing auloi. Later, auloi were also made from the Lybian lotos tree, whose wood was hard and especially suitable for manufacturing woodwind instruments. Auloi were also made from sycamore-wood, bone, and ivory and later, even from metal.

The various hypotheses for the "invention" of the aulos were discussed earlier.

The aulos was the cultic instrument of the "Great Mother," CYBELE. Together with her cult, adopted by the Greeks in the fifth century, auloi were supposed to have been introduced into the Greek musical practice, although—as we know—the Phrygian influence upon Greek music dates back to the seventh century B.C.E. The sharp and piercing sound of the auloi, so different from the soft timbre of the domestic stringed instruments, was considered *orgiastikos* by the Greeks and was strongly opposed by the philosophers. Only gradually could the aulos prevail, inasmuch as the people took a liking for the instrument. Nevertheless, a certain antagonism always remained against it. In 586 B.C.E. it was allowed at the Pythic plays but in the following contest it was discarded. It took a long time for it to resume its place in the festivals.

In spite of the saga of the importation of the aulos along with the cult of the CYBELE, the aulos must have had a longer history in Greek antiquity. It can be surmised that it was identical with the Egyptian double-pipe and was brought to Greece via Phoenicia and Crete. The aulos soon became the generic term for all woodwind instruments, with the exception of the syrinx, whose construction was based upon an entirely different principle. For some time, it was not evident whether the instrument used by the virtuosi in the *Mousic* agōns represented a clarinet- or oboe-type. FETIS and GEVAERT thought that it may have been a clarinet with a vibrating metal tongue, though it is generally assumed that it was the double-oboe, whose mouthpiece was a double reed. In most cases, the two pipes of the aulos were of the same length. The use of the instrument with two pipes of different lengths is not clear, especially when one of the pipes is depicted with fewer finger-holes than the other.

Despite the instrument's popularity with the masses, the strict followers of the ancient *Mousikē* looked askance upon the irresistible diffusion of the aulos in both of its applications—in the aulōdy (to accompany singing), and the aulētics (the solo playing of the instrument). The latter application was considered as abandoning the principle of the *Mousikē*. In addition, it took quite a long time before the aulos had shed the taint of its foreign origin. Notwithstanding, when the aulos was finally considered as sharing equal rights with the kithara and lyra, it was still somewhat subordinated to the *Mousic* instru-

ments. This is evidenced, for instance, by the fact that until the time of MELANIP-
PIDES, the poet of dithyrambs, the aulos-players received their wages from the
poets, evidently because the poets' work was considered to be the more important element of the agōn and the aulos-players were of minor importance
compared to the poets. In later times, this changed radically. The aulos-vir-
tuosi completely displaced the kithara-player. Until the fifth century, the
records of the *chorosdidaskaloi* (the list of the dramas containing the names
of the authors and the dates of the performances) mentioned only the poet and
the choir-master. In the fourth century, the names of the aulētes were added;
in the second half of the century, the names of the aulētes appear at the head
of the list.

Despite its growing importance, there were outstanding men, philosophers as well as politicians, who remained hostile to the aulos-play. ALCIBIADES
(ca. 450–404 B.C.E.), for instance, who in his youth received a thorough *Mousic*
education, refused to learn the aulos, because he considered it vulgar and not
congenial for a "free man." ARISTOTLE wanted it to be eliminated from the
education of the youth, alleging that it was not an ethical but an orgiastic
instrument.[95] PYTHAGORAS, according to tradition, considered the playing of
the aulos as licentious, ignoble, and harmful. On the other hand, PERICLES
(493–437 B.C.E.), in his youth, was instructed in music by DAMON, the most
famous teacher of the time, who taught him not only the lyra, but also the
playing of the aulos.

The struggle for appreciation of aulos-music was displayed in a satyr-play
by PRATINAS, a contemporary of AESCHYLOS. He presented on the stage two
choirs, one infavor of the aulos, the other against it. The latter group inveighed
against the former on account of its servility to the aulos; this instrument
should not dominate the song, but follow it.[96]

In Boeotia, the homeland of the aulos, the attitude toward the instrument
was, of course, quite different. PINDAR, in his twelfth Pythic song, devoted to
the victorious aulēte MIDAS, glorified the aulos as the invention of ATHENA
which openly contradicts the "official" mythology.

Even ARISTOPHANES declared the kithara the ideal *Mousic* instrument and
poured out witticisms upon the aulētes, especially those from Boeotia (*Birds*,
859 ff.). Later on ARISTOPHANES employed solo-singers accompanied by auloi,
and he inserted aulos-soli, as, for instance, in an intermezzo between two parts
of an aria, a kind of postlude to the first part (*Birds*, 222, and *Frogs*, 1263).
This is unmistakable proof of the increase of musical soloists in dramatic plays
dating from the end of the fifth century.

A minor remark of evaluation concerning the auloi can be seen in the haughty
saying of the Athenians:

The sons of Thebes should play the aulos, since it is not given to them to entertain
themselves in words.[97]

Nevertheless, the aulos soon became a very popular instrument. Because it
originated from Boeotia, it was natural that Boeotian musicians displayed remarkable proficiency on it. For the dramatic plays of Athens and other cities,
aulētes from Boeotia were preferred. Many of these are recorded by name,
which shows not only their popularity, but even more the appreciation accorded artistic aulos-playing by the people at large.

Owing to a period of temporary hostility between Athens and Boeotia (457–447 B.C.E.), the use of the auloi in dramatic performances of Athens may have been somewhat reduced; but even then, the playing of auloi in theatrical plays was considered indispensable. In most cases, aulētes other than Boeotians were employed.

The aulos had a relationship to singing that was quite different from that of the kithara. While the kitharōdos could accompany his own singing, this was impossible for the aulēte, who furnished the musical background for the choir-singing, or played during the pauses of the dramatic action. As a soloist, his role was restricted to the *anabolē*, or the *prooimion*, the instrumental preludes to the plays.

Like the stringed instruments, the aulos also had numerous variants, which —unlike the original—grew out of the Greek musical practice. They were of different sizes and had different names. *Parthēnioi*, the pipes for girls, were the soprano category of the auloi; *paidikoi*, representing the alto-range, were for boys; *teleioi*, the "complete ones," corresponding to the range of the tenor voice, and the *hyperteleioi*, the "super complete ones," were the lowest, the bass category, both for the accompaniment of male voices. There existed still other categories, such as the *kitharistērioi*, used in the agōns, and some others, which were merely modifications of the main types.

Auloi were generally composed of two pipes. Most of the pictorial representations show the pipes of equal length. There were also auloi with pipes of different lengths, called *elymoi* (the Phrygian auloi), which are frequently represented in pictures. The two pipes were not firmly connected to each other, not even with a common mouthpiece. Thus, each pipe could be played either alone or together. The pipe designed to play the melody originally had four finger holes; later, so that one could play them in various modes, the number of finger holes was increased. Also, the players utilized a practical device consisting of metal or bone rings, which were slid over the pipes so that the player was able to close or open any of the finger holes, as a prerequisite for the particular mode he wanted to perform. Such a device was already known to the ancient Egyptians. Several flutes, or flute-like instruments of this type are preserved in Egyptian museums.[98] POLLUX reported[99] that this innovation was introduced in Thebes by DIODOROS, who, it is said, provided the pipes with openings by which the air had lateral outlets. This is undoubtedly the device referred to as *bombyx*, which made pretuning possible, so that a scale could be played in any mode.

According to another version, PRONOMOS, the teacher of ALCIBIADES (450–404 B.C.E.) constructed a similar device, for which the finger holes not used could be closed. Preserved antiquities show that this device was applied only in later hellenistic times. It is, however, more probable that the innovation goes back to the Egyptian musical practice.[100]

The characteristic tone of the aulos was produced by a mouthpiece consisting of double reeds (like today's oboe). The reeds were made from blades of straw flattened by pressure. The embouchure employed for playing this instrument must have exerted much pressure upon the cheeks when they were inflated. As mentioned previously, when the goddess ATHENA saw her beautiful face become distorted by blowing the instrument "invented" by her, she flung it away in scorn (see above). To prevent inflating the cheeks as well as to regulate a uniform wind supply, the Greek aulētes employed a device called *phorbeia* (also *peristomion*). This consisted of a band that was wrapped around the mouth and tied behind the head in order to keep the cheeks from puffing out. In the front there was an orifice through which the mouthpiece of the instrument was inserted (Illus. 114).

It is not certain whether both pipes were used to play the melody, since pictorial relics show that the left pipe was without finger holes. It might be, therefore, that the left pipe produced a continuous drone, as was the case with the later Roman bagpipes.

Although Greek mythology attributes the invention of the aulos to the goddess ATHENA, there is a Peloponnesian legend, reported by PAUSANIAS,[101] in which the instrument was invented by ARDALOS of Athens, son of the god HEPHAESTOS.

More reliable are the historical records concerning the artistic use of the aulos by TERPANDROS (ca. 675–659 B.C.E.). The Phrygian OLYMPOS may have been another performer of the aulos, although it cannot be proven historically, therefore the nomoi attributed to him are probably apocryphal.

While the high Olympian gods rejected the playing of the aulos, the Muses, caretakers of the *Mousic* arts, were more sympathetic and had adopted the aulos for their own use. They played the instrument before APOLLO and among themselves as a solo instrument or part of an ensemble (Illus. 104).

The aulos was the instrument most generally employed for the rites of DIONYSOS. The sileni, sirens and maenads, who comprised the retinue of the god DIONYSOS, all played the aulos. At the thiasos, komos, and symposion, the auloi were the preferred instruments. They were also played at all festive occasions for dances, processions, masquerades, athletic events, and even at work (Illus. 102 and 113). They were the implements of the agōns, and became indispensable for accompanying the dramatic plays. That DIONYSOS himself never played the instrument is strange, since the legacy of preserved paintings depicts him always with a stringed instrument.

The aulos had a particularly important role at the sacrifices. The procession of the sacrificial animal to the sanctuary of ATHENA was accompanied by an aulos player. It was natural, therefore, that the sacrificial act itself should employ auloi for the musical background. ATHENA had to tolerate the playing of the aulos in her sanctuary even though she had repudiated it. To alleviate her hardship, stringed instruments were added in later times. The playing of the auloi was such an essential part of the sacrifice that HERODOTUS[102] considered their absence a "foreign" custom at Persian sacrifices.

Still other ritual usages were closely connected with the aulos, particularly those of DIONYSOS. Although he did not play the aulos, we have a report of DIONYSOS doing so at one occasion, namely, when he brought the drunken HEPHAESTOS back to Olympus to free HERA from her uncomfortable throne (see above).

Similar to those of the cult of DIONYSOS were the nocturnal feasts of the Phrygian goddess CYBELE, at which, beside the auloi, several other "orgiastic" instruments were used, such as the *tympana*, the *kymbala* and the *krotala*.

According to tradition, the cult of CYBELE, including the orgiastic instruments, had been introduced to Greece from Phrygia. However, the tympana and krotala were already mentioned in the Homeric hymn to the "Great Mother-Goddess" of Asia-Minor. Consequently, the cult with its accompanying instruments must have been much older than the historical records would have us believe.

Another tradition, which seems more reliable, holds that the adoption of the cult of CYBELE took place around 700 B.C.E. A new theory assumes that there were two different periods in which the playing of the aulos in Greek music can be ascertained: a primitive but very old one, and a newer, more artistic, imported from Phrygia.[103] Against this hypothesis the fact may be invoked that in the Homeric epos aulos-music was cultivated only by the Trojans, while at all other occasions, such as banquets and work, HOMER mentioned only the phorminx as an accompanying instrument.

The Hellenes did not fully accept the new artistic playing of the auloi. Numerous complaints were raised against these "naughty innovators," who introduced into the erstwhile "clean" music of the auloi all kinds of "twists," "ornamentations," and "changes of modoi." The poets of the later dithyrambs, who were at the same time their own composers, such as MELANIPPIDES, PHRYNIS, CINESIAS, TIMOTHEOS, PHILOXENOS, and their followers, were reproached for using the instrumental accompaniment more and more as an end in itself, thus neglecting the most important element of the song, the lyrics.

These innovations of the dithyrambic poets automatically led to *absolute* music, independent of the spoken word. With this, the principle of the *Mousikē*, the unity of *melos*, *rhythmos*, and *logos*, so highly praised by the ancient generation of poets, was completely obliterated.

The Egyptians had an aulos with only one pipe called *monaulos*, known to the Greeks as *photinx*. However, it is not clear whether this aulos was blown vertically, or horizontally as was the Lydian flute.[104] In Phrygia the diagonal flute may have also been known,[105] also in Etruria. A pictorial specimen of such an instrument was discovered on a stone-relief of an urn in a tomb at Perugia that dates from the second century B.C.E., and is considered the earliest pictorial representation of a transversal flute (see Illus. 126).

Greek funeral services ordinarily took place without musical accompaniment. Only wailing women were admitted to such ceremonies. Nevertheless, there are records that indicate that the deceased were at times honored by instrumental music. For instance, in two pictures we see aulos players accompanying the funeral cortege. It seems, however, that music was used to accompany the procession rather than to participate in the funeral ceremony proper.

On the other hand, there are frequent representations of instruments on tombs, especially chordophones. Here, they may signify gift offerings to the deceased rather than tokens of honor.

At funerals there were frequently plays produced in honor of the deceased. These plays were generally dances with weapons and with spear-throwing. Because the aulos played a prominent accompanying role at athletic events, this may have spurred the idea for the aulos participation at funeral ceremonies.

In sports the aulos had particular functions, and they were represented frequently in the *palaistra* as well as at agōns (Illus. 113). Auloi were not employed for racing events (horse, chariot, running), because the movements of the contestants would be disturbed by the use of any accompanying instrument. In all other athletic activities at which the participants did not have to change places drastically, as in spear and discos throwing, jumping, and the like, the use of auloi enhanced the evenness and harmonious aspect of the bodily move-ments. Only at boxing matches was instrumental accompaniment absent com-pletely, indicating that this activity did not solicit a *Mousic* practice.

In military life auloi were commonly used. On their way to battle, the soldiers marched to the sound of auloi. Aulos players were placed at strategic points on the battlefield, evidently to pass on signals to the troops. Prior to combat, an aulēte played a war song, which undoubtedly raised the morale of the soldiers. A specific tune was played as the signal for attack.

Finally, mention should be made of the healing power of music attributed to the playing of instruments by the Greeks and other peoples of Antiquity. For purposes of healing, the auloi were considered the most potent of all musical media. Their playing could heal madness as well as all the violent emotions, and even physical illness. In HOMER we read how ODYSSEUS, during a hunt on Parnassus, was attacked and severely wounded by a boar. His hunting companions, the sons of AUTOLYKOS, came to his rescue, and through their magic song were able to stop his bleeding, which led to his complete recovery.[106]

PLATO maintained that dancing and aulos playing can heal the korybantic frenzy.[107] ATHENAIOS explained that aulos playing, and even the choice of certain modoi, possessed effective healing power against physical ills (see above).[108]

Since the aulos originated in Phrygia, melodies in the Phrygian mode were used for their healing power.

The invention of the *syrinx*, according to legend, has been attributed to Pan, son of Hermes. Accordingly, it was called Pan's pipe. Since Pan was the god of the shepherds, this instrument was associated with pastoral life. The instrument comprised pipes of various lengths, tied together and held under the lower lip where the air stream was blown across the uniformly straight end of the pipes. We sometimes see a syrinx with pipes of equal length, the difference of pitch being produced by pouring wax into the reeds. On some pictures, the syrinx is seen with four pipes, on others with five or more. The Muses did not refrain from playing the syrinx, and even APOLLO played it while guarding the sheep of ADMETOS. PLATO recognized only the strings as *Mousic* instruments, yet among the wind instruments he accepted the syrinx, because it was closely connected with nature.[109]

The playing of the kithara was called *kitharizein;* the aulos, *aulein;* and the syrinx, *syrizein.* The Greeks had additional linguistic constructions to express the various kinds of musical activity, for instance, *peirozein* ("try" to make music), and *anaballein* (a technical term to "start singing the *prooimion*").

Prior to the appearance of the transverse flute, the syrinx was the only wind instrument that was played by "piping," while the auloi were played by "blowing." Originally, the Pan's pipes were made from reeds, later from wood, metal, clay, and, in some cases, a special kind of resin. We possess numerous pictorial representations of this instrument so that we are well informed about its shape. If these extant reproductions are correct, they always show the pipes in odd numbers: five, seven, and nine, which seem to correspond to the Greek scale of seven tones, with its normal extensions, following the system of tetrachords.

Another Greek wind instrument was the *salpinx*, a trumpet. It was a long metal tube with a bell- or funnel-shaped opening on one end. SOPHOCLES had another name for it, *kodōn* (funnel), describing the whole instrument in terms of this characteristic. The tube was made of iron or bronze, the mouthpiece of animal horn (*glotta ostinē*), which could be inserted into the tube. In the preserved pictures this mouthpiece is not clearly recognizable, and we know of its existence only from literary sources.

The salpinx was mentioned in the Iliad, and must therefore have belonged to the ancient instruments of the Greeks. As mentioned above, the legend attributed its invention to the goddess ATHENA. In Argos, she was worshipped as ATHENA SALPINX. The real inventors of the instrument may have been the Etruscans, the first bronze-casters in the Mediterranean. The Egyptians may have adopted the instrument through their commercial dealings with the Etruscans. In the tomb of TUT-ANKH-AMON two trumpets were found (Illus. 32) that were very similar to those of the Greeks. The Tyrrhenic nations, as well as the Assyrians and Hebrews, took over the trumpet from the Egyptians and introduced it to the Greeks.

The salpinx was both a festive and a war instrument. It was employed for all processions and sacrifices, at which it was blown by priests (cf. its analogous use by the Hebrews). Like the aulos, the salpinx was also blown with the phorbeia.

AESCHYLOS, in his *Eumenides*, called the sound of the trumpet *diatoros*, "yelling," "piercing," and it may be assumed that the average player indeed played it in such a manner. However, there may have been some professional players, who could skilfully handle the instrument to the point of virtuosity. There are records about a certain HERODORUS of Megara, whose playing of the salpinx earned him ten prizes in the Olympic games. We even know of a female virtuoso of the instrument, AGLAIS, the daughter of MEGALOKLES, as reported by POLLUX.[110]

This may convince us that some players could produce more than a few natural harmonics, otherwise no "virtuosity" would have been possible on the salpinx. This was confirmed by HERACLEIDES, when he stated that the salpinx also possessed "softer" tones. This can be understood only if we assume that there were some musically gifted players. A later parallel to this may be the "clarin-blowing" of the sixteenth and seventeenth centuries, an art that developed to a high degree of virtuosity on the natural instrument. Many trumpet passages of HANDEL and J. S. BACH are just as difficult on our more technically developed modern trumpets.

In later times in Greece, the salpinx also became the favored instrument of war. Soldiers marched to its sounds, it signaled the attack, and during combat it had important strategic functions (the aulos was similarly used). There is a characteristic anecdote in one of ARISTOPHANES' comedies, which deals with a salpinx player who lamented that his profession was ruined because the war ended and he was without work. NIKE, the goddess of victory, blew the salpinx at the close of war, and also at agōns, when she conferred the prize on the victor. Except for a few cases where the salpinx was blown in an artistic manner, it was not considered under the category of *Mousic* instruments.

Besides the salpinx, the Greeks employed another signal-instrument, the *keratinē*, whose etymology is clearly given by the word *keras*, the horn of cattle. It is shown in several pictures, and despite its markedly different form, it is interpreted as the "second kind of trumpet" of the Greeks.

Concerning percussive instruments, the Greeks possessed only those of the cult of CYBELE imported from Phrygia: the *tympana, kymbala,* and *krotala,* and an instrument whose proper origin cannot be determined with certainty, a kind of xylophone. In accordance with their orgiastic character, the percussion instruments did not belong to the *Mousikē.*

The tympanon was the hand-drum known to all peoples of Antiquity, and in Greece as in other countries, it was played mostly by women to accompany dances. It had a round or square frame, made of wood or metal, upon which animal skin was stretched on one or both sides. It was played with a clenched fist, or with the fingers of one hand. Sometimes bright ribbons were attached to the frame, merely as ornaments. The tympanon is usually and erroneously translated as "tambourine," a modern instrument with skin on only one side; the frame contains additional tinkling metal-plates, which the antique tympanon lacks.

HOMER did not mention the tympanon, which indicates that it was introduced to Greece later. In the Greek mythology it was the instrument of the Dionysian cult, played mostly by the nymphs, the sileni, and the raving maenads. Men and boys are never depicted with it.

The kymbala were metal cymbals (mostly bronze), struck together, appearing always in pairs. They were similar to today's cymbals, with a boss in the middle, through which there was an opening so that a loop of leather could be inserted in order to hold them.

The assumption that the kymbala were identical with another noise-making instrument, the *krembala,* is erroneous. The kymbala were metal cymbals, therefore instruments of percussion, while the krembala were shaking or rattling instruments. ATHENAIOS called them *chalkopara krembala,* "clappers with bronze cheeks," and used a specific term for their playing *krembalizein,* "to shake the *krembala.*"[111]

All these instruments were not Greek in the proper sense and were used only in the orgiastic rites of foreign religions.

The domestic clapper instruments were the *krotala,* hand-clappers with two movable arms fastened together, made of wood, bone, or metal. Struck together, they produced a sound used mainly as rhythmic accompaniment for dancing. Since they were always employed in pairs, the term appears mostly in the plural. While the Egyptians had quite a number of noise-making instruments (sistra, all kinds of clappers, etc.), the Greeks restricted themselves to a single type that had proved its usefulness, and they adhered to it through all the centuries despite all the foreign, especially Asiatic, influence.

The krotalon must have been an ancient instrument, since we find it mentioned by HOMER. As HERODOTUS reported, it was played mostly by women in the orgiastic rites of DIONYSOS and CYBELE. The maenads also employed it for their frenzied dances. It was frequently used in the komos and symposion, especially for dancing. However, for the refined artistic dances, it was completely absent.

Finally, there are serious doubts that an instrument such as the xylophone was known to the Greeks. The instrument, if the Greeks had one, may be that represented in a picture depicting a women's chamber, with female amateurs enjoying themselves by playing house-music (Illus. 105. 110). This so-called xylophone is not played by them, but appears to be lying, half hidden, behind the chair of a woman playing the harp. On a vase from Apulia, the instrument is again depicted, this time in a woman's hand. In another picture it is held by a flying EROS. In modern musicological works on instruments, it is termed "a small ladder," which is an appropriate definition. It has ten bars; in other pictures, originating from Southern Italic cultures, the bars number from ten to seventeen. They are believed to be metal slabs of different pitches; therefore the instrument, if there was one, could be considered a xylophone. But the name is erroneous, because the xylophone is supposed to have wooden bars (*xylon*=wood) of varying lengths and thicknesses, thus creating different pitches. The slabs of the Greek contraption are of equal length, and the available pictures do not indicate any difference in their thickness. Thus, the assumption that it represents a Greek percussion instrument is at least questionable, the more so since there is no specific term for it in Greek literature. In more recent writings, it is called "Apulian sistrum." This name is evidently more appropriate than that of xylophone, which has a trapeze-like shape, while the Greek instrument has the shape of a ladder with rungs of equal length. It was probably a sistrum- or a rattle-like instrument. If one should use rods of wood or metal and move them up and down over the rungs, it could indeed produce a rattle-like sound. Viewed from this angle, it could represent a Greek noise-making instrument. For lack of a more suitable explanation, this assumption seems to be the most plausible one.

Indisputable proof exists that the sistrum was known to the Greeks. A discovery of the Cretic culture period supports this fact. On a vase-relief of Hagia Triada from the Middle- to Late-Minoan period (ca. 2500 B.C.E.), there is a picture of a sistrum that has the exact form of the Egyptian spur-sistrum (Illus. 116). It cannot be assumed that an instrument imported from Egypt and used by the predecessors of the Greeks disappeared from their music practice. Even if there are no literary records about such an instrument, it can be taken for granted that some instrument producing a rattling sound was in use by the Greeks. This "small ladder" might have been the instrument used for such purposes, similar to the Egyptian sistrum, which disappeared for reasons unknown to us.

It would be more plausible to consider the existence of a xylophone-like instrument in Greek music, supposedly invented by a man named DIOCLES, and termed *oxybapha*. Of this instrument only very vague descriptions exist and there are no pictures at all. We know, however, that it had plates (or vessels of clay) in various sizes, which were struck by a wooden stick. The different sizes (or lengths) of the plates would probably come closer to the idea of our present xylophone. And if the assumption is correct that the sounding bodies of the instrument were vessels of clay, we have many parallels for it dating from primitive times up to our own day. *Oxybapha* might also have been the term of a percussive instrument in ARISTOPHANES' *Frogs*, with which the Muse of EURIPIDES enters the scene. However, lack of precise details concerning the instrument forces us to mere surmises.

Among archaeological discoveries, small or middle-sized bells of various material have been found, the use of which cannot be explained unequivocally from the existing literature. We know, for instance that, in the sacred grove of ZEUS in Dodona, bells were hung on chains and were sounded by the blowing wind. They represent a species of Aeol's harp. There is a Hebrew legend about King David, who was said to have had such an instrument sounded by the wind.

An instrument mentioned by POLLUX,[112] named *askaron*, seems to have been a kind of a rattle. He furnished no description of it, nor stated on what occasion it was played. The only information given by him is that it was of clay.

For the sake of completeness, it should be mentioned that EURIPIDES once referred to the *kochlos,* a hornlike instrument using a conch-shell, which

is played even today as a signal-instrument by the sea-farers of the Greek islands.[113]

Furthermore, PINDAR mentioned the *molossos* (an instrument from a city of the same name), which usually accompanied the dances of the Cretans. What kind of instrument it might have been cannot be determined from the incomplete record.

If there were no instruments to support dancing, it sufficed—as generally in the Orient—that the onlookers clapped their hands. The Greeks also made ample use of this makeshift.

Some writers include among Greek instruments a device known as the *kroupezion,* for marking the rhythm at dances, particularly of larger dance-groups. This consisted of two wooden plates connected with hinges. One of the plates was fastened like a sandal on the foot of the dance instructor or the dance leader, who alternately lifted and struck the lower plate, thus producing a clapper-like sound. With this rhythmic support, his hands were free to play an instrument at the same time, probably the aulos. Later, the sound of the kroupezion was increased by applying to the wooden plates small- or medium-sized bronze-cymbals (Illus. 115). This noise-making implement was taken over by the Romans, who called it *scabellum* and used it not only for dance-groups, but also for large choral ensembles. ST. AUGUSTINE, in his treatise on music, referred to the scabellum, mentioning that the leaders of music, the *symphoniaci,* use foot-clappers equipped with small cymbals.

We do not possess precise information about the timbre of the Greek instruments. We have only vague notions gained through pictorial representation. Generally speaking, the various stringed instruments (kithara, lyra, barbiton, harps) are depicted in homogeneous groups, and only once in a while shown with the aulos. In one picture, showing the Muses in an ensemble, two of them play auloi, the others the trigōn-harp, the phorminx, and the cradle-kithara, respectively (Illus. 104). It cannot be said unequivocally whether such various combinations of instruments warrant any deductions as to certain norms or customs. It is improbable, however, that the Dionysian noise-making instruments were ever played along with the Apollinian strings. The aesthetic approach toward music-making of the Greeks might not have tolerated the combination of the glaringly different tone qualities of the two types of instruments and, consequently, we never see in pictures the tympanon, kymbalon, krotalon, or syrinx shown with the *Mousic* instruments. Besides, there may have been some hesitant religious considerations against using the stringed instruments, hallowed by APOLLO, along with the orgiastic noise-making instruments.

THE DANCE

The dance is as old as music itself. SACHS considers the dance to be the mother of all arts.[114] According to modern views, singing originated from dancing. Dance was created out of the need of primitive man to transform his emotions into corporeal movements. When such emotions accumulated and reached a high degree of intensity, the body started to move instinctively.

From this primordial stage, manifesting itself mainly in inarticulated movements, the dance progressed in human civilization through various degrees of development until it reached a well-regulated form that may be characterized as dance in the proper sense of the word. PAUL HENRY LÁNG believes that Greek dance originated "probably as a form of witchcraft, demon enchantment, and sex symbolism."[115]

In its developed form, the dance had great significance in Greek culture. What distinguished Greek dance from that of all the other civilized nations of Antiquity was its decisive role in the education of the young. Dance was one of the most important elements of the *Mousic* education, and it remained a dominant factor in civic life long after the youth's education terminated. About the interrelationship between dance and the education of the youth, a later chapter will give more pertinent information.

In Greece, just as in all other countries of Antiquity, there were solo dances and communal dances. The difference between and the importance of each will be demonstrated presently.

As early as the Archaic period of Greek history, HOMER describes the singing and playing of instruments combined with the dance as representing a threefold artistic unity, belonging to the Greek form of *Mousic* education. In the round-dance of the choir, the *kyklios choros*, we witness the combination and blending of the three arts: the sung poem, the instrumental accompaniment, and the artfully regulated dance. To this artistic order one can add the other elements of the *Mousic* arts, namely, *logos*, the word; *harmonia*, the *modos* (or key, scale); and *rhythmos*, as determinative for the *melos*. This is clearly expressed as early as HOMER, who defines the singer as the "leader in the dance."

The instrument that usually accompanied dancing is the aulos. It was used both for solo-dances as well as for community dancing. The aulos-player did not participate in the dance; he is usually depicted as seated. Dancing girls employed the clappers, krotala, to support the dance rhythm. The maenads are also frequently represented playing their favorite instrument, the krotala.

On the shield of ACHILLES there is a representation of a round-dance accompanied by the aulos and the lyra. This seems to have been a new practice introduced into the musical culture, since from then on, stringed instruments appear as accompaniment for dances. HOMER mentions the phorminx as such an instrument when he describes the dance of the buffoons,[116] but in the Homeric epics it served as accompaniment for group dances only. ANACREON refers in one instance to the pēktis as an accompaniment to the round-dance.[117] In many pictures on vases, dancing men and women are accompanied by the lyra.

At festive and cultic occasions, the processions and the round-dance were not too different from each other, consequently their musical background was almost identical. The wedding cortege, which took place accompanied by dancing, was always led by a young aulos player. HOMER and HESIOD both report this as an ancient custom. HOMER, in describing the shield of ACHILLES, refers to such a bridal procession:[118]

They marched with the brides coming from their chambers, through the city, with torches, and everywhere there was rejoicing for the wedding. Young men whirled in dances, to the accompaniment of auloi and lyres.

The mother of the bridegroom received the bridal couple on the porch of her home, a ceremony accompanied by lyres.

At old-time popular festivities women were masked and sometimes disguised as men, and danced to the accompaniment of auloi.

Processions with sacrificial gifts were always led by auloi. The use of auloi in sacrifices, as well as in other cultic rites, has been mentioned above. It was natural that war dances, as well as sportive events and contests, should have a similar musical background. Sometimes dancing girls are represented as performing the dance with krotala, which replaced the auloi for indicating the dance-rhythm.

In ACHILLES' shield, which depicted many Greek customs, a peculiar dance is shown called the *kybistētēres*. It is a dance in which the performers did somersaults.[119] It may have been an ancient round-dance, in which the dancers ran toward each other, the one in the center executing the somersaults. This dance was accompanied by the singing and playing of lyres.

Evidently the Greeks brought with them such dances from their original homeland, for they show unmistakable Cretic-Mycenic features.[120] In Cretic statuary we see similar dances depicted. Even in legends the memory of such dances remained alive. THESEUS, after delivering at Delos the twice-seven victims, was known to have performed such a round-dance.

According to the native Cretic mythology, the infant ZEUS owed his life to dance. When he was menaced by his father, CHRONOS, who used to devour his own children, priestly *Courētai* danced around him, striking their shields with their weapons, in order to save him by making noise. This legend is evidently based upon the ancient Oriental belief that demons and evil spirits cannot endure loud noises and may be chased away by such. Yet, it is difficult to understand where, in those times, the warrior Courētes could have gotten these weapons. But mythology does not care much about such incongruities.

Cretic dances were very popular for a long time among the Greeks. The Dorians were the first to come to Crete, and they stayed there long enough to become familiar with the customs of the country, among them the dances. They brought these to continental Greece, and this explains why Greek dances were strongly influenced by those of the Cretans. The Spartans cultivated with particular zeal a Cretic form of war-dance, the *pyrrhichē*, so called because the participants were clad in red garments (*pyrrhos*=red). Even five-year-old children participated in it. The Spartans considered such dances as means of developing the military prowess of the youth. The skill gained in these dances was utilized in war. The belief was widespread that some of the warriors owed their valor in the battle to their skill in using the pyrrhichē. This gives credence to the famous saying of SOCRATES that the best dancer is also the best soldier. The Spartans proceeded to their battles in a specific marching order, called *embatēria*, which showed definite dancing features.[121] As time went on, the pyrrhichē was transformed into a pantomime that served merely as entertainment. Thus the term lost its original meaning. In a later epoch even women participated in the pyrrhichē, and once it became merely a show-piece it was performed only by professional dancers.

The pyrrhichē paved the way to the introduction of other choir-dances into

Greek life: the *paianēs*, already mentioned above; the *hyporchēmata*, honoring APOLLO; and the *gymnopaidia*, danced by naked youths, a dance-form imitating the movement of wrestlers.[122]

All of these dances were based on the *emmēleia* (melodious, harmonious), those dignified and solemn forms of the *Mousic* dance, so strongly contrasting to the martial war-dances of the Spartans. Therefore, the emmēleia was for the most part performed by women. The finest species of such dances took place in the *Partheniades*, at which young maidens, holding hands, executed a round-dance and sang hymns in honor of the gods.

The emmēleia was the origin of the later civic-life choir-dances, which took hold in family life also, such as the ritual on the tenth night after the birth of a child, the ceremonies at the reaching of manhood of the young boys, the roguish choir-singing of the girls before the bridal chamber, as well as the lamenting procession to the burial place.

Besides these domestic folk-dances, the ethnic groups living in Greece at the time preserved their own native dances. Among them one finds the dances of the Cretans, the Phrygians, the Thracians, and the Macedonians. ATHENAIOS records the names of some dancers who excelled in such native dances and became famous because of their specific skills.[123]

These polished dances were in strict contrast to the wild dances of the *thyoskooi mainadēs*, the raving maenads. These were persons of mythology used to demonstrate the drawbacks of the unbridled, orgiastic dance that led to depravity and the corrupting of public morals. In contrast to this disparagement caused by the wild ecstasy of the soul, stood *sophrosinē*, the teaching of wisdom, honoring the gods by moderation. Yet—and this is typical of the Greek approach to the *Mousic* spirit—the wild and unbridled activity of such dances eventually became the origin of the Greek drama. Maenads, sileni, satyrs—all unruly figures —were the active persons of the Dionysian cult and contributed to the basic elements from which the Greek drama emerged. The choir singers and their leaders were carried on a ship on wheels to the plays in which the death and resurrection of DIONYSOS were shown. On such a ship in the year 534 B.C.E. the singer and dancer THESPIS traveled to Athens, invited by PEISISTRATOS to present dance-performances in honor of DIONYSOS. The singers were dressed in goat-skins (*tragos*=goat), and their song was called the "goat-song," in Greek *tragoidia*. This is the origin of the first dramatic performances of the Greeks, bearing the name *tragedy*.

Dances played an important role in the social gatherings of the Greeks. As mentioned above, the symposion was always followed by the komos when the banquet was over. Once the food was cleared from the tables and the wine was poured into the goblets, followed by the usual singing "around" of the participants, the guests were entertained by professional singers and dancers. These dancers were mostly females, performing all kinds of fertility-dances, devoid, of course of all religious connotations. These were merely lascivious productions, designed to exhibit the bodily charms of the dancers. Thus, from the entertainment following the komos, there originated the theatrical play *komoidia*, and with it the second mighty pillar of the Greek Drama, leading— besides the great works of the philosophers—to unsuspected heights of Greek spiritual achievements. (A different interpretation of the origin of Greek comedy will be discussed in the next chapter.)

In conclusion, it can be stated that the dance of the Greeks, like other elements of their culture, was not an original achievement of their own. Everything in form, content, and in the movements of Greek dance was adopted from other, mostly Asiatic, nations. We witness in Greece the same rites—for initiation, fertility, wedding, war, and death—as in those of the Near East; the same dance-types, the same kinds of movements, of forms, of round-dances for both sexes, of dances in straight rows for men and women, the same pantomimes and processions with dancing evolutions, and, of course, all kinds of solo-dances. Only in a later period are records found of two persons dancing together.[124]

What was new and significant in Greek dance customs was the institution of ritual choric-dances, in which the performers lost their personal identity and consciousness, merging completely with the divine. This is the most outstanding characteristic of Greek dance, not to be found elsewhere in the ancient Orient. It therefore represents a unique manifestation of Greek spirituality.

THE DRAMA AND THEATER

In a historical essay about the music and poetry of ancient Greece, there is a statement according to which

> tragedy appears with Aeschylos, the first by whom entire dramas are preserved, as a completely developed literary form.[125]

Whereas this statement might be valid as far as the dramas of AESCHYLOS are concerned, it overlooks the general principle that no art-form can emerge suddenly in perfect form, but requires development before it attains its apogee.

In the preceding chapter I discussed the various arts that combined to produce the highest literary form of Greek poetry, the drama. In these, the dance, combined with singing, was the prime mover. Just as the *tragoidia* was born of the "goat-song," and the *komoidia* arose from the entertainment after the komos, the satyr drama also owes its existence to dance and singing.

As mentioned above, *komos* has a double meaning; first, it refers to the entertainment (music as well as dance) following the symposion. The other interpretation, however, which might have been decisive for the creations of the komoidia, was that which designated the *komoi* as groups of singers and dancers who, at the agricultural festivals, and in all kinds of disguises, roamed from village to village, performing all kinds of mischievous pranks. The term in Greek for village was *komē*. The verb designating the strolling from village to village was *komazein*, while the groups who did so were the komoi; their singing was termed *komoidia*, and these singers were the komoidoi. With this etymology, it becomes convincing that the drama—in this case, the komoidia—"was born out of the spirit of music." This is a generally accepted theory. But how about the *tragoidia*, which was supposed to have grown out of the same *Mousic* source?

The *tragoidia* originated with the continuation of the mimic presentations sung and danced by the satyr-like participants of Dionysian revelries clad in goat-skins. According to historical reports (mentioned above), the singer and dancer THESPIS was invited to Athens with his troupe by PEISISTRATOS in 534, to entertain the population with his rollicking performances. This might have been the ancient rural spring festival of Athens, introduced by PEISISTRATOS, out of which the germ of Greek drama emerged. To explain the origin of the goat-skin, there are historical records that state that at the birthplace of THESPIS in Icaria, every year a goat was sacrificed to DIONYSOS. It is possible, and even probable, that in the accompanying ceremony the singers of THESPIS were clad in goat-skins.

Originally, the main performer in the primitive tragoidia was the singing and dancing choir. Only a small, but significant, change was still needed to transform such a satyr-play into a real dramatic spectacle. This was the introduction of an *actor* with spoken dialogue. It seems that this was the innovation made by THESPIS, who, at the same time, was the speaker and actor of his play. Soon a second, and then a third, actor were added, by which artifice a real dramatic action could be developed in theatrical performances. The role of the choir also changed. Previously, the participants only sang and danced, but now they became, so to speak, the public opinion commenting upon and underscoring the dramatic action, taking sides for or against one of the acting characters. This juxtaposition of the protagonists and the singing choir provided the turning point in the development of the new art-form, the drama.

THESPIS, the dancing master and choir-leader (*chorosdidaskalos*), is considered to be the first writer of tragedy; he himself played the lyre and accompanied the singing of his choir. As such, he was the *hypokritēs*, the expounder, of the happenings on the stage; he recited the *prooimion*, the prologue, and the *rhēsis*, the verses connecting the various stanzas of the choir song. As the kitharōdos of the play, he stood outside and above the choir, either on a platform (*bēma*), or at the *thymēlē*, the small altar devoted to DIONYSOS, which was placed in the center of the stage or on the steps which the choir encircled. In a later period, the hypokritēs stood at the thymēlē, while the place assigned to the choir was on the ancient dancing floor, the *orchēstra*.

It is difficult to establish unequivocally whether THESPIS was a historical personage, or merely a legendary figure, the personification of the origin of the drama. His name is first mentioned by ARISTOPHANES in his *Wasps*, where "archaic dances" are mentioned similar to those in which THESPIS participated in the agōns. This interpretation refers to THESPIS merely as the kitharōdos, but not the author of tragedies. In a later epoch, especially after the complete efflorescence of the Greek drama, it becomes more difficult to imagine that it was the kitharōdos who inaugurated the tragedy. Yet, there are historical records indicating, even if in an indirect way, that THESPIS might have been the originator of drama. It is said about him:

He was the first to introduce the prologos, the rhēsis, and there was only one hypokritēs[126]

All these characteristics appear to allude to THESPIS.

At the various stages of the development of Greek drama as it presents itself between THESPIS and AESCHYLOS, several names deserve to be mentioned, such as PRATINAS (ca. 500 B.C.E.), CHOIRILOS (ca. 500 B.C.E.), and PHRYNICHES (end of the fifth century), the latter supposed to have been a disciple of THESPIS. All of them are known to have paved the way for the development of the great tragedies.

The golden period of the antique drama is represented by the names of three

great authors who all lived about the same time: Aeschylos (525–456), Sophocles (ca. 496–406), and Euripides (480–401). They are joined by the famous
satirical author of comedies, Aristophanes (ca. 448–380).

Euripides was the first to introduce the solo aria in a theatrical play. This was
done in his play *Alcestis* (438 b.c.e.), which, however, was not a tragedy, but,
rather curiously, a satyr-play. For this "innovation" he was chided by Aristophanes. In a later drama, *The Trojans*, (415 b.c.e.), Euripides further developed
the musical potentialities of the tragedy, and in a subsequent play, *Andromeda*,
he introduced, as a novelty, musical echo-effects.[127] Agathon, a younger contemporary of Euripides (ca. 448–407 b.c.e.) is credited with the introduction of
"chromatic" music into the tragedy, surely a "revolutionary" innovation for
those times.

As for the composition of the music in Greek tragedies, we cannot equate
this procedure with our modern conception of composing, where lyrics are
usually written first and the music set to them after. In Greece, the tragic
authors conceived the poem and the music together; it was a simultaneous
creative experience. Lyrics and melody constituted an indivisible unity. Therefore, the three great representatives of the attic tragedy were praised by the
Greeks not merely as poets but also as musicians.[128]

Is it not ironical that Aristophanes, who satirized everything obsolete, everything ossified in the social institutions of his time, was opposed to "new music"?
He denounced especially the "embellishments," which contributed, as he thought,
to the degeneration of the dignified old music. His antagonistic attitude against
"modern" music, however, did not last long, for he soon committed the same
"sins" in his own comedies. Another author of comedies, Pherecrates (a contemporary of Aristophanes), severely criticised the "music of the future," and
represented the Muse as a raped virgin. Hostility against the "music of the
future" is by no means a phenomenon of modern times. Almost every epoch
of music history had its "music of the future," which sooner or later became
the "music of the present," and, in due time, the "classical music." We need
recall only a few names in music history: Beethoven, Wagner, Richard Strauss,
Debussy, Stravinsky, and Bartók, among others, who suffered from the unjust
diatribes of the professional "judges" of music, the critics.

However, enmity in Greece against the "new music" remained ineffective;
the new musical types were acclaimed by the audiences, and thus a new nomos
and a new dithyrambos came into being, not to be readily discarded. The real
creator of the "music of the future" was Timotheos of Miletos (ca. 446–357).
He was soon followed by Melanippides of Melos (ca. 450–400 b.c.e.), Crexos
(ca. fifth century b.c.e.), Philoxenos (ca. fifth century b.c.e.), and Polyeidos
(ca. 440–380 b.c.e.). They all contributed to the development of, and found new
possibilities for, the "modern" style.[129]

The most outstanding representative of the new dithyrambos was Phrynis
of Mytilene, who obtained the victory in the *Panathenaean* plays in 446 b.c.e.
He introduced richer rhythms and unusual modulations into his performances,
and is credited to have developed an improved kind of kithara (or lyra). Not
all the contemporary musicians followed his example; Damon of Athens (ca.
450 b.c.e.), who was at the same time a politician, philosopher, and musical
theorist, held the view that the "old" music and its ethics were the sole guar-
antees of maintaining the institutions of the state. For him, revolution in the
music generates revolution in the state.[130] Plato, too, fought against "modern"

music; his opinions about the aesthetics of music are the most significant contributions to Greek music theory.

It is not the object of this succinct review of the Greek drama to reveal all its *Mousic* characteristics, but rather to examine merely its musical aspects since, according to modern theory, drama originated out of the spirit of music.

It was shown above that the tragedy developed from the kitharōdic satyr-play. ARISTOTLE says that "it took a long time before the tragedy, starting with short actions and funny language, arrived at its full dignity."[131] Until the appearance of EURIPIDES, the satyr-plays remained an integral part of the Dionysian drama. Every author of a tragic trilogy made concessions to the older style of composing, as noted in the fourth part of EURIPIDES' poem, a satyr-play in honor of DIONYSOS. The *dramatis personae* of such satyr-plays were the retinue of DIONYSOS: sileni, satyrs, tityretus, bacchants, lemnians, thiads, mimallones, naiads, nymphs, Courētes, as all these mythological figures were called. The actors in such plays were, of course, human beings, who, according to the conception of the Greeks, through *mimēsis,* were metamorphosed in the play into such mythical figures, to change again, after the play was over, into human beings.

This is demonstrated clearly in the hymn of the *Courētoi* of Palaikastro, in which the ritual dance of the Couroi represented an ancient cultic legend. The skipping (dancing) and the din made by striking their shields were interpreted in the mythology as the means of protecting the infant ZEUS from his pursuers.[132]

The musical accompaniment of the dramatic play was carried out by a single aulos-player, who used a double-reed instrument, but certainly had several species at his disposal in order to be able to change the modos required for a special solo or choir strain. Only rarely was the accompaniment entrusted to a stringed instrument, as in the dance of the buffoons in the Odyssey, at which, as we see in HOMER, the phorminx was used to accompany their dance. But this happened long before the emergence of the drama and, furthermore, it represents more myth than history. The aversion of the Athenians to the aulos as accompaniment for singing probably goes back to the myth about ATHENA that she repudiated the instrument. Most of the aulos-players were from Boeotia, probably because the country originated the instrument, and evidently because the Phrygians were the best aulos-players.

The poets of the classical epoch were at the same time the composers of the music for their plays. Yet, it is hard to understand how SOPHOCLES could have composed his own music, since, as he stated himself, he had no musical education. Despite the powerful figures he created in his plays, his tragedies could not do without music. When music does appear in his tragedies, it is always organically interlinked with the dramatic action. Music occupies a different position in the works of EURIPIDES. Here, it is more frequently used, but this tragedian avoids, as far as possible, the use of the aulos, preferring the sound of the softer stringed instruments. His favorite instrument was the syrinx, "the sweet shepherd's pipe."[133]

The choir, while singing, executed dance patterns, which were not merely rhythmic movements but represented carefully prepared mimetic gestures. They were supposed to underline the content of the dramatic action. The choir-dance of the drama, in contradistinction to the *kyklios choros,* the round dance in civic life, was not performed in a circle, but in a linear arrangement. The choir of the tragedy and of the satyr-plays was displayed in three rows of five singer-dancers (*choreutēs*) each. The statement of POLLUX that the choir of AESCHYLOS consisted of fifty choreutēs might have been prompted by the fact that in the *Eumenides,* besides the choir of the Erynnies, a second choir was introduced.

The singing of the choir was specialized in accordance with its function in the dramatic plays. Its various categories were: the entrance-choir (*parodos*), the choir standing without changing its place (*stasima*), and the choir of exit (*aphodos*). The solemn choir-dance of the tragedy was called *emmēleia.* That of the satyr-plays, which were fast and grotesque, was called *sikinnis,* while in the comedy a lascivious dance, the *kordax,* was frequently introduced, probably as a contrast to, and caricature of, the dignified and solemn dances of the tragedy.

Even the imitative forms of the archaic dances were preserved in the Classical period. There were animal-dances, in which the movements of bears, lions, foxes, and birds were imitated (Illus. 103). In all such dances, the *phorai* and the *schēmata* were the basic ingredients of the dance forms. The phorai were the gestures by which the emotions and actions of the play were expressed, while the schēmata were used for the characterization of a single person of the play. Several such movements are described or suggested in the literature; for instance, a hand at the head meant sorrow and suffering, the violent thrust of the arms signified war or fight, and the stretching of the hands upwards was supposed to describe worship of the gods.[134]

Originally, the choir did not take part in the dramatic action itself. The choir members stood above it as onlookers, commenting mostly on the action. Gradually, the use of the choir in the Greek drama increased, but diminished again as more and more actors were employed.

The kitharōdic choir-song of the fifth century was strictly regulated. Its main parts were:

1) The *prooimion,* a short group of verses, the prologue of the drama

2) The *agōn,* the choir-song proper, so termed because in it the acting choir competed with another part of the choir

3) The *epilogos.*

The prooimion was also called *archē;* the kitharōdos who intoned it was the *exarchon,* he who "started" the singing. He remained the leader throughout each choral section, accompanying the chorus on his instrument and singing to his own accompaniment.

The exarchon was not involved in the actions of the choir and was not a member of the choir itself. He stood at the thymēlē and recited the verses of the hypokritēs, the "interpreter." In the earliest tragedies he did not assume a role in the drama; the dramatic involvement came later, when the hypokritēs and the actor were unified in the person of the divine singer THESPIS, *Thespis aiōdos.*

The dramatic poems, whether tragedy, comedy, or satyr-play, were divided into two main categories: *mimēsis* and *dihegēsis;* but there were also some mixed forms. Mimēsis ordinarily represented a psychophysical action, in which "the musical happening was caused by the psychic happening, and vice versa"; mimēsis stands therefore as the physical expression of the soul.[135] Basically, in the mimēsis the myth and the actual play are merged in one. In the play, the actors are transformed into the demonic personalities of the myth; after the play they again become ordinary mortals. PLATO defines mimēsis accurately and rationally (*Republic*, 394 b, c). He maintains that it is the essence of the actions and feelings in the drama, while he regards the dihegēsis as the objective narratives and recited reports by the actors. The difference may be defined thus: tragedy and comedy are purely mimētic poems, in which the subject of the play is presented by acting persons. The dithyrambos is a purely dihegētic form; the epic poem is a mixed species in which the objective reports alternate with direct speeches of acting persons.[136] However, PHILODEMOS of Gedara (in Syria), a contemporary of CICERO (ca. 110–40 B.C.E.), rejected the mimēsis completely. He maintained that music has no faculty whatsoever to "imitate" or "describe" anything. This approach to music belongs to the later formalistic school, already far removed from the classic theory.

The cultic dithyramb was performed with auloi and belonged organically to the *kyklios choros* of the festive calendar. Such dithyrambic performances taken over from the liturgy were sponsored by wealthy citizens (see above) and recorded for posterity. Both the participants as well as the choreutēs were identified by name.

Another form of poetry, closely connected with music, was the ancient art of rhetoric, although the term seems to be used in contradiction to the facts. In its basic form, rhetoric is the art of words. The principle of it, however, goes back to the structure of the kitharōdic song. According to the *Rhetorics* of KORDAX of Sicily (confirmed also by QUINTILIANUS), its structure, just as in the choir song, consisted of the prooimion, agōn, and epilogos.

From this it becomes evident that not only the drama, but all the other *Mousic* arts, among them rhetoric, had their origin in song. This was the natural approach to the dithyrambic-aulētic character of the Greek drama and to the kitharōdic song, which became the germ of tragedy.

At this point a brief examination of the role of the audience and consideration of the effect that the music of the drama exerted on the public is in order.

There are scarcely any reports about this matter, but all writers are unanimous in their opinion that the tragic melodies deeply stirred the listeners. The powerful effect of the music, intensified by the passionate rendition of the actor-singers as well as by that of the instrumentalists, caused vehement opposition on the part of the philosophers. In the great tragedies, music expressed all degrees of passions, grief, sorrow, and all the other emotions of the human soul. The most solemn form of the music, that which penetrated most deeply into the sentiments of the audience, was that of the cultic song, performed by professional singers. Besides this highly effective art, there was a more popular way of advancing the popularity of music for big audiences. This was achieved by the citizens themselves, who enjoyed making music in their daily lives and used it not solely in work-songs to lighten their chores.

The most important musical presentations took place in connection with the great national festivals, at which occasions the unity of the entire nation achieved its overwhelming expression. It is well known that at these events music played an essential role and constituted the strongest unifying force of the nation, particularly when it was coupled with dramatic pantomime effects. The festivals were responsible for the creation of a uniform type of Greek music.[137] To them came musicians from all the districts of Greece to present to a Panhellenic audience the particular achievements of their respective tribes. The cultivation of all the arts was powerfully influenced by this intermingling of the different races, starting with the beginning of the fifth century. It led to the creation of the particularly strong sense of nationalistic consciousness, resulting in unification of the Hellenic people in the domain of the arts, especially of music. This synthesis of the dramatic and musical arts reached its greatest heights during the Golden Age of Greece and lasted until the Roman conquest.

EDUCATION OF THE YOUTH

The place where the Muses were worshipped was called *Mousaion*. It is significant that the school in which Greek *Mousic* education took place was also called Mousaion.

The Greek ideal of education was the *kalokagathia* (*kalos*=beautiful, *agathos*= good), the aim of which was to bring the beautiful and the good in every young man to the point of spiritual unity. Greek education was directed less to imparting knowledge to youth than to the formation of his character. The goal of the *Mousic* education was to provide a basic education for the free citizen through the *kyklios choros*, the communal round dance. Reading and writing were subordinated to the *Mousikē;* they were helpers of singing and playing the kithara. Consequently, "music" meant in classical Athens an all-embracing *Mousic* activity, which was not yet divided into "school subjects" such as literature, arithmetic, rhetoric, and so on. HOMER relates that he taught children "the *grammata* (i.e., reading and writing) as well as *all the other music.*"

Gradually, the comprehensive *Mousikē* was subdivided into several "school subjects," designated as artes liberales. The usual interpretation of the "free arts" is apt to create a wrong impression. They were not the arts performed "freely," but disciplines the exercise of which was considered vital for the education of free-born citizens. The choir of free citizens, the *kyklios choros*, created the term "free arts," because only free men could participate in the community dances and were therefore obliged to undergo the necessary education for this civic duty. This education was termed *enkyklios paideia*, "education in the circle" of the free choreutēs.

Not only in Athens, but everywhere in classic Greece, *Mousic* education and the participation in the choir dance was a civic duty. As stated above, PLATO mentions a friend of his, CLEINIAS, of Crete, who declared that the citizens of Crete knew only the songs they learned in their chorus.[139]

Familiarity with the choir songs was so widespread that any well-educated man could perform quite a number of them at the Symposion, accompanying himself on the lyra. "To intone the singing in the round" meant in Greek parlance to take up and continue the *skolion*, the "drinking song."

Such choir performances took place not only in their own cities. The *polis*, the community, frequently sent entire groups to another place, mostly to sanctuaries. The leader of such a delegation was called the *architheoros*, "the leader of the theory," and designated as being the ambassador of the festive group. Every year such a group was sent from Athens on a state ship to Delos. Before the return of this ship, no death sentence could be carried out in Athens. The origin of this custom was based upon a legendary event, which is related in extenso in an ode of BACCHYLIDES, a poet from Cheos (fifth century B.C.E.). This ode was usually sung by the civic choir of Cheos in honor of APOLLO, on the way from the place of disembarkation of the group to APOLLO's sanctuary. The essentials of this legend have been described earlier.

In the *Mousaion,* the children were taught reading, writing, and the technique of playing the kithara. All of these subjects enabled them to understand the meanings of the poems and to participate actively in the choir-dance. As soon as the body of the child was developed sufficiently, intellectual education was followed by physical training in the *palaistra.* Thus, intellectual and physical education went hand-in-hand, having as the ultimate goal that of blending the individual organically with the *kyklios choros.* Every child had to learn music, but, in order not to pervert the purpose of musical education and not to destroy its ethical values, the teaching of music was not permitted to degenerate into a specialization. In the opinion of many Greek thinkers, indulgence in music for the sake of virtuosity would produce softness of character.

In Athens, SOLON was the chief promoter of musical education. He considered the moral character of a responsible citizenry the fundamental basis of the state, and tried to inculcate civic virtues in the youth by *Mousic* education. The practice of music in Greece was prohibited to slaves (exactly the opposite was the case of the peoples of the ancient Orient, with the exception of the Hebrews). Familiarity with music was considered to be an important attribute of a noble person. Education in music was restricted to free-born Athenians. It was no shame to be uneducated in other fields of knowledge, but it was considered a disgrace to fail in singing, or even to refuse to participate in singing education. A well educated man was considered an *anēr mousikos,* a "musical man," while an uneducated person was simply called *anēr amousos,* an "unmusical man," or "a man without music."

In Sparta, the great lawgiver LYCOURGOS created an organization which possibly surpassed that of Athens. PLUTARCH reports that LYCOURGOS, on a trip to Crete, observed a number of customs and practices which, after his return, he introduced in Sparta. Among these customs was an extensive cultivation of music, which—strongly supported by King MINOS—made of the Cretans god-fearing and law-abiding citizens. LYCOURGOS introduced, among other rules, an obligatory and supervised music education, in which every Spartan—young or old, male or female, whatever his rank may have been—had to participate. Through this compulsory music instruction, he sought to increase the social and political responsibility of the Spartans and enable them to become useful citizens of the state.

According to PLATO and the other great philosophers, music had the leading role among the *Mousic* arts. He considered music as the most important element of education; its aim was to develop the character and the morals of the individual; consequently, the practice of music was not considered a "private" matter, but was the concern of the state. The other phase of education, gymnastics, was important, but was not to be the dominant factor—music should prevail. But not all kinds of music were apt for education of the youth; PLATO considered the music only in the Doric mode, which, due to its masculine aspect, was especially useful in developing character.

PLATO asked to have schools established and supervised by the state; but the Athenians preferred private schools, because, in their opinion, these provided a better type of education. Professional teachers opened schools, to which boys were admitted from the sixth year of age on. The term paidagōgos did not refer to the teacher, but mostly to a slave, or sometimes to an old woman, who accompanied the boy to the school and brought him home again (Illus. 118, 119). The pupils stayed in school until they were fourteen or sixteen, and boys of wealthy families even longer.[140] The teacher taught all the subjects himself; these embraced reading, writing, arithmetic (the Greeks used letters for numbers, just as did the Hebrews), music, and gymnastics; some "modernists" in ARISTOTLE's time added drafting and painting. Every pupil had to learn to play the lyra, and most of the instruction was carried out in a poetical and musical manner.[141] Foreign languages were not taught, but much care was devoted to correct use of the mother tongue. Gymnastics were taught in the gymnasion or palaistra. Nobody was considered well educated who could not swim or wrestle, or who was inept in archery and slinging.

The education of girls took place at home and was restricted to domestic and practical matters. In Sparta, even the girls had to take part in public gymnastic exercises. The mothers were the instructors of their daughters; they taught them reading, writing, and arithmetic, in addition to such practical activities as spinning, weaving, and embroidery. Also dancing, singing and, in most cases, playing an instrument were part of domestic education. Greek women on the average were rarely well educated; the few educated women were mostly *hetairai* who, besides their bodily charms, fascinated men by their intellectual qualities. "Respectable" women did not receive a higher education; this was reserved for men alone.

Higher education in Greece was carried out by private teachers, the Sophists, a class of well-paid, clever practitioners, who moved from city to city, giving public courses in philosophy, grammar, rhetoric, history, and other disciplines. There were quite a few ambitious young men who, not satisfied with what they learned in public schools, were avid in their desire for greater knowledge. Some of them procured the necessary money (sometimes quite substantial sums) by night work and other means, to be able to participate in such courses.[142]

In general, when a youth reached his sixteenth year, his further education was devoted to the fitness of his body as the necessary preparation for war. The gymnastic exercises were all aimed to develop military prowess. By his eighteenth year, the young man entered the second of four phases of Athenian citizenry (*pais, ephebos, anēr, geron*—child, youth, man, old person) and was accepted into the ranks of the young soldiers, the epheboi. Guided by special instructors, he was trained in the duties of both citizen and soldier. He lodged and had his meals together with the other young men, had a special uniform, and his moral life was supervised day and night. In the first year, he was subjected to hard drill. Furthermore, he had to take part in lectures on literature, music, geometry, and rhetoric. In the second year, he was sent to garrison border districts, where he was instructed in how to repel external attacks. As rewards, these young men had certain privileges, such as special seats in theatres, outstanding functions in religious processions, and others. They carried out relay races with torches, between Piräus and Athens, which took place at night, and in which, as onlookers, the entire population participated. When they reached their twenty-first year, their training as epheboi was completed; they were freed from the authority of their parents and were formally accepted with full rights and privileges as citizens of the state. However, in Athens

the complete education of the young man, his paideia, was brought about by his music instruction.

This was based on a principle established by SOLON, in which education in music was set up as a law of the state, just as it was in Sparta by LYCOURGOS.

This type of education had three purposes: utility, moral cultivation (*paideia*), and intellectual virtue (*diagōgē*). There was an element of utility in music; namely, when it served the purposes of entertainment. *Paideia,* the educational goal of music instruction, was different from *pàidia,* which indicated the utilitarian use of music: play or recreation. This, in turn, led to *anapausis,* relaxation or amusement, whereas *diagōgē,* containing pleasure of a higher kind, also had a moral element involved.

To these three functions of music was added a fourth, that of *katharsis,* the purifying or relieving of human emotions by art, an Aristotelian notion, the full impact of which will be discussed in connection with the effects of tragic drama upon the audience.

During PLATO's time, three years of musical education were considered sufficient. For the *paideia,* only the Apollinic lyre was the proper medium. Therefore, in vase pictures, mainly lyre-playing is shown. The music teacher, though he played the lyre, was called, nevertheless, kitharistēs. Although its popularity was far behind that of the lyre, playing the aulos was also taught in public schools. In Athens instruction in aulos playing was carried out for only a few decades. Around the middle of the fifth century it disappeared entirely, because it did not further the educational goals, which were directed toward developing a man's character. ARISTOTLE considered the aulos not an ethical but an orgiastic instrument.[144] In contradistinction to the "official" mythology, he held that ATHENA repudiated the aulos because it was unsuitable for developing the ethical disposition of mankind (*dianoia*). The main reason, however, for the aversion of the Greeks to the aulos was the fact that it originated in Boeotia—at that time still a "foreign" country—and thus it was opposed by the chauvinism of Greek patriots. Since the aulos was taught assiduously in Boeotia, the best players came from there, and were preferred at all public occasions, such as dramatic performances and processions, and even for the music for military purposes.

The other instruments, the kithara, the harp (trigōnon), and the instruments belonging to the percussion family, were not taught in public schools—the kithara, because it required too much skill in playing, the others because they were not regarded as *Mousic,* but as orgiastic instruments. The trigōnon, a species of the harp family, was rejected by PLATO[145] as well as ARISTOTLE[146] as not desirable for the education of the youth. From the opinions of the philosophers it becomes manifest that the goal of music instruction was not to insure mastery of an instrument, but to give the pupil a *Mousic* education.

We learn from ARISTOPHANES that the young pupils of the same quarter of the city were required to march in rank and file to the kitharistēs, with naked feet, in any weather, "even if snow fell as densely as sugar from a sieve." The master taught them hymns such as "Terrible Pallas, destroyer of cities," or patriotic songs such as "A call is heard from far away," and others.[147]

On many vase and wall paintings having music teaching as the subject, one frequently sees the teacher seated instructing a single pupil (Illus. 120, 121, 122). If each has an instrument in his hands, this seems to indicate that the pupil, guided by the teacher, is in the process of following his master's demonstration or advice. Usually the pupil is standing before the teacher in a rigid, disciplined attitude, with arms pressed close to his body, like soldiers standing before a superior officer (Illus. 101, 121). Sometimes we see the teacher holding a lyre in his hands, while the pupil reads from a scroll; this seems to indicate that a new song is being studied or rehearsed. (Illus. 118). When teaching the aulos, the teacher is depicted with a barbiton, seemingly accompanying the pupil, who is playing the wind instrument.

The kitharistēs may have given regular weekly or daily lessons. On some vase pictures, we see the next pupil with his instrument, waiting for the end of the previous lesson. For instance, the music master LINOS is thus represented, occupied with the boy IPHICLES, while young HERACLES waits to follow his brother's lesson. (The tragic end of LINOS by the raging HERACLES was mentioned earlier (see Illus. 92). Pupils of noble families were led to the music lesson by the *paidagōgos*, or *paidiotriben*, who carried the instrument. Sometimes this accompanying person was a female employee, or a female slave.

There was no special instruction in singing; the kitharistēs taught both playing and singing. Singing belonged to any music instruction, and was even the more important part of it.

Every well-educated Greek male was expected to be knowledgeable in the art of singing and competent in rhetoric. This raises an interesting question: what were the criteria in classical Greece for "beautiful" singing? There might have been in Athens as well as in Sparta (the two states in which music instruction was compulsory by law) quite a few men without any singing voice, at least according to our Western conception of "singing." In our civilization we often encounter people unable to sing, who are fully aware of this shortcoming. There must have existed such persons in all epochs and in all countries. We might assume that the Greeks did not put too much stress upon the artistic beauty of the singing voice; it seems that the "good will" of the singer was in most cases sufficient to cause people to overlook his vocal shortcomings. Therefore, singers with beautiful voices, such as ORPHEUS, AMPHION, ARION, and others, were highly praised and received almost divine honors.

ARISTOTLE believed that certain "high-sounding" *harmoniai* (or *modoi*) were favorable for the voices of old men. Here we must consider (as discussed earlier), that "high" and "low" in the Oriental conception does not correspond to our Western notions about pitch-relationship. Therefore, what we call downward in the scale was, for the Greek kithara- or harp-player, upward. The range of the Greek instruments corresponded to that of the human voices. If we follow ARISTOTLE's opinion in the light of the generally accepted conception of the Orient, we have to understand that his "high-sounding" *harmoniai* refer to the "bass range" of the human voice.

When the development of musical art in the later period of Greece started to deteriorate and virtuosity got the upper hand, it was PLATO's voice that warned about the dangers of the degeneration of the arts.[148] He considered himself as the advocate of the "good old music," which had the moral power to further *kalokagathia*. He saw music merely in the light of its ethical value, in the possibilities of its educational goals, and disavowed almost completely the pleasure it created and the entertainment it served. He also rejected instrumental music alone, and considered instruments useful merely for accompanying singing. PLATO believed that *harmonia* bestowed *enharmostia* on the leaders of the state and produced a well-disposed citizenry. He also maintained that the proper rhythm leads to *eurhythmia*, a well-balanced order of the state.[149]

PLATO's philosophy sought to curtail considerably the artistic pleasure and enjoyment of the musical performance. Fortunately, this conception of music had no general validity, since, despite the philosophical reservations, the people showed a great predilection for music; just the kind of music the philosophers castigated was for them an inexhaustible source of popular enjoyment. This becomes evident in the writings of ARISTOTLE, who, in contrast to PLATO, acknowledges, besides the educational value of music, its entertaining quality.

> For we all say that music belongs to the most enjoyable things, as well concerning music alone, as it is connected with song.

With this, he admits that besides the moral qualities of music, it also contains a sensually beautiful element.

In summary, it can be said that music, that is, the *Mousic* art, played an important role in Greek education. Philosophers who examined the methods and goals of education were at variance with one another as to whether the teacher should spread knowledge or concentrate on developing the character of youth. Despite the conflicting viewpoints, Greek education was an outstanding synthesis of the intellectual and physical, and provided the young citizen moral and aesthetic education of a high value. It was the first, and remained the unique, attempt in the history of mankind to introduce music as one of the strongest pillars of education. The results are shown in the spirituality that permeated the life of the Greek citizen, whose education was based upon the principle of the *kalokagathia,* a principle never before in Antiquity encountered with such far-reaching application, and never afterwards in the history of human civilization applied with the same ethical intent.

MUSIC AS A PROFESSION

In a state in which music assumed such important functions, there must have been a great demand for musicians of all categories: performers, teachers, builders of instruments, and so on. Consequently, there must have been a great number of professionals devoted to the art.

Such a profession must already have existed at an earlier period, since we know the names of kitharōdes and aulētes who performed in public. There must have been also teachers of music who were paid either by the pupils or by the state (as in Sparta), or by both. Builders of instruments are not mentioned specifically in the classical literature, but in a musical culture that required so great a variety of instruments, such a profession is self-evident.

In public performances, in the cult, in agōns, and the like, the kitharōdes and aulētes appeared in a specific dress, with rich flowing festive garments. This professional attire of performing musicians is represented on vase pictures around 550 B.C.E., but the custom was much more ancient and evidently goes back to archaic times. In that epoch the *aiōdos* was at the same time a poet and singer as well as a kithara player, and also "the leader of the joyous dances." Thus, a single musician might represent all the various facets of his profession. In later times, the profession was divided into different branches, and the musician restricted himself for the most part to his specialty and excelled in a particular field of his art.

In the agōn, the kitharōdos had his assigned place on the bēma; the same was true of the singer using an aulēte. The singer required to perform a solo aria was placed in the center of the stage along with his accompanist.

The poets, who were generally their own composers, usually rehearsed their own works, and received payment, probably from the state. The basic modos of their compositions was Doric, but as time went by, Ionic elements infiltrated, especially in Athens. The first musician who made such a change was SIMONEIDES of Cheos (536–468 B.C.E.), who developed his own style, and achieved victory in Athens even against AESCHYLOS. His nephew, BACCHYLIDES (505–450 B.C.E.), contributed but little to the new style of choir lyrics. The acme of this trend was reached by PINDAROS of Thebes (522–450 B.C.E.), whose four books of "*Epinikoi*" are preserved. These were songs of victory, used when the winners of the contests reentered their home city. Each song had its own melody and its specific poetical rhythm. Since in these songs the epic element prevails, these poems may be classified as choir-ballads.[150]

A special profession was that of the *chorosdidaskalos*, the poet of the choir songs, who at the same time was the composer of the music and the dancing master, who had to arrange the choreography. A similar profession, which had only superficial connection with music, was that of the *tragodidaskalos*, whose task was to rehearse the actors, the hypokritēs of the drama, for their role in the tragedy. This function was similar to that of the stage director (*Regisseur*) of the modern theater. Since, in tragedy as well as in comedy, long phrases were performed with singing, the *tragodidaskalos* had to rehearse these musical passages also with the actors. The poet PHRYNICHOS boasts about his ability as a dancing master:

My art has produced as many dance figures as a stormy night creates waves on the sea.[151]

The musical profession asserted itself mainly at the agōns. Here musicians vied with each other, not only out of love for art, but also to win prizes, the amount of which was sometimes considerable. The kitharōdos and singer AMOIBOS, received an attic talentum (about $6,000) whenever he performed.[152] The aulētes were also highly paid. According to an inscription from Corcyra (the modern Corfu), fifty Corinthian mines (about $5,000) was the reward for three aulētes and three tragic and three comic actors, besides their expenses. In addition, all competent artists received prizes of victory.[153] HERODORUS of Megara, the aulēte, was victorious ten times in the Olympic contests (according to POLLUX, even seventeen times, which is doubtful, however, considering the time element).

How valuable on occasion the prizes were for musicians becomes evident by an inscription, reported by EUCLEIDES, in which there is mention of a wreath for the victor in a kitharōdic contest for which 85 gold drachmas were paid.[154] The value of the drachma was normally $1, that of the gold drachma much higher. In another inscription, reported also by EUCLEIDES, the sums of the prizes for victorious kitharōdes and aulētes are mentioned. The prizes for the winning singers were 2500 drachmas and for winning instrumentalists, 500 drachmas.[155]

Even choirs received prizes. For the plays of Poseidon in the Piräus, LYCOURGOS decreed as recompense for the *cyclic* choir winning the contest at least ten mines; for the second winner, eight; for the third, six mines ($1000, $800, and $600, respectively).

Furthermore, the victor in the great national festivals was extolled as a national hero, and his name was sometimes recorded for posterity. Several cities allotted to the victors large sums of money; some elevated them to the rank of general. The population adored them to such a point that the philosophers had to raise their voices against such intensive adulation. Poets such as SIMONEIDES and PINDAROS were commissioned and highly paid by the admirers of the victors to compose poems in their honor, which were sung by choirs of young men at the processions leading the victor back to his home town. The aulos virtuoso MIDAS, of Agrigentum, was praised by PINDAROS as a conqueror. Sculptors were also commissioned to immortalize the victor in marble or bronze, and some cities gave them for life free quarters and board in the city hall.[156]

Among the kitharōdes who excelled in the agōns, OLYMPOS deserves to be mentioned first (ca. 700 B.C.E.).* He composed about a century before the establishment of the Pythian games in Delphoi, a song (or dithyramb) describing APOLLO's fight with the dragon, which was named *"Nomos Pythikos."*

One of the most famous kitharōdes was TERPANDROS (fl. between 676–659 B.C.E.). He hailed from Antissa on Lesbos and, according to STRABO,[157] he increased the number of strings of the four-stringed lyra to seven, with which he won the prize in the *Mousic* contest in 676.

Among his followers, the most outstanding was the aulēte SAKADAS, who was the victor in the Pythic games in 586 B.C.E., also with a *"Nomos Pythikos,"* the subject of which was similar to the nomos of OLYMPOS. However, while the latter described APOLLO's fight with the help of words, SAKADAS's nomos was a purely instrumental piece, performed on the aulos. POLLUX called it *dēloma,* "demonstration," i.e., the description of APOLLO's fight. It had five parts with the following titles: 1) Preparation for the fight, 2) Challenge, 3) The fight, 4) Song of victory, and 5) Victory dance. For centuries this famous nomos was played again and again in the Pythic plays.

This composition is generally considered as the very first example of "program music." This is true only with certain qualifications. The legend about APOLLO's fight with the dragon was universally known in Greece; everybody listening to its "description" in music could easily supply with his own imagination the well-known facts to the strains of the music. This might have been the cause of the unprecedented success of the nomos, which seems not to have diminished throughout the centuries.

It would be not too farfetched to assume that the presentation of APOLLO's fight might have been supported by dancing and pantomime (i.e., evolutions), and that SAKADAS was merely the composer of the music used to it. However, this is but a surmise.

It happened to the aulēte MIDAS, participating in a Pythic contest, that his mouthpiece was broken. He continued playing the instrument like a vertical flute, a monaulos. Despite this obstacle, he won the prize.

Following SAKADAS's pioneering achievement, there were in ancient Greece, beginning with the fourth century, numerous other attempts at describing "in

---

* As stated earlier, OLYMPOS seems not to have been a historical person. The song attributed to him was evidently spurious.

music" various "programs," by instrumental or vocal means, or both, such as a storm, or gale, or the singing of birds. Of these, the rendering of a sea storm by the aulēte virtuoso TIMOTHEOS was a prominent example. His dithyrambus *"Nauplios"* relied only upon the sounds of his aulos. A competitor of his, the aulēte DORION, mocked him, saying that he had heard bigger sea storms in boiling cooking vessels.[158] The trend of "program music" has continued throughout the Middle Ages until our day. Composers of all categories have tried to stimulate the imaginations of their audiences with associative means, such as titles and descriptions, sometimes supplementing their lyrics with the imitations of actual bird songs or other animal sounds, or with characteristic rhythms.

In the mythology of Greece a number of blind professional singer-musicians are mentioned. One of them was DEMODOKOS at the court of the Phaiakes, who had to be led by a herald, who also carried his instrument (*Odyssey*, VIII, 62 ff.). According to the legend, the gift of singing was bestowed upon him by the Muses as compensation for his blindness. Much worse was the fate of the singer THAMYRIS, the grandson of APOLLO and the son of the nymph ARGIOPE. He achieved such virtuosity in singing and playing that in his presumption he boasted that he surpassed even the Muses in singing. As punishment for his arrogance, the infuriated Muses blinded him and deprived him of his divine gift of singing and playing (*Iliad*, II, 595 ff.). The singer TEIRESIAS had to pay with his eyesight for having revealed in his songs things that humans should not know. According to another version of the myth, he lost his sight when in an unguarded moment he watched ATHENA bathing.

In general it was a dangerous undertaking—at least in mythology—for human beings to enter a *Mousic* contest with divine beings. A typical example of this is the contest between APOLLO and MARSYAS, in which the Muses awarded APOLLO the prize despite MARSYAS's superior performance. In this contest between APOLLO and MARSYAS it was agreed that the loser had to put himself completely in the power of the winner. In Greece, as in the other countries of Antiquity, there were in every contest a winner and a loser; the latter accepted his defeat in the spirit of good sportsmanship. Never was there, however, a more cruel victor than the divine APOLLO, who flayed the defeated MARSYAS alive. This myth is interpreted symbolically as the victory of the Apollinian lyre against the Boeotian, sensual, Asiatic aulos.

In the world of reality, the broadest and most important field for professional musicians was the theater; tragedy, comedy, and satyr-plays used kitharōdes and aulētes in increasing numbers. The dramatic plays took place in open air; the same was true for the ritual actions with music, which were usually held on the steps of the temples, in front of their entrance. The gymnastic exercises, as well as the athletic contests with musical accompaniment, also took place in the open. Thus, the activity of the professional musician was in most cases an open-air performance.

The exceptions were the musical entertainments at the symposia, and the other forms of house music; the latter, however, did not employ professional musicians, except in unusual cases—when, for instance, the thrēnos, the dirge at funerals, was held in the home instead of at the burial ground.

In early Antiquity, and also in Greek musical practice, there were no special buildings set aside for musical performances. These, for the most part, were held in cultic places, in which the participants were at the same time the worshippers and performers.

This changed radically as soon as the musical practice distinguished between active performers and an audience consisting of mere listeners. This necessitated the creation of specific places for concert-like performances, which became more and more frequent. For such purposes, the Hellenes built special halls, which they named *Odeion*. The most famous of such buildings was that erected by PERICLES (ca. 493–429 B.C.E.) on the southeast slope of the Acropolis, which was inaugurated in 442 B.C.E. It was destroyed by fire, but was rebuilt, since it constituted a public necessity for the Athenians. It was constructed in an oblong shape, the interior being broken up by two rows of columns carrying a tent-like roof. The audience was seated in circular rows, on stone seats, embellished by the arms of the city, showing the Athenian owl. A few of these seats remain as the only relics of this first concert hall in the history of human civilization.[159]

In this hall, all kinds of instrumental combinations were presented, such as auloi with kithara or lyra probably along with the syrinx, especially in the more developed form of this instrument, when it had already a substantial number of pipes. Except for the agōns, this was the place where musician-virtuosi gave solo performances in which they dazzled the audiences with their dexterity. However, noise-making instruments were not admitted to the Odeion; these were reserved for the great number of popular entertainments that took place in the streets.

In view of the strict order and lawfulness of Greek life, it was inevitable that the principle of organization should exert its sway upon the civic life of the states. Soon the various professions of the citizenry started to create specific guilds to protect their interests and to select spokesmen to exert their rights. One of these important guilds was that of the brotherhood of musicians, to which all the related professions, such as the dramatic poet-composers, and the music teachers, belonged. The name of this guild was "Dionysian artists" and quite a number of them and their helpers were employed by the municipal or state authorities. A thiasos of the thymēlic choir-dancers, because of being indispensable for dramatic performances, was even freed from military service. DIODOROS reports that thousands of the members of this Dionysian brotherhood were state employees, and that they were exempt not only from military service, but also from paying taxes. They were considered as simple workmen and did not possess citizenship; nevertheless, they constituted a useful segment of the citizenry and were respected accordingly.

Even wandering musicians were organized in guilds, as is proven by an inscription in Delphoi.[160] They were completely equipped with everything necessary for carrying out their itinerant profession: tents, mechanic's tools (evidently to keep their instruments in good shape), even water-skin bottles, provided for places where there was a lack of drinking water.[161] Other wandering groups of musicians also possessed their own professional equipment, and were able to move from place to place.

Historical records furnish us with highly relevant data about such wandering groups of musical and theatrical artists. At the celebration of ALEXANDER on the occasion of his victory over DARIUS, he employed no less than 3000 musicians and actors. The feast was organized by CHARES, one of ALEXANDER's generals, and it is significant that the guilds of musicians could muster in a relatively short time a great number of musical artists. The celebration took nine days; it is not difficult to imagine the extensive role the musicians evidently played in entertaining the troops.

When HEPHAISTION, a friend of ALEXANDER, died, a funeral celebration was

344 arranged, lasting three days. For this, also, a great number of musicians were engaged.

arranged, lasting three days. For this, also, a great number of musicians were engaged.

Besides ALEXANDER, the kings of Cyprus frequently summoned singers and musicians for their own entertainment, and also for the pubilc feasts and plays.

The musical guilds of the different regions of the country maintained close ties with each other and undertook frequent journeys to visit each other's countries. During such pilgrimages, they used to sing songs in the hypophrygian modos based upon their *Harmotios Nomos,* a passionate melody using the same mode as that in which the songs of the *Oresteia* were performed.[162]

The guilds provided also for the funerals of their members. In the chapter devoted to Roman musical life, it will be shown that there existed entire burial chambers, in which only members of the musicians' guild were entombed.

In the ruins of the theater at Teos, an inscription was found that seems to indicate that the general quarters of the Greek Dionysian brotherhood were located in this city. For some unknown reason, the guild of the theatrical poets and musicians of the city contracted debts and could not repay them at the appointed time, a circumstance that, according to the law, would have caused its members to lose the right to perform in public. Since the Dionysian festivities were approaching, the guild applied to the city fathers for help. In a secret session of the Synod, the leaders of the city found ways and means to assist the guild in its financial predicament, so that the festivities could take place without further complications.[163] The inscription lists the individuals who, after this solution, were employed for the festival: mechanics for the scenic apparatus (in our modern term, stage hands), a tragic poet, a tragic actor, a kitharōdos, two aulētes, two players of "melodramatics" (probably hypokritēs, additional actors) for the tragedy, two actors for the comedy, and an additional kithara player as accompanyist for a singer. Another passage of the inscription indicates that the number of these persons had to be multiplied by three, since these were only the foremen of each group.[164]

To these guilds belonged also the aulētridēs, the aulos-playing girls, mainly of Syrian origin, who in Antiquity flooded the entire Mediterranean basin. They were mostly girls of poor families, who made their living in this way. Their aulos-playing was merely a pretext for a less honorable trade. There were quite a number of them in Athens, and a great many in Piräus, Athens' port (as in all ports of all times). They had their own professional organization and, in order to exercise their trade, they had to pay a small tax and received a regular "license." In Rome they were called *ambubajae;* I will tell more about them in the following chapter.

As mentioned above, the main brotherhood of musical artists had its headquarters in Teos; it had branches everywhere in the antique world by which they maintained permanent connections with each other. Such branches existed in all larger cities of Greece, in Macedonia, Palestine, Phrygia, Syria, Italy, and even in Gaul.[165] The preserved inscriptions furnish the names of 53 places, large and small, in which such brotherhoods existed. According to its name and purpose, it was exclusively a musical and theatrical union designed to protect the interest of its members; in reality, there were more than a dozen different professional organizations, which were only loosely connected with music and art. For instance, the tent-makers belonged to it, because they made the necessary accommodations for the itinerant musicians and theatrical groups; also the masons, who worked on temple buildings; the manufacturers of instruments; the tailors, who made the theatrical costumes; the decorators, for the scenic apparatus, and others. The teachers of music, of course, also belonged to this organization.[166]

The patron saint of this widely spread union was the god DIONYSOS who, in the conception of the Greeks, ennobled humanity and spread enjoyment. Consequently, all the musicians and the related members of the huge organization called themselves "Dionysian" artists. The emperor HADRIAN (76–139 C.E.) amalgamated all the still-existing societies into a single union. These Dionysian guilds were the real carriers of musical practice in the post-classic era.

Thus, the musical profession in Greece shows a homogeneous and high standard of artistry, strict organization in guilds, joint liability, and care for the deceased. Although there are no records in this regard, it may be assumed that they had also some provision for the welfare of families of deceased members. In view of the social consciousness of the musicians, such an assumption is not unwarranted.

In conclusion, it can be said that the Dionysian artists represented an important segment of the economic structure of Greece. They received strong support by SOLON whose *ius coeundi* guaranteed their unity for the protection of their professional interests. Of all these brotherhoods, that of Athens was the most important and retained its importance even when Greece became a Roman province. The advent of Christianity put an end to the organization of musicians' unions, and only in our time do we encounter similar organizations having as their aim the economic protection of artists and the preservation of their rights. Thus, in all artistic matters, Greece paved the way also in the domain of the social welfare of the musicians and assumed in this respect a leading role in the history of mankind.

Could we in some mystic way resuscitate Greek music and reproduce it on our modern instruments, our ears, spoiled by centuries of advanced music-making, would probably be highly disappointed. The music of ancient Greece would sound to us primitive, monotonous, and possibly insignificant, and we would be unable to understand how a highly civilized nation could enjoy to such an extent this "primitive" music. If we deduce from the historical fact that the force of tradition compelled the Greek nation to cling to their once-established music practice, we might explain this phenomenon by the completely different perceptive ear (*Hörfähigkeit*) of the Orientals and their different psychological approach to their musical manifestations. In spite of the fact that Greece belonged geographically to Europe, it was inseparably connected with the civilization of the Near East, and had not only its own musical norms, but also its own music aesthetics. Just as it is not possible to reproduce ancient, or even modern, Oriental music (e.g., the Arabic) exactly, in our Western musical notation based on the tempered scale, so it is not given to the limited receptive capacity of our modern ears to discern the many micro-intervals of that period and apply to them our system of notation.

I have to omit in this investigation the complicated music system and the theory of the *harmoniai*, as well as the method of application of the Greek scales. This is a science in itself, outside the scope of my study, which is restricted to the social implications of music in the life of Greece. Its basic elements will be discussed later. Here it should be mentioned only that it is self-evident that a nation which developed such a complicated music theory could not do without a system of musical notation. In fact, Greek musical notation is the first in the history of civilization, one about which we are amply informed.[167] The Hellenes had even two different types of notation, one for singing and one for instrumental music. As signs for notes, they used mainly the letters of their alphabet and certain symbols of an ancient Oriental idiom. After the classical period, the usefulness of musical notation diminished, since, according to later views, the *note* had no direct relationship to the *tone*, just as the written letter was subordinate to the living word. The Greeks considered the word of mouth superior to the written text.

In Greek music, the symbols of notation were placed above the words in one straight line. In addition to the symbols representing the tones themselves, there were signs indicating the duration of tones (lengths of two, three, four, and five "beats"), as well as signs for pauses or rests. The meter and the rhythm of a melodic strain was determined not so much by these signs as by the prosody of the text.

Greek music was homophonous; polyphony and harmony as we understand them were generally unknown in the music of the Orient, and also in that of Greece. However, HICKMANN has discovered polyphony in the music of Egypt (see note 182); in the music of the Romans there are also some indications of a primitive kind of polyphony, called by them *paraphonia*, and some scholars think that some traces of polyphony can be detected also in Greek music; for instance, where heterophōnia is mentioned. However, it cannot be said unequivocally whether this term refers to real polyphony, or merely to a certain kind of interpretation. Thus, the question of whether Greek music knew any type other than monodic music must remain undecided, for the time being at least.

The accompaniment of singing with instruments must have been rather simple. If the accompaniment was furnished by stringed instruments, it consisted mainly in some isolated tones, stressing certain words, or marking the end of the verses. The seven (in later times eleven) strings of the lyra or barbiton were not sufficient to follow a melody note for note. Even the magadis with its twenty strings was not able to do this, since it had in fact only ten different tones, the others being duplicated in the octave (*dia pasōn*). Even less were the auloi capable of following a melody, since their few finger-holes did not afford a sufficiently wide melodic range.

Greek musical practice centered in singing; every class and rank sang, the aristocracy and the common people, professional singers, and amateurs without specific musical training, well-rehearsed choirs, and popular groups of the komoi. On the Olympus there was singing also; APOLLO sang with the accompaniment of the kithara. Singing was common with the Muses, who may be considered a divine choral society. The literature mentions even the singing of animals such as birds, swallows, and swans. But this kind of "singing" has to be understood as only metaphorical, as in other ancient Oriental languages.

POETS, COMPOSERS, AND WRITERS ABOUT MUSIC

We owe to HOMER everything we know about Greek music of archaic times. In his epics he preserved all the beautiful legends about musical art, gave a comprehensive picture of musical practices in his mythological narrations, thus transmitting the musical lore of ancient times to posterity.

Was HOMER a living person or a legend? Are the two great epics, the *Iliad* and *Odyssey*, his works, or were the poems transmitted orally from generation to generation and written down only in later times? For many centuries these questions have occupied the minds of innumerable scholars, who have never arrived at a definite solution. It is significant that even in Antiquity there were some doubts about HOMER's authorship. JOSEPHUS says, for instance:

> It is even thought that Homer did not leave his songs in a written form, but that they were preserved in the memory of many generations, before they were united in later times.[168]

As a matter of fact, we do not know anything about HOMER; either where he was born (five or six cities vied for this honor), or when he lived (the epoch of his lifetime oscillates between the fourteenth and eighth century B.C.E.). Just as his person is in doubt, his name seems not to be authenticated by any reliable record. There are all kinds of hypotheses concerning how the name could have come into being. One of them is that in the Greek *Theogony* the Muses sang together (in Greek *homēreusai*); less credible is the theory that a messenger was accompanied (*homērēsē*) to the city by a swineherd. It is more convincing that the name HOMER was not that of a single person, but the term for a poetic society, called Homēroi, so that the name could well have been used for one of its members.[169] There are also doubts about HOMER's blindness. It seems there is a mistaken identification with the blind singer DEMODOKOS at the court of the Phaiakes.

The first historical notice about the homeric text occurs in a legend reported by CICERO, PAUSANIAS, and others, according to which the songs of HOMER, originally scattered, were unified, ordered by PEISISTRATOS in Athens, in the sixth century B.C.E. In this way they received their final form as we know them today. An earlier Greek version asserts that HIPPARCHOS, the elder son of PEISISTRATOS, was the person first responsible for bringing the poems to Athens, and that he directed that they be read by rhapsōdes, in relays, in the Panathenic festivals.

In HERODOTUS's times, not only the *Iliad* and the *Odyssey* were ascribed to HOMER, but a number of anonymous poems, such as the "Cypria," the two epics about the war with Thebes, *Thebais* and *Epigonoi*, and also the *Hymns*. These last are attributed to HOMER even by modern scholarship. The Greeks did not like anonymity; thus, besides the two great epics, a number of anonymous poems were attributed to HOMER.

Besides HOMER, a more prosaically disposed epic poet, HESIOD (846–777 B.C.E.), deserves mention. Originally, he was an agricultural laborer and shepherd, who, while tending his sheep at the mountain of Helicon, dreamt that the Muses placed the soul of a poet in his body. Whether this dream is based on reality, or whether it was merely invented by him (or posterity) to justify his calling as a poet, cannot be ascertained. At any rate, he wrote poems and sang them with such marked success that it is asserted that he won victories in the agōns, even against HOMER.[170]

Other famous poets and singers of nomoi were the aulētes OLYMPOS (ca. 700 B.C.E.);[171] CLONAS of Tegea in Arkadia (fifth century B.C.E.), who is considered to be the creator of the aulōdic nomos; POLYMNESTOS of Colophon (sixth century B.C.E.); and SAKADAS of Argos (ca. 586 B.C.E.). Evidently, in this epoch, the ancient art of the aiōdos split into a declamatory-reciting branch (the rhapsōdos), and a more pronouncedly musical class (the kitharōdes).

The first and most important representative of the kitharōdic nomos-composers was TERPANDROS (literally: "the delighter of man," ca. 675–659 B.C.E.). He hailed from Antissa on Lesbos, where he created a school for kitharōdes. As STRABO reports,[172] he was the first to introduce a lyra with seven strings, replacing the one with the usual four strings, thus assuring its permanent acceptance in musical practice. It was a foregone conclusion that with this richer-sounding instrument he was able to earn the victory as a kitharōde in the *Mousic* agōns of 676 B.C.E.

He was already famous as a kitharōdos in Lesbos, but having killed a man in a fight, he was banned from the island.

About 700 B.C.E., allegedly due to an oracle of Delphoi, he was invited to Sparta to prepare the choir for a *Mousic* contest of APOLLO in Carneia. He was glad to accept the invitation, participated as a kitharōdos in this contest (in 676 B.C.E.), and won the victory. After this he settled in Sparta, where he lived out his remaining years as a music teacher and *chorosdidaskalos*. The powerful effect of his improved instrument is reflected in a tale based partly on history, partly on legend. According to this, TERPANDROS succeeded by playing his lyre to calm down a revolt of the citizenry of Sparta. It seems, however, that this event has to be understood merely symbolically, attesting to the ethico-political effect of music.

In spite of his merits as a musician, the archly conservative city fathers of Sparta censured him for having increased the number of strings on his lyre and—as a warning—ordered that the instrument be nailed to the wall. For how long, it is not said, but evidently this reprimand had no lasting effect. In a later epoch, TIMOTHEOS increased the number of strings to eleven, but—as PLUTARCH reports—he was not allowed to participate in the agōns of Sparta until he removed the "offensive" strings.

A pupil of TERPANDROS, the aulēte CAPION is credited with having changed the form of the kithara (or lyra) which, from then on, was built according to his improvement.

Whether this is merely an anecdote, or whether it represents a fact, there exists a tale about how TERPANDROS lost his life. In a drinking bout, while he was singing, one of his companions threw a fig at him which lodged in his trachea and on which he choked.[173]

At Lesbos there lived a group of important lyric poetesses, SAPPHO, MYRTIS of Anthedon, CORINNA of Thebes (or Corinth), and others, who accompanied their poems with stringed instruments. SAPPHO established a regular music school on the island, in which the curriculum consisted of lyre playing, singing, and dancing, besides—evidently—instruction in composing new songs.

In this epoch flourished, among other lyric poets, ALCAIOS (ca. 600 B.C.E.), ANACREON of Teos (ca. 560–475 B.C.E.), IBYCOS of Rhegium (middle of the sixth century), and PINDAROS of Thebes (522–450 B.C.E.). Of their numerous poems only fragments are preserved—without their music. This lesbic group of poet-singers wanted to create a new, more popular form of poem, which differed markedly from the older, classical style and meter.

PINDAROS was the scion of an aristocratic family of Thebes that traced its ancestors to archaic times, among which there were allegedly several heroes whom he glorified in his poems. He owed his knowledge in music to his uncle, a famous aulos-player. His odes were composed in honor of princes and rich people, and for a period he was singer in residence at several princely courts. He set his own poems to music and taught them to choral groups. His literary output was highly varied; he composed hymns and paianes for Dionysian feasts, partheniai for girls' choirs, enkomia for famous men, skolia for banquets, thrēnoi for funerals, and epinikia for the victors in the Panhellenic contests. Of all these, only forty of his odes are preserved; they carry the names of the winners in the contests. However, nothing remained of their music. He must have been rather wealthy, since it is related that the Athenians paid him 10,000 drachmas (about $10,000) for a dithyramb in which he glorified their city. He lived in Thebes and reached his 80th year. After his death Athens erected a monument in his honor at public expense. In 335 B.C.E. ALEXANDER punished the revolting Thebes by completely burning down the city; he gave orders to his soldiers, however, to spare the house in which PINDAROS lived and died.

The most famous of the lesbic poets was ANACREON (ca. 560–475 B.C.E.), who was born in the city of Teos in Ionia (Asia Minor). Like many of his contemporary poet-musicians, he lived at the courts of great tyrants. These showed an iron hand in state affairs, but were evidently ardent sponsors of art and artists. They kept for themselves real *"Mousic courts,"* and assembled artists of all categories. This may constitute an early parallel to Renaissance Italy, in which period autocratic princes were avid sponsors of the arts and sciences.

In the preserved fragments of ANACREON's poems, only stringed instruments are mentioned, the barbiton, pēktis, and magadis, a sign that these were the preferred instruments of the lesbic circle. In an epitaph it is said that ANACREON did not cease to use the barbiton even in the underworld.[174] According to questionable records he even invented this instrument; this is evidently a myth.

An ardent promoter of music was ARCHILOCHOS of Paros (675–630 B.C.E.). He led the life of a mercenary soldier and a singer at the same time, and was called accordingly a "singing hero." His biographical data are supported by the fact that he described correctly a solar eclipse that occurred on April 6, 648 B.C.E. His compositions are distinguished by more sprightly tempi, and he was also the first to introduce into his accompaniments elaborate ornamentations (*krousis hypo tēn ōdēn*). He is credited with being the creator of the iambic lyrics.

According to PLUTARCH's testimony, the period of the "new" music was inaugurated by THALETAS of Gortyn (ca. 670 B.C.E.), who was the first to compose and set to music hyporchēmata (choir songs to be danced). His home town seems to indicate that the music of Sparta was based upon that of Crete, as we know already by the journey of LYCOURGOS to this island. THUCYDIDES still mentions the old Spartan custom of marching into battle with the sound of auloi (V, 70), a custom LYCOURGOS might have observed in Crete. THALETAS was invited to Sparta by LYCOURGOS in order to combat an epidemic (pestilence?) with his string playing, a significant example of the superstitious belief in the healing power of music. Allegedly THALETAS was successful in his attempt. Throughout his life he remained in Sparta where he introduced gymnic choir dances (*gymnopaidia*).

TIMOTHEOS of Miletos (449–359 B.C.E.) was the typical representative of a new, richer musicality, proven by the fact that, in a report of ION of Chios (a contemporary of SOPHOCLES), he introduced the daring innovation of an eleven-stringed kithara (or lyra). According to PHERECRATES, there were even twelve strings. This could not go unpunished in an arch-conservative state such as Lacedaimonia. He was accused of being a "revolutionary." ATHENAIOS reports about this (see above).

The acquittal of TIMOTHEOS implied that he was allowed to play, and possibly to teach his instrument. At public contests, however, the additional strings had to be curtailed, probably owing to the sense of fairness of the Spartans, for a so much richer sounding instrument might have constituted a marked disadvantage for the other contestants.

TIMOTHEOS increased the differences between the kitharōdic nomos and the dithyrambos by introducing into his kitharōdy a technique of embellishments, which probably raised the idea of "heterophonia" in Greek music. This, however, was quite different from our notion of heteronomy or polyphony.

PHRYNIS of Mytilene, too, augmented the number of strings (to nine) and, furthermore, mixed several *harmoniai* without discrimination, causing him also to be considered a "revolutionary." (Every innovator was called so.) The new style must have been acclaimed by the audiences, since he won many contests in Athens. Another "sinner" against the classic trend was MELANIPPIDES; he was reproached for having endangered the poetic content of the songs by too greatly extending the musical forms and for using an exaggerated kind of ornamentation.[176]

Among TIMOTHEOS's followers were, besides MELANIPPIDES, CINESIAS (ca. 450–390 B.C.E.), CREXOS (fifth century B.C.E.) and the extremely popular TELESTES of Salinus, who was a famous aulos player. TELESTES won the victory for the first time with a dithyrambos in 402 B.C.E. in the *Panathenic* festival. However, he committed a heresy against the official mythology by declaring that it was a lie that ATHENA repudiated the aulos. Since, according to the mythology, APOLLO learned from ATHENA how to play the aulos, TELESTES' assertion might have had no serious consequences for him. His heresy was not an isolated case; the poetess of Boeotia (or Corinth), CORINNA, also maintained that the mythology might have been in error, since it explicitly states that APOLLO was taught to play the aulos by ATHENA.

Although the Greek nation as an entity held the *Mousic* arts in high honor, as time went by, several tribes of the nation developed different degrees of "musicality." In general, the Dorians were credited with the "classical" approach to the *Mousic* arts; therefore, the *Dorian* harmonia was considered as the most appropriate for the education of the youth. It seems, however, that the Ionians and the neighboring Aeolians manifested a more conspicuous musical spirit and a richer musical phantasy than the strictly conservative Dorians.

There is a widespread belief that the Spartans did not contribute anything of their own to the musical art, since in Sparta music was subordinated to the welfare of the state and the conduct of war. This is only partially true. Prior to LYCOURGOS, who introduced the warlike spirit to Sparta, Sparta was, just like any other Greek city, full of music and singing. In earlier times, probably, it might even have surpassed Athens in the love and practice of music. Only after the life of Sparta was transformed to a point where the highest virtue was the conduct of war, and everything else was subordinated to this goal, was music displaced from its previously dominant position. Not only were all others than the Doric *harmonia* banished and all other modoi prohibited, but any deviation from the Doric was punished by law. It is evident that under such restrictions the *Mousic* arts must have been strongly handicapped.

Most of the musicians who lived and worked in Sparta were foreigners. This is true of TERPANDROS, mentioned earlier, whose work was continued by TYRTAIOS (middle of the seventh century B.C.E.) of Aphidna in Lacedaimonia (or perhaps Attica). His songs were designed to impart to the youth of Sparta the idea that to die in war represented an enviable heroic fate. LEONIDAS, King of Sparta, said of him "that he understood how to inflame the souls of the youth."[177]

Among the younger generation of poet-composers, PHYLOXENOS of Cythera is outstanding (435–380 B.C.E.). His vocal works have the characteristics of fully developed choral cantatas, with inserted virtuoso solo-arias. The kitharōdic nomos, a form of vocal composition with several contrasting movements, was introduced by PHRYNIS of Mytilene (ca. 450 B.C.E.) referred to earlier for his "revolutionary" achievements in augmenting the number of strings of his instrument and some unorthodox methods of the style of his compositions.

The earliest representative of the fully developed choir-lyrics was ALCMAN of Sardes (fifth century B.C.E.). His official position in Sparta was that of chorosdidaskolos (choir-master). The Spartans particularly liked his *"Parthēniai,"* poems and compositions for women's choirs, certainly a peculiarity in a city in which the laws and the education were based upon military virtues. These choir-songs probably had a ritual-religious background, which might explain their popularity. Besides, he wrote a great number of secular songs, hymns and paianes, wedding songs, and songs for symposia, also love songs and drinking songs, with an amorous, even erotic, slant.

With him began the line of poets of love-songs, which reached its zenith with ANACREON. ALCMAN's name was at the head of the "nine lyric poets," designated by the literary clan of Alexandria as the foremost poets of the classical period: ALCMAN, ALCAIOS, SAPPHO, STESICHOROS, IBYCOS, ANACREON, SIMONEIDES, PINDAROS, and BACCHYLIDES.

We owe most of what we know about Greek music to the writings of the great philosophers. The golden age of writers on music started after the Persian wars. The pioneers in this field were DAMON of Athens, the music teacher and adviser of PERICLES, DEMOCRITOS (born ca. 460 B.C.E.), and GLAUCOS of Rhegium, a contemporary of DEMOCRITOS. GLAUCOS was considered the first historian of music in classical Greece.

The father of Greek musical science was PYTHAGORAS of Samos (570–500 B.C.E.), the founder of the mathematic and acoustic elements of music theory. Until his time, the Greek scale was based upon the strings of the kithara and the pitch relations as established by the holes of the aulos. PYTHAGORAS was the first to determine the acoustical basis of sound on a scientific basis by mathematical calculations. He developed his theories orally only, but his pupils recorded them, and while merely fragments are preserved (the authenticity of which is highly contested), the knowledge about the overtone series, or "chord of nature," is attributed to him. Among his pupils are PHILOLAOS (ca. second half of the fifth century B.C.E.), and HIPPASOS of Metapont. Another of these writers about PYTHAGORAS's findings was LASOS of Hermione (ca. 500 B.C.E.), who was a professional musician, but who also did research in music theory. Unfortunately, nothing is preserved of his work. We do not even know

its title. More is known about ARCHYTAS of Tarent (ca. 400–350 B.C.E.), who
also belonged to the school of the Pythagoraeans. The entire science of music
projected by this school has been summed up by CLAUDIOS PTOLEMAIOS (second
century C.E.) in his comprehensive *"Harmonika."* To him we owe our knowledge
of the early and the later approach of the Greeks to musical science. His treatise
was completed by numerous commentators, among whom PORPHYRIOS (233–
304 C.E.) and the Syrian JAMBLICHOS (second century C.E.) are the most note-
worthy.

Other followers of PYTHAGORAS were the mathematicians EUCLEIDES (ca. 300
B.C.E.), ERASTOTHENES (275–194 B.C.E.), GAUDENTIUS (second century C.E.),
and NICOMACHOS (second century C.E.). All these presented only the mathematical and acoustical side of music.

The greatest merit, however, for the creation and development of the musical
science of the Greeks belongs to the philosophers PLATO (427–347 B.C.E.),
ARISTOTLE (384–322 B.C.E.), and their pupil ARISTOXENOS of Tarent (ca. 320–
300 B.C.E.), called in Antiquity simply *ho mousikos,* "the musician." All these
writers have left us ample information about the classical period of Greek
musical science and practice. True, PLATO himself was no expert in music, yet
he developed basic thoughts about the influence of music upon the mind and
character of man, and is the originator of the doctrine of ethics in music.[178]

In contradistinction to PLATO, ARISTOTLE understood *Mousikē* as music in
the proper sense. According to his conception, music possessed by its very
nature the faculty to influence the soul of the listener in a specific way.

Among other writer-philosophers, who left us records about Greek musical
practice, THEOPHRASTUS (372–287 B.C.E.) should be mentioned, who attributed
to music special healing powers (see below).[179] A historical work on music by
HERACLEIDES PONTICUS (ca. 390–ca. 310 B.C.E.) was preserved in fragments by
PLUTARCH. Furthermore, works of PHILODEMOS of Gedara (ca. 110–40 B.C.E.)
and DIOGENES of Seleucia on the Tigris (ca. 240–ca. 130 B.C.E.) contain valuable
contributions for understanding of Greek music.

Outstanding among the later theorists was ARISTEIDES QUINTILIANUS (first to
second century C.E.). His work *"Peri Mousikē"* ("About Music") in three volumes
is one of our most important sources for the ancient aesthetics of music. PLU-
TARCH of Chaironeia (ca. 46–ca. 120 C.E.) left us an attempt at the history of
music in dialogue form, which, however, is rather confused; furthermore, his
authorship is contested. Yet, whether he was its author or not, the treatise contains much valuable information about the music of Antiquity.

In works of writers who were not professional musicians, as well as in dic-
tionaries and descriptions of the mores and customs of the Greeks, we find
much valuable information about their music, as, for example, in GALLIUS,
ATHENAIOS, JULIUS POLLUX, HESYCHIOS, SUIDAS, and others.

Numerous other writers of Antiquity have left works about the theory of
music; they belong, however, to Roman Antiquity. We will scrutinize them
in the subsequent section.

I mentioned earlier the belief in the magic power of music extant in the
Orient, and also in Greece. Music had a mystical displacing power (see the
myth of AMPHION (EURIPIDES, *Phönic,* 823 ff.), but more important in the consciousness of the Hellenes was its faculty of healing (*Odyssey* XIX, 457 ff.).

Prior to the Homeric epics, information about the magic powers of music was even more widely disseminated than was the case in the Homeric world. The divine physician in HOMER, the healer PAIEON, is merely the personification of the healing song (paian) which, as time went by, became, through hypostasis, the physician himself. The paian-call was, in the cult of the Delphic APOLLO, an invocation for healing.[180]

As mentioned above, the myth attributes to THALETAS of Gortyn, who was invited to Sparta by LYCOURGOS, the faculty of subduing an epidemic through his paian. Whether he succeeded is not divulged by our sources. The healing power of the aulos against bodily sickness, about which ATHENAIOS informs us,[181] has been attributed to THEOPHRASTUS.

Music that heals sicknesses also had the faculty of chasing away evil spirits, although—according to ancient belief—this could be achieved much more effectively by loud noise, especially by the use of noise-making instruments. At sacrificial rites, the chasing away of demons was originally supposed to be achieved by the loud outcry of the women, called *ololygō;* later, the sounds of piercing auloi were used for this purpose.

By its power of healing, music could also achieve moral purification and recovery (*katharsis*) (see below). The main instruments for this purpose were the Apollinian strings. Nevertheless, even auloi could be useful for subduing certain conditions of the mind and the soul, so, for instance, auloi could heal rage, madness, passionate love, and even bodily sickness, if properly used. PLATO mentions the healing of corybantic frenzy through dance and the music of auloi (*Laws,* 790 d–e), and in the *Symposium* (215 c) he mentions that ALCIBIADES compares the sayings of SOCRATES to the healing power of the aulosplaying of the mythic aulētes OLYMPOS and MARSYAS. Thus, the belief in this power of music survived until the rationally minded epoch of the Greek philosophers, and beyond.

The music of the Greeks was homophonous. True, polyphony of some kind was known in ancient Egypt,[182] but the writings of the Greek philosophers and theorists of music do not contain anything referring to playing or singing other than in unison. Alternating between solo and choir-singing was widely used, but nothing indicates that this was done in other than in a homophonic way. The choir groups were often divided into two half choirs; TYRTAIOS even used three choir groups on one occasion, as POLLUX reports, divided according to age (children, young men, and grownups). In this instance the singing was performed in unison.

The accompaniment by instruments did not always follow the vocal line— sometimes it was more or less independent, which created the idea of heterophōnia in Greek music which, however, cannot be compared with today's notion of heterophony. The instrumental accompaniment was called *krousis*, but this term cannot be identified with what we understand by "accompaniment."[183] A significant passage in ARISTOTLE's *Problems*[184] seems to indicate that the krousis was carried out in two voices. The lower voice followed the vocal line in unison; the upper voice was said to have its own accompanying "melody." This may refer only to certain embellishments or ornaments by the accompanying instrument, which were slightly different from the vocal melody. A second, independent melodic line cannot be assumed; this would be contrary to the basic conception of the Greeks about their music.

THE PRESERVED GREEK MUSICAL RELICS

Greek musical practice left us only a few, mostly incomplete documents. Their enumeration follows:

1) The beginning of PINDAR's First Pythian Ode (allegedly from the fifth century B.C.E.), first published by ATHANASIUS KIRCHER in his *Musurgia Universalis* (1650). No original source for it can be found; furthermore, the style of the piece belongs ostensibly to a time later than that of PINDAR. It is therefore assumed that it is spurious, or even a forgery.

2) A fragment of the first *stasimon* (choir-singing at the same place) from the *Orestes,* verses 330 ff. (fifth century B.C.E.), written on a papyrus, discovered in 1892 in the collection of the Austrian archduke RAINER.

3) A small instrumental exercise in an anonymous writing about music; published in 1841.

4) A fragment, possibly from a tragedy, written on papyrus (ca. 250 B.C.E.), in the Cairo Museum.

5) & 6) Two practically completely preserved hymns in honor of APOLLO, chiseled on a wall of the Athenian treasure house of Delphoi (ca. middle of the second century B.C.E.), discovered in 1893 (Illus. 123).

7) Skolion (drinking song) of the "Sicilian" SEIKILOS (second or first century B.C.E.), chiseled in stone on a stele of a tomb at Tralleis in Asia Minor. Discovered in 1883.

8) The so-called Berlin Papyrus, first published in 1918. It is written on the reverse side of a Latin military document dating from 156 C.E., according to the contents of the Latin text. The Greek text, on the reverse side, was evidently added some years later.

Besides this text, with which we will deal in the following chapter, the papyrus contains three musical fragments, the first a paian to APOLLO, the second a poem alluding to the suicide of AJAX the elder, caused by the deceit of ODYSSEUS, the third, containing only one line of music, which cannot be correctly deciphered.

The musical notes are partially vocal, partially instrumental, and are similar to those found in other musical relics. In the first fragment there are 12 lines of vocal notes, followed by three lines of instrumental notes; in the second, four lines of vocal melody and, similarly, three lines of instrumental notes (Illus. 124).

HERMANN ABERT made a thorough analysis of these musical fragments and added a transcription in modern notation, which gives us a clear idea of these musical relics:[185]

9) Hymn to Helios.

10) Hymn to Nemesis.

11) Hymn to the Muse. All three were composed in the second century C.E. by MESOMEDES (the last one may be by DIONYSIOS, and published—without musical transcription—in 1581 by VINCENZO GALILEO in his *Dialogo della Musica antica.*

12) An early Christian hymn with antique music notes, written on a papyrus (end of the third century C.E.), discovered at Oxyrhinchos in Egypt. Although very short, this hymn, the only preserved document from the time of the transition from Greece of Antiquity to Christian Hellenism, is highly important for the evaluation of the early period of Christian music.[186]

13) For the sake of completeness, the so-called Hibeh Papyrus should be mentioned. It was discovered at the Egyptian town Hibeh in 1906, and was written on the reverse side of a discarded Latin military document (dealt with already in no. 8 of this list) in the so-called Berlin Papyrus. It was written in 156 C.E., according to the contents of the Latin document; the Greek text was evidently added several years later.

The Hibeh Papyrus is an important contribution to the existing controversy between PLATO's and ARISTOTLE's theories concerning the psychological effect of music upon the attitude of humans and the different approach to this phenomenon developed by the Sophists. We will examine this document in greater detail in the following chapter.

THE ETHOS OF GREEK MUSIC

Greek music was, at least until the end of the classical period, exclusively utilitarian music, imbedded in every day life and of service to the various functions required by religious, state, and social institutions. Whether for ritualistic purposes, for the education of the youth, or for public or private festivities, music was specifically destined to be performed, rather than listened to. In the ritual, music was used by the individual for the purpose of honoring the gods. In education, musical activity served to develop the character of the youth and enabled him to participate in the *kyklios choros*, which subsequently helped him gain admittance to the community of citizens. Popular music-making was also based upon active rather than passive participation. In the *Mousic* agōns, listening to music for enjoyment was completely relegated to the background, since the main purpose was that of the contest. In every century of Greek life, music remained a heteronomous art phenomenon, in which both the individual and community participated as part of the social structure.

Because music in Greece was so connected with general life, we may legitimately speak of "musical life" in Greece. At the summit of their classical period, the Greeks considered their music as a life value and not as an art phenomenon for fostering sentiment and pleasure.[187]

This attitude shifted radically at the end of the classical period (at the turn of the fifth to the fourth century), when music changed from a utilitarian form to an art-form, mainly through the gradual rise of virtuosity. This was first manifested when instrumentalists began to display instrumental techniques of high achievement, and then it led to music as a profession. At this stage, music gradually lost its heteronomous characteristics, becoming a phenomenon destined to be listened to, at first in appreciation of the artist's achievement. Later, however, it was regarded merely as a means of pleasure. The basic approach of the audience to the musical art changed, thus creating an entirely new element in the enjoyment of music. It became an "autonomous" art product, to be listened to and enjoyed.

Through this mutation, the emphasis on musical performance shifted from active participation to the achievements of the soloist. Singing was governed, as before, by the unity of poetic text and melos, but in instrumental music, the performer was not bound to the accent and rhythmic structure of the lyrics;

thus, a new art-form was created. "Music without words" spread irresistibly, although eventually it was reduced to "music for amusement," at first hesitantly, but still based upon the Greek ideal of the intrinsic value of the *Mousic* art. Later, particularly in the Graeco-Roman period, it was completely detached from the original life values of Greek music. We could characterize this by the modern term, *absolute music,* if music at this stage had still followed artistic goals. As history shows, this was no longer the case. Music deteriorated to a mere sensual enticement (one of many others) and exclusively served the pleasure of the masses (more about this subject will be said in examining the music of the Romans).

All this must be emphasized before we turn to the examination of the ethos of Greek music.

The Greek term *ethos* has remained a foreign word in all other languages. While its derivatives (ethics, ethical, etc.) have become generally accepted and understood notions, the use of the term *ēthos* is still quite unclear. *Ēthos* expresses certain universal characteristics inherent in music, and also indicates the general or objective elements of an art phenomenon in contrast to its subjective characteristics, which express a basic philosophical attitude termed *pathos.*

The ethos of Greek music was defined by Greek philosophers in this way:

> music should not be judged for its faculty to afford entertainment, but according to its ability to create in man the 'moral-good.'[188]

As PLATO stipulated, the center of the entire doctrine of art is not the musically "beautiful," but the musically "good." A musical piece should not give the listener mere artistic pleasure, but it should contribute to his development in becoming a morally better human being. The presupposition of this entire doctrine is the assumption of the mysterious connection existing between the world of tones and the human psyche, which creates the wondrous effects that make music one of the most important factors in the moral education of man.[189]

Where are the historical sources for the doctrine of the ethos? Even a scholar such as HERMANN ABERT, who has delved into the problem more than anyone else, was unable to give an unequivocal answer to this question.[190] The fact that the Greeks were convinced that there existed a definite correlation between music and the human soul, and that this reciprocal effect was able to form the character of man, warranted the assumption of a certain medical basis for the ethos, which was later transferred from physical to psychic influence. Lately, this idea was abandoned and instead it was assumed that magic could have been the basis of the doctrine of the ethos. This theory seems to be more plausible, since we know about the Oriental, and especially the Egyptian, influences upon Greek musical thought. It might be, therefore, that the origin of the *ēthos* doctrine goes back to Oriental thinking in general. This, however, is merely a hypothesis, which to this day has not been corroborated by historical facts.

Despite its importance in Greek civilization, music was not regarded as an "art" in the popular sense until the zenith of the classical period, particularly if we consider music a "beautiful art." The Greeks looked upon it as "good art," or—if they assumed that the "good" is at the same time "beautiful"—then it was both a "good and beautiful art," in the sense of the Greek ideal of culture, the *kalokagathia*. ABERT stresses the point that music for the Hellenes, at least before the classical period, was never an "independent" art, at least as we understand it.[191] He emphasizes the difference between the musical life of our time, whose goal is enjoyment and entertainment, as compared with that of the Greeks, who considered it an indispensable part of their daily life and a normative element of their spiritual existence.

In these investigations we must pass over the highly complicated musical system of the Greeks and the theory of the Greek *harmoniai*, which deals with scales and modes (corresponding to our modern notions of "key" or "tonality"). Inasmuch as this was also considered to be a widespread acoustical science, it necessitates a special study beyond the scope of this essay, which deals mainly with the social implications of music. However, it may help to refer in broad outlines to the basis of Greek musical theory, the tetrachord, a sequence of four notes of whole and half tones. According to where the half-steps were inserted in the tetrachord, the *harmoniai* received specific characteristics and names. Our modern music utilizes mainly major and minor keys. The Greeks differentiated thirty "modes" ("keys"), the norms of which were strictly regulated and to be followed by composers as well as performers.

The three genres of tetrachords were divided into the diatonic, chromatic, and enharmonic species, the first using the diatonic scale, the second adding some chromatic intervals, and the third using transpositions, with a number of quarter tones as well. The scale patterns were divided into three main categories: the Dorian group,

     e f g a || b c d e ,

the Phrygian group,

     d e f g || a b c d ,

and the Lydian group,

     c d e f || g a b c .

In addition, the Greek musical system employed scales of transposition. All this is a complicated discipline, about which everyone interested in the subject may find ample information in numerous scholarly publications.

At this point it is enough to state that the Greeks attributed to their *harmoniai* various ethical properties. The philosophers defined these with much detail, though not in a homogeneous way. Their opinions were unanimous concerning only the Dorian *harmonia*, which was considered the most valuable for the education of the youth. It was characterized as being manly and serene, most favorable for the development of character. Among all the ancient writers, PLATO and ARISTOTLE were the main advocates of the educational potentialities of the Dorian *harmonia*.

PLATO included the Hypodorian mode, a variant of the Dorian *harmonia*. Originally, this mode belonged to the tribe of the Aeolians. Both terms have been used without much discrimination by the Greeks.[192] The Aeolian *harmonia* lacked the austerity of the Dorian mode; it had a milder, friendlier aspect, just as the Aeolian landscape had more pleasing features, which made it the country of origin of the lyric singing art, featuring such practitioners as TERPANDROS, ALCAIOS, and SAPPHO.

The opinions of the philosophers were far from unanimous with regard to the Phrygian *harmonia*. PLATO attributed to it a peaceful ethos, while ARISTOTLE, who held a contrary opinion, characterized it as orgiastic and pathetic, and considered it fit only for the Dionysian dithyrambos. The Greeks did not regard it as a national, autochtone *harmonia*, but one imported from Phrygia with the cult of CYBELE. Through the centuries, even when it was eventually accepted by the Greeks, it still remained in their subconscious as a "foreign" *harmonia*. ARISTOTLE pointed out a contradiction found in PLATO's writings, according to which he (PLATO) admitted the Phrygian *harmonia*, but rejected the aulos even though they belonged together being of the same origin. This antagonism between the Dorian and Phrygian manifested itself most conspicuously in Greek musical practice where the kithara was in opposition to the aulos. This dichotomy was maintained almost throughout the entire existence of classical Greece.

I should mention, in addition, a specific characteristic of the Phrygian *harmonia*, namely its faculty of enhancing the *enthousiasmos*, bringing about the discharge of the psychic effects, which resulted in *katharsis*, the purification of the soul. This important philosophical concept of Greek aesthetics was arrived at through the interplay of drama and music. Music alone could not bring about katharsis, not even to a limited degree. Only through its close association with the tragic poem could music achieve the highest goal of the musico-dramatic arts, being capable of "cleansing" the soul of unethical sentiments.

Besides the psychic katharsis, the aulos was supposed to heal physical illness (see above).

According to unanimous reports of the ancient writers, the introduction of the Lydian *harmonia* was parallel to that of the Phrygian. Yet, the "foreign" aspect, which was stamped upon the Phrygian, was likewise done away with, so that it was introduced into all branches of musical practice. Although the ethos of the Phrygian *harmonia* never lost its Oriental character, the Lydian gradually transformed into a Greek national mode.

The basic character of the Lydian was originally that of a threnodic mood. The reason for this may have been that it was employed at funeral lamentations, which were always accompanied by auloi. There was even a specific term for these types of instruments: *auloi thrēnētikoi*. The threnodic character of the Lydian *harmonia* is the more surprising, since in its Hypolydian variant it is identical with our Major key. Curiously enough, the major mode did not have the same meaning in Greek music as in our Western concept. In Greece, it had the character of softness, while the minor key—as we understand it—was considered appropriate solely for a free man.[194] Nevertheless, ARISTOTLE held that the Lydian *harmonia* was useful for the education of boys, because it could create a sense of integrity.

The fourth of the basic *harmoniai* was that of the Ionian (also called Iastian). According to the reports of ancient writers, it was identical with the Hypophrygian. This *harmonia*, which reflected the enjoyment of Ionian tribal life, imparted its main characteristic, which was softness bordering on laziness, "apt to blunt the energy of the listener and to drive him to pleasure."[195] For this reason, PLATO rejected it for the citizens of his state.[196] The Ionian *harmonia* was mostly used at drinking bouts and, since it led frequently to drunkenness, it was considered unbecoming for free citizens of the state. In principle, the Dorian austere manliness was in contrast to the Ionian softness.

In architecture there was, besides the Dorian and Ionian, an Aeolian, or Corinthian, style, but neither PLATO nor any other ancient writer has given us any information about its architectural characteristics.

Besides the main *harmoniai* there were a number of secondary forms, expressed by the suffix *"hyper"* or *"hypo,"* also some mixed (*"mixo . . . "*) forms, and even some transposing scales. All these constituted a veritable labyrinth of the Greek musical system, in which the uninitiated would be helplessly lost. Therefore, I do not consider this subject essential for this investigation.

The extraordinary possibilities of music for developing good or bad character were recognized by PLATO, who established rules for them that today may appear as odd, but were completely logical within his philosophical thinking. Since such demoniac powers were attributed to music that all thoughts and actions of mankind were believed to be held in its sway, music had to be considered as one of the guiding principles of public life, especially in education, as we have seen earlier.

ARISTOTLE made an important distinction between ethical and practical music on the one hand, and the enthusiastic on the other hand. This difference consisted mainly in the effect of music upon the emotional life of man, and was therefore more of secondary than primary significance.[197]

This reciprocal relationship between the ethical and aesthetic approach is the basic tenet of Greek musical practice.

From the experience that ARISTOTLE derived from the priesthood in certain religious rites, he developed his doctrine of the musical *katharsis*. He transferred his theory from the specific domain of religious ecstasy to psychic effects in general. Any effect could be brought to a climax by constantly increasing it, while at a certain point it will calm down naturally. Art alone has the capacity to bring about such a "cleansing" of the soul. This was the famous doctrine of *katharsis tōn pathēmatōn*. However, ARISTOTLE had in mind merely the *katharsis* effected by the musico-religious experience.

ARISTOTLE's doctrine about the effects of *katharsis* represents the acme of the role of music in the emotional life of mankind. In this theory, the one-sidedness of PLATO has been discarded, his harshness softened, his inconsistencies about the essence and aims of music eliminated. In the Aristotelian aesthetics of music there is a freer view, which approaches more closely the aesthetics of our day. The summary of ARISTOTLE's music philosophy is that music does not stand exclusively in the service of the state, but has equal importance for the development of the individual.

The ideas of PLATO and ARISTOTLE, recognized as general norms for music, did not remain unopposed. In view of the authority of their personalities, a contrary opinion in Athens would have amounted to heresy. The strict state laws would have prevented any open opposition, and the expected punishment would probably have discouraged any such attempt.

Yet, there were such wide opinions, as proven by a discovery, the musical aspect of which was discussed earlier, among the musical relics (no. 13). Its significance lies, however, in a different approach to the emotional possibilities of music. I refer here to the Hibeh Papyrus, the discovery of which was briefly reported above. According to its first publisher,[199] the relic was called the "Berlin Document"; it would, however, be more appropriate to call it the "Hibeh Papyrus," after the place where it was discovered.[200]

The village of Hibeh was once the ancient Egyptian town of Teuzoi, not far from Oxyrhinchos, where an important discovery of papyri was made. Whereas the papyri of Oxyrhinchos were found in a dump of rubbish, the Hibeh Papyrus was discovered in a burial tomb. The mummies were wrapped in long rolls of papyrus, on which there were writings of the most varied kinds, among them the present document.

The text of the papyrus is a fragment of an oration by a musical theorist and sophist of Athens, who aired a contrary opinion about the generally accepted theories of PLATO regarding the expressive power of music. Probably a contemporary of PLATO, such a public deviation from the accepted truth would have been a risky undertaking within the borders of Greece. For this reason, the unknown orator carried his Philippic to the relatively unknown Egyptian town of Hibeh, where he may have felt secure from possible persecution. It is the opinion of one of the first editors of the Hibeh Papyrus, FRIEDRICH BLASS, that the author of the papyrus was the sophist HIPPIAS of Elis—but there is no historical evidence for this assumption.

The "tenor" of this oration was the refutation of the theory that some melodies "make us equable, others reasonable, others righteous, others brave, and others cowardly."[201] As a proof of this theory, the orator cited the fact that the people living in the area of Thermopyle, as well as their neighbors, the Aeolians and Dolopeans, were braver than the tragedians, who used exclusively enharmonic melodies, which were supposed to produce courage, while the music of the Thermopyleans was diatonic. Similarly, as he asserted, chromatic music does not create fearfulness or cowardice, as was generally assumed. He went even further, denying that music has any effect upon emotions and he scoffed at the "specialists," who built elaborated systems upon such theories but nevertheless sang and played pitifully poor music. He ridiculed the theorists who asserted that "certain melodies are related to the Laurel tree and others to the ivy plant."[202] He also satirized the two musical symbols of APOLLO and DIONYSOS, by which music was divided into two categories, ethical and orgiastic, and he failed to appreciate all the other categories of music.

It is conceivable that the attack of the orator of Hibeh was directed against DAMON, whose work *Areopagiticus* seems to have caused his ire. He went even so far as to call DAMON an "amateur," although we know that DAMON had a thorough musical education (he was the music teacher of young PERICLES, among others, and besides had great political influence upon this illustrious statesman). With much more justification could PLATO and ARISTOTLE have been called musical "amateurs," since both stressed repeatedly their lack of a thorough musical education.

In contradistinction to the attitude of the orator of Hibeh against DAMON, it must be stated that DAMON was in his epoch the leading authority on music aesthetics and the protagonist of the specific influence of music upon the psyche. He maintained that there were indissoluble ties between music and society, and that each change of musical style must implicitly be followed by radical changes in the form of the state.

However we judge the attack of the orator of Hibeh, whether we consider it as the opinion of a single grumbler or whether it represents a cross-section of the opposition against the doctrines of PLATO, ARISTOTLE, and DAMON, the fact is not altered that besides the "official" position of music in the state, there might have been different currents of which the Hibeh Papyrus is a single, but certainly not a unique, example.

There are other questions related to the Hibeh Papyrus, which are, however, of only secondary importance but nevertheless must be mentioned. First of all, in opposing such illustrious contemporaries as PLATO and ARISTOTLE, the orator of Hibeh had certainly planned to address a larger audience. Why did he select for his oration a small town in Egypt? What might have been the size and the composition of his audience? Why did he write his oration (or part of it) on a discarded Latin military document? Papyrus was at those times certainly not a rare commodity, especially in the country where it was manufactured. All these are questions that cannot be answered; however, they do not detract from the importance of the orator's attitude against the "official" musical trend in Athens.

Besides the artful practice of music, there was in Greece a kind of "music for everyday use." This type did not belong to the *Mousic* art and—as folk music pure and simple—was not governed by the rules of the *Mousikē technē*. These were the work-songs, used for all professions requiring uniform rhythmical activity, such as we find in all the civilizations of Antiquity. Such work-songs must have existed in archaic Greece; we even know some of their names: *himaios, ioulos, lityersēs, eilinos,* all these being terms that were not properly understood even at Alexandria in later times.[203]

Once the philosophers discovered the close relationship between music and emotional life, the next step was to draw the consequences therefrom and to adapt the music to ethical purposes. Thus, as time went by, a complete musico-ethical system was developed, which examined all phases of musical life as to their usefulness for moral education and which sharply separated the good from the bad.

PLATO was the most zealous champion of the doctrine of ethos; he considered the *Mousikē* as an indispensable element for the preservation and development of a sound state order. He went so far as to postulate that a poet cannot be a useful member of the community before he displays appropriate political and social activity in the service of the state.[205] In this, he was followed by ARISTEIDES QUINTILIANUS, who maintained that one can disclose with certainty the character of entire states by the melodies and rhythms they use.[206]

According to PYTHAGORAS, musicians were the most useful members of the community for the education of the youth. The instruction of music should not have for its sole aim the development of virtuosity on an instrument. According to the Greek concept, the virtuoso is merely a workman who "sells" his art to anybody for lucrative purposes, earning by this the contempt of the free citizens.

There are numerous anecdote-like tales in literature that attest to the Greek's beliefs regarding the irresistible moral power of music. EMPEDOCLES is said to have prevented a murder by his lyre-playing. TIMOTHEOS, in playing the aulos, excited the great ALEXANDER to martial fervor. Especially numerous are the fabulous reports about PYTHAGORAS's musical activity.[207]

All these tales and legends, although manifestly embellished by the folklore, are testimonials to the strong belief of the Greeks in the close relationship between music and emotional life, exemplified in the ethical power of music.[208]

The doctrine of the ethos developed with the passage of time into a special discipline. To it belonged the faculty to evolve a sound judgment about the ethical value of a musical piece. This was by no means simple, since the ethos was determined not by one single factor alone, but by a blending of several elements, such as the melody, rhythm, and even the quality of the musician's performance. It was evident that the Greek musician, if he took his moral responsibilities seriously, had no easy position with regard to his audience, especially in view of the sprightly temperament of his countrymen, to whom any aesthetic-ethic blunder would immediately become apparent. This shows the great ethical and cultural impact of the musician upon the life of the nation.

Besides the choice of the *rhythmos,* it was mainly the *harmonia* that determined the ethos of a particular musical piece. Each mode (or key) possessed a specific character, not to be found in any other one. As mentioned above, the Greek writers attributed to the different *harmoniai* certain tribal characteristics, just as they did in the architecture, where they distinguished clearly among the Dorian, Ionian, and Corinthian styles of building.

This specialization in music according to the various tribes is significant in Greek music history, because prior to the fifth century, when philosophers and theorists established generally accepted rules for a musical system, the musical practice was in the hands of the tribes themselves. There was a Dorian, Ionian, and Aeolian music. Each tribe possessed its own characteristic musical features and its own national songs, which reflected the peculiarities of their landscapes. The main factor in this regard was the choice of a particular *harmonia,* which was later considered by the entire nation as a characteristic of a specific tribe.[210]

To this was added, even in ancient times, another important element, the intrusion of two non-Greek modoi, the Phrygian and the Lydian. However, it cannot be assumed that these modoi were new to the Greeks. It is more probable that both modoi, perhaps under different names, were known and practiced in several Greek districts, just as was the case with the aulos-music, which—according to general belief—originated in Asia Minor, although it was used in archaic times for Greek rites.[211]

As mentioned repeatedly, the aulos was connected with the cult of Cybele, but it also had its place in funeral services; thus, it had on the one hand an orgiastic, on the other hand a threnodic ethos, certainly a discrepancy with which the Greeks lived for a long time. Thus the ethos of Greek music developed on threefold lines: in the Dorian, music manifested itself through dignity and symmetry; in the Phrygian, the orgiastic element was predominant; in the Ionian, a more rational approach to music was manifest, which stressed enjoyment as its element, and thus music was regarded as an embellishment of daily life.

The synthesis of all three trends took place in the great national *Mousic* contests. Here, artists of all provinces converged, bringing with them the specialties of their own district and making them known to a Panhellenic audience. The unifying tendency of a long development created an admirable musical culture, as exemplified by names such as Terpandros, Thaletes, Sappho, Xenocritos, and others. Dorian and Phrygian were the two great poles, one standing for the Apollinian principle, the other representing the Dionysian. All other *harmoniai* were brought into closer relationships with these two principal modes, so that between Dorian and Aeolian, and Phrygian and Ionian the differences were straightened out, in giving them new names of Hypodorian and Hypophrygian and, in addition, new meanings and functions.[212]

Such a development did not occur suddenly. The compositions of the old school were maintained alongside those of the new. This is the reason why the writings of the philosophers sometimes show confusing vagueness about the ethos of the different modoi. This difficulty can easily be resolved if we consider the one report as referring to the ethos familiar to a specific tribe, and the other as the final generally accepted norm for the ethical values of Greek music.[213]

To summarize the principles of the ethos of Greek music, it is best to adopt the guiding norms of ARISTOTLE, who classified the various *harmoniai* according to their effect upon the emotions of the listener. ARISTOTLE distinguished among the modoi *ēthika, praktika,* and *enthousiastika.*

The term *ēthikos* is a common denominator for anything that may influence the ethos of a musical piece. This influence can be of different kinds: it can contribute to the strengthening of character, the development of virility, and to producing heroic impulses in the youth. This was the basic characteristic of the Dorian *harmonia.* Other *harmoniai* are apt to disturb the equilibrium of the psychic life, either by creating painful sensations or by going so far as to paralyze the energy and will-power of the individual.[214]

The practical *harmoniai* have the effect of creating immediate impressions upon the will power. The enthusiastic *harmoniai* are outside of the normal emotional receptivity, and cause its suspension, at least temporarily, at which time the individual arrives at the state of ecstasy.

The ethos of the various *harmoniai* was not an innate characteristic, but was developed during a long historical process. The principal difference between the main elements of the doctrine of the ethos are the scale-patterns (the modoi) and the rhythmos. The latter, representing the sensual element of music, carries a built-in ethos, while the melody is subjected to the fluctuations of performance which changes with the generations.

HERMANN ABERT cogently summarizes the four stages of the development of the doctrine of the ethos, from its beginning to its perfection.[215]

The first stage was characterized by the period in which the musical practice was exclusively in the hands of the various tribes.

The second phase began with the penetration of aulos-music from Asia Minor to Greece, represented by the half-mythical musician, OLYMPOS. It was mentioned earlier, however, that the aulos was by no means an exclusively Asiatic instrument; the Greeks must have known it even in archaic times.

The third phase was determined by the increased exchange of the musical peculiarities of the various tribes, which demonstrated their regional diversities in the Panhellenic musical agōns.

The last epoch was that of the burgeoning of the choral lyric and the glorious rise of the drama with all its important musical implications. This epoch also witnessed the combination of the *harmoniai* in one gigantic system of music theory, the like of which never existed before in human civilization, and which exerted its influence far into the Middle Ages and, through the music of the Church, down to our time.

This last epoch of Greek musical development was the golden age for musical science, in all its manifestations.[216] The circle of writers on music in Alexandria was especially fertile in this field (see the works of PTOLOMÄUS). Since this activity, however, is already part of the Graeco-Roman period, it will be discussed in detail in the section following.

What is so meaningful and admirable in this composite picture of Greek musical practice is the importance of music for the general life of a nation, a practice never before achieved on such a scale in the history of civilization. The entire nation represented itself in its music, based upon the participation of all elements of artistic, political, and social life, a unique phenomenon in the history of the civilization of mankind.

NOTES

1. *Koller*, p. 9.
2. *Ibid.*, p. 17.
3. *Ibid.*
4. *Ibid.*, p. 26.
5. Hesiod, *Theogony* 36–76.
6. *Koller*, p. 42.
7. *Ibid.*, p. 27.
8. *Ibid.*
9. *Ibid.*, p. 62.
10. *Ibid.*, p. 45.
11. *Wegner*, p. 13.
12. *Ibid.*
13. *Koller*, p. 93.
14. *Ibid.*
15. *Wegner*, p. 16.
16. Edward A. Pillman, *Musical Thought in Ancient Greece* (New York and London, 1964), p. 19.
17. *Wegner*, p. 16.
18. *Ibid.*, p. 18.
19. *Ibid.*
20. *Ibid.*, p. 25.
21. *Iliad*, II, 595 ff.
22. *Wegner*, p. 25.
23. *Koller*, p. 63.
24. *Ibid.*, p. 64.
25. *Ibid.*, p. 65.
26. *Durant*, 2:20.
27. *Ibid.*, p. 38.
28. *Wegner*, p. 129.
29. *WegnerGesch*, p. 44.
30. *Wegner*, p. 129.
31. *Ibid.*, p. 130.
32. *Ibid.*, p. 131.
33. Aristotle, *Politikē*, 1340 a.
34. *Koller*, p. 83.
35. *Wegner*, p. 131.
36. *Koller*, p. 82.
37. *Ibid.*, p. 66.
38. *Ibid.*, p. 86.
39. *Ibid.*, p. 87.
40. *Laws*, 666 d.
41. *Koller*, p. 93.
42. *Ibid.*, p. 96.

43. *Ibid.*, p. 96.
44. Thucydides, III, 104.
45. *Koller*, p. 101.
46. *Ibid.*, p. 104.
47. *Republic* VIII, 398 d.
48. *Odyssey*, XVII, 3838.
49. *Ibid.*, IX, 5 ff.
50. Plato, *Symposion*, 212 d.
51. *Wegner*, p. 174.
52. *Ibid.*, p. 76.
53. *Koller*, p. 112.
54. *Wegner*, p. 81.
55. *Ibid.*, p. 26.
56. *Athen*, XIV, 631.
57. *Koller*, p. 120.
58. *Ibid.*, p. 124.
59. *Riemann, Handbuch*, p. 116.
60. Suidas, *s.v. perideipnon.*
61. *Koller*, p. 126.
62. *Ibid.*, p. 128.
63. *Ibid.*, p. 129.
64. *Ibid.*, p. 130.
65. *Wegner*, p. 84.
66. Hesiod, *Wedding Ceremony.*
67. *Wegner*, p. 85.
68. A poem by the Roman poet Catullus affords much insight into the *hymenaios*. In it he vividly describes the wedding ceremony of a Roman couple, Vinia and Manlius. Except for the Roman names, everything in the poem is a reproduction of a Greek wedding. Literary history considers it an imitation of Greek customs (see Catullus, 61).
69. *Pollux*, IV, 52.
70. *Athen*, XIV, 10.
71. *Iliad*, XVIII, 604.
72. *Wegner*, p. 97.
73. *Athen*, XIV, 617 b.
74. Wegner furnishes a highly informative graphic reproduction (in drawings) of the development of the kithara, from the primitive to the most advanced species (pp. 136–37 of his book). It is strange, however, that he mentions the "plagi-aulos," the horizontal flute, among the stringed instruments (p. 68).
75. *Athen*, XIV, 535 f.
76. *Ibid.*, 636 f.
77. *Ibid.*, 635, a.
78. *Ibid.*, IV, 183 c.
79. *Ibid.*, 83 d.
80. *Ibid.*, XIV, 635 c.
81. *Ibid.*, 635 b, d.
82. *Ibid.*, 636 a.
83. *Ibid.*, 636 b.
84. *Ibid.*, 635 c.
85. *Ibid.*, 637 a.
86. *Ibid.*, 634 f.
87. *Ibid.*, 636 b.
88. *Ibid.*, 635 a.
89. In the bas-relief found at Kuyundchik (Illue. 66).
90. *Syrigma* is an exact parallel to harmonics on modern stringed instruments, called flageolet-tones, or simply flageolets. This is the French term for whistle-flutes.
91. *Athen*, XIV, 638–39.
92. *Ibid.*, 635 b.
93. *Ibid.*, 636 e,f.
94. *Wegner*, p. 100.
95. *Politeia*, VIII, 6, 5 ff.

96. *Wegner*, p. 154.
97. Plutarch, *Alcibiades*, 192 d,e.
98. *HickmannGesch*, pp.112–113.
99. *Pollux*, IV, 80.
100. *HickmannGesch*, pp. 112–113.
101. Pausanias, II, 31.
102. Herodotus, I, 132, 1.
103. *Wegner*, p. 139.
104. *Pollux*, IV, 74.
105. Pliny the Elder, *Historia naturalis*, VII, 204.
106. *Odyssey*, XIX, 457 ff.
107. Aristotle, *Laws*, 790 d.e.
108. *Athen*, XIV, 624, a,b.
109. *State*, 399 c-e.
110. *Athen*, IV, 88 f.
111. *Ibid.*
112. *Ibid.*, 60.
113. *Wegner*, p. 67.
114. *SachsDance*, p. 17.
115. Paul Henry Láng, *Music in Western Civilization* (New York, 1941), pp. 5, 7.
116. *Iliad*, XVIII, 604 ff.
117. Anacreon, 18 d.
118. *Iliad*, XVIII, 49 a.
119. *Ibid.*, XVIII, 590 ff.
120. *SachsDance*, p. 238.
121. *Athen*, XIV, 630 ff.
122. *SachsDance*, p 240.
123. *Athen*, XIV, 10.
124. *SachsDance*, p. 245.
125. *Koller*, p. 165.
126. *Ibid.*
127. *SchneiderKultur*, p. 549.
128. Hermann Abert, *Die Musik der Griechen.* In *Gesammelte Schriften und Vortäge*, ed. Fr. Blume (Halle, 1929), p. 26.
129. P. H. Láng, p. 10.
130. *SchneiderKultur*, p. 549.
131. Aristotle, *Poetika*, IV, 17.
132. *Koller*, p. 159.
133. *Iphigeneia in Aulis*, 1036 ff.
134. *SachsDance*, p. 234.
135. *Koller*, p. 154.
136. *Ibid.*, 168. *Cf.* Aristophanes, *Frogs*, 1031 ff.
137. Hermann Abert, p. 78.
138. Plutarch, *Vita Homeri*, 4.
139. Aristotle, *Laws*, 666 d.
140. Plato, *Protagoras*, 325.
141. *Durant*, 2:289.
142. James Henry Breasted, *The Conquest of Civilization* (New York and London, 1938), p. 345.
143. Aristotle, *Laws*, VII, 819 d.
144. *State*, 819 d, e.
145. *Politeia*, VIII, 6, 5.
146. *Ibid.*, XIII, 6, 7.
147. Hyppolite Taine, *Philosophie und Kunst* (Leipzig, 1902), 2:170.
148. *State*, 399 c-e.
149. *Ibid.*, 522 a.
150. Adler, *Handbuch*, p. 57.
151. *Koller*, p. 86.
152. Herodotus, V, 63; VI, 66.
153. August Böckh, *Die Staatshaltung der Athener* (Berlin, 1886), 1:153.

154. The value of the drachma was normally $1.00; that of the gold-drachma much higher.
155. Böckh, 1:270.
156. *Durant,* 2:216.
157. *Strabo,* XIII. 217.
158. *Athen,* VIII, 338 a.
159. *Wegner,* p. 116.
160. Ward, p. 250.
161. *Ibid.,* p. 248.
162. *Ibid.,* p. 251.
163. *Ibid.,* p. 265.
164. *Ibid.*
165. *Ibid.,* p. 232.
166. *Ibid.*
167. About the attempts to decipher Babylonian musical signs, see p. 22.
168. *JosApio,* I, 1, 2.
169. John Forsdyke, *Greece before Homer. Ancient Chronology and Mythology* (London, 1956), p. 13.
170. *Durant,* 2:98.
171. The historicity of Olympos is not certain.
172. Strabo, XIII, 2, 4.
173. *Lyra Graeca* (Loeb Classical Library, London), vol. 1, p. 29.
174. Wegner, p. 144.
175. *Athen,* XIV, 636 e,f.
176. *WegnerGesch,* p. 19.
177. G. Grote, *History of Greece* (Everyman's Library, London n.d.), 3:195.
178. *Athen,* XIV, 624 a.
179. *Wegner,* p. 181.
180. *Athen,* XIV, 624 a.
181. See Hickmann's findings about the subject in *Musicologie Pharaonique* (Kehl, 1956), pp. 97 ff.
182. Peter Wagner, *Über die Anfänge des mehrstimmigen Gesanges.* In ZMW (1926), 9:3 ff.
183. Abert, *Ethos,* p. 59.
184. See n. 16.
185. Hermann Abert, *Der neue griechische Papyrus mit Musiknoten.* In *Gesammelte Schriften und Vorträge,* ed. Fr. Blume, (Halle, 1929), pp. 59–82.
186. P. H. Láng, p. 28.
187. *WegnerGesch,* p. 22.
188. Plato, *Laws,* II, 1668 a.
189. *Republic,* III, 398 c.
190. Hermann Abert, *Der gegenwärtige Stand der Forschung über antike Musik.* In *Gesammelte Schriften und Vorträge,* ed. Fr. Blume (Halle, 1929), p. 50.
191. *Ibid., Die Lehre vom Ethos der griechischen Musik* (Leipzig, 1929), p. 57.
192. *Athen,* XIV, 625 a.
193. Abert, *Ethos,* p. 92.
194. *Ibid.,* p. 94
195. *Ibid.,* p. 87.
196. *Republic,* III, 398 e.
197. Abert, *Ethos,* p. 2.
198. *Ibid.,* p. 16.
199. Mommsen, In *Berliner griechische Urkunden* (1906), 2:696.
200. Grenfelt and Hunt, *The Hibeh Papyrus* (London, 1906).
201. Edward A. Lippman, p. 112.
202. *Ibid.*
203. Karl Bücher, *Arbeit und Rhythmus* (Leipzig, 1902), p. 49.
204. Abert, *Ethos,* p. 50.
205. *Republic,* 597 d – 602 c.
206. Abert, *Ethos,* p. 50.
207. *Ibid.,* p. 55.
208. *Ibid.*

209. *Ibid.,* p. 65.
210. *Ibid.,* p. 76.
211. *Ibid.,* p. 77.
212. *Ibid.,* p. 79.
213. *Ibid.*
214. *Ibid.,* p. 96.
215. *Ibid.*
216. Adler, *Handbuch,* p. 61.

11

Rome

THE ETRURIAN PRELUDE

One of the exceptional and almost unique phenomena in the history of civilization, where a conquering nation adopted, even completely absorbed, the cultural achievements of a defeated people, was the case of the Babylonians, who adopted *in toto* the religion, the institutions of the state, the economic system, and the music of the conquered Sumerians.

The same thing was repeated millennia later upon the adoption of the Greek civilization by the Romans. The cultural achievements of the Greeks must have exerted such an irresistible attraction upon the expanding Roman nation that the Romans almost totally absorbed the artistic and literary achievements of the older and more advanced civilization.

However, here the comparison ends. The Babylonians, prior to taking over the Sumerian achievements, had no culture of their own, at least in the field of music. Therefore, for the Babylonians, the adoption of the music of the Sumerians constituted a welcome enrichment of their own cultural life. The Romans, on the other hand, who conquered the Apennine peninsula step by step, had found there long-settled peoples, among them the Etruscans. This nation possessed a rich musical culture, which could have been of great import to the conquering nation. However, owing, on the one hand, to the difference between these peoples and, on the other hand, to their historic evolution, the Romans' goal was exclusively one of conquest. Their aim was solely the acquisition of war booty and material gain. Only after Etruscan resistance was completely broken did the Romans begin to appreciate Etruscan culture and music. This becomes evident when we consider both the religion and the military institutions of the Romans, in which elements of the Etruscan music played an increasingly important role. Generally speaking, Rome, after the consolidation of its political development, remained under the influence of Greek rather than Etruscan music. The penetration of Greek tonal art into the Roman cultural life was so far-reaching that we may very well call it the continuation, even the adoption, of Greek music by the Romans. The internal and external transformation that subjected Rome to Etruscan music does not alter the fact that the roots of Roman musical practice mingled deeply with those of the Greeks.

Prior to the conquest of Italy by Rome, the Etruscans were the most powerful people on the Italian Peninsula. They immigrated in the tenth century B.C.E. from the Aegaean provinces and settled originally on the western coast of the peninsula, in the region of today's Tuscany. According to tradition, they originated in Asia Minor; their language, too, points to the pre-Grecian dialects of the Near East. An ancient source[1] indicates that the Etruscans were an autochthonous, i.e., indigenous, people of Italy, an assumption not borne out by historical facts. According to other sources, they were considered Lydians,[2] Pelasgians,[3] or former inhabitants of the islands of Lemnos and Imbros.[4] As a matter of fact, the origin of the Etruscans is still not established beyond doubt. They were originally, in all probability, a mixture of several tribes who, under the favorable living conditions of the Apennine peninsula, united into a nation and developed their own culture.

As a war-loving people addicted to conquest, they gradually expanded northward until they reached the Alps and south into the Campagna. Around Rome they established numerous fortified settlements and—according to a not-very-reliable tradition—one of their resolute chieftains succeeded in conquering Rome itself (618 B.C.E.). For a century the Roman people remained under Etruscan domination and civilization.[5]

By extended trade with the nations of the Mediterranean, as well as by piracy (a legitimate profession of those days), they became wealthy and built cities in their territory, enriching their culture by close interrelationship with numerous Greek colonies in the Mediterranean, especially with Carthage.

They were called *Tyrrhenoi* or *Tyrsenoi* by the Greeks, *Tusci* or *Etrusci* by the Romans, while they called themselves *Rasna* or *Rasenna*. It is beyond the scope of this study to follow the political and social history of the Etruscans, but the end of their national existence may be briefly mentioned. In the year 88 B.C.E. they received Roman citizenship and in 27 B.C.E. (under AUGUSTUS) they were incorporated completely as part of the Roman civilization.[6]

The music of the Etruscans exerted a powerful influence upon the musical practices of the Romans, who in their military music followed the Etruscan pattern exclusively. Rich discoveries in Etruscan tombs (in ceramics and wall paintings) show forms of life and musical practices akin to that of the Greeks. Like the Greeks, the Etruscans accompanied all religious feasts, contests, and festive processions with music and dance.

A modern treatise considers that: "the music of the Etruscans could not have been unimportant."[7] This super-cautious statement is the more astonishing, since abundant antiquities discovered in Etruscan tombs testify to the intense musical practice of this people. From the rich archaeological material available, I refer merely to the most important ones giving insight into the elaborate musical culture of the Etruscans.

In Rome, the Etruscan "flutists" (*subulones*) were famous, long after the Etruscans gave up their national existence.[8] A significant episode in Roman history indicates the importance of the Etruscan flutists in the musical life of Rome, about which LIVY gives a detailed account[9] (see p. 382).

The Etruscans were credited with the "invention" of the trumpet (the Greek *salpinx*). This is supported by the historical fact that as early as 700 B.C.E. the Etruscans mined copper and iron in the Mediterranean basin, and brought lead and iron from northern Europe down the Rhine and Rhone. They sold their metal products in every major port of the Mediterranean.[10] It is evident that the Etruscans were the most ancient bronze-casters in the Mediterranean region, and as such could very well have been the first manufacturers of trumpets. The other peoples of the region, including the Egyptians, could have acquired the instrument from the Etruscans.

At any rate, metal trumpets are depicted in ancient Etruscan tombs in wall paintings. Among these one finds the trumpet with the straight tube with a wide bell, which the Romans adopted and called *tuba*. This was the only trumpet used by the Greeks, who called it the *"tyrsenic salpinx"* (Illus. 126). In addition, the Etruscans developed, evidently after a Hittite religious emblem, a long type of trumpet, having at the sounding end a hook-like curve; it entered the Roman military music under the name of *lituus* (Illus. 125). The word is supposed to have its origin in the Etruscan language, but this cannot be proven unequivocally. By dint of this curvature close to the bell of the instrument, its form resembles that of the Phrygian aulos, the *aulo elymos*. This, too, indicates that it might have originated in Asia Minor. The oldest picture of it has been found in the *Tomba della scimmia* (the "Tomb with the monkey") at Chiusi.[11]

Another species of Etruscan trumpet was a tube bent in circular form, narrower than the two aforementioned which, however, being considerably longer, could produce more natural harmonics and was possibly used also in the art music of the Romans. Its term in Rome was *cornu*. In order to carry it on the shoulder, it had a vertical pole that held both tubes together and gave the instrument the stability necessary to be played easily. In Pompeii, two well-preserved specimens of this instrument have been found (Illus. 125).

The *cornu* must have been an original creation of the Etruscans, since in no archaeological discovery of Antiquity can we find similarly built instruments. Another species of trumpet, possibly also created by the Etruscans, was adopted by the Romans under the name of *bucina*. It is a variety of *cornu*, with the difference that the tubes are not bent in a circle but in parallel form, by which it more resembles today's trombone than a trumpet (Illus. 135). It was the cavalry trumpet of the Romans, and it is reproduced on a tombstone of a Roman cavalryman,[12] called *bucinator* on the epitaph.

All four types of brass instruments were in use by the Etruscans. Whether they were invented by them cannot be ascertained. The fact remains, however, that they were manufactured by Etruscan craftsmen, thus they may be considered significant manifestations of the musical practice of this people (Illus. 126).

There is, however, an important invention that is to the credit of the Etruscans: a removable mouthpiece for brass instruments. We know that the Hebrews and the Greeks had removable mouthpieces for various wind instruments, but it seems that this device existed much earlier with the Etruscans. Consequently, we may consider it as a genuine Etruscan innovation. The Romans made wide use of this artifice. BEHN gives us very instructive pictures of Roman removable mouthpieces.[13] The Romans used them with the *tuba*, the *cornu*, and the *bucina*, but oddly enough, not with the *lituus;* this latter instrument was manufactured only with a permanent mouthpiece, cast with the tube.

The most important representation of a musical instrument from the Etruscan period was discovered in the family tomb of the Voluminers in Perugia (end of the second, beginning of the third century B.C.E.). It shows in stone relief a man playing the transversal flute (Illus. 126). The Greek term for this species of instruments was *plagiaulos;* the Romans called it *tibia vasca;* and its name among the Etruscans was *calamaulos.*

CURT SACHS believed that the transversal flute (at least in Europe) could not be found prior to the Middle Ages. He maintained that it was taken over by the Europeans from Asia. The earliest specimen of this instrument known to SACHS appears in an East Turkestanic fresco of the fifth century c.e. In his opinion, the earliest transversal flutes made their appearance in Byzanz, from whence (not before the end of the twelfth century c.e.) they made their way to western countries, particularly to Germany.[14]

This assertion was completely shattered by the discovery in Perugia. In a later work, SACHS admits this frankly, and considers this picture from the so-called *urna del flutista* the earliest representation of a transversal flute.[15] The instrument depicted has eight holes, for the fingers of both hands, possibly also holes for the thumb which, however, cannot be seen. In Etruscan antiquities a picture of the flute is reproduced several times.[16]

It cannot be ascertained whether the other musical instruments used by the Etruscans were creations of this people or imported from their primeval Asiatic country. In fact, they were very similar to analogous Greek instruments, which indicates a common Asiatic origin. Among the stringed instruments, we find on wall paintings of tombs the kithara and the lyra, but these are found only in the *Tomba della Pulcella* at Tarquinia. Another species of stringed instrument, the cradle kithara, can be found more frequently, especially in the *Tomba degli Scudi,* located also in Tarquinia.

In the picture of a musician in the *Tomba dei Leopardi* (so called because on the front part of the sarcophagus leopards are depicted), is included the picture of a lyra that is almost identical with the Greek lyra. However, the barbiton seems not to have been a favorite Etruscan instrument, because it appears only sporadically in wall paintings. The lute and the harp are almost completely missing in the Etruscan instrumentarium; there is only one picture of the harp, in Preneste, from a later period.

Among the woodwinds, the Etruscans used the double-aulos, which is similar to, if not identical with, the Greek instrument; evidently both nations imported it from Asia Minor (Illus. 128, 129). The syrinx is depicted in a "concert" performed by two musicians sitting on a couch or on a bench, one playing the syrinx, the other a kind of lyre. This scene is depicted on a hammered bronze bucket (*situla*) discovered in the Certosa of Bologna, dated sixth century B.C.E. (a syrinx is also shown on another *situla*). Both musicians depicted in the first-mentioned *situla,* as well as their audience, have large hats with broad brims. It might be that such hats were a special attire of professional musicians among the Etruscans (Illus. 130). If this assumption is correct, the "audience" in this picture could possibly be participants in the musical performance, either singers or dancers. A similar large hat, carried by an aulos player, can also be found in an Etruscan wall painting in Chiusi (Siena Province) from the sixth century B.C.E. (Illus. 131). There is also in this picture a female dancer who carries an especially showy headdress, which cannot be found in any other Etruscan paintings. It must be surmised that this headdress had some ritual significance.

JULIUS POLLUX mentions a curious Etruscan instrument of which he says, "The Tyrrhenses played the flute on a horn." If this is not based upon unauthenticated hearsay, it can be assumed that the Etruscans applied some fingerholes to the natural horn of an animal and provided this instrument with a mouthpiece so that it could, indeed, be played like a flute (or pipe).[17] However, since there is no pictorial representation of such an instrument, it is not possible to verify POLLUX's statement.

As for the percussive instruments of the Etruscans, they had only a few varieties, as far as we can judge from their preserved antiquities. Of all the Greek percussive instruments, we find in Etruria mainly the hand-clappers (the *krotala* of the Greeks) and clappers fastened on a rod, which were not in use in Greece and may have been introduced (directly or in a roundabout way) from Egypt.

We do not possess written records about the musical life of the Etruscans. Until now philology has not succeeded in deciphering Etruscan writings; we do not know, therefore, whether their writings contain anything concerning their musical practice.

This is the more astonishing since we know that Roman aristocrats sent their sons from the seventh to the fourth centuries B.C.E. to Etruscan cities to get higher education, among other things, in geometry, surveying, and architecture. Therefore a common language must have existed to understand each other, unless we assume that the Etruscans spoke Latin so fluently that they could transmit their knowledge in these disciplines to the Roman youth.

Thus, unless the key to the Etruscan language is found, our knowledge of Etruscan history and music is restricted to the art objects, paintings, and artifacts that are preserved in great numbers in burial chambers and sarcophagi.

We are more fortunate with regard to archaeological discoveries. The oldest preserved instruments date back to the early bronze period and were found in the so-called *terremares*. Among these, there is a primitive flute (*tibia*) made from the shinbone of a dog, as well as a horn of clay (43 cm. long) in the form of a cattle horn.

From more recent times, the so-called Villanova period, there are in tombs of central and upper Italy discs of bronze or clay that have the appearance of cross-sections of bells (Illus. 132). Several of these contain clappers, a sign that they were considered to be real bells, and therefore belong to the category of percussive instruments. These were symbolic reproductions of bells, placed in tombs in accordance with Etruscan belief in immortality. They had the practical function of keeping away evil demons from the deceased, according to the Oriental belief that evil spirits cannot stand noise. In later times, the Etruscans placed real bells in the tombs for the same purpose (Illus. 133).

According to literary sources, in the tomb of the Etruscan national hero, PORSENNA, the survivors hung up bells, which were activated by the blowing of the wind. The purpose was the same: to chase away hostile demons who might disturb the soul of the deceased.[18]

Furthermore, in northern Italy, there were discoveries of several *situles*, which depict various musical instruments. One of them, showing two musicians playing a syrinx and a lyre, has been mentioned above. On another *situla*, an Etruscan lituus-player is depicted. In wall paintings, cornu- and lituus-players are frequently represented (see Illus. 126). On the island of Sardinia, a bronze sculpture has been found showing a man with a large horn at his lips.[19] On a vase found in lower Italy, there is one picture of a tuba-player and another of a horn-player (see Illus. 125). The last mentioned instrument is a species of the tuba; it is slightly but not circularly curved, as is the cornu. The player has to hold it with both hands, as he does the straight tuba.

In numerous reproductions of cultic rites or official acts, the horns and trumpets are doubled. This is not accidental, since the doubling of trumpets in the cult was common usage of the peoples of Antiquity.[20] We see it with the Hebrews, whose sacred trumpets were always blown in pairs. In the tomb of TUT-ANKH-AMON two trumpets were found, which may indicate a similar custom among the Egyptians.

Belief in immortality played an important role in the musical practice of the Etruscans, and they shared it with the Sumerians and Egyptians. Not only did they believe that life continued after death, but they assumed that the deceased followed the same occupations and customs as in his lifetime. These activities included music and dance. It is for this reason that we find in many tombs numerous pictorial representations concerning music, which were supposed to reproduce the realities of the former life of the deceased.

Burial ceremonies were embellished with rich musical displays; the lying-in-state and the funeral lament were accompanied by aulos- and kithara-players; the deceased were also honored with dances. These musical displays had a hidden purpose: to keep the influence of demons away from the deceased.

Another way of honoring the dead was to hold funeral plays at the grave, coupled with athletic competitions. Included were chariot races, weapon dances, competitions of throwing the diskos and spears, as well as gymnastic displays. The athletic show was accompanied by aulos-players, the women honoring the deceased with dances. This type of funeral ceremony was customary even in earlier times, both in Asia Minor and in Greece; the Etruscans might have taken them over from there.

Not only athletic competitions for funerals were accompanied by the playing of the aulos. On an amphora found at Vulci is reproduced a boxing match with musical accompaniment,[21] a procedure considered by the Greeks to be incompatible with the *Mousic* arts. Even in kitchen activities the aulos was used as an accompaniment and as an aid to certain rhythmic functions[22] (Illus. 129).

On the other hand, there are no records (pictorial or other) indicating whether the Etruscans held *Mousic* agōns. This is by no means surprising, considering that their musical practice was dominated solely by practical necessities of everyday life.

All the representations in Etruscan monuments of gods' indulging in music (APOLLO's contest with MARSYAS, the aulos-playing ATHENA looking at herself in a mirror, and so on,) are those taken over from Greek mythology or are copies of Greek art products; thus, they do not enrich our knowledge of Etruscan musical practice.

In other archaeological discoveries from Etruscan times, kithara-players, as well as male and female dancers, are depicted. The forms of the kithara are similar to those of the Greeks; the interrelationship between the archaic music practice of the Greeks and that of the Etruscans is unmistakable. Another proof of this is a bas-relief on a tomb-stele of Chiusi, reproducing a musician who plays the double-aulos; he is using the *phorbeia* (in Latin *capistrum*), a device employed, as we know, by the Greek aulos-players.

Instrumental music is utilized in numerous Etruscan practices in Antiquity.

Illus. 125 Cornu- and lituus-players. Wall painting in the Tomba di Castel
Rubello, Orvieto. (End of the seventh century B.C.E.). Museo Archeologico,
Florence. (After Günther Fleischhauer, *Musikgeschichte in Bildern, Etrurien,*
Leipzig, 1964. Illus. 18.)

Illus. 126 Trumpet- and hornplayer on an Italic vase. (After Gerhard, *Apulische Vasen.*)

Illus. 127 Cross-flute (36x44 cm) from Perugia, the Tomb of the Volumniers (end of the second to beginning of the first century B.C.E.). (After Günther Fleischhauer, *Musikgeschichte in Bildern, Etrurien*, Leipzig, 1965. Illus. 20.)

Illus. 128 Tibia- and lyre players. Wall painting in the Tomba dei Leopardi, Tarquinia (480–470 B.C.E.). (After Günther Fleischhauer, *Musikgeschichte in Bildern, Etrurien,* Leipzig, 1965. Illus. 10.)

Illus. 129 Tibia-players in the kitchen. Wall painting in the Tomba Golini, I, Orvieto. Museo Archeologico, Florence. (After Günther Fleischhauser, *Musik- geschichte in Bildern, Etruria,* Leipzig, 1965. Illus. 11.)

Illus. 130 Concert on an Italic bronze vessel (*situla*). (After Montelius, *Civilisation primitive en Italie,* Paris, 1895–1904.)

Illus. 131 Dance-scene on a wall painting in an Etruscan tomb (sixth century B.C.E.). Museo Civico, Chiusi, Prov. Siena. (After Max Wegner, *Musik in Geschichte und Gegenwart, Etrurien,* vol. III. col. 1595.)

Illus. 132 Cross-sections of bells (bronze or clay). From Etruscan tombs of the Villanova period. (After Montelius, *Civilisation primitive en Italie,* Paris, 1895–1904.)

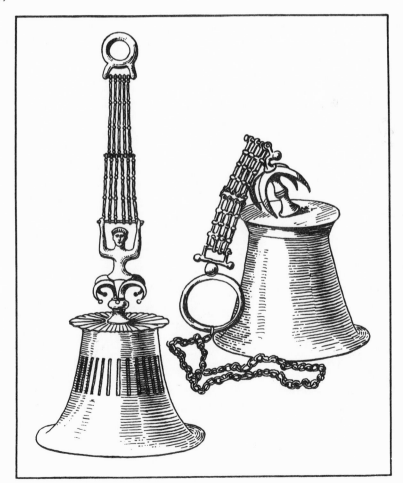

Illus. 133 Bronze bells from Etrurian tombs. (After Montelius, *Civilisation primitive en Italie,* Paris, 1895–1904.)

Illus. 134 Worksong. Roman marble relief. Villa Albani, Rome. Two satyrs tread grapes, another plays the aulos, and supports the rhythm of the working satyrs with the *scabellum.* (After Curt Sachs, *Musik der Antike,* in *Handbuch der Musikwissenschaft,* Potsdam, 1934.)

Illus. 135 Bucina as pictured on a stone-relief, and its reconstruction. (After Friedrich Behn, *Musikleben im Altertum . . . ,* Stuttgart, 1934.)

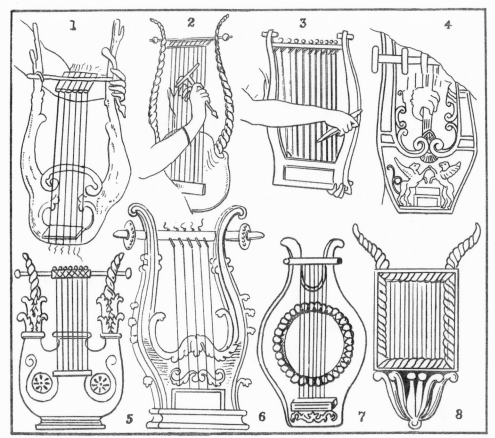

Illus. 136 Kitharas from the period of the Roman Emperors. (After *Archäologische Zeitung*, 1858.)

Illus. 137 Kithara player. Hellenistic terra-cotta figurine (25 cm). (third century B.C.E.). Collection Feuardent. (After Günther Fleischhauer, *Musikgeschichte in Bildern*, Rome, Leipzig, 1965. Illus. 54.)

Illus. 138 Lute player. Relief from a sarcophagus (65 cm). (second half of the third century C.E.). Lateran Museum, Rome. (After Günther Fleischhauer, *Musikgeschichte in Bildern, Rome*, Leipzig, 1965. Illus. 78.)

Illus. 139 Psyche. (After Baumeister, *Denkmäler des klassischen Altertums*, 1885–1888.)

Illus. 140 Lute-player. Relief from a sarcophagus (68 cm). (second half of the third century. C.E.). In St. Crisogono, Rome. (After Günther Fleischhauer, *Musik-geschichte in Bildern, Rome*, Leipzig, 1965. Illus. 77.)

Illus. 141 Players of tibia and lyra, at a funeral sacrifice (second half of the second century B.C.E.). British Museum. (After Günther Fleischhauer, *Musikgeschichte in Bildern, Rome*, Leipzig, 1965. Illus. 23.)

Illus. 142 Musicians and dancers. Mosaic (44x42 cm), from the so-called Villa of Cicero at Pompeii (end of the second century B.C.E.). Museo Nazionale, Naples. (After Günther Fleischhauer, *Musikgeschichte in Bildern, Rome*, Leipzig, 1965. Illus. 53.)

Illus. 143 Woman playing the pandura. Terra-cotta figurine from Tanagra (21 cm). Musée du Louvre. (After Günther Fleischhauer, *Musikgeschichte in Bildern, Rome,* Leipzig, 1965. Illus. 55.)

Illus. 144 Organ and cornu-player on a Mosaic (230–240 C.E.). (After Wilmow-ski, *Römische Villa von Hennig,* 1865.)

Illus. 145 Water-organ from Carthago. Terra-cotta. (After Dedering, *Die Orgel,* 1905.)

Illus. 146 Organ prospect from Pompeii. Drawing after the original. (After Friedrich Behn, *Musikleben im Altertum . . . ,* Stuttgart, 1954.)

Illus. 147 Roman litui, found in the Rheinlands. (After Friedrich Behn, *Musikleben im Altertum . . . ,* Stuttgart, 1954.)

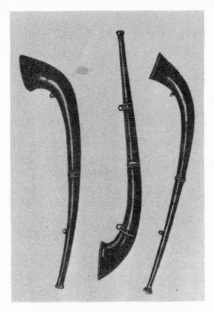

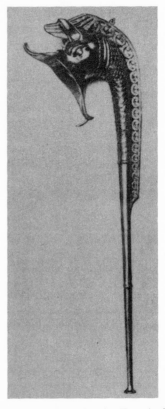

Illus. 148 Animal-headed carnyx, as shown on Trajan's column. In the Römisch-germanisches Zentralmuseum at Mainz. (After Friedrich Behn, *Musikleben im Altertum . . . ,* Stuttgart, 1954.)

Illus. 149 Fight of gladiators, accompanied by a water-organ, tuba- and cornu-players. Part of a mosaic at Zliten (Tripolis) (ca. 70 C.E.). (After Curt Sachs, *Musik der Antike,* in *Handbuch der Musikwissenschaft,* Potsdam, 1934, p. 27.)

Illus. 150 Dance Scene, marble relief (time of the Emperors). From a tomb of the Via Appia, Rome. Museum of the Thermae. Two dancing girls with clappers, accompanied by concussion sticks, with an applauding audience. (After Curt Sachs, *Musik der Antike,* in *Handbuch der Musikwissenschaft,* Potsdam, 1934. p. 28.)

Vocal music, on the other hand, is almost completely lacking. If we consider how arduously the Hellenes depicted singing in solo and in choirs, this lack in Etruscan monuments is quite surprising. However, it would be erroneous to conclude that singing in Etruscan musical life assumed only a minor role. In Etruria, as in other peoples of Antiquity, singing was a daily activity, in all classes of society as well as in all age categories. The difference between Etruria and Greece was that in the former nation the musicians, singers, and dancers belonged mainly to the class of slaves,[23] while in Greece they were members of the free society and constituted a privileged class.

The most important feature of the Etruscan musical culture, prior to the annihilation of their national existence, was the fact that, owing to their higher civilization, which they brought with them from their mother country in Asia Minor, they became the teachers of music to the Romans.

If Rome could claim the title of mother of the Italian people, let us not forget that Etruria could justly claim the name of grandmother.[24]

The Romans, having to build their institutions of state on Etruscan models, owe Etruria much of their religious cult, as well as their architecture. Even the name *Roma* is probably derived from the Etruscan *rumon* ("river").[25]

The most decisive influence the Etruscans exerted upon the Romans was in the field of religion. I will have more to say about this when we scrutinize the Roman practice of music.

Did the Etruscans have their own system of music? Did they make use of "keys" in music (*modoi*)? This could be assumed, considering the close relationship between Greek and Etruscan music. Unfortunately, no records exist supporting this possibility. In the later musical practices of the Romans, based originally on those of the Etruscans, the Greek influence probably erased the former Etrurian elements. Nevertheless, STRABO asserts that Roman music played on official occasions had been taken over from the Etruscans. This is correct insofar as public ceremonies are concerned. Whether for religious or political events, the musical background was supported mainly by the participation of brass instruments. The Etrurians were the principal manufacturers of various categories of brass instruments, and the Romans might well have used their music too, on solemn occasions. This practice changed only with the conquest by the Romans of Magna Graecia (281–266 B.C.E.). From then on, the penetration by Greek music into Rome's culture was irresistible, and probably erased any existing elements of the former Etrurian art. But as long as Etruria still preserved her national unity, her own musical culture is evidenced by numerous archaeological discoveries.

On a stone sarcophagus from Nefro (first half of the fourth century B.C.E.), there is the reproduction of a wedding ceremony. In the wedding cortege the bride is followed by a kithara-player, the groom by a cornu-player and a female aulos-player. In the home of the bride they play the lyre, as was usual in Greece. A stone sarcophagus from Caere (in the Vatican) shows a public procession accompanied by rich musical display. This pictorial representation has been placed in the fifth century B.C.E. It shows a festive couple followed by a chariot drawn by two horses; the procession is headed by a cornu-player and another musician blowing the lituus; then follows a herald, after him a player on the "cradle-kithara," and an aulos-player.

As mentioned above, LYCOURGOS invited THALETAS of Gortyn to Sparta to subdue an epidemic (probably the plague?) with his singing. Something like this also happened in Rome. According to LIVY,[26] Etruscan dancers and flutists were invited to Rome to "fight" against the plague of the year 393 B.C.E. As LIVY reports, this was a ritual healing ceremony; the pantomimic dances and plays were supposed to be an atonement to placate the ire of the gods. If we add to LIVY's report that of STRABO, it becomes evident that the Romans attributed to the Etruscan ritual music a specific healing power. About this more will be said later.

Further details about the musical life of the Etruscans may be culled from other archaeological discoveries. In the *Tomba dei leopardi* at Tarquinia, there are well-preserved wall paintings which, though under early Hellenistic influence, show genuine Etruscan features. The most beautiful among these paintings is a scene in which a cupbearer approaches a company of banqueteers, followed by an aulos-player and a musician with a stringed instrument very similar to the Greek barbiton (Illus. 128).

As in Greece, dancing Etruscan women are depicted with hand-clappers, wrongly called "castanets," although they served a similar purpose, that of supporting the dancers rhythmically.[27]

In public processions, especially at weddings, the aulos was the usual accompanying instrument, just as in Hellas. Brass instruments, too, gradually appear in Etruscan paintings, among them the cornu and the lituus. Fully developed pictures of these instruments have been found in a tomb of *Castel Rubello* in Orvieto (end of the fourth century B.C.E.).[28]

Other wall paintings in ancient tombs, such as those of the *Tomba del Triclinio* and the *Tomba del Citadoro*, show male and female dancers as well as musicians of both sexes. The most ancient of these tombs depicting dance-music is the *Tomba delle Leonesse* of the sixth century B.C.E. In other tombs, there are similarly vivid reproductions of musical scenes. These include the *Tomba della Caccia e Pesca*, *Tomba della Pulcella*, *Tomba del Morto*, *Tomba dei Leopardi*, *Tomba Golini* in Orvieto, *Tomba dei Baccanti*, *Tomba Prancesca Giustiniani*, and many more. All this proves how important and widespread music must have been in the life of the Etruscans.

The belief of the Etruscans concerning life after death has been extensively illustrated by wall paintings in which their "paradise" after death includes endless entertainment, with lightly clothed women dancing to the accompaniment of the aulos and the lyra. At banquets, weddings, and funerals, there were all kinds of instruments—pipes, lyres, syrinxes, and trumpets. Love of music and love of dance were important manifestations of the Etruscan civilization. Wall paintings in tombs show again and again symposia with richly clad participants of both sexes reclining in pairs on couches, served by slaves and entertained by dancers and musicians.[29]

In a tomb of Cervereti there were discovered among other implements numerous objects declared by archaeologists to be musical instruments. Among them a lengthy frame with cross-bars is believed to represent a xylophone. In discussing the Greek instruments, I raised some doubts about the existence of a similar xylophone-like instrument in Greece. The same doubts exist about this object. At any rate, this Etruscan instrument could belong to the type of noise-making implement that has been taken for the alleged Greek xylophone. The other object found in this tomb, having numerous holes, might possibly be regarded as the base of a syrinx, the pipes of which are missing, perhaps destroyed by age in the many centuries before the tomb's discovery.

The decline of Etruria started in the sixth century B.C.E. with the growing independence of its cities in Latium. On the sea, the Etruscans suffered two defeats by the Greeks (474 and 403), with the result that their trade was reduced. On the mainland, the Gallic invaders weakened their power and drove them out from the Po Valley. Jealousies and wars between rival cities contributed to the undermining of their strength. Thus, it needed only a decisive thrust by the Roman warriors to break the supremacy of the Etruscans in Italy (310 B.C.E.).

Whether Etruscan music and its practice originated on Italian soil cannot be unequivocally proven, owing to the lack of authentic historical records. It may be assumed, however, that during the migration from the country of their origin in Asia Minor, they might have brought with them many features of their ancient civilization, and also at least the basic elements of their music.

The love of music of the Etruscans may be inferred by the historical fact that during a famine, the leaders of the nation, TYRRHENUS and LYDUS, succeeded in appeasing the suffering of the population by offering them music and plays.[30] The ever-growing influence of Greek musical culture might have contributed to the amalgamation of the various trends of Etruscan art, so that a homogeneous Etruscan musical culture was the final result, one very different from that of the Hellenes. This can be inferred mainly through the predilection of the Etruscans for the penetrating sound of brass instruments, a fact that makes it quite unlike the music of the Greeks. Nevertheless, Etruscan military music played an important role in the music of the Romans, whose warlike character closely resembled that of the Etruscans.

It must be stressed that written records about Etruscan music were composed only centuries later by Romans whose statements were mostly hearsay and cannot be considered authentic information. Yet, it can be asserted that the role of the Etruscans as the immediate music masters of Rome is clearly evident. Their influence lasted in Rome for centuries, until Rome succumbed to the enchantment of the higher Greek musical culture, which first weakened, then extinguished almost completely, the former Etruscan music.

What remained permanently in Roman music from the Etruscan model was the predominance of brass instruments. Without the Etruscan forerunners in this domain, the Romans could not have developed their heavy military music, since this kind of sound was unknown—and foreign—to Greek musical art, which was based upon more delicate and less penetrating sound effects.

This was by no means merely an achievement of the Greeks. Southern Europe was unified culturally, having a homogeneous musical physiognomy, using the same instruments, which often bore the same names. In this milieu, Etruria was, so to speak, a foreign element having its own sound ideal, its own instruments, its own musical "aesthetics," if I may use this term. Rome could do no better than to take over the existing Etruscan musical achievements. But as soon as Greece became the leader of musical art, her influence and musical practice permeated the entire Italian peninsula through her colony of Magna Graecia, Sicily, and the southern part of the Apennine Peninsula. With the conquest of Magna Graecia by the Romans (281–266 B.C.E.), the inroads of Greek music upon Rome became decisive ones. Rome was wise enough not to evade the Greek cultural influences, and soon Greek tonal art supplanted the hitherto sole impact of Etruscan music. Nevertheless, Etruria can legitimately be considered as the forerunner of the later-blooming Graeco-Roman musical culture.

THE CHANGE-OVER

After all we know about the musical practice of the Etruscans, it is surprising that music historians generally consider the beginning of Roman music as not derived from the Etruscans, but rather as originating under the direct influence of Greece. Even then, Roman music is characterized not so much as an imitation of Greek music as being a "decadent" art that carries the seed of its later decay even at its inception. It has been generally denied that Roman music possessed its own physiognomy and it has been asserted that it completely lacked the high ethos that distinguished Greek music. In short, it seems that musical historians approached Roman music with preconceived ideas, which made an objective judgment difficult.

We frequently read in musicological works about the "sterility" and "degeneracy" of Roman music. In some of them, Roman music is not even treated in a special chapter, but is considered as belonging to a "Greek-Roman cultural entity."[31]

In a treatise on social history we find the following statement about the value of Roman music:

Rome and music; what antithesis! No other people were fundamentally less musical than the Romans.[32]

In one of the leading historical works about the civilization of Antiquity, there is the statement:

Roman music was really Greek, transformed to Roman soil and adapted to Roman condition.[33]

And another historian says:

There was never a Roman music, insofar as it refers to an art form in the higher sense of the word, but only a Greek music transplanted to Roman soil.[34]

Other antagonists have gone even farther, attributing to the music of the Romans complete sterility, lack of individuality as well as lack of independence. Some have stated that the Romans considered their music to be but a rhythmically organized noise. The eminent musicologist, P. H. LÁNG, maintained that the Romans had a "rather uncouth and vulgar" taste in music.[35] Even HERMANN ABERT, a scholar who, more than anybody else, delved into the depth of the music of Antiquity, considered Roman music basically nothing but a more or less degenerate Greek music.[36]

And, indeed, if we take the judgments of the Roman writers, especially those of the satirists, at their face value, Roman music appears to have been of inferior quality. SENECA the Elder (first century C.E.) complains that the size of orchestras and choral groups was of such gigantic proportions that sometimes there were more performers in the theaters than audience. HORACE asserts that the sound quality of the aulos could vie with that of the tuba.[37] AMMIANUS MARCELLINUS mentions that "there are now lyres as large as coaches."[38] (Illus. 33).

In general, contemporary records indicate that the tendency to practice music prevailed, at least in public life, in gigantic proportions. Music teachers and music schools furnished dilettantes *en masse;* it belonged to the *bon ton* of every bourgeois family to give their daughters instruction in lyre-playing. Rich people employed multitudes of slaves, who made music day and night, to the despair of their neighbors. At banquets there was no longer any conversation, since music drowned out every attempt at it. A veritable invasion of virtuosi of all kinds flooded the theaters and concert halls, bringing with them all their idiosyncrasies, vanities, and intrigues.

This is, at least, how the Roman writers characterize the state of music in the Rome of their time. Even CICERO complains of the loss of the "austere sweetness" of music as it could be heard in olden times on the stage. Furthermore, he says that the present use can create only *delectatio puerilis* ("childish pleasure"), but it is practically worthless because it cannot achieve any sentiment of happiness.[39]

We read with astonishment and regret that SACHS, eminent scholar and student of the music of Antiquity,

prefers to draw the curtain over this section of music history.[40]

I think it unjust to consider only the negative side of a cultural phenomenon; Roman music decidedly has positive values to its credit, as well.

And, indeed, in recent times voices appear in increasing number that attribute to Roman music a value of its own, if not its own physiognomy, despite its dependence on Etruscan and Greek patterns.

Among those who take up the cudgel for Roman musicality, GÜNTHER WILLE, in two treatises—one short,[41] and more recently in a full-sized book[42]—has become the champion of those who envisage in Roman music more than an object of entertainment. He refers justly to the fact that conclusions, especially wrong conclusions, based upon the personal opinion of individuals cannot establish a reliable picture of a cultural trend.[43]

As a principle, it must be stressed, on the contrary, that the musicality of an entire people cannot be judged solely by music history alone; it is necessary to invoke the principles based on a character study of the peoples in question. It is outside of the task of this essay to deal with this important facet in detail; therefore, it is mentioned cursorily.

The preconceived judgment about Roman music is the more astonishing, since there are in the Roman as well as the Greek literature more than four thousand passages referring to music. Therefore, it would have been necessary to separate the chaff from the grain and to try to peel off the many exaggerations and disfigurations that still blight critiques of Roman musical practice. This is the aim of my investigation. In looking at Roman music "too much under the ancient idealizing preconception about Greek music,[44] the other extreme should be avoided, that of attributing to Roman music features it did not or could not possess.

The basic principle of Roman music is generally considered to have been *solida utilitas*, "practical usefulness."[45]

With all ethical appreciation of Greek music, its sense and aim were basically the same; it was "music for practical use" (*Gebrauchsmusik*), just like the Roman, and this fact was not altered by the later developing notion of "art music" in Greek civilization. Maybe the practically inclined Romans recognized earlier the utilitarian value of their music; their enjoyment of music was not diminished by this, and I cannot agree with ABERT when he says that "the Roman character was basically no less than friendly toward music."[46]

In a satire by MARCUS TERENTIUS VARRO (116–26 B.C.E.), the contrast between lovers of music and those opposing it is aptly characterized. His poem entitled "Onos Lyras" ("The Donkey as a lyre-player") is a humorous comment on music, based upon the Greek proverb: *Onos lyras akouon kinei ta ota*, "The donkey, when he hears a lyra, moves his ears."[47] In it, VARRO describes a vivid controversy between two camps. Those against declared that music is not only effeminate but unnecessary; the others maintained that music is useful, since even working men sing at work and thereby alleviate their drudgery. The defenders use their arguments not merely to stress the enjoyment of music, but also its useful value. This, of course, is the principle of worksongs in all civilizations, ancient and recent. This still does not constitute an aesthetic approach to music, but represents the principle of utilitarianism, the *solida utilitas*. Such a satirical poem cannot, of course, be considered as a norm for the general approach of the Romans to music as an art. In those times, the adversaries of music had to be fought with sarcasm and satire. This was the aim of VARRO's little poem. In it, he aptly elucidates the musical situation of Rome, where there were not merely cynical opponents of music, but also defenders of it, even if only from the standpoint of its practical value.

Besides this humoristic diatribe, VARRO seems to have had a more positive approach to music. In his lost treatise, *Disciplinae*, an entire chapter (no. 7, entitled "De musica") was devoted to music as a science and an art.

There are other statements in the literature attesting to real music lovers, such as that of the younger SENECA, who says that there are people who prefer

to be awakened in the morning by peaceful music, instead of military signals,[48]

and OVID's statement

that he would like much more to play the lyra in peace of mind, than to be in a military camp.[49]

These opinions, by no means isolated, show that leading poets of the epoch, contrasting them to the all-embracing spirit of Roman military life, did not lose sight of the artistic values of music.

There are also many accusations about Roman "barbarism," supposedly inflicted upon the noble Greek music. Even if we were to assume that in the

Roman theater no art song was to be heard, and that anything offered there was but rhythmically organized noise, the facts are to the contrary.

There were a multitude of itinerant virtuosi of all categories, singers as well as instrumentalists, who through the centuries vivified Rome's musical life. These virtuosi served not merely the desire of the audiences for sensational stimulus, but gave music lovers a chance to enjoy "good music," or what was understood as such in this period.

Such observations of Roman writers are certainly no valid proof of Roman "musicality." Better than such literary statements will be an objective survey of Roman musical practice on the basis of actual facts. It will show that above the masses, who were addicted solely to amusement and pleasure-seeking, there were individuals as well as broad strata of society for whom music was not merely an enticement of the senses, but represented an aesthetic necessity. This was the case in the early republican period, and even more so in imperial Rome at a later time.

MUSIC IN THE RELIGION OF ROME

In order to understand the role of music in Roman ritual, we must examine the religious institutions of the Etruscans, from whom the Romans had taken over almost all the important elements.

The Etruscans had a central sanctuary, the grove of Voltumna, evidently the supreme god of the Etruscans, which was located in the district of Volsinii.[50] They developed in their religion an institution that the Romans greatly admired and called *disciplina Etrusca*. It consisted in observations of lightning and the flight of the birds, and in looking at and interpreting the inner organs, especially the liver, of the sacrificial animals, in order to learn from them the will of the gods. This custom probably goes back to the Babylonians, from whom the Etruscans might have taken it over. The Romans adopted the same custom and called these examiners of the animals' viscera *haruspices*. The augurs, too (*aves-gero*), the observers of the flight of the birds, as well as the auspices (*avis-scipio*), were taken over from the Etruscans and incorporated into the religious *Collegia* of the Romans. The augurs, haruspices, and soothsayers had such an importance in the Roman life, that they were an official party of every Roman army unit as late as JULIAN (363 C.E.). In addition to the priests, under the leadership of the high priest (*Pontifex maximus*), the nine augurs represented the most influential religious body in the Roman hierarchy. Their decisions were determined mostly by political necessities, whenever the government expected from them a favorable or unfavorable opinion. The priests as well as the augurs were frequently influenced by "donations," which tended to slant their oracular pronouncements. This gives insight into CICERO's statement that it might have been difficult for two augurs, meeting each other, not to laugh about their divinations.[51]

Gradually, the religion of Rome became increasingly the political tool of the state. This at least is how POLYBIUS characterized it about 150 B.C.E.[52] This, however, was nothing new, because a similar interrelationship between the reigning powers and the state religion can be observed in almost all the countries of the antique world.

Besides the direct influence of the Etruscan religion upon that of the Romans, one circumstance should not be discarded, that of the magic-ritual background present in all primitive religions. As shown earlier, the original purpose of the music in the cult was using magic to chase away demons and malevolent spirits through loud noises. "Music" consisted, at such an archaic stage of civilization, mainly of noises. The aim of ritual music was to

> build the bridge to the gods, insure their clemency and avert their enmity. . . . Therefore the priesthood was from ancient times on the carrier and administrator of this magic art.[53]

Among the Roman sodalities of priests, the Salii and the Arval brothers assumed, from ancient times on, the role of attending to the musical functions of the ritual. The Salii were installed according to the tradition by NUMA POMPILIUS himself, the creator of the Roman sacral rites, and his successor TULLUS HOSTILIUS. Their task was to honor the war gods Mars and Quirinus with war dances and appropriate songs.[54] Every year in March and October they held armed processions in the city, which were led by a dancer (*praesul*) and a singer (*vates*) performing archaic songs and ancient war dances. These ritual songs of the Arval brothers originated in the earliest period of Roman history, and their texts were so obsolete that, by the end of the Republic and the times of the emperors they could no longer be understood.

In their sacred music the Romans employed mainly the brass instruments taken over from the Etruscans. The use of the stringed instruments was introduced only after the adoption of the *ritus Graecus,* but from then on it held its place firmly in the cult.[55] For sacrifices the Romans used the *tibia;* it was never missing from sacrificial ceremonies.

Did the augurs and the other functionaries of the Roman ritual fulfill their religious duties with or without music? And did they perform the music, if any, themselves, or did they have professional musicians as helpers? In the extant literary sources there is no unequivocal answer to these questions. We can only surmise that they pronounced their oracles with a musical background, as was usual with the Greek oracles of Delphoi. An indirect proof for the participation of secular musicians in religious rites is the popularity of the "Etruscan flutists" (*subulones*). An event reported by LIVY is the proof thereof.[56]

The Etruscan flutists participated each year in the Feast of JUPITER. In 309 B.C.E., Rome was involved in a war, and the financial situation of the republic was at such a low level that the community could not pay the musicians as was the rule in former years. The musicians took a drastic step: they decided to strike, counting that the superstitious Roman aristocracy would not dare to offend JUPITER by lack of music. To insure their payment, they resolved to emigrate to Tibur (the present Tivoli) on the other side of the Tiber and refuse to return to Rome. They yielded to no persuasion and no threat, insisting on their ancient rights. Finally, they were outwitted by a ruse.

The Roman Senate sent a delegation to Tibur asking for help. The fathers of the community promised their cooperation, and a stratagem was agreed upon: the musicians were asked to give a concert in Tibur, to which they gladly agreed. During and after the concert they were treated copiously with wine until they were dead drunk. In this condition they were loaded upon carriages and brought back to Rome. When they awakened at daylight at the forum, the population received them jubilantly and praised them for their return to Rome.

Under these circumstances it was impossible for them to refuse their collaboration at the festival. But they made one condition, which was granted, namely, that they be entitled every year on the 13th of June (the date of the happening) to hold in Rome a solemn procession carrying a red flag (*vexillum russeum*), to arrange a kind of merry carnival with singing (*cum cantu*), and to collect donations for the benefit of their guild.

Besides this lively story, historical records furnish ample proofs for the role of music in the cult. The defeat of the Romans by HANNIBAL at Cannae (216 B.C.E.) caused such consternation in the Senate that it decided to appeal for help to the Greek gods. The Sibylline Books had prophesied that HANNIBAL would retreat from Roman soil if the Magna Mater, *i.e.*, the Phrygian goddess CYBELE, were brought to Rome, together with her cult. In 205 B.C.E. the Roman Senate sent an appeal to ATTALUS, king of Pergamon, who granted Rome's request. A black stone, supposedly the personification of the goddess, was brought with great pomp to Rome. In the same year, HANNIBAL did, in fact, retreat from Rome, and as thanks to CYBELE the Romans built in her honor a large temple on the Palatine. With the cult of CYBELE, the orgiastic rites connected with it also entered Rome.[57] The music in these rites exerted its influence upon other branches of the Roman religion in which—besides Greek and Phyrgian gods—the Egyptian Isis was particularly venerated; in the northwestern part of the city a large sanctuary was erected in her honor.

In the fourth century the cult of Isis came to Greece, in the third to Sicily, and in the second to Italy; from there, it spread everywhere in the Roman Empire. Not only foreign slaves, but hosts of Roman citizens, belonging to all strata of the population, joined her cult. In all larger cities sanctuaries in her honor were erected. She was called "The Queen of the Heaven," "Star of the Seas," "Mother of God." Statuettes of her have been found along the Danube, the Rhine, and the Seine. Even in London a temple devoted to her was excavated.[58] The Emperor DOMITIAN (51–96 C.E.) renovated and embellished the temples of Isis and SERAPIS.

The rites of Isis in Egypt took place with rich musical display; with her cult, the music pertaining to it was also introduced to Rome.

Besides the cults of CYBELE and Isis, many other mystery cults entered the Roman religion, among them that of DIONYSOS, who—according to the Greek custom—was honored with orgiastic rites. Members of all classes of Roman society, mainly, however, foreign slaves, participated in these rites, processions, and sacrifices. The Senate, and later several emperors, among them AUGUSTUS and TIBERIUS, tried to restrain the penetration and spread of the numerous mystery-cults, but in vain. For the great masses of the population, especially for those of the cities, the orgiastic rites and the music belonging to them exerted an irresistible attraction. With these cults, a great number of foreign musicians and dancers came to Rome. Their instruments and concert-music gained little by little a firm foothold in the theater, and were later copiously employed in the entertainment music of the Romans.

No other religion had as many gods as the Romans. There were specific gods for the various phenomena of public and private life—for natural events, for fertility, war, peace, honor, hope, virtue, superstition, and the innumerable other manifestations of human existence. VARRO estimated the number of Gods to exceed 30,000, which is certainly highly exaggerated; we have to consider, however, that many of them were so-called demi-gods. Almost all heroes as well as a number of emperors received the status of gods. The Roman gods (or most of them) are the equivalents of the saints of the Christian church; "canonization" was unknown in Rome. This is how the statement of PETRONIUS (the satirical author of NERO's times (7–66 C.E.) is to be understood when he says that some cities of Italy had more gods than inhabitants.[59] It is evident that with these numerous gods all kinds of musical practices penetrated into the Roman religion.

The overwhelming influence of music in religious rites will be even more significant when we deal with the festival cycle of the Romans.

With the invasion of all kinds of foreigners, such as prisoners of war, slaves, merchants, and returning legionnaires, further mystery and mixed religions came to Rome. These soldiers, sometimes being long absent from Rome, accepted foreign cults and brought them home with them.

From the south came the cult of PYTHAGORAS, whose tenets included vegetarianism and whose adherents believed in resurrection after death. From Hieropolis came ATARGATIS, known to the Romans as SYRIA DEA, (the Syrian Goddess), also AZIZ, the ZEUS of Dolichē. These cults were introduced to Rome by Syrian merchants and slaves. From Parthia came the cult of MITHRAS, of the sun-worshippers. From Judaea came the austere religion of YAHVEH, the god who did not tolerate other gods beside him, who gave his adherents severe moral laws, and isolated them completely from the rest of the population. Among the adherents of this stern god were believers, in increasing numbers, who worshipped his resurrected son whom they considered to be the long-awaited Messiah.

In all these ancient mystery-religions, with their elaborate ceremonies of expiation and purification, music played an essential role, either furnishing the tonal background for the sacrifices offered, or as a stimulant for the mass hysteria connected with these rites.

It does not require much imagination to realize that the music in the rituals of the numerous Roman religions oscillated between the exalted and the debased, thus giving, in its diversity, to Roman ritual music a multi-faceted physiognomy unique in the history of human civilization.

THE ROMAN FESTIVAL CYCLE

I have demonstrated that the Greek calendar consisted of an almost-uninterrupted succession of feasts, days of commemoration, and official and private festivities. Only the month of November was free from such events, due to the inclement weather.

The Roman festival cycle was, possibly, even more abundant. The year had over one hundred festive days (*feriae*); these were divided into *fasti consulares*, *libri magistratuum*, *annales maximi*, and *fasti calendares*. The difference between them was rather vague; some of them were strictly defined, others may have belonged to two or more categories.

The first, and sometimes the ninth and fifteenth, of each month were festive days. From the 11th to the 13th of May, Roman families celebrated the feast of the *Lemures*, the souls of the deceased. The *Parentalia* and *Feralia* in February served the same purpose, namely, to appease the dreaded shades of the dead. Some of the feasts of the cult of the deceased were mournful and gloomy; others, in a curious contrast and for no obvious reason, were joyous, frolicsome, even playful.

On February 15th the Roman celebrated the feast of the *Lupercalia,* dedicated to the god FAUNUS, to keep away the wolves (*lupus*) from the country folk. For this purpose goats and sheep were sacrificed. The priests were clad in goat-skins and ran around the Palatine and entreated FAUNUS to chase away, together with the wolves, the evil spirits. On the 15th of March, the poor left their hovels and built themselves tents on the Camp of Mars, celebrating the beginning of the new year and prayed to the goddess ANNA PERENNA (translated literally "the Ring of the Year") to grant them as many years of life as they could drink cups of wine.[60] In April the *Floralia,* the feast of FLORA, goddess of flowers and wells, took place; this feast lasted six days, with merriment and ample imbibing of wine. The May 1 was devoted to the *Bona Dea,* the Good Goddess; on the 9th, 11th, and 13th of May were celebrated the *Liberalia* of the god LIBER and the goddess LIBERA, the patron saints of grapes. At the end of May took place the joyous feast of the *Ambervalia.* The priests of the Arval brotherhood (*Arval*=Plower) marched singing in a procession along the borders of the adjoining farms and placed flowers on stones marking the boundaries of the farms, sprinkling upon themselves blood of the sacrificial animals while invoking MARS to bestow fertility on the land. In December the *Lares* (the deities) of the earth were honored with the *Compitalia;* in January rich sacrificial gifts were brought to the god TELLUS (the Earth) to secure a rich harvest.

The Oriental symbol of fertility, the phallus, was celebrated by honoring PRIAPUS, the Greek god of Procreation. This god was introduced rather late to Rome, but soon gained many adherents who celebrated his feast with scandalous customs, which St. AUGUSTINE sharply condemned.[61]

In most of these feasts and customs, the ancient Oriental belief (or superstition) was manifest, according to which human practices can overcome evil demons by magic means, fetishism and totemism.

The introduction of the rites of CYBELE (*Magna Mater*) enriched the Roman calendar in April with an additional festival, the *Megalesia,* the feast of the Great Mother. It started with wailings for her deceased son ATTIS, which was changed to a delirious frenzy after his "resurrection." This feast was symbolic of the rejuvenation of Nature after the winter sleep, just as in all the spring festivals of Antiquity the motive of the celebration was the rebirth of fertility.

The cult of DIONYSOS was celebrated with nocturnal orgiastic rites, known as the *Bacchanalia* (BACCHUS was the Roman equivalent of the Greek DIONYSOS). Since these rites took place at night and in secrecy, a rumor arose that human sacrifices were offered in them. Even LIVY gave credence to such hearsay.[62] Probably on account of such unfounded tales, the Senate, in 186 B.C.E. prohibited the cult, imprisoning 7000 of its adherents and condemning several hundreds of them to death. It is not certain whether the Senate succeeded by such draconic measures in suppressing the Bacchus cult, because the urge of the Orientals for mysticism and orgiastic rites was too deeply ingrained in the populace; it seems that the cult continued in secret after only a short interruption.

After the harvest was gathered, the gods were neglected for a while. This changed in December with the observance of the festival of the *Brumelia,* which lasted the whole month. According to contemporary descriptions, the whole town resembled a wine tavern. There was singing in the streets the whole night, and everywhere unbounded frolicking reigned.[63]

The summit of the festivities in December was the *Saturnalia*, lasting from the 17th to the 23rd of the month. In this festival the Romans celebrated the casting of the seed for the coming harvest—it was a festival in which all class differences were abolished, even reversed. The slaves sat with their masters at the same table, gave them orders, and made jokes about them; the masters served their slaves and did not start eating until the slaves had had their fill.[64]

In 17 B.C.E. AUGUSTUS introduced the so-called *ludi saeculares*, in which for three days theatrical plays were presented and competitions were held in honor of SATURN's golden age. The *ludi saeculares* were a misnomer—in reality they were religious feasts. Each day started with ritual ceremonies and sacred songs; their aim was return to friendly relations with the Roman gods, which were supposed to have deteriorated on account of the multitude of foreign religions that had inundated Rome.

AUGUSTUS, who banished the Egyptian and Asiatic cults from Rome, made only one exception: that of the Jewish religion. In all the provinces, the religious freedom of the Jews was maintained.

Among the festivals may be counted those on which *ludi*, plays, were offered. In the early Empire there were 76 such festival days, among them 55 on which *ludi scenici*, theatrical plays or pantomimes, were featured, and 22 on which performances in the circus, in the stadium, or in the amphitheater, were given. The number of the *ludi* was constantly increased, so that in the year 354 C.E. there were popular feasts on no fewer than 175 days.[65] These *ludi* embraced the most diversified presentations: recitations, concerts, pantomimes, scenic plays, but also athletic competitions, horse and chariot races, combats with wild animals, even sea battles on an artificial lake. Most of these latter presentations belong more in the domain of circus plays but, nevertheless, they were part and parcel of the festival cycle.

Besides the "official" festivals on a national scope, there were abundant local festivities in many provinces, especially in Asia Minor, such as, for instance, the feast of ARTEMIS in Ephesus, which was celebrated during the entire month of May; and a specific feast in honor of DEMETER in Eleusis, which lasted three days.

Twice a year, on the 23rd of March and the 25th of May, there was a ceremony called *Tubilustrium*, on which the sacred ritual trumpets, and also those employed in the army, especially the trumpets leading to battle, were symbolically cleaned. It was less a religious act than a demonstration of the importance of the trumpets (and the other brass instruments) in the ritual and the army.

MUSIC IN PUBLIC LIFE

The basic character of Roman music was utilitarian. Whether in the family, or at funerals, banquets, public festivities, and so on, music was a daily necessity. There was, indeed, no domain of public or private life in which music had no share.

The overwhelming majority of Romans considered music not as an art but as *solida utilitas*, an integral element of daily life, a means of amusement, which had the same importance as eating, drinking, and the other amenities of civic life. Some writers and poets (especially in the imperial period) expressed a more aesthetic approach to music. These isolated opinions do not alter the fact that the masses looked upon music mainly as a form of entertainment, a viewpoint which continued unchanged until the decline of the Empire.

A deeper appreciation of music could be found in Rome only in isolated cases. Even after the Romans adopted music first from the Etruscans, then from the Greeks, it had to strive against conservatism, which considered art music as degenerate. In 115 B.C.E. the censors prohibited playing any instruments, with the exception of the short Italian aulos, the tibia. Even a century later, the elder SENECA looked upon music as being unmanly. Meanwhile, MARCUS TERENTIUS VARRO (116–26 B.C.E.) published his famous book about music (*De musica,* one of his 74 books in 620 volumes), which contributed greatly to the abolition of the ancient prejudice against music. This book was the starting point for many similar treatises. Eventually, Greek music with its sensuous melodies and the artful use of delicate instruments broke through all resistance, so that around 50 C.E. music in Rome was recognized as an art form valued for itself. From then on, it became an essential element in the education of every distinguished Roman, male or female; women especially passed entire days practicing music, singing, and even composing new songs. Even the emperors were affected by the music mania, as will be shown presently.

Lyric poems had to be performed with musical accompaniment—art music was composed mainly for this purpose. Choir-singing increased in popularity, and even if it never achieved the artistic significance of the Greek *kyklios choros,* it was zealously employed at weddings, plays, and on religious occasions, as well as at funerals. HORACE was commissioned by AUGUSTUS to compose for his *ludi saeculares* a *carmen saeculare.* The reason for selecting HORACE for this *carmen* seems to have been that he was not only the *poeta laureatus* of the epoch, but also because he was well versed in music, as is evident from the fact that he accompanied the singing of this *carmen* on the lyre. Thus, HORACE can be considered the first creator of a Roman artistic innovation, being the author of the poem, the composer of the music, and the leader of the performance. The *carmen* was sung by 27 boys and as many girls on June third of the year 3 B.C.E. upon the steps of the entrance to the temple of APOLLO PALATINUS.

Following Greek custom, soon public concerts were given with the participation of soloists and choral groups. At public plays music contests were introduced. Even at modest banquets, music had its appropriate role. MARTIAL, for instance, promised to a friend whom he invited to dinner at least one tibia-player.[66] PETRONIUS mentions a man who put a clock in his banquet room, and placed close to it a bucina-player (trumpeter) in uniform who had to indicate how much time passed from his employer's life.[67]

The custom of adorning banquets with music was taken over first from the Etruscans, and later—on a more elaborate scale—after the penetration into Rome of Greek musical practice.

On the other hand, men of refinement condemned the excessive use of music. At another occasion, MARTIAL said that the best entertainment was that in which no tibia-player disturbed the conversation, and he considered that man happy who enjoyed his meal without music.[68] PETRONIUS, in his satire, *The Banquet of Trimalchio,* scoffs at the habits of a rich upstart, at whose banquets even the tables were wiped clean to the rhythm of a song.[69]

In the pantomimes, *symphoniae* were inserted, which meant that a choir sang and danced to the accompaniment of a group of instrumentalists. Sometimes an actor sang a solo aria; in other instances a professional singer (*cantor*) sang the lyrics, while a mime interpreted the words with gestures and appropriate dances. The pantomimes were frequently presented in gigantic proportions; sometimes 3000 singers and 3000 dancers participated in them.[70]

There were numerous instrumental virtuosi, and the number of good average artists was legion. From all parts of the empire musicians converged on Rome, attracted by the gold of the capital of the world. The huge number of musically educated slaves made it possible for their masters to maintain large choirs and orchestras with almost no expense.

In the long run, this led to a veritable trade of musically gifted slaves, which eventually took on such proportions that the Emperor THEODOSIUS, in 385, prohibited the selling and buying of kithara-playing girls, and also their employment in banquets and public performances.[71]

Many wealthy persons had their own permanent music groups. Some had their especially gifted musicians sent to famous teachers for further education (see "Music Instruction" below, where an apprentice contract between the owner of a young slave and a music teacher is described).

Professional virtuosi were in great demand and undertook extended concert tours in all parts of the empire. They were highly paid and often became the idols of the audiences. For several of them monuments or statues were erected. With this exaggerated veneration, musicians began to display more and more vanity, conceit, arrogance, and all other bad habits of the "privileged" few. Women of high society adored them and paid large sums for their love (see also p. 418); other female admirers fought for the possession of a plectrum the admired artist had used in the concerts; others offered sacrifices to the gods to insure victory for their favorites in the festival contests. The famous tibia player CANUS boasted that his music was able to chase away sorrow, increase joy, create piety, and kindle the flame of love.[72] The victors in poetical and musical contests received the coveted oak wreath from the hands of the Emperor.

The virtuosi seldom stayed long in one place; as soon as they "milked" one town, they changed their locality, especially since there was an insufficient number of rich music-lovers in one place; furthermore, they had many other engagements and were generally booked months ahead. Their agents sent them on lengthy tours, as is the custom in our time with celebrities.

The honoraria of some of the traveling virtuosi bordered on the fantastic. Records indicate that for the reopening by VESPASIAN of the theater of Marcellus, the tragic actor APELLES was paid 100,000 sesterces; the two kitharōdes participating on this occasion received 200,000 sesterces each.[73] VESPASIAN's thrift, even avarice, were well known; yet he paid his musical artists generously. Some of them, like APELLES, received 100,000 sesterces, none of them under 40,000; furthermore, several of them were honored with golden wreaths. An inscription from the city of Aphrodisias in Asia Minor states that in a musical contest the first prize for the victorious kitharōde was 3250 dinarii.

Despite the prohibition *in foro cantare*, to "make music in public,"[74] bands of musicians roamed the streets and places of Rome with tibias and cymbals and hand-drums. They sang and danced and passed the plate around. Jongleurs, acrobats, and all other figures of the popular fairs flooded the squares; some of these street musicians represented a one-man orchestra. One of these musicians may be seen in a terra-cotta figurine in which he plays a syrinx, which is connected by a pipe to an air bag that the player activates with his right foot

(Illus. 41). Some authorities doubt that the syrinx in this figurine is connected with the air bag, and interpret the contraption activated by the foot of the musician as a *scabellum*. This device (it can scarcely be termed an "instrument") served by its penetrating sound to keep larger groups of singers or dancers together. For a single musician to use a scabellum would have been senseless, the more so since the rhythm of the music performed was stressed by a cymbal-playing child or dwarf (see Illus. 41).

In a fresco of Herculaneum (now in the Naples Museum) a concert is depicted in the home of a wealthy man. It shows a female aulos-player using the *phorbeia*. The instrument has two rather long pipes and the player is accompanied by a kithara-player. That it is a real house concert and not merely a private musical entertainment is evident from the large audience depicted in this fresco.

In the closing years of the Republic, it was a widespread custom to arrange house concerts and musical entertainments at banquets at which all categories of hired musicians performed. Orchestral musicians (*symphoniaci*) belonged to the retinue of MILO, the people's tribune. CLODIA at Baiae arranged lectures and concerts for her guests, and CAESAR himself liked to be entertained at his meals by music.[75]

For the character of such music we are restricted to mere guesses since—despite the multitude of indications in the Roman literature—there are no positive records to describe their sound qualities. Occasionally statements occur indicating that the main thing in such performances was that the music be loud enough and that the chief merit of a musician was how long he could sustain a note on his instrument. It was therefore more of a question of lung power than of artistic achievement.[76]

Nevertheless, some of the performances must have had certain artistic qualities, since the competition between musicians was very keen, and the audiences were in general highly demanding. Not even the professional claque, used regularly by both famous and not-so-famous artists, could provide the expected success if the performance was lacking the necessary brilliance. And if the performers were guilty of mistakes, the audiences did not spare them signs of their obvious displeasure.[77]

As for professional claques, there were, as it seems, numerous loafers who were only too glad to hire out to contractors who used them to "applaud a CANUS or a GLAPHYRUS" or other celebrities.[78] This profession seems to have been rather lucrative, and there was never a lack of aspirants. In spite of such an effective organization, it sometimes happened that kitharōdes were booed in the Theatre of Pompejus.[79]

An event—which probably remained unique—is generally quoted as a proof of the "lack of musicality" of the *profanum vulgus*, as PLAUTUS characterized the general citizenry of Rome.

For the triumphal plays of the victorious LUCIUS ANICIUS GALLUS (167 B.C.E.), a group of famous Greek musicians was hired to give a concert in the arena. The audience revolted and insisted that in lieu of the concert a boxing match be held.[80] However grotesque this happening might appear, it cannot be overlooked that for this occasion the public was promised something "exalting," and the audience felt itself cheated by a simple musical performance.

On the other hand, there are records testifying that there were in Rome numerous connoisseurs of music who, hearing the first tones of a piece played by an aulēte, immediately recognized it and could name the play to which it belonged, a fact that surprised even CICERO.

In view of the great "consumption" of musical performances of all kinds, there must have been, in addition to a multitude of professional musicians, widespread amateurism. In earlier times, the free-born Romans repudiated all forms of musical activity. This they felt was the business of slaves; familiarity with singing and playing was not considered appropriate to a man of standing. Only later, and under the influence of Greek culture, did this attitude change, and the rising tolerance with regard to music shifted to acceptance. Soon, amateurism assumed such proportions that even the Greek professional practice was completely overshadowed by it and private music schools mushroomed in every larger city.

Familiarity with music was generally considered part of female education. STATIUS reports that his step-daughter found a husband through her mastery of the lyra, as well as through the fact that she could set his poems to music and sing them. PLINY the Younger says the same thing about his third wife. The paramour of LUCIUS VERUS, the beautiful girl PANTHEA of Smyrna, must have been, according to LUCIAN, an outstanding singer, who could accompany herself on the kithara. He compares her with the muses and sirens and says that her singing surpassed that of the nightingale.[81] Even assuming that LUCIAN used an exaggerated form of poetic imagery in his report, PANTHEA must have been a singer of extraordinary qualities. Just as in Greece, the *hetairai* in Rome understood that to entice men mere bodily charm was not enough. In addition to their intellectual qualities, it was necessary for the women to display mastery in music.

These are merely a few examples to prove the existence of a widespread love of music among the Roman women and girls.

But amateurism little by little gained a foothold among the men as well. The only writer who raised his voice against it was the older SENECA who—as is well known—was a protagonist of the ancient simple life and austere morals. He complained that the noble sciences were neglected, that the interests of the masses were focused on idleness, that their mentality was governed by ignoble occupations such as singing and dancing, all of which exerted an effeminate influence upon the youth.[82]

SENECA the Elder drastically expresses his attitude to the music of his day in saying:

> I am always ashamed of humanity, when I enter the school of the philosophers; the Neapolitans are interested in the theatre and are eager to find a good bagpiper . . . but where a man should receive a good education, there is nobody, there is no interest for such a purpose.[83]

SENECA the Younger rebukes the abuses and exaggerations of musical amateurism, pointing out that these so-called lovers of music spend their entire day in singing and composing songs, forcing their voices by artificial means to attain a different character from the natural sound[84]

In imperial Rome, musical amateurism is attested to by a multitude of literary sources. It was believed that a fine voice was a great help in enabling individuals to be accepted by the nobility,[85] and that mastery in music was greatly appreciated at the highest level of society.[86] It is therefore not surprising that OVID, along with his advice in the art of love, considered a fine voice as particularly appropriate for the artifices of love.[87] MARTIAL scoffs at the many-sided amateur who does everything "nicely": sings nicely, plays the lyra nicely, but does not do anything really well.[88]

In the above-mentioned satire of PETRONIUS, the host, TRIMALCHIO, asks one of his guests, known as a good singer, to give proof that he is, for the benefit of the general assemblage. This man regrets his inability to sing, since in his youth he sang so much that he almost had consumption. TRIMALCHIO then tries to sing himself, but distorts atrociously the airs of the kitharōde and composer MENECRATES, a famous musician in NERO's time.[89]

In high society, too, amateurism must have been very widely spread. CAIUS CALPURNIUS PISO, the leader of the conspiracy against NERO (65 C.E.), is praised so excessively in a poem composed honoring his excellence as a player of the lyra, that one would have thought that APOLLO himself was his teacher.[90] The consul LUCIUS NORBANUS FLACCUS was an expert as a tuba (trumpet) player; he practiced the instrument diligently, even on the very day on which he started his functions as a consul (January 1, 19 C.E.).

There are very few records available dealing with music from the last period of Roman Antiquity (third century to the end of the fourth). Among them is a report of the astronomer FIRMICUS MATERNUS (third century) mentioning "public musicians," who were honored by the people. His remarks refer to composers as "inventors" of melodies for theatrical plays.[91] AMMIANUS MARCELLINUS reports that the Roman palaces, formerly famous for disseminating sciences, now resound with the singing and playing of instruments. Where formerly the philosophers were welcome, there are now singers and music teachers in their place; everywhere one could hear music, but the libraries, the depositories of knowledge, were silent as the graves.[92]

With the growth of Christianity, musical practice assumed a religious and ethical character. As secular music became coarse and served exclusively the sensuous instincts of the masses, the music of the early Christians brought about the necessary balance in the direction of the simple and unsophisticated practice of music. Roman music, which at this time exclusively served the frivolous pleasures of the senses, went unchecked toward its complete decay. It was especially the music of the theater and the unlimited reign of the pantomime that led to the complete corruption of Roman music.

But even during the time of the Emperor THEODORIC (489–526), when the migration was in full swing, the musical culture of Rome retained, to a certain extent at least, its ancient vitality.[93]

That music as an art survived the destruction of the antique culture is due on one hand to the rising Christian religion, and on the other hand to the development of Byzantine civilization. We know today that the music of the early Christians was not only strongly influenced by, but was the immediate successor of, Hebrew temple and synagogue singing. The fact that the musical practice of the Romans did not follow the fate of their once mighty empire, is due mainly to the development of the early Christian music practice, influenced by the ancient Jewish music, which survived beneath the surface for centuries. Unmistakable proof of this is contained in numerous statements made by the early Church fathers, who spoke almost unanimously of the continuous influence of Jewish music upon the new religion.[94]

MUSIC AT THE IMPERIAL COURTS
(Musical Amateurs among the Roman Caesars)

The history of human civilization never knew so many crowned heads who practiced music with such diligence and even with ardor as did the Roman Caesars. Whether the reason for this was real love of music, or whether familiarity with music belonged to a "good education," to which members of princely families were exposed, cannot be answered unequivocally. Yet, it is remarkable how many of the Roman emperors practiced music and sometimes achieved results far above ordinary amateurism. This sheds a favorable light upon the quality of music instruction in Rome, because without it, it would not have been possible to impart to members of the high nobility, and even to families of emperors, the incentive to cultivate music seriously.

There is an anecdote about JULIUS CAESAR, a contemporary record (not mentioned, however, by his biographer SUETONIUS), which seems to shed some light upon his relationship to music. If true, it must be attributed to his desire for ostentation rather than to his love of the art. As this record, which is probably highly exaggerated, states, CAESAR ordered for some public festivity 22,000 tables placed on the streets of Rome, richly spread with food and drink. Every Roman citizen could participate at this gigantic banquet. The tables reserved for persons of higher standing were provided with individual groups of musicians. If the record is to be believed, there must have been hosts of prefects, or "masters of ceremonies," to keep the tables free for the privileged ones and to assign each musical group to its proper place. While this report can be used only with great caution, it is correct to assume that at this time there may have been about 10,000–12,000 male and female singers and musicians in Rome.

More plausible is SUETONIUS's report,[95] which states that at the cremation of the assassinated JULIUS CAESAR, the musicians of Rome threw their ornate professional garments into the pyre, expressing by this gesture their grief over his death. This seems to imply that CAESAR was instrumental in improving the conditions for the musicians of Rome, although there are no records to support such an assumption.

Another version asserts that the musicians threw their instruments into the funeral pyre. This is an obvious misstatement, based on a wrong translation of SUETONIUS's text.[96] As a matter of fact, there were many war veterans participating in CAESAR's campaigns who, on passing the funeral pyre, threw their weapons into the fire. Weapons, swords, and spears were at any rate less expensive than instruments of music, and it is logical to assume that the veterans of his wars sacrificed their weapons as a final tribute to their assassinated leader.

Similarly, we do not know anything concrete about the attitude of AUGUSTUS (53 B.C.E.–14 C.E.) toward music, despite the abundance of historical records about his life and reign. The only hint that he might have had some relationship to music was the fact that he commissioned HORACE to write the *carmen saeculare*, evidently set to music by the poet himself.

About TIBERIUS's attitude toward music, there are no records. That he spoke Greek fluently, and even composed poems in Greek verses, inspired by his preferred poets, EUPHOTION, RHIANUS, and PARTHENIUS, however, permits the conclusion that his Greek teachers implanted in him respect for the achievements of Greek culture, of which music was an integral part. Incidentally, the marble busts of his favorite Greek poets were placed by him in the public libraries of Rome.[97]

The efforts of his Greek educators seem to have remained without tangible results, since TIBERIUS did not attend performances of Greek dramas[98] and even reduced the salaries of the actors.[99] This might be ascribed less to his lack of love of art, than to the fact that the actors were highly overpaid. Otherwise, his tyrannical reign and even more his immoral conduct might indicate little incentive for his love of musical art.

More is known about CALIGULA (12–41 C.E.). He received a good education, which included singing and instrumental instruction. This may explain his infatuation with the theater and everything connected with it. He supported quite a number of actors, and probably musicians also, and, as for his personal pleasure, he indulged in acting and dancing. He was not immune to artistic vanity and was often eager to demonstrate his "art" to an audience. Since his imperial dignity forbade him to appear in public, he used a ruse, inviting some leading senators to "an important conference," and used it as a pretext to demonstrate his achievements in singing and dancing.[100] His biographers, however, recording the acts of his reign, divulge nothing about whether he tried to improve the state of music or the lot of the musicians.

A characteristic gesture that gives a picture of his "artistic" vanity is described by SUETONIUS.[101] CALIGULA ordered a great festival in honor of some god, in which he planned to present himself for the first time to a large audience as a theatrical actor. Curiously enough, this was the last day of his life; he was assassinated at the age of 27. Thus, the murderers robbed his people of the opportunity of witnessing their Emperor's first artistic performance.

About the history of music, the reigns of the succeeding emperors contain mainly empty pages. We know little of CLAUDIUS (10 B.C.E.–54 C.E.), GALBA (3–69 C.E.), VESPASIAN (9–79), TITUS (40–81), or the short-lived OTHO (32–69), who reigned only 95 days, or VITELLIUS (15–69), whose reign lasted briefly over a year, or finally PERTINAX (assassinated in 193, shortly after he ascended the throne). All these more or less powerful Emperors failed to promote music, to the detriment of Roman culture.

It is true that TITUS, brought up at the court of CLAUDIUS, together with his son BRITANNICUS, was educated by the same teachers and in the same subjects as the son of the Emperor; he is reported to have made rapid progress in his studies. He also had a good musical education; " . . . he was something of a musician too: sang pleasantly, and mastered the harp."[102] He might have done something for music while he was Emperor if his wars (especially the war against Judaea) and his early death (in his 42nd year) had not prevented him from doing so (he reigned exactly two years, two months and 20 days).

Shortly before his death, TITUS made the enigmatic remark that "only a single sin lay on his conscience."[103] It has been interpreted to mean that he may have repented his impious entry into the forbidden Holy of Holies of the Jerusalem Temple. It was a capital crime for a Roman even to trespass the Court of the Israelites of the Temple. At any rate, the Jews ascribed his early death to this cause, and even Queen BERENICE is said to have reproached him for this act.[104]

DOMITIAN's reign started with negative effect when he abolished the pantomimes on account of their licentiousness and because he considered them as exerting a degenerating influence upon the public morality. On the other hand, he vigorously sponsored literature and the arts. In order to promote the art of poetry, he installed in 86 the Capitolinian Plays, featuring literary and musical contests. For these plays, he erected a stadium and a large music hall on the Campus Martius. Thus, his reign was beneficial for music even if we do not know anything of his own musical activities.

In an impulse to improve the morals of the masses, he issued all kinds of prohibitions against sexual transgressions. In one instance this went so far that he expelled from the Senate a Quaestor who was a dance addict and who attended theatrical performances too often.[105] He ordered the execution of a sickly boy simply because he too greatly resembled the famous actor PARIS and imitated his manners.[106] His later reign was tainted by cruelty and unbridled violence. It is natural, therefore, that under such circumstances the arts could not prosper.

It would have been unusual had NERVA (39–98), one of the rare Emperors who reigned through benevolence, not done anything for the arts. MARTIAL called him "the TIBULLUS of our time," and indeed NERVA, besides being a good lawyer, was a talented poet. He distributed land among the poor worth sixty million sesterces, canceled overdue taxes, reduced the inheritance tax, freed the Jews from the tribute imposed upon them by VESPASIAN, and set in order, by appropriate measures, the state finances. And yet nothing is known as to whether he did anything for the arts and music. Whether this is a fact or is due merely to incomplete historiography, cannot be said unequivocally. Generally, the biographers of the emperors did not forget to put the artistic achievements of the rulers in the best light. In spite of all other attainments, NERVA's biography lacks the honorable and probably well-deserved epithet of "lover of arts."

TRAJAN (52–117) was a mighty conqueror and a passionate builder of cities. He constructed the *Forum Trajanum* in Rome, at the entrance of which, in his honor, the Trajan column was erected, which still stands today at the same place although in ruins. The bas-reliefs depict TRAJAN's campaigns, which include his conquest of Dacia (today's Romania). Besides temples and a library, he erected on the Forum a theater and a music-hall as evidence of his love of the arts.

His reign was also distinguished by his largess in the social field. From the booty of his campaign in Dacia, and from the gold mines of the conquered country, he distributed to all Roman citizens who requested it, 650 denarii (about $260.00); it is said that there were 500,000 such gifts. He established large public works in order to reduce unemployment created by the demobilization of the army. Among these works were roads and aquaducts; in Ostia he built a large port and connected it by a canal with the Tiber. Among other public works, he erected an amphitheater in Verona, supported every city that was damaged by fire, earthquake, or flood, and admonished the cities of his realm to spend the surplus of their income for the betterment of the living conditions of their poor.

It would be natural to assume that an emperor who had such outstanding merits as a conqueror and social reformer, besides erector of buildings for the exercise of the arts, would have been generous also to music and musical artists. But nothing has been recorded about NERVA or TRAJAN, either by their biographers or in contemporary documents.

More is known in this regard about TRAJAN's successor, HADRIAN (76–138 C.E.).

The family of this Emperor originated in the city of Adria, situated at the Adriatic Sea. From there the family emigrated to Spain, where HADRIAN was born in the city of Italica. When his father died, he came under the tutelage of his uncle TRAJAN, who gave him the most brilliant education, "brilliant" as understood in that period. It included a little of everything. TRAJAN inspired the youth with such a love of Greek literature that HADRIAN was nicknamed "Graeculus." He also received instruction in music, along with other disciplines, among them medicine, mathematics, painting, and sculpture. In spite of being the crowned head of a state, he was active as an amateur in all of these various arts.

The extensive education of his youth had its repercussions in his later years. He was a fairly good singer, dancer, and player of the harp, and a rather good painter, but he lacked talent for sculpture. He supported artists, writers, and philosophers, and was the author of several books, among them a treatise on grammar. He wrote an autobiography and composed a number of poems in Latin and Greek, some of them serious, some others obscene.[107] He used to surround himself with scholars and philosophers, often asking them difficult questions, and was amused by their disputations and contradictory opinions. HADRIAN founded a University and erected for it a splendid building, the *Athenaeum*, which outshone even the *Museum* of Alexandria.

His greatest ambition was to enhance Rome with splendid statuary, so that it would even surpass its old glamour. His artistic propensities always went hand in hand with his talent as an organizer. He erected, repaired, or reconstructed hundreds of buildings. But in his modesty, extremely rare among Roman emperors, he did not allow his name to be affixed to any of these buildings.

His most famous reconstruction was that of the *Pantheon*, the best-preserved building of ancient Rome. It is said that HADRIAN himself designed the plans of most of the buildings erected by him; it must be assumed, however, that he used the advice of professional architects. This does not diminish his merits as a city-planner of gigantic proportions.

He spent a winter in Athens, where he distinguished himself as a great lover of arts. The Athenians honored him by conferring on him the title of *Archōn*, a high distinction even for a Roman Emperor. He presided over plays and festivals and was pleased to be called the liberator, Helios, Zeus, and the Redeemer of the world. In order to beautify Athens, he developed an even more extended building program than in Rome. On a large square he erected a library with marble walls, encircled by colonnades. One hundred columns carried a golden roof; the library itself was richly dotted with reliefs and other sculptures. He built a temple for HERA, and for ZEUS PANHELLANICOS, "the god of all Hellenes." In 131, he completed the gigantic *Olympieion*, the temple of the OLYMPIAN ZEUS, started six centuries earlier by PEISISTRATOS, and which ANTIOCHUS EPIPHANES left unfinished. It is said of HADRIAN that when he left Athens, the city was cleaner and more beautiful than ever before.

In spite of his love of the arts and his sponsorship of artists and philosophers, HADRIAN is remembered in history merely as a conqueror and city-builder. This is one of the injustices of professional historiography, which emphasizes military successes and building activities more than spiritual achievements. HADRIAN asserted himself also in the intellectual field and deserves to be counted among the Roman emperors as an ardent sponsor of the arts and sciences.

His successor, ANTONINUS, called PIUS (86–161), was no intellectual, in the real sense of the word. He did not receive the usual education of members of princely families, and he preferred religion to philosophy. He looked disdainfully on the class of writers, philosophers, and artists. He did not understand them, but nevertheless supported them and invited them frequently to his court. His reign was so effective that the Senate called him, besides PIUS, OPTIMUS PRINCEPS, the best ruler. He had no love ncr understanding for music; thus his reign did not further the development of musical art.

If the administration of the "amousic" ANTONINUS represented an economic blessing for Rome, that of his successor, MARCUS ANNIUS VERUS (generally called MARCUS AURELIUS, 121–180), was far less successful. Rarely had a princely boy received a more "universal" education than the young AURELIUS. This education surpassed all normal limits, for seventeen teachers vied with each other to develop the mind and character of the young prince. Among them were four grammarians, four rhetoricians, a lawyer, and no less than eight philosophers. In addition, he was instructed in music by the famous musician ANDRONIUS, and in singing by the kitharōde GEMINUS. Furthermore, in his youth MARCUS had to perform religious services in a Roman temple. This required him to memorize every word of the ancient liturgy in a language that was already obsolete at that time and could no longer be understood by the people. He was called the "Emperor-Philosopher," since he did not value anything higher than philosophy, often even neglecting for it the urgent needs of his empire.

He hired gladiators for his campaign against the rebellious Marcomans, which caused widespread indignation among the people, who accused him of "curtailing our pleasure, compelling us to become philosophers."[108] His misfortune as a ruler was that he named his brother LUCIUS as co-regent and entrusted him with the supreme command of his war against the Parthians. During the campaign, LUCIUS met PANTHEA in Antiochia, a famous beauty of those times, by whom disaster struck the Empire. LUCIAN described her as a perfect masterpiece of sculpture, with an enchanting voice, which he compared with that of the Muses and Sirens, a voice that surpassed the singing of the nightingales. She was well versed in playing the lyra, could accompany her singing, had lofty intellectual qualities, and was familiar with literature and philosophy. With her charms she enticed LUCIUS to the degree that, for her sake, he forgot the Parthians, who became a serious menace to Syria. It was necessary for MARCUS to appoint another commander of the army, AVIDIUS CASSIUS, the lieutenant of LUCIUS, who succeeded in breaking the onslaught of the Parthians and who reconquered a sizable portion of the lost territory.

Nevertheless, MARCUS was generous and allowed LUCIUS to return as the victorious conqueror. LUCIUS insisted, however, that MARCUS take part in his triumphal procession.

Soon, however, another serious setback took place. LUCIUS's returning army brought an epidemic with it. Everywhere the army passed enormous ravages were inflicted. It was a kind of bubonic plague, against which there was no remedy. All infected with it died, so that entire cities and whole districts were depopulated. The happy *hilaritas*, which initially constituted the leitmotif of MARCUS's reign, was gone; as a result, the people had recourse to superstitious practices and sought salvation in a new religion, which promised resurrection and eternal life.

In addition, there were new wars with wild tribes of the Chattes, Marcomans, Jaziges, and others, on the Danube. In this imminent danger to the empire,

MARCUS gave up philosophy and personally assumed command of the army. He succeeded in welding his disorganized soldiers into a disciplined army, a fact that is the more remarkable since it was achieved by an "intellectual" Emperor, who loathed war on principle.

Toward the end of his life, MARCUS appointed his only surviving son, COMMODUS, as his successor, and engaged the best teachers of Rome to prepare him for his future responsibilities. The youth, however, preferred dancing, singing, hunting, and fencing, and developed a strong aversion to books and philosophy. He favored the company of athletes and gladiators, was an inveterate liar and user of foul language, and developed cruel habits, against which all the admonitions of the aging MARCUS remained fruitless.

Once more, MARCUS succeeded in subduing the barbarian tribes, and entered Rome triumphantly. During the campaign he found time in Athens to attend lectures of the most famous philosophers and to carry on discussions with them in Greek. During his sojourn in Athens, he instituted chairs for the leading philosophic trends, belonging to the Platonic, Aristotelian, Stoic, and Epicurean schools, and supported them with generous donations.

Difficulties with his family, as well as the long wars, afforded him little time for taking care of the arts and artists, and so it is an irony of fate that this highly intellectual emperor left few memories as a sponsor of the arts. The sole exception was his accomplishment in Athens and, to a lesser degree, that in Rome, where he established flourishing philosophical schools. In spite of all his troubles and wars, he did find time to write a book, entitled *Meditationes*, in which he dealt with problems of morals and fate. Better than any other of his accomplishments, this book has preserved his memory for posterity.

His successors distinguished themselves mainly through wars, political intrigues, and cruelties. They did little or nothing for the arts and artists.

SEPTIMIUS SEVERUS (146–211) studied literature and philosophy in Athens, and was later active as a lawyer in Rome. Although he was one of the best-educated Romans, and had poets and philosophers in his entourage, he did not allow his intellectual leanings to interfere with his wars. He was addicted to astrology and believed in dreams. When his first wife died, he married a Syrian woman, JULIA DONNA, the daughter of a rich priest of the god ELAGABAL. Her horoscope promised her a throne, and six years later, the prophecy became reality: SEPTIMIUS was elected Roman Emperor.

What SEPTIMIUS neglected in artistic activities, the Empress more than compensated. She created a literary circle around her, furthered the arts, and eagerly sponsored literary works. She erected the *Atrium Vestae* and built the beautiful temple of VESTA, still standing today on the Forum. Her Syrian origin, together with her strong will, brought about a monarchy that under her influence became more and more Oriental in character and further increased its power under the reign of her grandson ELAGABALUS.

The reign of CARACALLA (Emperor 188–217) was distinguished by violence and wars. His character is best described by the fact that he waited impatiently for the death of his father and urged the physicians to "finish off" the old man.[109] The only recorded intellectual fact of his reign is that he showed great admiration for his teacher on the kithara, MESOMEDES, for whom, after his death, he built a magnificent cenotaph.[110] Had he not built the grandiose bathhouse carrying his name, he would be mentioned merely among the barbarian Emperors. This gigantic bathhouse was finished under ALEXANDER SEVERUS and represents one of the outstanding ruins of Antiquity. In one part of these ruins, open air operatic performances today take place; this is the sole, if late, contribution of CARACALLA to music.

Following his example, other emperors also built huge bathhouses, the largest among them that of MAXIMIAN, started in 295. There, 3600 people could take baths at the same time; it contained a gymnasium, a concert-hall, and accommodations for lectures. In one of its rooms, the *Trepidarium*, MICHELANGELO directed the building of the Church of Santa Maria degli Angeli, the largest in Rome after that of the Basilica di San Pietro.[111]

ELAGABALUS (205–222) was fourteen years old when he ascended the throne. In his youth he was a priest of Baal, and his name was VARIUS AVILUS. Only after he became emperor did he change his name to ELAGABALUS, "the creative god." (Latin writers transformed his name into HELIOGABALUS, meaning "the Sun-god.")

As a priest of Baal, he played the aulos, the syrinx, and other instruments at the sanctuary in Emessa.[112] He did the same at the celebration of his ascending the throne as the Emperor.[113] Contemporary historians report that he sang, danced, acted dramatic scenes, played the tube (trumpet), the lute, and the organ. (*Ipse cantavit, saltavit, ad tibias dixit, tuba cecinit, pandurizavit, organo modulatus est.*)[114] His main pleasure, however, was that of entertainment, on which he squandered fabulous sums. A banquet given for his friends never cost less than 100,000 sesterces (about $10,000), and often as much as 3,000,000. He spent exorbitant sums for jewelry, clothing, and all kinds of extravaganzas. When he undertook a trip, he requested six hundred carriages[115] for the things he needed most to accompany him on his journey.

It is evident that, in view of such extravagant waste, nothing was left for the arts and artists. He was assassinated in his seventeenth year.

Like his predecessor, SEVERUS ALEXANDER (208–235) ascended the throne in his fourteenth year. His education was entrusted to his mother, who trained his body as well as his mind. He excelled in all sports, studied Greek and Latin literature, and was expected to become a good ruler. He painted and sang nicely, played the tibia, the lyre, and the organ, but allowed only his sons and his entourage to listen to his artistic accomplishments.[116] He showed respect for the Senate, invited its members to his palace, and often went to their homes. He was friendly with his subjects, visited sick people of the low classes, and gave an audience to anybody who seemed to be worthy of it. In this epoch of Roman history, a music-loving emperor was such a common occurrence that one who did not himself practice music created astonishment.

He soon recognized the absurdity of ELAGABALUS, who wanted to replace the religion of JUPITER with that of the Syrian god, and took all measures to reinstate the ancient Roman faith.

His religious beliefs were quite remarkable, and in his tolerance he surpassed even present times. He believed in a kind of monotheism; his "god" was a composite supreme being who could be worshipped in any way, following any rites. During his reign there was complete freedom of worship, a practice that was far ahead of his time. In his private chapel, he had ikons (his "holy pictures") of JUPITER, ORPHEUS, APOLLONIUS of Tyrana, ABRAHAM, and JESUS. He worshipped all of them every morning, considering them merely as mute symbols of a universal, all-embracing religion.

In this respect, he may be compared to the Egyptian Pharaoh IKHNATON (1375–1358 B.C.E.), who introduced his monotheism thousands of years earlier, worshipping ATON, the life-giving sun of the universe. The difference between him and SEVERUS ALEXANDER was, however, that while IKHNATON abolished all other Egyptian gods with fire and sword, ALEXANDER's reign was distinguished by complete freedom of worship.

ALEXANDER recommended that the Romans adopt the morals and ethics of the Jews and Christians. He followed the Biblical precept: "Do not do to others what you do not want to have done to yourself." He engraved this golden rule on the walls of his palace and on many public buildings. His tolerance toward the Jews caused the sarcastic witticism of the Alexandrians of naming him "the head of the Synagogue."

It would be logical to assume that this "Citizen-Emperor" would have supported the arts and artists. Again, we are left in the dark about this by historiography. The only fact alluding to his concern for the musicians of his realm was that he legalized, encouraged, and reorganized their guilds, just as he did those of the workmen and artisans. He gave them permission to select their own spokesmen from among their members, a social measure akin to those of modern times.[117] Thus, it can be said that the musicians benefited greatly from ALEXANDER's solicitude.

In spite of his exemplary, modest way of living, and all the blessings his reign brought for Rome, he did not escape the fate of the last emperors following SEPTIMIUS SEVERUS, all of whom were assassinated. MAXIMINUS, the general of the legions in Pannonia, covetous of the throne, ordered the murder of ALEXANDER (only twenty-seven years old), his mother, and all his adherents.

With ALEXANDER's death, the Roman Empire lapsed into anarchy, causing military, political, economic, and moral decay and, eventually, the decline and complete dissolution of the once-mighty world power of Rome.

I have left NERO for the end of this account, although chronologically he belongs to an earlier period. In his person are manifested all the worst instincts of a musical "artist": self-conceit, arrogance, vanity, jealousy, and a legion of other bad habits, so that, following NERO, the report about music-loving later Emperors would have been an anti-climax. For this reason, in the present survey, NERO is last in the gallery of amateur musicians among the ruling Roman potentates.

NERO CLAUDIUS CAESAR DRUSUS GERMANICUS (37–68 C.E.), whose name was originally LUCIUS DOMITIUS ABENOBARBUS, ascended the throne when he was seventeen years old. He was an only child and, consequently, was excessively spoiled by his mother AGRIPPINA. He received the surname NERO which, in the Sabinic dialect, meant "courageous," "strong." Despite the fact that he received a good education and that the first years of his reign showed high promise, he soon developed the most extravagantly debauched practices and cruelty without limits. He suspected that his mother, who took sides with his first wife, OCTAVIA, against POPPAEA, planned his downfall, and he ordered that she be poisoned. When this failed, owing to her vigilance, he suggested a boat ride for her in a collapsible boat, which ended in a prearranged shipwreck. But she swam safely to the shore. When all this misfired, he sent murderers to her villa, who killed her with their swords. He looked at her naked body soberly, without any emotion, just as a coroner would have done.[118] Indeed, this was quite an achievement for a youth of twenty-two!

Following the murder of his mother, he ordered the murder of his aunt, DOMITIA LEPIDA, under the same suspicion, and confiscated all her property.

The same treatment was meted out to other members of his family, including his adoptive-father CLAUDIUS, his daughter ANTONIA, who had refused to marry NERO, his step-son RUFRIUS CRISPINUS (the son of POPPAEA by her first marriage), and even his first wife, OCTAVIA, whom he accused of adultery. CLAUDIUS's son BRITANNICUS, met the same fate. He had been educated with TITUS and had an agreeable voice—reason enough for NERO to be jealous of him. He called an expert poisoner and stood by while this man concocted a fast-working poison. That night at dinner, NERO poured the poison into BRITANNICUS's cup; he dropped dead at the very first taste. NERO regretfully assured his dinner guests that the "poor boy had long been subject to these epileptic seizures."[119]

After the murder of his mother, AGRIPPINA, he induced his teacher SENECA to draft a letter to the Senate, in which he offered "proof" that AGRIPPINA had conspired against him, and that when this was discovered, she committed suicide. Until his own death (by suicide ordered by NERO), SENECA was ashamed of this letter.[120] SENECA's death parallels in dignity that of SOCRATES. At that time, SENECA accused his former pupil, saying:

> Who knew not Nero's cruelty? After a mother's and a brother's murder, nothing remains but to add the destruction of a guardian and a tutor.[121]

The Senate accepted NERO's "explanation," and thanked the gods that nothing had happened to the emperor.

Along with his vices and corrupt mind, he loved music, poetry, beaux-arts, the theater, and athletic contests. In 59 C.E. he introduced the *ludi juvenales,* "plays for the youth"; in the following year, he inaugurated the *Neronia,* which —after the prototype of the Greek Olympiades—were supposed to be held every four years. Besides horse-races and athletic contests in these festivals, there were contests in music. NERO decided to participate in these performances, despite SENECA's advice to the contrary. Nevertheless, NERO invited the populace to these plays, in which he participated as a musician, and the people came *en masse* to see and, as was to be expected, to applaud their emperor.

His greatest ambition was to be regarded as an outstanding artist. He practiced painting, sculpture, and poetry with particular fervor, but even more music.[122] Since he wanted to be heard in public more often, he arbitrarily shortened the frequency of the *Neronia,* just as it suited him.[123] One evening he invited the leading members of the Senate to his palace and passed the night with them demonstrating how to play, and explaining the mechanism of, a new water-organ.[124] The most famous lyre-player of the time, TERPNOS, instructed him in his art, and from then on, NERO spent whole nights practicing the lyre.[125]

NERO was a veritable slave of his own voice; he always had a voice teacher with him, who had to admonish him to save his voice and who held a napkin before his mouth to protect the precious possession from harmful influences. In order to improve his voice he used to lie on his back with plates of lead on his chest; he sought to achieve further improvement by frequent purges and emetics. He avoided apples and other fruits, and all foods that could be harmful to his voice.[126] On some days he did not take any other nourishment than garlic and olive oil. When an astrologer forecast that he would lose his throne, he answered gleefully that he would then live merely by his art.

He considered himself a great poet. He wrote humorous poems about GALBA's revolt, to which he composed the music and which he performed with obscene gestures.[127] His entourage presented these poems to the people, and thus NERO acquired fame as a great poet.[128]

For years his most ardent desire was to perform as a musical artist. In 59, he gave in his gardens on the Tiber a semipublic concert as a kitharōde. It took five more years for him to gain enough courage to perform before a huge audience. For this purpose he selected Naples, where—as he thought—the predominantly Greek spirit would be beneficial to his venture. His "success" was a foregone conclusion, since he employed a claque of more than five-thousand sturdy young men, who had to accompany him wherever he performed publicly. The demonstrations of approval were strictly regulated and appropriately rehearsed. They were divided into three grades: first came the *bombi*, a loud humming, like that of bees; then the *imbricus*, the noise of "roof tiles," produced by clapping with hollowed hands; finally, the *testae*, the "brickbats," applauding with flat hands.[129]

After his first successes in Naples, NERO dared to appear as a musical artist in the great theater of POMPEIUS in Rome (65 C.E.). In these recitals he performed his own poems, set to music by himself. SUETONIUS maintains that he saw the manuscripts of these compositions, with corrections by NERO's own hand.[130] To give proof of his various talents, NERO also presented himself as a tragic actor. According to the custom of the time, he had—like any other actor—to kneel down at the beginning of the play and ask the adience for its applause. The people of Rome were enchanted to see their emperor kneeling before them and did not withhold their enthusiastic approval of his performance.

To make such presentations more popular, he persuaded, or forced, several senators to appear publicly as actors, musicians, athletes, and even gladiators. Those who refused were either exiled or secretly killed. Even his old tutor, SENECA, was banished (62 C.E.), because he opposed NERO's extravagances and criticized them in private circles. As mentioned before, NERO later ordered him to commit suicide.

The zenith of his artistic career was an extended concert-tour in Greece (in 66 C.E.). He was convinced "that the Greeks alone are worthy of my genius; they really listen to music."[131] On the first possible occasion he sailed to Greece, and, scarcely arriving at Cassiope, gave a concert in the temple of JUPITER CASSIUS. This was his first performance in a lengthy tour in the land of "connoisseurs of music."

He gave orders that the great national festivals with *Mousic* contests, which took place at regular intervals, should all be held during his sojourn in Greece, in order to give him opportunity to participate in them. This amounted to a break with the hallowed tradition, but he did not care in the least that some of these festivals had just been held recently; they had to be repeated.

During these concerts the gates were tightly closed and strictly guarded. Nobody was allowed to leave under any circumstances, even for the most urgent needs. Men simulated death in order to be carried out; women in the audience even gave birth to children.

Yet, the curious fact is that NERO was prone to nervousness before every appearance. In spite of his ever-present claque, he was afraid that the expected success would not materialize. He was extremely friendly and affable to his competitors; in secret, he ordered that they be killed. Not only did the living ones encounter his jealousy; he destroyed every sign of the winners of former contests. He ordered that the statues and busts erected in their honor be removed, and they were pulled down with hooks and thrown into the public sewers.[132]

During the rebellion of VINDEX CAIUS JULIUS (March of 68 C.E.), nothing annoyed NERO more than VINDEX's contemptuous opinion of his kithara-playing. He was even induced to refer to it in the Senate: "He replied that he could hardly deserve VINDEX's taunt . . . after his long painstaking cultivation of this art. . . . He asked several senators whether they knew of any better performer than himself."[133] It is not difficult to imagine the fate of a senator who would dare to give NERO a negative answer.

The judgment of VINDEX might to a great extent have been the reason for NERO's putting such an exceedingly high reward—2,500,000 sesterces—on his head.[134] Even before preparing the campaign against VINDEX, he took good care that there should be carriages in sufficient numbers for his musical instruments and his theatrical accessories. Then he started recruiting his army for the campaign.[135]

Returning from Greece to Italy, he stayed for a while in Naples, the place of his earliest triumphs. He ordered that a segment of the city wall be broken, as was usual in Greece when a victor returned from a festival. He ordered the same thing in Antium, then in Alba Longa, and finally in Rome. His entrance into Rome took place with great pomp. To make his return even more impressive, sacrifices were offered in his honor while he approached Rome. In his triumphal cortege he displayed with pride the 1808 prizes that he had won on his Greek *tournée*.

In spite of the numerous murders of his family (mother, wife, aunt, step-son, etc.), as well as the unscrupulous elimination of countless of his artistic competitors and political adversaries, the greatest crime that NERO committed was, in the opinion of posterity, the burning of Rome, a crime of which he was probably innocent. True, historians accuse him almost unanimously of setting Rome on fire.[136] Yet, there is no positive proof that he was responsible for this tragedy.

The fire started in the Circus Maximus on July 18, 64 C.E., and lasted six days and seven nights. NERO was at that time in Antium, and when he hurriedly returned, Rome was already a single sea of flames. NERO's palace on the Palatine was also completely destroyed. The only "proof" for NERO's guilt is the fact that he put on his costume of a tragic actor and, mounting the tower of MAECENAS's palace, declaimed "The Fall of Ilium" to the accompaniment of a kithara. This might have been more of a histrionic gesture, caused by his self-conceit, than real proof of his guilt in the conflagration. For what he did for Rome after the great fire was extraordinary and highly praiseworthy. After the rubbish was removed, NERO devoted himself passionately to rebuilding the city. He asked all cities of the realm to contribute to this purpose. And indeed, after the rebuilding, Rome was more beautiful and healthier than before.

Had NERO, after the fire, changed his private life with the same zeal as that with which he planned the reconstruction of Rome, he would perhaps not be judged as a monster by history. But his life and behavior went from bad to worse. As his debauchery and senseless wastefulness increased from year to year, his enemies became more numerous and more infuriated. Especially, they could not forget the murder of his mother. The state coffers were empty; in addition, the bad news from the various theaters of war multiplied. Soon no man in Rome was more hated than NERO. Popular dirty jokes, hateful satirical pamphlets, and venomous outbursts were the order of the day. Finally, the Senate issued a resolution for NERO's removal and demanded the death penalty for him as an enemy of the state. When even his own bodyguards deserted, he flew from his palace, accompanied only by his scribe EPAPHRODITUS, and hid himself in the lowly shack of a poor freed slave on the Via Salaria.

When he learned of the Senate's decision and the impending death penalty (which at those times was carried out with utmost cruelty), he wanted to commit suicide but had not the necessary willpower to thrust the dagger into his body. Eventually, the last one of the faithful who stood with him, EPAPHRO-DITUS, did this service for him and administered the death-stroke.

Until the last minute of his life he was "acting." He deplored his cruel fate with the words: *"Qualis artifex pereo!"* (another version says: *"Quam artistam morio"*), "what an artist dies with me!".

Shortly before the Senate decided upon his demise, he made the public vow that, if he retained his power, he would celebrate his victory with a great musical festival, in which he would perform on the water-organ, the aulos, and the bagpipe, and would, on the last day of the festival, dance the role of Tarnus in VIRGIL's *Aenaeis*. In order not to endanger his success, he ordered, in the last days of his reign, the murder of the actor PARIS, whom he considered a serious rival for the planned festival.[137]

NERO died at the age of thirty-two, on the anniversary of the murder of his first wife, OCTAVIA. Rome learned about his death with delirious joy. The people ran in the streets with caps of liberty on their heads, as though they were newly freed slaves. Thus an "artistic career" came to an end, the career of a self-conceited, grandiloquent, cruel, and unscrupulous amateur musician, who sacrificed his family, his friends, and even the welfare of the Empire for his alleged "art," until he came to a miserable end, which he brought on himself through his egomaniacal behavior.

MUSIC INSTRUCTION

In no other branch of Greek and Roman music is the difference between the two more conspicuous than in the field of music instruction. Music in Greece was not merely the handmaiden of religious rites, nor an element of entertainment, neither was it exclusively subordinate to aesthetic requirements, but was part and parcel of the civic duties of every freeborn man. Without a thorough musical education, the citizen was not considered to be a member with full rights of the commonwealth. The goal of music education in Greece was to lead the individual from the state of *amousia*, "the lack of *Mousic* education," to *eumousia*, "the perfect education," the main avenue of which was instruction in music.

Musical practices in Rome were quite different, since they served different purposes. Accordingly, music instruction followed dissimilar lines. The main difference between the two was that music instruction in Greece aimed at quality, in Rome at quantity. How did this manifest itself in the field of teaching?

Due to the wide usage of music (serious as well as popular), the profession of the Roman music teacher must have been a rather busy one. Historically speaking, the first music teachers of the Romans were the Etruscans. When Greek culture took an increasingly stronger hold on Roman life, this role was

taken over by immigrant Greek musicians. Only when Greek culture permeated Roman life completely was music instruction assumed by their own
Roman musicians. This fact is the more plausible since the greater number of
musical amateurs, especially girls and women, could not be served by Greek
teachers exclusively.

In Antiquity, and similarly in the Roman Empire, every good musician was
at the same time a music teacher. Thus there was evidently no shortage of them.
The instrumental virtuosi, especially those touring the country, might have
been too busy to fulfill their concert engagements, hence were probably not as
active as teachers remaining in one locale. The virtuosi, in some special instances, might have consented to teach, privately, singing and lyre-playing to
some persons of high standing.[138] This was the case of the most famous kithara-
player of imperial Rome, TERPNOS, who was NERO's teacher.[139] Whether NERO
exercised some "soft" persuasion in this instance is not divulged by his biographers. At any rate, TERPNOS could not resist instructing such an outstanding
pupil as the Emperor. Who taught NERO to play the water-organ and the bagpipe is not known. Likewise, little is known about the music teachers of other
emperors, for there are no historical records in this respect.

The profession of teaching music must have been a highly lucrative one in
Rome. Some records about this have been found in the city of Teos in Asia
Minor, which was the center of the musicians' guilds of Greece as well as of the
organization of all Dionysian artists in the Near East (see below). Therefore,
these records have a high credibility.

They inform us that, in the late third and the early second centuries B.C.E.,
three teachers of reading and writing were paid between 500 and 600 drachmas,
two teachers of gymnastics 500 each, and the music teacher 700 drachmas.[140]
The functions of the music teacher included kithara-playing (with the fingers
or with a plectrum), and instruction in the theory of music. Teaching the tibia
or other wind instruments is not mentioned. Instruction in music seems not to
have been compulsory in public schools, since not all the boys participated in
it. At the end of the school year, there were examinations to determine the
progress of the pupils.

This information, although scant, gives us at least some insight into music
teaching in public schools. What might have been the situation in private
instruction? A recent discovery provides information in this regard.

In 1922 a papyrus was found in Alexandria, dated in the year 206 B.C.E. It
is an apprentice contract, in Greek, between the owner of a young slave named
NARCISSUS and a music teacher.[141] The slave boy must have been particularly
talented in music, so that his master felt induced to afford him opportunity
for further education. The young man already had a sufficient knowledge of
music. The apprentice contract provided for the perfection of his skill on several
instruments: he had to learn four tunes on the double Lydian aulos, two of them
to be arranged as accompaniments to other instruments. He also had to master
five tunes on the syrinx and on another Egyptian instrument of the aulos-type,
called *aigyptios tereitē*. Two of these had to be adapted as accompaniments
(for singing or instruments?). Further, he had to learn two accompaniments
to go with kithara performances for the SERAPIS festival; four more accompaniments and six more musical numbers for solo rendition. Two of these were for
the Phrygian aulos, mentioned in the contract as a special instrument. Two of
the compositions had to be arias (*kroumata*) played on the longer, or left-

hand, reed of the double-aulos, which usually carried the *krousis* or accompaniment.[142]

The period of training stipulated in this contract seems to have covered not more than six months, implying that the slave boy already had some preliminary knowledge in music before entering upon this special training. The contract called for a testing of the candidate by three experts who were to be selected by agreement between the master of NARCISSUS and his teacher. The remuneration received by the teacher amounted to one hundred drachmas, payable in two installments (this last detail is not included in the contract, but can be inferred by similar musical and dancing contracts based upon businesslike methods found in other papyri).

This contract allows us to draw three conclusions:

1) Even in unmusical Rome, true talent was recognized and furthered;

2) A wealthy Roman, evidently possessing quite a number of slaves, appreciated and sponsored one of them, who showed exceptional talent for music;

3) Talent for music was not restricted to certain classes or social strata, but was recognized whether it appeared in a free citizen or a slave.

As we have seen, in the early Republican period Romans of the high society considered it beneath their dignity to practice music themselves, and left this activity to their slaves. Only gradually did this attitude change, when familiarity with music became widespread, to be eventually a part of the *bon ton* of society.

Besides music instruction in the lower grades of the public schools, instruction on a higher level soon became a norm, in which both sexes participated, particularly the numerous amateurs among girls and women. Their musical curriculum embraced lyra-playing, singing, and dancing.[143] These schools of advanced learning might also have prepared the virtuosi for their future careers.

CICERO was one of the protagonists of general musical education; he emphasized that "human education is only conceivable with the help of the Muses" (*"cum Musis, id est cum humanitate et doctrina"*).[144] He understood the phrase *help of the Muses* to embrace all *Mousic* arts, including music.

Instrumental music in the army was entirely under Etruscan influence. All the brass instruments of the Roman legions, the *tuba, lituus, cornu*, and *bucina* were taken over from the Etruscans. Considering the size of the Roman army, there must have been many hundreds, even thousands of players of brass instruments in the military installations. All the larger units had some, or all types of them. True, the "art" of these musicians consisted mainly in giving certain signals, but even these had to be learned, because the success or failure of a military action depended on the correct use of them. The teachers for these instruments were experienced players themselves, just as today the signal-instruments in military use are taught by the old hands in this profession.

Unfortunately, we have no records of how these military signals may have sounded, especially about their rhythmical characteristics. JULIUS POLLUX informs us simply that there were four different signals: for the attack, for encouragement during the battle, for the retreat, and for the stop and the establishment of the camp for the night;[145] but he does not furnish any information about their characteristics. Yet there must have been marked differences between them, because we know that frequently these signals were used purposely in a deceitful way in order to mislead the adversary. For instance, sometimes a signal was given for retreat, encouraging the enemy to attack, thus luring him into a trap. In some cases, the trumpet-players were placed far away from the army in order to deceive the enemy about the location of the troops. In other cases, the centurions, after leaving the camp, left behind some trumpeters to mislead the enemy by their signals.

In literary works, the customs during the battle as well as when resting in the camp, were characterized by the name of some of the wind instruments. So, for instance, *in medias tubas* had the meaning "during the battle," and *post lituos* meant "after the battle was over." The *cornu*-player used to stay close to the army emblems. This is how they are depicted in Trajan's column in the campaign against the Daciers.

The ceremony of the *tubilustrium*, the symbolic ritual cleaning of the trumpets has been mentioned above. In a later epoch, the Romans used a collective term, *Aeneatores*, for the players of brass instruments.

In the navy, the use of trumpets was less frequent than in the army. Sometimes the instrument was employed to keep the oarsmen in uniform rhythm, but this function was better served by the *symphoniacus*, who had to beat the rhythm on a metal plate placed on the stern of the vessel.

Like the other musicians of the Empire, the army-trumpeters were organized in special guilds (see below).

SINGING

As shown earlier, singing was for the Greeks an educational *necessity* and an integral part of a good education. Furthermore, singing in Greece had a highly ethical significance.

All these requirements were lacking in Rome. Here singing had merely a utilitarian value, *solida utilitas*, with no aim other than entertainment. The quantity of singing in Rome had to supplant the quality in Greece. The quantity grew larger with the ever-spreading amateurism and it eventually took on gigantic proportions. With the increase of all artistic media (orchestras and choir groups), musical practice became coarser and coarser, which, however, did not diminish the pleasure of the Romans in singing or listening to it. In spite of the attitude of the Romans toward vocal art, so different from that of the Greeks, their pleasure in listening was no less intensive. This will be clear if we scrutinize the various occasions on which singing was an essential element of Roman life.

Prior to the adoption of Greek customs and Greek musical practice, Roman prejudice considered that singing, for a freeborn man, especially for one of high standing, was not suitable. Not only was the playful practice of music improper, but the professional use of it was considered indecent for a free citizen. The spread of Greek culture resulted little by little in a certain tolerance toward music. The result was that in the time of the Gracchi (second–first century B.C.E.) there were already schools for singing and dancing in Rome, frequented by boys and girls of well-to-do families, even of the nobility. This caused the deep displeasure of the younger Scipio (first century B.C.E.).[146] As time passed, however, the art of singing was looked upon more favorably. In a conversation with Cicero in the year 91, one of the leading personalities of Rome of that time, Lucius Licinius Crassus, mentions without disapproval that his friend, the knight Numerius Furius, a good family father, was practising singing, which he had studied as a boy (*puer didicit quod discendum fuit*).[147]

Even SULLA (138–78 B.C.E.), whose government was characterized by harsh dictatorial measures, did not disdain the acquaintance of actors and singers, and was very susceptible to praise as a good singer.[148] But the historian COR- NELIUS NEPOS (100–22 B.C.E.) still maintained that, according to Roman customs, practising music, especially singing, was not appropriate to a man of distinc- tion.[149]

Nevertheless, love of music spread more and more in the Roman society. The historian SALLUSTIUS (86–35 B.C.E.) reports about SEMPRONIA, the paramour of CATILINA (108?–62 B.C.E.), that she sang more artfully than was suitable for an honorable woman.[150] The younger PLINY (61–114? C.E.) had high praise for the singing of his third wife.[151] We have records about girls with extraor- dinarily fine voices. LUCIAN (100?–200? C.E.) informs us about such a singer, PANTHEA, the beautiful girl of Smyrna. For her sake, the supreme commander of the Roman army in the war against the Parthians forgot his duties and brought serious danger to the Empire. (LUCIAN's opinion about PANTHEA's voice has been quoted earlier.)

Beginning with the second century B.C.E., the Hellenistic art song made its triumphant entry into Rome. Female kithara-players and virtuosi from Greece, Egypt, and Asia Minor, accompanying their singing on stringed instruments, were welcome in the public as well as private homes of the Romans. The public singing of lyric poems accompanied by instruments became so popular that lovers of music, mainly amateurs, from all classes of the society, devoted them- selves with ardor to this art form, and sometimes even entered contests with professional singers. Of course they took private instruction before such a ven- ture, as was the case with the Emperor NERO.

As in Greece, singing was never omitted at a banquet. The difference was that, among the Greeks the participants themselves provided the musical enter- tainment, while in Rome this role was assigned to professional singers, mainly girls, who were at the same time dancers. In the households of the nobles and the wealthy there were numerous slaves who were specially trained for singing and dancing.

In the streets, at work, and while tilling the land, one could hear continuous singing. In processions, boys and girls sang hymns; brides and grooms were escorted with singing.

As in other nations of Antiquity, work in Rome, if based upon a regular rhythmic activity, was alleviated by appropriate songs. Frequently mentioned in literary sources are songs of the oarsmen on riverboats, songs of the galley- slaves, as well as work songs of weavers, spinners, vintagers, treaders of the grapes, and songs of the reapers, of the sheaf-binders, the shepherds, the fishers, the hunters, the watchmen, and so on.

The Romans also had quite a number of folksongs, drinking songs, songs of the nurses, songs for anniversaries and weddings, love songs, and a special kind of satirical song called *carmina famosa*. The street-vendors in Rome had spe- cific melodious calls, which cannot be termed songs in the proper sense, but each category of them—the vendors of drinks, sausages, cakes, and also the itinerant cooks and others—offered their merchandise with a characteristic *mod- ulatio*, mentioned in literary works.[152]

For a more artistic use of songs in the imperial period, the odes of the Greek lyric poets (ANACREON, SAPPHO, ALCAIOS, etc.) used to be performed with sing- ing. At first, this was true merely of Greek poems, but soon it was also extended to the odes of HORACE, who called them "lyrics, combined with string instruments."[153]) His *carmen seculare*, commissioned by AUGUSTUS, which he set to music himself, was sung by him in the customary festival attire of the kitharōdes on the steps of the Temple of APOLLO PALATINUS. According to another version, it was sung by a choir of young boys and maidens, with the poet furnishing the accompaniment on the kithara.

Poems of PLINY the Younger were also sung to the accompaniment of lyres and kitharas.[154] HORACE's phrase *cantare Catullum*[155] refers to the poems of CATULLUS performed with singing. OVID expressed the hope that his *Heroides* would be sung in the future with musical accompaniment,[156] which later became fact.

AULUS GELLIUS (c. 117–c. 180 C.E.) described a banquet given by a wealthy music lover from Asia Minor in the rustic countryside of Rome.[157] At this occasion, excellent choral groups of boys and girls were displayed who, after the meal, sang poems of ANACREON and SAPPHO, as well as love-elegies of contemporary poets, accompanied by lyres. VIRGIL's *Eclogues* were performed in theatrical plays by professional singers.[158]

When OVID was in exile, he was pleased to learn that his poems were "danced" successfully on the stage, implying that they were also sung.[159] His *Heroides* were also "danced" in pantomimes, while the choir sang an accompaniment to them.

Other Roman songs for special occasions were, besides those mentioned above, marching songs, triumphal songs, and certain satirical and lampooning songs. Such satirical songs were already used in Greece, and were, as a rule, performed in iambic rhythms, because—as the Greeks believed—this rhythm was most appropriate for this type of poetry. This custom seems to have been taken over by the Romans; Roman literary sources reveal the existence of such abusive poems, which frequently contained personal invective that, as in Greece, was written in iambic meters. Such poems (with or without singing) even had special names; HORACE called them *iambi criminosi*,[160] CATULLUS *truces*,[161] and APOLLINARIS SIDONIUS *feroces*.[162]

Roman art songs were accompanied either by kitharas or auloi, in the cult as well as in funeral ceremonies and, in domestic use, they honored the souls of the deceased.

Throughout Antiquity singing was homophonous. Harmony, as we understand it today, was unknown, and counterpoint, which requires the independent moving of several vocal or instrumental parts was probably unknown. The few examples that seem to indicate the existense of polyphony in Antiquity (see above) consisted more or less of heterophonic variations or embellishments of the melody, but no "second," or independent parts. Monophony was the guiding principle of ancient singing; it was governed by the interrelationship between lyrics and music. The ancients considered the words more important than the underlying melody. In vocal music, the melody had no independent life; "its value was the manner with which it was adapted to the lyrics, its strength was to underline appropriately the declamation."[163] Singing was always performed in unison, meaning that the voices of male and female singers, as well as of boys and girls, sang the melody in their vocal range, usually in the interval of an octave.

The choir was led by a conductor, placed in the middle, who was also the precentor. To keep the singers together rhythmically, especially large choir-masses, the Romans, like the Greeks, used the *scabellum* (Illus. 115), and in large groups, several of them.

In Rome there was not much difference between sacred and secular music. Both served practical purposes, the *solida utilitas*, the utilitarian principle. In both Greece and Rome, the range of the instruments, as well as that of solo and choir singing, was governed by that of the human voice. Anything exceeding this range belonged to the domain of individual virtuosity, had no artistic value, and was counted among the "tricks" of the profession.

Next to Rome, Alexandria was the most important music center of the Empire. Instrumentalists and singers coming from there to Rome stood in high esteem and had big success. A singer of Alexandria who accompanied himself on the trigōn-harp, came to Rome at the end of the second or the beginning of the third century c.e., and was enthusiastically received. Many music lovers knew the songs performed by him by heart.[164] Scarcely thirty years after the final conquest of Egypt (30 b.c.e.), Roman women sang melodies originating from Alexandria, as well as songs heard in theatrical plays.[165] Sometimes these foreign singers accompanied themselves with the tibia. Tacitus mentions, for instance, *"Eucaerus natione Alexandrinus canere tibiis doctus,"* ("Eucaerus, an Alexandrian by birth, skilled in singing to the tibia.").[166] At the end of the first century b.c.e., the Roman *jeunesse dorée* was just as familiar with the melodies of the pantomimes as with the arias sung in the theater[167] and with the songs performed by the pretty Andalusian girls (*gaditanae*) who used castanetes as accompaniment, and embellished with their singing the banquets of the nobles.[168]

Originally considered to be merely an added attraction to festive meals, musical performances developed to the point where they became the main purpose of social gatherings. Martial asks the question, how can a banquet best be arranged? By eliminating the singing of the choir and its accompaniment, was his answer.[169] Pliny the Younger, inviting a single friend to a simple dinner, gave him a choice among a lecture, a scene from a comedy, or lyre-playing.[170] Even the puritanically minded Martial, who lived as a tenant on the third floor of a building, on one occasion inviting a friend to a simple meal felt induced to make amends for the meagre food offered by playing the short tibia.[171]

It was easy for wealthy Romans to entertain large choirs and orchestras. Among the hundreds of slaves of the noble families were numerous individuals trained in music, who brought with them their musical skill acquired in their homeland. Their masters encountered no difficulties in making them perform their musical duties, and they were certainly more pleased with this kind of work than doing hard labor. Besides, the more gifted among them received special instruction by professionals, as was described earlier in a particular case (see above).

Chrysogonos, a wealthy freed man of Sulla, had so many musicians among his slaves that his entire home reverberated day and night with music.[172] On outings and picnics to neighboring places, the singers and musicians accompanied their masters.[173] In the resorts, frequented by aristocrats, one could hear singing and instrumental playing in their luxurious villas from morning to evening, and especially at night.[174] How this mania for music eventually degenerated becomes evident from *The Banquet of Trimalchio*, by Petronius, conceived as a satire, but certainly containing some truth about the manner of living of the rich upstarts. In this pastiche, intended to be a biting caricature, the author shows that the offering, carrying, and carving of the food, and even the clearing and wiping of the tables, took place to the rhythm of music and singing. PETRONIUS observed sarcastically that "one could imagine being not in a private home, but at a theatrical performance."[175]

A more serious use of music took place at funerals. The Roman funeral rites remained under Etruscan influence. Every funeral cortege was led by songs, and the lowering of the coffin was also accompanied by singing. The funeral wailing of women alternated with playing the tibia. When AUGUSTUS was incinerated at the Campus Martius, boys and girls of noble families performed the funeral songs for the deceased Emperor. Sometimes even trumpets were added to funeral ceremonies.

In the *Banquet of Trimalchio* the heavily drunken master of the house orders, as a joke, a mock-funeral, at which trumpets had to play a loud funeral march (*"consonare cornicines funebri strepitu"*).[176] Therefore, the saying *"ad tubicines mittas"* ("send for the trumpets") implied in Roman parlance "prepare the funeral."

In ancient times, there were in Rome no special regulations for funeral ceremonies. The first ones we encounter are contained in the Twelve-Tables-Laws (middle of the fifth century B.C.E.). There, the number of tibia-players is limited to five; also it prohibited women, while performing funeral wailings, to scratch their cheeks.[177] In a later period, professional wailing women were employed for funeral lamenting, as was the Greek custom.

The music at funerals, especially the vocal part, originally had a magic purpose, as in all ancient Oriental religions. Loud music (or noise) was supposed to chase hostile spirits and malevolent demons away from the deceased, as well as from the participants in the rites. The Romans had a specific ritual honoring the souls of their ancestors, the *"Lemuries,"* at which the head of the family scattered black beans about and made loud noises by hitting tools of metal.[178] The lamenting songs of funeral ceremonies were an ancient Roman custom, called "Nenies," or "Exequies."

Summarizing these scattered informations, we note that in Rome the intensive practice of singing was mainly for the purpose of entertaining and that it was on a gigantic scale. Later on, singing was used mostly for sensuous pleasure, as a concomitant phenomenon of the decaying mores. This led gradually to the degeneration, and eventually to the complete decline of the once-flourishing vocal art.

The ancient ethical character of the musical art was preserved mainly by the new religion of Christianity. It was Byzantium's musical culture that provided the transition from Antiquity to the Middle Ages and thus gained merit for saving an age-old tradition.

THE MUSICAL INSTRUMENTS OF THE ROMANS

None of the nations of Antiquity have been given so little credit for their own creations in the field of musical instruments as the Romans.

Their stringed instruments—the kithara, lyra, and barbiton—were taken over directly from Greece, or in a roundabout way from Etruria. The same is true about the monaulos (called by the Romans *tibia*) and the double-aulos. The brass instruments, which played so great a role in the Roman army, were of Etruscan origin, adopted by the Romans for their own use.

In the preserved pictorial representations, too, the instruments are scarcely different from those of Greece. The only contribution the Romans made to the history of musical instruments is that—as indicated by their musical practice—they developed everything on a gigantic scale, making the instruments coarser, less refined. Thus we encounter string instruments of huge size, sometimes having eighteen strings. Some lyres were of the size of coaches, so that is was necessary for two people to play them[179] (Illus. 33).

Besides the stringed instruments imported from Greece, Rome imported quite a number of Oriental harps, similar to the Assyrian and Jewish psalterium. In concert practice, the harp-like instruments enjoyed only a minor role; the instruments of the virtuosi, also of the amateurs, were the kithara and lyra, and their variants (Illus. 135–140).

In both Greece and Rome, pipes of different species were used, such as the Phrygian aulos, which corresponded to the male voices, while the choraulos was used mainly for female voices. Just as TERPNOS (NERO's teacher) was unrivaled as a kithara-player, so was CANUS (second half of the first century C.E.) admired as the most outstanding tibia-virtuoso. He himself said that "if the audiences knew how much pleasure his playing affords him, they would not pay for it, but should be paid themselves."[180] As early as AUGUSTUS's times, the tibia became, by lengthening its pipes, an instrument capable of competing with the sound of the tuba (trumpet).[181]

As the Greek historian POLYBIUS states, the Roman shepherds used a specific instrument, called *bucina pastoralis*, which might be a misnomer, since the ordinary *bucina* was a trumpet. The shepherds' *bucina* is mentioned also by VARRO.[182] It might have been a variant of the tibia with a larger sounding bell, giving a louder sonority, hence the name *bucina*. The Greeks sometimes called the tuba a tyrrhensic instrument. VIRGIL also mentions the "tyrrhenic sound" of the tuba.[183]

Besides enlarging their instruments and their sonority, the Romans' main aim was directed toward mass effects. Huge choirs and large orchestras destroyed the intimate charm of Greek musical practice. In Alexandria, in the time of PTOLEMAEUS PHILADELPHUS (283–246 B.C.E.), a gigantic procession took place in which a choir of 600 singers and 300 kithara-players participated.[184]

St. AUGUSTINE distinguishes between an instrumental soloist and a player in an orchestra saying that "a bad choraulēs is a good symphoniacus."[185] The latter term refers to the average player in an orchestra or in an ensemble group.

In the last period of the Republic, "symphonies" are often mentioned, performed by large groups of instrumentalists, called *"symphoniaci"*.[186] In Roman Antiquity, "symphony" meant something entirely different from what is understood by today's term. It was applied to the playing together of several musicians, or groups of musicians, in what we call today an ensemble group or an orchestra. The *collegium symphoniacorum* was the *collegium tibicinum et fidicinum Romanum*, the professional guild of the Roman musicians, players of string and wind instruments.[187]

The ensemble playing of several or many instruments appears only in Hellenistic times; "monster"-concerts, performed by hundreds of kitharists and aulētes, are not reported prior to the period of the Emperors.[188]

In Roman musical practice, the ensemble playing of numerous instruments of different categories was a normal procedure, while in Greece (except for using the kithara with the aulos), it was unusual and even contrary to real art. Some examples of ensemble playing in large groups among the Romans are included in a report of HORACE (65–8 B.C.E.), according to which, in the temple of VENUS, songs were accompanied by numerous lyres, tibias, and the berenycian aulos.[189] Another report reveals that in the *Aprilies,* established by HADRIAN for the 21st of April in honor of the goddess ROMA, the whole city reverberated with songs, accompanied by tibias, cymbals, and hand-drums.[190] MAXIMUS of Tyrus compared the Homeric poetry, on account of the diversity of its characteristics and effects, with a *panharmonic* instrument, that is, with an orchestra, in which the aulos, lyra, tuba, syrinx, and other instruments accompanied a singing choir.[191]

In the description of the wedding music in the *Epithalamium Laurentii Anthologia Latina* (742 B.C.), all the usual instruments and their ensembles are listed separately: *tympana, chorda simul, symphonia, tibia, buxus* (?), *cymbala, bambilium* (?), *cornus et fistula, sistrum, quaeque per aeratas inspirant carmina fauces, humida folligenes exclament organe voces.* Among the names of these instruments, *buxus* and *bambilium* cannot be identified unequivocally. *Buxus* might be the *gaita gallega*—the bagpipe of Galicia, the northwestern province of Spain—some parts of the instrument being called *buxas.* But this is merely a surmise. As for *bambilium,* modern research assumes that the correct spelling should be *bombalium* which, in this case, would be a low-sounding flute (perhaps the Etruscan *plagiaulos,* the transversal flute). It might also be that it refers to an instrument mentioned in the spurious letter to Dardanus[192] under the name of *bombulum,* which would be, in this case, a shaking instrument. At any rate, the Romans may have employed remarkably large orchestras for wedding ceremonies.

In the rites of DIONYSOS there were bells to be shaken, and in the cult of ISIS the sistrum was used, which was certainly imported from Egypt. The syrinx, the instrument of the shepherds and peasants, was frequently employed in the pantomimes. Most of the noise-making instruments may have been introduced to Rome through commercial exchange, as well as the result of the general cultural interrelationship between the nations of the Mediterranean basin.

Choral performances in imperial Rome took place on a gigantic scale. SENECA reports, as was noted before, that there were sometimes more performers on the stage than people in the audience.[193] The singers and musicians not only occupied the stage, but were sometimes placed within the audience itself, where room for them was especially reserved. Brass instruments were also frequently placed in the audience, because there was no room for them on the stage, already occupied by numerous tibia-players and several water-organs (*hydraules*). In imperial Rome there were no difficulties in placing such huge masses of performers, because the theaters of those times could seat 12,000 people and more.

In 284 C.E., CARINUS presented a series of plays in which one hundred trumpet players participated. Other groups in these plays comprised one hundred horn-blowers and two hundred choraulos- and pythaulos-players. These plays were the most outstanding events of the year.[194]

Much more difficult than that of seating such masses of performers must have been the problem of keeping the musicians together melodically as well as rhythmically. This was achieved by the *scabellum,* or several of them, fastened at the sole of the choir leader.

There is an early reference to the possibility of conducting by other than acoustical means. St. AUGUSTINE explains the metric notions of *levatio* and *positio,* which he clearly differentiates from the melic *arsis* and *thesis.* From this QUIN-TILIANUS infers[195] that there might have existed a kind of leading the music with motions of the hands. But this is merely his own assumption, not corroborated by other coeval or later sources. Whether this refers to cheironomy, as used in Antiquity, is not clear from QUINTILIANUS's statement.

Hand in hand with the increase in number of performers, music gradually lost its artistic values, which loss eventually reached such proportions that bereft of ethical qualities, it served merely external effects. Degeneration and decay of music were the result, induced and hastened by the ever-expanding pantomime, which completely corrupted the aesthetic approach to music even for the few real music lovers who still remained (see the following chapter).

A survey of Roman instruments would be incomplete without mentioning two species which, though not created by Romans, enjoyed a great popularity and gave the imprint, so to speak, of the music practice of imperial Rome. These are the water-organ (*hydraulis*) and the bagpipe (generally called *utricularium*).

We do not know who invented the organ. Its primitive form was the wind-organ, which already existed in a nutshell in the syrinx—the Pan's pipe of Antiquity—with its row of pipes of different length, which the player held under his lower lip and into which he blew from above. It was only necessary for a resourceful man to apply a pumping mechanism, replacing the human breath, and the pneumatic organ was born.

After several improvements, KTESIBIOS, an engineer at Alexandria (fl. 246–221 B.C.E.), invented a mechanism that regulated the flow of air to the pipes by water pressure. This was the water-organ, which constituted a definite progress compared with the pneumatic organ. In its first phase it was loud, and this was the reason the Romans used it in their circus and theatrical plays.

It is not my aim to give a survey of the development of the organ from the pneumatic to the hydraulic, and back to the pneumatic stage. This has been done in special essays, especially by KATHLEEN SCHLESINGER and GEORGE HENRY FARMER.[196] It is sufficient to refer only to its chief characteristics: sounding pipes of different lengths, a duct to lead the air to the pipes, and a mechanism (some kind of a keyboard) by which the pipes produced their sounds. These principles were equally valid for the pneumatic as well as the hydraulic organ.

All the so-called historical records about the early organs—in the Bible (Gen. 4:21), in the early rabbinical writings,[196a] and in the Christian writings—attributing the "invention" of the instrument to the patron saint of music, SANTA CAECILIA, are merely legends without any historical foundation.

When the organ first appeared in historical records in the form of the *hydraulis,* it was already a rather highly developed instrument. Although its invention (or perfection) was ascribed in the classical literature to PLATO, ARISTOTLE, PYTHAGORAS, and ARCHIMEDES (this last indication according to TERTULLIAN), the most credible assumption is that this honor belongs to the Alexandrian KTESIBIOS.

The instrument *magrephah,* mentioned in the Talmud, has created extensive discussion among the rabbinical Sages, who did not arrive at an unequivocal conclusion as to whether such an instrument existed at all in the Temple of Jerusalem. Nor do we know whether the term referred to the *hydraulis* or to another organ-like instrument.

The first historical evidence of the *hydraulis* appears in the musical practice of the Romans. Since in its early, imperfect stage it was rather loud and coarse, the Romans considered it to be the appropriate musical accompaniment in the circus for the combats of gladiators and other exciting events, such as the fights of humans with animals, chariot-races, and the like. Gradually, the mechanism of the instrument was improved, so that it could, to a certain extent, serve musical purposes. The great lover of music NERO was enthralled by the hydraulis and spent much time and effort in learning to play it. In this epoch it must have been improved to a point where the famous orator MARCUS FABIUS QUINTILIANUS (ca. 35 ca. 118 C.E.), who possessed good discernment in the arts, was strongly impressed by its versatility and expressive tone.

In NERO's time several types of the hydraulis must already have existed. SUETONIUS reports that when in Antium (where NERO lived at that time) bad news arrived about the rebellion of VINDEX, the Emperor hurriedly returned to Rome. But instead of summoning the Senate for a review of the military situation, he ordered the leading senators to his palace, where he talked with them only cursorily about the war, but spent most of the time demonstrating a new type of water-organ to them. He explained the differences between the various types, of which he possessed all, and declared that he planned to introduce the organ into theatrical plays.[198] He wanted to present himself, along with his other talents, as a player of the organ.

In later times, there seems to have been, for use in homes, a smaller and softer-sounding variety of the hydraulis, about which ATHENAIOS informs us: "We heard from a neighboring house the sound of a water-organ (*hydraulis*); it was very sweet and joyous (*hēdys kai terpnos*), so that we all turned our attention to it, charmed by its tunefulness (*emmelais*)."[199] During this period there were certainly quite a number of such house-organs. They were introduced to Byzantium and, improved still further by the Byzantines, were used as well for artistic purposes. There are a number of pictorial representations of them (Illus. 144, 145). As time went by, their mechanism might have become too complicated, so that they were replaced by the less involved, therefore more practical, pneumatic organ, leading through the development of the Middle-Ages to our present-day organ.

The other instrument closely connected with the musical practice of imperial Rome was the bagpipe. It is a species of pipe-like instrument which, however, did not get its air-supply directly from the mouth of the player, but through the intermediary of an air bag made of animal skin. Since such an air-reservoir contained more air than was necessary to make the pipes sound, the player did not need to stop the melody to take a breath; he supplied the necessary air by pressure upon the bag, placed under his left elbow.

On this air-bag were fastened, beside the pipe through which the player filled the bag with air, several sounding pipes, chanters, generally two or three, sometimes more. One or two of these had finger holes and were destined for the melody proper; the others produced a bourdon sound, which gave the characteristic tone quality of the instrument. The Romans had several terms for the instrument: *tibia utricularis, chorus, pythaules,* but mostly *utricularium.*

JULIUS CAESAR was the first to introduce the bagpipe into the circus. The instrument became the favorite of NERO, who also employed it in the Roman army. He was proud to be a virtuoso on the instrument and—as has been told before—made a public vow that if he retained his power, he would arrange a great musical festival in which he would perform on the lyra, the tibia, the bagpipe and the hydraulis, and furthermore, present himself as a dancer. This grandiose plan fell through on account of his pitiful demise.

Like everything else in Rome's musical practice, which was carried out on an enormous scale, bagpipes were used in gigantic numbers. CARINUS reports that in one giant-sized orchestra there were one hundred bagpipers. This suggests that the bagpipes of the Romans must have had a uniform tuning, otherwise such a mass of bagpipes would not have harmonized properly with the rest of the orchestra, but would have created unbearable confusion.

Contrary to the water-organ, which disappeared soon after the fall of the Roman Empire, to be supplanted by the more practical pneumatic organ, the bagpipe appeared in almost all the nations under different names. In French it was called *cornemuse* or *musette*, in Italian *cornamusa*, in Spanish *gaita*, in Slavonic and Hungarian *duda, dude*, or *dudy*, and still other names. It has been most colorfully retained in the Scottish Highlands, where it has become the national instrument.

THE DANCE

Anthropology, the history of civilization, psychology, and all related disciplines are unanimous in the opinion that the dance is as old as human cultivation itself. No nation since earliest Antiquity could dispense with dance. It was used in cultic rites, in public or private life, and it expressed both joy and sorrow, as well as the innumerable other emotions of the individual and collective society. In Rome this practice was no different from that of other peoples; it served the same purposes and was the product of the same practical and psychological necessity.

And yet it appears as though the Romans made only a minor contribution to the dance among the arts. The main reason for this is found in an inconsiderate statement of CICERO: *"nemo fere saltat sobrius, nisi forte insanit"* ("only a lunatic would dance when sober").[200] This *aperçu* of CICERO, uttered in the heat of a court litigation, made it appear as though the dance in Rome were proscribed (especially the dancing of men), and considered a vice.

Another statement of CICERO seems to confirm this attitude. He characterized the young men belonging to the followers of CATILINA as addicts of low behavior in love affairs, interested only in singing, playing of instruments, and dancing.[201] This statement, too, should not be taken literally; it arose from his opposition to CATILINA.

For dance was an indispensable attribute of Roman life, from ancient times on. CURT SACHS gives an illuminating survey of the history of Roman dance customs from ancient times to that of the Empire. He distinguishes three specific periods and emphasizes the fact that the development of the Roman dance follows the civilizing trends of history.

In the first, old Roman period, dance served the ritual almost exclusively; the spring procession of the sowing priests, the purification of the fields, the weapon dances of the warriors and of the priests of Mars (the *Salii*), all were more or less manifestations of religious rites. The term *Salii* was equivalent to *saltantes* (dancers), although their productions might have contained little dancing other than choric evolutions, walking around in a circle, beating rhythmically their shields, and the like. PLUTARCH, who could not have witnessed such archaic dances, nevertheless praised the grace and suppleness of their movements as preserved in the tradition. LUCIAN's description is more credible. He characterizes them as "the most majestic of dances." The dancers stamped their feet in a ternary rhythm, hence this dance was called *tripudium,* dance of three steps.

The second period of the history of Roman dance begins around the year 200 B.C.E. It was dominated by Etruscan and Greek dances, which gradually entered public as well as private life. In spite of the aversion of some statesmen, dance schools became more and more numerous, as dance became considered a "social" obligation. Citizens, and even patricians, sent their sons and daughters to such schools, since dance was increasingly considered a fashionable trend in private life.

The conservatives warned against the new propensity. The younger SCIPIO (AEMILIUS AFRICANUS PUBLIUS CORNELIUS, ca. 185–129 B.C.E.), in about 150, closed the schools that taught singing and dancing,[202] but to no avail; they were opened soon again. CORNELIUS NEPOS (100–29 B.C.E.) maintained that leading men of the state never practiced music or dance. If dance was indulged in by men alone, it was especially considered a vice.[203] Other men in public life were more understanding, thus the famous orator, MARCUS FABIUS QUINTILIANUS (ca. 35–ca. 118 C.E.), who was on principle a strict adherent of puritanical mores, advocated that future orators should study music in order to train their ear to harmony, and take dance lessons to be able to stress their eloquence by the grace and rhythm of their movements. The satire of JUVENAL (ca. 60–ca. 140 C.E.) does not deal with the dance itself, but rather with its abuses and its exaggerated influence among the reigning circles. Moreover, DIO CHRYSOSTOMOS, contemporary of the Emperor TRAJAN (52–117 C.E.), characterizes the life in Alexandria as a "continuous revel of dancers, whistlers [i.e., pipers], and murderers."[204]

In the third period, that of the Empire, Roman dances were increasingly dominated by Greek and Oriental customs. Greek choreography prevailed, but was soon spoiled by theatrical dances, and especially by the spreading of the pantomime, dramatic actions without words, which became the favorite art phenomenon of this period.

If we disregard the few unfavorable, or hostile, opinions of leading persons against the dance, it can be stated that public opinion overwhelmingly favored dance. For valid proof of this, we may refer to the fact that in the education of princes and future emperors, music, singing, and dancing were essential requirements. I mention only some of the Roman princely persons, such as CALIGULA, BRITANNICUS (the son of the Emperor CLAUDIUS, whom NERO poisoned out of jealousy), HADRIAN, MARCUS AURELIUS, his son COMMODUS, the Empress JULIA DONNA (the wife of SEPTIMIUS SEVERUS), ELAGABALUS, SEVERUS ALEXANDER, and last but not least, NERO, the famous musician, actor, and dancer among the emperors.

In aristocratic families as well as in bourgeois circles, dancing belonged to good education. MACROBIUS refers to three members of the high nobility: MARCUS CAELIUS, GABINIUS, and to the son of CRASSUS, whose dancing was of an artistic quality.[205] Apart from the pleasure dancing offered to the Roman society, it was considered, just as among the Greeks, the best means for the harmonious development of the body. The Roman ladies, especially, indulged with fervor in the pleasure of dancing, besides other artistic occupations such as poetry, music, and singing. In public schools the girls received the same education as the boys, with additional courses in music and dancing. To the pleasures that a host offered his invited guests belonged, besides a good meal, music, dancing, recitation of poems, and theatrical plays.

Italy, especially Rome, offered a wide field of activity to the numerous foreign groups of dancers who flooded all provinces of the Empire. Egypt, Syria, and Spain sent famous female dancers (*saltatrices*) for guest performances, who eventually settled permanently in Rome. They brought with them their Oriental instruments, which took root in Roman musical practice. Their major role, however, was in the pantomime, which gave such foreign dancers their real popularity.

In order to realize the impact of pantomime not only upon the general public, but sometimes upon distinguished visitors, we have to refer to the type of performance that NERO offered one of his guests, the cynic DEMETRIUS (see below).

To fully understand such pantomimic presentations, the audience had, of course, to be familiar with the "story" of the play, which generally was borrowed from the mythology, which most persons knew. The pantomime was the *ballett* of the Romans, eclipsing not only all other theatrical productions, but completely eliminating them. Through the pantomime, the dance became the fashion, and was passionately practiced by the Romans. Every private home had a dance floor; for wealthy Romans it was a social obligation to have in their household a cook, a philosopher, and a dancing master.

In addition, the Romans assiduously cultivated war dances, ritual dances, and work dances. At festivals and in plays, folk-dances were indispensable for enhancing the joy of the occasion. With all their predilection for the dance, the Romans adhered more to the technical perfection of it than to its refinement, in contradistinction to the Hellenes, for whom dance had a deeper artistic significance and a higher ethical value, qualities that remained unadulterated during the entire existence of Greek cultural life.

As mentioned earlier, for choral performances in which a multitude of singers took place, the *scabellum* was a necessity in order to keep the masses rhythmically together by acoustical means. This was an even more important requirement for group dances, because without a loud marking of the time the rhythmic precision of the dancers could not be maintained. Even when the dances were accompanied by musical instruments, the most necessary implement for keeping the dancers together was the *scabellum*.

MUSIC AS A PROFESSION

Even more than in Greece, music as a profession was regarded as an important element of the Roman economy. In Greece, the general musical education was carried out in groups, in the *kyklios choros,* which was supported by the state itself and entrusted to teachers who were public functionaries. Only individuals for whom the general instruction was insufficient and who aspired to higher aims with their musical knowledge—be it for their own pleasure or for professional purposes—resorted to private instruction. Individual music instruction served higher aims; therefore private teachers in Greece were in the minority.

In Rome, there was no state-regulated *public* music instruction; anything a music lover wanted to acquire had to be done through private teachers. Their numbers must have been considerable throughout the entire history of Rome, and since they were well paid, their class was an essential part of Roman economic life.

In addition, there was the often-mentioned predilection of the Romans for mass music productions and, in general, for grandiose effects in musical performances. There must have been hundreds, even thousands of musicians in Rome, as well as in other places, to satisfy the demand for music teachers.

From the mass of performers some outstanding artists emerged whose names are preserved for posterity. I restrict myself to quoting the names of only those who were important enough to be immortalized in records of historiography. There were certainly many more, no less important ones, whose names appear only occasionally in the literature.

I have already referred to the most famous kithara-virtuoso of the time, TERPNOS, who was honored by being the teacher of NERO. It is not impossible that the "sacred" festivals, the *Neronia*, in which music and poetry were the main subjects, owe their creation to TERPNOS's influence upon the Emperor. These festivals, inaugurated in the year 60, served more to satisfy the Emperor's craving to present himself as a performer than to his love of art.

Among other famous virtuosi, the singer and aulēte TIGELLIUS HERMOGENES, deserves mention. Son of a slave in Sardinia, he flourished at the court of AUGUSTUS. HORACE calls him *cantor atque optimus modulator* ("singer and the best composer").[206] The kitharōde MENECRATES was rewarded by NERO with a palace and an estate "worthy of men who had celebrated triumphs."[207] MESOMEDES of Crete, a freed man, was the luminary at HADRIAN's court. He is the only poet-composer of whom the music of three hymns is preserved (see p. 354). HADRIAN allowed him such a high salary that the Emperor's successor, ANTONINUS PIUS, had to reduce it.[208]

Other kitharōdes also received princely rewards. The virtuoso ANAXERON was honored by his birthplace, Magnesia on the river Meander, with a priesthood and a monument erected on a public square. MARCUS ANTONIUS, one of the triumvirs, transferred to him the tax-income of four cities and elected him commander of a military unit.[209]

APELLES, a dramatic singer of Askalon, a favorite of the Emperor CALIGULA, met a curious fate. Asked by the Emperor whether he considered him or JUPITER greater, the singer committed the *faux pas* of hesitating with his answer. For this, CALIGULA ordered that he be scourged; but the Emperor praised even his cries of pain as "attractive."[210]

CANUS and GLAPHYRUS were famous tibia- and kithara-players. In spite of their well-established reputation, they kept a well-paid claque for their own adulation.[211]

The notorious *chronique scandaleuse* of the Roman actors and musical virtuosi was no different from that of other Oriental civilizations of Antiquity. Everywhere, famous artists had been the spoiled favorites of rich and frivolous women. Numerous coeval records of Rome testify about women of high nobility, who "bought" the love of a renowned actor, dancer, or singer. This seems to have been quite common, as neither the public at large, nor the families in which such happenings occurred, showed much concern about it.

This licentiousness even spread into the imperial courts. It was an open secret that the wife of the Emperor Pertinax had a liaison with a famous kitharōdos. Best known are the amorous escapades of Valeria Messalina, the third wife of the Emperor Claudius, whom he married when he was forty-eight and she was sixteen. She soon fell in love with the dancer Mnester, and after him lovers succeeded one another almost uninterruptedly. While the Emperor was in Ostia in the year 48, Messalina went through a formal marriage, "with pomp and with accustomed rites," to a handsome youth, Caius Silius.[212] It seems that until then Claudius tolerated her profligacy, but bigamy was too much, even for the most "understanding" Emperor. One of her former lovers, Narcissus, her accomplice in many vicious acts, betrayed her to the Emperor. Claudius rushed back to Rome, ordered Silius and other lovers of Messalina slain, and summoned her "to plead her case." Narcissus, fearing that the Emperor would forgive her once more and turn against him, dispatched soldiers with the instruction to kill her. They found her alone with her mother and killed her in her mother's arms. She was then only twenty-six years old.

The way of life of vain musical artists has been repeatedly chastised by satiric poets and writers, without, however, in the least changing the prevailing situation. It is evident that the blame should be ascribed more to the lascivious women than to the virtuosi themselves. Besides, such satirical onslaughts must frequently have been tainted by the poets' personal dislikes of certain artists, and they do not refer to the great number of honestly striving musicians.

On the other hand, it must be stated that even among the famous performers envy and jealousy were rampant. Competitors closely observed the public and private behavior of their rivals and, although externally friendly toward each other, they did not refrain from insidious calumnies of their adversaries. Inveighing publicly against a competitor occurred only rarely, because this would have been considered contrary to the spirit of the fraternity and would have turned mostly against the aggressor himself. There were subtler means of getting rid of a dangerous rival, mostly by bribing him, or in some cases eliminating him by assassination, a prerogative of the Emperor Nero. Shortly before his own ignominious end, Nero ordered the murder of the famous singer and actor Paris, whom he considered a dangerous rival in the planned celebration of his victory.[213]

Vanity and capriciousness were at all times characteristic of the profession of musical artists. This was no different in Rome from in Greece. The more an artist was admired and praised, the more his vanity, arrogance, and whimsicality became predominant. Phaedrus, the writer of fables, reports a humorous incident about a conceited artist who became the butt of derision through his ridiculous vanity.

The tibia-player Princeps Cappa (the word in Latin means "prince"), who used to be the accompanist of the famous dancer of pantomimes, Bathyllus, broke his leg during a change of scenery. He had to stay in bed several months, and his playing was missed by the art-loving public. When he could walk again, even with some difficulty, a wealthy man who wanted to organize a play persuaded him to participate in it. In this play, the choir sang a new song that was unknown to the tibia-player, the lyrics of which contained the phrase: "Rome should exult, since its prince (*princeps*) is well off." (This referred to some princely person who recovered from a sickness). At this moment, the audience rose to its feet and applauded vigorously. The musician took this acclaim as referring to his person and blew kisses to the audience. The amused audience soon discovered the mistake and, in fun, demanded that the song be repeated. Again, the artist thanked them rapturously. Of course, the musician PRINCEPS was innocent in this case; nevertheless, he was accused of having accepted the honors due an imperial prince, and was thrown out with much indignation.[214]

Even more obvious was the whimsicality of the aforementioned TIGELLIUS HORMOGENES, who provoked the ire of CICERO in the year 45.[215] If he did not feel disposed, nobody could induce him to sing. Even AUGUSTUS, who was used to giving orders, frequently received the "cold-shoulder treatment" from the capricious singer, but seems to have tolerated his temperamental excesses with good humor.

When, however, he was seized by the "spirit," he sang all the stanzas of *Io Bacchus,* from the first until the last course of a banquet without stopping. His instability and whimsicality appeared not only in his artistic, but also in his private life. HORACE describes his erratic behavior:

> Now he ran around as if obsessed, now he walked solemnly, as in a procession. Today he had two hundred slaves, the next day only ten. Sometimes he talked grandiloquently, at other times he wanted only a three-legged table and a salt-shaker and a rough toga to keep him warm. If he received a million one day as a present, in five days he had nothing left of it. He squandered the easily won wealth with both hands; he assembled around himself a court of quack-doctors, beggars, dancing girls, street-musicians and wags. He passed his nights in carousing, and slept the whole day.[216]

Thus, TIGELLIUS is the perfect example of a conceited, sybaritic, whimsical, and neurotic, almost irresponsible artist. There must have been several other hedonistic musicians in Rome, but about none of them do we possess such a detailed report as appears in HORACE's description of TIGELLIUS.

These and similar cases, even if they happened more frequently, were the exceptions. In general, the profession of the musicians in Rome had a solid civic appearance; sociologically and economically, the musicians were a privileged class in the Roman society, a class governed by the demand and supply of their members. Although a sizable number of the musicians were slaves, the authorities did not treat them as such, but considered them as members worthy of full civic rights in Roman society. It is a curious fact that despite this tolerant attitude, the profession of the musician was considered as *infamia* by the populace, unless the artist was one of the protagonists of the profession. But the great mass of musicians did not suffer under such a humiliating classification. They owed their protection mainly to their fraternities or guilds, which gave them the necessary moral strength and human self-consciousness.

The professional organizations of the Roman musicians had different aspects and aims, according to the nationality, the social standing of their members, and also to the purpose they pursued in their professions. Following their historical development and the practical necessities of the guilds, we have to distinguish between:

1) The priestly sodalities of the Salii and Arval brothers
2) the collegia of the sacral tibia- and kithara-players
3) the fraternities of the military musicians
4) the guilds of the musicians employed at funerals

5) the organization of the members of the theatrical professions
6) the unions of the various secular instrumentalists
7) the fraternities of the singing groups, which called themselves, after Greek models, "*Societas cantorum Graecorum,*" having branches in all larger cities.[217]

In the historical records, professional musicians first appeared in the cult, as is proven by the Twelve-Table-Laws, in the fifth century B.C.E.[218]

The social standing of the musicians in Rome, although high ranking in general, was nevertheless divided into several strata. The Salii and the Arval brothers belonged to the nobility. The musicians employed in the cult, the tibia- and lyra-players, were in the last century of the Republic freed slaves. During the period of the Emperors, the musicians of the army held the rank of "noncommissioned officers," while the musicians of the navy remained slaves. Greek virtuosi, actors and musicians, who settled permanently in Rome, belonged to the fraternity of the Dionysian artists. In contrast to Greek actors, who were all free citizens, a great many of the Roman actors were freed slaves, while the majority of the foreign dancers and musicians, who provided the necessary entertainment for the populace, were slaves. Thus, the social standing of Rome's musical artists shows a picture that is far from homogeneous, oscillating between citizenship and slavery, and tainted—even if theoretically—by *infamia.*

This situation was thoroughly changed when the union of the Greek Dionysian artists was taken over by the Romans. Their guilds accepted anyone whose professional competence was established. In these *collegia,* all the members were "brothers," the women "sisters." Religion, race, and social standing were no handicaps to be accepted by these fraternities; at the *agapē* (as the community meal was called after Greek model), slaves sat at the same table with the freeborn. Among them were, until the fourth century, quite a few professional Jewish singers, actors, and poets.[219] Wealthy Romans frequently furthered these guilds by donations, and sometimes included them in their last wills.[220] Every member in good standing was given a dignified funeral.[221]

According to Greek custom, these fraternities called themselves "Dionysian artists," although the god DIONYSOS did not in Rome have the same significance as in Greece. Nevertheless, they enjoyed great esteem and had branches in Athens, Teos, Pergamon, Alexandria, and other places, although probably not so many as in ancient Greece, where they existed in almost every large city. In the Roman Empire, they were a continuation of the Greek guilds which, as in Greece, embraced all the personnel needed for public performances: poets and actors for the tragedy and comedy, stage directors, choir-singers, dancers (male and female), rhapsōdes and kitharōdes, musicians (aulētes and trumpeters). The guilds also included the other helpers needed to present a play, such as stagehands and seamstresses for the costumes.

After the conquest of Macedonia (167 B.C.E.) and the destruction of Corinth (144 B.C.E.), Greek actors and musicians flooded the Italian peninsula. At the triumphal return of victorious generals, they took part in the festival plays organized in Rome for MARCUS FULVIUS NOBILIS (186 B.C.E.), LUCIUS ANICIUS GALLUS (167 B.C.E.), and LUCIUS MUMMIUS (146 B.C.E.).

This invasion of Greek actors and musicians exerted a powerful influence upon the Roman theater. It brought about the presentation of Greek theatrical plays (serious and comic) in the original form and language but adapted for Roman taste. Furthermore—and this was even more important—it fertilized Roman dramatic creativity.

Among the Roman musical fraternities, those of the players of brass instruments were the most important, owing to the prevalence of these instruments in the army. All categories had their guilds: the *tubicines* (trumpeters), *cornicines* (horn-blowers), to which evidently also the *bucinatores* and *liticines* belonged. Another term for the *tubicen* was *tubicantius*. The *tubicen artifex organorum*[222] was sometimes interpreted as designating an organ virtuoso. This is highly improbable, because the organ of those times was technically a rather undeveloped instrument that probably did not permit "virtuoso" performances. Furthermore, in no musical contest of the epoch is an organ player ever mentioned as a victor. It is better to explain the term as applying to a manufacturer of organs, as indicated by the noun *artifex*.

The fraternity of the tibia-players embraced the *pythaules, protaules,* and *hypaules*. The difference in terminology might have been caused by the various types of the tibia. Suetonius mentions the fraternities of the *psylokitharistae* and *chorokitharistae*,[223] indicating the two main species of musicians playing stringed instruments—solo lyre-players, and accompanists of choir-singing. All categories of orchestral musicians were organized in the all-embracing *collegium tibicinum et fidicinum Romanorum*, also called *Collegium symphoniacorum*.[224] This collegium was already mentioned by Plutarch; he states that it was created by Numa Pompilius himself.[225] Allegedly, the priesthood of the Salii was also created by Numa Pompilius. He selected twelve Salii who, with brass shields and sacred lances, marched in solemn procession through the streets of Rome, sang old songs, and performed rhythmical dances.[226]

The *Collegium tibicinum* enjoyed from ancient times on such special privileges as, among others, being fed at public expense in the temple of Jupiter,[227] and holding a carnival-like festival, the *quinquatrus minusculae*, at which the players roamed the city in fancy dress,[228] singing ancient melodies.[229]

The Roman actors created their own fraternity about the middle of the second century B.C.E., and called themselves, rather modestly, *Parasiti Apollinis*.

The concert artists also had their own guild which, however, was not called a collegium, but—rather grandiloquently—*Synodus magna psaltum*.[230]

A stone inscription found at Cabelli informs us of the existence of a *Collegium utricularium*, the fraternity of the bagpipers, whose leader had the title *magister*.

The musicians participating in theatrical performances united in their own guild, to which the "players" of the *scabellum* belonged, and which, curiously enough, was called *Collegium scabillariorum*.

After the conquest of Macedonia and the destruction of Corinth, the Roman authorities took over the protectorate of the fraternities that flourished in Greece, but applied a stricter economic surveillance over them.

Besides safeguarding their professional interests and helping each other, these fraternities also extended assistance to the families of the deceased. The poor among them were buried at the expense of the fraternity. There were large cemeteries in Rome in which mainly musicians and their families were laid to rest. At the Via Appia, a large mausoleum was also found, with niches for the urns of cremated musicians.

It is strange that the members of these fraternities, despite their social achievements, did not have the right to own real estate. Their buildings as well as their other possessions were the common property of the guilds, which means that their members were considered as collective owners of their buildings.

In every large city organized (or unorganized) prostitution was a social necessity. This was the case in Rome, Alexandria, and all the other urban areas of the Empire. The entire basin of the Mediterranean was flooded by mostly Syrian girls of poor families, whose only chance for a living lay in their bodily charm. They played a domestic instrument called the *abub*, a short pipe with one tube, which became their trade-mark. In Greece they were called *aulētridēs*, in Rome *ambubajae*. Their playing the pipe was not done for artistic reasons; it mainly helped them to solicit customers. I mentioned earlier that in Greece they had to pay a small fee and received a license from the authorities, which gave them the right to exercise their profession. In Rome there was a similar custom; the tax was collected by special officials (*vectigalarii*), who sometimes used cruel methods of extortion—torture or even prison—to collect the tax from the girls. Therefore, many of them preferred to be sold as slaves, and used this pretext to enjoy a carefree life with a wealthy Roman as his legalised concubine.

As long as they lived in freedom, they congregated in the basements of the Roman circuses, which were called *ambubajarum collegia*. This term had an additional meaning; it indicated that these pariahs of human society also had their professional guilds.[231] It is not known whether their guilds could protect them in any way, or permit them any social advantages. Probably this was not the case, but it is characteristic that even these girls felt the necessity of having some kind of professional organization.

It was mentioned above that the Emperor HADRIAN (76–138 c.e.) assembled all existing workmen's guilds in one all-embracing union. He recognized the important role that these fraternities played in the economic life of the Empire and understood the advantage of consolidating them.

Rising Christianity was hostile toward the fraternities of workmen; the Church tolerated no association's having any influence on the great masses other than that of the priesthood. As the power of the Church increased, all secular institutions were abolished. The decisive step in this direction was the Council of Laodicea (363 c.e.), which abrogated SOLON's *jus coeundi*, by which the demise of the workmen's unions was made final and irrevocable.

The abolition of the workmen's fraternities had an immediate and unfavorable economic result. The Fathers of the Church also inflicted grievous damage on the singing of hymns and psalms, which in this period was not exclusively confined to liturgical use. In the secular life of early Christianity, psalm-singing was identical with today's custom of folksinging. There must have been a great number of "psalms," so titled in every-day parlance, that had nothing in common with the canonical Book of Psalms. However, since their usage was widespread throughout the population, they were considered harmful by the Church authorities. The clergy maintained that these "psalms" were composed by laymen, therefore were not "inspired" by the Holy Spirit. They were declared *psalmoi idiōtikoi*, and were prohibited from being sung in the churches, and subsequently even in private life.[232] By this draconic measure, the priests afflicted severe damage on popular singing but were unable to wipe out completely a practice dear to the masses. The people looked for and found other sources to satisfy their inborn urge for singing, and, after only a short interruption, popular song and the pleasure of singing were reborn.

THEATER AND DRAMA

Drama came to Rome by chance and, as it were, through the back door. In 272 B.C.E., the Romans conquered Tarentum on the Calabrian Peninsula and slaughtered a sizable part of its Greek defenders. LIVIUS ANDRONICUS (fl. ca. 240 B.C.E.) was spared such a fate, but was enslaved and sold to a wealthy Roman, who took him to Rome and entrusted him with the education of his children. He taught them, and others, Greek and Latin. He was poetically gifted and ventured to translate the Odyssey into Latin, an undertaking that earned him great acclaim. Very soon he was freed and was commissioned by the Aediles to write a tragedy and a comedy for the *ludi* (the plays) of 240 B.C.E. He used Greek models for this purpose, directed the plays, played the principal role, and sang the songs he had inserted, accompanied by auloi. After a number of performances his voice failed, so that he was compelled to entrust the songs to another singer, while he underscored the singing with mimical gestures, a procedure later imitated by many dramatic poets that led step by step to the creation of the pantomime. The Aediles were so enchanted with the introduction of literary drama that, honoring ANDRONICUS, they conferred on dramatic authors the privilege of forming a guild and holding their conventions in the temple of MINERVA on the Aventine hill. From then on, it became the custom to present dramatic plays at all *ludi scenici.*[233]

Public theatrical performances had been presented in Rome even before ANDRONICUS's appearance. In 389 B.C.E., Etruscan actors (more appropriately termed buffoons) performed simple theatrical plays with music. These plays were devoid of any dramatic content and consisted mainly of dances accompanied by tibias.[234] Such attempts were short-lived and were soon displaced by the Latin version of Greek dramas. The creation of Roman drama therefore rightfully belongs to ANDRONICUS.

It did not take more than five years after this first attempt to bring forth various limitations. A plebeian veteran soldier from Campania, CORAEUS NAEVIUS (ca. 202 B.C.E.), wrote a comedy in which, after the model of ARISTOPHANES, he chastised the abuses rampant in the Roman society. High-placed persons who felt that they were pilloried by his sarcasm took action against the author and sent him to prison. He recanted and gained his liberty, but soon wrote another satire, just as biting as the first, after which he was banned from Rome. In exile he continued his literary activity, but narrow-minded censors for a long time retarded the development of the Roman drama which, in the meanwhile, was compelled to follow the worn-out path of Greek mythological subjects.

CICERO called the character of the music of the theatrical plays of ANDRONICUS and NAEVIUS *severitas iucundus,* "gentle severity," consequently it must have differed from the until-then-prevalent rough and coarse music.[235] HORACE bestows high praise on the *Mousikē,* the art of the Muses; he says that it was given to humanity as an exaltation of life, as *requies laborum,* "recreation after toil."[236]

Eventually Roman talent prevailed, and the poet QUINTUS ENNIUS (239–169 B.C.E.) created exquisite works in almost all branches of literary productivity. He wrote several comedies, however, that had no marked acclaim. He earned more success with his twenty tragedies, which paved the way for the later dramatic authors PLAUTUS (ca. 254–184 B.C.E.) and TERENCE (ca. 190–ca. 159). Another dramatic author whose plays dominated the Roman theater of those times was CAECILIUS STATIUS (d. 168 B.C.E.). PLAUTUS wrote or adapted one hundred and thirty plays, twenty of which are preserved.[237] TERENCE, who died at the age of twenty-five, left to posterity his principal works,[238] but all the plays of CAECILIUS STATIUS have been lost.

The prose literature of Rome, however outstanding, does not belong in this investigation unless it contains musical references. More important here are the records of the Roman authors that deal with the music of the dramatic plays, since they represent the personal observations of the writers and consequently must be considered authentic material for the history of Roman music.

When music was called for in Roman plays, the tibia-player, who was generally also the composer of the music, intoned a prelude before the play began, and filled the pauses between the acts with his playing. Furthermore he had to underscore musically the arias and melodramatic portions of the play, and accompany the dances with his instrument, the dances being essential parts of the dramatic plays. HORACE, however, in a letter, states unequivocally that in tragedy, especially for accompanying solo singing, the aulos was not used, but stringed instruments exclusively.[239]

At the time of PLAUTUS and TERENCE, Roman actors every year performed in the festivals organized by the state, the *Ludi Romani, Ludi Plebei, Ludi Apollinares, Ludi Megalenses*, and also in the funeral ceremonies of leading state functionaries.

Among the directors of the plays were several who were particularly gifted and who gained wide recognition. One of them, LUCIUS AMBIVIUS TURPIO, who was highly successful in producing comedies of CAECILIUS and TERENCE, was sent by the state on several *tournées* with his troupe.[240]

To correctly appreciate the dramatic practice of the Romans, we have to realize the dimensions of their theaters. A rich upstart, AEMILIUS SCAURUS, built a theater with 8000 seats; the building had 360 columns and 300 statues; the stage was divided into three stories; the theater had three colonnades, one of wood, the other of marble, the third of glass.[241] SCAURUS's slaves rebelled against the hard work imposed upon them by their master and burned down the building. The owner suffered a loss of 100,000,000 sesterces.

One of CAESAR's generals, SCRIBONIUS CURIO, built two theaters of wood, each in a half-circle, back to back; they were put on wheels and could be turned around, so that they could be used as an arena for fights of gladiators.

In spite of the huge theatrical buildings, erected either by rich individuals or by the Caesars, using state funds, the Roman drama was intended to be read and not performed. In its first period the Roman stage repertoire consisted of ancient Greek or adapted works; the play was merely the frame for the actors, who were the real attraction of the theatrical art. Many of them had huge earnings and were just as admired and adored by the public as today's movie stars. It can be said that the Roman drama died in the arena, sacrificed by the Roman *circenses*, the showy and exciting presentations in the circus.

Most of the burlesque actors hailed from Istrio in Etruria, and accordingly were called *istriones*; hence the Latin term *histrio* for actors of any category.

The theater structures of PLAUTUS and TERENCE were made of wood; in the background was a kind of backdrop called *scaena*, while the foreground was a circle-shaped space, where the dances were performed. The part next to the stage, the *orchestra*, was the *proscenium*, where the actors played their roles. The audience stood or sat on chairs brought by themselves. The wooden scaffoldings of the building were torn down after each festival, to be constructed anew at the next. Not before 145 B.C.E. was a permanent theater built in Rome, still of wood and without a roof, but with seats arranged in a semicircle, as in the Greek amphitheater. There was no entrance fee; slaves were admitted, but were not allowed to sit; women were relegated to the back rows. The audience was the roughest and most unrestrained in the history of the theater. During the prologue, as well as during the play itself, there were frequent admonitions to keep quiet. Sometimes, for the amusement of the audience, fistfights or rope-walkers were inserted, during which time the play was interrupted, to be continued after the amusement was over. When the play ended, one of the actors pronounced the formula *nunc plaudite omnes,* or something similar, to indicate that the audience could give vent to their approval of the actors.

The production in the amphitheater always started with a colorful procession. At the head of it marched trumpeters and hornblowers, playing the *cornu* and *lituus.* They were followed by the principal actors, wearing ornate helmets. The beginning of the play was announced by a trumpet blast: for musical background, the play was accompanied by an instrumental group composed of a water-organist, a tuba-player, and two cornu-players. As the dimensions of the theaters and arenas were gradually enlarged, more musicians were employed for the accompaniment.

As long as the theaters were of medium size, it sufficed that the actors indicate the characters of the persons by make-up and appropriate wigs. Around 100 B.C.E., when the theaters became increasingly larger, this was no longer sufficient. From then on the actors wore masks, called *personae,* a term derived probably from the Etruscan *phersu,* meaning "mask." Thus, *dramatis personae* signified the "masks of the drama." As in Greece, the tragic actors used high shoe-like footwear (*cothurns*), the comic actors low shoes (*soccus*). The audience preferred uncouth jokes to real humor, buffoons were more in demand than serious actors, and vulgar writings eclipsed real poetry. Therefore PLAUTUS was more popular than TERENCE.

It was a peculiarity of the Roman theater that adaptations of ancient comedies, especially those of ARISTOPHANES, were prohibited by law. The Twelve-Tables-of-Laws punished political satire with the death penalty.[242] Thus, most of the Roman comedies were imitations or adaptations of Greek mythological subjects.

This is the background against which music in the Roman theater must be understood. As in the Greek drama, parts of the Roman plays were sung, accompanied by the aulos (or the Latin tibia); later (exactly as ANDRONICUS had improvised when he lost his voice) the singer performed his song while another actor underscored the words with mimical gestures. As time passed, this led to the creation of a new art form, the pantomime, ("all mimicry").

There was still another reason behind the origin of pantomime. Its subjects were chosen mainly from the Greek classical literature, which, in view of the polyglot population of Rome, had the advantage that the spoken dialogue could be omitted, leaving the carrying out of the action solely to mimic presentation. In 21 B.C.E. two actors came to Rome, PYLADES from Cilicia and BATHYLLUS from Alexandria, who were the real creators of the Roman pantomime; they simply introduced the Hellenistic art form, long used in Greece, presenting one-act plays consisting merely of music, visual action, mimicry, and dancing. At that time, Rome had become tired of the ancient dramas with their pompous verses and stereotyped characters and welcomed the new art form.

Roman audiences were delighted by the physical grace of the two actors, by their showy costumes, the humor of their masks, the quick and adroit change of the personified characters, and by the new kind of orientalism projected in these plays. Soon there were numerous fans of the new art form, as well as imitators in increasing numbers. Pantomime eventually killed Roman drama, and, to a certain degree, even displaced comedy. The pantomime became the *ballet* of the Romans, making all other theatrical art obsolete. Not until the reign of the sun-king, Louis XIV, did ballet again attain the importance in human society that it enjoyed in Roman life.

In addition to pantomime, another specific art form developed, that of the mimic play, in which the spoken word was not completely excluded. In these plays the stage director had the most important function. His direction was the controlling factor whenever the various competing members of the play—the actors, singers, dancers, and musicians—wanted to go their own way. These mimic plays vied in popularity with the pantomimes. In them thrashing scenes were frequently introduced, as well as sarcastic allusions to actual happenings, sometimes accompanied by unmitigated ribaldry, obscene words and gestures. The actors of the mimic plays performed barefooted, without masks and in coarse attire. Usually, they improvised the plays, inserting copious dances and songs, making use of the latest hit songs among the ditties. In a preserved text of such a mimic play from the second century C.E., entitled *Charition*,[243] we find at several points, and especially in the dance scenes, instructions for the stage director, and a request for the use of percussion instruments (*kroumata*), among them frame-drums and clappers.[244]

CURT SACHS vividly describes the effect of the pantomime upon the audience, as reported by LUCIAN:

Once in the time of Nero, a pantomime was danced before the Cynic Demetrius. The time-beaters [i.e., the *scabelli*], the flutes, even the chorus, were ordered to preserve a strict silence; the pantomime, left to his own resources, represented the loves of Ares and Aphrodite, the telltale Sun, the craft of Hephaestus, his capture of the two lovers in the net, the surrounding gods, each in his turn, the blushes of Aphrodite, the embarrassment of Ares, his entreaties,—in fact the whole story. Demetrius was ravished at the spectacle; nor could there be higher praise than that which he accorded to the performers. "Man," he shrieked at the top of his voice, "this is not seeing, but hearing and seeing, both: 'tis as if your hands were tongues!"[245]

SACHS also quotes another statement of LUCIAN, who tells

of the high tribute paid to the art by a foreigner of the royal family of Pontus, who was visiting the Emperor on business, and had been among the spectators of this same pantomime. So convincing were the artists' gestures, as to render the subject intelligible even to one who (being half Greek) could not follow the vocal accompaniment. When he was about to return to his country, Nero, in taking leave of him, bade him to choose what present he would have, assuring him that his request should not be refused. "Give me," said the Pontian, "your great pantomime; no gift could delight me more." "And of what use can he be to you in Pontus?" asked the Emperor. "I have foreign neighbors, who do not speak our language; and it is not easy to procure interpreters. Your pantomime could discharge that office perfectly, as often as required, by means of his gesticulations." So profoundly had he been impressed with the extraordinary clearness of pantomimic representation.[246]

With the tendency of the Romans to develop all art forms on a gigantic scale, it was not uncommon that in some pantomimes as many as 3000 singers and 3000 dancers participated.[247]

Certain arias or songs presented in these theatrical performances were widely known by the populace and were sung everywhere; the same was true with various musical sections of the pantomimes. They were so well known that connoisseurs of music could tell after the first few notes to which production and to what scene they belonged.

There is no better way to characterize the Roman pantomime than by comparing it with today's enthusiasm for motion pictures. The pantomime was the "movie" of the Romans.

Like every other art form of the Romans, the pantomime eventually degenerated into a mere showpiece for obscenities. It so happened that the puritanically minded Emperor DOMITIAN (reign 81–96 C.E.) disavowed these abuses in the public life and prohibited such immoral pantomimes. For this purpose he called on the ancient Julian laws, which abolished, among other things, adultery, children's prostitution, homosexuality, and castration. In no other domain of his reforms did he obtain such far-reaching results as in that of the pantomime, much to the displeasure of the populace. No sooner was DOMITIAN dead than the pantomime was revived, with all its moral decay, and it remained the main entertainment of the people until the end of the Roman Empire.

WRITERS ON THE SCIENCE OF MUSIC

It is difficult to determine whether the early theorists on the music of Antiquity belong in the Greek or Roman period. In no other domain of musical practice were the Romans so dependent upon Greek cultural achievements as in the science of music. It is a well-known fact that the Romans borrowed their musical culture where they could find it: from the Etruscans, the Egyptians, the Cretans, the Phrygians, and later—directly or indirectly—from the Greeks. Since, however, only the Hellenes developed their own musical system and science, the Romans had no easier way than to adopt, continue, and develop the accomplishments of the Greeks. This created the situation where all, or most, of the Roman writings about music were based upon the Greek achievements in this domain.

In examining Roman literature about music, it is striking how contradictory their writings are; they follow mostly the verified, and sometimes unverified tradition, without referring too much to the musical practices of their own time. In most cases, the Roman writers merely took over, or commented upon, the Greek theories, thus the overall picture of Roman musical science remains merely the image of the Greek accomplishments.

Among the "Roman" writers on music, ARISTOXENOS of TARENTUM (ca. 350–ca. 300 B.C.E.), who is mentioned briefly among the Greek scientists, is outstanding as a pathfinder. He was the first to take into consideration not only the acoustical, but also the physiological side of music. Furthermore, he is credited with being the creator of music aesthetics, a discipline that he enlarged and developed into an independent science. Allegedly, he wrote 452 treatises, from which only two books are preserved, *Elements of the Harmonics* and fragments of the *Elements of Rhythmics*.

ARISTOXENOS can be considered the first psychologist of music, since he investigated and analyzed not merely the origin of the sound, but also the effect of music upon the human soul through the auditory senses.

In spite of the fact that the music theorist KLEIONIDES, a contemporary of the Emperor TRAJAN (55–117 C.E.), appeared several centuries after ARISTOXENOS, he may be considered his disciple. His treatise *Eisagōgē* is strongly influenced by ARISTOXENOS's theories.

EUCLID of Alexandria has already been briefly mentioned among the Greek writers. He was basically a mathematician, who developed, according to Pythagorean principles, the system of the Greek scales, which also became the basis of Roman music theory. One of his treatises, *Katatomē kanonos*, (in Latin *Sectio canonis*), has been preserved and was first printed 1557 in Paris, then repeatedly reprinted.

Another renowned mathematician and music theorist was ERASTOTHENES of Cyrene (276–195 B.C.E.), whose preserved work, *Katasterismos*, contains valuable information about Greek music and instruments. He introduced a new order of tetrachords, transmitted to posterity by PTOLEMAIOS.

The theoreticians mentioned up to here belong basically to the Greek school. The Greek-Roman musical science starts with PTOLEMAIOS CLAUDIUS of Alexandria (ca. 100–170 C.E.), famous as a mathematician, astronomer, and geographer. Among others, he wrote a work in three books about music, *Harmonika*, which, comprising the older theories, belongs to the most important sources of music theory of Antiquity.

DIDYMOS of Alexandria (b. 63 C.E.) was originally a grammarian, but he wrote books about the theory of overtones, preserved in fragments by PORPHYRIUS and in some quotations of PTOLEMAIOS. He was the first to establish the difference between the large and small whole tone, called after him the *didymic comma* (81:80).

The Neo-Pythagorean NICOMACHOS of Gerasia in Syria (second century C.E.) was also a mathematician, whose tractate *Harmonices Enchiridion* deals mainly with the musical symbolism of numbers.

The historian PAUSANIAS, a contemporary of HADRIAN (177–138 C.E.), left us a description of Greece that contains useful information of a musicological nature. The writings of LUCIUS APULEIUS of Madaura (second to third century C.E.) are distinguished by frequent references to music.

PORPHYRIUS of Tyros (ca. 232–304 C.E.) was a disciple of PLOTINUS (230–ca. 270 C.E.). The former's musicological activity is reduced to a commentary of the *Harmonics* by PTOLEMAIUS. No other work of his is preserved.

PLUTARCH of Chaironeia (ca. 46–120 C.E.), who flourished under HADRIAN's reign, is the author of a highly valuable biographical compendium of Greek and Roman generals and emperors. Furthermore, he wrote an outline summarizing the practices found in the earliest period of Greek music. Since it is based upon oral tradition, it cannot be considered an authentic history of Greek tonal art. Nevertheless, it has the merit of being the very first attempt at recording the history of the music of the Hellenes. He died in a government office as a consul in the year 120.

PHILODEMOS of Gedara in Syria (first century C.E.), a contemporary of CICERO, was a frequent house-guest of PISO, a Roman consul in 58 B.C.E.[248] His treatise, *Peri mousikē*, is preserved only in fragments. Curiously, he showed in this work an antagonistic attitude toward music, especially rejecting *Mimēsis*, because— as he asserted—music has no faculty whatsoever to express physical actions or happenings.[249] His treatise is characterized by a formalistic presentation of the aesthetics of music, outlined earlier by the sophists; but PHILODEMOS greatly enlarged this approach and gave it philosophical meaning. His work was discovered in a papyrus found at Pompeii, and was first printed in 1795.

The most important musicological treatise of this epoch was *De musica libri septem* by ARISTEIDES QUINTILIANUS of Smyrna (ca. 35–95 C.E.), who established a scientific system of music theory and musical education. In it he stated that music in ancient times was not only assiduously cultivated, but enjoyed actual veneration. Musicians were considered to be seers (*vates*) and wise men (*sapientes*). Furthermore, he maintained that orators must be instructed in music as well, so that they might always be able to use the proper pitch when speaking.[250]

CICERO also stressed the importance of musical education for orators,[251] as did another QUINTILIANUS, whose first names were MARCUS FABIUS (ca. 35–96 C.E.), the author of a textbook on rhetoric, *Institutio oratoria*. In the chapter "Eurhythmy," its author emphasizes the interrelationship between oratory and dance, maintaining that the harmonious movements of an orator may be developed by dancing.

In scrutinizing the approach of Roman writers to music, one may find many references to the belief in the healing power of music, an extension of the ancient conception, found in all nations of Antiquity, that music affects not only the soul, but is also capable of curing physical illnesses. Among the numerous ancient statements about music's healing power a few should be mentioned: the historical (or semi-historical) tale of THALETAS's healing by music during an epidemic of plague in Sparta; an analogous tale in Rome, as reported by LIVY; descriptions by TERPANDROS and ARION of the healing of several illnesses; the tale of ISMENIAS's playing the aulos to cure ischias, various advice of THEOPHRASTUS on how to use music to cure illnesses; VARRO's recommendation to play the aulos to ward off snakebites; and the curious advice of ASCLEPIADES on healing deafness by playing the tuba.

Contrary to the views of the philosophers and theoreticians of music, who recognized the positive value of music, SEXTUS EMPIRICUS (second to third century C.E.) was one of the Sceptics, who denied the ethical importance of music. He maintained that music has merely an entertaining and diverting influence upon humans, and is apt to reduce young people to weakness and licentiousness.[252] (A similar approach is presented, based upon the recently discovered Hibeh papyrus).

To the writers on music belong also those who describe, in more or less detail, the water-organ (*hydraulis*) invented by the engineer KTESIBIOS of Alexandria (ca. 246–ca. 221 B.C.E.). Some of these are APOLLONIUS of Perga (ca. 247–205 B.C.E.), PHILO in his treatise *Pneumatica*, and HERON of Alexandria in his *Mechanica*. MARCUS VITRUVIUS POLLIO's book *De architectura* is our most valuable source about the architecture of his time. In it he deals occasionally with musical science, and investigates the mathematical theory of the diatonic scale. His work contains an essay about *Automatic Wind Instruments*, in which he provides a fairly accurate description of the *hydraulis*.

Other musical theorists belonging to a later period were ALYPIOS (fl. 380 C.E.), and BACCHEIOS (fourth century C.E.), whose writings contain relevant disclosures about the tonal system of classical Antiquity, and about acoustics as well as musical notation. ALYPIOS wrote an *Introduction to Music*. BACCHEIOS's treatise, *Isagoge musicae artis,* is in the form of a dialogue and contains a synopsis of the knowledge about music during the fourth century.

Although contemporary records have gaps about the system of musical notation used by the Romans, we may assume that they adopted the Greek system of musical notation. Indirect proof of this may be found in the few pictorial representations that survive, showing singers holding in their hands some kind of notebook. Whether these books contained merely the lyrics of the songs or musical symbols as well is a matter of conjecture. It would be logical, however, to believe that the art of musical notation had been adopted in some form from the Greeks, like other elements of their musical practice and science. There is a single reference to musical notation in QUINTILIANUS's *De musica* where he considers the familiarity with musical notation a specific feature of musical education.[253]

Other works of less importance for transmitting musical science are *Fragmentum de musica* by CENSORINUS (fl. 230 c.e.), a lost treatise of ALBINUS, Roman consul in 335 and town-prefect in 336, and *Disputatio de somnis Scipionis* by FAVONIUS EULOGIUS, a disciple of St. AUGUSTINE. A contemporary of ALBINUS was the grammarian CHALCIDICUS, who held that the foundation of a good education was the knowledge of harmonics and arithmetic. He based his theories upon the close relationship between the musical intervals and the principles of mathematics. Further insight into music is afforded us by MACROBIUS, a contemporary of St. AUGUSTINE, who, in commenting upon Scipio's dreams, also contributes some ideas about the harmony of the spheres (see below).

For the sake of curiosity, FULGENTIUS (fifth century c.e.) should be mentioned. He deserves to be considered a "mythograph" rather than a writer on music. In his treatise, he indiscriminately mixed mythology and music, based upon the tale of APOLLO's contest with MARSYAS, and considered the myth of ORPHEUS and EURYDICE, as an important symbol of the art of music.

Of greater value for the propagation of musical science is a textbook by MARTIANUS CAPELLA of Carthage (fifth century c.e.), although in it musical science is also treated in a mystical and allegorical manner, as when he describes the wedding of MERCURY with PHILOLOGY. At least the entire ninth chapter is devoted to music.

Passing in review the achievements of Roman writers in the domain of musical science, one facet, inherited from ancient peoples, should not be overlooked, namely, the theory about the Harmony of the Spheres, as developed mainly by the Pythagorean school.

This theory is based upon the assumption that cosmic influences are expected upon terrestrial music. According to this conception, just as the tones of the musical scale have a strong relationship to one another, there is a corresponding parallel between the revolving time of the celestial bodies, a notion that later developed into a complicated esoteric-mystical science. Roman writers other than musical theoreticians also expressed their ideas about the celestial harmonies. CICERO, for instance, considered the music of the spheres as a "loud, and at the same time, sweet song."[254] In his opinion mundane music was a heavenly gift, a conception akin to that of the Hebrews. Other Roman writers treated the harmony of the Spheres more or less cursorily, among them PLINY the ELDER, CENSORINUS, MACROBIUS, and FAVONIUS EULOGIUS. MARTIANUS CAPELLA and BOETHIUS discussed the subject more elaborately.

Besides our knowledge gained from these writers who dealt with specifically musical matters, we find useful insights into the musical life of Rome in the works of the leading literary men of the epoch. Marcus Terentius Varro (116–27 B.C.E.), in his treatise about the free arts, *Disciplinarum libri IX*, stresses the importance of music as a strong component of general instruction, by which he approaches the Greek ideal of education. Julius Pollux of Naucratis in Egypt (second century C.E.) sums up the knowledge of his time in an encyclopedic work entitled *Onomasticon*, which he dedicated to the Emperor Commodus (161–192 C.E.). It contains valuable insights, and definitions of music in general, as well as descriptions of instruments and music theory in particular.

A special class of informative literature about music is the half-historical, half-narrative book of the grammarian Athenaios of Naucratis (second to third century C.E.), who spent most of his life in Rome. His work, entitled *Deipnosophistēs* ("Sophists at Dinner"), is presented in the form of imaginary dialogues between philosophers and sophists participating at a banquet. This literary dialogue is particularly important for a special reason: it contains numerous quotations of other writings of Antiquity that have been lost and about which there are no other records.

The works of Marcus Tullius Cicero (106–43 B.C.E.), without attempting to deal with music directly, shed some light upon the social conditions relating to the musical practices of Rome.[255] In later Roman times, a cleavage gradually developed between music as a science and the actual practice of music. It entailed a growing disdain of the Roman society for professional musicians, which is clearly reflected in Cicero's writings.

There are also statements about the practice of music to be found in the works of the poets, such as Ovid, Horace, Martial, Juvenal, Lucian of Samosata, and others of this period, who represented "public opinion." The essays of the historians and biographers (Pliny the Elder, Tacitus, Suetonius, and others), contribute relevant information about our subject. If we add to this the innumerable details found in the writings of minor literary persons and poets, as well as the statements of public officials, we gain a clear composite picture of Roman musical life.

The practice of music in Rome degenerated along with the political, social, and economic importance of the once-so-powerful state. After the collapse of the Roman Empire, nothing was left of its flourishing musical practice but the miserable profession of wandering musicians, jugglers, and buffoons at fairs, who degraded the musical profession for centuries. This situation changed only with the emergence in the twelfth and thirteenth centuries of the medieval troubadours and jongleurs in France, and their counterpart, the *juglares* in Iberian lands and the Minnesingers in Germany. Due to their artistry, music again became socially acceptable. Thus, at a much later date they were responsible for inaugurating the trend toward achieving a nobler and more artistic use of the musical profession.

After the fall of Rome, music as an art was preserved by the Christian Church, in the West through the new liturgy of the Christian faith, in the East through the musical achievements of the Byzantine (East Roman) Empire.

The late Roman writers, and especially the Fathers of the Church, tried to transmit the achievements of the Graeco-Roman musical culture to posterity. Of these, special importance must be assigned to St. Augustine (354–430 C.E.), who furnished valuable insight into the music of his time. His approach to the tonal art was laid down in his treatise *De musica,* in which he tried to blend the antique theory (Books 1–5) with Christian theology (Book 6), giving mystico-religious interpretations to many a musical term.

Other Church Fathers who made more or less significant incursions into the science of music were CLEMENT of ALEXANDRIA (d. ca. 215 C.E.), whose essays on various topics, *Strōmata,* contain some information about music, and CASSIODORUS (ca. 480–ca. 575 C.E.), whose *Institutiones divinarum et humanorum rerum* paved the way for BOETHIUS. The fifth chapter of this work is a veritable compendium about the theory of music.

CASSIODORUS, a high official at the court of King THEODORIC, addressed a letter to BOETHIUS in the fall of the year 506, asking him to procure a kitharōdos for the King of the Franks, CHLODWIG. The letter, which is preserved, contains besides this request a lengthy eulogy of music.

The last one of the early Church Fathers who tried to synthesize the musical knowledge of his time and preserve it for coming generations was ISIDORE of SEVILLA (580–636 C.E.). In his two treatises, *De ecclesiasticis officiis,* and *Etymologiae sive origines,* he presents valuable insights into the musical science of the period. His chapter on rhythm is mainly a catalogue of percussive instruments, which he does not always describe correctly.

The individual whose influence upon the Middle Ages had the greatest impact was ANCIUS MANLIUS TORQUATUS BOETHIUS (ca. 475–524 C.E.). He was the scion of an ancient noble family, who during his political career as consul was for many years the close advisor of THEODORIC, King of the Visigoths. The king suspected him of entertaining treacherous connections with the Byzantine Court and executed him.

BOETHIUS left us a philosophical and mathematical treatise, *De institutione musica,* in five books. This opus exerted an unusually strong influence upon the music of the early Middle Ages, because it faithfully transmitted the Greek theory and aesthetics of music to posterity. It became and remained the basis of both musical practice and the science of music throughout the Middle Ages. As HERMANN ABERT writes of this great work of BOETHIUS,

Thus, the entire musical credo of the Pythagorean school, with its ethical dogmas, with its mystico-symbolical teachings, even with the numerous anecdotes about the miraculous deeds of its originator, were preserved through the entire Middle Ages, and influenced considerably the aesthetic views of coming times.[256]

NOTES

1. Dionysos of Halicarnassos, *Roman Antiquities,* 1:28–30.
2. Herodotus, I, 94.
3. Hellanikos.
4. *Durant,* 3:11.
5. Antikleides; see *Fleischhauer,* p. 7.
6. *Fleischhauer,* p. 8.
7. Max Wegner, in *MGG,* 2:1595.
8. Ovid, *Fasti,* VI, 653 ff.
9. Livy, IX, 30 59.
10. Paul-Louis, *Ancient Rome at Work* (New York, 1927), p. 66. J. Toutain, *Economic Life of the Ancient World* (New York, 1930), p. 111.
11. Friedrich Behn, *Musikleben im Altertum und frühen Mittelalter* (Stuttgart, 1954), p. 132.

12. *Ibid.,* p. 140.
13. *Ibid.,* Plate 79, Illus. 181.
14. *SachsReal,* p. 311.
15. *SachsHist,* p. 142.
16. Behn, p. 130.
17. *Ibid.,* p. 131.
18. *Ibid.,* p. 135.
19. *Ibid.,* p. 129.
20. *Ibid.,* p. 132.
21. *Fleischhauer,* p. 31, Illus. 7.
22. *Ibid.,* p. 37, Illus. 128.
23. Livy, V, 1.
24. L. Home, *Primitive Italy and the Beginning of Roman Imperialism* Trans. from the French by V. Gordon Child (New York, 1926), p. 128.
25. W. J. Duff, *Literary History of Rome* (London, 1909), p. 6.
26. Livy, VII, 2, 4 ff.
27. See the bronze statuette from Chiusi, reproduced in *Fleischhauer,* p. 31.
28. *Fleischhauer,* p. 45, Illus. 18.
29. G. Dennis, *Cities and Cemeteries in Etruria* (Everyman's Library, 1933–37), 1:321.
30. Servius, In *Vergilii carmina commentarii,* 69.
31. Behn, p. 79.
32. Th. Birt, *Das Kulturleben der Griechen und Römer* (Leipzig, 1929), p. 370.
33. Albert Trevor, *History of Ancient Civilization* (New York, 1939), 2:590.
34. Ludwig Friedländer, *Darstellungen der Sittengeschichte Roms* (Leipzig, 1920), 2:163.
35. Paul Henry Láng, *Musik in Western Civilization* (New York, 1941), p. 31.
36. Hermann Abert, "Der gegenwärtige Stand der Forschung über antike Musik," in *Jahrbuch der Musikbibliothek Peters* 28 (Leipzig 1921–22).
37. Horace, *Ars poetica,* 202.
38. Ammianus Marcellinus, *Rerum gestarum,* XIV, 6, 18.
39. Cicero, *De finibus,* I, 21 ff.
40. *SachsRise,* p. 273.
41. Günther Wille, "Die Musikalität der alten Römer," in *AfMW* 11 (1954):71–83.
42. *Ibid., Musica Romana* (Stuttgart, 1963).
43. *Ibid.,* "Die Musikalität . . . ," p. 77.
44. *Ibid.,* p. 76.
45. Cicero, *De finibus,* I, 21 ff.
46. Abert, "Der gegenwärtige Stand . . . ," p. 56.
47. Varro, *Menippae*(fragment), 348.
48. Seneca the Younger, *Epistulae morales,* 51, 12.
49. Ovid, *Epistulae ex Ponto,* 3, 117 ff.
50. Pauly, *Realencyclopedie der klassischen Altertumswissenschaft* 2, ser. 17, (Stuttgart, 1894–). W. Eisenhut, *Voltumna.*
51. Cicero, *De divinatione,* II, 24–50.
52. Polybius, *History,* VI, 56.
53. Hermann Abert, "*Musik und Politik im klassischen Altertum,*" in *Neue Musikzeitung* (1924), no. 1, p. 4.
54. Dionysos of Halicarnassos, *Roman Antiquities,* 2:70, 1; Livy, I, 20, 4.
55. Horace, *Carmina,* 3, 11, 5 ff.
56. Livy, IX, 30, 9.
57. Sir John Frazer, *Adonis, Attis, Osiris* (London, 1907), pp. 34, 219–24.
58. James Breasted, *Ancient Times* (Boston, 1916), p. 660.
59. *Durant,* 3:60.
60. Ovid, *Fasti,* III, 523.
61. St. Augustine, *City of God,* VI, 9.
62. Livy, XXXIX, 8.
63. *CAH* 2 (New York, 1924):638.
64. *Athen,* XIV, 44.
65. Sir J. Sandys, *Companion to Latin Studies* (Cambridge, 1926), p. 502.
66. Martial, *Liber Spectaculorum,* IX, 72.
67. Petronius, *Satyricon,* 26.
68. Martial, *Liber Spectaculorum,* IX, 72.

69. Petronius, *Cena Trimalchionis*, IV.
70. Ammianus Marcellinus, *Rerum gestarum*, XIV, 6.
71. *Codex Theodosianus*, 15, 7.
72. Philostratos, *The Life of Apollonius of Tyrana*, V, 21.
73. Suetonius, *Vespasian*, 19.
74. Cicero, *De officiis*, I, 40, 145.
75. Macrobius, *Satirae*, II, 4, 28.
76. Galen, *Of the Use of the Parts of the Human Body*, VIII, 187.
77. Cicero, *De oratore*, III, 98.
78. Martial, *Liber Spectaculorum*, IV, 5, 6.
79. *Ibid.*, XIV, 166.
80. Polybius, *Historiae*, XXX, 14.
81. Lucian, *Imagines*, 13 ff.
82. Abert, *Römische Musik*, p. 186.
83. Seneca, *Controversiae*, I, proem.
84. *Ibid.*, *De brevitate vitae*, 12, 4.
85. Horace, *Saturae*, 9, 25.
86. Manilius, IV, 525 ff.
87. Ovid, *Ars amatoria*, I, 595.
88. Martial, II, 7, 5 ff.
89. Petronius, *Cena Trimalchionis*, 64, 2 ff.
90. *Laus Pisonis*, 166–177.
91. Firmicus Maternus, *Matheseos*, III, 6, 2.
92. Ammianus Marcellinus, XIV, 6, 18.
93. Apollinaris Sidonius, *Carmina*, 23, 300–306.
94. See the author's *Music in Ancient Israel* (New York, 1969), chapter *"Christian Psalm Singing in Talmudic Times."*
95. Suetonius, *Julius Caesar*, 84.
96. *Ibid.*
97. *Ibid.*, *Tiberius*, 7.
98. *Ibid.*
99. *Ibid.*, 34.
100. *Ibid.*, *Caligula*, 54.
101. *Ibid.*
102. *Ibid.*, *Titus*, 3.
103. *Ibid.*, 10.
104. *Ibid.*, 10n.
105. *Ibid.*, *Domitian*, 8.
106. *Ibid.*, 10
107. Martial, VIII, 70; IX, 26.
108. Historiae Augustae, *Marcus*, XXIII, 4.
109. Herodianus, III, 139.
110. Dio Cassius, 77, 13, 7.
111. *Durant*, 3:635.
112. Herodianus, V, 3, 8.
113. *Ibid.*, V, 3, 9.
114. Lampridius, *Historiae Augustae. Antoninus Heliogabalus*, 32, 8.
115. Dio Cassius, LXXX, 13.
116. Lampridius, *Historiae Augustae. Alexander Severus*, 17.
117. *Ibid.*, 33.
118. Suetonius, *Nero*, 34.
119. *Ibid.*, 33.
120. Tacitus, *Annales* XIV, 10.
121. *Ibid.*, XV, 62.
122. *Ibid.*, XIII, 3.
123. Suetonius, *Nero*, 21.
124. *Ibid.*, 41.
125. *Ibid.*, 20.
126. *Ibid.*
127. *Ibid.*, 40, 42.
128. *Ibid.*, 42.

129. *Ibid.*, 20.
130. *Ibid.*, 52.
131. *Ibid.*, 22.
132. *Ibid.*, 24.
133. *Ibid.*, 41.
134. Dio Cassius, LVIII, 23.
135. Suetonius, *Nero*, 44.
136. Tacitus, XV, 38; Suetonius, *Nero*, 38; Dio Cassius, LXXII, 16; and others.
137. Suetonius, *Nero*, 54.
138. Horace, *Saturae*, 1, 10, 90 ff.
139. Suetonius, *Nero*, 20.
140. Esther Violet Hansen, *Attalids of Pergamon* (Ithaca, N. Y., 1947), p. 354.
141. W. L. Westermann, "The Castanet Dancers of Arsinoe," in *Journal of Egyptian Archaeology*, 10:143–44.
142. *Cf.* Varro, *tibia dextra* and *tibia sinistra*. In *De re rustica*, I, 2, 15–16.
143. K. Britten, *Roman Women* (Philadelphia, 1907), p. 95.
144. Cicero, *Tusculanae disputationes*, V, 23.
145. Pollux, *Onomasticon*, IV, 85.
146. Macrobius, *Saturae*, III, 14, 7.
147. Cicero, *De oratore*, III, 86 ff.
148. Macrobius, *Saturae*, II, 14, 10.
149. Cornelius Nepos, *Epaminondas*, 1, 2.
150. Sallustius, *Catilina*, 25.
151. *Friedländer*, 1:270.
152. Seneca, *Epistulae*, 58, 2.
153. Horace, *Carmina*, IV, 9, 4.
154. Pliny, *Epistulae*, VII, 4, 9; IV, 19, 4.
155. Horace, *Saturae*, I, 10, 13.
156. Ovid, *Ars amatoria*, III, 345.
157 Aulus Gellius, XIX, 9, 3–5.
158. Aelius Donatus, *Vita Vergilii*, 6.
159. Ovid, *Tristia*, II, 519; V, 7, 25.
160. Horace, *Carmina*, I, 16, 2.
161. Catullus, *Carmina*, 36, 5.
162. Apollinaris Sidonius, *Epistulae*, IX, 14.
163. Abert, in Friedländer, *Darstellungen* . . . , 2:165.
164. *Athen*, IV, 183 c.
165. Ovid, *Ars amatoria*, III, 318; Tacitus, *Annales*, XIV, 66.
166. Tacitus, *Annales*, XIV, 66.
167. Martial, III, 63, 5.
168. Aulus Gellius, XIX, 9, 3 ff.
169. Martial, III, 63, 5.
170. Pliny, *Epistulae*, I, 15, 2.
171. Martial, V, 78, 30.
172. Cicero, *Pro Roscio Amerino*, 134.
173. *Ibid.*, *Pro Annio Milone*, 55.
174. *Ibid.*, *Pro Caelio*, 35; Seneca, *Epistulae*, 53, 4.
175. Petronius, *Cena Trimalchionis*, 31, 4 ff.
176. *Ibid.*, 26.
177. Cicero, *De legibus*, 2, 23, 59.
178. Ovid, *Fasti* 5, 441 ff.
179. Ammianus Marcellinus, XIV, 6, 18.
180. Plutarch, *Moralia, an seni resp. ger. sit*, 5; Martial, IV, 5, 8; III, 3, 8.
181. Horace, *Ars poetica*, 202.
182. Varro, *Res rustica* 2, 4, 30; 3, 13, 1.
183. Virgil, *Aeneis*, 8, 526.
184. *Athen*, V, 201 f.
185. St. Augustine, *Epistola* 60.
186. Cicero, *In Verrem*, II, 3, 105; V, 31, 92; II, 5–64.
187. *Symphonia* was the name given in the Graeco-Roman period to an entertainment company that hired out musicians and dancers for festivals in the smaller neighboring

cities or villages. See W. L. Westerman, "The Castanet Dancers of Arsinoe," in *Journal of Egyptian Archaeology* 10 (1924):137–38.

188. Abert, "Die Musik der Griechen," in *Gesammelte Schriften* (1929), p. 28.

189. Horace, *Carmina*, IV, 1, 22.

190. *Athen*, VII, 362 a.

191. Maximus Tyrus, *Dissertationes*, 26, 4.

192. St. Jerome, *Ad Dardanum de diversis musicorum instrumentis epistola*. In *Patrologia Latina*, XXX.

193. Seneca, *Epistolae*, 84, 10.

194. *Vita Carini*, XIX.

195. Quintilianus, 9, 4, 51.

196. Kathleen Schlesinger, "Researches into the Origin of the Organs of the Ancients," in *SIMG* (Leipzig, 1901); Abdy Williams, *The Story of the Organ* (London, 1906); George Henry Farmer, *The Organs of the Ancients* (London, 1931).

197. Mishnah, *'Arakin*, II:6; *Tamid*, III:8; Tal. Bab., *'Arakin* 10 b, 11 a; Tal. Yer., *Sukkah*, V:3; V:6.

198. Suetonius, *Nero*, 41.

199. *Athen*, IV, 174 a.

200. Cicero, *Pro Murena*, 6, 13.

201. *Ibid., In Catilinam* II, 23.

202. Gaston Boissier, *La réligion romaine* (Paris, 1874), 2:215.

203. Cornelius Nepos, *Vitae. Epaminondas*, 15, 1.

204. Dio Chrysostomos, XXXII, 69.

205. Macrobius, *Saturae*, 3, 14, 15.

206. Horace, *Saturae*, 1, 3, 129.

207. Suetonius, *Nero*, 30, 2.

208. Suidas, *Historia Anton. Pius*, 7, 7.

209. Strabo, 14, 1, 31; *Friedländer*, 1:291.

210. *Friedländer*, 1:63.

211. Martial, IV, 5, 8.

212. Tacitus, XI, 25.

213. Suetonius, *Nero*, 54.

214. Abert, in *Friedländer, Darstellungen* . . . , p. 182.

215. Cicero, *Ad familiares*, VIII, 24.

216. Horace, *Saturae*, 1, 3, 1–19; 2, 1–4.

217. *Corpus Inscriptionum*, 1 and 2, no. 2519.

218. *Lex* XII, table 10.

219. Abraham Berliner, *Geschichte der Juden in Rom*, (Frankfurt, 1893), 1:98.

220. *Durant*, 3:335.

221. *Ibid.*

222. *Corpus Inscriptionum* . . . , 9:171 a.

223. Suetonius, *Domitian*, 4, 4.

224. *Corpus Inscriptionum* . . . , 6, no. 2193.

225. Plutarch, *Numa*, 17, 3.

226. Livy, 1, 20, 4.

227. *Ibid.*, 9, 30, 5.

228. Varro, *De lingua latina*, 6, 3, 17.

229. Ovid, *Fasti*, 6, 691 ff.

230. *Corpus Inscriptionum* . . . , no. 33968.

231. William Sanger, *History of Prostitution* (New York, 1939), p. 46.

232. Agobardus, *De ritu canendi Psalmos in Ecclesia*.

233. Livy, VII, 2.

234. *Ibid.*

235. Cicero, *De legibus*, II, 34.

236. *Koller*, p. 92.

237. Adelphoe Andria, Eunuchus, *Heautontomirenus, Hecyra, Phormio*, etc.

238. Achilleis, *Silvae, Thebeis*.

239. Horace, *Ars poetica*.

240. R. Taylor, *The Opportunities for Dramatic Performances in the Time of Plautus and Terence*, in *Transactions and Proceedings of the Americal Philological Association* 68 (Lancaster, 1937):285 ff., 300.

241. Pliny, XXXVI, 24.
242. Cicero, *De re publica*, IV, 10.
243. *Papyrus Oxyrhinchos*, II, 413.
244. Friedländer, *Sittengeschichte Roms* (Vienna, 1934), 2:144 ff.
245. *SachsDance*, p. 247.
246. *Ibid.*
247. Ammianus Marcellinus, XIV, 6.
248. Strabo, *Geōgraphikōn*, XVI, 2, 29.
249. Abert, *Ethos*, p. 29.
250. Quintilianus, *De musica*, I, 12, 14.
251. Cicero, *De oratore*, 3, 15, 58.
252. Sextus Empiricus.
253. Quintilianus, *De musica*.
254. Cicero, *De re publica*, 6, 5, 18.
255. *Ibid.*
256. Abert, *Ethos*, p. 38.

Epilogue

While this study has dealt primarily with the function of music in society and religion by examining the various theories connected with the origin of music, it has been possible to determine the approximate stage of human existence at which music assumed importance in daily life. At first, the interrelationship of the social and religious aspects of human behavior appeared quite vague, because the musical usage that began in prehistoric times gained a foothold only during the long and arduous development of mankind. Since the earliest facets of this development continue to remain obscure, historians of civilization can only surmise what music's beginnings were like.

Civilizations do not crop up suddenly. They are the result of a long and continuous evolution, beginning with the most primitive and moving through more advanced stages. To an even greater extent this is valid for music, particularly for the musical instruments of ancient times. Between the primitive sound-producing artifacts of the proto-historic epoch and the more sophisticated instruments of such recorded civilizations as the Sumerians and Egyptians, there is a hiatus that can be explained only by the assumption that during this period there must have existed a number of now-extinct civilizations[1].

The various stages of human civilizations (paleolithic, neolithic, bronze age, etc.) were undoubtedly established as man moved from nomad-hunter through dweller-farmer, constantly in search of a better and more secure way of life. We may assume that social life in primitive civilizations began when men first gathered together in caves or other shelters for protection against wild animals and severe climatic conditions. Whether at such an early level of civilization we can speak of a conscious social behavior, with particular regard to music, is at best hypothetical.

As to the earliest manifestations of religion, scientists are unanimous in the opinion that religion originated when men began to fear the very gods they created. A fear of the hidden forces of nature and of the elements, which men did not understand but attributed to higher beings, led to the worship of these forces, placating them with sacrifices, offerings, prayers, and incantations. In the most primitive religions, such ceremonies undoubtedly included music. It is even possible to associate the function of the *shaman*, the archaic prototype of the priest, with "music." Here, music meant the incantation of the magic formula. The term *incantation* already carries the germinal connotation of the musical rendering of such primitive ceremonies.

Contemporary science assumes that human life, as we understand it, originated about one million years ago, at a time when the animal instincts of the dwellers of our globe gradually evolved into instincts of reasoning. This is the time when individuals began to act consciously. Discoveries in caves, where evidence of human habitations were found, date back about 50,000 years, making it difficult to assume that at such an early age music existed in some form. CHAILLEY estimates the first musical manifestations of mankind (in the form of dance) to have occurred 40,000 years ago. This assumption, of course, lacks proof.[2]

It may well be that the earliest remnants of human life, especially its artifacts, are those which were found near Peking. Their age, estimated to be about one million years old, still does not allow us to come to any well-defined conclusions concerning the time when music first made its appearance. With the discovery of the "Neanderthal man," placed at about 40,000 years ago, we are nearer to CHAILLEY's estimation; however, as pointed out above, his figure is to be considered arbitrary and does not furnish us with any further clues for dating correctly the "earliest appearance" of music in human existence.

We do not know exactly when man passed from the hunting stage—that is from the period of food gathering—to agriculture. Perhaps this took place a half a million years ago, during the neolithic age. Most probably this is the period in which we may place the first forms of social behavior, that is, when people began living together in a kind of social environment.

Historiography assumes that the Chinese are the most ancient of the civilized peoples.[3] In 1907, pottery and other remains of an ancient culture were excavated at Anau, in southern Turkestan, which were ascribed to the period between 8,000 and 10,000 years B.C.E.[4] These discoveries were attributed to a time in this period when the culture of Turkestan was already at its height.

"The arts, if not the race, reached eastward to China and Mandchuria," says DURANT.[5] I would like here to offer a contrary opinion, that we see in these discoveries in Turkestan the radiation of Chinese culture *toward the West*. One look at a map of the Far East will suffice to show the bridges that might have connected the nations of high Antiquity, placing them directly or indirectly under the influence of the Chinese culture. The Chinese-Mongolian empire—including the intermediate areas of Tibet and Afghanistan—bordered on Media-Persia to the west, and India to the south. Chinese culture exerted its influence, commercially and intellectually, on the neighboring countries, and this may also have been the case with music.

It would be a too far-fetched assumption to attribute the foundation of all Oriental musical cultures solely to the Chinese. However, it is undeniable that the elements of music throughout the Orient appear to exhibit common traits; this may support the supposition that the conception of music throughout this area had its source in a mighty and enduring civilization such as the Chinese.

This influence was even more widespread, especially when we consider the many remarkable similarities between the music of the Chinese and that of the Babylonians (who, as we know, took over their music from the Sumerians). A most conspicuous feature, a concept to be found in both cultures, is that of the interrelationship between the seasons and the musical intervals.

In view of the manifestly greater age of the Chinese civilization, it can be assumed that the Chinese were responsible for the very first instruments that *consciously* served music as an art. Furthermore, according to Chinese tradition, music was considered not only an art but a "science." This notion is remarkable, in that music was conceived not only as sound, but was also believed to possess transcendental power.[6] Moreover, this notion is demonstrated in a legend which, according to tradition, originated in the third millennium B.C.E., but—judging from its mystical and esoteric character—is probably much older.

This legend has two parts: one, describing how the Chinese scale was "discovered," the other, disclosing how Chinese music was regulated by a uniform (and unalterable) pitch-norm, undoubtedly the earliest precursor of the modern "Kammerton" (or fixed pitch).

According to this legend, HUANG-TI, the "Yellow Emperor," was very eager to develop the arts and sciences throughout his empire. He focused his attention primarily on musical culture, and sought to establish it as an exact science. For this purpose, he sent his Master of Music, LING-LUN, to the legendary country of So-Young, a sort of Promised Land situated at the head waters of the river Huan-Ho. (So-Young was discovered thousands of years earlier by King Mou, who found such happiness there that he never returned to his native land).

High on a mountain, LING-LUN discovered a dense forest of bamboo reeds, all nearly the same height. He cut one of the stems between two knots and blew into it. The tone thus produced was similar to the sound of his own voice when he spoke softly, and also that of the river Huang-Ho. Thus he was assured that this must be the "Ur-tone," the absolute pitch, *huang-chung* (the "yellow bell"), the basic sound of all music.

Nearby he saw two birds, one male and one female, perched upon a bamboo tree. These were the miraculous *Foung-Hoang* (phoenix) birds, whose appearance reveals good tidings. The male *Foung*, who imitated the sound produced by the bamboo, sang six "perfect" sounds, while the female *Hoang* continued with six other, "accidental" sounds, all together comprising the twelve semi-tones of the octave (octave according to Western musical theory). Therefore, LING-LUN cut eleven more bamboo tubes of different sizes, to match the sounds of the miraculous birds.

Upon his return, LING-LUN presented the Emperor this series of tones, which were henceforth elevated to *lüs*, meaning "laws," thereby constituting the basis of Chinese music as well as the empire's musical science.[7]

But how did LING-LUN "scientifically" establish the dimensions of the twelve bamboo tubes? He resorted to the expedient of filling the tubes with grains of a millet, called *chou*, which are black, very hard, and not prone to attack by insects. The number of the grains in the tube of the basic pitch, *huang*, was exactly one hundred, which henceforth became the norm for establishing the length and width of the standard pipe. The dimensions of the other pipes were related proportionately to that of the basic tube.

With regard to the invention of the various musical instruments, the Chinese offer several traditional accounts. One of them asserts that most of their popular instruments originated during the period when China was ruled by a heavenly spirit called KI. This epoch antedates China's historical existence by several millennia. Another account assigns the invention of stringed instruments to the great Fo-HI, called the "Son of Heaven," who supposedly was the founder of the empire and who lived about 3000 B.C.E. Again, this is ostensibly too late a period for the establishment of the Chinese empire which, according to historical records, is many thousands of years older.

Another account attributes the creation of the most important musical instruments, as well as the systematic arrangement of the tones, to NUI-VA, a supernatural female and a virgin mother, who supposedly lived at the time of Fo-HI.

Here, too, the Chinese reckoning of such "miracles" does not agree chronologically with historical evidence, because during the supposed epoch of Fo-Hi, the highly developed Sumerian and Egyptian civilizations were already flourishing in the east.

According to reliable sources, the Chinese had more than two hundred types of instruments.[8] These, however, might have been mere variants of some basic types of stringed, wind, and percussion instruments. Which of these can be traced back to archaic times remains a matter of conjecture.

Nonetheless, this wealth of instruments attests to a continuous musical tradition, spread over several millennia, and suggests that Chinese music exerted an important influence throughout Asia.

Additional historical light is thrown on Chinese musical science by the compilation of the Jou-Lü, the "Ceremonial of the State of Jou," a system relating musical sounds to the order of Nature, which dates to the third century B.C.E. This system was supposed to "regulate the Harmony of the Universe, in general, and of the State, in particular," so that the first duty of a new ruler became that of insuring the maintenance of tradition in the musical and ritualistic practice of the State.[9]

With the passage of time, this concept brought about the creation of a Board of Rites, whose structure was identical with the Board of Music. This institution, unique at so early a period in human history, was comprised of an indefinite number of officers, whose duties were directed "to the study of the principles of Harmony and Melody, the Composition of musical pieces, and their adaptation for the various occasions on which they were required."[10]

It is remarkable how closely this mutual relationship between ritual and music resembles that of the Greek musical system, which originated thousands of years later.

The parallel with the music of the Hellenes is even more startling if we observe the attitude of the Sage and ethical teacher KUNG-FU-TSE, known popularly as CONFUCIUS, toward music as the essential element of human betterment. Indeed, CONFUCIUS lived relatively close to the Christian era (ca. 551–ca. 479 B.C.E.), but his teachings represent a derivative and summary of an earlier moral code that dominated Chinese thought for many centuries. This may have led to the development of a religion based on his ethical teachings. This religion—combined with ancestor worship and the belief in the two guiding principles of nature, called *ying* (evil, darkness, cold, negative forces, passivity) and *yang* (good, positives of light, heat, activity)—developed into the movement called Confucianism and became one of the great ethical pillars of Chinese religious thought (the others being Taoism and Buddhism). Most remarkable among CONFUCIUS's teachings is the negative Golden Rule, "do not do unto others that you would not like done to yourself," a moral precept stated about five centuries before the time of Christ.

CONFUCIUS's philosophy likewise based the arts and music upon moral and ethical principles. "If a man is without moral character, what good can the use of the fine arts do him? If a man is without moral character, what good can the use of music do him?" Describing a musical piece he had heard, he mused: "It has all the excellence of the physical beauty of harmony, and it has also all the excellence of moral greatness."[11]

These norms, however, applied solely to ritual music. China's popular music, on the other hand, was opposed to the established aesthetic principles, since there was no recognized precedent for it; thus, the doctrine of ethos was simply ignored.[12] Popular music was generally considered "vulgar." CONFUCIUS felt that a vulgar-minded man's performance "is loud and fast, . . . his heart is not harmonically balanced; mildness and graceful movements are foreign to him." Thus, the "noisy" music of the tyrants of *Hia* and *Yin* was considered vulgar and was so described by LÜ -PU-WE, the poet of *Spring and Fall:* "They deemed the loud sounds of big drums, bells, stones, pipes and flutes beautiful. . . . They aimed at new and strange timbres, at never heard of tones, . . . they tried to outdo one another and overstepped the limits."[13]

In contrast to such excesses of musical noise, CONFUCIUS held that "the noble-minded man's music is mild and delicate, keeps a uniform mood, enlivens and moves." Music should be serene; accordingly, the graphic symbol for *yüo,* "music," and *lo,* "serenity," was the same.[14]

Here again we witness analogous ethical conceptions between the music of China and that of the ancient Greeks. CONFUCIUS himself, after listening to several old hymns, became so enraptured that he could not eat for three months. The legendary character of the ethos of Chinese music becomes even more pronounced in the account that KOUEI, a kind of ORPHEUS of Chinese lore, constructed from slabs of sonorous stones an instrument called *ch'ing,* the sound of which could draw wild animals around him and make them subservient to his will.[15] Such sonorous stone-slabs were excavated on the famous Shang sites and in An-Yang, in the plains of northeast China. This tends to suggest that the musical lore of the Chinese was not merely an outgrowth of fantasy but was based upon some valid facts.

Another aspect of the musical conception of ancient China was the belief that the changes of the seasons corresponded to certain musical facts and tones. Thus, the four seasons were separated from one another not only by time, but also by precise musical intervals, *e.g.,* a fifth from autumn to spring, a fourth back to winter, and so on, as shown in the following sequence:

Autumn	= F
Spring	= C
Winter	= G
Summer	= D

These relationships were taken over by the Babylonians, though somewhat modified:

Summer	= C'
Winter	= G
Autumn	= F
Spring	= C

As SACHS points out, "there is agreement except for the position of summer. Why? Here, I think, is the reason: The Chinese arrangement follows a cycle of fifths and fourths (F, C, G, D, or D, G, C, F), while the Babylonian, the division of strings into ground tone (1:1), octave (1:2), fifth (2:3), and fourth (3:4)." SACHS attributed this principle of division in Babylonia to the fact that this country knew of the acoustical laws governing the divisions of the strings, and thereby Babylonia became the earliest home of the fretted lute.[16] "This system was extended and worked out in a manner analogous to that of similar systems in India, Islam, ancient Greece, and even to the Christian Middle Ages."[17]

How did these cosmological theories migrate from China to India and Babylonia? I have already referred to those geographical bridges that made this possible—the routes for commercial and intellectual exchange between China and the countries located farther west and south. Thus, the Babylonians (through the intermediary of their predecessors, the Sumerians) may have been acquainted with the Chinese cosmological notions, symbolizing the relationship of the seasons with musical intervals, and adapted them to their own conception.

A further indication concerning the Chinese attitude toward music becomes apparent through the maxim of Confucius: "If you want to know whether a country is well governed and has good mores, listen to its music." The numerous historical records about Chinese emperors prove how fond they were of music and how they tried to enact special legislation to improve the musical culture of their empire.

For several centuries, the extinction of a dynasty was invariably attributed to its failure to secure the true *huang-chung*. Therefore, when a new ruler ascended the throne, "it was a matter of prime concern to regain the exact measurements of the bamboo pipe of absolute pitch."[18]

There are still other significant concepts that the Chinese maintained with regard to music, for example: "Music hath the power of making heaven descend upon earth,"[19] a thought that approximates the belief that the Israelites entertained about the divine origin of music. Moreover, the idea that "human song is generally attributed to be the basis or origin of instrumental music,"[20] is also Chinese.

Similarly, the attitude of Egypt toward the relationship between the State and its music can be traced back to China, proving that the Chinese notions concerning music radiated far beyond their immediate boundaries, permeating the entire area of the Oriental world.

While it would be misleading to pretend that Chinese music establishes the basis for all Oriental music, it may be said that the age of Chinese culture far surpasses all the historically recorded civilizations, thus giving support to such an assumption.

Passing from the Far East to the Near East, we find three civilizations,—Mesopotamia, Egypt, and Cretic-Mycaene—which, although seemingly independent of one another, stand out as having created their music spontaneously, without the help of obvious extraneous influences. The Cretic-Mycaenic culture had particular impact upon the entire Mediterranean basin. The music of all the nations living in this area has in common an evolution that may be traced to their religious beliefs about prehistoric times. This evolution manifested itself in several more or less analogous practices, centering on the belief that the supernatural powers (gods, demons, spirits) had to be appeased by "music," whatever the word may have meant during this archaic stage of human existence.

Along with religious motivation, there are unmistakable signs of Chinese influence to be found throughout most Oriental musical cultures. Even the Cretic-Mycaenic civilization, which was separated from China by half of a huge continent, appears to have developed independently, but it too has been proven to be of Asiatic origin. At least this fact indicates the possibility of its having absorbed some Chinese traits.

Therefore it is not surprising that Media-Persia, geographically close to China, sums up its religious and social conduct in the succinct phrase "good thoughts, good deeds."[21] This approximates the Chinese concept that the sacred music constitutes the very foundation of the state and the social order.[22]

Even the Hindu tradition maintained that "music was in the beginning an essentially sacred art, the discovery of which was attributed to SARASVATI, goddess of eloquence and the arts."[23] Here, again, the link with the Chinese attitude toward music is unmistakable. Both China and India conceived the idea that the essence of music lay not solely in the sound but also in the possession of transcendent power.[24]

Similarly, the Hebrews attributed supernatural power to music, endowing their tonal art with ethical qualities that were previously unknown in the music of the Fertile Crescent. They stressed "inspiration," and the divine influence upon music practice, which were held in common by poets, singers, and musicians alike. True, the Hebrews might have adopted, or taken over, most of the elements of their music directly from the Egyptians, their "teachers" in musical art. But with regard to the spiritual qualities of their music, the pupils then by far surpassed their masters. The musical practice of the Egyptians was mainly that of a "utilitarian" art, despite its strong connection with religion. While the music of the Hebrews followed the same principle at the beginning, it soon succeeded in freeing itself from utilitarian shackles and developed, in later times, into an autonomous art, the first such phenomenon in the history of mankind. Its guiding force was emotion, abandoning the Chinese belief in the power to sustain or, if improperly used, to destroy universal harmony.[25] Nonetheless, the Chinese as well as the Hebrews maintained the belief in the magic power of sounds.

In the "pyramid of civilization," various elements are superimposed upon one another rather than progressively developed.[26] Thus we witness that civilizations do change. But do they die? Not quite. "Nations die, but resilient man picks up his tools and his arts and moves on, taking his memories with him. Civilization migrates with him, and builds another home somewhere else. An aging culture hands its patrimony down to its heirs across the years and the seas."[27]

This explains how we find, suddenly, without any apparent connecting links, such highly developed and sophisticated instruments as the gold and mosaic kithara of the Sumerians (Illus. 5), found in the Great Death Pit of ʾUr; the magnificent bow harps of the Egyptians (Illus. 21); the *kinnorot* and *nebalim* of King Solomon, "made of precious wood," such as were not seen before in Israel; and the many other highly developed Babylonian and Assyrian tools of music.

All this presupposes the existence of many previous civilizations, which had had to build their own way of life and their own experiences and skills upon the ruins of former ones. Only in this way can we explain how musical instruments grew from their primitive and crude forms into highly sophisticated and artistically meaningful implements in a constantly changing and evolving musical culture.

The prehistoric man who populated the Nile valley already employed various kinds of musical instruments, as is evidenced in excavations found at Badari and Negadah in Upper-Egypt, and in Merinde and El-Omari in Lower-Egypt. These instruments must be regarded basically as noise-making implements for primitive ritual ceremonies, but they may also be designated as "musical instruments" in the proper sense. With the Negadah-period (ca. 3300 B.C.E.) the recorded history of Egypt begins, and during the first Dynasty of kings, real musical instruments were discovered.[28]

In Greek music, an entirely new element entered musical history, the science of music, properly speaking, which was based upon physical discoveries, experimentation, and reflection; up to this time these procedures were unknown. Thus the interrelation of Chinese and Greek musical thought becomes even more evident. The establishment of the basic pitch-tone in China, together with the consciously constructed twelve tones of the "octave," may be regarded as a parallel to the elaborate musical science of the Hellenes. The teaching of the "doctrine of ethos" in music is still another achievement of the Greek musical culture.

In contrast to the highly intellectual and educational value of Greek music, the Romans merely transformed their tonal art into a utilitarian scheme which declined to the same degree as Roman life. Music served mainly pleasure and sybaritism, constituting entertainment for the individual and the masses. By this change of approach, the high ethos of Greek music, the most important spiritual creation of the Hellenes toward their musical art, was lost, and degenerated to a mere titillation of the senses. Thus, the music of the Romans was deprived of all the lofty qualities with which its predecessors, the Greeks, originally sought to infuse it. There appears to be little relationship between Chinese and Roman musical thought.

With the fall of the Roman empire, the once vigorous tonal art of Antiquity not only lost its meaning, but was menaced by total extinction. Christianity, and particularly Byzantium, saved music from such a fate. The transition to the musical art of the Middle Ages was carried out not by the peoples, nor by the temporal governing powers, but by the new religion, which sought a conscious return to the ethical principles involved in the performance of divine service.

Whether this evolution may still be traced back to ancient China is a question that cannot be answered unequivocally. One fact, however, clearly emerges from this succinct survey of the tonal art of Antiquity: when Europe was still a cultural wasteland, when her intellectual potentialities were as yet unborn, the Orient created through its own initiative a musical culture that not only influenced the nations living in it, but also radiated its own intrinsic energy to the music of the whole civilized world of Antiquity.

Only when we place the role that China played in this evolution in its proper perspective can we appreciate the almost miraculous burgeoning of the intense Asiatic musical culture that exerted such a strong influence upon the music of the civilized nations, past and present.

Whether or not we accept the theory that the Chinese musical culture was predominant in its influence upon all, or most, of the coeval or succeeding civilizations, we cannot escape the empirical truth that serves as the guiding principle of this study:

EX ORIENTE MUSICA.

NOTES

1. Extinct either from geological causes, or because of feuds between humans, for necessities of food-gathering for survival, which, in these primitive and savage times might have resulted in the total annihilation of a people, or a tribe, and its supposed civilization.
2. See Prologue.
3. Demetrius Charles Bulger, *A Short History of China* (London, 1900), p. 1.
4. *CAH*, 1 (New York, 1924):108.

5. *Durant*, 1:108.
6. *New Oxford History of Music* (1957), 1:57.
7. Some other translations of *Lü:* rule, statute; musically: tube, pitch-pipe, or standard pitch. The fundamental tone upon which the whole musical system of the Chinese was based was called *huang-chung*, the "Yellow Bell," or "Imperial Bell," since yellow was the symbolic color of the emperor, his robes, and insignia (See Fritz A. Kuttner, "Musicological Interpretation of the Twelve Lüs in China's Traditional Tone System," in *Ethnomusicology* 9 (Jan. 1965).
8. *Grove's Dictionary of Music*, 2:232.
9. *New Oxford History of Music* (1957), 1:88.
10. C. Frank Brinkley, *China, its Arts and Literature* (Boston, 1902), 10:57.
11. *Ibid.*, 11:8
12. R. H. van Gulik, *The Lore of the Chinese Lute* (Tokyo, 1940), p. 39.
13. *SachsRise*, p. 106.
14. *Ibid.*
15. Carl Engel, *Musical Myths and Facts* (London, 1866), 1:75–76.
16. *SachsRise*, p. 77.
17. *New Oxford History of Music* (1957), 1:87.
18. Willi Apel, in *Harvard Dictionary of Music* (Cambridge, Mass., 1953), p. 136.
19. Charles Darwin, *The Descent of Man* (New York, 1871), p. 879.
20. *Ibid.*, p. 878.
21. James Breasted, *The Conquest of Civilization* (New York and London, 1938), p. 218.
22. Apel, p. 136.
23. Lavignac, *Encyclopédie*, 1:169.
24. *New Oxford History of Music*, 1:86.
25. *Ibid.*, 1:88.
26. *Ibid.*, 1:28.
27. Will Durant, *The Lessons of History* (New York, 1968), p. 94.
28. Hans Hickmann, *Musikgeschichte in Bildern*, vol. 2, *Ägypten* (Leipzig, 1961), p. 18.

Bibliography

Abert, Hermann. "Der gegenwärtige Stand der Forschung über antike Musik." In *Gesammelte Schriften und Vorträge,* edited by Friedrich Blume. Halle, 1929.

——. *Die Lehre vom Ethos in der griechischen Musik.* Leipzig, 1899.

——. *Der neue griechische Papyrus mit Musiknoten.* In *Gesammelte Schriften und Vorträge.* Edited by Friedrich Blume. Halle, 1929.

——. "Ein neuer musikalischer Papyrusfund." In *Zeitschrift der Internationalen Musikgesellschaft,* 1906. 8. Jahrg., Heft 3.

Adler, Guido. *Handbuch der Musikgeschichte.* 2 vols. Berlin, 1929.

Agobardus. *De ritu canendi psalmos in Ecclesia.* Incomplete.

Alexander, J. A. *The Psalms translated and explained.* 2 vols. New York, 1855.

Ambros, August Wilhelm. *Geschichte der Musik.* 2 vols. Breslau, 1862–1882.

Ammianus, Marcellinus. *Rerum gestarum Libri XXXI* (only 18 vols. preserved).

Apuleius, Lucius. *Metamorphoses (The Golden Ass).* New York, 1927.

Aristeides Quintilianus. *De Musica.* Edited by Marcus Meibohm. Amsterdam, 1652.

Aristophanes. "Thesmophoriazusae." In *Eleven Comedies.* 2 vols. New York, 1943.

Aristotle. *Politikē,* VIII.

Athenaios. *Deiphnosophistēs (Sophists at Dinner).*

Augustinus, Friedrich. *Beiträge zur semitischen Religionsgeschichte.* Berlin, 1888.

——. *Die Psalmen Übersetzt und erklärt.* (Göttingen, 1897).

Barnett, Lionel D. *Antiquities of India.* New York, 1914.

Baron, Salo Wittmayer. *The Jewish Community.* 3 vols. Philadelphia, 1942.

——. *A Social and Religious History of the Jews.* 3 vols. New York, 1937. Enlarged ed. 8 vols. Philadelphia, 1957.

Barry, Phillips. "On Luke 15:25, Symphonia, Bagpipe." In *JBL* 1904.

Beda Venerabilis. "Interpretatio Psalterii artis cantilenae," in *PL* 92.

Behn, Friedrich. *Musikleben im Altertum und frühen Mittelalter.* Stuttgart, 1954.

Berliner, Arthur. *Geschichte der Juden in Rom.* Frankfurt, 1893.

Bertholet, Alfred. *A History of Hebrew Civilization.* London, 1926.

Bezold, Carl. *Ninive und Babylon.* Bielefeld and Leipzig, 1926.

Birt, Theodor. *Das Kulturleben der Griechen und Römer.* Leipzig, 1928.

Böckh, August. *Die Staatshaltung der Athener.* 2 vols. Berlin, 1886.

Boissier, Gaston. *La réligion romaine.* Paris, 1874.

Braun, O. "Ein Brief des Katholikos Timotheos I über biblische Studien des 9. Jahrhunderts." In *Oriens Christianus,* I, 1901.

Boulger, Demetrius Charles. *A Short History of China.* London, 1900.

Breasted, James Henry. *Ancient Times.* Boston, 1916.

————. The Conquest of Civilization. New ed. New York & London, 1938.

Brittain, A. *Roman Women.* Philadelphia, 1907.

Brondi, Maria Ritta. *Il Liuto e la Chitarrone.* Torino, 1926.

Bücher, Karl. *Arbeit und Rhythmus.* Leipzig, 1924.

Büchler, A. "The Zadokite Fragments." In *JQR,* 1913.

Budde, Karl. "Das hebräische Klagelied." In *Zeitschrift für alttestamentliche Wissenschaft.* 1882.

————. Geschichte der althebräischen Literatur. Leipzig, 1906.

Calmet, Augustin. *Dictionnaire historique, critique, chronologique et litteral de la Bible.* Geneva, 1780. Enlarged ed. Boston, 1832.

Cambridge Ancient History. 2 vols. New York, 1923–1939.

Cassel, David. *Die Pesachhaggada.* Berlin, 1895.

Cassiodorus. "Expositio in Psalterium, Ps. CIX." In *PL.* LXX.

————. "In Psalterium praefatio." In *PL.* LXX.

Chailley, Jacques. *40,000 Years of Music: Man in Search of Music.* Translated from the French by Rollo Myers. London, 1964.

Chantepie de la Saussaye, Pierre Daniel. *Lehrbuch der Religionsgeschichte.* 2 vols. Tübingen, 1925.

Cicero, Marcus Tullius. *Ad familiares.*

————. *Pro Caelio.*

————. *Catilina.*

————. *De Divinatione.*

————. *De legibus.*

————. *De officiis.*

————. *De oratore.*

————. *De finibus.*

————. *Pro Milone.*

————. *Pro Roscio.*

————. *In Verrem.*

Clement of Alexandria. "Paidagōgos, II, 4. Quomodo in Conviviis se recreare oportet." In *PGL* 8. Also in *PG* 7.

"Clitarchos, *Scholia in Platonis Minoem.*" In Siebenkees, J. PH, *Anecdota graeca e prestantissimis italicarum bibliothecarum codicibus descriptis,* 1798.

Cornelius Nepos. *Epaminondas.*

Cyclopedia of Biblical Literature. New York, 1883.

Daremberg, C. and Saglio, E. *Dictionnaire des Antiquités Grecques et Romaines.* 3 vols. Paris, 1875–1919.

Dennis, G. *Cities and Cemeteries in Etruria.* Everyman's Library.

Dio Cassius Cocceianus. *Romaika (The History of Rome).*

————. *De Regno* (addressed to Trajan).

Donatus Aelius. *Vita Virgilii*.

Darwin, Charles Robert. *The Descent of Man*. 2nd ed., New York, 1874.

Delitzch, Franz Julius. *Biblical Commentary on the Psalms*. 2 vols. Edinburgh, 1892.

Dimont, Max. *Jews, God and History*. New York, 1962.

Diodorus, Siculus. *Historia Bibliotheca*.

Duff, W. J. *Literary History of Rome*. London, 1909.

Durant, Will. *The History of Civilization*. Vol. 1, *Our Oriental Heritage*. New York, 1935.

————. *The History of Civilization*. Vol. 2. *The Life of Greece*. New York, 1939.

————. *The History of Civilization*. Vol. 3, *Caesar and Christ*. New York, 1944.

Ebeling, Erich. "Ein Hymnenkatalog aus Assur." In *JRAS*, 1923.

————. *Religiöse Keilinschrifttexte aus Assur*. Leipzig, 1918.

Engel, Carl. *Musical Myths and Facts*. 2 vols. London, 1864.

————. *The Music of the Most Ancient Nations*. London, 1864.

Erman, Adolf. *Aegypten und aegyptisches Leben im Altertum*. New bearb. von Hermann Ranke. Tübingen, 1923.

————. *Die Ägyptische Religion*. Berlin, 1905.

Euripides. "Cyclops." In *The Complete Greek Drama*. 2 vols. New York, 1938.

Eusebius Pamphilius of Caesarea. "Ekklēsiastikēs historias." In *PGL*, 20.

————. "Praeparatio Evangelica." In *PG*, 13, also in *PGL*, 21.

Ewald, Heinrich August. *The Antiquities of Israel*. Boston, 1876.

————. *Die Dichter des Alten Bundes*. Göttingen, 1866.

Farmer, Henry George. *The Organ of the Ancients. From Eastern Sources (Hebrew, Syriac and Arabic)*. London, 1931.

Finesinger, Sol Baruch. "The Shofar." In *HUCA* (1931–32). Vols 8–9.

Firmicus Maternus. *Matheseos Libri VIII*.

Fleischer, Oskar. *Neumenstudien*. 2 vols. Leipzig, 1895.

Fleischhauer, Günther. *Musikgeschichte in Bildern*. Vol. II, *Etrurien und Rom*. Leipzig, 1964.

Flood, Wm. H. Grattan. *The Story of the Bagpipe*. London, 1911.

Forkel, Johann Nicholaus. *Allgemeine Geschichte der Musik*. 2 vols. Leipzig, 1788–1801.

Forsdyke, John. *Greece before Homer: Ancient Chronology and Mythology*. London, 1956.

Frazer, Sir James. *Adonis, Attis, and Osiris*. London, 1907.

Friedländer, L. *Darstellungen aus der Sittengschichte Roms*. 2 vols. Leipzig, 1920.

Galen. *On the Use of the Parts of the Human Body*.

Gallé, A. F. *Daniel avec Commentaires de R. Saadia, Aben-Ezra, Rashi*. Paris, 1900.

Galpin, Francis William. *The Music of the Sumerians and Their Immediate Successors the Babylonians and Assyrians*. Cambridge, 1937.

Gaster, Moses. *Daily and Occasional Prayers*. London, 1901.

Gaster, Theodor Herzl. *The Dead Sea Scriptures in English Translation.* Garden City, N. Y., 1956.

———. "Psalm 29." In *JOR* 37 (1946–47).

Gellius Aulus. *Noctes Atticae* (only one book extant).

Gesenius, Wilhem. *Hebräisches und chaldäisches Handwörterbuch über das A.T.* Leipzig, 1915.

———. *A Hebrew and English Lexicon of the Old Testament, including the Biblical Chaldee.* Boston, 1906.

———. *Thesaurus philologicus criticus linguae Hebraicae et Chaldaeae Veteris Testamenti.* 3 vols. Vol. II edited by Aemilius Roediger. Leipzig, 1829–1858.

Geuaert, François Auguste. *Histoire et théorie de la musique dans l'Antiquité.* Ghent, 1881.

Ginzberg, Louis. "Genizah-Studies." In *JOR* 16 (1903–1904).

Goldziher, Ignaz. *Abhandlungen zur arabischen Philologie.* Leiden, 1896–1899.

Goodspeed, Edgar J. "The Shulammite," In *American Journal of Semitic Languages and Literature* 50 (1933–34).

Gordon, Cyrus Herzl. *Before the Bible: The Common Background of Greek and Hebrew Civilizations.* (New York and London, 1962).

Graetz, Heinrich Hirsch. "Eine Strafmassnahme gegen die Leviten." In *MGWJ* 35 (1886).

———. *History of the Jews.* English ed. 6 vols. Philadelphia, 1898.

Grenfelt, Bernard Pyne and Hunt, Arthur S. *The Hibeh Papyri.* Vol. 2. London, 1906.

Gressman, Hugo. *Musik und Musikinstrumente im Alten Testament.* Giessen, 1903.

Grimme, Hubert. *Psalmenprobleme.* Freiburg, 1902.

Grote, George. *History of Greece.* New York, 1846.

Grünhut Lazar. *Die Rundreise des R. Petachjah aus Regensburg.* Frankfurt, 1904.

Gur (Grasowsky) Jehudah. *Milon 'Ibri* (Hebrew Lexicon). 2 ed. Tel-Aviv, 1947.

Hansen, Esther Violet. *Attalids on Pergamon.* Ithaca, N. Y., 1947.

Harper, R. F., ed. *Assyrian and Babylonian Literature.* New York, 1904.

Hartmann, Henrike. *Die Musik der sumerischen Kultur.* Frankfurt, 1960.

Harkavy, Alexander, trans. *The Twenty-Four Books of the Old Testament.* 2 vols. New York, 1916.

Harris, C. W. *The Hebrew Heritage, a Study of Israel's Cultural and Spiritual Origins.* New York, 1935.

Hastings, James. *A Dictionary of the Bible.* 4 vols. New York, 1898–1904.

———. *Encyclopedia of Religion and Ethics.* 12 vols. New York, 1908–1921.

Heracleides Ponticus. See Athen. XVI, 614 c ff.

Herder, Johann Gottfried. *The Spirit of Hebrew Poetry.* 2 vols. Translated by James March. Burlingtom, 1833.

Herodotus. *Historia.* Translated by G. Rawlinson.

Hesiod. *Theogony.*

Hickmann, Hans. *Musicologie Pharaonique. Etudes sur l'évolution de l'art dans l'Egypte ancienne.* Kehl, 1956.

————. *Musikgeschichte in Bildern.* Vol. II. Ägypten. Leipzig, 1961.

Hieronymus, St. "Ad Dardanum de diversis generibus musicorum instrumentis Epistola XXVIII." In *PL.* 30.

————. "Breviarium in Psalmos, Ps. XXXII." In *PL.* 26.

————. "Commentarium in Epistolam ad Galatas, I, cap. 1." In *PL.* 26.

Hyppolitus. *Tractatus contra omnes haereses* (only two fragments are preserved).

The Holy Scriptures According to the Masoretic Text. A new translation. Philadelphia, 1971.

Homer. *Iliad.*

————. *Odyssey.*

Hommel, Fritz. *Geschichte Babyloniens und Assyriens.* Berlin, 1885–1888.

Horace (Quintus Horatius Flaccus). *Ars Poetica.*

————. *Carmina.*

————. *Satirae.*

Ibn Ezra, Abraham ben Meir. *Commentary to Isaiah.*

————. *Commentary to Psalm 8.*

Ibn Khallikan. *Biographical Dictionary.* (English ed.).

Idelsohn, Abraham Zevi. *Hebräisch-Orientalischer Melodienschatz* (Jerusalem, Berlin, Vienna), 10 vols. (Also English and Hebrew eds.)

————. *Jewish Music in its Historical Development.* New York, 1929.

Isidore of Sevilla. "Etymologiae." In *PL.* 82.

Jahn, Johann. *Biblical Archaeology.* New York, 1833.

Jahrbuch der Musikbibliothek Peters. Vol. 28. Leipzig, 1922.

Jakob, B. "Beiträge zu einer Einleitung in die Psalmen." In ZAW 16.

Jastrow, Marcus. *A Dictionary of the Targumim, the Talmud Babli and Yerushalmi and the Midrashic Literature.* New York, 1943.

Jastrow, Morris Jr., *Die Religion Babyloniens und Assyriens.* 2 vols. Giessen, 1905–1912.

Jeremias, Alfred. *Handbuch der altorientalischen Geisteskultur.* Leipzig, 1913.

————. *The Old Testament in the Light of the Ancient East.* 2 vols. English ed. London, 1911.

Jerome, St. See Hieronymus, St.

Jewish Encyclopedia. 12 vols. Edited by Isidore Singer. New York, 1901–1906.

Jewish Quarterly Review. New York.

John Chrysostom. "Eis tōn Psalmōn XLI." In *PGL* 55.

————. "Prooimia tōn Psalmōn." In *PGL* 60.

Joost, J. M. *Geschichte des Judentums und seiner Sekten.* Leipzig, 1857.

Josephus Flavius. *Antiquitatum Judaeorum Libri XX.* (*The Antiquities of the Jews*).

————. *Contra Apionem* (*Against Apion*).

————. *De bello Judaico Libri VII* (*The Wars of the Jews*).

Journal of Biblical Literature. Syracuse, N. Y.

Journal of Egyptian Archaeology. Vol. 10 (1924).

Journal of the Royal Asiatic Society. London.

Justin Martyr. *"Cohortatio ad Graecos."* In *PL.* 11.

Kees, Hermann. *Der Opfertanz des ägyptischen Königs.* Leipzig, 1912.

Keil, Karl Friedrich. *Kommentar zur Chronik.* 1870.

Keyserling, Hermann. *Das Reisetagebuch eines Philosophen.* Darmstadt, 1921.

Koller, Hermann. *Musik und Dichtung im Alten Griechenland.* Bern and Munich, 1963.

Komroff, Manuel. *The Contemporaries of Marco Polo.* New York, 1928.

Kramer, Samuel Noah. *From the Tablets of Sumer.* Indian Hills, Col., 1956.

Krauss, Samuel. *Synagogale Altertümer.* Berlin, Vienna, 1922.

————. *Talmudische Archäologie.* 3 vols. Leipzig, 1910–12.

Kuttner, Fritz A. "Musicological interpretation of the Twelve Lüs in China's Traditional Tone System." In *Ethnomusicology* 9 (1965).

Lach, Robert. *Die Musik der Natur- und der orientalischen Kulturvölker,* in *Adler's Handbuch der Musikgeschichte.* 2 vols. Berlin, 1929.

Lagarde, Paul Anton. *Übersicht über die im Aramäischen, Arabischen und Hebräischen übliche Bildung im der Nomina.* Göttingen, 1889.

Land, S. I. N. P. *Anecdota Syriaca.* 4 vols. Leiden, 1870.

Láng, Paul Henry. *Music in Western Civilization.* New York, 1941.

Langdon, Stephen Herbert. *Babylonian Liturgies.* Paris, 1913.

————. "Babylonian and Hebrew Musical Terms." In *JRAS* (1921), part 2.

————. *Sumerian Liturgical Texts.* Philadelphia, 1917.

Leitner, Franz. *Der gottesdienstliche Volksgesang im Jüdischen und Christlichen Altertum.* Freiburg, 1906.

Lewy, Julius. "The Feast of the 14th Day of Adar." In *HUCA* 14. 1939.

Lippman, Edward A. *Musical Thought in Ancient Greece.* New York and London, 1964.

Lombroso, Cesare. *Klinische Beiträge zur Psychiatrie.* Leipzig, 1869.

Longford, W. W. *Music and Religion.* London, 1916.

Löw, Leopold. *Beiträge zur jüdischen Alterthumskunde.* Szeged, 1875.

Lucian of Samosata. *De Syria Dea.*

Lucius Apuleius, see Apuleius, Lucius.

Lyra Graeca. (London, Loeb's Classical Library).

Macrobius, Ambrosius Theodosius. *Satirae.*

Manilius, Marcus. *Astronomica Libri V.*

Martial, Marcus Valerius. *Liber Spectaculorum.*

Mauduit, Jacques. *40.000 ans d'art moderne.* Paris, 1900.

Maximus of Tyrus. *Dissertationes.*

Mielziner, M. *Introduction to the Talmud.* New York, 1925.

Moffat, James. *A New Translation of the Bible.* New York and London, 1922.

Monatsschrift für die Geschichte und Wissenschaft des Judentums. Krotoschin.

Moore, George. "Symphonia Not a Bagpipe." In *JBL* 24 (1903).

Moortgatt, A. *Der Unsterblichkeitsglaube in der altorientalischen Bildkunst.* Berlin, 1949.

Moser, Hans Joachim. *Dokumente der Musikgeschichte.* Vienna, 1954.

Movers, Franz Karl. *Die Phönizier.* 2 vols. Bonn, 1841–1856.

Mowinckel, Sigmund. *Psalmenstudien.* 6 vols. Christiania, 1924.

Nadel, Siegfried. "The Origin of Music." In *JQ* 16 (1931).

Nägelsbach, K. W. E. *Der Prophet Isaiah.* New York, 1906.

Neefe, Konrad. "Die Tonkunst der Babylonier und Assyrer." In *Monatshefte für Musikgeschichte* 22 (1890).

Neilos (Nilus). "Narratio V." In *PLG* 7.

New Oxford History of Music. New York and London, 1927.

Oesterley, Emil Oscar William. *The Psalms in the Jewish Church.* London, 1910.

———. *The Sacred Dance.* New York, 1923.

Ovid. *Ars amatoria.*

———. *Epistulae.*

———. *Fasti.*

———. *Tristia.*

Peritz, Ismar. "Women in the Ancient Hebrew Cult." In *JBL* (1898).

Petronius, Caius (1st century, c.e.) *Cena Trimalchionis.*

Pfeiffer, Augustus Friedrich (1640–1698), *Über die Musik der alten Hebräer.* Erlangen, 1779.

Pfeiffer, Robert H. *Introduction to the Old Testament.* New York, 1941.

PG. (Patrologia Graeca).

PGL. (Patrologia Graeco-Latina).

PL. (Patrologia Latina).

Philo, Judaeus. *De legatione ad Caium.*

———. *In Flaccum.*

———. *Peri biou Mouseōs (About the Life of Moses).*

———. *Peri biou Mouseōs (About the Life of Moses).*

———. *Peri biou theorētikou hē ikēton (About the Contemplative Life).*

———. *Peri tōn en merei diatagmatōn (On the Special Laws).*

———. *Peri tōn menetezōmenōn (On the Change of Names).*

Philostratus. *The Life of Apollonius of Tyrana.*

Piso, Caius Calpurnius. *Laus Pisonis.*

Plato. *Dialogues.* Translated by B. Jewett. Vol. V. Oxford, 1924.

———. *Phaedrus.*

———. *Protagoras.*

———. *Symposium.*

Pliny the Elder. *Historia naturalis.*

Plutarch. *Lives (Vitae).*

———. *De superstitione.*

Pollux, Julius of Naucratis. *Onomasticon.*

Porphyry. *Peri apochēs empsychōn (On the Abstinence from Animal Food).*

Portaleone, Abraham da. *Shilṭe ha-Gibborim*. Mantua, 1612.

Prätorius, Michael. *Syntagma musicum*. Wolfenbüttel, 1614–1619.

Pratt, Waldo Selden. *The History of Music*. New York, 1935.

Quasten, J. *Musik und Gesang in den Kulten der heidnischen Antike und der christlichen Frühzeit*. Münster, 1930.

Rackham, Richard B. *The Acts of the Apostles*. London, 1912.

Realenzyclopedie der classischen Altertumswissenschaft. 34 vols. Edited by Pauly. Stuttgart, 1894.

Reinach, Solomon. *Orpheus*. New York, 1941.

Reisner, George Andrew. *Sumerisch-babylonische Hymnen nach Tontafeln aus griechischer Zeit*. Berlin, 1896.

Renan, Ernest. *Mission de Phénice*. Paris, 1864.

——. *The Song of Songs*. Translated by William M. Thomson. London, 1860.

Riehm, Eduard Carl August. *Handwörterbuch des biblischen Altertums*. Bielefeld and Leipzig, 1893–1894.

Riemann, Hugo. *Handbuch der Musikgeschichte: Altertum und Mittelalter*. Vol. I. Leipzig, 1904.

Robertson, Smith W. *The Prophets in Israel*. New York, 1882.

——. *The Religion of the Semites*. New York, 1894.

Roth, Cecil. *History of the Jews*. New York, 1961.

Sa'adia ben Naḥmani. *Commentary on Daniel*.

Sabatier, Paul. See Jakob, B.

Sacher, Abram Leon. *A History of the Jews*. New York, 1965.

Sachs, Curt. "Die Entzifferung einer babylonischen Notenschrift." In *Sitzungsberichte der Preussischen Akademie der Wissenschaften, XVIII. 1924.*

——. *Geist und Werden der Musikinstrumente*. Berlin, 1929.

——. *The History of Musical Instruments*. New York, 1940.

——. *Die Musik der Antike*. In *Handbuch der Musikwissenschaft*. Potsdam, 1934.

——. *Die Musik des Altertums*. Breslau, 1924.

——. *Rhythm and Tempo*. New York, 1953.

——. *The Rise of Music in the Ancient World East and West*. New York, 1943.

——. *The Wellsprings of Music*. Edited by Jaap Kunst. The Hague, 1962.

——. *World History of the Dance*. New York, 1937.

Sallustius, Gaius Crispus. *Catilina*.

Sandys, Sir John. *Companion in Latin Studies*. Cambridge, 1925.

Sanger, William. *History of Prostitution*. New York, 1939.

Schäfke, Rudolf. *Aristeides Quintilianus*. Berlin, 1937.

Schechter, Solomon. *Studies in Judaism, 1st Series*. Philadelphia, 1896.

Schlesinger, Kathleen. "Researches into the Origin of the Organ of the Ancients." In *Sammelbände der Internationalen Musikgesellschaft*. Leipzig, 1901.

Schletterer, H. M. *Geschichte der geistlichen Dichtung und kirchlichen Tonkunst*. Hannover, 1869.

Schneider, Hermann. *The History of World Civilisation from Prehistoric Times to the Middle Ages.* 2 vols. Translated by Margaret M. Green. New York, 1931.

———. *Kulturleistungen der Menschheit.* 3 vols. Leipzig, 1931.

———. *Kultur und Denken der Babylonier und Juden.* Leipzig, 1910.

Schneider, Marius. "Primitive Music." In *New Oxford History of Music.* 1957.

Schneider, Peter Joseph. *Biblisch-geschichtliche Darstellung der hebräischen Musik, deren Ursprung, Zunahme.* Bonn, 1837.

Scholz, P. *Götzendienst und Zauberwesen bei den alten Hebräern.* Regensburg, 1877.

———. *Die heiligen Altertümer des Volkes Israel.* 2 vols. Regensburg, 1868.

Schrader, Eberhard. *Die Keilinschriften und das Alte Testament.* Giessen, 1882.

Schumacher, Gottlieb. *Tell el-Muteselim.* 2 vols. Leipzig, 1908.

Schürer, Emil. *Gemeindeverfassung der Juden in Rom.* Leipzig, 1879.

Sendrey, Alfred. *Bibliography of Jewish Music.* New York, 1951.

———. *Music in Ancient Israel.* New York, 1969.

———. *Rundfunk und Musikpflege.* Leipzig, 1931.

Seneca, Lucius Annaeus. *De brevitate vitae.*

———. *Controversiones.*

———. *Epistulae.*

Sethe, Kurt Heinrich. "Urgeschichte und älteste Religionen der Agypter." In *Abhandlungen für die Kunde des Morgenlandes.* XVIII, no. 4 (Leipzig, 1930).

Shabbetai Bass. *Sidur Amsterdam.* Amsterdam: 1680.

Siebenkees, Johann Philipp. *Anecdota graeca.* See Clitarchos.

Sievers, Eduard. "Metrische Studien. Part I. Studien zur hebräischen Metrik." In *Abhandlungen der philologisch-historischen Klasse der Königlich Sächsischen Gesellschaft der Wissenschaften.* XXI, no. 1. 1901.

Spencer, Herbert. "The Origins and Function of Music." In *Essays.* 2 vols. New York, 1904.

Stainer, Sir John. *The Music of the Bible.* New ed. by F. W. Galpin. London, 1914.

Strabo. *Geōgraphikōn.*

Stumpf, Carl. *Die Anfänge der Music.* Leipzig, 1911.

Suetonius, Gaius. *The Twelve Caesars.* Translated by Robert Graves. London, 1957.

———. "Nero." In *Vitae Imperatorum Romanorum.*

Suidas. *Historia Antonini Pii.*

Tacitus, Cornelius. *Annales.*

———. *Historia.*

Tagore, Rabindranath. *My Reminiscences.* New York, 1917.

Taine, Hippolyte Adolphe. *Philosophie und Kunst.* 2 vols. Leipzig, 1902.

Thirtle, James William. *Old Testament Problems.* London, 1916.

———. *The Titles of the Psalms.* London, 1904.

Thucydides. *Historia.*

Trevor, Albert. *The Roman World, History of Ancient Civilization.* Vol. II. New York, 1939.

Unger, Hermann. *Musikgeschichte in Selbstzeugnissen.* Munich, 1928.

Universal Jewish Encyclopedia. 10 vols. Edited by Isaac Landmann. New York, 1939–1942.

Villoteau, Guillaume André. *Description de l'Egypte.* 13 vols. Paris, 1809.

Wallanschek, Richard. *Anfänge der Tonkunst.* Leipzig, 1903.

————. *Primitive Music.* London, 1893.

Ward, Cyrus Osborn. *The Ancient Lowly.* 2 vols. Chicago, 1907.

Waterman, Leroy. *The Song of Songs, translated and interpreted as a Dramatic Poem.* Ann Arbor, Mich., 1948.

Wegner, Max. *Musikgeschichte in Bildern.* Vol. II, *Musik des Altertums. Griechenland.* Leipzig, 1962.

————. *Die Musikinstrumente des Alten Orients.* Münster, 1950.

————. *Das Musikleben der Griechen.* Berlin, 1949.

Weiss, Johann. *Die musikalischen Instrumente in den heiligen Schriften des Alten Testaments.* Graz, 1895.

Wellesz, Egon. *Byzantinische Musik.* Breslau, 1927.

Wellhausen, Julius. *The Book of the Psalms.* New York, 1898.

Werner, Eric. "*Musical Aspects of the Dead Sea Scrolls.*" In *MQ* 43 (Jan. 1957).

Westphal Rudolph. *Geschichte der alten und mittelalterlichen Musik.* Breslau, 1865.

Wetzstein, Johann Gottfried. "Die syrische Dreschtafel." In Bastian's *Zeitschrift für Ethnologie,* vol. 5. 1873.

Wilkinson, Sir Gardner. *The Manners and Customs of the Ancient Egyptians.* 2 vols. London, 1878.

Wiedemenn, A. *Die Religion der alten Ägypter.* Münster, 1890.

Wille, Günther. *Musica Romana.* Stuttgart, 1967.

————. "*Die Musikalität der alten Römer.*" In *AfMW* 11.

Williams, Abdy. *The Story of the Organ.* London, 1906.

Winckler, Hugo. *Keilinschriftliches Textbuch zum A. T.* 2 vols. Leipzig, 1909.

Wolf, A. A. *Der Prophet Habakkuk.* Darmstadt, 1822.

Wright, W. "Some Apocryphal Psalms in Syriac." In *Proceedings of the Society of Biblical Archaeology* (June 1887).

Yasser, Joseph. *The Magrephah of the Herodian Temple; A Fivefold Hypothesis.* In *Journal of the American Musicological Society* 13 (1960).

————. "Restoration of Ancient Hebrew Music." *Abstract in First Ten Years of the Annual Three Choir-Festival.* New York, 1946.

Zeitlin, Solomon. "The Dead Sea Scrolls and Modern Scholarship." In *JQR. Monograph Series no. 3.* Philadelphia, 1956.

Zeitschrift für alttestamentliche Wissenschaft.

Zeitschrift für neutestamentliche Wissenschaft.

Zenner, K. J. *Die Chorgesänge im Buche der Psalmen.* Freiburg, 1896.

Zunz, Leopold. *Die gottesdienstlichen Vorträge der Juden.* Berlin, 1832.

————. *Die Ritus des synagogalen Gottesdienstes geschichtlich entwickelt.* Berlin, 1859.

Index